UNITED STATES FOREIGN TRADE HIGHLIGHTS

UNITED STATES FOREIGN TRADE HIGHLIGHTS

TRENDS IN THE GLOBAL MARKET

2017

THIRD EDITION

EDITED BY SUSAN OCKERT

Bernan Press

Lanham • Boulder • New York • London

Published in the United States of America by Bernan Press, a wholly owned
subsidiary of The Rowman & Littlefield Publishing Group, Inc.
4501 Forbes Boulevard, Suite 200
Lanham, Maryland 20706

Bernan Press
800-462-6420
www.rowman.com

ISBN-13: 978-1-59888-886-7
eISBN-13: 978-1-59888-887-4

∞™ The paper used in this publication meets the minimum requirements
of American National Standard for Information Sciences—Permanence
of Paper for Printed Library Materials, ANSI/NISO Z39.48-1992.

Manufactured in the United States of America.

CONTENTS

List of Tables vii
List of Figures xiii
Preface xv
Introduction...xvii

SECTION A: U.S. INTERNATIONAL TRANSACTIONS AND INVESTMENT POSITION...................1
Highlights...3
About the Data 4
Tables 6

SECTION B: U.S. FOREIGN TRADE IN GOODS AND SERVICES 19
Highlights...21
About the Data 25
Tables 26

SECTION C: U.S. COMMODITY TRADE BY GEOGRAPHIC AREA..135
Highlights...137
About the Data 139
Tables 140

SECTION D: U.S. COMMODITY TRADE..167
Highlights...169
About the Data 173
Tables 176

SECTION E: IMPORTS AND EXPORTS BY STATE...205
Highlights...207
About the Data 209
Tables 212

Index...315

LIST OF TABLES

SECTION A: U.S. INTERNATIONAL TRANSACTIONS AND INVESTMENT POSITION

Table A-1. International Transactions, 2005–2015 6
Table A-2. U.S. Net International Investment Position, 2005–2015 10
Table A-3A. First Year Expenditures for New Foreign Direct Investment in the United States, 2005–2015 12
Table A-3B. First Year Expenditures and Planned Total Expenditures for Investments Initiated in 2015,
             Industry of Affiliate by Type of Investment 13
Table A-3C. First Year Expenditures and Planned Total Expenditures for Investments Initiated in 2015,
             Country of UBO by Type of Investment 14
Table A-4. Foreign Exchange Rates, 2005–2015 15

SECTION B: U.S. FOREIGN TRADE IN GOODS AND SERVICES

Part I: Trade in Goods and Services
Table B-1. U.S. International Trade in Goods and Services, 1960–2015...26
Table B-2. International Trade in Goods and Services, 1967–2015...27
Table B-3. U.S. Trade in Goods — Balance of Payments (BOP) Basis vs. Census Basis, 1960–2015 28
Table B-4. U.S. Trade in Services by Type of Service, 1999–2015..29
Table B-5. Exports and Imports of Goods by Principal End-Use Category, 1992–2015 30

Part II: Exports and Imports in Selected Categories
Table B-6. U.S. Exports with World by Harmonzied System (HS) for Total Merchandise, 2010–2015.....................32
Table B-7. U.S. Imports with World by Harmonzied System (HS) for Total Merchandise, 2010–2015.....................34
Table B-8. Top U.S. Imports, Exports, Deficit, and Surplus for Total Merchandise, 2010–2015 36
Table B-9. U.S. Imports from World Total by 5-Digit End-Use Code, 2006–2015 37
Table B-10. U.S. Exports to World Total by 5-Digit End-Use Code, 2006–2015 40
Table B-11. Exports with World by Standard International Trade Classification (SITC), 2005–2015 42
Table B-12. Total All Merchandise Exports to World, 2010–2015...44
Table B-13. Top 10 Trade with World for SITC Total All Merchandise, 2010–2015 45
Table B-14. U.S. Top Ten Exports, Imports, Deficit, and Surplus by Standard International Trade
             Classification (SITC), 2010–2015...46
Table B-15. U.S. Exports of Total Merchandise by North American Industry Classification
             System (NAICS), 2010–2015..47
Table B-16. U.S. Imports of Total Merchandise by North American Industry Classification
             System (NAICS), 2010–2015..48
Table B-17. U.S. Balance of Payments with World by North American Industry Classification
             System (NAICS), 2005–2015..49
Table B-18. Top 10 Imports, Exports, Deficit, and Surplus by North American Industry Classification
             System (NAICS), 2010–2105..51
Table B-19. Real Exports of Goods by Principal End-Use Category, 1995–2015 52
Table B-20. Real Imports of Goods by Principal End-Use Category, 1995–2015 53

Part III: U.S. Trade with Countries and Regions
Table B-21. U.S. Exports of Total Merchandise to Individual Countries by Harmonized System, 2005–2015 54
Table B-22. U.S. Imports of Total Merchandise from Individual Countries by Harmonized System, 2005–2015......62
Table B-23. U.S. Imports of Goods from Regions and Individual Countries, Selected Years, 2000–2015 70
Table B-24. U.S. Total Exports of Goods to Regions and Individual Countries, Selected Years, 2000–2015 74
Table B-25. U.S. Total Balance of Payments of Goods by Region and Individual Country,
             Selected Years, 2000–2015 78

Table B-26. U.S. Exports of North American Industry Classification System (NAICS) Manufactures by Region and Individual Country, 2010–2015 82

Table B-27. U.S. Imports of North American Industry Classification System (NAICS) Manufactures by Region and Individual Countries, 2005–2015..86

Table B-28. U.S. Balance of Payments of North American Industry Classification System (NAICS) Manufactures by Region and Individual Countries, 2005–2015...94

Table B-29. U.S. Exports by North American Industry Classification System (NAICS) by Region and Country, 2005–2015 102

Table B-30. U.S. Agricultural Imports by North American Industry Classification System (NAICS) from Regions and Individual Countries, 2005–2015...110

Table B-31. U.S. Agricultural Balance of Payments by Regions and Individual Countries, 2005–2015....................118

Table B-32. Top 30 Purchasers and Suppliers of U.S. Agricultural Products by North American Industry Classification System (NAICS), 2005–2015 126

Table B-33. Top 30 Suppliers of U.S. Agricultural Products by North American Industry Classification System (NAICS), 2005–2015...128

Table B-34. U.S. Total Exports, Imports, and Balances by Area, 2000–2015...130

Table B-35. U.S. Trade in Services, by Type of Service and by Country or Affiliation, 2005–2015..........................131

SECTION C: U.S. COMMODITY TRADE BY GEOGRAPHIC AREA

Table C-1.   Top U.S. Trade Partners Ranked by 2015 U.S. Export Value for Goods, 2014–2016 140
Table C-2.   U.S. Trade by Commodity with Canada, 2010–2015 141
Table C-3.   U.S. Trade by Commodity with Mexico, 2010–2015..142
Table C-4.   U.S. Trade by Commodity with China, 2010–2015..143
Table C-5.   U.S. Trade by Commodity with Japan, 2010–2015..144
Table C-6.   U.S. Trade by Commodity with United Kingdom, 2010–2015 145
Table C-7.   U.S. Trade by Commodity with Germany, 2010–2015..146
Table C-8.   U.S. Trade by Commodity with South Korea, 2010–2015..147
Table C-9.   U.S. Trade by Commodity with Netherlands, 2010–2015 148
Table C-10. U.S. Trade by Commodity with Hong Kong, 2010–2015...149
Table C-11. U.S. Trade by Commodity with Belgium, 2010–2015..150
Table C-12. U.S. Trade by Commodity with France, 2010–2015..151
Table C-13. U.S. Trade by Commodity with Brazil, 2010–2015...152
Table C-14. U.S. Trade by Commodity with Singapore, 2010–2015 153
Table C-15. U.S. Trade by Commodity with Taiwan, 2010–2015...154
Table C-16. U.S. Trade by Commodity with Switzerland, 2010–2015...155
Table C-17. U.S. Trade by Commodity with United Arab Emirates, 2010–2015..156
Table C-18. U.S. Trade by Commodity with Australia, 2010–2015...157
Table C-19. U.S. Trade by Commodity with India, 2010–2015 158
Table C-20. U.S. Trade by Commodity with Saudi Arabia, 2010–2015...159
Table C-21. U.S. Trade by Commodity with Italy, 2010–2015...160
Table C-22. U.S. Trade by Commodity with Israel, 2010–2015..161
Table C-23. U.S. Trade by Commodity with Columbia, 2010–2015 162
Table C-24. U.S. Trade by Commodity with Chile, 2010–2015 163
Table C-25. U.S. Trade by Commodity with Malyasia, 2010–2015...164
Table C-26. U.S. Trade by Commodity with Thailand, 2010–2015 165

SECTION D: U.S. COMMODITY TRADE

Table D-1.   U.S. Selected Agriculture Exports, 2005–2015..176
Table D-2.   U.S. Selected Agriculture Imports, 2005–2015...177
Table D-3.   Exports and Imports by Country: Beverages and Spirits, 2010–2015...178
Table D-4.   Exports and Imports by Country: Cereal and Grains, 2010–2015..179

Table D-5.   Exports and Imports by Country: Cocoa, 2010–2015 180
Table D-6.   Exports and Imports by Selected Country: Coffee and Tea, 2010–2015 181
Table D-7.   Exports and Imports by Country: Dairy Products, 2010–2015 182
Table D-8.   Exports and Imports by Country: Fruits and Nuts, 2010–2015..183
Table D-9.   Exports and Imports by Country: Live Trees and Cut Flowers, 2010–2015..184
Table D-10.   Exports and Imports by Country: Meat, 2010–2015 185
Table D-11.   Exports and Imports by Country: Oilseeds and Soybeans, 2010–2015 186
Table D-12.   Exports and Imports by Country: Sugar, 2010–2015 187
Table D-13.   Exports and Imports by Country: Tobacco, 2010–2015 188
Table D-14.   Exports and Imports by Country: Vegetables, 2010–2015...189
Table D-15.   Exports and Imports by Country: Aircraft, Spacecraft, and Parts, 2010–2015 190
Table D-16.   Exports and Imports by Country: Electric Machinery, 2010–2015 191
Table D-17.   Exports and Imports by Country: Furniture, 2010–2015..192
Table D-18.   Exports and Imports by Country: Nuclear Reactors, 2010–2015 193
Table D-19.   Exports and Imports by Country: Optic-Photo, Medical or Surgical Instruments, 2010–2015 194
Table D-20.   Exports and Imports by Country: Organic Chemicals, 2010–2015..195
Table D-21.   Exports and Imports by Country: Pharmaceutical Products, 2010–2015 196
Table D-22.   Exports and Imports by Country: Precious Stones, Diamonds, Etc. 2010–2015......................................197
Table D-23.   Exports and Imports by Country: Vehicles and Parts, 2010–2015 198
Table D-24.   Crude Oil Imports by Country: 2010–2015...199
Table D-25.   Crude Oil Exports by Country: 2010–2015...200
Table D-26.   Sources of Rare Earth Elements Imports 201
Table D-27.   Trade Balance: Advance Technology Products, 1990–2016...202
Table D-28.   U.S. Trade in Advance Technology Products: Biotechnology, 2014 and 2015 203

SECTION E: IMPORTS AND EXPORTS BY STATE

Part I: State Trade by Country

Table E-1.   State Trade by Country: Alabama, 2012–2015..212
Table E-2.   State Trade by Country: Alaska, 2012–2015 213
Table E-3.   State Trade by Country: Arizona, 2012–2015 214
Table E-4.   State Trade by Country: Arkansas, 2012–2015 215
Table E-5.   State Trade by Country: California, 2012–2015..216
Table E-6.   State Trade by Country: Colorado 2012–2015..217
Table E-7.   State Trade by Country: Connecticut, 2012–2015 218
Table E-8.   State Trade by Country: Delaware, 2012–2015...219
Table E-9.   State Trade by Country: District of Columbia, 2012–2015...220
Table E-10.   State Trade by Country: Florida, 2012–2015...221
Table E-11.   State Trade by Country: Georgia, 2012–2015 222
Table E-12.   State Trade by Country: Hawaii, 2012–2015 223
Table E-13.   State Trade by Country: Idaho, 2012–2015 224
Table E-14.   State Trade by Country: Illinois, 2012–2015...225
Table E-15.   State Trade by Country: Indiana, 2012–2015 226
Table E-16.   State Trade by Country: Iowa, 2012–2015...227
Table E-17.   State Trade by Country: Kansas, 2012–2015 228
Table E-18.   State Trade by Country: Kentucky, 2012–2015..229
Table E-19.   State Trade by Country: Louisiana, 2012–2015..230
Table E-20.   State Trade by Country: Maine, 2012–2015 231
Table E-21.   State Trade by Country: Maryland, 2012–2015..232
Table E-22.   State Trade by Country: Massachusetts, 2012–2015..233
Table E-23.   State Trade by Country: Michigan, 2012–2015..234
Table E-24.   State Trade by Country: Minnesota, 2012–2015..235
Table E-25.   State Trade by Country: Mississippi, 2012–2015...236

Table E-26.   State Trade by Country: Missouri, 2012–2015 237
Table E-27.   State Trade by Country: Montana, 2012–2015..238
Table E-28.   State Trade by Country: Nebraska, 2012–2015...239
Table E-29.   State Trade by Country: Nevada, 2012–2015 240
Table E-30.   State Trade by Country: New Hampshire, 2012–2015...241
Table E-31.   State Trade by Country: New Jersey, 2012–2015..242
Table E-32.   State Trade by Country: New Mexico, 2012–2015..243
Table E-33.   State Trade by Country: New York, 2012–2015..244
Table E-34.   State Trade by Country: North Carolina, 2012–2015...245
Table E-35.   State Trade by Country: North Dakota, 2012–2015...246
Table E-36.   State Trade by Country: Ohio, 2012–2015...247
Table E-37.   State Trade by Country: Oklahoma, 2012–2015..248
Table E-38.   State Trade by Country: Oregon, 2012–2015..249
Table E-39.   State Trade by Country: Pennsylvania, 2012–2015..250
Table E-40.   State Trade by Country: Rhode Island, 2012–2015...251
Table E-41.   State Trade by Country: South Carolina, 2012–2015...252
Table E-42.   State Trade by Country: South Dakota, 2012–2015...253
Table E-43.   State Trade by Country: Tennessee, 2012–2015..254
Table E-44.   State Trade by Country: Texas, 2012–2015..255
Table E-45.   State Trade by Country: Utah, 2012–2015..256
Table E-46.   State Trade by Country: Vermont, 2012–2015 257
Table E-47.   State Trade by Country: Virginia, 2012–2015...258
Table E-48.   State Trade by Country: Washington, 2012–2015..259
Table E-49.   State Trade by Country: West Virginia, 2012–2015...260
Table E-50.   State Trade by Country: Wisconsin, 2012–2015..261
Table E-51.   State Trade by Country: Wyoming, 2012–2015...262

Part II: State Trade by Commodity

Table E-52.   State Trade by Commodity: Alabama, 2014–2015 263
Table E-53.   State Trade by Commodity: Alaska, 2014–2015..264
Table E-54.   State Trade by Commodity: Arizona, 2014–2015 265
Table E-55.   State Trade by Commodity: Arkansas, 2014–2015 266
Table E-56.   State Trade by Commodity: California, 2014–2015..267
Table E-57.   State Trade by Commodity: Colorado, 2014–2015..268
Table E-58.   State Trade by Commodity: Connecticut, 2014–2015 269
Table E-59.   State Trade by Commodity: Delaware, 2014–2015..270
Table E-60.   State Trade by Commodity: District of Columbia, 2014–2015 271
Table E-61.   State Trade by Commodity: Florida, 2014–2015...272
Table E-62.   State Trade by Commodity: Georgia, 2014–2015..273
Table E-63.   State Trade by Commodity: Hawaii, 2014–2015...274
Table E-64.   State Trade by Commodity: Idaho, 2014–2015...275
Table E-65.   State Trade by Commodity: Illinois, 2014–2015...276
Table E-66.   State Trade by Commodity: Indiana, 2014–2015...277
Table E-67.   State Trade by Commodity: Iowa, 2014–2015..278
Table E-68.   State Trade by Commodity: Kansas, 2014–2015...279
Table E-69.   State Trade by Commodity: Kentucky, 2014–2015..280
Table E-70.   State Trade by Commodity: Louisiana, 2014–2015..281
Table E-71.   State Trade by Commodity: Maine, 2014–2015..282
Table E-72.   State Trade by Commodity: Maryland, 2014–2015..283
Table E-73.   State Trade by Commodity: Massachusetts, 2014–2015..284
Table E-74.   State Trade by Commodity: Michigan, 2014–2015..285
Table E-75.   State Trade by Commodity: Minnesota, 2014–2015...286
Table E-76.   State Trade by Commodity: Mississippi, 2014–2015..287
Table E-77.   State Trade by Commodity: Missouri, 2014–2015...288

Table E-78.   State Trade by Commodity: Montana, 2014–2015 289
Table E-79.   State Trade by Commodity: Nebraska, 2014–2015..290
Table E-80.   State Trade by Commodity: Nevada, 2014–2015 291
Table E-81.   State Trade by Commodity: New Hampshire, 2014–2015 292
Table E-82.   State Trade by Commodity: New Jersey, 2014–2015..293
Table E-83.   State Trade by Commodity: New Mexico, 2014–2015 294
Table E-84.   State Trade by Commodity: New York, 2014–2015..295
Table E-85.   State Trade by Commodity: North Carolina, 2014–2015..296
Table E-86.   State Trade by Commodity: North Dakota, 2014–2015..297
Table E-87.   State Trade by Commodity: Ohio, 2014–2015 298
Table E-88.   State Trade by Commodity: Oklahoma, 2014–2015...299
Table E-89.   State Trade by Commodity: Oregon, 2014–2015 300
Table E-90.   State Trade by Commodity: Pennsylvania, 2014–2015 301
Table E-91.   State Trade by Commodity: Rhode Island, 2014–2015...302
Table E-92.   State Trade by Commodity: South Carolina, 2014–2015 303
Table E-93.   State Trade by Commodity: South Dakota, 2014–2015...304
Table E-94.   State Trade by Commodity: Tennessee, 2014–2015..305
Table E-95.   State Trade by Commodity: Texas, 2014–2015 306
Table E-96.   State Trade by Commodity: Utah, 2014–2015 307
Table E-97.   State Trade by Commodity: Vermont, 2014–2015..308
Table E-98.   State Trade by Commodity: Virginia, 2014–2015 309
Table E-99.   State Trade by Commodity: Washington, 2014–2015..310
Table E-100. State Trade by Commodity: West Virginia, 2014–2015..311
Table E-101. State Trade by Commodity: Wisconsin, 2014–2015...312
Table E-102. State Trade by Commodity: Wyoming, 2014–2015..313

LIST OF FIGURES

INTRODUCTION

Figure 1.   U.S. GDP and Total Trade, 1997–2016...xvii
Figure 2.   Total U.S. Exports and Imports, 1995–2015 xviii

SECTION A: U.S. INTERNATIONAL TRANSACTIONS AND INVESTMENT POSITION

Figure A-1.   U.S. Assets and Liabilities, 2005–2014 3
Figure A-2.   Foreign Exchange Rates, Local Currency Unit per Dollar, 2005–2015...4

SECTION B: U.S. FOREIGN TRADE IN GOODS AND SERVICES

Figure B-1.   International Trade in Goods and Services, 1960–2015...21
Figure B-2.   Top 2005 Imports...22
Figure B-3.   Top 2015 Imports...22
Figure B-4.   Top 2005 Exports...23
Figure B-5.   Top 2015 Exports...23
Figure B-6.   U.S. Exports in Total Services by Selected Year and Country, 2000–2015 24

SECTION C: U.S. COMMODITY TRADE BY GEOGRAPHIC AREA

Figure C-1.   Top 15 Trade Surpluses by Country, 2015 137
Figure C-2.   Top 15 Trade Deficits by Country, 2015 138
Figure C-3.   Top Trading Partners of the United States (Exports), 2015 138
Figure C-4.   Top Trading Partners of the United States (Imports), 2015 139

SECTION D: U.S. COMMODITY TRADE

Figure D-1.   U.S. Trade in Goods and Services, 2005–2015..169
Figure D-2.   Exports and Imports of Agricultural Products, 2005–2015...170
Figure D-3.   Top Ten Imports, 2015 170
Figure D-4.   Top Ten Exports, 2015 171
Figure D-5.   U.S. Crude Oil Imports: OPEC and Non-OPEC Countries, 1995–2015 172
Figure D-6.   U.S. Exports of Advanced Technology Products, 2015 173
Figure D-7.   U.S. Imports of Advanced Technology Products, 2015 174

SECTION E: IMPORTS AND EXPORTS BY STATE

Figure E-1.   U.S. Imports from Top 10 Countries, 2012–2015 208
Figure E-2.   Top 10 Exporting States 2012–2015..208
Figure E-3.   Destination of U.S. Exports, 2012–2015 209

PREFACE

Bernan Press is pleased to introduce the third edition of *United Foreign Trade Highlights*—the first edition since 2007. This publication brings together a wide variety of government data to assist the user in assessing trends in U.S. international trade. In June 2014, the Bureau of Economic Analysis (BEA) introduced a comprehensive restructuring of the U.S. international economic accounts, the most significant change in the presentation of these accounts since 1976. The comprehensive restructuring represents the culmination of a multi-year effort to modernize and enhance the accounts by introducing changes recommended by new international statistical guidelines along with other improvements.

This publication includes the following information:

- U.S. international transactions data (the most comprehensive measure of international trade), including the external position of the United States with respect to its financial balances with the rest of the world

- U.S. international investment data which highlights U.S. owned assets and liabilities where a negative net investment position represents a U.S. net liability to the rest of the world (i.e. net borrower)

- U.S. aggregate foreign trade data, which include trade balances in goods and services and information on the U.S. trade performance with regard to its top trading partners

- U.S. commodity trade by geographical region and with its largest trading partners

- U.S. commodity trade by detailed product groups

- State exports of goods and imports, including figures that show the distribution of exported goods among manufactured, agricultural, and other goods services

The uses of these data are numerous. They show historic trends in trade in goods and services, reveal how well the United States is doing in trade with its chief foreign competitors, and provide a source of information on how trade affects both the country as a whole and each individual state.

Public policy analysts use these data to evaluate and plan programs, to measure the impact of tariff and trade concessions under the World Trade Organization (formerly General Agreement of Tariffs and Trade) and the General System of Preferences (GSP), and to analyze operations under various trade agreements, including the North American Free Trade Agreement (NAFTA). These trade data are also useful for analyzing market share and product penetration and for determining general marketing policies and product development.

This publication has five sections, each of which highlights a particular facet of U.S. foreign trade. Sections A—D provide information on the U.S. economy as a whole, while Section E examines export and import activity at the state level.

Section A provides information on U.S. international transactions—the "balance of payments" data—and the international investment position, a statistical balance sheet that presents the dollar value of U.S. external financial assets and liabilities. The data are provided by the BEA and the U.S. Census Bureau (both are part of the U.S. Department of Commerce) and are available on a quarterly and annual bases from two different data systems. The international transactions accounts (ITAs) provide information on the exchange of goods and services plus primary income (investment income and compensation) and secondary income (current transfers such as U.S. government grants, withholding taxes, and insurance-related transfers). In addition, this publication includes a sharper focus on the components of the international financial flows, including cross-border securities transactions.

A widely used statistic from the accounts is the current account balance—the most comprehensive measure of trade and goods and services—and its accumulation, which determines the net international position (whether the United States is a net lender or borrower nation.)

The global economic crisis that started in late 2007 highlighted the importance of economic statistics that provide a clear and timely depiction of major developments in both the real and the financial sectors of economies around the world. In some respects, the responses of policymakers to the crisis were hampered by a lack of detailed, timely, and international comparable information about financial asset and liability flows and their impact on production, employment, and income.

Section B provides aggregate data on foreign trade in goods and services on a balance of payment basis; these data are available monthly, quarterly, and annually from the BEA and Census Bureau and are compatible with the international transactions accounts. The national income and products (NIPAs), an alternate data system, provide data that differ somewhat in concept, scope, and definitions from the international transaction accounts. The NIPAs are published each quarter with the release of the gross domestic product (GDP) data—the broadest measure of U.S. domestic economy activity in the United States. Annual NIPA data is released annually the end of July.

The balance of payments data are the most prominent source of information relating to trade in services, including maintenance and repair services; transport; travel (for all purposes including education); insurance services; financial services; charges for the use of intellectual property; telecommunications, computer, and information services; other business services; and government goods and services. The main focus of Section B is the export and import of goods or merchandise. These are shown in several detailed product groupings and in terms of bilateral trade with the other countries. The data in this volume appear on an annual basis.

Section C presents U.S. commodity trade with the top trading partners of the United States. The data is collected by the Census Bureau and compiled by Office of Trade and Economic Analysis (OTEA) in the International Trade Administration (ITA). These data appear as annual data in this publication.

Section D provides highlights of these commodity trade data, cross-classified by the top countries exported and imported, as well as detail about the trade balances between the United States and other nations. Additional commodities detailed include agricultural commodities, rare earth elements, and Advanced Technology Products.

Section E focuses on trade activity at the state level. It includes data on exports and imports of goods by state, including information about each state's top export and import products and commodities and the countries that purchase and supply these products.

As noted above, the data in this volume are annual time series, supplemented in several tables by information on recent changes. The data cover different time spans due to variations in data availability. The data in this volume are presented through 2015. These data are the most recent available and were released in June 2016.

All statistical data are subject to errors due to sample variability, incomplete coverage, reporting and classification errors, and other causes. The responsibility of the editor and publisher of this volume is limited to reasonable care in the reproduction and presentation of the data obtained from established government sources.

Susan Ockert has worked as an economist in the military, for the federal government, and at regional and state levels. She earned her Masters of Economics at George Mason University in Fairfax, Virginia as well as her Masters of International Management at the Thunderbird University in Glendale, Arizona. She also has taught economics at the collegiate level.

As always, special thanks are due to the many federal agency personnel who assisted us in obtaining the data, provided excellent resources on their websites, and patiently answered our questions.

INTRODUCTION

As the 21st century began, the U.S. economy was riding high as the tech-bubble expanded. However, by 2001, the dotcom[1] bubble burst. The National Bureau of Economic Research (NBER) pronounced that a recession occurred between March 2001 to November 2001, lasting just eight months. Equity markets grew exponentially by speculation in unproven internet-based companies. The technology-dominated NASDAQ nearly doubled then lost 10 percent of its value by mid-April 2001. Both U.S. exports and imports declined in 2000–2001, 6.8 percent and 5.5 percent respectively.

By 2007, the U.S. and global economies had recovered and even prospered. However, according to NBER, another economic downturn started in December 2007 and lasted until January 2009 for a total of 18 months. The Great Recession became the deepest global recession since the Great Depression. The world including the European Union, Japan, and the United States experienced low growth rates while Russia's GDP contracted.

As the financial sector melted down, global stock markets tumbled as did producer and consumer confidence and demand for exports. Unemployment, inflation, and foreclosures rose. Only the falling oil prices had a positive impact on the global economy. World output declined to near historic lows at 2.2 percent while the U.S. economy fell 2.1 percent in 2009. Countries such as the U.S. implemented public sector stimulus programs to counteract the falling global demand for goods and services.

Recovery from the Great Recession was sluggish, unbalanced, and weak. Further shocks to the world output included the continuing uncertainty in the financial sector, instability in the euro area, the U.K. vote to leave the European Union, and the incoming administration in the United States.

As shown below, the U.S. GDP declined in 2009 during the Great Recession. Total trade, exports plus imports, fluctuated between 23.3 percent and 29.9 percent until

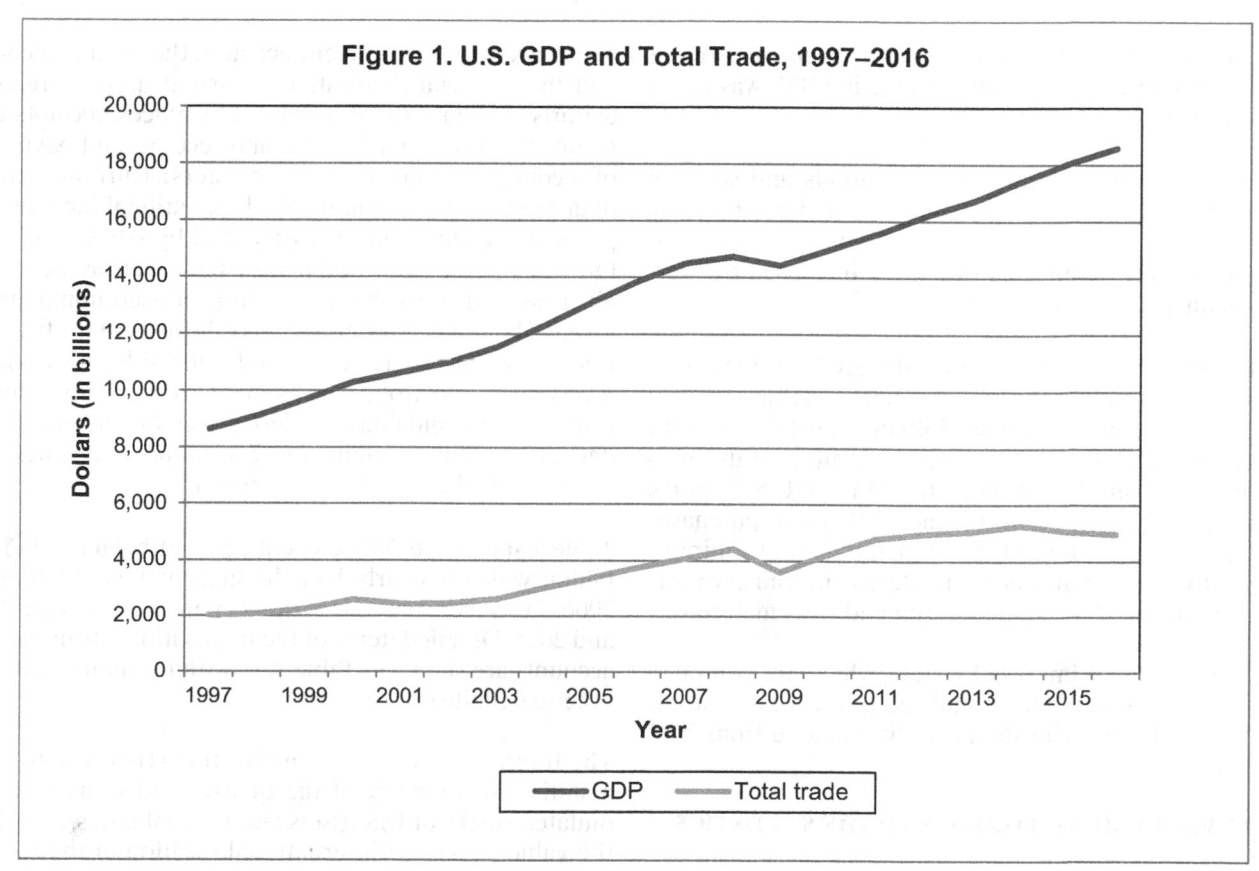

Figure 1. U.S. GDP and Total Trade, 1997–2016

---

[1] A dotcom is a company that embraces the internet as the key component in its business.

xvii

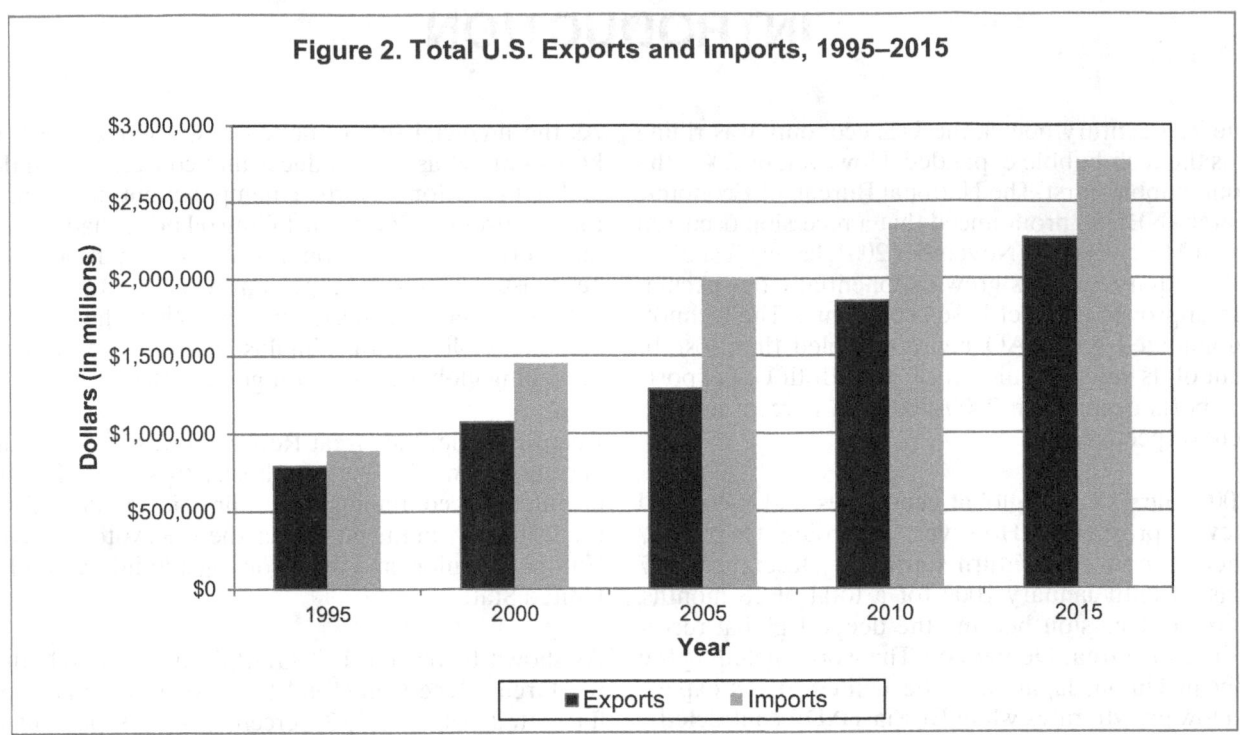

Figure 2. Total U.S. Exports and Imports, 1995–2015

2010. Total trade accounted for 30+ percent in 2011 to 2014. The only year where the change in GDP was negative was 2009.

The U.S. continues to import more goods and services that it exports, resulting in a trade deficit since the early 1970s. As seen in the figure above, exports have grown 5.6 percent annually while imports have increased 6.2 percent on an average annual rate.

The U.S.'s top 25 trade partners in 2015 are listed in Section C. The composition of the top importers has changed over the years. Vietnam was ranked 56th in imports in 2000 but moved all the way up to 13th in 2015. United Arab Emirates moved from 38th ranked to 15th for U.S. imports. Vietnam supplies cotton to the U.S. then purchases apparel articles from the U.S. The United Arab Emirates (AE) provides aircraft parts and electric machinery parts while importing aluminum and iron and steel materials.

Part E includes of imports by state which are compiled from the automated data submitted to the U.S. Customs and Border Patrol. This data is only available from 2012 to present.

UNDERSTANDING FOREIGN TRADE STATISTICS

The International Transaction Accounts (ITAs) are a quarterly statistical summary of transactions between U.S. residents and nonresidents organized into three major accounts: the current account, the capital account, and the financial account. The current account records exports and imports of goods and services, receipts and payments of primary income, and receipts and payments of secondary income (current transfers). Current account data are used in compiling the U.S. national income and product accounts (NIPAs) prepared by BEA. The capital account records capital transfers, such as debt forgiveness, and transactions in non-produced nonfinancial assets. The financial account records investment transactions between U.S. residents and nonresidents for direct investment, portfolio investment, other investment, reserve assets, and financial derivatives. Financial account data are used in compiling the flow of funds statistics prepared by the Federal Reserve Board.

Table 1 shows the 2015 current account balance of -$463 billion which is nearly half the high of $806.7 billion in 2006. However, the CA rose 18 percent between 2014 and 2015. Detailed items of the international transactions accounts are shown in Table A-1, with footnotes that give precise definitions.

The International Investment Position (IIP) accounts are a statistical summary of the quarter-end value of accumulated stocks of U.S. assets and U.S. liabilities, as well as the value of the net international position of the United States. Separate statistics are available for the value of accumulated stocks of direct investment, portfolio investment, other investment, reserve assets, and financial

Table 1. U.S. International Transactions, 2015

Item	Billions of Dollars
Current Account Balance	−$463.0
Trade balance in goods	−$762.6
Exports	$1,510.3
Imports	$2,272.9
Trade balance in services	$262.2
Exports	$750.9
Imports	$488.7
Balance on primary income	$182.4
Balance on secondary income	−$145.0
Financial Account balance	−$169.9
Direct Investment assets (net)	−$30.8
Portfolio investment (net)	−$97.0
Other	−$42.1
Capital account balance (net)	−$0.0
Statistical discrepancy*	$267.8

* The statistical discrepancy is the difference between net acquisition of assets and net incurrence of liabilities in the financial account (including financial derivatives) less the difference between total credits and total debits recorded in the current and capital accounts.

Table 2. U.S. International Investment Position, 2015

Type of Investment (billions of dollars)	Amount
U.S. Assets	$23,341
Direct investment	$6,978
Portfolio investment	$9,606
Financial derivatives	$2,292
Other investment	$3,977
Reserve assets	$384
U.S. Liabilities	$30,621
Direct investment	$6,544
Portfolio investment	$166,767
Financial derivatives	$2,338
Other investment	$5,063
Net international investment position	−$7,281

derivatives. Changes in positions arise from financial transactions, asset valuation changes, and other changes in the volume of assets. Data from the IIP accounts are used in compiling national balance sheet statistics prepared by the Federal Reserve Board. Table 2 provides the 2015 IIP for the United State and shows these components.

Net lending (borrowing) measures the balance of funds supplied to the rest of the world. Net lending means that, an economy supplies funds to the rest of the world. Net borrowing means the opposite. Net lending (borrowing) can be measured by current- and capital-account transactions or by financial transactions. Conceptually, the two measures are equal, in practice, the two measures differ by the statistical discrepancy. The United States was last a lender to the world was 1988. Since then, the U.S. depends on other countries to buy U.S. assets.

Comprehensive Restructuring of U.S. International Economic Accounts

The comprehensive restructuring that BEA released in June 2014 represents the culmination of a multi-year effort to modernize and enhance the accounts by introducing changes recommended by international statistical guidelines along with other improvements. While selected changes have been introduced over the last several years, the June 2014 release features a new presentation of the accounts that not only conforms more closely to international guidelines but also brings the U.S. accounts into closer alignment with those of other countries. These changes improve the overall comparability of international economic statistics and provide policymakers and others with a stronger statistical foundation for understanding and responding to international economic events.

The major changes, which are briefly described below, include changes in sign convention and income presentation, the use of functional investment categories and sector detail, and the presentation of direct investment on an asset/liability basis.

Notes and Definitions

Sign convention. The uniform use of negative signs for debit entries is eliminated.

Under the new presentation, positive signs are used to show exports and imports, income receipts and payments, transfers made and received, and increases in assets and liabilities. Negative signs are used only to indicate negative investment income (losses) and decreases in assets or in liabilities (as occur, for example, if investments are sold off). Current-account and capital-account balances are calculated as the difference between the underlying gross flows (exports minus imports, for example). For the financial account, net lending/borrowing is calculated as the difference between the acquisition of assets and the incurrence of liabilities. These new conventions should not only make the ITAs easier to understand and interpret, but should also simplify understanding their relationship to the corresponding changes in asset and liability positions in the IIP accounts.

Income presentation. The new tables adopt the nomenclature of primary income and secondary income introduced for the current account in BPM6.[2] Primary income is income generated from current production and is equivalent to income receipts and income payments as shown in BEA's previous presentation. Secondary income is equivalent to current transfers and is presented on a gross basis—that is, secondary income receipts and secondary income payments are shown separately rather than combined and presented on a net basis.

Functional categories. The new presentation reflects significant changes to the presentation of the financial account and the IIP accounts. Financial account transactions and positions in the IIP accounts are classified according to five functional categories—direct investment, portfolio investment, other investment, reserve assets, and financial derivatives other than reserves—and then according to the type of instrument. Investment income in the current account is also classified by functional category.

Sector detail. The new presentation introduces additional detail on portfolio investment and, in the future, other investment by sector. BPM6 defines four main sectors: central bank, deposit-taking corporations except the central bank, general government, and "other sectors," which includes the two subsectors "other financial corporations" and "nonfinancial corporations, households, and NPISHs" (nonprofit institutions serving households). BEA has eliminated the summary category "other sectors" and presents the two subsectors in its place.

Two basic changes to the names in the new presentation have been made. First, the term "corporations" is replaced with the term "institutions" to include enterprises such as partnerships that belong in this category but that are not organized as publicly held corporations. Second, because BEA has little source data on the transactions of households and NPISHs with foreign residents, BEA uses the label "nonfinancial institutions."

Asset/liability basis. Direct investment is presented on the asset/liability basis recommended by BPM6, to the extent that source data allow, in addition to the directional basis recommended by earlier guidelines. On the directional basis, direct investment statistics are organized according to whether the direct investment is outward (U.S. direct investment abroad) or inward (foreign direct investment in the United States). On the asset/liability basis, direct investment statistics are organized according to whether the investment relates to an asset or a liability. The U.S. international transactions accounts, or "balance of payment" accounts, provide a comprehensive and detailed view of the economic and financial transactions between the United States and foreign nations, as well as of the accumulated value of U.S.-owned assets and U.S.-owned liabilities in the United States. This is known as the "net international investment positions of the United States."; that is, whether the nation is a net creditor or debtor to the rest of the world. Major transactions include merchandise trade, travel, transport, other services, and governmental and private capital flows.

Classification of Transactions and Positions

The international economic accounts disaggregate and classify resident-nonresident transactions and positions in various ways to provide greater insight into their economic significance and to present the statistics in the broader context of integrated economic accounts. Classifications are used to group similar components and to separate components with different characteristics.

Current and Capital Accounts

The current account of the ITAs consists of resident-nonresident transactions in produced assets, primary income, and secondary income (current transfers). The capital account of the ITAs consists of resident-nonresident transactions in nonproduced nonfinancial assets and capital transfers. Major current account classifications include goods vs. services and primary income vs. secondary income (current transfers). Distinctions between goods and services, between current and capital transfers, and between primary income and services are not always straightforward.

Goods vs. Services

In economic accounts, goods and services are the two major categories of outputs of productive activities. Goods are physical items with ownership rights that can be exchanged among institutional units through transactions. The production of a good can be separated from its subsequent sale or resale. Services are the result of activities that change the condition of the consumer or that facilitate the exchange of products and financial assets. In general, ownership rights cannot be established for services and they cannot be separated from their production. Exceptions occur for some intellectual property products, such as computer software and audio-video recordings, that can be traded separately from their production.

---

[2] The International Monetary Fund's 6th edition of the Balance of Payments and International Investment Position Manual influenced BEA's comprehensive restructuring of the U.S. International Economic Accounts.

Primary Income vs. Services

Primary income includes both investment income such as interest, dividends, and reinvested earnings and compensation of employees. An important issue for distinguishing compensation of employees from services trade is the existence of an employer-employee relationship between a resident and nonresident. Provision of certain types of services may pose classification problems because firms may choose to purchase a service, such as legal services, from a self-employed person or may hire an employee to provide the service. If an employer-employee relationship exists between the worker and the producing entity, the payment represents compensation of employees. If an employer-employee relationship does not exist, the payment constitutes a purchase of services.

Current vs. Capital Transfers

Secondary income in the current account consists of current transfers between residents and nonresidents. The capital account includes capital transfers along with transactions in non-produced nonfinancial assets. Unlike an exchange, a transfer is a transaction that provides a good, service, or asset to another institutional unit without a corresponding return of economic value (quid pro quo).

Capital transfers represent change in ownership of an asset between parties. Current transfers include items such as personal remittances, government grants, cross-border fines and penalties, and institutional remittances. Capital transfers include debt forgiveness, non-life insurance payments resulting from catastrophic events, and investment grants.

FOREIGN TRANSACTIONS IN THE NATIONAL INCOME AND PRODUCT ACCOUNTS (NIPA)

In addition to the ITAs and the net investment status of the United States, the BEA also produces quarterly data on foreign transactions that are compatible with the domestic-based national income and product accounts (NIPAs). Unlike the international transactions accounts, these data show trends in price and quantity. Because of differences in scope, concept, and definitions, the aggregate value of the foreign transactions in the NIPA accounts are not exactly the same as the estimates from the international transactions accounts. The chief differences consist of the NIPA's of only the 50 states and the District of Columbia (the international transactions also include Puerto Rico and the U.S. territories) and different treatment of gold and of some services) these differences are detailed in the 21st edition of *Business Statistics of the United States*, also published by Bernan Press. A reconciliation of the two sets of international transactions can be found in the *Survey of Current Business*, with the most recent update in the July edition.

U.S. INTERNATIONAL TRADE IN GOODS AND SERVICES

The key building blocks for the aggregate foreign trade statistics are the data on exports and imports of goods and services produced monthly by the BEA and the Census Bureau. Their monthly publication provides an earlier view of U.S. trade patterns than the quarterly trade aggregates. However, as noted previously, they exclude income flows and unilateral transfers but are available in considerably more detail. This greater detail allows the user to look at specific industry products, such as petroleum or advanced technology. These and many other products can be cross-classified to show U.S. trade with individual countries and regions. Exports and imports of goods are also available by state.

Trade in Goods

Monthly data on exports and imports of goods are compiled by the Census Bureau and are said to be measured on a "Census basis." Unlike the census economic survey data, which are based on solicited responses such as the population and labor force data, the trade data are compiled from the U.S. Customs Service reports on virtually all goods shipments leaving or entering the United States.[3] Since 1990, exports to Canada are compiled using Canadian import data.[4]

---

[3] Data on U.S. exports of merchandise from the U.S. to all countries is compiled from the Electronic Export Information (EEI) filed by the USPPI or their agents through the Automated Export System (AES). The EEI is unique among Census Bureau data collection methods since it is not sent to respondents soliciting responses as in the case of surveys. Each EEI represents a shipment of one or more kinds of merchandise from one exporter to one foreign importer on a single carrier. Filing the EEI is mandatory under Chapter 9, Title 13, United States Code. Qualified exporters or their agents submit EEI data by automated means directly to the U.S. Census Bureau.

[4] The United States is substituting Canadian import statistics for U.S. exports to Canada in accordance with a 1987 Memorandum of Understanding signed by the Census Bureau, U.S. Customs and Border Protection, Canadian Customs, and Statistics Canada. Similarly, under this Memorandum of Understanding, Canada is substituting U.S. import statistics for Canadian exports to the United States. This data exchange includes only U.S. exports destined for Canada and does not include shipments destined for third countries by routes passing through Canada or shipments of certain grains and oilseeds to Canada for storage prior to exportation to a third country. These shipments are reported on and compiled from EEIs.

The data reflect the exports and imports of the 50 states, the District of Columbia, Puerto Rico, the U.S. Virgin Islands, and U.S. Foreign Trade Zones (FTZ) (enclosed area under control of U.S. Customs with facilities for handling, storing, assembling, manufacturing, and processing goods that are not subject to formal customs entry procedures and payment of duties and tariffs until the foreign merchandise enters customs territories for domestic consumption).

In general, the statistics record the physical movement of merchandise between the United States and foreign countries. The data include both government and nongovernment shipments but exclude transactions between U.S. territories and possessions (treated as domestic trade); transactions with the military, diplomatic, and consular installations abroad; U.S. goods returned to the United States by the armed forces; the personal and household belongings of travelers; and in-transit shipments. Imports are arrivals of merchandise from foreign countries that enter consumption channels (such as stores), warehouses or foreign trade zones.

Valuation. The value of merchandise exports and imports is measured in accordance with census definitions. Exports are valued at "f.a.s.," or "free alongside of ship," at the port of exportation. This value excludes the cost of loading the goods aboard the ship and other costs beyond the port of exportation.

For imports of goods, the value is measured by the appraised value reported to the customs services, which is generally the price paid for the merchandise for export to the United States. U.S. import duties, freight, insurance, and other charges incurred in bringing the merchandise to the United States are excluded.

Statistical month. The month of exportation is based on the date upon which the merchandise leaves the United States. The month of importation is the month in which U.S. Custom Service released the merchandise to the importer.

Classification of goods exports and imports. The export statistics are initially collected and compiled in terms of about 8,000 commodity classifications in Schedule B, as determined by the Census Bureau. Classifications are based on the Harmonized Commodity Description and Coding System (also known as the Harmonized System, or HS), which describes and measures the characteristics of the goods. The Harmonized System is an international system established by the United Nation to classify products for tariff and statistical purposes and to enhance comparability of data among nations. The import statistics are initially collected and compiled in terms of about 14,000 commodity classifications, as determined by the

U.S. International Commission: these are also based on the HS.

Under the Harmonized System, individual product categories are represented by 6-digit codes (the number of digits represents the level of detail for a product) and are aggregated to higher levels of classification. The United States defines products using 10-digit codes, which is allowed HS as long as the country definitions are within the HS 6-digit framework. In this volume, statistics are shown at the 2-digit level for United States as a whole and at the 6-digit level for states. (More information on the HS, can be found at unstats.un.org.)

The HS and Schedule B are summarized into six "end-use" categories that allow the examination of goods by principal uses: food, feeds and beverages; industrial supplies and materials; capital goods except automobile products; vehicles, parts and engines; consumer goods except foods and autos; and other merchandise. The end-use demand concept was developed by the BEA for the purpose of estimating balance of payment data. These data are supplied by the Census Bureau for use in the international transactions accounts and the NIPAs.

Another universal grouping is the Standard International Trade Classification (SITC), a statistical classification of commodities designed by the United Nations and compatible with the HS. It is designed to provide commodity aggregations that are needed for the purposes of economic analysis and to facilitate the international comparison of trade by commodity. There are 10 broad groupings under the SITC system: (1) foods and live animals; (2) beverages and tobacco; (3) crude materials; (4) minerals, fuels, lubricants, and related materials; (5) animal and vegetable oils, fats and waxes; (6) chemicals and related products; (7) manufactured goods classified chiefly by material; (8) machinery and transport equipment; (9) miscellaneous manufactured articles; and (10) commodities and transactions not classified elsewhere. These 10 classes of commodities represent the aggregation of approximately 3,000 5-digit SITC codes that reflect detailed products in each of the broad categories. Section B provides data by end-use, HS, NAICS, and SITC.

Goods are also classified according to the North American Industry Classification System (NAICS), which was jointly produced by the United States, Canada, and Mexico following the ratification of the North American Free Trade Agreement (NAFTA). This system is designed to promote comparability of data with North America and is not strictly comparable to the SITC system, because product descriptions under NAICS may not fit neatly into the SITC classification scheme. Twenty categories are identified in NAICS.

Due to the growing importance of technology goods in the U.S. economy and in world trade, the Census Bureau also provides a separate classification of "advanced technology products," which are discussed in Section D. About 500 of the Schedule B and HS commodity classification codes used in reporting U.S. exports and imports are identified as "high technology," indicating that the products are from a high technology field (such as biotechnology) and represent leading-edge technology in that field; such products constitute a significant part of all items covered in that classification code.

To highlight trade with other areas of the world, merchandise trade data are presented both bilaterally (trade between individual countries and the United States) and in regional groupings; both classification are presented in this volume. These groupings and individual countries can be found in Section C.

For the purposes of bilateral trade, the country of destination for exports is defined as the country in which the goods are to be consumed, further processed, or manufactured (as known to the shipper at the time of exportation). If the shipper does not know the ultimate destination of the goods, the shipment is credited to the last country to which the shipper knows that the merchandise shipped in the same form as it was in when it exported. The country or origin of imports is the country where the goods are grown, manufactured, or mined. When the country of origin cannot be identified, transactions are credited to the country of shipment.

Merchandise export and imports are also available by state and are shown in Section E of this publication. They denote the state from which the export actually starts its journey to the port of exportation. This may not be where the product is actually grown or produced or the actual location of the exporter. For imports, the country from which the import actually starts starts its journey to port of importation.

Merchandise trade on a census basis is adjusted to a balance of payments basis by the BEA in its monthly FT900 release to bring the data in line with the concepts and definitions used to prepare the international transactions accounts and the NIPAs. Generally, these adjustments include changes in ownership that occur without the goods passing into or out to the customs territory of the United States. These adjustments are necessary to supplement the basic census data, to eliminate the duplication of transactions recorded elsewhere in the international accounts, and to the value transactions according to a standard definition.

The adjustments to exports include the following:

- The deduction of military sales contracts is made because census data include these contracts as goods, while the BEA data includes them as services.

- An addition is made for the private gift parcels mailed to foreigners by individuals mailed though the U.S. Postal Services, because only commercial shipments are covered in census goods exports.

- Gold (nonmonetary) exports purchased by foreign official agencies from private dealers in the United States and held at the Federal Reserve Bank of New York are added to census figures because census data only include gold that leaves the customs territory.

Adjustments for imports include the following:

- An addition is made to imports for inland freight in Canada. Imports of goods from all countries are valued at the port of exportation, including inland freight charges (customs value). In the case of Canada, this should be the cost of the goods at the U.S. border. However, the customs value for certain Canadian goods is their point origin in Canada. The BEA therefore makes an addition for the inland freight charges of transporting these goods to the U.S. border to make value comparable to the customs value reported by all the countries.

- An addition is made for gold sold by official foreign agencies to private purchasers out of the stock of gold held at the Federal Reserve Bank of New York. Census data only include gold that enters the customs territory.

- Imports by U.S. military agencies are deducted because these military sales contracts are included in the Census Bureau's goods data, while the BEA includes them in its services data.

Each month, the aggregate goods data published in the FT900 release contain current-month preliminary estimates together with revisions of the prior month's estimates. The revisions reflect additional data that have become available since the previous month's release. Trade classified by "end-use" category is similarly revised. SITC and country detail are not revised monthly. In this volume, all of these data appear on annual basis. Annual revisions for the monthly data are made in June of each year.

Trade in Services

The new international standards for trade in services provide new guidance in light of the major changes in how services are delivered and growth in the trade of new types of services. The international standards also reflect the recognition of expenditures on research and development (R&D) and on artistic originals as fixed investment.

Maintenance and repair services n.i.e (not included elsewhere) covers maintenance and repair services by residents of one country for goods that are owned by residents of another country. The repairs may be performed at the site of the repair facility or elsewhere.

Maintenance and repair of ships, aircraft, and other transport equipment are currently included in transport because these transactions cannot be separately identified in BEA's source data for transport services. Construction maintenance and repairs, including renovation, repair, or extension of fixed assets in the form of buildings, and repairs of railway facilities, harbors, and airfield facilities are included in the construction component of other business services. Computer maintenance and repairs are included in the computer services component of telecommunications, computer, and information services.

Transport consists of transactions associated with moving people and property from one location to another and includes related supporting and auxiliary services. Transport is classified by mode of transport—sea, air, or other mode—and by what is transported (passengers or freight). Under sea transport and air transport, BEA presents port services, which include cargo handling, storage and warehousing, and other related transport services.

Travel (for all purposes including education). Travel consists of transactions involving goods and services acquired by nonresidents while visiting another country. A traveler is defined as a person who stays, or intends to stay, for less than one year in a country of which he or she is not a resident or a nonresident whose purpose is to obtain education or medical treatment, no matter how long the stay. Purchases can be either for own use or for transfer to others. Travel is a transactor-based component that covers a variety of goods and services, primarily lodging, meals, transportation in the country of travel, amusement, entertainment, and gifts. Travel excludes goods for resale, which are included in goods under general merchandise. All passenger service for travel between the United States and other countries is included in transport.

Insurance services include the direct insurance services of providing life insurance (including annuities) and nonlife (property and casualty) insurance, reinsurance, and auxiliary insurance services. Direct insurance and reinsurance are measured as gross premiums earned plus premium supplements less claims payable, with an adjustment for claims volatility. Premium supplements represent investment income from insurance reserves attributed to policyholders who are treated as paying the income back to the insurer. Auxiliary insurance is measured separately and includes agents' commissions, brokerage services, insurance consulting services, actuarial services, and other insurance services.

Financial services include financial intermediary and auxiliary services, except insurance services. These services include those normally provided by banks and other financial institutions. Services primarily include those for which an explicit commission or fee is charged; implicit fees for bond transactions are also included.

Charges for the use of intellectual property n. i. e. include (1) charges for the use of proprietary rights (such as patents, trademarks, copyrights, industrial processes and designs including trade secrets, and franchises) that can arise from research and development as well as from marketing and (2) charges for licenses to reproduce or distribute (or both) intellectual property embodied in produced originals or prototypes (such as copyrights on books and manuscripts, computer software, cinematographic works, and sound recordings) and related rights (such as for live performances and television, cable, or satellite broadcast).

Telecommunications, computer, and information services include these three sectors. Telecommunications services include the broadcast or transmission of sound, images, data, or other information by electronic means. These services do not include the value of the information transmitted. Computer services consists of hardware- and software-related services and data processing services. It includes sales of customized software and related use licenses as well as licenses to use non-customized software with a periodic license fee. This item also includes software downloaded on the Internet, fees and subscriptions for online gaming, licensing agreements, and end-user fees associated with downloading applications. Cross-border transactions in non-customized packaged software with a license for perpetual use are included in goods. Information services includes news agency services, database services, and web search portals.

Other business services consist of research and development services, professional and management consulting services, and technical, trade-related, and other business services.

Research and development services consist of services associated with basic and applied research and experimental development of new products and processes. Professional and management consulting services include legal services, accounting, management consulting, managerial services, public relations services, advertising, and market research. Included are amounts received by a parent company from its affiliates for general overhead expenses related to these services. Technical, trade-related, and other business services include architectural and engineering services, waste treatment, operational leasing services, trade-related, and other business services.

Government goods and services n .i. e covers goods and services supplied by and to enclaves, such as embassies, military bases, and international organizations; goods and services acquired from the host economy by diplomats, consular staff, and military personnel located abroad and their dependents; and services supplied by and to governments that are not included in other services categories. Services supplied by and to governments are classified to specific services categories when source data permits.

Services estimates are based on quarterly, annual, and benchmark surveys and partial information generated from monthly reports. Service transactions are estimated at market prices. Estimates are seasonally adjusted when statistically significant seasonal patterns are present. No country or area detail is available due to the lack of adequate source data upon which to base estimates.

Revision policy. Each month, a preliminary estimate for the current month and a revised estimate of preceding month are released. After a revision is released, no further changes are made to that month's estimate until more complete data become available (in March, June, September, and December of each year). When these data become available, the estimates are then revised for the six preceding months. Further information on trade in services can found on the BEA website at www.bea.gov.

WORLD TRADE STATISTICS

In addition to U.S. foreign trade data, there are many sources of information on foreign trade trends of other countries. The World Trade Organization (WTO) publishes an annual report on world global trade (data for 2015 were released in July 2016), which contains detailed analysis and tables for most countries, leading trading nations, trade by sector and production and regional trade. These data are supplemented by the WTO's press releases. Further information is available on the WTO's website at www.wto.org.

The Organizational for Economic Co-operation and Development (OECD) provides detailed trade data on both goods and services on their 35 member countries, including Australia, Austria, Belgium, Canada, Chile, Czech Republic, Denmark, Estonia, Finland, France, Germany, Greece, Hungary, Iceland, Ireland, Israel, Italy, Japan, Korea, South, Latvia, Luxembourg, Mexico, Netherlands, New Zealand, Norway, Poland, Portugal,

Slovak Republic, Slovenia, Spain, Sweden, Switzerland, Turkey, United Kingdom and United States. The OECD website www.oecd.org also provides links to the trade databases of other key international organizations such as the World Bank, the International Monetary Fund (IMF), and various regional development banks and organization. The site also links to non-governmental sources, such as research institutions that produce trade data and analysis.

The World Bank provides financial and technical assistance to developing countries around the world to reduce poverty and support development. The primary World Bank publication is the *World Development Indicators* which include development indicators such as population and population growth, GNI, GDP, GDP growth, exports and imports, and gross capital formation, deforestation, water use, energy use and electricity use per capita and more. For more information, see www.worldbank.org.

The International Monetary Fund (IMF) is a source of international statistics on all aspects of international finance. For most countries of the world, it provides data on international transactions, government accounts, exchange rates, and other relevant data needed in analyses of balance of payments issues. For more information, see www.imf.org.

In addition, the Office of Trade and Economic Analysis (OTEA) in the U.S. Department of Commerce's International Trade Administration provides the data for Trade Stats Express at tse.export.gov. This website provides national trade data and state export data. Information is presented on global patterns of U.S. merchandise trade and product profiles of U.S. merchandise trade with a selected market plus global patterns of state's exports, state-by-state exports to a selected market and export product profile to a selected market. The U.S. Census Bureau provides state exports and imports at www.census.gov.

COUNTRY GROUPINGS

Africa—Algeria, Angola, Benin, Botswana, Burkina Faso, Burundi, Cameroon, Cabo Verde, Central African Republic, Chad, Comoros, Congo (Brazzaville), Congo (Democratic Republic of - Kinshasa), Djibouti, Egypt, Equatorial Guinea, Eritrea, Ethiopia, Gabon, Gambia, Ghana, Guinea, Guinea-Bissau, Ivory Coast (Cote d'Ivoire), Kenya, Lesotho, Liberia, Libya, Madagascar, Malawi, Mali, Mauritania, Mauritius, Morocco, Mozambique, Namibia, Niger, Nigeria, Rwanda, Sao Tome and Principe, Senegal, Seychelles, Sierra Leone, Somalia, South Africa, South Sudan, Sudan, Swaziland, Tanzania, Togo, Tunisia, Uganda, Zambia, and Zimbabwe.

Asia—Afghanistan, Armenia, Azerbaijan, Bangladesh, Bhutan, Brunei, Cambodia, China, Georgia, Hong Kong, India, Indonesia, Japan, Korea (North), Korea (South), Laos, Macau, Malaysia, Maldives, Mongolia, Myanmar Nepal, Pakistan, Philippines, Singapore Sri Lanka, Taiwan, Thailand, Turkey, and Vietnam.

Central Asia: Kazakhstan, Kyrgyzstan, Tajikistan, Turkmenistan, and Uzbekistan.

Middle East—Bahrain, Iran, Iraq, Israel, Jordan, Kuwait, Lebanon, Oman, Qatar, Saudi Arabia, Syria, United Arab Emirates, and Yemen.

Australia and Oceania: Australia, Fiji, Kiribati, Marshall Islands, Micronesia, Nauru, New Zealand, Palau, Papua New Guinea, Samoa, Solomon Islands, Tonga, Tuvalu, and Vanuatu.

EUROPE

European Union—Austria, Belgium, Bulgaria, Croatia, Cyprus, Czech Republic, Denmark, Estonia, Finland, France, Germany, Greece, Hungary, Ireland, Italy, Latvia, Lithuania, Luxembourg, Malta, Netherlands, Poland, Portugal, Romania, Slovakia, Slovenia, Spain, Sweden, and United Kingdom.[5]

Euro Area—Austria, Belgium, Cyprus, Estonia, Finland, France, Germany, Greece, Ireland, Italy, Latvia, Lithuania, Luxembourg, Malta, Netherlands, Portugal, Slovakia, Slovenia, and Spain.

---

[5] Membership in the EU is set to decline in 2018 since the United Kingdom (Britain) populace voted to leave the EU. This action is called "Brexit." Over 52% of votes were cast to withdraw the United Kingdom from the EU.

Non-EU Europe—Albania, Andorra, Belarus, Bosnia-Herzegovina, Iceland, Kosovo, Liechtenstein, Macedonia, Moldova, Monaco, Montenegro, Norway, Russia, San Marino, Serbia, Switzerland, Ukraine, and Vatican City.

North America/Caribbean Islands—Anguilla, Antigua and Barbuda, Aruba, Bahamas, Bermuda, Barbados, British Virgin Islands, Canada, Cayman Islands, Cuba, Curacao, Dominica, Dominion Republic, Greenland, Grenada, Guadeloupe, Haiti, Jamaica, Martinique, Mexico, Montserrat, St. Kitts and the Grenadines, Sint Maarten, Trinidad and Tobago, Turks and Caicos Islands, and United States.

South/Central America—Argentina, Belize, Bolivia, Brazil, Chile, Colombia, Costa Rica, Ecuador, El Salvador, Falkland Islands (Islas Malvinas), French Guiana, Guatemala, Guyana, Honduras, Nicaragua, Panama, Paraguay, Peru, Suriname, Uruguay, and Venezuela.

REGIONAL ASSOCIATIONS

ASEAN (Association of Southeast Asian Nations)—Brunei, Cambodia, Indonesia, Laos, Malaysia, Myanmar, Philippines, Singapore, Thailand, and Vietnam.

OECD (Organization for Economic Cooperation and Development)—Australia, Austria, Belgium, Canada, Chile, Czech Republic, Denmark, Estonia, Finland, France, Germany, Greece, Hungary, Iceland, Ireland, Israel, Italy, Japan, Korea (South), Latvia, Luxembourg, Mexico, Netherlands, New Zealand, Norway, Poland, Portugal, Slovakia, Slovenia, Spain, Sweden, Switzerland, Turkey, United Kingdom, and United States.

OPEC (Organization of the Petroleum Exporting Countries)—Algeria, Angola, Ecuador, Equatorial Guinea Gabon, Iran, Iraq, Kuwait, Libya, Nigeria, Qatar, Saudi Arabia, United Arab Emirates, and Venezuela.

SECTION A

U.S. INTERNATIONAL TRANSACTIONS
AND INVESTMENT POSITION

SECTION A: U.S. INTERNATIONAL TRANSACTIONS AND INVESTMENT POSITION

HIGHLIGHTS

Since 1994, the United States has run a current account trade deficit of over $100 billion annually. This account is a net measure of transactions between the U.S. and the rest of the world. The highest deficit occurred in 2006 at over $807 billion while the lowest occurred in 2013 at $377 billion, a decline of 114 percent. This deficit was primarily due to a deficit in goods, meaning that U.S. imports of goods outstripped U.S. exports.

The U.S.'s current account deficit closely emulated the balance of goods until 2009. However, as the world suffered the worst recession since the Great Depression of the 1930's, U.S. exports declined at a much faster rate.

Exports in 2009, in the midst of the Great Recession, fell 18 percent from 2008. Exports of cars and their parts declined 32.7 percent but then recovered in 2010 with exports increasing 37.1 percent. Travel, a major service, declined 17.1 percent in 2009 then increased 15.2 percent. In other words, Americans decreased their international travels.

As part of the comprehensive restructuring in 2014, the use of the balance sheet analysis was implemented. This led to a better understanding of international economic developments. Instead of U.S.-owned assets abroad and foreign-owned assets in the United States categories, foreign-owned assets are now called liabilities.

Figure 1 demonstrates the widening difference between assets and liabilities. In 2014, the difference rose to over $700 million. Before the financial collapse of the global financial began, the smallest different between these assets and liabilities was $128 billion. This represents more than a four-fold increase.

To finance the current account deficit, the United States needs to borrow from the rest of the world. This net borrowing consists of foreigners purchasing U.S. stocks, bonds, companies or some other asset. Between 1999 and 2000, the deficit doubled. Between 2009 and 2010, the deficit fell 89 percent.

Table 1 displays the United States net borrowing. As can be seen, United States need for borrowing began in 2012.

The Great Recession's impact on the U.S. dollar was contrary to contemporary international economic theory. With global equity values plunging, bank loans nearly impossible to obtain, and commodity prices crashing, the predictable direction for the dollar would also be declining. However, the dollar has appreciated against major currencies beyond expectations, i.e. becoming stronger and stronger. A strong dollar makes imports and travel

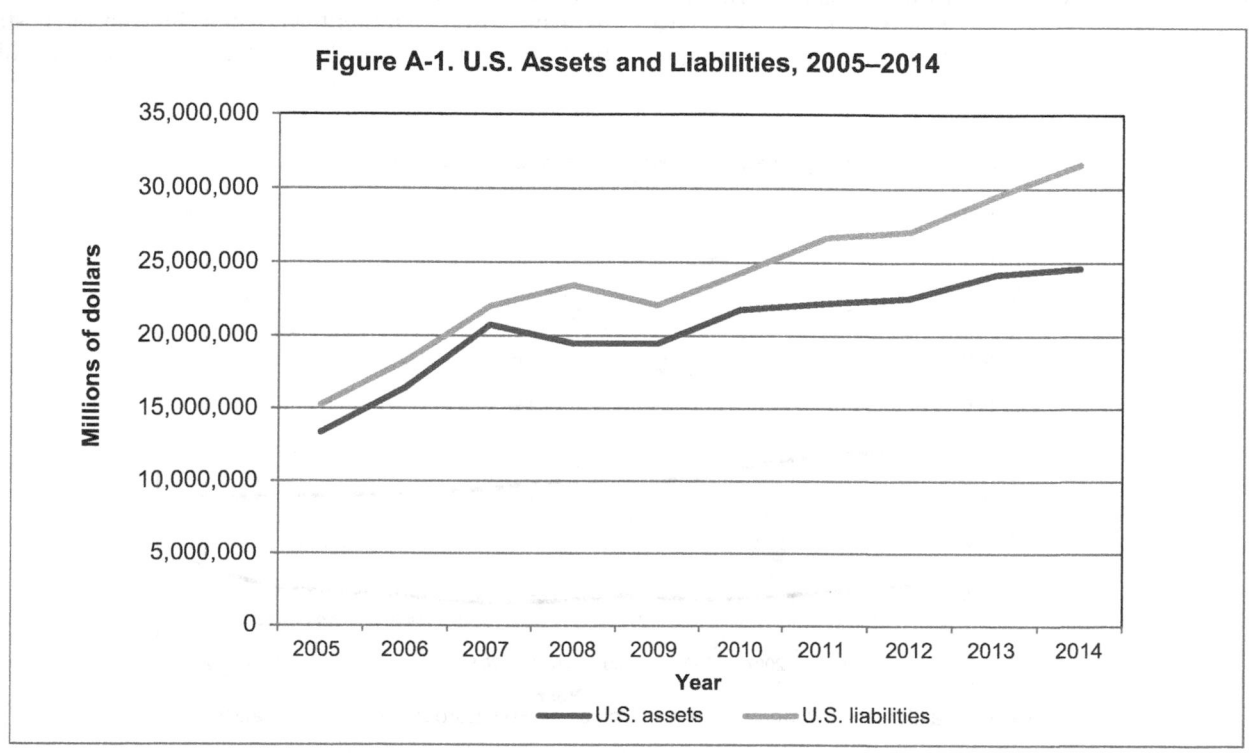

Figure A-1. U.S. Assets and Liabilities, 2005–2014

abroad less expensive. On the other hand, a strong dollar makes U.S. exports more expensive and fewer foreign tourists coming to the United States.

Table 1. U.S. Net Borrowing (Millions of dollars)

Year	Amount	Percent change
1999	-$238,148	
2000	-$477,701	101%
2001	-$400,254	-16%
2002	-$500,515	25%
2003	-$532,883	6%
2004	-$532,334	0%
2005	-$700,721	32%
2006	-$809,148	15%
2007	-$617,251	-24%
2008	-$730,572	18%
2009	-$230,962	-68%
2010	-$436,972	89%
2011	-$515,759	18%
2012	-$441,249	-14%
2013	-$395,831	-10%
2014	-$239,648	-39%
2015	-$209,203	-13%

ABOUT THE DATA

Section A provides an overview of U.S. international transactions and the net international investment position of the United States. In addition, Section A provides foreign exchange rates for over 220 countries. This data is important background for understanding the foreign trade data throughout the rest of this volume.

Table A-1 shows U.S. international transactions: the current account balance, the restructured assets and liabilities, and net borrowing.

Table A-2 displays the net international investment position of the United States. This position is presented as a statistical balance sheet that shows the dollar value of U.S. external financial assets and liabilities.

Table A-3 displays expenditures for investments.

Table A-4 displays over 220 foreign exchange rates in their local exchange unit. An exchange rate is the conversion rate of one currency of one currency in another. This rate depends on the local demand for foreign currencies and their local supply, country's trade balance, strength of its economy, and other such factors.

The data are shown on an annual basis from 2005–2015. Annual revisions are made to the data in June of each year and are published in the July edition of the Survey of Current Business. The data are also available on the Bureau of Economic Analysis (BEA) web site at www.bea.gov.

The comprehensive restructuring of the international economic account was implemented in 2014. This multiple-year project modernized the accounts to bring the data in closer alignment with new international statistical guidelines. Since 2014, an annual revision will be

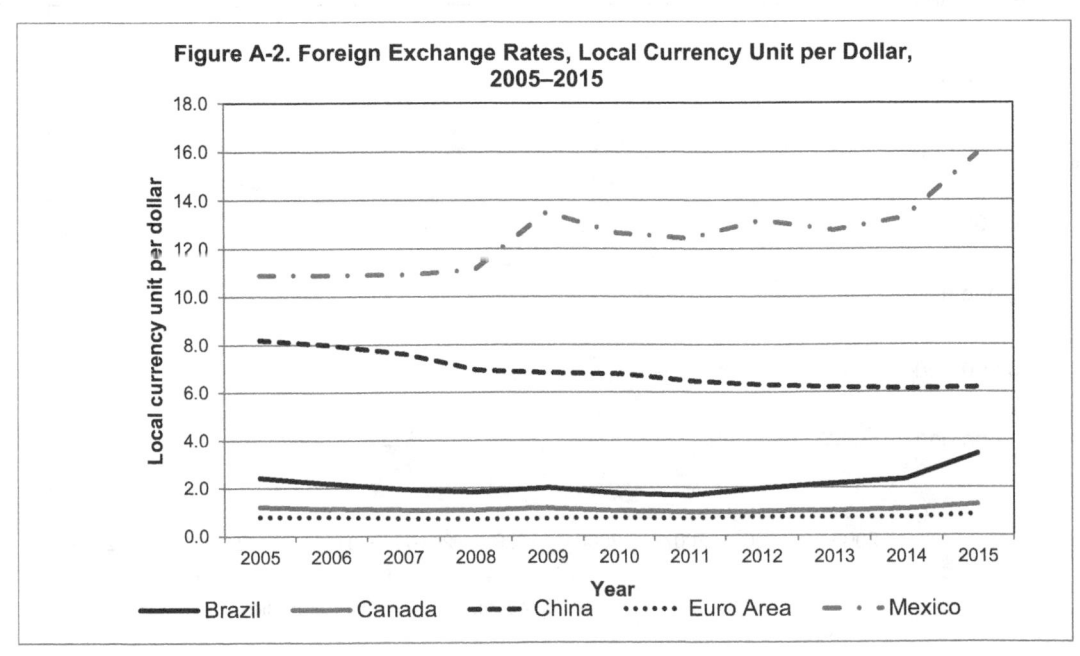

Figure A-2. Foreign Exchange Rates, Local Currency Unit per Dollar, 2005–2015

published. BEA's goal is to provide as long a time series as possible for the restructured accounts. For some data, source material is not available until 2011, however others are available back to 1999, therefore BEA will be publishing data in different time series.

Table A-1 contains the many footnotes published by the BEA that specifically define the components of the U.S. international transactions accounts.

Data may not add to total because of rounding.

Table A-1.   International Transactions, 2005–2015

(Millions of dollars.)

Item	2005	2006	2007	2008	2009	2010
Exports of goods and services and income receipts (credits)	1,895,983	2,222,124	2,569,492	2,751,949	2,285,922	2,630,799
Exports of goods and services	1,286,022	1,457,642	1,653,548	1,841,612	1,583,053	1,853,606
Goods	913,016	1,040,905	1,165,151	1,308,795	1,070,331	1,290,273
General merchandise	906,104	1,030,589	1,150,198	1,288,516	1,055,433	1,271,966
Foods, feeds, and beverages	58,955	65,962	84,264	108,349	93,908	107,719
Industrial supplies and materials	236,812	279,120	316,284	386,917	293,540	388,561
Capital goods except automotive	358,426	404,026	433,019	457,655	391,498	447,839
Automotive vehicles, parts, and engines	98,406	107,263	121,264	121,451	81,715	112,008
Consumer goods except food and automotive	115,228	129,034	145,863	161,157	149,287	164,909
Other general merchandise	38,276	45,184	49,505	52,987	45,486	50,931
Net exports of goods under merchanting	1,330	1,499	1,547	1,465	797	411
Nonmonetary gold	5,582	8,817	13,406	18,813	14,101	17,896
Services	373,006	416,738	488,396	532,817	512,722	563,333
Maintenance and repair services n.i.e.	7,624	8,235	10,020	10,586	12,863	14,549
Transport	52,622	57,462	65,824	74,973	62,189	71,656
Travel (for all purposes including education)[1]	101,470	105,140	119,037	133,761	119,902	137,010
Insurance services	7,566	9,445	10,841	13,403	14,586	14,397
Financial services	39,878	47,882	61,376	63,027	64,437	72,348
Charges for the use of intellectual property n.i.e.	74,448	83,549	97,803	102,125	98,406	107,521
Telecommunications, computer, and information services	15,515	17,184	20,192	23,119	23,816	25,038
Other business services	58,302	68,619	82,382	92,738	95,984	101,029
Government goods and services n.i.e.	15,582	19,222	20,921	19,084	20,538	19,784
Primary income receipts	543,982	693,089	844,033	823,707	614,379	684,915
Investment income	539,186	688,020	838,814	818,342	608,639	678,984
Direct investment income	301,184	333,235	380,844	423,365	370,301	447,773
Portfolio investment income	129,691	166,146	221,610	241,329	184,417	194,852
Other investment income	107,126	187,414	234,910	152,076	53,140	35,660
Reserve asset income	1,185	1,226	1,449	1,572	781	699
Compensation of employees	4,796	5,069	5,219	5,364	5,740	5,931
Secondary income (current transfer) receipts[2]	65,980	71,393	71,912	86,630	88,491	92,278
Imports of goods and services and income payments (debits)	2,641,418	3,028,851	3,288,135	3,442,738	2,669,945	3,072,759
Imports of goods and services	2,000,267	2,219,358	2,358,922	2,550,339	1,966,827	2,348,263
Goods	1,695,820	1,878,194	1,986,347	2,141,287	1,580,025	1,938,950
General merchandise	1,691,201	1,872,316	1,977,283	2,127,790	1,569,630	1,924,446
Foods, feeds, and beverages	69,072	76,081	82,974	90,439	82,861	92,492
Industrial supplies and materials	533,686	613,242	648,412	798,796	469,641	610,268
Capital goods except automotive	382,833	422,611	449,117	458,698	374,054	450,406
Automotive vehicles, parts, and engines	238,715	255,962	258,497	233,204	159,188	225,641
Consumer goods except food and automotive	412,734	447,647	479,758	485,679	429,853	485,121
Other general merchandise	54,161	56,773	58,524	60,974	54,034	60,519
Nonmonetary gold	4,618	5,878	9,064	13,497	10,395	14,504
Services	304,448	341,165	372,575	409,052	386,801	409,313
Maintenance and repair services n.i.e.	3,015	4,583	5,209	5,742	5,938	6,909
Transport	75,643	77,962	79,326	83,988	64,133	74,628
Travel (for all purposes including education)[1]	79,988	84,206	89,235	92,545	81,421	86,623
Insurance services	28,710	39,382	47,517	58,913	63,801	61,478
Financial services	12,126	14,733	19,197	17,218	14,415	15,502
Charges for the use of intellectual property n.i.e.	25,577	25,038	26,479	29,623	31,297	32,551
Telecommunications, computer, and information services	15,975	19,776	22,384	24,655	25,784	29,015
Other business services	35,960	48,130	54,968	67,488	68,553	70,646
Government goods and services n.i.e.	27,454	27,353	28,260	28,880	31,460	31,960
Primary income payments	476,349	649,752	743,429	677,561	490,794	507,254
Investment income	460,441	633,326	727,707	660,500	476,376	493,292
Direct investment income	127,979	159,189	136,261	139,073	112,610	159,757
Portfolio investment income	238,558	304,934	381,788	400,032	332,495	313,527
Other investment income	93,904	169,203	209,658	121,395	31,271	20,008
Compensation of employees	15,909	16,426	15,722	17,061	14,418	13,962
Secondary income (current transfer) payments[2]	164,801	159,740	185,784	214,839	212,324	217,242
Capital account						
Capital transfer receipts and other credits	15,462	0	494	6,170	0	0
Capital transfer payments and other debits	2,346	1,788	110	159	140	157
Financial account						
Net U.S. acquisition of financial assets excluding financial derivatives (net increase in assets/financial outflow (+))	572,317	1,336,866	1,572,509	-309,468	132,204	963,449
Direct investment assets	61,925	296,059	532,939	351,724	313,726	354,575
Equity	51,621	266,312	431,378	360,130	262,058	343,040
Debt instruments	10,304	29,748	101,561	-8,406	51,669	11,535
Portfolio investment assets	267,290	493,366	380,807	-284,269	375,883	199,620
Equity and investment fund shares	186,684	137,331	147,782	-38,550	63,696	79,150
Debt securities	80,606	356,035	233,025	-245,720	312,186	120,469
Short term	18,822	115,742	15,190	-82,645	136,127	62,279

⁰ Transactions are possible but are zero for a given period.
(*) = Transactions between zero and +/- $500,000.
D = Suppressed to avoid disclosure of individual companies.
n.a. = Transactions are possible, but data are not available.
Quarterly estimates are not annualized and are expressed at quarterly rates.
[1] All travel purposes include 1) business travel, including expenditures by border, seasonal, and other short-term workers and 2) personal travel, including health-related and education-related travel.
[2] Secondary income (current transfer) receipts and payments include U.S. government and private transfers, such as U.S. government grants and pensions, fines and penalties, withholding taxes, personal transfers (remittances), insurance-related transfers, and other current transfers.

Table A-1.   International Transactions, 2005–2015—*Continued*

(Millions of dollars.)

Item	2011	2012	2013	2014	2015	2005-2015 Average Annual Percent
Exports of goods and services and income receipts (credits)	2,987,571	3,098,059	3,201,282	3,306,574	3,138,696	3.4
Exports of goods and services	2,127,021	2,218,989	2,279,937	2,343,205	2,223,618	3.7
Goods	1,499,240	1,562,578	1,592,043	1,632,639	1,513,453	3.4
General merchandise	1,463,990	1,524,738	1,557,698	1,609,715	1,491,817	3.4
Foods, feeds, and beverages	126,247	133,049	136,160	143,751	127,704	5.3
Industrial supplies and materials	485,258	483,232	492,296	500,007	419,378	3.9
Capital goods except automotive	494,202	527,459	534,524	551,321	538,603	2.8
Automotive vehicles, parts, and engines	133,036	146,158	152,670	159,690	151,563	2.9
Consumer goods except food and automotive	174,719	180,994	188,370	198,300	197,387	3.7
Other general merchandise	50,529	53,846	53,678	56,646	57,182	2.7
Net exports of goods under merchanting	511	552	462	296	252	-10.5
Nonmonetary gold	34,739	37,289	33,883	22,628	21,385	9.4
Services	627,781	656,411	687,894	710,565	710,165	4.4
Maintenance and repair services n.i.e.	16,436	17,186	18,648	22,389	24,123	8.0
Transport	79,830	83,944	87,415	90,031	84,225	3.2
Travel (for all purposes including education)[1]	150,867	161,632	172,901	177,241	178,297	3.8
Insurance services	15,114	16,790	17,058	17,417	18,665	6.2
Financial services	78,271	76,692	84,091	87,290	86,286	5.3
Charges for the use of intellectual property n.i.e.	123,333	124,440	127,927	130,362	126,210	3.6
Telecommunications, computer, and information services	29,171	32,510	35,035	35,885	36,989	6.0
Other business services	112,568	120,382	121,873	129,514	135,260	5.8
Government goods and services n.i.e.	22,191	22,835	22,946	20,438	20,110	1.7
Primary income receipts	759,727	769,479	794,763	823,353	783,077	2.5
Investment income	753,622	763,177	788,007	816,445	775,989	2.5
Direct investment income	477,415	466,330	478,051	476,617	423,504	2.3
Portfolio investment income	237,343	260,429	278,439	308,205	319,157	6.2
Other investment income	38,018	35,944	31,144	31,321	33,114	-7.5
Reserve asset income	846	474	374	301	214	-10.8
Compensation of employees	6,105	6,302	6,756	6,909	7,088	2.6
Secondary income (current transfer) receipts[2]	100,822	109,590	126,582	140,016	132,001	4.7
Imports of goods and services and income payments (debits)	3,447,924	3,547,729	3,578,042	3,696,100	3,622,774	2.1
Imports of goods and services	2,675,646	2,755,762	2,758,331	2,851,529	2,763,374	2.2
Goods	2,239,886	2,303,749	2,294,630	2,374,101	2,272,760	2.0
General merchandise	2,221,911	2,284,535	2,276,882	2,358,653	2,260,172	2.0
Foods, feeds, and beverages	108,257	111,127	116,004	126,683	128,916	4.2
Industrial supplies and materials	765,553	734,803	686,692	672,611	492,287	-0.5
Capital goods except automotive	513,430	551,777	557,893	595,732	605,909	3.1
Automotive vehicles, parts, and engines	255,226	298,498	309,572	328,499	350,189	2.6
Consumer goods except food and automotive	515,868	518,821	533,957	559,392	598,157	2.5
Other general merchandise	63,578	69,508	72,764	75,736	84,714	3.0
Nonmonetary gold	17,975	19,214	17,748	15,448	12,589	6.9
Services	435,761	452,013	463,700	477,428	490,613	3.2
Maintenance and repair services n.i.e.	8,236	8,015	7,486	7,468	9,251	7.8
Transport	81,377	84,985	90,634	94,219	96,893	1.7
Travel (for all purposes including education)[1]	89,700	100,338	104,107	110,787	120,471	2.8
Insurance services	55,654	55,513	53,420	50,096	48,331	3.5
Financial services	17,368	16,703	18,519	19,503	20,134	3.4
Charges for the use of intellectual property n.i.e.	36,087	38,661	38,999	42,124	39,157	2.9
Telecommunications, computer, and information services	32,756	32,779	33,812	33,314	33,155	5.0
Other business services	83,289	87,157	91,389	95,752	101,716	7.2
Government goods and services n.i.e.	31,293	27,861	25,334	24,163	21,505	-1.6
Primary income payments	538,766	557,301	570,220	585,369	591,753	1.5
Investment income	524,582	542,356	554,392	569,031	574,498	1.5
Direct investment income	178,862	176,081	176,347	176,152	153,274	1.2
Portfolio investment income	324,944	345,249	361,750	378,705	405,468	3.6
Other investment income	20,776	21,026	16,295	14,174	15,757	-11.2
Compensation of employees	14,184	14,946	15,828	16,339	17,255	0.5
Secondary income (current transfer) payments[2]	233,512	234,665	249,492	259,202	267,647	3.3
Capital account						
Capital transfer receipts and other credits	0	7,668	0	0	0	-100.0
Capital transfer payments and other debits	1,186	764	412	45	45	-23.2
Financial account						
Net U.S. acquisition of financial assets excluding financial derivatives (net increase in assets/financial outflow (+))	496,320	167,398	643,915	792,145	242,234	-5.6
Direct investment assets	440,405	377,899	399,203	357,190	345,115	12.1
Equity	401,533	322,558	336,930	355,622	312,849	12.8
Debt instruments	38,872	55,341	62,273	1,568	32,266	7.9
Portfolio investment assets	85,365	238,763	476,237	538,058	186,344	-2.4
Equity and investment fund shares	6,950	95,755	284,303	436,526	172,524	-0.5
Debt securities	78,415	143,008	191,935	101,531	13,820	-11.1
Short term	-51,256	-6,611	47,020	15,299	67,254	8.9

° Transactions are possible but are zero for a given period.
(*) = Transactions between zero and +/- $500,000.
D = Suppressed to avoid disclosure of individual companies.
n.a. = Transactions are possible, but data are not available.
Quarterly estimates are not annualized and are expressed at quarterly rates.
[1] All travel purposes include 1) business travel, including expenditures by border, seasonal, and other short-term workers and 2) personal travel, including health-related and education-related travel.
[2] Secondary income (current transfer) receipts and payments include U.S. government and private transfers, such as U.S. government grants and pensions, fines and penalties, withholding taxes, personal transfers (remittances), insurance-related transfers, and other current transfers.

Table A-1. International Transactions, 2005–2015—*Continued*

(Millions of dollars.)

Item	2005	2006	2007	2008	2009	2010
Long term	61,784	240,293	217,835	-163,075	176,059	58,190
Other investment assets	257,196	549,814	658,641	-381,770	-609,662	407,420
Currency and deposits	82,879	154,026	375,146	123,493	-394,461	150,249
Loans	173,031	392,255	272,812	-501,550	-215,735	251,128
Insurance technical reserves	n.a.	n.a.	n.a.	n.a.	n.a.	n.a.
Trade credit and advances	1,286	3,534	10,683	-3,712	535	6,043
Reserve assets	-14,094	-2,373	122	4,848	52,256	1,835
Monetary gold	0	0	0	0	0	0
Special drawing rights	-4,511	223	154	106	48,230	31
Reserve position in the International Monetary Fund	-10,200	-3,331	-1,021	3,473	3,357	1,293
Other reserve assets	617	735	989	1,269	669	511
Currency and deposits	224	309	517	587	138	55
Securities	309	308	288	443	480	439
Financial derivatives	0	0	0	0	0	0
Other claims	84	118	184	239	51	17
Net U.S. incurrence of liabilities excluding financial derivatives (net increase in liabilities/financial inflow (+))	1,273,038	2,116,304	2,183,538	454,051	318,350	1,386,345
Direct investment liabilities	138,328	294,289	340,066	332,734	153,787	259,345
Equity	112,459	184,143	190,418	294,861	148,465	203,148
Debt instruments	25,869	110,146	149,648	37,874	5,322	56,197
Portfolio investment liabilities	832,037	1,126,735	1,156,612	523,683	357,352	820,434
Equity and investment fund shares	89,258	145,481	275,617	126,804	219,302	178,952
Debt securities	742,779	981,254	880,995	396,879	138,050	641,481
Short term	-45,310	22,756	158,983	287,226	-124,007	-53,031
Long term	788,088	958,498	722,012	109,652	262,056	694,513
Other investment liabilities	302,673	695,280	686,860	-402,367	-192,789	306,566
Currency and deposits	-124,782	224,386	239,302	74,441	-74,225	115,678
Loans	415,824	465,221	426,981	-483,554	-172,464	172,256
Insurance technical reserves	n.a.	n.a.	n.a.	n.a.	n.a.	n.a.
Trade credit and advances	11,632	5,673	20,576	6,746	6,301	18,632
Special drawing rights allocations	0	0	0	0	47,598	0
Financial derivatives other than reserves, net transactions[3]	n.a.	-29,710	-6,222	32,947	-44,816	-14,076
Statistical discrepancy						
Statistical discrepancy[4]	31,597	-634	101,008	-45,793	153,201	5,146
Of which: Seasonal adjustment discrepancy	.....	.....	.....	.....	.....	.....
Balances						
Balance on current account (line 1 less line 31)[5]	-745,434	-806,726	-718,643	-690,789	-384,023	-441,961
Balance on goods and services (line 2 less line 32)	-714,245	-761,716	-705,375	-708,726	-383,774	-494,658
Balance on goods (line 3 less line 33)	-782,804	-837,289	-821,196	-832,492	-509,694	-648,678
Balance on services (line 13 less line 42)	68,558	75,573	115,821	123,765	125,920	154,020
Balance on primary income (line 23 less line 52)	67,632	43,337	100,604	146,146	123,584	177,661
Balance on secondary income (line 30 less line 58)	-98,822	-88,347	-113,872	-128,209	-123,833	-124,964
Balance on capital account (line 59 less line 60)[5]	13,116	-1,788	384	6,010	-140	-157
Net lending (+) or net borrowing (-) from current- and capital-account transactions (line 101 plus line 107)[6]	-732,319	-808,514	-718,260	-684,779	-384,163	-442,118
Net lending (+) or net borrowing (-) from financial-account transactions (line 61 less line 84 plus line 99)[6]	-700,721	-809,148	-617,251	-730,572	-230,962	-436,972

[0] Transactions are possible but are zero for a given period.
(*) = Transactions between zero and +/- $500,000.
D = Suppressed to avoid disclosure of individual companies.
n.a. = Transactions are possible, but data are not available.
..... = Not applicable, or for data periods 1960-1997, transactions that are 0, not available, or not applicable.
Quarterly estimates are not annualized and are expressed at quarterly rates.
[3] Transactions for financial derivatives are only available as a net value equal to transactions for assets less transactions for liabilities. A positive value represents net U.S. cash payments arising from derivatives contracts, and a negative value represents net U.S. cash receipts.
[4] The statistical discrepancy, which can be calculated as line 109 less line 100, is the difference between total debits and total credits recorded in the current, capital, and financial accounts. In the current and capital accounts, credits and debits are labeled in the table. In the financial account, an acquisition of an asset or a repayment of a liability is a debit, and an incurrence of a liability or a disposal of an asset is a credit.
[5] Current- and capital-account statistics in the international transactions accounts differ slightly from statistics in the National Income and Product Accounts (NIPAs) because of adjustments made to convert the international transactions statistics to national economic accounting concepts. A reconciliation between annual statistics in the two sets of accounts appears in NIPA "http://www.bea.gov/iTable/iTableHtml.cfm?reqid=9&step=3&isuri=1&903=136">table 4.3B.
[6] Net lending means that U.S. residents are net suppliers of funds to foreign residents, and net borrowing means the opposite. Net lending or net borrowing can be computed from current- and capital-account transactions or from financial-account transactions. The two amounts differ by the statistical discrepancy.

Table A-1.   International Transactions, 2005–2015—*Continued*

(Millions of dollars.)

Item	2011	2012	2013	2014	2015	2005-2015 Average Annual Percent
Long term	129,671	149,620	144,914	86,232	-53,434	-199.0
Other investment assets	-45,327	-453,724	-228,426	-99,520	-282,933	-200.6
Currency and deposits	-89,161	-519,346	-121,540	-147,354	-207,783	-206.3
Loans	39,821	64,933	-116,691	54,595	-73,189	-194.4
Insurance technical reserves	n.a.	n.a.	n.a.	n.a.	n.a.	
Trade credit and advances	4,013	689	9,805	-6,761	-1,962	-202.9
Reserve assets	15,877	4,460	-3,099	-3,583	-6,292	-5.2
Monetary gold	0	0	0	0	0	
Special drawing rights	-1,752	37	22	23	9	-166.1
Reserve position in the International Monetary Fund	18,079	4,032	-3,438	-3,849	-6,485	-3.0
Other reserve assets	-450	391	317	243	185	-7.7
Currency and deposits	110	24	3	5	-20	-185.1
Securities	-598	365	313	234	205	-2.7
Financial derivatives	0	0	0	0	0	
Other claims	39	3	1	4	0	-100.0
Net U.S. incurrence of liabilities excluding financial derivatives (net increase in liabilities / financial inflow (+))	977,073	615,711	1,041,959	977,421	426,036	-7.0
Direct investment liabilities	257,411	232,001	287,163	131,831	409,872	7.5
Equity	185,051	193,797	211,762	68,854	302,908	6.8
Debt instruments	72,361	38,204	75,401	62,977	106,965	9.9
Portfolio investment liabilities	311,626	746,988	501,975	705,030	263,360	-7.4
Equity and investment fund shares	123,357	239,065	-67,486	155,077	-171,253	-204.4
Debt securities	188,269	507,923	569,461	549,953	434,613	-3.5
Short term	-86,722	16,266	45,374	22,935	44,308	-199.9
Long term	274,991	491,658	524,087	527,019	390,305	-4.6
Other investment liabilities	408,036	-363,278	252,821	140,559	-247,197	-198.7
Currency and deposits	475,678	-245,669	201,981	51,031	36,752	-192.2
Loans	-84,789	-129,242	38,503	75,265	-293,883	-197.7
Insurance technical reserves	n.a.	n.a.	n.a.	n.a.	n.a.	
Trade credit and advances	17,147	11,633	12,337	14,263	9,934	
Special drawing rights allocations	0	0	0	0	0	
Financial derivatives other than reserves, net transactions[3]	-35,006	7,064	2,213	-54,372	-25,401	
Statistical discrepancy						
Statistical discrepancy[4]	-54,219	1,516	-18,658	149,923	274,920	15.5
Of which: Seasonal adjustment discrepancy	.....	.....	.....	.....	.....	
Balances						
Balance on current account (line 1 less line 31)[5]	-460,354	-449,670	-376,760	-389,526	-484,078	-2.8
Balance on goods and services (line 2 less line 32)	-548,625	-536,773	-478,394	-508,324	-539,756	-1.9
Balance on goods (line 3 less line 33)	-740,646	-741,171	-702,587	-741,462	-759,307	-0.2
Balance on services (line 13 less line 42)	192,020	204,398	224,193	233,138	219,551	8.1
Balance on primary income (line 23 less line 52)	220,961	212,178	224,543	237,984	191,323	7.2
Balance on secondary income (line 30 less line 58)	-132,690	-125,075	-122,910	-119,185	-135,645	2.1
Balance on capital account (line 59 less line 60)[5]	-1,186	6,904	-412	-45	-45	-168.5
Net lending (+) or net borrowing (-) from current- and capital-account transactions (line 101 plus line 107)[6]	-461,540	-442,765	-377,172	-389,571	-484,123	-2.7
Net lending (+) or net borrowing (-) from financial-account transactions (line 61 less line 84 plus line 99)[6]	-515,759	-441,249	-395,831	-239,648	-209,203	-7.7

[0] Transactions are possible but are zero for a given period.
(*) = Transactions between zero and +/- $500,000.
D = Suppressed to avoid disclosure of individual companies.
n.a. = Transactions are possible, but data are not available.
..... = Not applicable, or for data periods 1960-1997, transactions that are 0, not available, or not applicable.
Quarterly estimates are not annualized and are expressed at quarterly rates.
[3] Transactions for financial derivatives are only available as a net value equal to transactions for assets less transactions for liabilities. A positive value represents net U.S. cash payments arising from derivatives contracts, and a negative value represents net U.S. cash receipts.
[4] The statistical discrepancy, which can be calculated as line 109 less line 108, is the difference between total debits and total credits recorded in the current, capital, and financial accounts. In the current and capital accounts, credits and debits are labeled in the table. In the financial account, an acquisition of an asset or a repayment of a liability is a debit, and an incurrence of a liability or a disposal of an asset is a credit.
[5] Current- and capital-account statistics in the international transactions accounts differ slightly from statistics in the National Income and Product Accounts (NIPAs) because of adjustments made to convert the international transactions statistics to national economic accounting concepts. A reconciliation between annual statistics in the two sets of accounts appears in NIPA "http://www.bea.gov/iTable/iTableHtml.cfm?reqid=9&step=3&isuri=1&903=136">table 4.3B.
[6] Net lending means that U.S. residents are net suppliers of funds to foreign residents, and net borrowing means the opposite. Net lending or net borrowing can be computed from current- and capital-account transactions or from financial-account transactions. The two amounts differ by the statistical discrepancy.

Table A-2.   U.S. Net International Investment Position, 2005–2015

(Millions of dollars.)

Type of investment	2005	2006	2007	2008	2009
U.S. net international investment position (line 4 less line 35)	-1,857,865	-1,808,474	-1,279,493	-3,995,303	-2,627,626
Net international investment position excluding financial derivatives (line 5 less line 36)	-1,915,780	-1,868,310	-1,350,965	-4,154,938	-2,753,961
Financial derivatives other than reserves, net (line 6 less line 37)	57,915	59,836	71,472	159,635	126,335
U.S. assets	13,357,001	16,409,857	20,704,503	19,423,416	19,426,459
Assets excluding financial derivatives (sum of lines 7, 10, 21, and 26)	12,166,972	15,170,862	18,145,171	13,295,966	15,936,680
Financial derivatives other than reserves, gross positive fair value (line 15)	1,190,029	1,238,995	2,559,332	6,127,450	3,489,779
By functional category:					
Direct investment at market value	4,047,170	4,929,892	5,857,923	3,707,211	4,945,292
Equity	3,449,302	4,294,301	5,090,968	2,928,147	4,097,179
Debt instruments	597,868	635,591	766,955	779,064	848,113
Portfolio investment	4,628,978	6,017,080	7,262,045	4,320,819	6,058,554
Equity and investment fund shares	3,317,705	4,328,960	5,247,990	2,748,428	3,995,295
Debt securities	1,311,273	1,688,120	2,014,055	1,572,391	2,063,259
Short term	274,002	388,839	383,890	314,103	437,491
Long term	1,037,271	1,299,281	1,630,165	1,258,288	1,625,768
Financial derivatives other than reserves, gross positive fair value	1,190,029	1,238,995	2,559,332	6,127,450	3,489,779
Over-the-counter contracts	1,171,172	1,213,354	2,526,075	6,065,174	3,460,696
Single-currency interest rate contracts	853,993	793,057	1,463,086	4,053,356	2,596,825
Foreign exchange contracts	147,057	176,267	290,943	497,234	277,387
Other contracts	170,122	244,030	772,046	1,514,584	586,484
Exchange-traded contracts	18,857	25,641	33,257	62,276	29,083
Other investment	3,302,781	4,004,037	4,747,993	4,974,204	4,529,030
Currency and deposits	1,661,683	1,960,739	2,316,936	2,813,073	2,539,562
Loans	1,607,542	2,005,912	2,382,672	2,116,729	1,944,389
Trade credit and advances	33,556	37,386	48,385	44,402	45,079
Reserve assets	188,043	219,853	277,211	293,732	403,804
Monetary gold	134,175	165,267	218,025	227,439	284,380
Special drawing rights	8,210	8,870	9,476	9,340	57,814
Reserve position in the International Monetary Fund	8,036	5,040	4,244	7,683	11,385
Other reserve assets	37,622	40,676	45,466	49,270	50,225
Currency and deposits	16,036	17,614	19,886	18,025	21,562
Securities	17,732	18,637	20,487	23,095	23,482
Other claims	3,854	4,425	5,093	8,150	5,181
U.S. liabilities	15,214,866	18,218,331	21,983,996	23,418,718	22,054,085
Liabilities excluding financial derivatives (sum of lines 38, 41, and 56)	14,082,752	17,039,172	19,496,136	17,450,903	18,690,641
Financial derivatives other than reserves, gross negative fair value (line 50)	1,132,114	1,179,159	2,487,860	5,967,815	3,363,444
By functional category:					
Direct investment at market value	3,227,144	3,752,602	4,134,239	3,091,240	3,618,630
Equity	2,483,696	2,895,531	3,097,513	2,000,508	2,513,901
Debt instruments	743,448	857,071	1,036,726	1,090,732	1,104,729
Portfolio investment	7,337,835	8,843,523	10,326,974	9,475,873	10,463,234
Equity and investment fund shares	2,304,013	2,791,893	3,231,651	2,132,433	2,917,681
Debt securities	5,033,822	6,051,630	7,095,323	7,343,440	7,545,553
Short term	588,894	621,409	800,047	1,099,788	977,437
Treasury bills and certificates	264,728	253,331	302,698	758,010	750,437
Other short-term securities	324,166	368,078	497,349	341,778	227,000
Long term	4,444,928	5,430,221	6,295,276	6,243,652	6,568,116
Treasury bonds and notes	1,719,663	1,872,847	2,073,744	2,494,964	2,920,160
Other long-term securities	2,725,265	3,557,374	4,221,532	3,748,688	3,647,956
Financial derivatives other than reserves, gross negative fair value	1,132,114	1,179,159	2,487,860	5,967,815	3,363,444
Over-the-counter contracts	1,116,479	1,156,241	2,456,093	5,904,724	3,333,846
Single-currency interest rate contracts	815,068	749,009	1,434,083	3,977,190	2,532,612
Foreign exchange contracts	132,101	151,046	240,138	481,833	245,230
Other contracts	169,310	256,186	781,872	1,445,701	556,004
Exchange-traded contracts	15,635	22,918	31,767	63,091	29,598
Other investment	3,517,773	4,443,047	5,034,923	4,883,790	4,608,777
Currency and deposits	1,437,342	1,764,543	2,020,793	2,331,692	2,248,451
Loans	2,020,101	2,611,946	2,926,354	2,458,056	2,211,894
Trade credit and advances	53,327	59,187	80,034	86,495	93,068
Special drawing rights allocations	7,003	7,371	7,742	7,547	55,364

Table A-2.   U.S. Net International Investment Position, 2005–2015—*Continued*

(Millions of dollars.)

Type of investment	2010	2011	2012	2013	2014	2015
U.S. net international investment position (line 4 less line 35)	-2,511,788	-4,454,997	-4,518,300	-5,372,654	-7,046,149	-7,280,637
Net international investment position excluding financial derivatives (line 5 less line 36)	-2,622,170	-4,541,036	-4,576,076	-5,450,211	-7,131,655	-7,337,870
Financial derivatives other than reserves, net (line 6 less line 37)	110,382	86,039	57,776	77,557	85,506	57,233
U.S. assets	21,767,827	22,208,896	22,562,162	24,144,775	24,717,536	23,340,771
Assets excluding financial derivatives (sum of lines 7, 10, 21, and 26)	18,115,514	17,492,318	18,942,401	21,127,675	21,503,427	20,945,418
Financial derivatives other than reserves, gross positive fair value (line 15)	3,652,313	4,716,578	3,619,761	3,017,100	3,214,109	2,395,353
By functional category:						
Direct investment at market value	5,486,391	5,214,826	5,969,502	7,120,688	7,133,132	6,978,349
Equity	4,620,850	4,320,052	4,983,895	6,054,227	6,045,074	5,811,120
Debt instruments	865,541	894,774	985,607	1,066,461	1,088,058	1,167,229
Portfolio investment	7,160,366	6,871,732	7,983,961	9,206,105	9,704,259	9,606,176
Equity and investment fund shares	4,900,246	4,501,438	5,321,857	6,472,877	6,770,629	6,828,231
Debt securities	2,260,120	2,370,294	2,662,104	2,733,228	2,933,630	2,777,945
Short term	472,810	416,631	414,909	449,683	447,190	486,243
Long term	1,787,310	1,953,663	2,247,195	2,283,544	2,486,440	2,291,702
Financial derivatives other than reserves, gross positive fair value	3,652,313	4,716,578	3,619,761	3,017,100	3,214,109	2,395,353
Over-the-counter contracts	3,621,801	4,668,527	3,585,781	2,980,312	3,143,987	2,346,708
Single-currency interest rate contracts	2,844,526	3,861,581	2,973,245	2,388,410	2,451,091	1,807,354
Foreign exchange contracts	330,298	323,413	280,217	307,972	415,446	342,289
Other contracts	446,977	483,533	332,319	283,930	277,450	197,065
Exchange-traded contracts	30,512	48,051	33,980	36,788	70,122	48,645
Other investment	4,980,084	4,868,723	4,416,570	4,352,549	4,231,785	3,977,292
Currency and deposits	2,767,247	2,581,531	2,061,681	1,975,717	1,785,516	1,628,574
Loans	2,161,759	2,232,094	2,299,165	2,323,462	2,399,237	2,303,984
Trade credit and advances	51,078	55,098	55,724	53,370	47,032	44,734
Reserve assets	488,673	537,037	572,368	448,333	434,251	383,601
Monetary gold	367,537	400,355	433,434	314,975	315,368	277,189
Special drawing rights	56,824	54,956	55,050	55,184	51,941	49,688
Reserve position in the International Monetary Fund	12,492	30,080	34,161	30,750	25,164	17,609
Other reserve assets	51,820	51,646	49,723	47,424	41,778	39,115
Currency and deposits	21,847	26,673	24,934	20,889	19,003	17,555
Securities	25,039	24,973	23,471	21,436	22,775	21,560
Other claims	4,934	0	1,318	5,099	0	0
U.S. liabilities	24,279,615	26,663,893	27,080,461	29,517,429	31,763,685	30,621,408
Liabilities excluding financial derivatives (sum of lines 38, 41, and 56)	20,737,684	22,033,354	23,518,476	26,577,886	28,635,082	28,283,288
Financial derivatives other than reserves, gross negative fair value (line 50)	3,541,931	4,630,539	3,561,985	2,939,543	3,128,603	2,338,120
By functional category:						
Direct investment at market value	4,099,097	4,199,225	4,662,434	5,814,935	6,350,052	6,543,809
Equity	2,927,753	2,968,362	3,415,843	4,443,216	4,884,081	4,979,264
Debt instruments	1,171,344	1,230,863	1,246,591	1,371,719	1,465,971	1,564,545
Portfolio investment	11,869,262	12,647,243	13,978,865	15,541,251	16,919,795	16,676,993
Equity and investment fund shares	3,545,769	3,841,901	4,545,361	5,864,600	6,642,507	6,218,865
Debt securities	8,323,493	8,805,342	9,433,504	9,676,651	10,277,288	10,458,128
Short term	919,271	830,725	844,743	891,646	911,791	955,166
Treasury bills and certificates	710,280	647,673	661,654	685,527	671,636	724,705
Other short-term securities	208,991	183,052	183,089	206,119	240,155	230,461
Long term	7,404,223	7,974,617	8,588,761	8,785,005	9,365,497	9,502,962
Treasury bonds and notes	3,748,544	4,356,681	4,909,828	5,107,089	5,484,398	5,423,369
Other long-term securities	3,655,679	3,617,936	3,678,933	3,677,916	3,881,099	4,079,593
Financial derivatives other than reserves, gross negative fair value	3,541,931	4,630,539	3,561,985	2,939,543	3,128,603	2,338,120
Over-the-counter contracts	3,512,342	4,581,255	3,527,668	2,903,000	3,062,604	2,291,128
Single-currency interest rate contracts	2,787,529	3,799,720	2,912,113	2,319,871	2,398,776	1,755,400
Foreign exchange contracts	304,088	330,141	295,181	306,521	393,617	344,038
Other contracts	420,725	451,394	320,374	276,608	270,211	191,690
Exchange-traded contracts	29,589	49,284	34,317	36,543	65,999	46,992
Other investment	4,769,325	5,186,886	4,877,177	5,221,699	5,365,235	5,062,486
Currency and deposits	2,364,754	2,838,712	2,601,672	2,674,496	2,886,739	2,914,267
Loans	2,238,430	2,165,106	2,080,724	2,344,810	2,265,606	1,923,642
Trade credit and advances	111,754	128,849	140,504	148,007	161,724	175,639
Special drawing rights allocations	54,387	54,219	54,277	54,386	51,166	48,938

Table A-3A.   First Year Expenditures for New Foreign Direct Investment in the United States, 2005–2015

(Millions of dollars.)

Item	2005	2006	2007	2008	2009-2013	2014	2015
Total Expenditures	91,390	165,603	251,917	260,362	...	250,581	420691
By type of investment:							
Acquisitions	73,997	148,604	223,616	242,799	...	235,799	408056
Establishments...........................	17,393	16,999	28,301	17,564	...	12,473	11,249
Expansions................................	...	...	...	...	...	2,309	1387

Note: Data on expansions started in 2014. First year expenditures include expenditures in the year in which the transaction occurred.
... = Data may not be shown for several reasons:
  • The data appear on another line in this table.
  • The data are not shown in this table but may be available in detailed country- or industry-level tables in this interactive system or in other BEA published tables on direct investment.
  • The data are not available, do not apply, or are not defined.

Table A-3B. First Year Expenditures and Planned Total Expenditures for Investments Initiated in 2015, Industry of Affiliate by Type of Investment

[Millions of dollars.]

Industry	First year expenditures[1]				Planned total expenditures[2]			
		By type of investment				By type of investment		
	Total	U.S. businesses acquired	U.S. businesses established	U.S. businesses expanded	Total	U.S. businesses acquired	U.S. businesses established	U.S. businesses expanded
All Industries	420,691	408,056	11,249	1,387	439,209	408,056	24,509	6,644
Manufacturing	281,410	280,234	458	718	287,294	280,234	1,843	5,218
Food	3,160	3,089	(D)	(D)	(D)	3,089	(D)	(D)
Beverages and tobacco products	673	(D)	1	(D)	673	(D)	1	(D)
Paper	436	(D)	(D)	78	(D)	(D)	(D)	(D)
Petroleum and coal products	0	0	0	0	0	0	0	0
Chemicals	150,288	149,884	107	298	154,400	149,884	538	3,978
Basic chemicals	(D)	(D)	3	274	(D)	(D)	(D)	(D)
Pharmaceuticals and medicines	122,060	122,043	(D)	(D)	(D)	122,043	(D)	(D)
Other	(D)	(D)	(D)	(D)	(D)	(D)	(D)	(D)
Plastics and rubber products	3,811	3,566	(D)	(D)	3,896	3,566	(D)	(D)
Nonmetallic mineral products	(D)	(D)	(D)	0	(D)	(D)	(D)	0
Primary and fabricated metals	4,735	4,713	(D)	(D)	(D)	4,713	(D)	(D)
Primary metals	4,614	(D)	5	(D)	(D)	(D)	(D)	7
Fabricated metal products	121	(D)	(D)	(D)	(D)	(D)	(D)	(D)
Machinery	(D)	(D)	5	26	(D)	(D)	5	27
Computers and electronic products	5,461	5,452	(*)	8	5,461	5,452	(*)	8
Semiconductors and other electronic components	(D)	(D)	(*)	1	(D)	(D)	(*)	1
Navigational, measuring, and other instruments	(D)	(D)	(*)	0	(D)	(D)	(*)	0
Other	1,000	993	(*)	7	1,000	993	(*)	7
Electrical equipment, appliances, and components	3,180	3,176	(D)	(D)	(D)	3,176	(D)	(D)
Transportation equipment	(D)	(D)	37	130	14,370	(D)	(D)	381
Motor vehicles, bodies and trailers, and parts	(D)	(D)	(D)	(D)	(D)	(D)	(D)	(D)
Other	656	633	(D)	(D)	(D)	633	(D)	(D)
Other	(D)	(D)	73	32	(D)	(D)	137	139
Wholesale trade	2,009	1,825	96	88	2,170	1,825	(D)	(D)
Motor vehicles and motor vehicle parts and supplies	(D)	(D)	12	6	(D)	(D)	12	9
Electrical goods	27	(D)	(D)	(*)	27	(D)	(D)	(*)
Petroleum and petroleum products	3	0	(*)	3	4	0	(*)	4
Other	(D)	(D)	(D)	78	(D)	(D)	(D)	(D)
Retail trade	10,687	10,618	69	(*)	10,687	10,618	69	(*)
Food and beverage stores	(D)	(D)	1	0	(D)	(D)	1	0
Other	(D)	(D)	68	(*)	(D)	(D)	68	(*)
Information	11,258	10,969	215	74	11,592	10,969	(D)	(D)
Publishing industries	6,042	6,031	(D)	(D)	(D)	6,031	(D)	(D)
Telecommunications	774	(D)	(D)	0	774	(D)	(D)	0
Other	4,442	(D)	(D)	(D)	(D)	(D)	(D)	(D)
Finance and insurance	44,420	41,811	2,598	11	44,668	41,811	2,842	14
Depository credit intermediation (banking)	(D)	(D)	6	3	(D)	(D)	6	4
Finance, except depository institutions	23,203	(D)	(D)	3	23,447	(D)	(D)	3
Insurance carriers and related activities	(D)	14,726	(D)	5	(D)	14,726	(D)	7
Real estate and rental and leasing	34,043	27,877	6,050	116	43,063	27,877	(D)	(D)
Real estate	(D)	(D)	(D)	(D)	(D)	(D)	(D)	(D)
Rental and leasing (except real estate)	(D)	(D)	(D)	(D)	(D)	(D)	(D)	(D)
Professional, scientific, and technical services	20,350	20,287	50	13	20,414	20,287	(D)	(D)
Architectural, engineering, and related services	397	394	3	0	397	394	3	0
Computer systems design and related services	10,696	10,678	14	4	10,696	10,678	14	4
Management, scientific, and technical consulting	(D)	(D)	2	0	903	(D)	(D)	0
Other	(D)	(D)	32	9	8,418	(D)	(D)	(D)
Other industries	16,515	14,435	1,713	367	19,322	14,435	(D)	(D)
Mining	312	(D)	13	(D)	(D)	(D)	(D)	(D)
Utilities	2,674	2,220	(D)	(D)	3,063	2,220	165	678
Construction	274	264	10	0	278	264	14	0
Transportation and warehousing	1,954	1,906	22	26	1,954	1,906	22	26
Administration, support, and waste management	2,753	2,736	9	9	2,757	2,736	(D)	(D)
Health care and social assistance	1,794	(D)	4	(D)	(D)	(D)	(D)	(D)
Accommodation and food services	1,613	(D)	43	(D)	(D)	(D)	(D)	(D)
Other	5,140	3,656	(D)	(D)	6,136	3,656	2,441	40

* = Less than +/- $500,000.
D = Suppressed to avoid disclosure of data on individual companies.
[1]First year expenditures include expenditures in the year in which the transaction occurred.
[2]Planned total expenditures include first year expenditures for all investments plus planned future expenditures (and expenditures from past years, if any) for establishments and expansions that are multiyear investments. For acquired U.S. businesses, first year expenditures and planned total expenditures are the same.

Table A-3C.   First Year Expenditures and Planned Total Expenditures for Investments Initiated in 2015, Country of UBO[1] by Type of Investment

(Millions of dollars.)

Country	First year expenditures[2] Total	By type of investment U.S. businesses acquired	U.S. businesses established	U.S. businesses expanded	Planned total expenditures[3] Total	By type of investment U.S. businesses acquired	U.S. businesses established	U.S. businesses expanded
All Countries...	420,691	408,056	11,249	1,387	439,209	408,056	24,509	6,644
Canada	84,938	83,692	933	313	89,754	83,692	5,409	653
Europe	284,807	279,274	4,987	546	288,100	279,274	7,661	1,165
Belgium...	(D)	(D)	1	6	(D)	(D)	1	(D)
Denmark...	154	154	1	0	154	154	1	0
Finland...	9	(D)	(D)	0	9	(D)	(D)	0
France..	12,744	12,652	44	48	(D)	12,652	44	(D)
Germany...	47,000	45,522	1,422	56	47,172	45,522	1,491	159
Ireland..	176,480	176,401	80	0	176,480	176,401	80	0
Italy...	(D)	(D)	131	(D)	6,799	(D)	(D)	(D)
Netherlands..	6,515	(D)	(D)	3	(D)	(D)	(D)	3
Spain...	1,104	1,090	10	4	(D)	1,090	(D)	4
Sweden..	1,296	1,290	5	(*)	1,296	1,290	5	(*)
Switzerland..	3,975	3,838	52	84	4,130	3,838	(D)	(D)
United Kingdom..	19,796	19,545	200	51	(D)	19,545	(D)	90
Other..	3,107	856	(D)	(D)	(D)	856	(D)	(D)
Latin America and Other Western Hemisphere .	3,298	3,027	241	30	3,483	3,027	(D)	(D)
South and Central America	241	122	(D)	(D)	(D)	122	(D)	133
Brazil..	117	(D)	(D)	0	234	(D)	20	(D)
Mexico..	67	1	57	9	84	1	(D)	(D)
Venezuela..	(*)	(*)	(*)	0	(*)	(*)	(*)	0
Other...	57	(D)	41	(D)	(D)	(D)	(D)	(D)
Other Western Hemisphere...........................	3,056	2,905	(D)	(D)	(D)	2,905	(D)	(D)
Bermuda..	(D)	1,108	(D)	0	(D)	1,108	(D)	0
United Kingdom Islands, Caribbean[4]...........	1,840	1,796	36	8	(D)	1,796	(D)	8
Other...	(D)	0	(D)	(D)	(D)	0	(D)	(D)
Africa	(D)	(D)	3	0	490	(D)	(D)	0
South Africa...	(D)	(D)	(D)	0	(D)	(D)	4	0
Other..	(D)	85	(D)	0	(D)	85	(D)	0
Middle East	5,858	(D)	(D)	(D)	(D)	(D)	(D)	(D)
Israel...	(D)	(D)	11	2	(D)	(D)	11	5
Saudi Arabia..	54	(D)	(*)	(D)	54	(D)	(*)	(D)
United Arab Emirates	(D)	(D)	1	(*)	(D)	(D)	1	(*)
Other..	708	(D)	(D)	(D)	(D)	(D)	(D)	(D)
Asia and Pacific	40,405	34,972	5,026	406	49,481	34,972	11,062	3,447
Australia..	(D)	(D)	69	(D)	1,830	(D)	(D)	(D)
China...	7,038	5,845	(D)	(D)	12,303	5,845	(D)	(D)
Hong Kong...	1,162	(D)	(D)	(D)	1,189	(D)	(D)	(D)
India..	585	569	(D)	(D)	(D)	569	(D)	(D)
Japan...	26,923	23,806	2,855	262	30,427	23,806	5,839	781
Korea, Republic of......................................	481	473	(D)	(D)	(D)	473	(D)	(D)
Singapore..	2,224	1,515	708	0	2,224	1,515	709	0
Taiwan...	61	59	(D)	(D)	63	59	(D)	(D)
Other..	(D)	(D)	(D)	(D)	202	(D)	(D)	(D)
United States[5]	(D)	(D)	(D)	(D)	(D)	(D)	(D)	(D)

* = Less than +/- $500,000.
D = Suppressed to avoid disclosure of data on individual companies.
[1]The Ultimate Beneficial Owner (UBO) is the entity, proceeding up the foreign ownership chain, which is not more than 50 percent owned by another entity. The UBO is the entity that ultimately owns or controls and thus ultimately derives the benefits and assumes the risks from owning or controlling an affiliate.
[2]First year expenditures include expenditures in the year in which the transaction occurred.
[3]Planned total expenditures include first year expenditures for all investments plus planned future expenditures (and expenditures from past years, if any) for establishments and expansions that are multiyear investments. For acquired U.S. businesses, first year expenditures and planned total expenditures are the same.
[4]The "United Kingdom Islands, Caribbean" consists of the British Virgin Islands, the Cayman Islands, Montserrat, and the Turks and Caicos Islands.
[5]The United States is the country of ultimate beneficial owner for businesses newly acquired, established, or expanded by foreign investors that are ultimately owned by persons located in the United States.

Table A-4.   Foreign Exchange Rates, 2005–2015

Official exchange rate (LCU per US$, period average.)

Country Name	Local Currency Unit per $dollar	2005	2006	2007	2008	2009	2010	2011	2012	2013	2014	2015
Afghanistan	afghanis (AFA) per US dollar	49.5	49.9	50.0	50.2	50.3	46.5	46.7	50.9	55.4	57.2	63
Albania	leke (ALL) per US dollar	99.9	98.1	90.4	83.9	95.0	103.9	100.9	108.2	105.7	105.5	126.6
Algeria	Algerian dinars (DZD) per US dollar	73.3	72.6	69.3	64.6	72.6	74.4	72.9	77.5	79.4	80.6	100.6
American Samoa	the US dollar is used											
Andorra	euros (EUR) per US dollar	0.8	0.8	0.7	0.7	0.7	0.8	0.7	0.8	0.8	0.8	0.89
Angola	kwanza (AOA) per US dollar	87.2	80.4	76.7	75.0	79.3	91.9	93.9	95.5	96.5	98.3	121.9
Antigua and Barbuda	East Caribbean dollars (XCD) per US dollar	2.7	2.7	2.7	2.7	2.7	2.7	2.7	2.7	2.7	2.7	2.7
Argentina	Argentine pesos (ARS) per US dollar	2.9	3.1	3.1	3.1	3.7	3.9	4.1	4.5	5.5	8.1	9.2
Armenia	drams (AMD) per US dollar	457.7	416.0	342.1	306.0	363.3	373.7	372.5	401.8	409.6	415.9	480.9
Aruba	Aruban guilders/florins per US dollar	1.8	1.8	1.8	1.8	1.8	1.8	1.8	1.8	1.8	1.8	1.8
Australia	Australian dollars (AUD) per US dollar	1.3	1.3	1.2	1.2	1.3	1.1	1.0	1.0	1.0	1.1	1.3
Austria	euros (EUR) per US dollar	0.8	0.8	0.7	0.7	0.7	0.8	0.7	0.8	0.8	0.8	0.89
Azerbaijan	Azerbaijani manats (AZN) per US dollar	0.9	0.9	0.9	0.8	0.8	0.8	0.8	0.8	0.8	0.8	1
Bahamas, The	Bahamian dollars (BSD) per US dollar	1.0	1.0	1.0	1.0	1.0	1.0	1.0	1.0	1.0	1.0	1
Bahrain	Bahraini dinars (BHD) per US dollar	0.4	0.4	0.4	0.4	0.4	0.4	0.4	0.4	0.4	0.4	0.4
Bangladesh	taka (BDT) per US dollar	64.3	68.9	68.9	68.6	69.0	69.6	74.2	81.9	78.1	77.6	77.4
Barbados	Barbadian dollar is pegged to the US dollar	2.0	2.0	2.0	2.0	2.0	2.0	2.0	2.0	2.0	2.0	2
Belarus	Belarusian rubles (BYB/BYR) per US dollar	2,153.8	2,144.6	2,146.1	2,136.4	2,793.0	2,978.5	4,974.6	8,336.9	8,880.1	10,224.1	15,713
Belgium	euros (EUR) per US dollar	0.8	0.8	0.7	0.7	0.7	0.8	0.7	0.8	0.8	0.8	0.9
Belize	Belizean dollars (BZD) per US dollar	2.0	2.0	2.0	2.0	2.0	2.0	2.0	2.0	2.0	2.0	2
Benin	Communaute Financiere Africaine francs (XOF) per US dollar	527.5	522.9	479.3	447.8	472.2	495.3	471.9	510.5	494.0	494.4	580.5
Bermuda	Bermudian dollars (BMD) per US dollar	1.0	1.0	1.0	1.0	1.0	1.0	1.0	1.0	1.0	1.0	1.0
Bhutan	ngultrum (BTN) per US dollar	44.1	45.3	41.3	43.5	48.4	45.7	46.7	53.4	58.6	61.0	63.9
Bolivia	bolivianos (BOB) per US dollar	8.1	8.0	7.9	7.2	7.0	7.0	6.9	6.9	6.9	6.9	6.9
Bosnia and Herzegovina	konvertibilna markas (BAM) per US dollar	1.6	1.6	1.4	1.3	1.4	1.5	1.4	1.5	1.5	1.5	1.8
Botswana	pulas (BWP) per US dollar	5.1	5.8	6.1	6.8	7.2	6.8	6.8	7.6	8.4	9.0	10
Brazil	reals (BRL) per US dollar	2.4	2.2	1.9	1.8	2.0	1.8	1.7	2.0	2.2	2.4	3.4
Brunei Darussalam	Bruneian dollars (BND) per US dollar	1.7	1.6	1.5	1.4	1.5	1.4	1.3	1.2	1.3	1.3	1.4
Bulgaria	leva (BGN) per US dollar	1.6	1.6	1.4	1.3	1.4	1.5	1.4	1.5	1.5	1.5	1.7
Burkina Faso	Communaute Financiere Africaine francs (XOF) per US dollar	527.5	522.9	479.3	447.8	472.2	495.3	471.9	510.5	494.0	494.4	580.5
Burundi	Burundi francs (BIF) per US dollar	1,081.6	1,028.7	1,081.9	1,185.7	1,230.2	1,230.7	1,261.1	1,442.5	1,555.1	1,546.7	1,578.2
Cabo Verde	Cabo Verdean escudos (CVE) per US dollar	88.7	87.9	80.6	75.3	79.4	83.3	79.3	85.8	83.1	83.1	97.6
Cambodia	riels (KHR) per US dollar	4,092.5	4,103.3	4,056.2	4,054.2	4,139.3	4,184.9	4,058.5	4,033.0	4,027.3	4,037.5	4,080.3
Cameroon	Cooperation Financiere en Afrique Centrale francs (XAF) per US dollar	527.5	522.9	479.3	447.8	472.2	495.3	471.9	510.5	494.0	494.4	580.5
Canada	Canadian dollars (CAD) per US dollar	1.2	1.1	1.1	1.1	1.1	1.0	1.0	1.0	1.0	1.1	1.3
Cayman Islands	Caymanian dollars (KYD) per US dollar	0.8	0.8	0.8	0.8	0.8	0.8	0.8	0.8	0.8	0.8	0.8
Central African Republic	Cooperation Financiere en Afrique Centrale francs (XAF) per US dollar	527.5	522.9	479.3	447.8	472.2	495.3	471.9	510.5	494.0	494.4	580.5
Chad	Cooperation Financiere en Afrique Centrale francs (XAF) per US dollar	527.5	522.9	479.3	447.8	472.2	495.3	471.9	510.5	494.0	494.4	580.5
Chile	Chilean pesos (CLP) per US dollar	559.8	530.3	522.5	522.5	560.9	510.2	483.7	486.5	495.3	570.3	653.6
China	Renminbi yuan (RMB) per US dollar	8.2	8.0	7.6	6.9	6.8	6.8	6.5	6.3	6.2	6.1	6.2
Colombia	Colombian pesos (COP) per US dollar	2,320.8	2,361.1	2,078.3	1,967.7	2,158.3	1,898.6	1,848.1	1,796.9	1,868.8	2,001.8	2,721.9
Comoros	Comoran francs (KMF) per US dollar	395.6	392.2	359.5	335.9	354.1	371.5	353.9	383.9	370.8	370.8	447.3
Congo, Dem. Rep.	Congolese francs (CDF) per US dollar	473.9	468.3	516.7	559.3	809.8	905.9	919.5	919.8	919.8	925.2	972
Congo, Rep.	Cooperation Financiere en Afrique Centrale francs (XAF) per US dollar	527.5	522.9	479.3	447.8	472.2	495.3	471.9	510.5	494.0	494.4	580.5
Costa Rica	Costa Rican colones (CRC) per US dollar	477.8	511.3	516.6	526.2	573.3	525.8	505.7	502.9	499.8	538.3	535
Cote d'Ivoire	Communaute Financiere Africaine francs (XOF) per US dollar	527.5	522.9	479.3	447.8	472.2	495.3	471.9	510.5	494.0	494.4	610.6
Croatia	kuna (HRK) per US dollar	5.9	5.8	5.4	4.9	5.3	5.5	5.3	5.9	5.7	5.7	6.9
Cuba	Cuban pesos (CUP) per US dollar							1.0	1.0	22.7	22.7	18.4
Curacao	Netherlands Antillean guilders (ANG) per US dollar							1.8	1.8	1.8	1.8	
Cyprus	euros (EUR) per US dollar	0.5	0.5	0.4	0.7	0.7	0.8	0.7	0.8	0.8	0.8	0.89
Czech Republic	koruny (CZK) per US dollar	24.0	22.6	20.3	17.1	19.1	19.1	17.7	19.6	19.6	20.8	24.2
Denmark	Danish kroner (DKK) per US dollar	6.0	5.9	5.4	5.1	5.4	5.6	5.4	5.8	5.6	5.6	6.6
Djibouti	Djiboutian francs (DJF) per US dollar	177.7	177.7	177.7	177.7	177.7	177.7	177.7	177.7	177.7	177.7	177.77
Dominica	East Caribbean dollars (XCD) per US dollar	2.7	2.7	2.7	2.7	2.7	2.7	2.7	2.7	2.7	2.7	2.7
Dominican Republic	Dominican pesos (DOP) per US dollar	30.5	33.3	33.3	34.9	36.1	37.3	38.2	39.3	41.8	43.6	45
Ecuador	the US dollar became Ecuador's currency in 2001											
Egypt, Arab Rep.	Egyptian pounds (EGP) per US dollar	5.8	5.7	5.6	5.4	5.5	5.6	5.9	6.1	6.9	7.1	7.7
El Salvador	the US dollar is used	8.8	8.8	8.8	8.8	8.8	8.8	8.8	8.8	8.8	8.8	8.8
Equatorial Guinea	Cooperation Financiere en Afrique Centrale francs (XAF) per US dollar	527.5	522.9	479.3	447.8	472.2	495.3	471.9	510.5	494.0	494.0	580.5
Eritrea	nakfa (ERN) per US dollar	15.4	15.4	15.4	15.4	15.4	15.4	15.4	15.4	15.4	15.4	15.4
Estonia	kroon (EEK) per US dollar	12.6	12.5	11.4	10.7	11.3	11.8		0.8		0.8	0.93
Ethiopia	birr (ETB) per US dollar							16.9	17.7	19.8	19.8	21.5
Euro Area	euros per US dollar	0.8	0.8	0.7	0.7	0.7	0.8	0.7	0.8	0.8	0.8	0.89
Falkland Islands	Falkland pounds (FKP) per US dollar	0.8	0.8	0.7	0.7	0.7	0.8	0.7	0.8	0.8	0.8	0.6
Faeroe Islands	Danish kroner (DKK) per US dollar							5.4	5.8	5.4	5.4	6.6

Table A-4. Foreign Exchange Rates, 2005–2015—*Continued*

Official exchange rate (LCU per US$, period average.)

Country Name	Local Currency Unit per $dollar	2005	2006	2007	2008	2009	2010	2011	2012	2013	2014	2015
Fiji	Fijian dollars (FJD) per US dollar	1.7	1.7	1.6	1.6	2.0	1.9	1.8	1.8	1.8	1.9	2.1
Finland	euros (EUR) per US dollar	0.8	0.8	0.7	0.7	0.7	0.8	0.7	0.8	0.8	0.8	0.89
France	euros (EUR) per US dollar	0.8	0.8	0.7	0.7	0.7	0.8	0.7	0.8	0.8	0.8	0.89
French Polynesia	Comptoirs Francais du Pacifique francs (XPF) per US dollar							85.7	90.6	85.7		
Gabon	Cooperation Financiere en Afrique Centrale francs (XAF) per US dollar	527.5	522.9	479.3	447.8	472.2	495.3	471.9	510.5	494.0	494.4	596.3
Gambia, The	dalasis (GMD) per US dollar	28.6	28.1	24.9	22.2	26.6	28.0	29.5	32.1	36.0	41.7	41
Georgia	laris (GEL) per US dollar	1.8	1.8	1.7	1.5	1.7	1.8	1.7	1.7	1.7	1.8	2.2
Gaza Strip	see entry for West Bank							3.6	3.9	3.6	3.6	3.9
Germany	euros (EUR) per US dollar	0.8	0.8	0.7	0.7	0.7	0.8	0.7	0.8	0.8	0.8	0.89
Ghana	cedis (GHC) per US dollar	0.9	0.9	0.9	1.1	1.4	1.4	1.5	1.8	2.9	2.9	3.7
Gibraltar	Gibraltar pounds (GIP) per US dollar							0.6	0.6	0.8	0.8	0.89
Greece	euros (EUR) per US dollar	0.8	0.8	0.7	0.7	0.7	0.8	0.7	0.8	0.8	0.8	0.89
Greenland	Danish kroner (DKK) per US dollar							5.4	5.8	5.4	5.6	6.6
Grenada	East Caribbean dollars (XCD) per US dollar	2.7	2.7	2.7	2.7	2.7	2.7	2.7	2.7	2.7	2.7	2.7
Guam	the US dollar is used											
Guatemala	quetzales (GTQ) per US dollar	7.6	7.6	7.7	7.6	8.2	8.1	7.8	7.8	7.9	7.7	7.7
Guinea	Guinean francs (GNF) per US dollar	3,644.3	5,148.8	4,197.8	4,601.7	4,801.1	5,726.1	6,658.0	6,985.8	6,907.9	7,014.1	7,305
Guinea-Bissau	Communaute Financiere Africaine francs (XOF) per US dollar	527.5	522.9	479.3	447.8	472.2	495.3	471.9	510.5	494.0	494.4	580.5
Guyana	Guyanese dollars (GYD) per US dollar	199.9	200.2	202.3	203.6	204.0	203.6	204.0	204.4	205.4	206.4	206.5
Haiti	gourdes (HTG) per US dollar	40.4	40.4	36.9	39.1	41.2	39.8	40.5	41.9	43.5	45.2	47.6
Honduras	lempiras (HNL) per US dollar	18.8	18.9	18.9	18.9	18.9	18.9	18.9	19.6	21.1	21.1	22.3
Hong Kong SAR, China	Hong Kong dollars (HKD) per US dollar	7.8	7.8	7.8	7.8	7.8	7.8	7.8	7.8	7.8	7.8	7.8
Hungary	forints (HUF) per US dollar	199.6	210.4	183.6	172.1	202.3	207.9	201.1	225.1	223.7	232.6	273.8
Iceland	Icelandic kronur (ISK) per US dollar	63.0	70.2	64.1	87.9	123.6	122.2	116.0	125.1	122.2	116.8	130.1
India	Indian rupees (INR) per US dollar	44.1	45.3	41.3	43.5	48.4	45.7	46.7	53.4	58.6	61.0	64.7
Indonesia	Indonesian rupiah (IDR) per US dollar	9,704.7	9,159.3	9,141.0	9,699.0	10,389.9	9,090.4	8,770.4	9,386.6	10,461.2	11,865.2	13,577.6
Iran, Islamic Rep.	Iranian rials (IRR) per US dollar	8,964.0	9,170.9	9,281.2	9,428.5	9,864.3	10,254.2	10,616.3	12,175.5	18,414.4	25,941.7	28,948
Iraq	Iraqi dinars (IQD) per US dollar	1,472.0	1,467.4	1,254.6	1,193.1	1,170.0	1,170.0	1,170.0	1,166.2	1,213.7	1,213.7	1,247.6
Ireland	euros (EUR) per US dollar	0.8	0.8	0.7	0.7	0.7	0.8	0.7	0.8	0.8	0.8	0.89
Isle of Man	Manx pounds (IMP) per US dollar							0.6	0.6	0.7	0.6	0.65
Israel	new Israeli shekels (ILS) per US dollar	4.5	4.5	4.1	3.6	3.9	3.7	3.6	3.9	3.6	3.6	3.9
Italy	euros (EUR) per US dollar	0.8	0.8	0.7	0.7	0.7	0.8	0.7	0.8	0.8	0.8	0.89
Jamaica	Jamaican dollars (JMD) per US dollar	62.3	65.7	69.2	72.8	87.9	87.2	85.9	88.8	100.2	110.9	116.8
Japan	yen (JPY) per US dollar	110.2	116.3	117.8	103.4	93.6	87.8	79.8	79.8	97.6	105.9	121.1
Jordan	Jordanian dinars (JOD) per US dollar	0.7	0.7	0.7	0.7	0.7	0.7	0.7	0.7	0.7	0.7	0.7
Kazakhstan	tenge (KZT) per US dollar	132.9	126.1	122.6	120.3	147.5	147.4	146.6	149.1	152.1	179.2	214.1
Kenya	Kenyan shillings (KES) per US dollar	75.6	72.1	67.3	69.2	77.4	79.2	88.8	84.5	86.1	87.9	99.7
Kiribati	Australian dollars (AUD) per US dollar	1.3	1.3	1.2	1.2	1.3	1.1	1.0	1.0	1.0	1.1	1.3
Korea, Dem. Rep.	North Korean won (KPW) per US dollar							140.0	133.5	98.5	7,900.0	8,200
Korea, Rep.	South Korean won (KRW) per US dollar	1,024.1	954.8	929.3	1,102.0	1,276.9	1,156.1	1,108.3	1,126.5	1,094.9	1,053.0	1,130
Kosovo	euros (EUR) per US dollar	0.8	0.8	0.7	0.7	0.7	0.8	0.7	0.8	0.8	0.8	0.89
Kuwait	Kuwaiti dinars (KD) per US dollar	0.3	0.3	0.3	0.3	0.3	0.3	0.3	0.3	0.3	0.3	0.3
Kyrgyz Republic	soms (KGS) per US dollar	41.0	40.2	37.3	36.6	42.9	46.0	46.1	47.0	48.4	53.7	60.1
Lao PDR	kips (LAK) per US dollar	10,655.2	10,159.9	9,603.2	8,744.2	8,516.1	8,258.8	8,030.1	8,007.8	7,860.1	8,049.0	8,151.6
Latvia	lati (LVL) per US dollar	0.6	0.6	0.5	0.5	0.5	0.5	0.5	0.6	0.8	0.8	0.9
Lebanon	Lebanese pounds (LBP) per US dollar	1,507.5	1,507.5	1,507.5	1,507.5	1,507.5	1,507.5	1,507.5	1,507.5	1,507.5	1,507.5	1,507.5
Lesotho	maloti (LSL) per US dollar	6.4	6.8	7.0	8.3	8.5	7.3	7.3	8.2	9.7	10.9	12.6
Liberia	Liberian dollars (LRD) per US dollar	57.1	58.0	61.3	63.2	68.3	71.4	72.2	73.5	77.5	83.9	86.1
Libya	Libyan dinars (LYD) per US dollar	1.3	1.3	1.3	1.2	1.3	1.3	1.2	1.3	1.3	1.3	1.4
Liechtenstein	Swiss francs (CHF) per US dollar							0.9	0.9	0.9	0.9	0.94
Lithuania	litai (LTL) per US dollar	2.8	2.8	2.5	2.4	2.5	2.6	2.5	2.7	0.8	0.8	0.91
Luxembourg	euros (EUR) per US dollar	0.8	0.8	0.7	0.7	0.7	0.8	0.7	0.8	0.8	0.8	0.89
Macao SAR, China	patacas (MOP) per US dollar	8.0	8.0	8.0	8.0	8.0	8.0	8.0	8.0	8.0	8.0	8
Macedonia, FYR	Macedonian denars (MKD) per US dollar	49.3	48.8	44.7	41.9	44.1	46.5	44.2	47.9	46.4	46.4	57.4
Madagascar	Malagasy ariary (MGA) per US dollar	2,003.0	2,142.3	1,873.9	1,708.4	1,956.2	2,090.0	2,025.1	2,195.0	2,206.9	2,414.8	2,872.7
Malawi	Malawian kwachas (MWK) per US dollar	118.4	136.0	140.0	140.5	141.2	150.5	156.5	249.1	364.4	424.9	520.5
Malaysia	ringgits (MYR) per US dollar	3.8	3.7	3.4	3.3	3.5	3.2	3.1	3.1	3.2	3.3	3.9
Maldives	rufiyaa (MVR) per US dollar	12.8	12.8	12.8	12.8	12.8	12.8	14.6	15.4	15.4	15.4	15.4
Mali	Communaute Financiere Africaine francs (XOF) per US dollar	527.5	522.9	479.3	447.8	472.2	495.3	471.9	510.5	494.0	494.4	580.5
Malta	euros (EUR) per US dollar	0.3	0.3	0.3	0.7	0.7	0.8	0.7	0.8	0.8	0.8	0.89
Marshall Islands	the US dollar is used											
Mauritania	ouguiyas (MRO) per US dollar	265.5	268.6	258.6	238.2	262.4	275.9	281.1	296.6	300.7	303.3	301.5
Mauritius	Mauritian rupees (MUR) per US dollar	29.5	31.7	31.3	28.5	32.0	30.8	28.7	30.0	30.7	30.6	36.8
Mexico	Mexican pesos (MXN) per US dollar	10.9	10.9	10.9	11.1	13.5	12.6	12.4	13.2	12.8	13.3	15.9
Micronesia, Fed. Sts.	the US dollar is used	1.0	1.0	1.0	1.0	1.0	1.0	1.0	1.0	1.0	1.0	1
Moldova	Moldovan lei (MDL) per US dollar	12.6	13.1	12.1	10.4	11.1	12.4	11.7	12.1	12.6	14.0	18.8
Monaco	euros (EUR) per US dollar	0.8	0.8	0.7	0.7	0.7	0.8	0.7	0.8	0.8	0.8	0.89

Table A-4. Foreign Exchange Rates, 2005–2015—*Continued*

Official exchange rate (LCU per US$, period average.)

Country Name	Local Currency Unit per $dollar	2005	2006	2007	2008	2009	2010	2011	2012	2013	2014	2015
Mongolia	togrog/tugriks (MNT) per US dollar	1,205.2	1,179.7	1,170.4	1,165.8	1,437.8	1,357.1	1,265.5	1,357.6	1,523.9	1,817.9	1,970.4
Montenegro	euros (EUR) per US dollar	0.8	0.8	0.7	0.7	0.7	0.8	0.7	0.8	0.8	0.8	0.89
Morocco	Moroccan dirhams (MAD) per US dollar	8.9	8.8	8.2	7.8	8.1	8.4	8.1	8.6	8.4	8.4	9.6
Mozambique	meticais (MZM) per US dollar	23.1	25.4	25.8	24.3	27.5	34.0	29.1	28.4	30.1	31.4	37.8
Myanmar	kyats (MMK) per US dollar	5.8	5.8	5.6	5.4	5.6	5.6	5.4	640.7	933.6	984.3	1,171.8
Namibia	Namibian dollars (NAD) per US dollar	6.4	6.8	7.0	8.3	8.5	7.3	7.3	8.2	9.7	10.9	12.6
Nepal	Nepalese rupees (NPR) per US dollar	71.4	72.8	66.4	69.8	77.6	73.3	74.0	85.2	93.0	99.5	102.4
Netherlands	euros (EUR) per US dollar	0.8	0.8	0.7	0.7	0.7	0.8	0.7	0.8	0.8	0.8	0.89
New Caledonia	Comptoirs Francais du Pacifique francs (XPF) per US dollar							85.7			89.8	89.8
New Zealand	New Zealand dollars (NZD) per US dollar	1.4	1.5	1.4	1.4	1.6	1.4	1.3	1.2	1.2	1.2	1.4
Nicaragua	cordobas (NIO) per US dollar	16.7	17.6	18.4	19.4	20.3	21.4	22.4	23.5	24.7	26.0	27.3
Niger	Communaute Financiere Africaine francs (XOF) per US dollar	527.5	522.9	479.3	447.8	472.2	495.3	471.9	510.5	494.0	494.4	480.5
Nigeria	nairas (NGN) per US dollar	131.3	128.7	125.8	118.5	148.9	150.3	153.9	157.5	157.3	158.6	196.9
Northern Mariana Islands	the US dollar is used											
Norway	Norwegian kroner (NOK) per US dollar	6.4	6.4	5.9	5.6	6.3	6.0	5.6	5.8	5.9	6.3	7.9
Oman	Omani rials (OMR) per US dollar	0.4	0.4	0.4	0.4	0.4	0.4	0.4	0.4	0.4	0.4	0.4
Pakistan	Pakistani rupees (PKR) per US dollar	59.5	60.3	60.7	70.4	81.7	85.2	86.3	93.4	101.6	102.9	101.4
Palau	the US dollar is used											
Panama	balboas (PAB) per US dollar	1.0	1.0	1.0	1.0	1.0	1.0	1.0	1.0	1.0	1.0	1
Papua New Guinea	kina (PGK) per US dollar	3.1	3.1	3.0	2.7	2.8	2.7	2.4	2.1	2.2	2.5	2.8
Paraguay	guarani (PYG) per US dollar	6,178.0	5,635.5	5,032.7	4,363.2	4,965.4	4,735.5	4,191.4	4,424.9	4,320.7	4,462.2	5,087.7
Peru	nuevo sol (PEN) per US dollar	3.3	3.3	3.1	2.9	3.0	2.8	2.8	2.6	2.7	2.8	3.2
Philippines	Philippine pesos (PHP) per US dollar	55.1	51.3	46.1	44.3	47.7	45.1	43.3	42.2	42.4	44.4	45.5
Poland	zlotych (PLN) per US dollar	3.2	3.1	2.8	2.4	3.1	3.0	3.0	3.3	3.2	3.2	3.7
Portugal	euros (EUR) per US dollar	0.8	0.8	0.7	0.7	0.7	0.8	0.7	0.8	0.8	0.8	0.89
Puerto Rico	the US dollar is used											
Qatar	Qatari rials (QAR) per US dollar	3.6	3.6	3.6	3.6	3.6	3.6	3.6	3.6	3.6	3.6	3.6
Romania	lei (RON) per US dollar	2.9	2.8	2.4	2.5	3.0	3.2	3.0	3.5	3.3	3.3	4
Russia	Russian rubles (RUB) per US dollar	28.3	27.2	25.6	24.9	31.7	30.4	29.4	30.8	31.8	38.4	61.3
Rwanda	Rwandan francs (RWF) per US dollar	557.8	551.7	547.0	546.8	568.3	583.1	600.3	614.3	646.6	681.9	726.9
Samoa	tala (SAT) per US dollar	2.7	2.8	2.6	2.6	2.7	2.5	2.3	2.3	2.3	2.3	2.6
San Marino	euro (EUR) per US dollar	0.8	0.8	0.7	0.7	0.7	0.8	0.7	0.8	0.8	0.8	0.89
Sao Tome and Principe	dobras (STD) per US dollar	10,558.0	12,448.6	13,536.8	14,695.2	16,208.5	18,498.6	17,622.9	19,068.4	18,450.0	18,466.4	21,681
Saudi Arabia	Saudi riyals (SAR) per US dollar	3.7	3.7	3.7	3.8	3.8	3.8	3.8	3.8	3.8	3.8	3.8
Senegal	Communaute Financiere Africaine francs (XOF) per US dollar	527.5	522.9	479.3	447.8	472.2	495.3	471.9	510.5	494.0	494.4	580.5
Serbia	Serbian dinars (RSD) per US dollar	66.7	67.1	58.5	55.7	67.6	77.7	73.3	88.0	85.2	88.4	106.6
Seychelles	Seychelles rupees (SCR) per US dollar	5.5	5.5	6.7	9.5	13.6	12.1	12.4	13.7	12.1	12.7	13.4
Sierra Leone	leones (SLL) per US dollar	2,889.6	2,961.9	2,985.2	2,981.5	3,385.7	3,978.1	4,349.2	4,344.0	4,332.5	4,524.2	4,923.8
Singapore	Singapore dollars (SGD) per US dollar	1.7	1.6	1.5	1.4	1.5	1.4	1.3	1.2	1.3	1.3	1.4
Sint Maarten (Dutch part)	Netherlands Antillean guilders (ANG) per US dollar	1.8	1.8	1.8	1.8	1.8	1.8	1.8	1.8	1.8	1.8	1.79
Slovak Republic	euros (EUR) per US dollar	31.0	29.7	24.7	21.4	0.8	0.7	0.8	0.8	0.8	0.75	0.89
Slovenia	euros (EUR) per US dollar	192.7	191.0	0.7	0.7	0.7	0.8	0.7	0.8	0.8	0.8	0.89
Solomon Islands	Solomon Islands dollars (SBD) per US dolla	7.5	7.6	7.7	7.7	8.1	8.1	7.6	7.4	7.3	7.4	7.9
Somalia	Somali shillings (SOS) per US dollar									19,276.0	20,227.0	
South Africa	rand (ZAR) per US dollar	6.4	6.8	7.0	8.3	8.5	7.3	7.3	8.2	9.7	10.9	12.6
South Sudan	South Sudenese oiunds (SSP) per US dollar							0.7	0.8	0.8	0.8	0.89
Spain	euros (EUR) per US dollar	0.8	0.8	0.7	0.7	0.7	0.8	0.7	0.8	0.8	0.8	0.89
Sri Lanka	Sri Lankan rupees (LKR) per US dollar	100.5	103.9	110.6	108.3	114.9	113.1	110.6	127.6	129.1	130.6	140
St. Barthelemy	euros per US dollar	0.8	0.8	0.7	0.7	0.7	0.8	0.7	0.8	0.8	0.8	0.89
St. Helena, Ascension, and Tristan da Cunha	Saint Helenian pounds (SHP) per US dollar							0.6	0.6	0.6	0.6	0.65
St. Kitts and Nevis	East Caribbean dollars (XCD) per US dollar	2.7	2.7	2.7	2.7	2.7	2.7	2.7	2.7	2.7	2.7	2.7
St. Lucia	East Caribbean dollars (XCD) per US dollar	2.7	2.7	2.7	2.7	2.7	2.7	2.7	2.7	2.7	2.7	2.7
St. Martin (French part)	euros (EUR) per US dollar	0.8	0.8	0.7	0.7	0.7	0.8	0.7	0.8	0.8	0.8	0.89
St. Pierre and Miquelon	euros (EUR) per US dollar	0.8	0.8	0.7	0.7	0.7	0.8	0.7	0.8	0.8	0.8	0.89
St. Vincent and the Grenadines	East Caribbean dollars (XCD) per US dollar	2.7	2.7	2.7	2.7	2.7	2.7	2.7	2.7	2.7	2.7	2.7
Sudan	Sudanese pounds (SDG) per US dollar	2.4	2.2	2.0	2.1	2.3	2.3	2.7	3.6	4.8	5.7	6.5
Suriname	Surinamese dollars (SRD) per US dollar	2.7	2.7	2.7	2.7	2.7	2.7	3.3	3.3	3.3	3.3	3.3
Svalbard	Norwegian kroner (NOK) per US dollar							5.6	5.8	5.9	5.9	7.4
Swaziland	emalangeni per US dollar	6.4	6.8	7.0	8.3	8.5	7.3	7.3	8.2	9.7	10.9	12.6
Sweden	Swedish kronor (SEK) per US dollar	7.5	7.4	6.8	6.6	7.7	7.2	6.5	6.8	6.5	6.9	8.2
Switzerland	Swiss francs (CHF) per US dollar	1.2	1.3	1.2	1.1	1.1	1.0	0.9	0.9	0.9	0.9	0.9
Syrian Arab Republic	Syrian pounds (SYP) per US dollar #	11.2	11.2	11.2	11.2	11.2	11.2	48.4	64.4	153.7	153.7	234.5
Taiwan	New Taiwan dollars (TWD) per US dollar								29.5	29.6	30.4	31.9
Tajikistan	Tajikistani somoni (TJS) per US dollar	3.1	3.3	3.4	3.4	4.1	4.4	4.6	4.7	4.8	4.9	6.2
Tanzania	Tanzanian shillings (TZS) per US dollar	1,128.9	1,251.9	1,245.0	1,196.3	1,320.3	1,409.3	1,572.1	1,583.0	1,600.4	1,654.0	2,039.4
Thailand	baht per US dollar	40.2	37.9	34.5	33.3	34.3	31.7	30.5	31.1	30.7	32.5	34.1

Table A-4.   Foreign Exchange Rates, 2005–2015—*Continued*

Official exchange rate (LCU per US$, period average.)

Country Name	Local Currency Unit per $dollar	2005	2006	2007	2008	2009	2010	2011	2012	2013	2014	2015
Timor-Leste..........................	the US dollar is used..............											
Togo...................................	Communaute Financiere Africaine francs (XOF) per US dollar	527.5	522.9	479.3	447.8	472.2	495.3	471.9	510.5	494.0	494.4	580.5
Tonga.................................	pa'anga (TOP) per US dollar.................	1.9	2.0	2.0	1.9	2.0	1.9	1.7	1.7	1.8	1.8	2
Tokelau...............................	New Zealand dollars (NZD) per US dollar...................							1.2	1.2	1.2	1.2	1.5
Trinidad and Tobago..............	Trinidad and Tobago dollars (TTD) per US dollar	6.3	6.3	6.3	6.3	6.3	6.4	6.4	6.4	6.4	6.4	6.4
Tunisia...............................	Tunisian dinars (TND) per US dollar...........................	1.3	1.3	1.3	1.2	1.4	1.4	1.4	1.6	1.6	1.7	1.9
Turkey................................	Turkish liras (TRY) per US dollar........................	1.3	1.4	1.3	1.3	1.5	1.5	1.7	1.8	1.9	2.2	2.7
Turkmenistan	Turkmen manat (TMM) per US dollar..................							2.9	2.9	2.9	2.9	3.5
Turks and Caicos Islands	the US dollar is used..............											
Tuvalu	Tuvaluan dollars or Australian dollars (AUD) per US dollar...........................							1.0	1.0	1.1	1.7	1.3
Uganda...............................	Ugandan shillings (UGX) per US dollar....................	1,780.7	1,831.5	1,723.5	1,720.4	2,030.5	2,177.6	2,522.7	2,504.6	2,586.9	2,599.8	3,396.6
Ukraine...............................	hryvnia (UAH) per US dollar.............	5.1	5.1	5.1	5.3	7.8	7.9	8.0	8.0	8.0	11.9	15.5
United Arab Emirates	Emirati dirhams (AED) per US dollar..........................	3.7	3.7	3.7	3.7	3.7	3.7	3.7	3.7	3.7	3.7	3.7
United Kingdom	British pounds (GBP) per US dollar...........................	0.5	0.5	0.5	0.5	0.6	0.6	0.6	0.6	0.6	0.6	0.7
United States.......................	US dollar................................	1.0	1.0	1.0	1.0	1.0	1.0	1.0	1.0	1.0	1.0	1
Uruguay	Uruguayan pesos (UYU) per US dollar........................	24.5	24.1	23.5	20.9	22.6	20.1	19.3	20.3	20.5	23.2	27
Uzbekistan	Uzbekistani soum (UZS) per US dollar.......................							1,715.8	1,890.1	2,311.4	2,311.4	2,565.8
Vanuatu	vatu (VUV) per US dollar...................	109.2	110.6	102.4	101.3	106.7	96.9	89.5	92.6	94.5	97.1	107.8
Venezuela, RB	bolivars (VEB) per US dollar.................	2.1	2.1	2.1	2.1	2.1	2.6	4.3	4.3	6.0	6.3	6.3
Vietnam..............................	dong (VND) per US dollar................	15,858.9	15,994.3	16,105.1	16,302.3	17,065.1	18,612.9	20,509.8	20,828.0	20,933.4	21,148.0	21,928
Virgin Islands (U.S.).............	the US dollar is used..............											
West Bank and Gaza.............	new Israeli shekels (ILS) per US dollar.....................							3.6	3.9	3.6	3.6	3.9
Yemen, Rep........................	Yemeni rials (YER) per US dollar.............................							214.9	214.9	214.9	214.9	214.9
Zambia...............................	Zambian kwacha (ZMK) per US dollar......................	4.5	3.6	4.0	3.7	5.0	4.8	4.9	5.1	5.4	6.2	
Zimbabwe*	Zimbabwean dollars (ZWD) per US dollar...................	22.4	164.5	9,686.8	6,723,052,073.3							

= Estimates from CIA World Factbook
* = The dollar was adopted as a legal currency in 2009; since then the Zimbabwean dollar has experienced hyperinflation and is essentially worthless.
Official exchange rate refers to the exchange rate determined by national authorities or to the rate determined in the legally sanctioned exchange market. It is calculated as an annual average based on monthly averages (local currency units relative to the U.S. dollar).

SECTION B

U.S. FOREIGN TRADE IN GOODS AND SERVICES

SECTION B: U.S. FOREIGN TRADE IN GOODS AND SERVICES

HIGHLIGHTS

Part I: Trade in Goods and Services

Even though the U.S.'s international trade data involves three different collections methodologies, the trends are similar. The last time the U.S. trade balance (exports – imports) was positive was in 1975. As Figure B-1 illustrates, U.S. exports have continued to rise but at a slower pace than imports. The largest deficit occurred in 2006 at -$762 billion then declined 50 percent by 2009. In 2015, the balance was $540 billion.

Part II: Exports and Imports

Of the U.S. largest ten exports and imports, eight are in same category. These products include vehicles, nuclear reactors, and precious stones. For example, the U.S. exported over $127.4 billion but imported over $280 billion of vehicles in 2015. Top six exports and imports charts are shown on the following pages which compare 2005 and 2015 data. The composition of U.S. exports has changed slightly between 2005 and 2015. For example,

imports of nuclear reactors fell from 30 percent in 2005 to 25 percent of the total in 2015.

Data for goods on a Census basis are compiled from the documents collected by the U.S. Customs and Border Protection and reflect the movement of goods between foreign countries and the 50 states, the District of Columbia, Puerto Rico, the U.S. Virgin Islands, and U.S. Foreign Trade Zones.

Goods on a Census basis are adjusted by BEA to a Balance of Payments (BOP) basis to align the data with the concepts and definitions used to prepare the international and national economic accounts. These adjustments, which are applied separately to exports and imports, are necessary to supplement coverage of the census data, to eliminate duplication of transactions recorded elsewhere in the international accounts, and to value transactions at market prices.

The National Income and Products Account (NIPA) are a set of economic accounts that provide information on the value and composition of output produced in the United

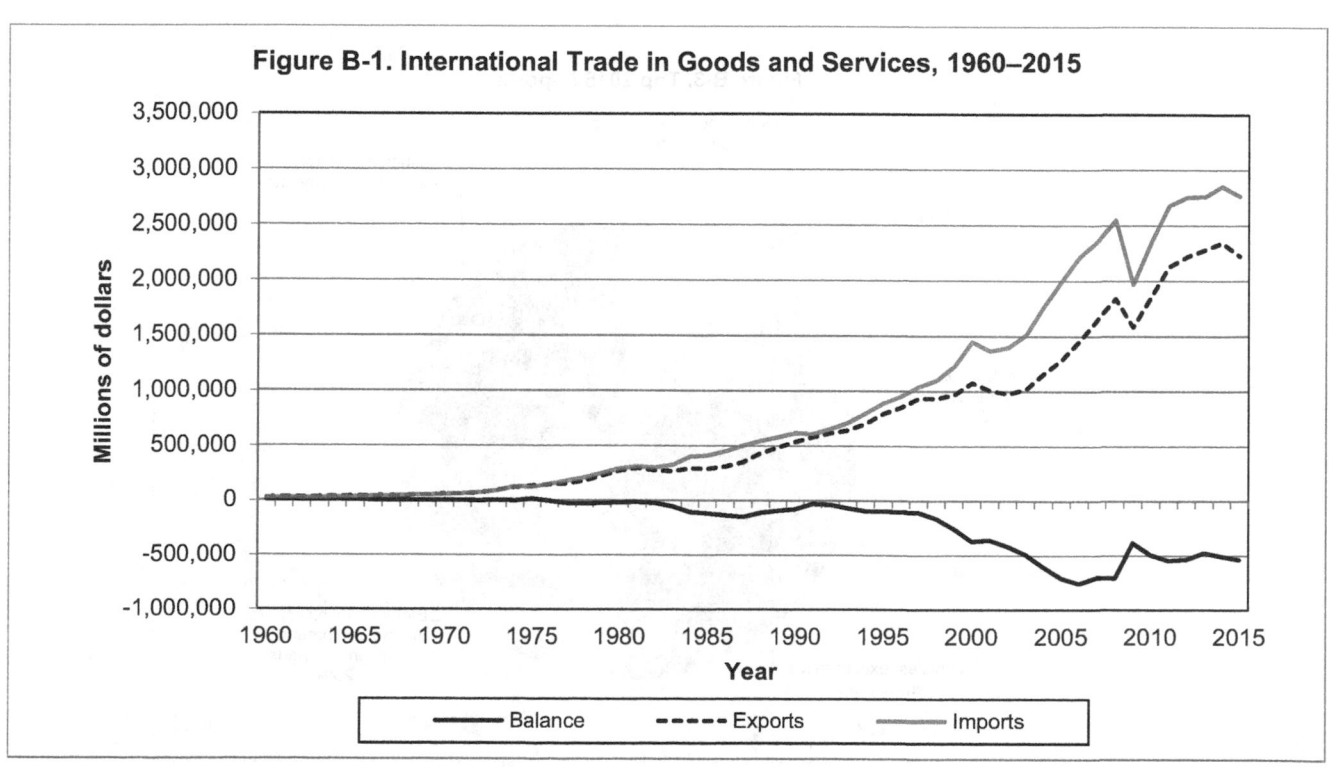

Figure B-1. International Trade in Goods and Services, 1960–2015

Source: U.S. Census Bureau and Bureau of Economic Analysis.

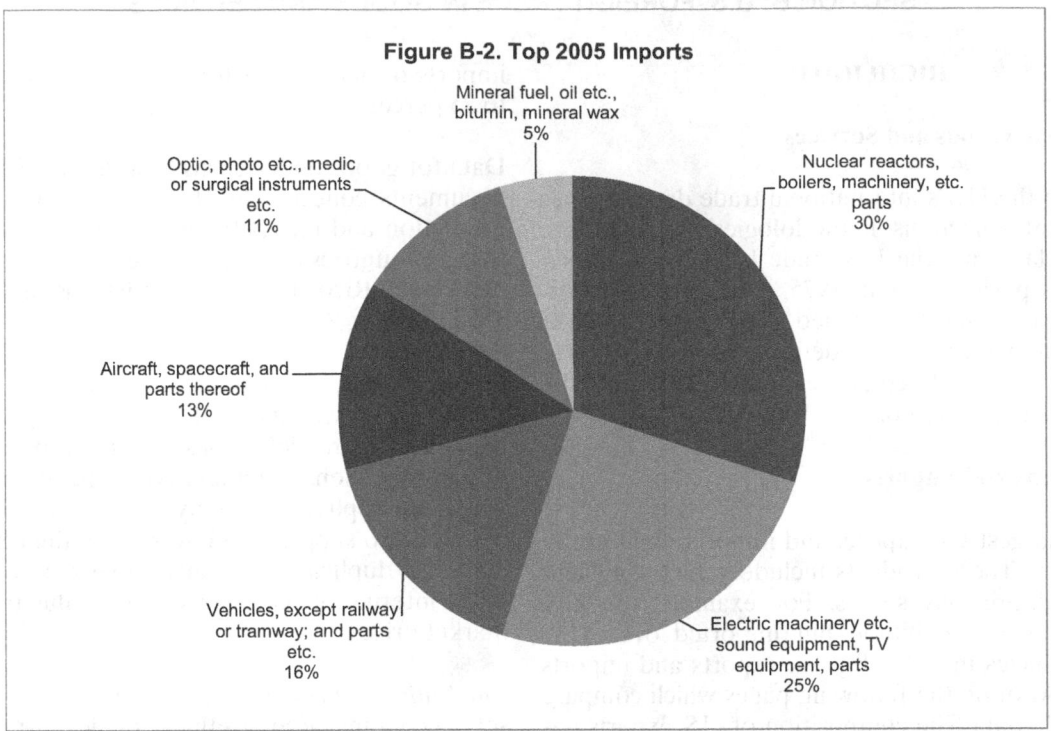

Figure B-2. Top 2005 Imports

Note: The residual category represents the difference between total Census Basis exports or imports and the sum of the components. *Source:* U.S. Census Bureau and Bureau of Economic Analysis.

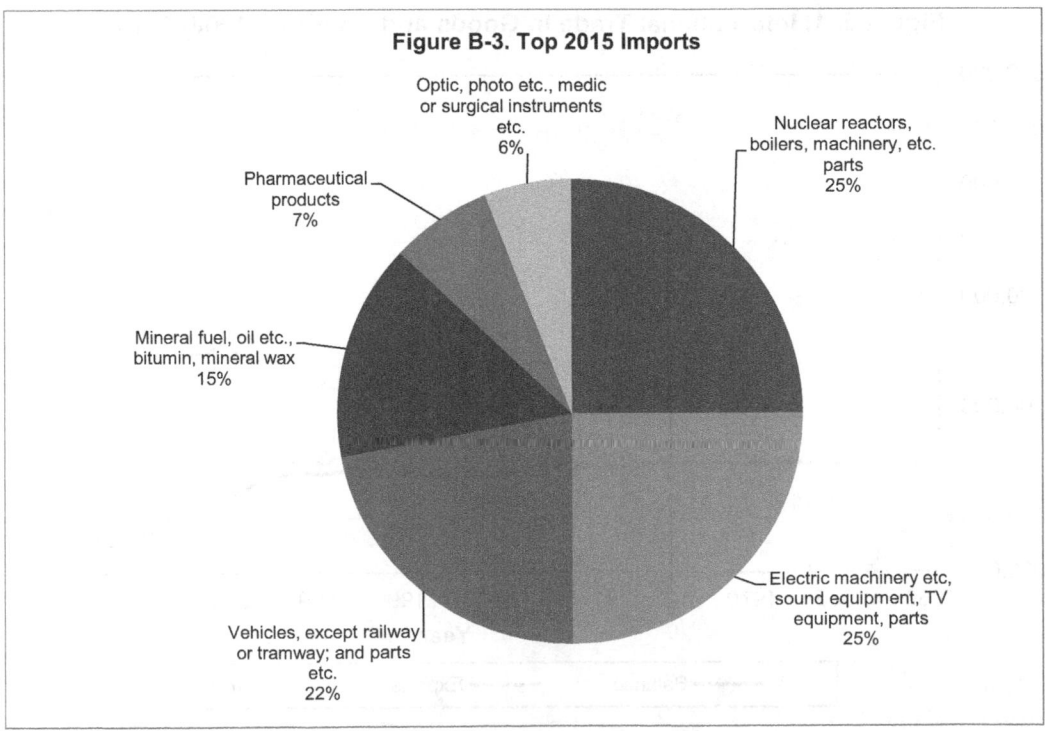

Figure B-3. Top 2015 Imports

Note: The residual category represents the difference between total Census Basis exports or imports and the sum of the components. *Source:* U.S. Census Bureau and Bureau of Economic Analysis.

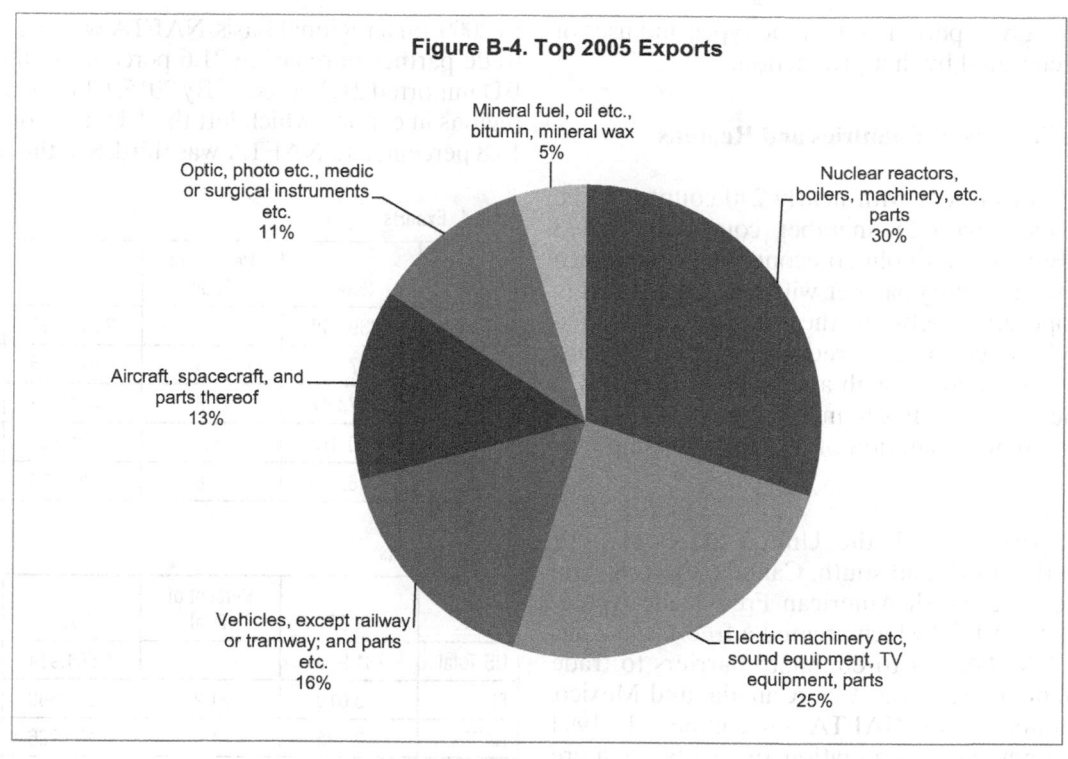

Figure B-4. Top 2005 Exports

Mineral fuel, oil etc., bitumin, mineral wax 5%

Optic, photo etc., medic or surgical instruments etc. 11%

Nuclear reactors, boilers, machinery, etc. parts 30%

Aircraft, spacecraft, and parts thereof 13%

Vehicles, except railway or tramway; and parts etc. 16%

Electric machinery etc, sound equipment, TV equipment, parts 25%

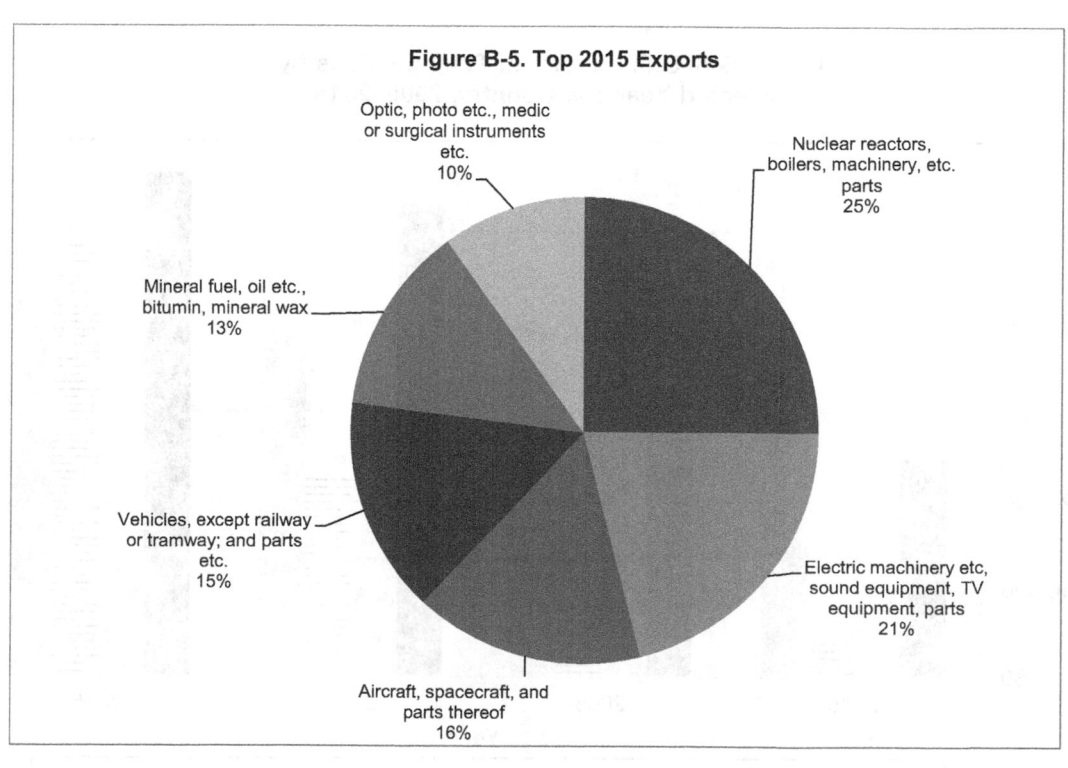

Figure B-5. Top 2015 Exports

Optic, photo etc., medic or surgical instruments etc. 10%

Mineral fuel, oil etc., bitumin, mineral wax 13%

Nuclear reactors, boilers, machinery, etc. parts 25%

Vehicles, except railway or tramway; and parts etc. 15%

Electric machinery etc, sound equipment, TV equipment, parts 21%

Aircraft, spacecraft, and parts thereof 16%

States during a given period and on the types and uses of the income generated by that production.

Part III: U.S. Trade with Countries and Regions

The United States trades with nearly 240 countries. The European Union, with 28 member countries located basically in Europe, is a politico-economic union which has been a major trading partner with the United States. Customs cooperation between the EU and the United States (U.S.) is based on an agreement of 1997 and has been further expanded through an agreement of 2004, a Joint Statement on Supply Chain Security of 2011 and a decision on mutual recognition of trade partnership programs of 2012.

Other trade partners with the United States are our neighbors to the north and south. Canada, the U.S., and Mexico signed the North American Free Trade Agreement (NAFTA) in 1992 which created a free-trade zone. The goal of NAFTA was to eliminate barriers to trade and investment between the U.S., Canada, and Mexico. The implementation of NAFTA on January 1, 1994 brought the immediate elimination of tariffs on more than one-half of Mexico's exports to the U.S. and more than one-third of U.S. exports to Mexico.

In 2000, on a regional basis, NAFTA was the U.S.'s largest trade partner purchasing 21.6 percent of all exports. The EU imported 21.2 percent. By 2015, China surpassed both regions in exports which left the EU in second place with 18.8 percent, and NAFTA was third. See the tables below.

Table 1. Exports

	2000	Percent of Total	2015	Percent of Total
US Total	1,239,449		2,271,117	
EU	227,751	18.4	426,006	18.8
NAFTA	207,047	16.5	421,603	18.5
China	100,018	8.1	481,881	21.2
Japan	146,479	11.8	131,120	5.8

Table 2. Imports

	2000	Percent of Total	2015	Percent of Total
US Total	781,918		1,504,914	
EU	168,619	21.2	272,688	18.1
NAFTA	169,195	21.6	159,266	10.6
China	16,185	2.1	116,186	7.7
Japan	64,924	8.3	62,472	4.2

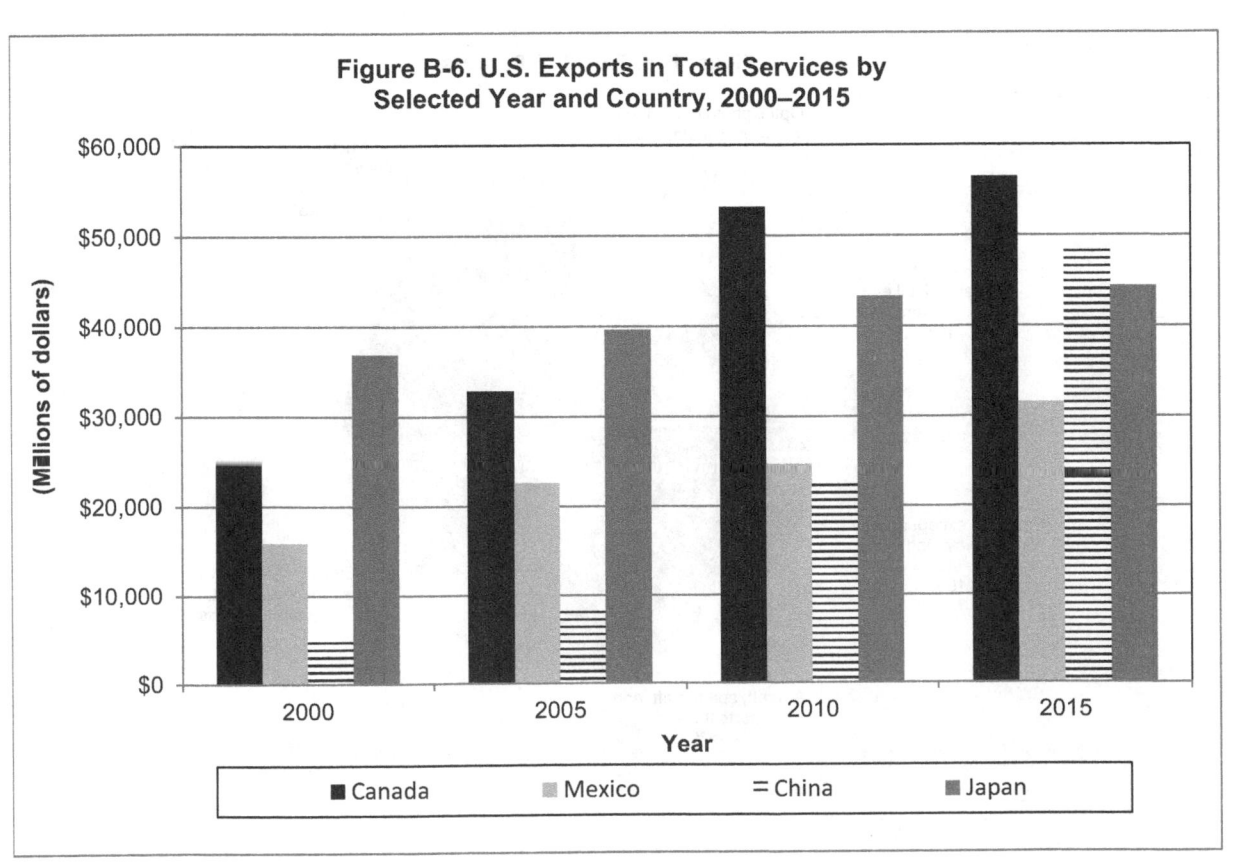

Figure B-6. U.S. Exports in Total Services by Selected Year and Country, 2000–2015

Table 3. Top Three Purchasers of US Exports (billions dollars)

	2005	2015	% of Total (2005)	Percent Change 2005–2015	% of Total (2015)
TOTAL	$716.20	$1,157.90		492%	
Canada	$192.40	$2,46.3	26.90%	250%	21.30%
Mexico	$110.50	$214.20	15.40%	685%	18.50%
China	$31.90	$89.10	4.50%	1081%	7.70%

The U.S. purchases (imports) nearly 30 percent of total from just three countries, the same as the above but in different order. Canada fell from second to third between 2005–2015.

Table 4. Top Three Sellers of US Imports (billions dollars)

	2005	2015	% of Total (2005)	Percent Change 2005–2015	% of Total (2015)
TOTAL	$1,231.90	$1,813.70		394%	
China	$237.70	$473.30	19.30%	473%	26.10%
Mexico	$134.40	$260.80	10.90%	685%	14.40%
Canada	$207.80	$208.50	16.90%	3%	11.50%

ABOUT THE DATA

This section provides a detailed picture of the overall U.S. foreign trade situation. Aggregate statistics appear first in this section, starting by major category for both goods and services. Table B-2 is based on the National Income and Product Accounts and differs from the totals shown on the balance of payments basis, as explained in "Understanding Foreign Trade Statistics."

Data for goods on a Census[1] basis are compiled from the documents collected by the U.S. Customs and Border Protection and reflect the movement of goods between foreign countries and the 50 states, the District of Columbia, Puerto Rico, the U.S. Virgin Islands, and U.S. Foreign Trade Zones.

Goods on a Census basis are then adjusted by BEA to a Balance of Payments (BOP) basis to align the data with the concepts and definitions used to prepare the international and national economic accounts. These adjustments, which are applied separately to exports and imports, are necessary to supplement coverage of the census data, to eliminate duplication of transactions recorded elsewhere in the international accounts, and to value transactions at market prices.

---

[1] U.S. export and import statistics are provided by the Foreign Trade Division and is responsible for issuing regulations governing the reporting of all export shipments from the United States. For import or export statistics, information on export regulations, commodity classifications, or a host of other trade related topics, go to www.census.gov/foreign-trade/index.html.

PART I: TRADE IN GOODS AND SERVICES

Table B-1. U.S. International Trade in Goods and Services, 1960–2015

(In millions of dollars. Detail may not equal totals due to seasonal adjustment and rounding.)

Year	Balance			Exports			Imports		
	Total	Goods	Services	Total	Goods	Services	Total	Goods	Services
1960	3,508	4,892	-1,384	25,940	19,650	6,290	22,432	14,758	7,674
1961	4,195	5,571	-1,376	26,403	20,108	6,295	22,208	14,537	7,671
1962	3,370	4,521	-1,151	27,722	20,781	6,941	24,352	16,260	8,092
1963	4,210	5,224	-1,014	29,620	22,272	7,348	25,410	17,048	8,362
1964	6,022	6,801	-779	33,341	25,501	7,840	27,319	18,700	8,619
1965	4,664	4,951	-287	35,285	26,461	8,824	30,621	21,510	9,111
1966	2,939	3,817	-878	38,926	29,310	9,616	35,987	25,493	10,494
1967	2,604	3,800	-1,196	41,333	30,666	10,667	38,729	26,866	11,863
1968	250	635	-385	45,543	33,626	11,917	45,293	32,991	12,302
1969	91	607	-516	49,220	36,414	12,806	49,129	35,807	13,322
1970	2,254	2,603	-349	56,640	42,469	14,171	54,386	39,866	14,520
1971	-1,302	-2,260	958	59,677	43,319	16,358	60,979	45,579	15,400
1972	-5,443	-6,416	973	67,222	49,381	17,841	72,665	55,797	16,868
1973	1,900	911	989	91,242	71,410	19,832	89,342	70,499	18,843
1974	-4,293	-5,505	1,212	120,897	98,306	22,591	125,190	103,811	21,379
1975	12,404	8,903	3,501	132,585	107,088	25,497	120,181	98,185	21,996
1976	-6,082	-9,483	3,401	142,716	114,745	27,971	148,798	124,228	24,570
1977	-27,246	-31,091	3,845	152,301	120,816	31,485	179,547	151,907	27,640
1978	-29,763	-33,927	4,164	178,428	142,075	36,353	208,191	176,002	32,189
1979	-24,565	-27,568	3,003	224,131	184,439	39,692	248,696	212,007	36,689
1980	-19,407	-25,500	6,093	271,834	224,250	47,584	291,241	249,750	41,491
1981	-16,172	-28,023	11,851	294,398	237,044	57,354	310,570	265,067	45,503
1982	-24,156	-36,485	12,329	275,236	211,157	64,079	299,391	247,642	51,749
1983	-57,767	-67,102	9,335	266,106	201,799	64,307	323,874	268,901	54,973
1984	-109,072	-112,492	3,420	291,094	219,926	71,168	400,166	332,418	67,748
1985	-121,880	-122,173	294	289,070	215,915	73,155	410,950	338,088	72,862
1986	-138,538	-145,081	6,543	310,033	223,344	86,689	448,572	368,425	80,147
1987	-151,684	-159,557	7,874	348,869	250,208	98,661	500,552	409,765	90,787
1988	-114,566	-126,959	12,393	431,149	320,230	110,919	545,715	447,189	98,526
1989	-93,141	-117,749	24,607	487,003	359,916	127,087	580,144	477,665	102,479
1990	-80,864	-111,037	30,173	535,233	387,401	147,832	616,097	498,438	117,659
1991	-31,135	-76,937	45,802	578,344	414,083	164,261	609,479	491,020	118,459
1992	-39,212	-96,897	57,685	616,882	439,631	177,251	656,094	536,528	119,566
1993	-70,311	-132,451	62,141	642,863	456,943	185,920	713,174	589,394	123,780
1994	-98,493	-165,831	67,338	703,254	502,859	200,395	801,747	668,690	133,057
1995	-96,384	-174,170	77,786	794,387	575,204	219,183	890,771	749,374	141,397
1996	-104,065	-191,000	86,935	851,602	612,113	239,489	955,667	803,113	152,554
1997	-108,273	-198,428	90,155	934,453	678,366	256,087	1,042,726	876,794	165,932
1998	-166,140	-248,221	82,081	933,174	670,416	262,758	1,099,314	918,637	180,677
1999	-258,617	-337,068	78,450	969,867	698,524	271,343	1,228,485	1,035,592	192,893
2000	-372,517	-446,783	74,266	1,075,321	784,940	290,381	1,447,837	1,231,722	216,115
2001	-361,511	-422,370	60,858	1,005,654	731,331	274,323	1,367,165	1,153,701	213,465
2002	-418,955	-475,245	56,290	978,706	698,036	280,670	1,397,660	1,173,281	224,379
2003	-493,890	-541,643	47,754	1,020,418	730,446	289,972	1,514,308	1,272,089	242,219
2004	-609,883	-664,766	54,882	1,161,549	823,584	337,966	1,771,433	1,488,349	283,083
2005	-714,245	-782,804	68,558	1,286,022	913,016	373,006	2,000,267	1,695,820	304,448
2006	-761,716	-837,289	75,573	1,457,642	1,040,905	416,738	2,219,358	1,878,194	341,165
2007	-705,375	-821,196	115,821	1,653,548	1,165,151	488,396	2,358,922	1,986,347	372,575
2008	-708,726	-832,492	123,765	1,841,612	1,308,795	532,817	2,550,339	2,141,287	409,052
2009	-383,774	-509,694	125,920	1,583,053	1,070,331	512,722	1,966,827	1,580,025	386,801
2010	-494,658	-648,678	154,020	1,853,606	1,290,273	563,333	2,348,263	1,938,950	409,313
2011	-548,625	-740,646	192,020	2,127,021	1,499,240	627,781	2,675,646	2,238,886	400,701
2012	-536,773	-741,171	204,398	2,218,989	1,562,578	656,411	2,755,762	2,303,749	452,013
2013	-478,394	-702,587	224,193	2,279,937	1,592,043	687,894	2,758,331	2,294,630	463,700
2014	-508,324	-741,462	233,138	2,343,205	1,632,639	710,565	2,851,529	2,374,101	477,428
2015	-539,755	759,307	219,552	2,223,618	1,513,453	710,165	2,763,374	2,272,760	490,613

Note: Data are presented on a balance of payments (BOP) basis.

Table B-2.   International Trade in Goods and Services, 1967–2015

(Billions of dollars; National Income and Product Accounts [NIPA] Basis.)

Year	GDP	Net Exports	Exports of goods and servcies				Imports of goods and services			
			Total	Durable goods	Nondurable goods	Exports of services	Total	Durable goods	Nondurable goods	Imports of services
1967	861.7	3.6	9.409	20.823	16.909	10.981	10.098	37.145	---	17.919
1968	942.5	1.4	10.151	24.541	18.839	11.784	11.602	46.546	26.54	18.241
1969	1019.9	1.4	10.646	27.133	19.014	12.247	12.263	42.433	27.73	19.391
1970	1075.9	4	11.781	30.861	21.063	13.349	12.787	42.709	28.84	20.403
1971	1167.8	0.6	11.986	23.246	21.218	14.324	13.469	46.755	31.905	19.822
1972	1282.4	-3.4	12.919	24.684	22.637	14.264	14.985	51.754	36.331	20.662
1973	1428.5	4.1	15.354	33.506	26.376	14.513	15.68	52.897	42.71	19.965
1974	1548.8	-0.8	16.567	32.035	28.282	15.303	15.325	51.3	41.415	19.943
1975	1688.9	16	16.462	26.769	25.326	16.207	13.622	40.793	40.051	19.078
1976	1877.6	-1.6	17.181	28.406	27.591	16.381	16.285	47.686	49.149	20.395
1977	2086	-23.1	17.595	27.413	28.398	17.119	18.065	53.454	56.724	21.412
1978	2356.6	-25.4	19.45	33.125	30.061	19.037	19.631	59.055	55.45	22.938
1979	2632.1	-22.5	21.377	38.879	33.98	20.39	19.957	55.888	55.678	23.254
1980	2862.5	-13.1	23.68	46.19	37.601	21.243	18.631	45.928	46.579	22.735
1981	3211	-12.5	23.972	37.359	37.747	23.322	19.124	48.541	43.096	24.066
1982	3345	-20	22.14	32.634	38.285	22.303	18.883	39.646	38.634	25.346
1983	3638.1	-51.6	21.569	32.324	35.832	22.258	21.265	49.409	39.748	27.394
1984	4040.7	-102.7	23.329	32.751	38.237	24.879	26.442	62.315	43.971	34.263
1985	4346.7	-114	24.109	32.493	38.668	25.577	28.158	61.109	42.693	36.871
1986	4590.2	-131.9	25.963	33.545	40.591	29.25	30.564	65.022	49.199	37.283
1987	4870.2	-144.8	28.79	36.545	40.498	31.462	32.373	61.146	51.464	41.678
1988	5252.6	-109.4	33.457	44.522	43.974	35.205	33.644	60.102	55.389	43.091
1989	5657.7	-86.7	37.329	50.284	48.502	39.428	35.126	57.601	57.732	45.179
1990	5979.6	-77.9	40.622	54.191	50.879	43.186	36.382	57.64	58.826	48.129
1991	6174	-28.6	43.309	56.807	54.883	45.929	36.328	54.966	58.896	46.877
1992	6539.3	-34.7	46.31	55.479	57.196	48.401	38.875	60.364	62.979	45.611
1993	6878.7	-65.2	47.827	53.352	56.061	50.022	42.236	66.306	68.325	46.828
1994	7308.8	-92.5	52.056	56.536	58.725	53.515	47.274	79.484	74.056	49.321
1995	7664.1	-89.8	57.406	63.723	61.837	57.143	51.056	82.371	75.535	50.807
1996	8100.2	-96.4	62.103	67.547	64.656	60.726	55.496	88.217	80.363	53.463
1997	8608.5	-102	69.501	73.741	70.126	63.921	62.971	94.992	85.439	58.11
1998	9089.2	-162.7	71.125	74.978	68.243	65.694	70.331	109.645	91.129	64.432
1999	9660.6	-256.6	73.006	77.47	70.314	64.786	77.463	115.33	97.572	62.471
2000	10284.8	-375.8	79.259	88.654	74.313	67.802	87.547	123.007	102.306	70.353
2001	10621.8	-368.7	74.628	80.892	73.39	64.4	85.064	115.753	103.511	69.9
2002	10977.5	-426.5	73.341	75.624	76.659	66.145	88.181	121.902	102.468	72.183
2003	11510.7	-503.7	74.635	77.573	78.911	67.129	92.119	123.011	107.343	73.71
2004	12274.9	-619.2	81.914	84.076	83.541	75.66	102.63	147.632	116.159	83.078
2005	13093.7	-721.2	87.036	90.396	83.486	78.508	109.129	157.83	120.082	86.821
2006	13855.9	-770.9	94.9	99.055	88.679	84.863	116.028	172.802	118.037	94.297
2007	14477.6	-718.5	103.694	104.603	93.293	96.462	118.951	156.288	117.174	100.156
2008	14718.6	-723.1	109.642	115.623	103.716	101.082	115.907	143.052	112.284	103.91
2009	14418.7	-395.4	100	100	100	100	100	100	100	100
2010	14964.4	-512.7	111.895	117.017	114.937	106.77	112.716	114.905	103.995	103.79
2011	15517.9	-580	123.158	119.488	124.452	120.398	107.585	119.472	137.998	110.756
2012	16155.3	-565.7	125.461	119.607	131.831	119.415	102.971	118.004	147.876	116.653
2013	16663.2	-508.4	130.483	120.743	132.856	121.191	99.38	118.802	150.946	116.169
2014	17348.1	-530	134.931	120.034	136.274	121.765	99.958	120.887	161.568	123.722
2015	17942.9	-530.3	135.513	119.287	132.849	121.316	101.248	120.587	166.083	128.582

Table B-3.   U.S. Trade in Goods—Balance of Payments (BOP) Basis vs. Census Basis, 1960–2015

(Millions of dollars.)

Year	Balance BOP Basis	Balance Percent Change	Balance Census Basis	Balance Percent Change	Exports BOP Basis	Exports Percent Change	Exports Census Basis	Exports Percent Change	Imports BOP Basis	Imports Percent Change	Imports Census Basis	Imports Percent Change
1960	4,892	(X)	4,608	(X)	19,650	(X)	19,626	(X)	14,758	(X)	15,018	(X)
1961	5,571	13.9	5,476	18.8	20,108	2.3	20,190	2.9	14,537	-1.5	14,714	-2.0
1962	4,521	-18.8	4,583	-16.3	20,781	3.3	20,973	3.9	16,260	11.9	16,390	11.4
1963	5,224	15.5	5,289	15.4	22,272	7.2	22,427	6.9	17,048	4.8	17,138	4.6
1964	6,801	30.2	7,006	32.5	25,501	14.5	25,690	14.5	18,700	9.7	18,684	9.0
1965	4,951	-27.2	5,333	-23.9	26,461	3.8	26,699	3.9	21,510	15.0	21,366	14.4
1966	3,817	-22.9	3,837	-28.1	29,310	10.8	29,379	10.0	25,493	18.5	25,542	19.5
1967	3,800	-0.4	4,122	7.4	30,666	4.6	30,934	5.3	26,866	5.4	26,812	5.0
1968	635	-83.3	837	-79.7	33,626	9.7	34,063	10.1	32,991	22.8	33,226	23.9
1969	607	-4.4	1,289	54.0	36,414	8.3	37,332	9.6	35,807	8.5	36,043	8.5
1970	2,603	328.8	3,224	150.1	42,469	16.6	43,176	15.7	39,866	11.3	39,952	10.8
1971	-2,260	-186.8	-1,476	-145.8	43,319	2.0	44,087	2.1	45,579	14.3	45,563	14.0
1972	-6,416	183.9	-5,729	288.1	49,381	14.0	49,854	13.1	55,797	22.4	55,583	22.0
1973	911	-114.2	2,389	-141.7	71,410	44.6	71,865	44.2	70,499	26.3	69,476	25.0
1974	-5,505	-704.3	-3,884	-262.6	98,306	37.7	99,437	38.4	103,811	47.3	103,321	48.7
1975	8,903	-261.7	9,551	-345.9	107,088	8.9	108,856	9.5	98,185	-5.4	99,305	-3.9
1976	-9,483	-206.5	-7,820	-181.9	114,745	7.2	116,794	7.3	124,228	26.5	124,614	25.5
1977	-31,091	227.9	-28,352	262.6	120,816	5.3	123,182	5.5	151,907	22.3	151,534	21.6
1978	-33,927	9.1	-30,205	6.5	142,075	17.6	145,847	18.4	176,002	15.9	176,052	16.2
1979	-27,568	-18.7	-23,922	-20.8	184,439	29.8	186,363	27.8	212,007	20.5	210,285	19.4
1980	-25,500	-7.5	-19,696	-17.7	224,250	21.6	225,566	21.0	249,750	17.8	245,262	16.6
1981	-28,023	9.9	-22,267	13.1	237,044	5.7	238,715	5.8	265,067	6.1	260,982	6.4
1982	-36,485	30.2	-27,510	23.5	211,157	-10.9	216,442	-9.3	247,642	-6.6	243,952	-6.5
1983	-67,102	83.9	-52,409	90.5	201,799	-4.4	205,639	-5.0	268,901	8.6	258,048	5.8
1984	-112,492	67.6	-106,702	103.6	219,926	9.0	223,976	8.9	332,418	23.6	330,678	28.1
1985	-122,173	8.6	-117,711	10.3	215,915	-1.8	218,815	-2.3	338,088	1.7	336,526	1.8
1986	-145,081	18.8	-138,279	17.5	223,344	3.4	227,159	3.8	368,425	9.0	365,438	8.6
1987	-159,557	10.0	-152,119	10.0	250,208	12.0	254,122	11.9	409,765	11.2	406,241	11.2
1988	-126,959	-20.4	-118,526	-22.1	320,230	28.0	322,426	26.9	447,189	9.1	440,952	8.5
1989	-117,749	-7.3	-109,399	-7.7	359,916	12.4	363,812	12.8	477,665	6.8	473,211	7.3
1990	-111,037	-5.7	-101,719	-7.0	387,401	7.6	393,592	8.2	498,438	4.3	495,311	4.7
1991	-76,937	-30.7	-66,723	-34.4	414,083	6.9	421,730	7.1	491,020	-1.5	488,453	-1.4
1992	-96,897	25.9	-84,501	26.6	439,631	6.2	448,164	6.3	536,528	9.3	532,665	9.1
1993	-132,451	36.7	-115,568	36.8	456,943	3.9	465,091	3.8	589,394	9.9	580,659	9.0
1994	-165,831	25.2	-150,630	30.3	502,859	10.0	512,626	10.2	668,690	13.5	663,256	14.2
1995	-174,170	5.0	-158,801	5.4	575,204	14.4	584,742	14.1	749,374	12.1	743,543	12.1
1996	-191,000	9.7	-170,214	7.2	612,113	6.4	625,075	6.9	803,113	7.2	795,289	7.0
1997	-198,428	3.9	-180,522	6.1	678,366	10.8	689,182	10.3	876,794	9.2	869,704	9.4
1998	-248,221	25.1	-229,758	27.3	670,416	-1.2	682,138	-1.0	918,637	4.8	911,896	4.9
1999	-337,068	35.8	-328,821	43.1	698,524	4.2	695,797	2.0	1,035,592	12.7	1,024,618	12.4
2000	-446,783	32.5	-436,104	32.6	784,940	12.4	781,918	12.4	1,231,722	18.9	1,218,022	18.9
2001	-422,370	-5.5	-411,899	-5.6	731,331	-6.8	729,100	-6.8	1,153,701	-6.3	1,140,999	-6.3
2002	-475,245	12.5	-468,263	13.7	698,036	-4.6	693,103	-4.9	1,173,281	1.7	1,161,366	1.8
2003	-541,643	14.0	-532,350	13.7	730,446	4.6	724,771	4.6	1,272,089	8.4	1,257,121	8.2
2004	-664,766	22.7	-654,830	23.0	823,584	12.8	814,875	12.4	1,488,349	17.0	1,469,704	16.9
2005	-782,804	17.8	-772,373	18.0	913,016	10.9	901,082	10.6	1,695,820	13.9	1,673,455	13.9
2006	-837,289	7.0	-827,971	7.2	1,040,905	14.0	1,025,967	13.9	1,878,194	10.8	1,853,938	10.8
2007	-821,196	-1.9	-808,763	-2.3	1,165,151	11.9	1,148,199	11.9	1,986,347	5.8	1,956,962	5.6
2008	-832,492	1.4	-816,199	0.9	1,308,795	12.3	1,287,442	12.1	2,141,287	7.8	2,103,641	7.5
2009	-509,694	-38.8	-503,582	-38.3	1,070,331	-18.2	1,056,043	-18.0	1,580,025	-26.2	1,559,625	-25.9
2010	-648,678	27.3	-635,362	26.2	1,290,273	20.5	1,278,495	21.1	1,938,950	22.7	1,913,857	22.7
2011	-740,646	14.2	-725,447	14.2	1,499,240	16.2	1,482,508	16.0	2,239,886	15.5	2,207,954	15.4
2012	-741,171	0.1	-730,446	0.7	1,562,578	4.2	1,545,821	4.3	2,303,749	2.9	2,276,267	3.1
2013	-702,244	-5.3	-689,470	-5.6	1,592,002	1.9	1,578,517	2.1	2,294,247	-0.4	2,267,987	-0.4
2014	-752,169	7.1	-735,194	6.6	1,633,320	2.6	1,621,172	2.7	2,385,489	4.0	2,356,366	3.9
2015	-762,565	1.4	-745,660	1.4	1,510,303	-7.5	1,502,572	-7.3	2,272,868	-4.7	2,248,232	-4.6

Table B-4. U.S. Trade in Services by Type of Service, 1999–2015

(Millions of dollars.)

Year	Total Services			Maintenance and Repair			Transport			Travel			Insurance		
	Exports	Imports	Balance	Exports	Imports	Balance	Exports	Imports	Balance	Exports	Imports	Balance	Exports	Imports	Balance
1999	271,343	192,893	78,450	4,089	1,278	2,811	43,218	49,620	92,838	92,338	59,592	151,930	3,052	9,389	12,441
2000	290,381	216,115	74,266	5,011	2,569	2,442	45,758	57,606	103,364	100,187	65,787	165,974	3,631	11,284	14,915
2001	274,323	213,465	60,858	5,897	1,999	3,898	41,716	53,840	95,556	86,733	60,730	147,463	3,424	16,706	20,130
2002	280,670	224,379	56,291	6,019	2,217	3,802	41,912	51,491	93,403	81,869	59,942	141,811	4,415	21,927	26,342
2003	289,972	242,219	47,753	5,699	2,246	3,453	41,446	57,863	99,309	80,332	61,884	142,216	5,974	25,233	31,207
2004	337,966	283,083	54,883	5,714	2,395	3,319	47,723	69,158	116,881	92,387	74,024	166,411	7,314	29,089	36,403
2005	373,006	304,448	68,558	7,624	3,015	4,609	52,622	75,643	128,265	101,470	79,988	181,458	7,566	28,710	36,276
2006	416,738	341,165	75,573	8,235	4,583	3,652	57,462	77,962	135,424	105,140	84,206	189,346	9,445	39,382	48,827
2007	488,396	372,575	115,821	10,020	5,209	4,811	65,824	79,326	145,150	119,037	89,235	208,272	10,841	47,517	58,358
2008	532,817	409,052	123,765	10,586	5,742	4,844	74,973	83,988	158,961	133,761	92,545	226,306	13,403	58,913	72,316
2009	512,722	386,801	125,921	12,863	5,938	6,925	62,189	64,133	126,322	119,902	81,421	201,323	14,586	63,801	78,387
2010	563,333	409,313	154,020	14,549	6,909	7,640	71,656	74,628	146,284	137,010	86,623	223,633	14,397	61,478	75,875
2011	627,781	435,761	192,020	16,436	8,236	8,200	79,830	81,377	161,207	150,867	89,700	240,567	15,114	55,654	70,768
2012	656,411	452,013	204,398	17,186	8,015	9,171	83,944	84,985	168,929	161,632	100,338	261,970	16,790	55,513	72,303
2013	687,894	463,700	224,194	18,648	7,486	11,162	87,415	90,634	178,049	172,901	104,107	277,008	17,058	53,420	70,478
2014	710,565	477,428	233,137	22,389	7,468	14,921	90,031	94,219	184,250	177,241	110,787	288,028	17,417	50,096	67,513
2015	750,860	488,657	262,203	24,036	8,996	15,040	87,221	97,050	-9,829	204,523	112,873	91,650	17,142	47,772	-30,630

Table B-4. U.S. Trade in Services by Type of Service, 1999–2015—*Continued*

(Millions of dollars.)

Year	Financial			Change for use of intellectual property			Telecommunications			Other business services			Government goods and services		
	Exports	Imports	Balance	Exports	Imports	Balance	Exports	Imports	Balance	Exports	Imports	Balance	Exports	Imports	Balance
1999	19,433	8,280	27,713	47,731	13,302	61,033	12,287	13,332	25,619	40,976	23,887	64,863	8,218	14,212	22,430
2000	22,117	10,936	33,053	51,808	16,606	68,414	12,215	12,397	24,612	40,497	24,414	64,911	9,156	14,516	23,672
2001	21,899	10,157	32,056	49,489	16,661	66,150	12,829	12,421	25,250	44,146	25,629	69,775	8,191	15,322	23,513
2002	24,496	8,963	33,459	53,859	19,493	73,352	12,451	11,721	24,172	47,996	29,274	77,270	7,653	19,353	27,006
2003	27,840	8,948	36,788	56,813	19,259	76,072	14,061	13,063	27,124	48,775	30,103	78,878	9,033	23,619	32,652
2004	36,389	11,156	47,545	67,094	23,691	90,785	14,962	14,210	29,172	54,398	33,065	87,463	11,985	26,296	38,281
2005	39,878	12,126	52,004	74,448	25,577	100,025	15,515	15,975	31,490	58,302	35,960	94,262	15,582	27,454	43,036
2006	47,882	14,733	62,615	83,549	25,038	108,587	17,184	19,776	36,960	68,619	48,130	116,749	19,222	27,353	46,575
2007	61,376	19,197	80,573	97,803	26,479	124,282	20,192	22,384	42,576	82,382	54,968	137,350	20,921	28,260	49,181
2008	63,027	17,218	80,245	102,125	29,623	131,748	23,119	24,655	47,774	92,738	67,488	160,226	19,084	28,880	47,964
2009	64,437	14,415	78,852	98,406	31,297	129,703	23,816	25,784	49,600	95,984	68,553	164,537	20,538	31,460	51,998
2010	72,348	15,502	87,850	107,521	32,551	140,072	25,038	29,015	54,053	101,029	70,646	171,675	19,784	31,960	51,744
2011	78,271	17,368	95,639	123,333	36,087	159,420	29,171	32,756	61,927	112,568	83,289	195,857	22,191	31,293	53,484
2012	76,692	16,703	93,395	124,440	38,661	163,101	32,510	32,779	65,289	120,382	87,157	207,539	22,835	27,861	50,696
2013	84,091	18,519	102,610	127,927	38,999	166,926	35,035	33,812	68,847	121,873	91,389	213,262	22,946	25,334	48,280
2014	87,290	19,503	106,793	130,362	42,124	172,486	35,885	33,314	69,199	129,514	95,752	225,266	20,438	24,163	44,601
2015	102,461	25,162	77,299	124,664	39,495	85,169	35,895	36,440	-545	134,648	99,354	35,294	20,270	21,515	*-1,245*

Table B-5. Exports and Imports of Goods by Principal End-Use Category, 1992–2015

(In millions of dollars. Details may not equal totals due to seasonal adjustment and rounding.)

| Period | Total Census Basis | | | End-Use Commodity Category | | | | | | | | |
| | | | | Foods, Feeds, Beverages | | | Industrial Supplies | | | Capital Goods | | |
	Exports	Imports	Balance	Exports	Imports	Balance	Exports	Imports	Balance	Exports	Imports	Balance
1992	448,164	532,665	980,828	40,270	27,610	67,880	95,490	138,644	234,134	175,915	134,253	310,168
1993	465,091	580,659	1,045,750	40,628	27,867	68,495	96,362	145,606	241,968	181,696	152,365	334,061
1994	512,626	663,256	1,175,882	41,956	30,958	72,914	103,872	162,114	265,986	205,022	184,368	389,390
1995	584,742	743,543	1,328,285	50,473	33,176	83,649	116,825	181,849	298,674	233,046	221,431	454,477
1996	625,075	795,289	1,420,364	55,534	35,710	91,244	126,954	204,482	331,436	252,977	228,074	481,051
1997	689,182	869,704	1,558,886	51,507	39,694	91,201	130,895	213,767	344,662	294,549	253,282	547,831
1998	682,138	911,896	1,594,034	46,397	41,243	87,640	128,883	200,140	329,023	299,350	269,451	568,801
1999	695,797	1,024,618	1,720,415	45,977	43,602	89,579	133,181	221,386	354,567	310,794	295,717	606,511
2000	781,918	1,218,022	1,999,940	47,871	45,979	93,850	139,829	298,980	438,809	356,934	347,025	703,959
2001	729,100	1,140,999	1,870,099	49,407	46,641	96,048	142,689	273,870	416,559	321,714	297,993	619,707
2002	693,103	1,161,366	1,854,469	49,616	49,687	99,303	148,990	267,693	416,683	290,437	283,323	573,760
2003	724,771	1,257,121	1,981,892	55,026	55,831	110,857	166,688	313,818	480,506	293,673	295,867	589,540
2004	814,875	1,469,704	2,284,579	56,570	62,143	118,713	180,856	412,772	593,628	327,540	343,582	671,122
2005	901,082	1,673,455	2,574,537	58,955	68,094	127,049	195,143	523,771	718,914	358,426	379,331	737,757
2006	1,025,967	1,853,938	2,879,905	65,962	74,938	140,900	215,838	601,988	817,826	404,026	418,259	822,285
2007	1,148,199	1,956,962	3,105,161	84,264	81,683	165,947	247,630	634,746	882,376	433,019	444,508	877,527
2008	1,287,442	2,103,641	3,391,083	108,349	88,997	197,346	286,343	779,481	1,065,824	457,655	453,743	911,398
2009	1,056,043	1,559,625	2,615,668	93,908	81,615	175,523	257,138	462,380	719,518	391,242	370,480	761,722
2010	1,278,495	1,913,857	3,192,352	107,719	91,748	199,467	291,215	603,104	894,319	447,537	449,387	896,924
2011	1,482,508	2,207,954	3,690,462	126,247	107,476	233,723	341,199	755,784	1,096,983	493,956	510,799	1,004,755
2012	1,545,821	2,276,267	3,822,088	133,049	110,271	243,320	353,591	730,639	1,084,230	527,178	548,708	1,075,886
2013	1,578,439	2,268,370	3,846,809	136,160	115,126	251,286	366,412	681,552	1,047,964	534,177	554,573	1,088,750
2014	1,620,532	2,347,685	3,968,217	143,751	125,757	269,508	395,265	666,751	1,062,016	551,056	591,115	1,142,171
2015	1,504,914	2,240,933	3,745,847	127,704	127,689	255,393	383,082	485,908	868,990	538,341	599,156	1,137,497

Note: Detailed data are presented on a Census basis. The information needed to convert to a BOP basis is not available.

Table B-5.   Exports and Imports of Goods by Principal End-Use Category, 1992–2015—*Continued*

(In millions of dollars. Details may not equal totals due to seasonal adjustment and rounding.)

Period	End-Use Commodity Category								
	Automotive Vehicles, etc.			Consumer Goods			Other Goods		
	Exports	Imports	Balance	Exports	Imports	Balance	Exports	Imports	Balance
1992	47,028	91,788	138,817	51,425	122,657	174,082	24,385	17,713	42,098
1993	52,404	102,420	154,824	54,656	134,015	188,671	23,893	18,386	42,279
1994	57,775	118,271	176,046	59,981	146,274	206,255	26,495	21,272	47,767
1995	61,828	123,795	185,623	64,425	159,905	224,330	28,723	23,387	52,110
1996	65,021	128,938	193,959	70,056	171,983	242,039	33,836	26,102	59,938
1997	74,029	139,812	213,841	77,366	193,811	271,177	33,505	29,338	62,843
1998	72,387	148,680	221,067	80,294	216,996	297,290	35,444	35,387	70,831
1999	75,256	178,964	254,220	80,922	241,905	322,827	35,324	43,044	78,368
2000	80,356	195,875	276,231	89,377	281,832	371,209	34,765	48,331	83,096
2001	75,435	189,782	265,217	88,331	284,293	372,624	34,110	48,421	82,531
2002	78,942	203,743	282,685	84,359	307,842	392,201	32,937	49,078	82,015
2003	80,633	210,139	290,772	89,908	333,878	423,786	32,487	47,587	80,074
2004	89,213	228,163	317,376	103,238	372,938	476,176	34,404	50,106	84,510
2005	98,406	239,449	337,855	115,285	407,237	522,522	36,964	55,572	92,536
2006	107,263	256,627	363,890	129,081	442,639	571,720	43,589	59,487	103,076
2007	121,264	256,666	377,930	145,975	474,552	620,527	47,300	64,806	112,106
2008	121,451	231,242	352,693	161,281	481,643	642,924	50,673	68,536	119,209
2009	81,715	157,652	239,367	149,455	427,332	576,787	43,215	60,165	103,380
2010	112,008	225,097	337,105	165,228	483,225	648,453	54,341	61,296	115,637
2011	133,036	254,619	387,655	175,304	514,108	689,412	52,888	65,169	118,057
2012	146,158	297,780	443,938	181,683	516,918	698,601	56,575	71,953	128,528
2013	152,670	308,803	461,473	189,101	532,755	721,856	58,251	75,562	133,813
2014	159,690	327,651	487,341	198,906	557,783	756,689	62,014	78,629	140,643
2015	151,563	348,283	499,846	197,817	595,175	792,992	61,317	84,721	146,038

Note: Detailed data are presented on a Census basis. The information needed to convert to a BOP basis is not available.

PART II: EXPORTS AND IMPORTS BY SELECTED CATEGORIES

Table B-6. U.S. Exports with World by Harmonzied System (HS) for Total Merchandise, 2010–2015

HS	Export	2010	2011	2012	2013	2014	2015
	TOTAL	1,278,494,525,839	1,482,507,755,226	1,545,820,839,892	1,578,516,879,950	1,621,171,618,259	1,502,572,229,518
	Foods, feeds and beverages	**114,532,975,095**	**136,081,252,881**	**141,937,475,915**	**144,975,003,617**	**153,016,419,858**	**136,223,883,774**
1	LIVE ANIMALS	814,890,071	1,038,251,364	1,189,530,232	1,019,514,929	944,295,813	757,360,691
2	MEAT AND EDIBLE MEAT OFFAL	12,051,903,134	15,357,261,104	16,096,226,509	16,274,745,442	17,665,168,093	14,278,381,054
3	FISH; CRUSTACEANS & AQUATIC INVERTEBRATES	4,028,222,279	5,082,222,129	5,024,708,727	5,134,076,513	5,257,079,440	5,087,845,483
4	DAIRY PRODS; BIRDS EGGS; HONEY; ED ANIMAL PR NESOI	3,223,273,009	4,113,779,080	4,252,529,967	5,769,222,235	6,160,374,243	4,447,901,155
5	PRODUCTS OF ANIMAL ORIGIN; NESOI	741,570,691	842,573,928	894,878,929	1,024,144,142	1,123,366,972	1,131,658,335
6	LIVE TREES; PLANTS; BULBS ETC.; CUT FLOWERS ETC.	416,042,869	423,746,283	400,532,063	417,596,816	421,378,448	411,245,226
7	EDIBLE VEGETABLES & CERTAIN ROOTS & TUBERS	3,784,499,541	3,939,248,155	4,044,613,580	4,404,427,386	4,511,818,098	4,363,056,510
8	EDIBLE FRUIT & NUTS; CITRUS FRUIT OR MELON PEEL	10,142,478,585	11,767,712,352	13,263,744,191	14,532,740,414	14,856,806,331	14,459,437,122
9	COFFEE; TEA; MATE & SPICES	888,103,008	1,226,518,123	1,295,237,452	1,184,247,043	1,224,696,955	1,219,454,066
10	CEREALS	20,036,820,271	28,347,941,016	20,616,227,140	20,301,036,516	22,825,948,714	18,799,966,274
11	MILLING PRODUCTS; MALT; STARCH; INULIN; WHT GLUTEN	830,992,496	870,422,650	955,146,084	912,478,271	936,329,821	886,704,661
12	OIL SEEDS ETC.; MISC GRAIN; SEED; FRUIT; PLANT ETC	21,959,179,277	21,231,783,916	29,688,506,908	26,955,408,692	28,876,576,254	23,619,245,783
13	LAC; GUMS; RESINS & OTHER VEGETABLE SAP & EXTRACT	566,016,918	602,082,724	743,281,020	619,071,942	605,322,090	572,970,645
14	VEGETABLE PLAITING MATERIALS & PRODUCTS NESOI	168,396,693	97,829,548	48,825,826	55,649,035	32,180,329	32,047,543
15	ANIMAL OR VEGETABLE FATS; OILS ETC. & WAXES	4,648,763,492	4,993,032,870	4,627,662,400	3,789,555,906	3,404,697,885	3,167,254,091
16	EDIBLE PREPARATIONS OF MEAT; FISH; CRUSTACEANS ETC	1,658,406,384	1,859,173,780	1,965,869,661	2,227,412,479	2,407,703,600	2,298,754,137
17	SUGARS AND SUGAR CONFECTIONARY	1,741,252,237	2,166,356,133	2,560,099,709	2,476,526,283	2,267,383,043	1,970,833,844
18	COCOA AND COCOA PREPARATIONS	1,385,233,144	1,592,859,889	1,717,000,953	1,870,791,003	2,118,581,220	1,949,866,177
19	PREP CEREAL; FLOUR; STARCH OR MILK; BAKERS WARES	3,087,156,331	3,505,309,232	3,887,706,293	4,193,985,012	4,254,275,203	4,279,738,369
20	PREP VEGETABLES; FRUIT; NUTS OR OTHER PLANT PARTS	3,778,290,784	4,404,190,110	4,750,358,967	5,071,531,595	5,190,017,079	5,425,107,865
21	MISCELLANEOUS EDIBLE PREPARATIONS	5,535,697,518	6,253,896,507	7,118,791,782	8,006,244,294	8,342,552,855	8,239,968,342
22	BEVERAGES; SPIRITS AND VINEGAR	4,712,806,821	7,814,659,221	6,887,352,486	6,952,722,650	7,624,827,163	7,562,243,238
23	FOOD INDUSTRY RESIDUES & WASTE; PREP ANIMAL FEED	8,332,979,542	8,550,402,767	9,908,645,036	11,781,875,019	11,965,040,209	11,262,843,163
	Industrial supplies and materials	**502,184,503,719**	**617,852,735,214**	**623,950,806,904**	**637,754,203,784**	**641,260,564,295**	**560,842,610,304**
24	TOBACCO AND MANUFACTURED TOBACCO SUBSTITUTES	1,671,101,643	1,695,718,949	1,657,584,481	1,909,886,988	1,805,463,578	2,077,517,416
25	SALT; SULFUR; EARTH & STONE; LIME & CEMENT PLASTER	2,264,617,154	2,501,859,883	2,616,724,431	2,596,545,666	2,855,091,104	2,677,884,697
26	ORES; SLAG AND ASH	5,558,830,773	7,700,074,023	7,019,870,423	7,320,982,174	8,362,919,547	6,811,997,450
27	MINERAL FUEL; OIL ETC.; BITUMIN SUBST; MINERAL WAX	81,692,031,854	130,566,667,652	137,332,528,657	148,902,536,669	155,851,665,718	104,105,881,821
28	INORG CHEM; PREC & RARE-EARTH MET & RADIOACT COMPD	12,853,530,080	15,295,628,726	13,658,258,339	12,438,817,099	12,681,947,927	12,367,717,904
29	ORGANIC CHEMICALS	40,928,206,521	45,682,439,840	46,079,294,886	46,599,579,308	42,326,082,876	38,755,176,681
30	PHARMACEUTICAL PRODUCTS	40,788,229,885	38,341,460,576	40,129,282,726	39,707,839,099	43,983,359,926	47,293,310,441
31	FERTILIZERS	4,667,397,891	6,308,950,329	5,378,724,892	5,022,023,701	4,632,388,913	4,394,457,750
32	TANNING & DYE EXT ETC; DYE; PAINT; PUTTY ETC; INKS	7,629,809,819	8,826,327,747	8,161,700,258	7,825,159,842	7,974,884,779	7,588,429,386
33	ESSENTIAL OILS ETC; PERFUMERY; COSMETIC ETC PREPS	9,094,028,878	9,633,632,802	10,452,105,120	11,132,291,730	11,556,765,395	11,808,302,041
34	SOAP ETC; WAXES; POLISH ETC; CANDLES; DENTAL PREPS	5,861,892,788	6,476,645,697	6,860,865,796	7,120,108,867	7,384,235,369	7,108,662,216
35	ALBUMINOIDAL SUBST; MODIFIED STARCH; GLUE; ENZYMES	2,709,811,018	2,973,427,825	3,064,813,377	3,275,747,077	3,475,600,656	3,391,488,510
36	EXPLOSIVES; PYROTECHNICS; MATCHES; PYRO ALLOYS ETC	804,463,297	812,259,777	874,116,036	840,472,857	863,294,570	865,067,862
37	PHOTOGRAPHIC OR CINEMATOGRAPHIC GOODS	2,832,929,568	2,760,976,978	2,573,655,290	2,560,790,120	2,375,018,595	2,364,571,383
38	MISCELLANEOUS CHEMICAL PRODUCTS	21,197,592,716	23,881,041,834	25,327,714,357	27,030,926,329	27,262,553,612	25,914,213,809
39	PLASTICS AND ARTICLES THEREOF	53,625,263,449	58,743,604,827	59,006,434,035	61,045,249,532	63,091,433,153	60,268,037,778
40	RUBBER AND ARTICLES THEREOF	12,121,181,293	14,889,441,268	15,724,934,830	14,855,918,049	14,993,588,816	13,663,647,885
41	RAW HIDES AND SKINS (NO FURSKINS) AND LEATHER	2,905,251,880	3,326,712,444	3,233,356,438	3,757,798,824	3,833,739,719	3,186,945,011
42	LEATHER ART; SADDLERY ETC; HANDBAGS ETC; GUT ART	1,214,459,171	1,365,038,987	1,539,721,780	1,643,391,401	1,624,687,416	1,684,273,884
43	FURSKINS AND ARTIFICIAL FUR; MANUFACTURES THEREOF	289,218,455	423,006,652	614,271,029	702,471,756	583,202,858	533,536,786
44	WOOD AND ARTICLES OF WOOD; WOOD CHARCOAL	7,076,308,910	7,914,476,070	7,890,641,014	8,963,166,683	9,744,606,733	8,927,937,190
45	CORK AND ARTICLES OF CORK	37,805,961	36,098,349	31,126,099	28,936,490	30,501,423	30,993,767
46	MFR OF STRAW; ESPARTO ETC.; BASKETWARE & WICKERWRK	23,093,597	21,323,964	23,596,575	22,121,014	21,168,312	18,467,603
47	WOOD PULP ETC; RECOVD (WASTE & SCRAP) PPR & PPRBD	8,861,531,583	10,102,765,689	9,311,759,470	8,965,421,214	8,965,406,799	8,704,333,323
48	PAPER & PAPERBOARD & ARTICLES (INC PAPR PULP ARTL)	15,784,736,540	16,945,425,340	16,057,949,059	16,414,411,631	16,350,561,941	15,697,909,371
49	PRINTED BOOKS; NEWSPAPERS ETC; MANUSCRIPTS ETC	5,758,555,541	5,747,146,007	5,700,094,128	5,580,855,708	5,219,028,641	4,860,935,291
50	SILK; INCLUDING YARNS AND WOVEN FABRIC THEREOF	26,349,246	23,610,584	16,866,833	13,484,999	12,584,366	12,628,402
51	WOOL & ANIMAL HAIR; INCLUDING YARN & WOVEN FABRIC	87,680,929	84,842,281	84,303,326	99,683,176	83,123,523	86,014,969
52	COTTON; INCLUDING YARN AND WOVEN FABRIC THEREOF	7,544,221,258	11,067,176,820	8,284,411,815	7,636,531,878	6,520,879,133	5,873,207,781
53	VEG TEXT FIB NESOI; VEG FIB & PAPER YNS & WOV FAB	23,544,314	19,079,402	17,113,594	16,791,784	20,048,517	22,375,194
54	MANMADE FILAMENTS; INCLUDING YARNS & WOVEN FABRICS	1,570,872,418	1,740,539,317	1,754,243,177	1,775,869,233	1,878,766,240	1,789,266,487
55	MANMADE STAPLE FIBERS; INCL YARNS & WOVEN FABRICS	2,257,754,014	2,635,624,168	2,632,974,957	2,741,206,059	2,710,426,078	2,463,755,889

Table B-6. U.S. Exports with World by Harmonzied System (HS) for Total Merchandise, 2010–2015—*Continued*

HS	Export / TOTAL	2010	2011	2012	2013	2014	2015
	TOTAL	1,278,494,525,839	1,482,507,755,226	1,545,820,839,892	1,578,516,879,950	1,621,171,618,259	1,502,572,229,518
56	WADDING; FELT ETC; SP YARN; TWINE; ROPES ETC.	2,098,667,959	2,257,364,076	2,295,695,733	2,445,142,454	2,512,908,814	2,339,159,674
57	CARPETS AND OTHER TEXTILE FLOOR COVERINGS............	1,006,280,928	1,077,286,820	1,105,466,032	1,124,815,762	1,118,647,226	1,032,245,082
58	SPEC WOV FABRICS; TUFTED FAB; LACE; TAPESTRIES ETC .	526,852,816	509,007,472	494,488,434	485,600,426	502,489,374	493,218,756
59	IMPREGNATED ETC TEXT FABRICS; TEX ART FOR INDUSTRY	1,745,418,973	1,902,258,918	2,033,214,794	2,115,293,613	2,239,813,642	2,241,201,603
60	KNITTED OR CROCHETED FABRICS	1,062,234,571	1,059,612,522	1,032,259,706	1,075,447,051	1,058,789,039	1,060,538,510
61	APPAREL ARTICLES AND ACCESSORIES; KNIT OR CROCHET	2,169,167,249	2,332,334,327	2,448,878,587	2,645,216,260	2,728,641,146	2,736,153,223
62	APPAREL ARTICLES AND ACCESSORIES; NOT KNIT ETC.	1,821,093,737	2,129,571,917	2,350,755,298	2,419,146,053	2,572,364,529	2,592,487,088
63	TEXTILE ART NESOI; NEEDLECRAFT SETS; WORN TEXT ART	1,650,142,390	1,894,217,155	1,999,850,036	2,165,964,188	2,225,651,708	2,182,667,357
64	FOOTWEAR; GAITERS ETC. AND PARTS THEREOF	1,105,454,224	1,290,038,604	1,332,305,334	1,391,282,682	1,456,188,127	1,463,617,789
65	HEADGEAR AND PARTS THEREOF	200,428,648	232,940,306	272,702,473	263,832,268	272,573,306	298,813,486
66	UMBRELLAS; WALKING-STICKS; RIDING-CROPS ETC; PARTS	22,538,416	30,253,103	31,806,985	29,476,564	32,214,815	33,419,746
67	PREP FEATHERS; DOWN ETC; ARTIF FLOWERS; H HAIR ART	88,391,338	102,704,432	111,383,109	120,779,273	128,346,978	138,346,309
68	ART OF STONE; PLASTER; CEMENT; ASBESTOS; MICA ETC.	2,829,960,773	3,174,045,168	3,343,968,102	3,512,032,347	3,856,186,032	3,867,715,186
69	CERAMIC PRODUCTS..	1,523,913,311	1,734,982,502	1,714,201,895	1,765,655,951	1,900,464,049	1,814,218,378
70	GLASS AND GLASSWARE	4,996,740,876	5,338,931,730	5,295,622,114	5,602,208,122	5,779,263,321	5,786,542,411
71	NAT ETC PEARLS; PREC ETC STONES; PR MET ETC; COIN ...	52,137,973,983	72,611,396,268	72,995,044,704	72,487,187,993	64,895,567,418	58,733,878,893
72	IRON AND STEEL	19,825,319,622	25,361,376,296	22,838,005,653	19,679,341,955	18,562,450,400	14,547,198,648
73	ARTICLES OF IRON OR STEEL..	16,197,383,923	18,519,856,556	21,154,320,200	22,049,195,857	22,603,649,908	19,631,695,087
74	COPPER AND ARTICLES THEREOF..................................	7,886,532,311	9,654,622,798	9,695,969,247	9,119,645,273	8,664,373,205	7,074,500,312
75	NICKEL AND ARTICLES THEREOF	1,702,240,449	2,231,076,340	2,170,239,613	2,107,195,997	2,206,032,299	2,187,395,162
76	ALUMINUM AND ARTICLES THEREOF	10,625,015,790	12,975,642,409	12,783,556,217	13,053,059,534	12,736,160,539	12,047,473,641
78	LEAD AND ARTICLES THEREOF......................................	186,821,487	179,812,078	154,786,547	189,229,573	207,644,751	158,507,721
79	ZINC AND ARTICLES THEREOF	289,233,020	323,615,789	395,246,263	322,867,465	443,052,132	347,865,445
80	TIN AND ARTICLES THEREOF...	222,216,705	243,649,075	197,526,915	189,956,941	207,596,133	158,736,086
81	BASE METALS NESOI; CERMETS; ARTICLES THEREOF	2,040,799,746	2,611,946,411	2,720,940,969	2,735,758,998	2,868,541,775	2,696,953,790
82	TOOLS; CUTLERY ETC. OF BASE METAL & PARTS THEREOF	4,711,937,467	5,392,654,619	5,464,841,638	5,496,446,721	5,457,382,295	4,957,451,081
83	MISCELLANEOUS ARTICLES OF BASE METAL	3,749,440,563	4,138,512,716	4,406,693,078	4,615,407,506	4,948,545,101	4,871,663,862
	Capital goods, except automotive.............................	**419,429,354,983**	**458,924,476,008**	**489,437,249,832**	**500,698,476,937**	**524,947,489,253**	**515,000,051,002**
84	NUCLEAR REACTORS; BOILERS; MACHINERY ETC.; PARTS .	182,902,860,899	205,826,159,717	215,180,487,807	213,440,918,266	219,842,558,893	206,100,142,194
85	ELECTRIC MACHINERY ETC; SOUND EQUIP; TV EQUIP; PTS	151,776,704,354	159,468,543,383	162,434,694,242	165,818,048,345	172,363,626,713	169,956,050,124
86	RAILWAY OR TRAMWAY STOCK ETC; TRAFFIC SIGNAL EQUIP	2,502,803,122	3,269,555,937	3,848,119,872	3,875,225,395	4,050,564,161	4,182,997,104
88	AIRCRAFT; SPACECRAFT; AND PARTS THEREOF	79,617,922,992	87,757,246,448	104,440,079,691	114,886,824,530	125,291,175,809	131,627,865,014
89	SHIPS; BOATS AND FLOATING STRUCTURES......................	2,629,063,616	2,602,970,523	3,533,868,220	2,677,460,401	3,399,563,677	3,132,996,566
	Automotive vechicels, parts, and engines	**99,148,692,588**	**120,011,780,504**	**133,078,052,912**	**134,090,149,318**	**136,021,387,004**	**127,396,967,732**
87	VEHICLES; EXCEPT RAILWAY OR TRAMWAY; AND PARTS ETC	99,148,692,588	120,011,780,504	133,078,052,912	134,090,149,318	136,021,387,004	127,396,967,732
	Consumer goods	**102,825,127,525**	**110,259,517,186**	**116,778,509,214**	**118,858,987,380**	**122,662,900,529**	**121,669,633,698**
90	OPTIC; PHOTO ETC; MEDIC OR SURGICAL INSTRMENTS ETC	73,960,066,842	79,383,778,894	83,367,062,357	84,344,595,248	84,976,899,318	83,444,556,553
91	CLOCKS AND WATCHES AND PARTS THEREOF....................	918,042,799	1,134,291,512	1,253,767,147	1,230,606,023	1,326,222,534	1,317,248,822
92	MUSICAL INSTRUMENTS; PARTS AND ACCESSORIES THEREOF	707,512,077	815,050,698	858,184,035	828,997,617	822,229,890	774,475,163
93	ARMS AND AMMUNITION; PARTS AND ACCESSORIES THEREOF	3,976,384,055	3,936,050,053	4,055,538,561	4,634,784,363	4,550,411,447	5,026,023,396
94	FURNITURE; BEDDING ETC; LAMPS NESOI ETC; PREFAB BD	8,591,937,170	9,552,824,362	10,622,789,543	11,103,413,945	11,842,773,619	11,558,116,682
95	TOYS; GAMES & SPORT EQUIPMENT; PARTS & ACCESSORIES	6,928,634,899	7,202,434,087	7,056,863,617	6,734,732,883	6,600,301,426	6,197,088,195
96	MISCELLANEOUS MANUFACTURED ARTICLES	1,290,442,834	1,325,913,287	2,176,674,913	2,284,255,077	2,340,065,503	2,321,383,962
97	WORKS OF ART; COLLECTORS' PIECES AND ANTIQUES.......	6,452,106,849	6,909,174,293	7,387,629,041	7,697,602,224	10,203,996,792	11,030,740,925
	Other goods..	**40,373,871,929**	**39,377,993,433**	**40,638,745,115**	**42,140,058,914**	**43,262,857,320**	**41,439,083,008**
98	SPECIAL CLASSIFICATION PROVISIONS; NESOI	40,373,871,929	39,377,993,433	40,638,745,115	42,140,058,914	43,262,857,320	41,439,083,008

Table B-7.   U.S. Imports with World by Harmonzied System (HS) for Total Merchandise, 2010–2015

HS	Import	2010	2011	2012	2013	2014	2015
	TOTAL	1,913,856,594,014	2,207,954,346,316	2,276,267,147,199	2,267,986,733,622	2,356,365,502,725	2,248,232,395,233
	Industrial supplies and materials	**5,669,820,617,806**	**6,581,918,542,080**	**6,755,171,664,520**	**6,740,149,477,795**	**6,995,178,529,966**	**6,667,144,652,491**
	Capital goods, except automotive................................	**1,864,902,906,852**	**2,165,873,588,673**	**2,246,465,047,786**	**2,240,681,802,487**	**2,322,744,327,576**	**2,220,831,311,275**
85	ELECTRIC MACHINERY ETC; SOUND EQUIP; TV EQUIP; PTS ...	258,235,732,124	278,578,502,864	291,562,129,068	298,482,465,393	315,812,496,521	328,286,273,785
84	NUCLEAR REACTORS; BOILERS; MACHINERY ETC.; PARTS	249,797,039,140	287,635,771,553	308,088,220,073	304,838,343,715	325,171,903,843	322,848,429,149
	Automotive vehicles, parts and engines	**182,789,210,416**	**202,618,529,448**	**240,003,940,732**	**249,017,542,957**	**261,650,574,600**	**279,899,687,298**
87	VEHICLES; EXCEPT RAILWAY OR TRAMWAY; AND PARTS ETC	182,789,210,416	202,618,529,448	240,003,940,732	249,017,542,957	261,650,574,600	279,899,687,298
	Consumer goods	**1,249,527,446,880**	**1,473,000,758,224**	**1,458,368,946,249**	**1,437,808,372,858**	**1,474,271,274,533**	**1,338,183,507,530**
27	MINERAL FUEL; OIL ETC.; BITUMIN SUBST; MINERAL WAX....	355,070,549,606	453,932,881,724	423,991,873,335	379,894,747,602	347,712,892,468	190,658,012,180
	Foods, feed and beverages	**599,006,284,833**	**682,804,691,783**	**696,726,095,390**	**711,928,410,673**	**760,088,760,547**	**769,547,210,799**
30	PHARMACEUTICAL PRODUCTS	61,628,685,081	65,748,306,910	64,563,002,548	62,908,417,125	72,613,258,128	85,507,993,837
90	OPTIC; PHOTO ETC; MEDIC OR SURGICAL INSTRMENTS ETC.	58,876,075,643	66,081,084,213	68,810,632,221	71,136,644,228	75,440,937,299	77,441,367,524
71	NAT ETC PEARLS; PREC ETC STONES; PR MET ETC; COIN	54,219,642,145	69,178,026,504	64,374,267,835	66,526,207,513	64,880,065,213	59,309,039,710
94	FURNITURE; BEDDING ETC; LAMPS NESOI ETC; PREFAB BD ..	37,821,166,238	39,790,724,984	44,365,466,241	47,661,903,375	51,938,811,977	56,924,568,716
29	ORGANIC CHEMICALS..	47,935,644,015	56,054,589,618	53,460,389,819	53,524,821,737	53,675,599,652	50,922,104,608
39	PLASTICS AND ARTICLES THEREOF................................	34,969,399,319	39,410,452,488	42,077,218,860	44,227,220,605	47,920,949,249	47,873,210,156
61	APPAREL ARTICLES AND ACCESSORIES; KNIT OR CROCHET .	38,316,334,691	41,839,331,101	41,135,839,681	42,952,295,181	45,104,869,951	46,866,345,975
62	APPAREL ARTICLES AND ACCESSORIES; NOT KNIT ETC.	34,207,011,914	36,935,341,560	36,785,258,653	38,016,754,783	37,877,249,839	39,236,575,107
73	ARTICLES OF IRON OR STEEL..	26,671,348,283	32,116,083,112	37,691,099,974	34,337,100,138	37,758,775,376	36,583,434,582
88	AIRCRAFT; SPACECRAFT; AND PARTS THEREOF	18,784,788,012	21,483,415,291	24,257,975,352	29,419,871,919	34,353,639,069	35,144,698,242
64	FOOTWEAR; GAITERS ETC. AND PARTS THEREOF	20,902,633,394	22,653,549,332	23,886,572,587	24,811,248,202	26,017,377,215	27,649,844,861
40	RUBBER AND ARTICLES THEREOF	21,749,991,222	27,998,242,374	28,599,703,724	27,400,759,313	27,662,389,636	26,443,658,417
72	IRON AND STEEL...	21,461,519,994	28,375,123,982	29,012,849,534	25,314,342,619	34,203,285,494	26,289,270,829
22	BEVERAGES; SPIRITS AND VINEGAR	15,742,262,869	17,858,296,224	19,821,707,487	20,210,982,056	20,359,060,077	21,260,302,926
76	ALUMINUM AND ARTICLES THEREOF	14,355,749,688	15,861,837,715	15,575,540,824	15,286,135,414	16,689,654,653	17,382,348,080
44	WOOD AND ARTICLES OF WOOD; WOOD CHARCOAL............	11,386,537,562	11,220,073,267	12,893,501,261	15,205,274,047	16,490,867,324	16,971,041,344
48	PAPER & PAPERBOARD & ARTICLES (INC PAPR PULP ARTL)	15,586,079,040	16,126,081,782	15,099,214,541	15,414,329,274	16,084,220,605	15,756,975,592
3	FISH; CRUSTACEANS & AQUATIC INVERTEBRATES	11,197,991,407	12,701,385,815	12,645,826,048	13,891,782,780	15,835,760,654	14,612,653,240
63	TEXTILE ART NESOI; NEEDLECRAFT SETS; WORN TEXT ART..	11,200,629,583	11,865,139,339	12,082,493,428	12,762,112,103	13,247,401,021	14,179,906,079
8	EDIBLE FRUIT & NUTS; CITRUS FRUIT OR MELON PEEL	8,863,914,318	9,732,655,918	10,184,784,760	11,191,993,575	12,641,969,818	14,021,023,338
42	LEATHER ART; SADDLERY ETC; HANDBAGS ETC; GUT ART.....	9,934,058,287	11,150,876,775	12,140,288,972	12,851,471,820	13,310,919,396	13,854,026,928
38	MISCELLANEOUS CHEMICAL PRODUCTS	8,775,007,058	10,751,302,226	11,112,474,157	12,002,299,921	12,266,851,441	12,707,805,811
28	INORG CHEM; PREC & RARE-EARTH MET & RADIOACT COMPD	14,419,815,070	17,872,771,253	16,149,986,883	14,874,442,945	13,714,847,460	12,609,014,897
33	ESSENTIAL OILS ETC; PERFUMERY; COSMETIC ETC PREPS ...	8,068,431,425	8,951,588,288	9,571,001,409	10,596,869,673	11,376,809,009	11,882,458,200
83	MISCELLANEOUS ARTICLES OF BASE METAL	7,877,729,294	8,739,259,474	9,434,148,332	9,993,130,712	10,493,936,595	11,080,583,356
82	TOOLS; CUTLERY ETC. OF BASE METAL & PARTS THEREOF ...	6,841,067,716	7,750,776,673	8,374,735,450	8,778,565,247	9,264,424,722	9,527,703,763
2	MEAT AND EDIBLE MEAT OFFAL	4,585,951,969	5,121,401,309	5,607,532,690	5,844,460,135	8,224,549,543	9,133,814,388
7	EDIBLE VEGETABLES & CERTAIN ROOTS & TUBERS	6,485,965,249	7,248,756,396	7,418,333,310	8,203,380,402	8,335,125,958	8,656,616,920
74	COPPER AND ARTICLES THEREOF..................................	8,834,965,805	11,436,094,881	10,227,434,926	10,612,714,185	9,606,009,913	8,289,292,741
9	COFFEE; TEA; MATE & SPICES	5,741,806,507	9,117,179,534	8,066,032,970	6,978,424,824	7,686,909,615	7,967,179,631
31	FERTILIZERS..	6,711,212,206	9,219,283,746	8,848,441,587	8,038,747,639	8,200,676,370	7,964,990,538
70	GLASS AND GLASSWARE	5,354,697,806	5,709,885,598	5,961,750,465	6,185,727,615	6,969,628,238	7,312,901,538
20	PREP VEGETABLES; FRUIT; NUTS OR OTHER PLANT PARTS...	5,477,096,549	6,484,731,091	6,777,311,469	6,801,427,394	6,986,990,186	7,220,193,188
68	ART OF STONE; PLASTER; CEMENT; ASBESTOS; MICA ETC.	4,658,780,626	5,091,937,544	5,501,071,999	6,193,785,646	6,730,698,222	7,214,288,589
19	PREP CEREAL; FLOUR; STARCH OR MILK; BAKERS WARES....	4,422,988,811	4,910,215,210	5,167,381,945	5,451,852,934	5,673,588,563	6,054,729,664
69	CERAMIC PRODUCTS...	4,522,547,706	5,104,213,219	5,190,326,483	5,398,890,652	5,838,308,480	5,871,018,967
15	ANIMAL OR VEGETABLE FATS; OILS ETC. & WAXES	4,374,859,810	6,638,792,996	6,042,608,727	5,905,672,020	5,970,535,583	5,826,591,692
91	CLOCKS AND WATCHES AND PARTS THEREOF.....................	3,746,831,906	4,831,612,401	4,836,163,495	5,118,979,540	5,411,277,429	5,680,097,332
18	COCOA AND COCOA PREPARATIONS................................	4,299,538,823	4,686,269,266	4,102,624,842	4,164,281,075	4,734,473,290	4,865,669,172
16	EDIBLE PREPARATIONS OF MEAT; FISH; CRUSTACEANS ETC..	3,866,806,599	4,439,517,039	4,540,419,644	4,602,701,370	4,984,849,579	4,825,152,055
49	PRINTED BOOKS; NEWSPAPERS ETC; MANUSCRIPTS ETC	4,284,326,714	4,183,133,649	4,186,138,644	4,199,361,794	4,278,969,202	4,463,765,074
21	MISCELLANEOUS EDIBLE PREPARATIONS	3,370,312,969	3,715,935,345	4,000,844,072	4,148,756,291	4,193,679,603	4,229,704,075
17	SUGARS AND SUGAR CONFECTIONARY................................	3,762,060,410	4,754,501,578	4,366,563,699	3,799,136,792	3,946,737,027	4,044,445,204
32	TANNING & DYE EXT ETC; DYE; PAINT; PUTTY ETC; INKS........	3,112,247,264	3,458,598,929	3,769,560,623	3,831,983,966	3,975,737,859	3,811,012,710
47	WOOD PULP ETC; RECOVD (WASTE & SCRAP) PPR & PPRBD	3,886,976,165	4,020,371,730	3,354,190,916	3,619,478,090	3,588,051,861	3,293,007,445
1	LIVE ANIMALS	2,354,616,668	2,300,010,320	2,611,313,578	2,638,841,764	3,541,982,508	3,285,639,477
25	SALT; SULFUR; EARTH & STONE; LIME & CEMENT PLASTER..	2,354,752,836	2,951,894,137	2,955,796,390	2,778,765,607	3,093,466,458	3,232,431,199
34	SOAP ETC; WAXES; POLISH ETC; CANDLES; DENTAL PREPS ..	2,410,355,723	2,617,304,778	2,826,044,609	2,897,416,613	3,102,535,614	3,103,036,708
93	ARMS AND AMMUNITION; PARTS AND ACCESSORIES THEREOF	2,736,743,389	2,637,094,790	3,141,426,153	3,670,602,502	3,242,414,813	3,001,319,136
23	FOOD INDUSTRY RESIDUES & WASTE; PREP ANIMAL FEED...	1,423,962,733	1,992,528,672	2,560,863,035	2,790,343,644	3,023,721,464	2,872,148,430
26	ORES; SLAG AND ASH..	3,127,419,028	3,937,707,987	3,795,314,303	3,307,540,354	3,510,877,027	2,733,531,186
4	DAIRY PRODS; BIRDS EGGS; HONEY; ED ANIMAL PR NESOI..	1,706,975,184	1,962,942,676	2,095,308,219	2,216,876,558	2,515,092,618	2,714,952,745
35	ALBUMINOIDAL SUBST; MODIFIED STARCH; GLUE; ENZYMES	2,013,531,003	2,293,763,476	2,471,890,165	2,456,032,333	2,686,439,198	2,701,151,643
89	SHIPS; BOATS AND FLOATING STRUCTURES........................	1,588,483,865	1,189,031,564	1,864,623,584	1,814,440,986	1,440,664,166	2,690,705,363
10	CEREALS	1,849,610,344	2,192,368,590	3,125,699,176	4,088,513,813	3,296,850,091	2,654,759,087
75	NICKEL AND ARTICLES THEREOF	3,243,888,150	4,037,596,321	3,315,046,073	2,837,837,199	3,431,792,341	2,607,655,930
12	OIL SEEDS ETC.; MISC GRAIN; SEED; FRUIT; PLANT ETC	1,650,274,918	2,054,018,052	2,325,827,557	2,955,427,187	3,606,373,372	2,568,847,191
57	CARPETS AND OTHER TEXTILE FLOOR COVERINGS..............	1,742,136,352	1,919,240,275	2,042,290,370	2,171,580,127	2,454,114,537	2,518,740,115

Table B-7.   U.S. Imports with World by Harmonzied System (HS) for Total Merchandise, 2010–2015—*Continued*

HS	Import / TOTAL	2010	2011	2012	2013	2014	2015
	TOTAL	1,913,856,594,014	2,207,954,346,316	2,276,267,147,199	2,267,986,733,622	2,356,365,502,725	2,248,232,395,233
59	IMPREGNATED ETC TEXT FABRICS; TEX ART FOR INDUSTRY .	1,896,276,227	2,123,661,625	2,174,236,917	2,267,491,736	2,420,742,056	2,416,270,623
65	HEADGEAR AND PARTS THEREOF	1,657,292,049	1,999,509,350	1,984,595,169	1,935,461,474	2,123,549,303	2,366,460,853
81	BASE METALS NESOI; CERMETS; ARTICLES THEREOF	2,232,064,297	2,693,895,306	2,836,558,005	2,387,685,074	2,674,794,629	2,330,429,199
54	MANMADE FILAMENTS; INCLUDING YARNS & WOVEN FABRICS	1,975,567,395	2,270,532,495	2,319,635,221	2,354,728,298	2,313,540,678	2,314,125,642
86	RAILWAY OR TRAMWAY STOCK ETC; TRAFFIC SIGNAL EQUIP	1,405,488,117	1,818,144,787	1,965,108,640	1,602,931,937	2,024,587,039	2,197,016,355
56	WADDING; FELT ETC; SP YARN; TWINE; ROPES ETC.	1,529,703,347	1,665,779,936	1,712,353,012	1,835,158,819	1,952,638,779	2,098,464,263
24	TOBACCO AND MANUFACTURED TOBACCO SUBSTITUTES	1,422,376,429	1,531,838,624	1,829,461,939	2,175,452,989	2,056,564,826	2,058,013,843
67	PREP FEATHERS; DOWN ETC; ARTIF FLOWERS; H HAIR ART..	1,531,813,430	1,824,787,648	1,854,555,596	1,785,159,356	1,749,168,492	2,047,257,905
55	MANMADE STAPLE FIBERS; INCL YARNS & WOVEN FABRICS	1,585,379,192	1,882,255,961	1,767,519,755	1,734,779,261	1,850,800,378	1,904,299,350
79	ZINC AND ARTICLES THEREOF	1,689,644,497	1,930,919,240	1,669,283,696	1,656,202,339	1,804,948,561	1,755,312,786
6	LIVE TREES; PLANTS; BULBS ETC.; CUT FLOWERS ETC.	1,483,246,259	1,547,076,287	1,620,977,702	1,677,547,625	1,727,651,483	1,735,015,801
13	LAC; GUMS; RESINS & OTHER VEGETABLE SAP & EXTRACT..	883,036,082	1,726,965,300	4,335,790,939	2,649,411,576	2,225,773,494	1,663,167,175
37	PHOTOGRAPHIC OR CINEMATOGRAPHIC GOODS..................	1,709,291,285	1,800,309,986	1,603,164,334	1,580,100,263	1,632,819,289	1,615,595,897
11	MILLING PRODUCTS; MALT; STARCH; INULIN; WHT GLUTEN .	1,102,580,191	1,214,212,465	1,295,768,228	1,417,446,726	1,544,106,611	1,557,312,378
92	MUSICAL INSTRUMENTS; PARTS AND ACCESSORIES THEREOF	1,206,240,235	1,254,488,638	1,260,205,558	1,238,315,053	1,295,269,591	1,265,738,029
60	KNITTED OR CROCHETED FABRICS	729,741,881	850,323,781	965,401,400	963,712,716	1,062,420,103	1,077,057,064
52	COTTON; INCLUDING YARN AND WOVEN FABRIC THEREOF....	1,082,405,621	1,253,390,682	1,137,205,657	1,099,033,218	1,077,316,171	1,056,198,410
5	PRODUCTS OF ANIMAL ORIGIN; NESOI................................	729,737,057	780,885,204	885,696,380	979,067,622	1,080,585,222	1,031,498,882
78	LEAD AND ARTICLES THEREOF	629,717,040	779,634,406	762,017,330	1,062,216,860	1,267,516,450	1,030,720,064
41	RAW HIDES AND SKINS (NO FURSKINS) AND LEATHER.........	598,431,814	619,335,816	683,679,410	720,629,920	799,386,940	803,895,675
36	EXPLOSIVES; PYROTECHNICS; MATCHES; PYRO ALLOYS ETC	603,947,335	622,152,532	635,906,730	650,174,042	752,955,814	782,272,698
58	SPEC WOV FABRICS; TUFTED FAB; LACE; TAPESTRIES ETC	633,738,725	699,419,069	728,878,166	739,395,359	761,095,014	774,226,603
80	TIN AND ARTICLES THEREOF.................................	808,488,955	1,023,036,389	883,811,339	927,066,192	916,403,589	668,347,293
66	UMBRELLAS; WALKING-STICKS; RIDING-CROPS ETC; PARTS	479,956,257	500,683,693	522,333,116	526,013,417	533,529,760	573,996,285
46	MFR OF STRAW; ESPARTO ETC.; BASKETWARE & WICKERWRK	392,810,686	470,480,996	496,862,671	491,320,459	510,384,276	532,147,298
43	FURSKINS AND ARTIFICIAL FUR; MANUFACTURES THEREOF .	303,949,350	359,810,148	370,022,804	428,473,227	497,065,224	447,320,760
51	WOOL & ANIMAL HAIR; INCLUDING YARN & WOVEN FABRIC.	235,344,955	281,169,616	313,883,906	302,606,736	315,842,031	320,668,630
45	CORK AND ARTICLES OF CORK	216,150,488	237,723,886	239,980,466	241,137,434	270,588,069	282,003,226
53	VEG TEXT FIB NESOI; VEG FIB & PAPER YNS & WOV FAB	166,913,160	201,199,561	208,297,181	209,196,819	214,482,204	241,030,445
50	SILK; INCLUDING YARNS AND WOVEN FABRIC THEREOF	153,639,428	176,602,151	162,593,610	141,043,757	133,285,695	116,635,289
14	VEGETABLE PLAITING MATERIALS & PRODUCTS NESOI.........	72,498,061	72,300,368	78,235,532	79,048,750	91,237,208	101,491,786
95	TOYS; GAMES & SPORT EQUIPMENT; PARTS & ACCESSORIES	29,770,537,155	27,748,482,557	27,032,770,021	26,645,366,162	27,640,386,170	29,851,031,239
96	MISCELLANEOUS MANUFACTURED ARTICLES	3,674,830,250	3,904,974,335	5,040,589,472	5,243,157,771	5,617,338,614	6,073,532,255
97	WORKS OF ART; COLLECTORS' PIECES AND ANTIQUES..........	6,247,591,682	6,894,183,981	7,791,234,894	9,061,466,121	9,184,211,002	11,678,311,490
	Other goods	**55,626,496,441**	**59,924,244,591**	**66,250,212,896**	**69,924,677,491**	**78,387,598,927**	**84,325,782,079**
98	SPECIAL CLASSIFICATION PROVISIONS; NESOI	41,899,513,889	45,880,960,912	53,264,490,596	56,481,960,061	61,344,177,621	67,191,350,050
99	SPECIAL IMPORT PROVISIONS; NESOI	13,726,982,552	14,043,283,679	12,985,722,300	13,442,717,430	17,043,421,306	17,134,432,029

Table B-8.   Top U.S. Imports, Exports, Deficit, and Surplus for Total Merchandise, 2010–2015

TOP 10 IMPORTS	2010	2011	2012	2013	2014	2015
HS						
TOTAL IMPORTS	1,913,856,594,014	2,207,954,346,316	2,276,267,147,199	2,267,986,733,622	2,356,365,502,725	2,248,232,395,233
85 ELECTRIC MACHINERY ETC; SOUND EQUIP; TV EQUIP; PTS....	258,235,732,124	278,578,502,864	291,562,129,068	298,482,465,393	315,812,496,521	328,286,273,785
84 NUCLEAR REACTORS; BOILERS; MACHINERY ETC.; PARTS....	249,797,039,140	287,635,771,553	308,088,220,073	304,838,343,715	325,171,903,843	322,848,429,149
87 VEHICLES; EXCEPT RAILWAY OR TRAMWAY; AND PARTS ETC	182,789,210,416	202,618,529,448	240,003,940,732	249,017,542,957	261,650,574,600	279,899,687,298
27 MINERAL FUEL; OIL ETC.; BITUMIN SUBST; MINERAL WAX....	355,070,549,606	453,932,881,724	423,991,873,335	379,894,747,602	347,712,892,468	190,658,012,180
30 PHARMACEUTICAL PRODUCTS	61,628,685,081	65,748,306,910	64,563,002,548	62,908,417,125	72,613,258,128	85,507,993,837
90 OPTIC; PHOTO ETC; MEDIC OR SURGICAL INSTRMENTS ETC.	58,876,075,643	66,081,084,213	68,810,632,221	71,136,644,228	75,440,937,299	77,441,367,524
98 SPECIAL CLASSIFICATION PROVISIONS; NESOI	41,899,513,889	45,880,960,912	53,264,490,596	56,481,960,061	61,344,177,621	67,191,350,050
71 NAT ETC PEARLS; PREC ETC STONES; PR MET ETC; COIN	54,219,642,145	69,178,026,504	64,374,267,835	66,526,207,513	64,880,065,213	59,309,039,710
94 FURNITURE; BEDDING ETC; LAMPS NESOI ETC; PREFAB BD ..	37,821,166,238	39,790,724,984	44,365,466,241	47,661,903,375	51,938,811,977	56,924,568,716
29 ORGANIC CHEMICALS........	47,935,644,015	56,054,589,618	53,460,389,819	53,524,821,737	53,675,599,652	50,922,104,608

Top 10 EXPORTS	2010	2011	2012	2013	2014	2015
HS						
TOTAL............	1,278,494,525,839	1,482,507,755,226	1,545,820,839,892	1,578,516,879,950	1,621,171,618,259	1,502,572,229,518
84 NUCLEAR REACTORS; BOILERS; MACHINERY ETC.; PARTS...	182,902,860,899	205,826,159,717	215,180,487,807	213,440,918,266	219,842,558,893	206,100,142,194
85 ELECTRIC MACHINERY ETC; SOUND EQUIP; TV EQUIP; PTS...	151,776,704,354	159,468,543,383	162,434,694,242	165,818,048,345	172,363,626,713	169,956,050,124
88 AIRCRAFT; SPACECRAFT; AND PARTS THEREOF	79,617,922,992	87,757,246,448	104,440,079,691	114,886,824,530	125,291,175,809	131,627,865,014
87 VEHICLES; EXCEPT RAILWAY OR TRAMWAY; AND PARTS ETC	99,148,692,588	120,011,780,504	133,078,052,912	134,090,149,318	136,021,387,004	127,396,967,732
27 MINERAL FUEL; OIL ETC.; BITUMIN SUBST; MINERAL WAX....	81,692,031,854	130,566,667,652	137,332,528,657	148,902,536,669	155,851,665,718	104,105,881,821
90 OPTIC; PHOTO ETC; MEDIC OR SURGICAL INSTRMENTS ETC.	73,960,066,842	79,383,778,894	83,367,062,357	84,344,595,248	84,976,899,318	83,444,556,553
39 PLASTICS AND ARTICLES THEREOF	53,625,263,449	58,743,604,827	59,006,434,035	61,045,249,532	63,091,433,153	60,268,037,778
71 NAT ETC PEARLS; PREC ETC STONES; PR MET ETC; COIN	52,137,973,983	72,611,396,268	72,995,044,704	72,487,187,993	64,895,567,418	58,733,878,893
30 PHARMACEUTICAL PRODUCTS	40,788,229,885	38,341,460,576	40,129,282,726	39,707,839,099	43,983,359,926	47,293,310,441
98 SPECIAL CLASSIFICATION PROVISIONS; NESOI	40,373,871,929	39,377,993,433	40,638,745,115	42,140,058,914	43,262,857,320	41,439,083,008

TOP 10 DEFICITS	2010	2011	2012	2013	2014	2015
TOTAL DEFICIT GOODS.............	-635,362,068,175	-725,446,591,090	-730,446,307,307	-689,469,853,672	-735,193,884,466	-745,660,165,715
98 SPECIAL CLASSIFICATION PROVISIONS; NESOI	-1,525,641,960	-6,502,967,479	-12,625,745,481	-14,341,901,147	-18,081,320,301	-25,752,267,042
64 FOOTWEAR; GAITERS ETC. AND PARTS THEREOF	-19,797,179,170	-21,363,510,728	-22,554,267,253	-23,419,965,520	-24,561,189,088	-26,186,227,072
62 APPAREL ARTICLES AND ACCESSORIES; NOT KNIT ETC.	-32,385,918,177	-34,805,769,643	-34,434,503,355	-35,597,608,730	-35,304,885,310	-36,644,088,019
30 PHARMACEUTICAL PRODUCTS	-20,840,455,196	-27,406,846,334	-24,433,719,822	-23,200,578,026	-28,629,898,202	-38,214,683,396
61 APPAREL ARTICLES AND ACCESSORIES; KNIT OR CROCHET .	-36,147,167,442	-39,506,996,774	-38,686,961,094	-40,307,078,921	-42,376,228,805	-44,130,192,752
94 FURNITURE; BEDDING ETC; LAMPS NESOI ETC; PREFAB BD ..	-29,229,229,068	-30,237,900,622	-33,742,676,698	-36,558,489,430	-40,096,038,358	-45,366,452,034
27 MINERAL FUEL; OIL ETC.; BITUMIN SUBST; MINERAL WAX....	-273,378,517,752	-323,366,214,072	-286,659,344,678	-230,992,210,933	-191,861,226,750	-86,552,130,359
84 NUCLEAR REACTORS; BOILERS; MACHINERY ETC.; PARTS....	-66,894,178,241	-81,809,611,836	-92,907,732,266	-91,397,425,449	-105,329,344,950	-116,748,286,955
87 VEHICLES; EXCEPT RAILWAY OR TRAMWAY; AND PARTS ETC	-83,640,517,828	-82,606,748,944	-106,925,887,820	-114,927,393,639	-125,629,187,596	-152,502,719,566
85 ELECTRIC MACHINERY ETC; SOUND EQUIP; TV EQUIP; PTS ...	-106,459,027,770	-119,109,959,481	-129,127,434,826	-132,664,417,048	-143,448,869,808	-158,330,223,661

TOP 10 SURPLUSES	2010	2011	2012	2013	2014	2015
TOTAL SURPLUS GOODS	-635,362,068,175	-725,446,591,090	-730,446,307,307	-689,469,853,672	-735,193,884,466	-745,660,165,715
88 AIRCRAFT; SPACECRAFT; AND PARTS THEREOF	60,833,134,980	66,273,831,157	80,182,104,339	85,466,952,611	90,937,536,740	96,483,166,772
12 OIL SEEDS ETC.; MISC GRAIN; SEED; FRUIT; PLANT ETC	20,308,904,359	19,177,765,864	27,362,679,351	23,999,981,505	25,270,202,882	21,050,398,592
10 CEREALS	18,187,209,927	26,155,572,426	17,490,527,964	16,212,522,703	19,529,098,623	16,145,207,187
38 MISCELLANEOUS CHEMICAL PRODUCTS	12,422,585,658	13,129,739,608	14,215,240,200	15,028,626,408	14,995,702,171	13,206,407,998
39 PLASTICS AND ARTICLES THEREOF............	18,655,864,130	19,333,152,339	16,929,215,175	16,818,028,927	15,170,483,904	12,394,827,622
23 FOOD INDUSTRY RESIDUES & WASTE; PREP ANIMAL FEED...	6,909,016,809	6,557,874,095	7,347,782,001	8,991,531,375	8,941,318,745	8,390,694,733
90 OPTIC; PHOTO ETC; MEDIC OR SURGICAL INSTRMENTS ETC.	15,083,991,199	13,302,694,681	14,556,430,136	13,207,951,020	9,535,962,019	6,003,189,029
47 WOOD PULP ETC; RECOVD (WASTE & SCRAP) PPR & PPRBD	4,974,555,418	6,082,393,959	5,957,568,554	5,345,943,124	5,377,354,938	5,411,325,878
2 MEAT AND EDIBLE MEAT OFFAL	7,465,951,165	10,235,859,795	10,488,693,819	10,430,285,307	9,440,618,550	5,144,566,666
52 COTTON; INCLUDING YARN AND WOVEN FABRIC THEREOF....	6,461,815,637	9,813,786,138	7,147,206,158	6,537,498,660	5,443,562,962	4,817,009,371
26 ORES; SLAG AND ASH........	2,431,411,745	3,762,366,036	3,224,556,120	4,013,441,820	4,852,042,520	4,078,466,264

Table B-9.   U.S. Imports from World Total by 5-Digit End-Use Code, 2006–2015

(In thousands of dollars)

	2006	2007	2008	2009	2010	2011	2012	2013	2014	2015
(END USE CODE) TOTAL	1,853,938,475	1,956,961,843	2,103,640,711	1,559,624,813	1,913,856,594	2,207,954,346	2,276,267,147	2,268,370,483	2,347,685,229	2,241,663,715
(00000) Green coffee	2,829,397	3,236,773	3,804,443	3,375,157	4,054,979	6,906,364	5,807,726	4,669,941	5,228,597	5,120,888
(00010) Cocoa beans	714,002	660,206	878,337	1,178,525	1,250,897	1,424,902	996,081	1,110,630	1,312,308	1,429,546
(00020) Cane and beet sugar	1,349,352	825,990	1,097,895	1,192,671	1,983,604	2,789,693	2,279,516	1,589,150	1,607,820	1,738,353
(00100) Meat products	7,467,816	8,009,648	7,419,473	6,381,711	7,175,311	7,710,549	8,524,837	8,821,833	12,077,668	12,786,025
(00110) Dairy products and eggs	1,443,500	1,579,748	1,680,926	1,421,506	1,409,699	1,585,701	1,689,623	1,744,194	1,962,011	2,136,123
(00120) Fruits, frozen juices	7,542,971	9,038,096	9,742,015	9,517,966	10,404,996	11,687,023	12,259,964	13,166,610	14,359,547	15,497,571
(00130) Vegetables	6,579,198	7,210,946	7,773,461	7,488,533	8,769,872	9,699,434	9,943,706	10,746,218	10,920,674	11,263,800
(00140) Nuts	1,114,083	1,222,908	1,393,366	1,306,974	1,477,549	1,883,761	2,008,684	2,019,859	2,378,985	2,798,983
(00150) Food oils, oilseeds	2,682,228	3,377,689	5,335,555	3,807,038	4,233,743	6,247,286	5,932,353	6,334,255	7,004,773	6,060,311
(00160) Bakery products	5,631,284	6,014,757	6,437,277	6,372,062	7,632,515	8,482,687	8,813,830	8,981,471	9,335,062	9,584,674
(00170) Tea, spices, etc.	975,870	1,129,117	1,280,477	1,203,575	1,442,806	1,753,348	1,851,713	1,987,785	2,141,668	2,414,903
(00180) Other foods	7,984,745	8,528,619	8,986,122	8,536,871	9,387,330	10,554,584	11,478,030	12,160,919	12,684,262	13,515,690
(00190) Wine, beer, and related products	7,834,133	8,353,650	8,396,895	7,433,225	7,889,776	8,533,194	8,913,637	9,128,035	9,684,721	10,155,671
(00200) Feedstuff and foodgrains	2,201,208	2,940,215	4,539,572	3,662,489	3,655,991	4,602,327	5,868,804	6,961,862	6,671,764	6,139,127
(01000) Fish and shellfish	13,202,892	13,547,094	14,023,220	13,011,241	14,635,413	16,575,259	16,621,795	17,911,796	20,213,233	18,697,691
(01010) Alcoholic beverages, excluding wine	4,929,948	5,546,173	5,498,552	5,034,960	5,647,838	6,297,280	6,561,153	6,966,177	7,114,706	7,306,350
(01020) Nonagricultural foods, etc.	455,128	461,826	709,417	679,509	682,566	729,688	719,879	824,847	1,059,501	1,058,752
(10000) Crude oil	216,627,331	237,211,653	341,912,489	188,711,775	252,160,511	331,582,054	313,174,962	272,807,177	246,407,742	125,819,431
(10010) Fuel oil	27,072,340	31,325,175	40,567,373	27,078,781	33,789,398	46,878,848	45,511,224	44,332,681	40,070,728	22,821,670
(10020) Petroleum products, other	44,232,158	48,324,067	52,305,853	28,806,356	38,002,414	50,918,067	50,116,224	48,378,292	43,551,052	31,307,506
(10030) Liquefied petroleum gases	14,498,098	14,118,010	18,494,596	9,091,834	12,158,078	9,963,079	6,366,286	4,160,379	3,980,429	2,028,324
(10100) Coal and related fuels	2,696,636	2,492,404	4,653,603	2,160,257	2,143,386	2,944,161	3,258,001	3,327,650	2,068,533	2,235,032
(10110) Gas-natural	28,277,948	32,033,504	34,454,222	16,056,377	17,402,100	13,533,118	8,621,801	10,308,807	13,790,089	8,347,456
(10300) Nuclear fuel materials	3,989,466	5,540,363	6,084,956	5,362,727	5,640,852	5,657,684	4,664,894	4,326,105	3,704,657	3,259,597
(10400) Electric energy	2,167,400	2,968,899	3,644,115	2,074,691	2,071,451	2,015,438	1,913,698	2,429,281	2,669,710	2,398,986
(11000) Pulpwood and woodpulp	3,189,112	3,743,108	4,011,841	2,445,714	3,891,105	4,024,405	3,360,058	3,623,226	3,593,459	3,300,874
(11100) Newsprint	3,073,249	2,383,543	2,364,763	1,441,706	1,377,086	1,463,910	1,344,162	1,290,437	1,316,415	1,068,437
(11110) Paper and paper products	8,185,618	7,960,039	7,700,917	6,013,754	6,668,395	6,887,589	6,913,099	7,085,079	7,464,704	7,525,962
(12000) Cotton, natural fibers	81,384	79,176	80,463	56,970	66,383	94,120	85,661	69,871	76,049	86,864
(12030) Hides and skins	149,059	151,744	156,656	114,340	172,763	187,571	226,399	286,003	304,967	241,816
(12050) Natural rubber	2,029,314	2,119,119	2,856,254	1,273,947	2,820,085	4,772,574	3,382,189	2,558,770	1,954,696	1,501,765
(12060) Farming materials, livestock	1,031,467	1,188,622	1,257,020	1,101,896	1,146,160	1,354,268	1,701,374	1,977,251	1,851,357	1,690,168
(12070) Tobacco, waxes, etc.	4,804,665	5,286,636	6,520,984	5,561,562	6,121,582	7,809,219	10,439,876	8,941,688	9,098,970	8,345,029
(12100) Cotton cloth, fabrics	1,739,301	1,487,272	1,287,393	922,646	1,198,927	1,357,415	1,259,412	1,228,879	1,185,178	1,171,983
(12110) Wool, silk, etc.	858,434	873,812	868,763	507,138	571,915	680,654	758,494	725,430	797,236	810,403
(12135) Synthetic cloth	5,413,842	5,636,183	5,372,960	4,059,885	5,109,830	5,894,471	6,008,832	6,069,411	6,315,910	6,314,425
(12140) Hair, waste materials	769,907	790,670	796,651	567,280	759,321	855,678	939,551	919,681	1,009,359	1,018,341
(12150) Finished textile supplies	3,324,957	3,571,803	3,585,864	2,954,617	3,665,861	4,018,593	4,222,292	4,468,604	4,703,001	4,799,205
(12160) Leather and furs	825,833	801,067	678,877	446,333	566,599	590,258	654,582	687,133	760,843	773,724
(12320) Materials, excluding chemicals	1,385,720	1,357,418	1,339,047	1,112,655	1,284,998	1,435,951	1,454,142	1,410,414	1,519,511	1,483,428
(12500) Plastic materials	13,453,399	12,828,397	13,379,805	9,137,107	12,077,487	14,105,852	14,581,261	15,308,548	17,277,692	16,152,783
(12510) Chemicals-fertilizers	7,667,513	9,524,343	15,094,894	8,140,219	11,494,774	15,817,203	16,115,386	15,456,869	14,985,352	14,417,036
(12530) Chemicals-inorganic	5,739,407	6,192,902	7,889,555	5,108,259	6,357,590	8,644,605	7,980,268	7,350,627	7,526,349	7,150,942
(12540) Chemicals-organic	18,850,340	19,145,436	22,690,819	16,156,537	20,429,765	25,409,587	24,773,148	26,504,850	28,074,188	23,255,782
(12550) Chemicals-other, n.e.c.	8,075,861	8,529,329	9,067,385	7,562,707	9,349,695	11,071,118	11,830,141	11,823,787	12,608,758	12,354,959
(13000) Lumber	8,698,276	6,768,682	4,577,546	2,743,649	3,513,885	3,498,014	4,123,304	5,199,967	5,895,057	5,599,992
(13010) Plywood and veneers	3,119,998	2,927,443	2,401,822	1,660,548	1,947,995	1,929,656	2,221,494	2,388,466	2,679,716	3,020,287
(13020) Stone, sand, cement, etc.	6,702,684	6,294,302	5,188,743	3,484,871	3,684,421	3,798,233	4,122,009	4,683,632	5,095,025	5,711,940
(13100) Glass-plate, sheet, etc.	1,262,102	1,185,038	1,107,843	900,611	1,090,452	1,107,167	1,203,106	1,337,589	1,571,694	1,722,428
(13110) Shingles, wallboard	12,225,584	9,965,169	8,146,905	6,180,769	6,810,921	6,879,013	7,802,861	8,991,227	9,455,412	9,867,789
(13120) Nontextile floor tiles	2,982,324	2,806,364	2,546,948	1,913,462	2,162,256	2,372,957	2,484,117	2,886,686	3,175,145	3,515,639
(14000) Steelmaking materials	6,513,384	7,294,619	10,797,226	3,806,178	7,314,571	9,001,617	8,581,955	7,315,378	8,751,627	5,977,780
(14100) Iron and steel mill products	22,370,042	18,512,616	21,742,687	8,665,168	14,392,830	19,794,926	20,870,226	18,106,877	25,693,386	20,211,854
(14200) Bauxite and aluminum	14,530,259	13,442,753	13,077,035	8,302,397	10,482,373	11,532,444	10,873,057	10,403,339	11,656,759	12,083,006
(14220) Copper	8,167,828	7,787,940	6,879,687	3,780,796	5,087,035	6,770,482	5,816,719	6,237,196	5,091,717	4,540,714
(14240) Nickel	3,216,144	4,727,249	3,406,760	1,613,922	2,946,258	3,604,580	2,884,676	2,330,791	2,962,416	2,136,172
(14250) Tin	435,478	553,292	762,105	481,018	760,468	978,561	833,543	853,391	868,673	626,721
(14260) Zinc	2,260,663	2,781,517	1,706,997	1,232,990	1,584,878	1,810,265	1,513,228	1,480,453	1,618,220	1,557,193
(14270) Nonmonetary gold	5,643,324	4,677,372	6,138,676	8,841,800	13,107,326	16,401,421	17,833,096	15,945,549	14,381,880	11,411,867
(14280) Other precious metals	8,326,151	11,083,009	11,398,193	5,840,478	9,579,153	15,674,713	12,574,998	11,823,041	10,798,391	8,843,214
(14290) Nonferrous metals, other	3,145,853	3,721,433	4,305,359	2,433,144	3,548,205	4,346,299	4,368,753	4,120,619	4,568,467	3,792,106
(15000) Iron and steel products, n.e.c.	8,553,103	9,179,464	10,387,084	6,042,157	6,846,409	8,724,556	9,999,157	9,321,710	10,236,765	9,511,150
(15100) Iron and steel, advanced	7,574,547	7,822,036	8,291,555	5,382,979	7,120,307	8,509,929	9,459,634	9,178,176	9,970,448	10,097,162
(15200) Finished metal shapes	16,372,731	17,032,770	17,672,081	12,203,775	14,315,451	16,720,714	17,388,143	16,842,341	17,602,494	17,992,266
(16040) Sulfur, nonmetallic minerals	863,354	890,758	1,834,206	723,897	1,099,656	1,581,074	1,645,875	1,438,303	1,356,364	1,263,018
(16050) Synthetic rubber–primary	2,030,206	1,973,076	2,388,688	1,564,318	2,292,144	3,133,779	3,243,919	2,812,983	2,974,716	2,527,272
(16110) Blank tapes, audio & visual	4,400,026	2,151,704	1,708,983	1,422,800	1,298,132	1,239,414	987,049	772,588	644,757	566,222
(16120) Industrial supplies, other	22,500,025	23,502,582	23,895,565	19,262,149	23,737,348	26,561,008	28,150,211	29,224,658	31,034,546	31,747,218
(20000) Generators, accessories	16,281,490	19,462,947	20,755,338	16,877,118	18,468,837	20,623,426	22,142,825	21,203,911	22,685,183	23,176,441

Table B-9.   U.S. Imports from World Total by 5-Digit End-Use Code, 2006–2015—*Continued*

(In thousands of dollars)

	2006	2007	2008	2009	2010	2011	2012	2013	2014	2015
(END USE CODE) TOTAL	1,853,938,475	1,956,961,843	2,103,640,711	1,559,624,813	1,913,856,594	2,207,954,346	2,276,267,147	2,268,370,483	2,347,685,229	2,241,663,715
(20005) Electric apparatus	33,598,566	35,561,026	35,659,122	27,436,113	36,814,974	41,545,845	42,856,812	45,677,871	48,500,054	48,318,819
(21000) Drilling & oilfield equipment	6,129,598	7,956,250	12,492,171	6,883,450	7,347,708	9,047,326	11,697,082	9,008,609	9,779,870	7,636,046
(21010) Specialized mining	843,423	855,070	941,066	584,767	574,503	768,508	704,479	692,463	699,640	667,799
(21030) Excavating machinery	10,357,932	8,730,429	8,446,227	3,914,347	5,929,947	9,775,630	12,707,256	10,406,211	11,243,803	10,819,115
(21040) Nonfarm tractors and parts	1,628,968	1,614,739	1,591,280	964,830	1,500,872	2,235,481	2,577,158	2,268,383	2,341,070	1,915,606
(21100) Industrial engines	14,089,534	15,738,713	18,296,577	13,628,575	16,804,185	21,362,160	23,804,118	22,097,455	24,745,001	24,161,211
(21110) Food, tobacco machinery	2,073,001	2,364,040	2,526,946	2,188,330	2,528,370	3,046,412	3,092,938	3,375,063	3,582,828	3,688,238
(21120) Metalworking machine tools	9,572,338	8,669,439	9,567,247	5,715,516	6,434,696	9,738,556	11,658,315	11,330,621	11,390,742	11,432,792
(21130) Textile, sewing machines	1,181,014	1,344,848	1,397,514	1,147,087	1,593,581	1,843,510	1,728,746	2,038,808	2,157,505	2,285,151
(21140) Wood, glass, plastic	6,622,222	6,400,403	5,948,736	4,301,427	4,864,604	5,511,336	6,157,573	6,917,612	7,237,070	8,018,334
(21150) Pulp and paper machinery	5,334,856	5,522,058	5,313,633	3,227,267	3,350,010	4,134,239	4,302,533	4,235,927	4,611,139	4,651,019
(21160) Measuring, testing, control instruments	13,356,058	14,602,284	14,850,140	11,520,770	14,823,745	17,512,180	18,411,310	18,773,560	20,003,393	20,380,071
(21170) Materials handling equipment	11,626,771	11,482,411	11,979,979	8,081,705	8,132,777	11,098,325	13,302,245	13,631,192	15,210,879	15,928,179
(21180) Industrial machines, other	29,065,609	34,818,385	36,599,660	28,759,833	35,658,919	45,091,657	48,061,285	47,300,601	53,815,854	51,176,816
(21190) Photo, service industry machinery	14,580,813	13,896,070	14,025,075	11,390,763	13,825,284	15,160,583	15,843,762	16,392,958	17,403,615	18,253,601
(21200) Agricultural machinery, equipment	6,793,688	7,108,474	7,886,389	5,534,372	6,485,686	8,060,605	9,323,096	9,933,582	10,425,876	9,678,302
(21300) Computers	33,771,286	40,765,812	40,668,451	40,762,433	55,285,628	64,899,780	65,770,055	64,690,704	63,698,262	63,048,419
(21301) Computer accessories	67,575,179	63,034,870	60,206,352	53,099,222	61,952,201	54,804,256	56,470,353	56,503,319	57,945,884	56,888,969
(21320) Semiconductors	27,375,040	26,614,593	25,654,959	21,322,030	29,438,386	37,950,320	40,234,847	41,439,853	43,721,860	45,999,342
(21400) Telecommunications equipment	40,209,308	44,333,950	44,800,333	37,272,950	47,581,762	48,475,079	52,802,049	54,409,523	58,638,045	66,118,293
(21500) Business machines and equipment	8,716,698	7,735,217	5,067,479	4,088,604	4,432,016	4,579,749	4,739,283	4,602,405	4,812,129	5,086,199
(21600) Laboratory testing instruments	3,007,437	3,657,552	4,351,364	3,696,478	4,531,490	5,438,631	5,644,570	5,344,546	5,743,267	5,713,362
(21610) Medicinal equipment	23,246,179	24,836,132	26,572,346	24,292,192	27,360,348	30,430,233	31,558,156	32,510,010	34,411,567	35,860,324
(22000) Civilian aircraft	10,606,713	13,280,139	12,389,767	9,530,481	8,774,076	9,845,999	10,163,289	14,068,667	16,727,464	18,296,299
(22010) Parts-civilian aircraft	6,621,739	8,258,743	8,920,155	8,767,221	9,868,862	11,369,640	13,440,721	15,345,926	17,576,060	17,389,455
(22020) Engines-civilian aircraft	11,156,193	12,868,637	14,103,358	12,312,424	12,639,752	14,306,212	16,517,527	17,527,342	18,849,849	19,454,611
(22100) Railway transportation equipment	1,602,857	1,553,170	1,647,349	1,143,169	1,179,105	1,411,866	1,695,018	1,398,317	1,628,696	1,838,989
(22200) Vessels, except scrap	28,982	446	457	1,945	2,675	1,817	13,333	11,418	15,463	2,834
(22210) Commercial vessels, other	72,454	289,081	90,510	89,097	104,444	165,987	112,419	147,399	152,756	164,599
(22220) Marine engines, parts	916,865	1,040,023	1,000,791	755,947	887,472	969,093	1,041,946	1,161,098	1,173,718	1,152,612
(22300) Spacecraft, excluding military	108,355	118,040	63,135	45,159	96,362	165,533	132,424	136,857	185,971	226,913
(30000) Passenger cars, new and used	135,508,635	133,858,747	125,605,565	81,073,453	114,841,010	122,347,245	146,360,337	152,482,388	153,350,473	166,085,101
(30100) Trucks, buses, and special purpose vehicles	23,396,934	22,334,053	15,192,878	11,437,224	15,651,955	19,525,835	22,676,935	25,403,703	31,606,259	34,126,482
(30110) Bodies and chassis for trucks and buses	986,664	980,653	819,524	580,560	646,027	729,860	940,909	789,525	762,755	906,995
(30200) Engines and engine parts (carburetors, pistons, rings, and valves)	19,988,906	20,798,903	19,054,742	12,968,631	19,176,095	24,409,736	26,840,648	26,382,939	29,313,993	29,464,499
(30210) Bodies and chassis for passenger cars	24,171	28,833	20,356	12,921	21,996	13,616	21,281	11,177	15,669	18,313
(30220) Automotive tires and tubes	6,958,120	7,567,045	7,823,063	6,721,477	8,655,057	10,561,849	11,418,942	11,740,227	12,170,689	12,289,071
(30230) Other parts and accessories of vehicles	69,812,461	73,379,942	64,936,699	47,346,628	66,060,701	76,819,819	89,520,517	91,993,294	100,431,620	105,447,583
(40000) Apparel, household goods - cotton	48,711,128	50,860,854	49,487,621	43,933,344	49,135,919	50,389,488	47,434,435	48,645,163	47,177,158	47,228,688
(40010) Apparel, household goods - wool	3,549,182	3,853,632	3,706,912	2,754,871	3,057,230	3,326,731	3,241,522	3,218,414	3,534,581	3,276,671
(40020) Apparel, textiles, nonwool or cotton	31,134,943	31,604,170	30,254,642	27,027,513	31,728,949	36,962,987	39,376,936	41,877,449	45,177,406	49,536,752
(40030) Apparel,household goods-nontextile	7,781,351	8,021,445	8,086,410	6,924,233	8,228,245	8,050,918	8,463,868	8,971,475	9,354,046	9,705,806
(40040) Footwear	14,704,371	15,255,691	15,462,556	14,013,538	16,887,984	18,349,629	19,111,578	19,536,386	20,363,612	20,971,365
(40050) Camping apparel and gear	8,010,180	7,780,492	7,730,256	6,749,880	7,715,432	8,630,952	9,036,726	9,526,354	10,265,417	11,774,930
(40100) Pharmaceutical preparations	64,345,595	71,733,278	78,911,316	81,475,881	85,453,679	91,767,582	87,808,292	83,956,287	91,924,898	108,305,982
(40110) Books, printed matter	4,318,850	4,636,175	4,475,780	3,508,815	3,737,767	3,648,726	3,622,864	3,658,402	3,746,621	3,948,583
(40120) Toiletries and cosmetics	5,832,059	6,336,732	6,785,686	6,004,414	7,043,424	7,934,891	8,692,060	9,559,288	10,177,096	10,260,652
(40140) Other consumer nondurables	12,443,926	13,141,289	13,412,564	11,552,837	12,526,056	13,151,645	13,409,622	13,929,376	14,488,075	14,931,070
(41000) Furniture, household goods, etc.	24,619,828	25,135,461	23,694,820	18,932,622	23,001,445	23,630,045	25,612,712	27,583,763	29,976,521	33,503,466
(41010) Glassware, chinaware	2,396,101	2,368,843	2,168,502	1,650,369	2,033,669	2,062,301	2,137,478	2,255,347	2,346,735	2,466,306
(41020) Cookware, cutlery, tools	6,352,192	6,607,672	6,684,513	5,854,020	7,067,386	7,460,358	7,811,906	8,383,856	8,664,297	9,417,704
(41030) Household appliances	18,436,314	19,793,677	19,361,401	17,129,652	19,845,459	20,892,926	22,265,429	23,395,029	25,210,758	26,954,528
(41040) Rugs	2,135,035	2,120,324	1,918,248	1,489,719	1,745,007	1,923,219	2,047,523	2,178,587	2,463,461	2,531,388
(41050) Cell phones and other household goods, n.e.c.	51,871,743	56,022,263	61,576,235	60,289,647	68,558,993	77,688,059	81,286,225	90,201,409	95,966,498	98,661,382
(41100) Motorcycles and parts	4,629,982	4,083,648	4,117,508	2,504,153	1,781,182	2,606,548	3,058,783	3,023,137	2,939,704	2,967,488
(41110) Pleasure boats and motors	2,983,314	2,945,370	2,563,019	1,429,049	1,874,876	2,146,346	2,315,722	2,431,236	2,646,193	3,276,999
(41120) Toys, games, and sporting goods	28,789,857	34,359,167	35,970,004	31,393,214	34,840,498	32,953,784	33,473,500	33,250,695	33,981,730	36,396,114
(41130) Photo equipment	928,353	7,429,386	7,164,621	5,494,807	5,946,471	5,343,235	5,362,253	3,937,043	3,489,834	3,640,104
(41140) Musical instruments	1,650,528	1,618,384	1,705,577	1,297,727	1,511,953	1,582,765	1,621,928	1,612,175	1,691,529	1,669,435
(41200) Televisions and video equipment	41,781,478	39,789,394	40,983,124	36,129,919	37,779,071	33,495,146	32,861,882	28,761,587	28,182,822	28,346,336
(41210) Stereo equipment, etc.	10,391,472	8,071,048	6,504,950	5,025,476	6,059,456	5,974,135	6,761,754	6,838,155	6,760,425	6,316,162
(41220) Recorded media	1,279,582	3,332,211	3,113,524	2,454,896	2,587,281	3,006,244	906,893	832,992	757,124	943,471
(41300) Numismatic coins	339,767	341,436	1,258,393	1,778,254	1,717,110	2,537,904	1,933,133	2,624,143	1,797,026	1,991,934
(41310) Jewelry	13,202,408	13,545,787	11,357,507	8,622,431	10,422,511	12,338,842	12,073,277	12,942,882	13,506,974	13,880,684
(41320) Artwork, antiques, stamps, etc.	8,673,540	10,860,462	9,466,276	6,547,502	8,069,678	8,798,301	9,799,248	11,046,179	11,159,371	13,709,084

Table B-9. U.S. Imports from World Total by 5-Digit End-Use Code, 2006–2015—*Continued*

(In thousands of dollars)

	2006	2007	2008	2009	2010	2011	2012	2013	2014	2015
(END USE CODE) TOTAL	1,853,938,475	1,956,961,843	2,103,640,711	1,559,624,813	1,913,856,594	2,207,954,346	2,276,267,147	2,268,370,483	2,347,685,229	2,241,663,715
(42000) Nursery stock, etc.	1,456,999	1,548,761	1,470,219	1,350,242	1,483,246	1,547,076	1,620,978	1,677,548	1,725,542	1,725,368
(42100) Gem diamonds........................	17,291,363	18,942,890	19,743,929	12,736,481	18,598,814	22,298,831	20,195,757	23,387,855	24,602,679	23,402,218
(42110) Gem stones, other...................	2,540,906	2,696,046	2,746,620	2,323,794	2,839,686	3,113,662	3,404,237	3,508,648	3,704,424	3,652,486
(50000) Military aircraft and parts	1,566,513	1,855,597	2,043,935	2,122,636	2,368,481	2,620,368	3,279,467	2,948,243	3,278,802	3,066,643
(50010) Other military equipment........	1,429,663	2,018,102	2,278,852	2,840,732	2,982,648	2,385,881	2,287,477	2,213,616	1,814,292	1,650,910
(50020) U.S. goods returned, and reimports	34,869,936	35,688,596	37,352,633	34,416,819	38,511,103	41,524,554	48,702,208	52,292,705	57,219,506	61,342,421
(50030) Minimum value shipments	20,190,454	21,185,697	22,788,431	16,962,755	13,726,983	14,043,284	12,985,722	13,442,717	11,642,462	13,208,059
(50040) Other (movies, miscellaneous imports, and special transactions)	1,430,909	1,486,363	1,549,582	1,310,096	3,706,918	4,587,657	4,691,784	4,659,408	4,673,727	5,525,854

Table B-10. U.S. Exports to World Total by 5-Digit End-Use Code, 2006–2015

(In thousands of dollars)

End-use product group	2006	2007	2008	2009	2010	2011	2012	2013	2014	2015
TOTAL	1,025,967,497	1,148,198,722	1,287,441,997	1,056,042,963	1,278,494,526	1,482,507,755	1,545,820,840	1,578,439,231	1,620,531,900	1,504,597,471
(00000) Wheat	4,256,669	8,450,461	11,445,584	5,515,311	6,914,427	11,307,755	8,343,707	10,668,357	7,905,041	5,735,476
(00010) Rice	1,337,293	1,471,002	2,311,533	2,274,187	2,441,313	2,233,784	2,155,275	2,304,894	2,148,509	2,198,534
(00100) Soybeans	7,288,375	10,443,447	16,031,502	16,905,202	19,019,850	18,086,113	26,157,536	22,980,698	25,107,824	19,810,893
(00110) Oilseeds, food oils	1,329,691	2,034,425	3,190,447	2,525,373	3,209,369	3,298,100	3,251,400	2,999,132	2,834,564	2,713,327
(00200) Corn	8,226,378	11,209,235	14,611,992	9,680,733	10,930,665	14,820,359	10,538,991	7,766,151	11,946,863	9,383,338
(00210) Sorghum, barley, oats	707,276	1,226,515	1,487,777	728,478	804,452	1,054,388	596,904	629,937	1,807,995	2,383,317
(00220) Animal feeds, n.e.c.	3,813,842	4,567,605	5,931,953	6,350,471	6,707,911	6,792,077	8,079,791	8,976,891	8,989,424	8,620,941
(00300) Meat, poultry, etc.	7,830,539	9,803,526	13,473,914	12,056,081	13,640,713	17,143,934	18,019,088	18,467,285	20,085,896	16,626,547
(00310) Dairy products and eggs	1,491,901	2,452,990	3,245,250	1,880,555	3,164,846	4,042,142	4,224,161	5,755,893	6,194,585	4,417,609
(00320) Fruits, frozen juices	5,565,404	6,204,632	7,147,122	6,888,310	7,769,770	8,821,102	9,250,533	9,498,211	9,396,225	8,887,459
(00330) Vegetables	3,852,542	4,320,698	5,091,865	4,942,980	5,430,433	5,874,086	6,217,169	6,755,766	6,991,046	6,808,962
(00340) Nuts	3,226,764	3,449,396	3,898,846	4,183,367	4,902,649	5,808,531	7,031,159	8,468,564	8,810,867	9,240,517
(00350) Bakery products	2,997,266	3,458,496	3,972,302	4,057,777	4,788,057	5,598,845	6,192,895	6,481,165	6,481,215	6,269,932
(00360) Other foods	6,585,524	7,282,239	8,312,435	8,116,537	9,131,686	10,695,800	11,941,614	12,829,726	13,287,350	12,870,968
(00370) Wine, beer, and related products	1,098,847	1,217,621	1,299,056	1,273,536	1,529,236	1,770,907	1,885,134	2,141,218	2,103,359	2,273,971
(01000) Fish and shellfish	4,350,747	4,374,738	4,373,778	4,088,512	4,575,567	5,703,758	5,657,735	5,824,443	5,977,404	5,772,932
(01010) Alcoholic beverages, excluding wine	958,548	1,176,751	1,280,937	1,169,517	1,398,285	1,727,999	1,898,759	1,917,883	2,022,211	2,017,200
(01020) Nonagricultural foods, etc.	1,044,775	1,120,494	1,242,933	1,270,889	1,359,497	1,467,096	1,607,319	1,694,023	1,660,722	1,676,620
(10000) Cotton, raw	4,516,513	4,590,808	4,814,406	3,368,670	5,892,131	8,467,841	6,253,750	5,629,604	4,412,393	3,911,056
(10100) Tobacco, unmanufactured	1,134,076	1,201,464	1,231,004	1,133,193	1,133,009	1,122,007	1,107,693	1,183,876	1,117,534	1,130,687
(10120) Hides and skins	2,055,688	2,182,541	2,066,608	1,465,990	2,286,714	2,663,995	2,785,288	3,136,304	2,932,076	2,443,182
(10130) Agric. industry-unmanufactured	1,578,557	2,126,111	3,270,157	2,781,143	3,964,065	4,481,918	4,618,075	5,006,770	4,941,465	4,640,734
(10140) Agric. farming-unmanufactured	1,848,596	2,082,180	2,470,796	2,358,184	2,517,680	2,921,733	3,292,393	3,337,932	3,320,099	3,102,542
(10150) Agriculture-manufactured, other	1,733,912	1,917,364	2,219,799	2,087,976	2,377,653	2,603,805	2,791,589	2,797,540	3,032,757	2,950,297
(11010) Metallurgical grade coal	2,563,510	2,937,949	5,810,995	4,455,228	8,260,363	13,011,987	10,661,508	7,787,250	6,064,075	4,192,113
(11020) Coal and fuels, other	1,337,047	1,676,376	2,793,453	2,066,459	2,201,816	3,793,373	7,113,470	6,527,032	5,814,355	4,698,465
(11100) Crude oil	567,086	751,092	1,031,499	972,228	1,206,553	2,061,866	2,499,915	4,905,421	11,591,677	7,683,498
(11110) Fuel oil	12,060,896	15,573,765	34,894,056	23,670,220	32,659,872	52,918,588	59,890,998	64,706,491	59,722,167	37,517,425
(11120) Petroleum products, other	17,316,831	19,325,281	27,995,137	21,731,464	33,228,174	54,656,438	56,752,177	60,813,412	62,224,329	46,096,919
(11130) Natural gas liquids	1,623,363	2,107,542	3,260,336	2,803,344	3,732,888	4,069,998	4,317,862	6,966,565	10,763,499	8,177,211
(11200) Gas-natural	2,241,159	3,163,501	4,892,249	3,286,064	5,110,942	6,439,250	4,918,913	6,070,892	7,771,840	4,775,089
(11300) Nuclear fuel materials	1,827,382	2,430,288	2,177,672	2,283,340	1,896,056	2,695,300	1,866,354	1,220,240	1,093,195	1,627,928
(11400) Electric energy	1,036,051	991,907	1,263,886	561,929	630,811	374,637	233,067	356,160	564,140	246,716
(12000) Steelmaking materials	6,801,742	9,882,359	14,193,933	8,548,322	11,056,398	14,854,669	12,501,720	10,658,591	9,393,901	5,851,131
(12100) Iron and steel mill products	7,280,901	8,857,734	11,471,121	7,063,152	10,126,104	12,502,927	12,253,845	11,140,077	11,330,139	9,461,193
(12110) Iron and steel products, other	5,161,823	5,779,523	7,264,146	5,412,567	6,340,167	7,136,864	7,535,166	7,389,822	7,649,234	6,870,633
(12200) Aluminum and alumina	7,293,397	8,029,016	8,569,567	5,691,779	7,551,167	9,524,167	9,279,403	9,386,743	8,918,634	8,240,450
(12210) Copper	4,701,430	5,378,672	6,125,726	4,085,511	6,226,275	8,488,430	8,740,748	8,563,143	8,757,667	7,304,678
(12260) Nonmonetary gold	8,783,018	13,307,357	18,689,079	13,932,512	17,576,949	33,985,486	36,599,536	33,152,876	22,022,663	20,955,090
(12270) Precious metals, other	7,041,535	8,438,360	10,564,281	8,007,692	12,645,463	11,195,456	8,715,240	7,390,143	7,583,665	6,255,476
(12290) Nonferrous metals, other	6,601,440	8,060,264	7,765,131	5,825,561	7,743,076	8,888,029	7,867,795	6,990,709	8,077,628	7,443,260
(12300) Finished metal shapes	13,941,026	15,288,523	16,918,626	13,091,337	15,857,383	18,022,491	19,499,568	20,133,212	21,045,956	19,512,471
(12420) Pulpwood and woodpulp	5,907,916	7,112,556	7,940,832	6,848,862	8,903,733	10,143,396	9,365,563	9,076,084	9,051,916	8,830,458
(12430) Newsprint	10,567,425	11,543,605	12,462,794	10,759,362	12,462,739	13,506,719	13,165,277	13,399,609	13,442,334	12,921,242
(12500) Plastic materials	27,923,880	29,118,286	31,639,545	25,543,801	32,797,362	36,062,915	35,297,880	36,228,166	36,853,875	34,102,712
(12510) Chemicals-fertilizers	5,299,442	6,292,134	10,760,304	7,034,570	7,965,498	9,985,818	9,436,127	9,664,708	9,487,635	8,717,769
(12530) Chemicals-inorganic	6,660,376	7,014,514	8,356,994	6,018,503	7,507,983	8,888,077	8,917,996	9,120,556	9,209,297	8,835,782
(12540) Chemicals-organic	27,124,997	31,622,940	33,351,324	24,602,598	34,134,677	39,568,652	35,578,969	35,053,183	32,836,472	30,018,461
(12550) Chemicals-other	18,518,081	20,421,169	23,176,664	20,785,260	25,563,548	28,825,610	29,513,968	30,342,134	30,923,637	29,814,639
(12600) Cotton fiber cloth	3,131,450	2,857,846	2,777,619	2,115,630	2,454,301	3,228,491	2,562,275	2,500,285	2,525,975	2,301,663
(12620) Manmade cloth	5,772,104	5,872,791	6,046,710	4,743,467	6,016,010	6,799,763	6,938,676	7,220,385	7,359,694	6,970,900
(12630) Hair, waste materials	552,491	606,774	617,950	488,015	627,345	661,784	628,480	659,844	660,912	687,503
(12640) Finished textile supplies	2,630,262	2,467,721	2,440,976	2,072,266	2,539,785	2,665,306	2,757,928	3,046,055	3,227,827	3,135,228
(12650) Leather and furs	1,051,872	1,150,922	935,118	568,783	875,211	1,045,322	1,015,355	1,273,897	1,428,863	1,229,808
(12700) Synthetic rubber-primary	3,188,402	3,609,603	3,763,748	2,792,362	3,852,523	4,917,657	4,761,896	4,038,443	3,959,737	3,375,881
(12720) Nonmetallic minerals	605,025	581,999	825,002	481,209	716,385	904,119	1,023,396	874,126	1,006,045	904,229
(12750) Industrial rubber products	2,929,954	3,249,079	3,372,866	2,864,700	3,649,591	4,327,053	4,949,693	4,981,959	5,276,350	4,985,677
(12760) Mineral supplies-manufactured	4,513,271	4,932,509	4,994,114	4,027,656	5,272,539	5,569,058	5,313,823	5,582,589	5,929,741	5,977,667
(12765) Tapes, audio and visual	1,796,091	584,404	505,783	696,209	593,922	547,678	359,095	284,022	233,565	193,854
(12770) Other industrial supplies	16,415,191	19,854,838	20,443,435	17,932,452	21,490,015	23,080,593	23,763,315	24,777,800	26,023,794	26,045,992
(13100) Logs and lumber	4,604,286	4,730,702	4,417,280	3,523,549	4,913,702	5,638,686	5,444,683	6,302,211	6,878,333	5,888,319
(13110) Wood supplies, manufactured	1,221,734	1,279,670	1,399,805	1,014,437	1,207,213	1,349,481	1,427,653	1,412,655	1,435,939	1,238,056
(13200) Glass-plate, sheet, etc.	1,279,408	1,475,229	1,628,697	1,344,362	1,534,207	1,608,839	1,523,063	1,650,211	1,619,537	1,518,824
(13210) Shingles, molding, wallboard	3,022,113	3,413,712	3,875,079	3,341,640	4,075,091	4,538,562	4,736,713	4,741,905	4,969,735	4,807,469
(13220) Nontextile floor tiles	415,826	462,505	498,880	425,461	495,134	553,410	593,812	591,878	627,696	573,942
(20000) Generators, accessories	9,467,357	10,415,345	12,125,075	10,296,288	12,364,270	13,055,163	14,670,841	14,241,885	14,758,458	13,454,961
(20005) Electric apparatus	29,809,799	30,884,798	30,835,619	26,062,564	32,143,063	35,363,853	38,295,626	40,238,038	42,491,991	42,708,988
(21000) Drilling & oilfield equipment	10,779,975	12,611,364	15,064,587	11,467,010	10,508,021	10,878,242	12,391,427	12,292,878	11,909,581	8,628,442
(21010) Specialized mining	838,723	1,059,037	1,436,270	1,123,268	1,394,461	1,886,543	2,093,337	1,745,987	1,584,736	1,236,575
(21030) Excavating machinery	9,870,857	12,790,982	15,079,628	9,810,299	12,665,771	16,693,839	17,546,616	14,765,062	13,046,433	10,396,039
(21040) Nonfarm tractors and parts	1,859,599	2,102,594	3,410,665	2,048,417	2,404,491	3,496,278	4,205,182	3,093,099	3,020,633	2,793,858

Table B-10. U.S. Exports to World Total by 5-Digit End-Use Code, 2006–2015—*Continued*

(In thousands of dollars)

End-use product group	2006	2007	2008	2009	2010	2011	2012	2013	2014	2015
(21100) Industrial engines	15,976,883	19,147,306	21,848,649	21,916,203	24,345,863	28,188,986	30,049,641	29,256,148	29,713,789	27,349,915
(21110) Food, tobacco machinery	2,193,266	2,610,392	3,055,859	2,722,159	3,018,026	3,330,492	3,655,513	3,921,350	4,006,981	3,937,689
(21120) Metalworking machine tools	9,497,605	6,715,081	7,442,813	5,298,367	6,523,564	7,771,126	7,866,250	7,676,707	7,621,607	7,273,932
(21130) Textile, sewing machines	1,273,208	1,384,618	1,323,294	965,597	1,172,175	1,162,335	1,162,997	1,163,947	1,183,415	1,086,891
(21140) Wood, glass, plastic	3,628,075	3,510,729	4,139,420	3,414,628	3,642,097	4,346,399	4,451,632	4,059,760	4,065,654	4,125,811
(21150) Pulp and paper machinery	2,852,539	2,701,033	2,955,993	2,311,204	2,460,274	2,682,000	2,580,908	2,454,725	2,539,648	2,373,294
(21160) Measuring, testing, control instruments	19,151,971	20,629,956	20,984,430	16,939,642	21,200,936	23,899,200	24,823,086	24,758,246	25,152,152	23,961,557
(21170) Materials handling equipment	9,919,919	11,985,740	14,728,350	9,722,423	11,730,546	15,762,259	18,074,169	15,293,210	14,493,173	12,865,215
(21180) Industrial machines, other	32,697,001	38,364,090	38,138,302	30,876,273	42,708,125	45,387,809	46,170,254	48,899,434	54,265,618	53,518,255
(21190) Photo, service industry machinery	8,192,305	9,191,558	9,846,793	7,888,360	9,333,760	10,254,009	11,121,366	11,107,639	10,825,599	10,354,516
(21200) Agricultural machinery, equipment	5,312,437	6,268,756	8,297,054	6,253,057	6,802,794	8,784,487	10,059,577	9,253,603	8,462,269	7,206,388
(21300) Computers	11,470,423	13,535,351	14,560,866	12,314,744	14,702,392	16,864,353	16,944,755	16,720,000	16,891,893	15,940,578
(21301) Computer accessories	36,109,996	29,403,993	29,336,861	25,402,179	29,111,454	31,595,237	32,270,948	31,367,132	31,896,967	30,871,208
(21320) Semiconductors	52,429,936	50,444,550	50,603,102	37,487,996	47,178,008	43,872,156	42,073,416	42,599,478	43,480,028	42,536,805
(21400) Telecommunications equipment	28,930,842	31,424,350	32,865,982	28,683,134	31,937,458	35,948,035	38,466,836	39,734,036	40,669,416	41,862,153
(21500) Business machines and equipment	2,702,010	5,392,134	4,246,641	2,973,575	3,138,484	3,187,221	3,183,609	2,977,583	2,976,641	2,649,057
(21600) Laboratory testing instruments	7,280,227	8,128,335	9,011,278	8,693,696	9,959,068	10,724,036	10,902,360	10,980,170	11,295,897	11,043,734
(21610) Medicinal equipment	22,702,165	23,825,242	27,023,260	26,879,276	29,806,763	32,106,731	33,642,384	34,121,663	34,914,416	34,419,432
(22090) Civilian aircraft, engines, equipment, and parts	64,502,981	73,019,297	73,998,632	74,755,438	71,921,297	80,352,575	94,309,320	104,990,544	113,071,133	118,918,133
(22100) Railway transportation equipment	2,939,640	3,013,878	3,430,978	2,500,782	2,799,601	3,585,256	4,131,936	4,198,284	4,251,912	4,360,364
(22200) Vessels, excluding scrap	51,701	108,920	88,165	22,016	34,201	96,916	52,817	102,317	374,900	158,425
(22210) Commercial vessels, other	222,441	293,268	372,734	395,242	418,316	419,977	498,485	627,126	575,496	656,122
(22220) Marine engines, parts	1,127,719	1,267,760	1,450,095	1,188,961	1,174,308	1,280,356	1,438,188	1,473,875	1,439,984	1,587,329
(22300) Spacecraft, excluding military	26,879	30,336	26,555	48,362	30,857	31,578	44,515	63,057	76,026	61,776
(30000) Passenger cars, new and used	33,977,613	43,743,138	49,568,671	27,501,371	38,354,297	47,397,769	53,510,565	56,248,789	60,572,963	54,493,884
(30100) Trucks, buses and special purpose vehicles	15,104,176	17,033,187	15,753,472	12,472,506	16,626,718	19,373,891	20,059,999	20,877,240	19,863,036	17,936,649
(30200) Engines and engine parts carburetors, pistons, rings, and valves)	12,197,079	13,222,680	12,860,797	8,775,176	12,469,355	14,705,701	15,914,444	16,481,697	18,353,727	16,951,241
(30210) Bodies and chassis for passenger cars	58,906	187,253	193,100	65,257	85,872	112,151	117,637	233,753	399,873	606,522
(30220) Automotive tires and tubes	2,487,460	2,733,607	3,076,308	2,768,978	3,161,778	3,783,536	4,117,945	3,988,341	4,137,080	3,758,813
(30230) Other parts and accessories of vehicles	43,336,184	44,330,344	39,850,620	30,131,644	41,309,616	47,662,895	52,437,671	54,840,367	56,363,680	57,816,881
(40000) Apparel, household goods - textile	5,199,401	4,744,950	4,913,001	4,767,587	5,372,016	6,027,837	6,492,050	6,866,767	7,188,161	7,158,323
(40030) Apparel, household goods-nontextile	1,839,910	1,953,582	2,232,846	2,117,895	2,342,950	2,699,664	2,939,634	3,008,698	3,047,709	3,109,845
(40050) Sports apparel and gear	588,789	565,214	607,659	520,298	579,318	693,664	710,406	731,973	829,767	800,297
(40100) Pharmaceutical preparations	30,919,365	35,164,635	40,422,158	46,122,661	46,625,248	45,056,547	47,798,606	48,365,179	50,958,434	55,046,476
(40110) Books, printed matter	5,205,957	5,586,630	5,808,117	5,183,642	5,420,857	5,367,728	5,379,343	5,336,879	5,042,084	4,712,489
(40120) Toiletries and cosmetics	6,760,241	7,615,193	8,715,182	8,436,427	9,410,757	9,877,924	10,651,875	11,323,473	11,789,068	11,874,137
(40130) Tobacco, manufactured	1,362,074	1,157,107	858,340	533,247	495,766	536,846	526,755	696,495	667,587	866,124
(40140) Other consumer nondurables	5,835,270	6,182,716	6,743,648	5,942,634	6,893,323	7,169,789	7,390,612	7,583,046	7,542,685	7,557,435
(41000) Furniture, household goods, etc.	3,209,952	3,591,487	4,045,732	3,221,439	3,756,686	4,124,996	4,667,394	4,918,598	5,143,355	4,968,615
(41010) Glassware, chinaware	433,268	493,571	521,438	395,705	464,936	498,100	558,228	572,543	602,917	580,486
(41020) Cookware, cutlery, tools	871,885	1,003,808	1,029,246	840,518	910,439	1,004,151	1,055,674	1,092,799	1,183,101	1,173,755
(41030) Household appliances	6,636,064	6,940,036	7,376,021	5,919,684	6,612,368	6,890,161	7,255,107	7,511,257	7,535,914	7,284,515
(41040) Rugs	1,008,340	1,023,943	1,090,418	849,025	995,913	1,080,733	1,103,086	1,113,963	1,113,222	1,028,413
(41050) Cell phones and other household goods, n.e.c.	14,078,144	15,458,272	17,020,468	16,629,750	19,262,770	20,495,501	21,628,067	23,602,946	24,668,725	24,779,721
(41110) Pleasure boats and motors	2,784,741	3,149,061	3,423,537	2,050,067	2,479,285	2,536,704	2,613,960	2,450,784	2,437,440	2,143,212
(41120) Toys, games, and sporting goods	9,044,514	11,288,684	11,615,803	9,839,225	10,494,228	10,528,231	10,451,871	10,288,804	10,391,321	9,386,546
(41140) Musical instruments	1,066,449	2,110,834	2,182,878	2,108,088	2,343,299	2,445,159	2,336,270	2,176,305	2,046,312	1,772,232
(41200) Televisions and video equipment	3,867,843	3,858,229	3,747,936	3,904,324	5,161,785	5,708,804	5,051,649	4,359,802	4,580,554	4,799,902
(41210) Stereo equipment, etc.	2,460,028	2,469,801	2,272,000	1,786,163	1,845,349	1,945,634	2,077,189	2,037,881	2,127,467	2,023,580
(41220) Recorded media	3,543,387	4,962,046	5,135,017	4,035,140	4,210,746	4,223,504	3,884,535	3,090,456	2,679,899	2,264,258
(41300) Numismatic coins	155,242	244,792	321,107	282,087	520,989	1,033,050	1,105,419	1,029,355	926,737	853,702
(41310) Jewelry, etc.	6,150,140	6,974,894	7,189,366	6,807,589	7,613,718	9,082,199	10,297,413	11,676,942	12,576,298	11,794,026
(41320) Artwork, antiques, stamps, etc.	5,952,850	7,497,948	8,448,043	6,861,140	6,838,590	7,325,160	7,686,155	7,943,240	10,395,029	11,220,915
(42000) Nursery stock, etc.	388,513	422,700	444,337	405,493	416,043	423,746	400,532	417,632	421,387	409,855
(42100) Gem diamonds	9,986,079	12,328,131	15,250,311	10,483,995	14,870,135	19,255,706	18,121,092	20,905,270	23,010,340	20,207,911
(50000) Military aircraft, complete	4,464,053	4,174,989	4,580,069	2,381,208	2,058,325	1,770,279	3,446,309	2,822,440	5,057,878	3,738,216
(50010) Aircraft launching gear, parachutes, etc.	344,801	329,905	393,594	452,002	340,753	315,277	358,144	471,797	395,631	414,334
(50020) Engines and turbines for military aircraft	1,643,263	1,780,258	1,772,342	1,912,519	1,990,308	1,991,838	2,175,815	2,286,167	2,545,886	2,584,754
(50030) Military trucks, armored vehicles, etc.	845,650	1,031,680	926,068	1,012,332	1,069,520	967,936	920,647	1,035,528	875,291	1,184,336
(50040) Military ships and boats	5,170	23,310	8,624	0	0	0	0	28,400	297,162	3,129
(50050) Tanks, artillery, missiles, rockets, guns and ammunition	2,714,832	2,935,530	2,881,743	3,121,615	3,605,513	3,514,532	3,619,080	4,137,926	4,048,464	4,563,896
(50060) Military apparel and footwear	693,126	654,518	540,713	434,997	577,555	674,227	625,333	689,489	1,179,000	1,241,282
(50070) Parts for military-type goods	5,917,827	5,963,682	5,490,903	5,481,298	5,661,570	5,677,039	6,057,562	6,145,477	6,159,541	6,339,647
(60000) Minimum value shipments	21,595,289	24,277,382	27,830,906	22,610,420	33,090,006	32,298,884	33,624,674	34,712,194	34,936,229	29,876,686
(60010) Miscellaneous domestic exports and special transactions	5,365,184	6,128,446	6,237,098	5,799,825	5,936,431	5,677,796	5,724,824	5,926,214	6,519,402	6,973,888
(60040) Undocumented exports to Canada	0	0	0	0	0	0	0	0	0	4,086,239

Table B-11.   Exports with World by Standard International Trade Classification (SITC), 2005–2015

SITC	Item	2005	2006	2007	2008	2009
0	Live Animals	664,021,676	755,490,005	749,438,097	860,115,282	796,487,078
1	Meat And Meat Preparations	6,737,867,517	7,281,659,721	9,152,539,624	12,607,479,532	11,637,005,791
2	Dairy Products And Birds' Eggs	1,398,635,385	1,589,525,376	2,572,929,714	3,352,675,675	2,011,245,764
3	Fish (Except Marine Mammal)	4,101,559,447	4,268,207,353	4,303,918,299	4,289,811,955	4,007,873,429
4	Cereals And Cereal Preparation	13,451,838,591	15,812,706,272	23,949,041,902	31,877,312,467	20,460,548,621
5	Vegetables And Fruit	11,344,188,324	12,329,911,103	13,581,641,849	15,702,599,520	15,641,066,205
6	Sugars; Sugar Preparations	840,236,364	1,056,876,116	1,413,521,168	1,323,533,216	1,239,621,897
7	Coffee; Tea; Cocoa	1,475,638,468	1,691,897,944	1,916,914,822	2,216,996,239	2,188,058,893
8	Feeding Stuff For Animals	4,222,219,120	4,710,003,268	5,737,090,145	7,892,247,500	8,035,632,438
9	Miscellaneous Edible	4,234,752,467	4,690,517,866	4,915,631,931	5,627,936,745	5,585,040,317
11	Beverages	2,153,144,539	2,579,313,797	3,005,525,423	3,369,068,725	3,303,089,017
12	Tobacco And Tobacco	2,334,302,943	2,507,307,300	2,369,837,326	2,099,171,644	1,695,694,839
21	Hides; Skins And Furskins	1,812,386,170	2,060,368,819	2,185,919,565	2,070,136,247	1,468,494,202
22	Oil Seeds And Oleaginous	7,080,763,781	7,809,979,401	11,110,312,821	16,854,443,705	17,602,225,027
23	Crude Rubber	2,312,180,696	2,740,575,882	3,116,163,494	3,195,085,660	2,388,002,285
24	Cork And Wood	4,176,151,285	4,407,117,126	4,551,794,996	4,364,528,292	3,579,571,019
25	Pulp And Waste Paper	5,201,428,464	5,863,049,402	7,065,247,736	7,890,871,206	6,796,439,514
26	Textile Fibers	5,459,942,338	6,171,668,254	6,477,864,374	6,837,277,594	5,213,213,768
27	Crude Fertilizers	1,771,020,670	2,020,163,696	2,105,769,670	2,517,694,881	1,842,453,376
28	Metalliferous Ores	11,367,696,927	16,839,545,402	23,313,370,600	29,754,205,470	20,217,631,127
29	Crude Animal And Vegetable Materials	2,089,096,890	2,241,215,394	2,546,939,124	2,977,779,511	2,587,713,864
32	Coal; Coke And Briquettes	3,484,077,656	3,680,935,495	4,304,262,671	8,232,882,150	6,206,447,466
33	Petroleum; Petroleum Products	18,100,641,323	26,721,150,546	32,162,179,366	60,744,716,393	43,073,251,582
34	Gas; Natural And Manufactured	4,014,622,074	3,399,396,508	4,731,134,780	6,500,228,458	5,006,684,230
35	Electric Current	1,046,509,118	1,036,051,436	991,906,979	1,263,885,805	561,928,652
41	Animal Oils And Fats	496,329,044	530,980,128	871,288,897	1,146,023,563	728,601,530
42	Fixed Veg. Fats & Oils	1,048,721,314	1,237,854,593	1,689,616,223	2,797,733,577	2,114,090,567
43	Animal/Veg Fats/Oils Process/Waste	215,334,666	214,443,813	297,059,493	486,442,850	374,192,708
51	Organic Chemicals	27,300,896,667	30,628,856,880	34,666,545,643	35,161,847,545	28,416,543,803
52	Inorganic Chemicals	7,919,356,710	9,214,049,262	10,945,233,825	13,092,394,480	10,428,265,949
53	Dyeing; Tanning and Coloring Materials	5,053,098,727	5,467,790,465	5,941,851,029	6,389,551,347	5,719,670,562
54	Medicinal And Pharmaceutical Products	25,937,598,531	29,265,390,993	33,610,430,332	38,338,490,357	44,231,628,701
55	Essential Oils	8,448,986,208	9,502,177,698	10,667,597,528	12,161,166,180	11,679,011,024
56	Fertilizers	3,287,510,730	3,180,606,210	3,730,066,392	7,437,357,384	4,088,423,785
57	Plastics In Primary Form	21,542,543,401	24,486,600,409	28,521,289,394	30,988,889,655	25,014,947,256
58	Plastics In Nonprimary Form	8,047,692,366	8,787,091,527	9,325,538,088	10,099,603,910	8,882,611,482
59	Chemical Materials	16,438,639,603	18,512,534,725	21,383,738,536	26,067,263,096	21,430,887,869
61	Leather; Leather Mfr	1,416,252,153	1,364,124,700	1,360,316,511	1,146,086,212	708,091,174
62	Rubber Manufactures	6,059,683,925	6,685,000,852	7,394,276,701	8,090,821,812	7,073,802,069
63	Cork And Wood Manufactures	2,004,803,335	2,217,490,271	2,338,019,787	2,486,034,848	1,913,664,779
64	Paper; Paperboard	11,841,697,129	12,706,030,369	13,859,555,694	15,048,286,401	13,241,161,455
65	Textile Yarn; Fabrics	12,397,850,274	12,679,722,582	12,425,526,640	12,496,082,561	9,930,566,834
66	Nonmetallic Mineral	15,483,673,967	17,598,020,652	20,742,026,517	24,058,576,525	17,873,910,880
67	Iron And Steel	11,504,323,174	12,773,281,146	15,164,291,304	20,143,337,719	13,242,207,563
68	Nonferrous Metals	10,920,623,675	16,899,112,825	16,856,309,136	17,178,284,242	11,418,459,309
69	Manufactures Of Metals	17,387,783,830	20,351,702,293	22,282,694,060	24,116,882,442	19,318,232,315
71	Power Generating Machinery	27,926,268,862	29,972,763,609	33,669,551,385	36,007,206,548	30,438,438,831
72	Machinery Specialized	35,479,493,319	40,056,061,179	51,464,843,465	55,607,785,596	40,070,258,308
73	Metalworking Machinery	7,057,784,134	8,892,063,259	6,000,213,909	6,759,631,498	4,794,417,902
74	General Industrial Machinery	41,641,122,731	47,076,118,667	52,005,348,393	59,013,819,808	48,764,495,137
75	Office Machines And ADP equipment	46,928,307,387	49,192,549,907	46,258,437,226	46,111,554,377	38,811,080,198
76	Telecommunications Equipment	29,997,259,571	33,979,183,415	38,022,538,576	40,604,747,599	36,114,595,246
77	Electrical Machry; Apparatus & Appliances	94,781,227,397	106,795,498,628	104,804,070,442	105,917,039,988	85,566,195,752
78	Motor Vehicles	80,532,444,582	88,993,798,624	103,023,980,783	106,535,443,413	69,806,497,712
79	Transport Equipment	67,553,916,309	80,550,342,668	89,607,295,360	90,457,994,737	87,061,324,991
81	Prefab Buildings; Sanitary; Plumbing; etc.	1,910,800,474	2,117,050,010	2,255,691,297	2,832,046,218	2,413,901,291
82	Furniture & Bedding	5,021,585,385	5,519,084,750	5,995,979,417	6,127,186,777	4,808,751,963
83	Travel Goods; Handbags	560,136,886	651,229,569	669,812,206	761,775,854	787,558,058
84	Articles Of Apparel and Clothing	5,006,021,903	4,885,378,335	4,320,006,301	4,448,634,157	4,186,147,437
85	Footwear	730,509,993	829,374,500	890,079,045	1,039,484,676	944,783,077
87	Professional Scientific Instruments	37,767,824,574	42,992,375,511	46,544,697,749	49,118,961,449	44,806,046,538
88	Photo Appt; Equipment & Optical Goods	7,888,327,892	8,355,117,817	8,467,387,837	8,221,882,967	7,711,665,906
89	Miscellaneous Manufactured Articles	43,946,439,250	49,571,894,029	56,739,730,765	60,124,248,175	54,284,675,782
93	Special Transactions	5,946,227,362	6,140,532,402	6,782,682,133	7,290,107,590	6,868,784,073
95	Coin Including Gold	40,401,289	114,405,792	168,003,284	237,136,877	219,903,672
96	Coin (Other Than Gold)	9,109,052	16,249,495	30,879,469	35,733,203	26,299,321
97	Gold; Nonmonetary	5,548,818,492	8,811,805,215	13,381,638,941	18,858,550,900	13,972,250,823
99	Low Value Shipments	19,179,326,039	21,886,223,268	24,591,686,002	27,977,183,745	22,610,498,995

Table B-11. Exports with World by Standard International Trade Classification (SITC), 2005–2015—Continued

SITC	Item	2010	2011	2012	2013	2014	2015
0	Live Animals	814,890,071	1,038,251,364	1,189,530,232	1,019,514,929	944,295,813	757,360,691
1	Meat And Meat Preparations	13,232,848,767	16,670,361,859	17,538,184,898	17,970,066,177	19,502,697,950	16,045,384,944
2	Dairy Products And Birds' Eggs	3,298,093,485	4,198,020,356	4,378,195,328	5,943,924,942	6,344,121,905	4,632,561,203
3	Fish (Except Marine Mammal)	4,477,426,924	5,594,626,642	5,514,109,963	5,637,599,056	5,780,845,761	5,590,736,172
4	Cereals And Cereal Preparation	23,196,666,429	31,849,195,753	24,538,950,679	24,450,635,452	27,056,063,249	22,950,507,421
5	Vegetables And Fruit	17,733,998,361	20,183,322,228	22,126,466,666	24,081,042,203	24,664,636,630	24,392,011,915
6	Sugars; Sugar Preparations	1,774,586,438	2,198,079,994	2,592,636,244	2,512,480,037	2,303,959,381	2,011,338,482
7	Coffee; Tea; Cocoa	2,604,596,238	3,193,140,382	3,431,620,993	3,498,332,925	3,759,190,544	3,523,844,386
8	Feeding Stuff For Animals	9,316,124,267	9,653,567,646	11,280,486,755	13,220,134,634	13,240,994,606	12,641,034,850
9	Miscellaneous Edible	6,178,577,157	7,011,403,610	7,814,253,707	8,676,363,885	9,017,892,364	8,964,241,435
11	Beverages	3,787,971,325	4,473,307,041	4,897,157,643	5,313,793,561	5,483,522,674	5,721,368,501
12	Tobacco And Tobacco	1,671,101,643	1,695,718,949	1,657,584,481	1,909,886,988	1,805,463,578	2,077,517,416
21	Hides; Skins And Furskins	2,288,550,267	2,665,618,123	2,787,527,858	3,141,065,518	2,933,024,721	2,442,684,840
22	Oil Seeds And Oleaginous	19,810,696,583	18,824,005,855	27,021,352,070	24,132,864,539	26,166,929,706	20,765,379,074
23	Crude Rubber	3,381,956,952	4,471,493,187	4,186,804,038	3,481,016,692	3,372,016,446	2,783,879,688
24	Cork And Wood	4,862,997,842	5,650,777,713	5,604,200,424	6,630,696,239	7,389,195,886	6,691,091,492
25	Pulp And Waste Paper	8,861,531,583	10,102,765,689	9,311,759,470	8,965,421,214	8,965,406,799	8,704,333,323
26	Textile Fibers	7,992,722,202	10,912,053,619	8,716,138,107	8,262,027,516	6,987,996,688	6,183,445,683
27	Crude Fertilizers	2,471,551,467	2,731,215,417	2,710,910,770	2,645,964,272	2,927,890,079	2,691,867,975
28	Metalliferous Ores	28,584,371,054	33,176,284,376	28,197,540,806	26,030,274,556	24,714,183,604	19,440,381,763
29	Crude Animal And Vegetable Materials	2,830,086,650	3,110,003,392	3,285,595,762	3,394,194,964	3,513,011,562	3,509,205,393
32	Coal; Coke And Briquettes	10,098,408,917	16,172,733,619	15,084,107,252	11,467,301,706	8,720,824,735	5,898,840,124
33	Petroleum; Petroleum Products	62,778,360,744	103,482,926,654	113,021,664,042	124,399,361,748	128,971,429,074	86,246,439,294
34	Gas; Natural And Manufactured	7,940,869,343	10,272,800,006	8,800,654,288	12,531,080,018	17,403,268,170	11,585,404,640
35	Electric Current	630,810,860	374,637,165	233,067,299	356,159,864	564,139,834	241,128,045
41	Animal Oils And Fats	1,086,502,417	1,309,796,560	909,137,766	780,970,432	747,570,146	559,171,969
42	Fixed Veg. Fats & Oils	2,763,867,700	2,708,866,172	2,739,584,610	2,117,118,190	1,832,101,839	1,878,188,321
43	Anml/Veg Fats/Oils Process/Waste	430,896,950	536,198,683	546,556,310	446,304,631	403,037,359	347,747,464
51	Organic Chemicals	38,834,670,944	45,598,902,007	44,341,072,767	44,553,645,459	40,848,133,295	36,379,501,289
52	Inorganic Chemicals	12,156,100,482	14,447,594,989	12,893,874,262	11,549,313,738	11,787,445,564	11,519,165,850
53	Dyeing; Tanning and Coloring Materials	7,621,405,676	8,823,066,608	8,170,350,005	7,837,536,906	8,028,393,218	7,630,909,732
54	Medicinal And Pharmaceutical Products	44,596,610,771	42,736,504,420	44,767,836,351	44,354,980,785	48,675,111,460	52,591,609,869
55	Essential Oils	13,172,324,999	14,030,705,769	15,069,020,284	15,864,503,162	16,479,565,343	16,420,983,288
56	Fertilizers	4,642,039,469	6,280,485,603	5,348,582,691	4,984,470,575	4,594,451,433	4,351,588,917
57	Plastics In Primary Form	32,136,023,534	35,359,464,521	34,544,037,366	35,523,072,179	36,057,827,490	33,250,334,811
58	Plastics In Nonprimary Form	10,885,130,507	11,944,561,464	12,155,952,651	12,662,149,196	13,491,577,785	13,637,495,366
59	Chemical Materials	25,228,414,238	28,239,648,147	30,034,834,536	31,974,582,410	32,299,307,821	30,854,119,790
61	Leather; Leather Mfr	1,055,754,537	1,250,477,985	1,264,683,071	1,530,383,265	1,675,997,733	1,481,821,407
62	Rubber Manufactures	8,576,528,488	10,221,678,020	11,347,281,570	11,199,226,741	11,463,971,718	10,714,841,152
63	Cork And Wood Manufactures	2,251,117,029	2,299,796,706	2,317,566,689	2,361,406,934	2,385,912,270	2,267,839,465
64	Paper; Paperboard	15,281,069,970	16,422,725,365	16,293,908,792	16,660,080,581	16,588,253,181	15,929,057,407
65	Textile Yarn; Fabrics	12,169,488,470	13,851,895,023	13,499,838,508	13,936,614,132	14,387,607,502	13,947,478,618
66	Nonmetallic Mineral	24,140,768,935	29,485,006,219	28,520,963,616	31,765,004,949	34,573,270,554	31,618,309,629
67	Iron And Steel	17,223,719,616	20,342,941,172	20,852,340,827	19,907,781,935	19,991,330,951	16,058,389,159
68	Nonferrous Metals	16,037,764,574	19,622,138,758	19,185,661,290	17,907,538,824	18,604,083,205	16,507,144,101
69	Manufactures Of Metals	23,001,782,513	26,452,493,114	28,632,975,026	29,669,459,818	30,877,880,934	29,256,430,365
71	Power Generating Machinery	36,025,805,146	39,659,936,176	43,026,958,677	41,995,753,074	44,061,494,817	41,193,273,670
72	Machinery Specialized	51,127,078,744	57,132,024,800	58,884,879,621	54,226,820,593	54,044,143,462	48,637,447,773
73	Metalworking Machinery	5,952,103,336	7,052,135,277	7,175,358,640	6,978,459,361	6,965,879,054	6,539,057,632
74	General Industrial Machinery	56,571,507,382	66,202,700,136	71,716,299,749	74,484,067,519	78,890,623,555	74,855,878,758
75	Office Machines And ADP equipment	44,535,244,974	48,920,127,682	49,834,012,945	48,786,744,512	49,507,989,603	47,035,672,526
76	Telecommunications Equipment	42,587,324,832	48,241,585,343	49,160,527,092	50,604,067,279	53,327,421,711	53,167,234,890
77	Electrical Machry; Apparatus & Appliances	105,378,484,390	107,089,376,378	108,080,048,026	110,777,990,833	114,116,976,318	112,843,402,396
78	Motor Vehicles	95,173,296,044	115,046,743,155	127,193,493,855	129,593,425,666	131,955,287,793	123,710,528,244
79	Transport Equipment	84,549,841,615	93,358,488,568	111,417,957,850	120,971,841,314	132,160,681,263	138,300,713,980
81	Prefab Buildings; Sanitary; Plumbing; etc.	2,852,711,577	3,240,185,897	3,494,861,772	3,659,167,682	3,851,798,306	3,608,751,593
82	Furniture & Bedding	5,891,878,549	6,415,864,499	7,197,989,349	7,584,623,031	8,106,078,343	8,029,962,154
83	Travel Goods; Handbags	847,926,900	971,719,811	1,096,032,219	1,175,497,598	1,173,344,780	1,229,816,010
84	Articles Of Apparel and Clothing	4,693,724,758	5,240,500,492	5,606,519,291	5,856,704,868	6,105,288,495	6,127,662,190
85	Footwear	1,105,454,224	1,290,038,604	1,332,305,334	1,391,282,682	1,456,188,127	1,463,617,789
87	Professional Scientific Instruments	51,848,230,732	56,877,814,520	59,780,821,847	60,834,246,490	61,623,613,941	60,336,014,771
88	Photo Appt; Equipment & Optical Goods	8,542,679,866	8,765,239,508	8,919,778,325	8,643,713,559	8,688,883,668	8,570,648,210
89	Miscellaneous Manufactured Articles	58,230,239,670	61,092,752,242	64,333,040,591	67,356,933,219	70,592,121,963	70,124,838,414
93	Special Transactions	7,283,865,990	7,079,109,114	7,014,070,727	7,427,864,615	8,317,087,483	8,952,709,117
95	Coin Including Gold	395,338,448	825,553,465	888,825,535	851,978,365	790,940,278	726,365,679
96	Coin (Other Than Gold)	71,646,697	136,378,011	78,900,734	50,559,244	45,113,097	52,036,012
97	Gold; Nonmonetary	17,828,358,638	33,899,339,285	36,606,924,562	33,295,595,670	22,119,059,805	20,886,107,100
99	Low Value Shipments	33,090,005,939	32,298,884,319	33,624,674,388	34,712,194,299	34,945,769,837	32,486,373,891

Table B-12.   Total All Merchandise Exports to World, 2010–2015

SITC	Item	2010	2011	2012	2013	2014	2015
	TOTAL....................	1,278,494,525,839	1,482,507,755,226	1,545,820,839,892	1,578,516,879,950	1,621,171,618,259	1,502,572,229,518
79	Transport Equipment..................	84,549,841,615	93,358,488,568	111,417,957,850	120,971,841,314	132,160,681,263	138,300,713,980
78	Motor Vehicles..................	95,173,296,044	115,046,743,155	127,193,493,855	129,593,425,666	131,955,287,793	123,710,528,244
77	Electrical Machry; Apparatus & Appliances......	105,378,484,390	107,089,376,378	108,080,048,026	110,777,990,833	114,116,976,318	112,843,402,396
33	Petroleum; Petroleum Products..................	62,778,360,744	103,482,926,654	113,021,664,042	124,399,361,748	128,971,429,074	86,246,439,294
74	General Industrial Machry..................	56,571,507,382	66,202,700,136	71,716,299,749	74,484,067,519	78,890,623,555	74,855,878,758
89	Miscellaneous Manufactured Articles..........	58,230,239,670	61,092,752,242	64,333,040,591	67,356,933,219	70,592,121,963	70,124,838,414
87	Professional Scientific Instruments	51,848,230,732	56,877,814,520	59,780,821,847	60,834,246,490	61,623,613,941	60,336,014,771
76	Telecommunications Equipment	42,587,324,832	48,241,585,343	49,160,527,092	50,604,067,279	53,327,421,711	53,167,234,890
54	Medicinal And Pharmaceutical Products..........	44,596,610,771	42,736,504,420	44,767,836,351	44,354,980,785	48,675,111,460	52,591,609,869
72	Machinery Specialized..................	51,127,078,744	57,132,024,800	58,884,879,621	54,226,820,593	54,044,143,462	48,637,447,773
75	Office Machines And ADP equipment..........	44,535,244,974	48,920,127,682	49,834,012,945	48,786,744,512	49,507,989,603	47,035,672,526
71	Power Generating Machinery..........	36,025,805,146	39,659,936,176	43,026,958,677	41,995,753,074	44,061,494,817	41,193,273,670
51	Organic Chemicals	38,834,670,944	45,598,902,007	44,341,072,767	44,553,645,459	40,848,133,295	36,379,501,289
57	Plastics In Primary Form..................	32,136,023,534	35,359,464,521	34,544,037,366	35,523,072,179	36,057,827,490	33,250,334,811
99	Low Value Shipments	33,090,005,939	32,298,884,319	33,624,674,388	34,712,194,299	34,945,769,837	32,486,373,891
66	Nonmetallic Mineral	24,140,768,935	29,485,006,219	28,520,963,616	31,765,004,949	34,573,270,554	31,618,309,629
59	Chemical Materials	25,228,414,238	28,239,648,147	30,034,834,536	31,974,582,410	32,299,307,821	30,854,119,790
69	Manufactures Of Metals..................	23,001,782,513	26,452,493,114	28,632,975,026	29,669,459,818	30,877,880,934	29,256,430,365
5	Vegetables And Fruit..................	17,733,998,361	20,183,322,228	22,126,466,666	24,081,042,203	24,664,636,630	24,392,011,915
4	Cereals And Cereal Preparation..........	23,196,666,429	31,849,195,753	24,538,950,679	24,450,635,452	27,056,063,249	22,950,507,421
97	Gold; Nonmonetary..................	17,828,358,638	33,899,339,285	36,606,924,562	33,295,595,670	22,119,059,805	20,886,107,100
22	Oil Seeds And Oleaginous	19,810,696,583	18,824,005,855	27,021,352,070	24,132,864,539	26,166,929,706	20,765,379,074
28	Metalliferous Ores..................	28,584,371,054	33,176,284,376	28,197,540,806	26,030,274,556	24,714,183,604	19,440,381,763
68	Nonferrous Metals	16,037,764,574	19,622,138,758	19,185,661,290	17,907,538,824	18,604,083,205	16,507,144,101
55	Essential Oils..................	13,172,324,999	14,030,705,769	15,069,020,284	15,864,503,162	16,479,565,343	16,420,983,288
67	Iron And Steel	17,223,719,616	20,342,941,172	20,852,340,827	19,907,781,935	19,991,330,951	16,058,389,159
1	Meat And Meat Preparations..........	13,232,848,767	16,670,361,859	17,538,184,898	17,970,066,177	19,502,697,950	16,045,384,944
64	Paper; Paperboard	15,281,069,970	16,422,725,365	16,293,908,792	16,660,080,581	16,588,253,181	15,929,057,407
65	Textile Yarn; Fabrics	12,169,488,470	13,851,895,023	13,499,838,508	13,936,614,132	14,387,607,502	13,947,478,618
58	Plastics In Nonprimary Form	10,885,130,507	11,944,561,464	12,155,952,651	12,662,149,196	13,491,577,785	13,637,495,366
8	Feeding Stuff For Animals	9,316,124,267	9,653,567,646	11,280,486,755	13,220,134,634	13,240,994,606	12,641,034,850
34	Gas; Natural And Manufactured	7,940,869,343	10,272,800,006	8,800,654,288	12,531,080,018	17,403,268,170	11,585,404,640
52	Inorganic Chemicals	12,156,100,482	14,447,594,989	12,893,874,262	11,549,313,738	11,787,445,564	11,519,165,850
62	Rubber Manufactures	8,576,528,488	10,221,678,020	11,347,281,570	11,199,226,741	11,463,971,718	10,714,841,152
9	Miscellaneous Edible..................	6,178,577,157	7,011,403,610	7,814,253,707	8,676,363,885	9,017,892,364	8,964,241,435
93	Special Transactions	7,283,865,990	7,079,109,114	7,014,070,727	7,427,864,615	8,317,087,483	8,952,709,117
25	Pulp And Waste Paper	8,861,531,583	10,102,765,689	9,311,759,470	8,965,421,214	8,965,406,799	8,704,333,323
88	Photo Appt; Equipment & Optical Goods	8,542,679,866	8,765,239,508	8,919,778,325	8,643,713,559	8,688,883,668	8,570,648,210
82	Furniture & Bedding..................	5,891,878,549	6,415,864,499	7,197,989,349	7,584,623,031	8,106,078,343	8,029,962,154
53	Dyeing; Tanning and Coloring Materials..........	7,621,405,676	8,823,066,608	8,170,350,005	7,837,536,906	8,028,393,218	7,630,909,732
24	Cork And Wood	4,862,997,842	5,650,777,713	5,604,200,424	6,630,696,239	7,389,195,886	6,691,091,492
73	Metalworking Machinery..................	5,952,103,336	7,052,135,277	7,175,358,640	6,978,459,361	6,965,879,054	6,539,057,632
26	Textile Fibers	7,992,722,202	10,912,053,619	8,716,138,107	8,262,027,516	6,987,996,688	6,183,445,683
84	Articles Of Apparel and Clothing	4,693,724,758	5,240,500,492	5,606,519,291	5,856,704,868	6,105,288,495	6,127,662,190
32	Coal; Coke And Briquettes..........	10,098,408,917	16,172,733,619	15,084,107,252	11,467,301,706	8,720,824,735	5,898,840,124
11	Beverages	3,787,971,325	4,473,307,041	4,897,157,643	5,313,793,561	5,483,522,674	5,721,368,501
3	Fish (Except Marine Mammal)	4,477,426,924	5,594,626,642	5,514,109,963	5,637,599,056	5,780,845,761	5,590,736,172
2	Dairy Products And Birds' Eggs..........	3,298,093,485	4,198,020,356	4,378,195,328	5,943,924,942	6,344,121,905	4,632,561,203
56	Fertilizers	4,642,039,469	6,280,485,603	5,348,582,691	4,984,470,575	4,594,451,433	4,351,588,917
81	Prefab Buildings; Sanitary; Plumbing; etc.	2,852,711,577	3,240,185,897	3,494,861,772	3,659,167,682	3,851,798,306	3,608,751,593
7	Coffee; Tea; Cocoa..................	2,604,596,238	3,193,140,382	3,431,620,993	3,498,332,925	3,759,190,544	3,523,844,386
29	Crude Animal And Vegetable Materials	2,830,086,650	3,110,003,392	3,285,595,762	3,394,194,964	3,513,011,562	3,509,205,393
23	Crude Rubber..................	3,381,956,952	4,471,493,187	4,186,804,038	3,481,016,692	3,372,016,446	2,783,879,688
27	Crude Fertilizers	2,471,551,467	2,731,215,417	2,710,910,770	2,645,964,272	2,927,890,079	2,691,867,975
21	Hides; Skins And Furskins	2,200,550,207	3,005,619,122	2,797,527,959	3,141,065,518	2,933,024,721	2,442,684,840
63	Cork And Wood Manufactures	2,251,117,029	2,299,796,706	2,317,566,689	2,361,406,934	2,385,912,270	2,267,839,465
12	Tobacco And Tobacco	1,671,101,643	1,695,718,949	1,657,584,481	1,909,886,988	1,805,463,578	2,077,517,416
6	Sugars; Sugar Preparations	1,774,586,438	2,198,079,994	2,592,636,244	2,512,480,037	2,303,959,381	2,011,338,482
42	Fixed Veg. Fats & Oils	2,763,867,700	2,708,866,172	2,739,584,610	2,117,118,190	1,832,101,839	1,878,188,321
61	Leather; Leather Mfr	1,055,754,537	1,250,477,985	1,264,683,071	1,530,383,265	1,675,997,733	1,481,821,407
85	Footwear..................	1,105,454,224	1,290,038,604	1,332,305,334	1,391,282,682	1,456,188,127	1,463,617,789
83	Travel Goods; Handbags	847,926,900	971,719,811	1,096,032,219	1,175,497,598	1,173,344,780	1,229,816,010
0	Live Animals	814,890,071	1,038,251,364	1,189,530,232	1,019,514,929	944,295,813	757,360,691
95	Coin Including Gold	395,338,448	825,553,465	888,825,535	851,978,365	790,940,278	726,365,679
41	Animal Oils And Fats	1,086,502,417	1,309,796,560	909,137,766	780,970,432	747,570,146	559,171,969
43	Anml/Veg Fats/Oils Process/Waste	430,896,950	536,198,683	546,556,310	446,304,631	403,037,359	347,747,464
35	Electric Current	630,810,860	374,637,165	233,067,299	356,159,864	564,139,834	241,128,045
96	Coin (Other Than Gold)	71,646,697	136,378,011	78,900,734	50,559,244	45,113,097	52,036,012

Table B-13.   Top 10 Trade with World for SITC Total All Merchandise, 2010–2015

EXPORTS	Item	2010	2011	2012	2013	2014	2015
SITC							
	TOTAL	1,278,494,525,839	1,482,507,755,226	1,545,820,839,892	1,578,516,879,950	1,621,171,618,259	1,502,572,229,518
79	Transport Equipment	84,549,841,615	93,358,488,568	111,417,957,850	120,971,841,314	132,160,681,263	138,300,713,980
78	Motor Vehicles	95,173,296,044	115,046,743,155	127,193,493,855	129,593,425,666	131,955,287,793	123,710,528,244
77	Electrical Machry; Apparatus & Appliances	105,378,484,390	107,089,376,378	108,080,048,026	110,777,990,833	114,116,976,318	112,843,402,396
33	Petroleum; Petroleum Products	62,778,360,744	103,482,926,654	113,021,664,042	124,399,361,748	128,971,429,074	86,246,439,294
74	General Industrial Machry	56,571,507,382	66,202,700,136	71,716,299,749	74,484,067,519	78,890,623,555	74,855,878,758
89	Miscellaneous Manufactured Articles	58,230,239,670	61,092,752,242	64,333,040,591	67,356,933,219	70,592,121,963	70,124,838,414
87	Professional Scientific Instruments	51,848,230,732	56,877,814,520	59,780,821,847	60,834,246,490	61,623,613,941	60,336,014,771
76	Telecommunications Equipment	42,587,324,832	48,241,585,343	49,160,527,092	50,604,067,279	53,327,421,711	53,167,234,890
54	Medicinal And Pharmaceutical Products	44,596,610,771	42,736,504,420	44,767,836,351	44,354,980,785	48,675,111,460	52,591,609,869
72	Machinery Specialized	51,127,078,744	57,132,024,800	58,884,879,621	54,226,820,593	54,044,143,462	48,637,447,773

IMPORTS		2010	2011	2012	2013	2014	2015
SITC							
	TOTAL	1,913,856,594,014	2,207,954,346,316	2,276,267,147,199	2,267,986,733,622	2,356,365,502,725	2,248,232,395,233
78	Motor Vehicles	178,948,802,298	198,711,226,140	235,323,167,911	244,464,616,488	257,482,125,323	275,771,843,077
33	Petroleum; Petroleum Products	329,755,040,175	431,866,352,670	408,508,831,976	363,140,895,567	326,708,773,207	177,446,478,154
77	Electrical Machry; Apparatus & Appliances	119,638,323,105	137,944,330,782	144,323,118,411	149,914,557,207	159,574,370,730	164,560,004,595
76	Telecommunications Equipment	137,306,562,273	137,951,886,255	143,882,935,840	146,206,727,661	152,762,067,751	159,521,624,204
75	Office Machines And ADP equipment	113,477,444,030	116,498,856,271	118,866,437,401	117,471,649,152	118,224,059,127	116,858,540,051
89	Miscellaneous Manufactured Articles	91,950,233,799	94,074,649,656	96,292,929,583	100,560,190,275	103,934,207,758	112,350,285,480
84	Articles Of Apparel and Clothing	78,522,073,403	85,565,858,572	84,916,580,960	87,909,651,495	90,153,601,959	93,616,623,410
74	General Industrial Machry	60,433,137,590	74,183,685,750	81,669,938,327	83,473,147,229	92,803,512,495	93,240,610,374
54	Medicinal And Pharmaceutical Products	65,170,819,738	69,708,367,403	68,886,686,113	66,800,781,829	76,179,049,904	89,257,813,482
71	Power Generating Machinery	46,164,891,144	56,038,830,686	62,864,318,019	60,713,433,631	66,480,593,543	67,301,597,023

SURPLUS		2010	2011	2012	2013	2014	2015
SITC							
1	Meat And Meat Preparations	8,160,837,327	10,934,542,309	11,311,863,979	11,462,596,209	10,582,505,586	6,057,367,341
25	Pulp And Waste Paper	4,974,555,418	6,082,393,959	5,957,568,554	5,345,943,124	5,377,354,938	5,411,325,878
32	Coal; Coke And Briquettes	8,074,145,794	14,039,949,090	13,575,876,937	10,448,648,996	7,522,002,994	4,759,822,968
26	Textile Fibers	6,801,536,357	9,426,872,841	7,313,924,102	6,967,709,723	5,568,749,345	4,737,165,136
9	Miscellaneous Edible	2,701,705,384	3,182,860,372	3,723,192,697	4,303,838,672	4,607,173,139	4,489,458,962
58	Plastics In Nonprimary Form	3,998,627,919	4,057,376,096	3,719,777,303	3,720,414,110	3,860,654,908	3,998,582,350
53	Dyeing; Tanning and Coloring Materials	4,516,265,889	5,364,595,936	4,413,264,951	4,024,741,843	4,056,769,114	3,802,133,901
72	Machinery Specialized	20,187,465,154	15,716,085,678	13,874,956,676	11,945,398,094	6,660,479,513	3,720,122,469
55	Essential Oils	3,608,567,688	3,416,890,396	3,689,915,240	3,384,811,872	3,123,569,149	2,569,475,971
2	Dairy Products And Birds' Eggs	1,844,062,303	2,578,946,696	2,644,993,787	4,175,916,994	4,355,418,058	2,459,535,637
21	Hides; Skins And Furskins	2,114,079,640	2,476,048,067	2,559,278,140	2,852,818,585	2,625,701,013	2,200,207,070
34	Gas; Natural And Manufactured	-13,190,482,847	-7,551,180,954	-3,128,840,952	-638,298,118	506,743,262	2,197,447,683

DEFICIT		2010	2011	2012	2013	2014	2015
SITC							
54	Medicinal And Pharmaceutical Products	-20,574,208,967	-26,971,862,983	-24,118,849,762	-22,445,801,044	-27,503,938,444	-36,666,203,613
82	Furniture & Bedding	-25,232,425,335	-25,950,338,104	-28,413,865,971	-30,420,259,033	-33,369,796,335	-37,508,593,514
89	Miscellaneous Manufactured Articles	-33,719,994,129	-32,981,897,414	-31,959,888,992	-33,203,257,056	-33,342,085,795	-42,225,447,066
77	Electrical Machry; Apparatus & Appliances	-14,259,838,715	-30,854,954,404	-36,243,070,385	-39,136,566,374	-45,457,394,412	-51,716,602,199
93	Special Transactions	-34,587,910,353	-38,788,104,895	-46,208,606,592	-49,012,595,380	-52,938,709,582	-58,145,419,818
75	Office Machines And ADP equipment	-68,942,199,056	-67,578,728,589	-69,032,424,456	-68,684,904,640	-68,716,069,524	-69,822,867,525
84	Articles Of Apparel and Clothing	-73,828,348,645	-80,325,358,080	-79,310,061,669	-82,052,946,627	-84,048,313,464	-87,488,961,220
33	Petroleum; Petroleum Products	-266,976,679,431	-328,383,426,016	-295,487,167,934	-238,741,533,819	-197,737,344,133	-91,200,038,860
76	Telecommunications Equipment	-94,719,237,441	-89,710,300,912	-94,722,408,748	-95,602,660,382	-99,434,646,040	-106,354,389,314
78	Motor Vehicles	-83,775,506,254	-83,664,482,985	-108,129,674,056	-114,871,190,822	-125,526,837,530	-152,061,314,833

Table B-14.   U.S. Top Ten Exports, Imports, Deficit, and Surplus by Standard International Trade Classification (SITC), 2010–2015

EXPORTS	Item	2010	2011	2012	2013	2014	2015
SITC	TOTAL	1,278,494,525,839	1,482,507,755,226	1,545,820,839,892	1,578,516,879,950	1,621,171,618,259	1,502,572,229,518
79	Transport Equipment	84,549,841,615	93,358,488,568	111,417,957,850	120,971,841,314	132,160,681,263	138,300,713,980
78	Motor Vehicles	95,173,296,044	115,046,743,155	127,193,493,855	129,593,425,666	131,955,287,793	123,710,528,244
77	Electrical Machry; Apparatus & Appliances	105,378,484,390	107,089,376,378	108,080,048,026	110,777,990,833	114,116,976,318	112,843,402,396
33	Petroleum; Petroleum Products	62,778,360,744	103,482,926,654	113,021,664,042	124,399,361,748	128,971,429,074	86,246,439,294
74	General Industrial Machry	56,571,507,382	66,202,700,136	71,716,299,749	74,484,067,519	78,890,623,555	74,855,878,758
89	Miscellaneous Manufactured Articles	58,230,239,670	61,092,752,242	64,333,040,591	67,356,933,219	70,592,121,963	70,124,838,414
87	Professional Scientific Instruments	51,848,230,732	56,877,814,520	59,780,821,847	60,834,246,490	61,623,613,941	60,336,014,771
76	Telecommunications Equipment	42,587,324,832	48,241,585,343	49,160,527,092	50,604,067,279	53,327,421,711	53,167,234,890
54	Medicinal And Pharmaceutical Products	44,596,610,771	42,736,504,420	44,767,836,351	44,354,980,785	48,675,111,460	52,591,609,869
72	Machinery Specialized	51,127,078,744	57,132,024,800	58,884,879,621	54,226,820,593	54,044,143,462	48,637,447,773

IMPORTS		2010	2011	2012	2013	2014	2015
SITC	TOTAL	1,913,856,594,014	2,207,954,346,316	2,276,267,147,199	2,267,986,733,622	2,356,365,502,725	2,248,232,395,233
78	Motor Vehicles	178,948,802,298	198,711,226,140	235,323,167,911	244,464,616,488	257,482,125,323	275,771,843,077
33	Petroleum; Petroleum Products	329,755,040,175	431,866,352,670	408,508,831,976	363,140,895,567	326,708,773,207	177,446,478,154
77	Electrical Machry; Apparatus & Appliances	119,638,323,105	137,944,330,782	144,323,118,411	149,914,557,207	159,574,370,730	164,560,004,595
76	Telecommunications Equipment	137,306,562,273	137,951,886,255	143,882,935,840	146,206,727,661	152,762,067,751	159,521,624,204
75	Office Machines And ADP equipment	113,477,444,030	116,498,856,271	118,866,437,401	117,471,649,152	118,224,059,127	116,858,540,051
89	Miscellaneous Manufactured Articles	91,950,233,799	94,074,649,656	96,292,929,583	100,560,190,275	103,934,207,758	112,350,285,480
84	Articles Of Apparel and Clothing	78,522,073,403	85,565,858,572	84,916,580,960	87,909,651,495	90,153,601,959	93,616,623,410
74	General Industrial Machry	60,433,137,590	74,183,685,750	81,669,938,327	83,473,147,229	92,803,512,495	93,240,610,374
54	Medicinal And Pharmaceutical Products	65,170,819,738	69,708,367,403	68,886,686,113	66,800,781,829	76,179,049,904	89,257,813,482
71	Power Generating Machinery	46,164,891,144	56,038,830,686	62,864,318,019	60,713,433,631	66,480,593,543	67,301,597,023

SURPLUS		2010	2011	2012	2013	2014	2015
SITC							
1	Meat And Meat Preparations	8,160,837,327	10,934,542,309	11,311,863,979	11,462,596,209	10,582,505,586	6,057,367,341
25	Pulp And Waste Paper	4,974,555,418	6,082,393,959	5,957,568,554	5,345,943,124	5,377,354,938	5,411,325,878
32	Coal; Coke And Briquettes	8,074,145,794	14,039,949,090	13,575,876,937	10,448,648,996	7,522,002,994	4,759,822,968
26	Textile Fibers	6,801,536,357	9,426,872,841	7,313,924,102	6,967,709,723	5,568,749,345	4,737,165,136
9	Miscellaneous Edible	2,701,705,384	3,182,860,372	3,723,192,697	4,303,838,672	4,607,173,139	4,489,458,962
58	Plastics In Nonprimary Form	3,998,627,919	4,057,376,096	3,719,777,303	3,720,414,110	3,860,654,908	3,998,582,350
53	Dyeing; Tanning and Coloring Materials	4,516,265,889	5,364,595,936	4,413,264,951	4,024,741,843	4,056,769,114	3,802,133,901
72	Machinery Specialized	20,187,465,154	15,716,085,678	13,874,956,676	11,945,398,094	6,660,479,513	3,720,122,469
55	Essential Oils	3,608,567,688	3,416,890,396	3,689,915,240	3,384,811,872	3,123,569,149	2,569,475,971
2	Dairy Products And Birds' Eggs	1,844,062,303	2,578,946,696	2,644,993,787	4,175,916,994	4,355,418,058	2,459,535,637
21	Hides; Skins And Furskins	2,114,079,640	2,476,048,067	2,559,278,140	2,852,818,585	2,625,701,013	2,200,207,070
34	Gas; Natural And Manufactured	-13,190,482,847	-7,551,180,954	-3,128,840,952	-638,298,118	506,743,262	2,197,447,683

DEFICIT		2010	2011	2012	2013	2014	2015
SITC							
54	Medicinal And Pharmaceutical Products	-20,574,208,967	-26,971,862,983	-24,118,849,762	-22,445,801,044	-27,503,938,444	-36,666,203,613
82	Furniture & Bedding	-25,232,425,335	-25,950,338,104	-28,413,865,971	-30,420,259,033	-33,369,796,335	-37,508,593,514
89	Miscellaneous Manufactured Articles	-33,719,994,129	-32,981,897,414	-31,959,888,992	-33,203,257,056	-33,342,085,795	-42,225,447,066
77	Electrical Machry; Apparatus & Appliances	-14,259,838,715	-30,854,954,404	-36,243,070,385	-39,136,566,374	-45,457,394,412	-51,716,602,199
93	Special Transactions	-34,587,910,353	-38,788,104,895	-46,208,606,592	-49,012,595,380	-52,938,709,582	-58,145,419,818
75	Office Machines And ADP equipment	-68,942,199,056	-67,578,728,589	-69,032,424,456	-68,684,904,640	-68,716,069,524	-69,822,867,525
84	Articles Of Apparel and Clothing	-73,828,348,645	-80,325,358,080	-79,310,061,669	-82,052,946,627	-84,048,313,464	-87,488,961,220
33	Petroleum; Petroleum Products	-266,976,679,431	-328,383,426,016	-295,487,167,934	-238,741,533,819	-197,737,344,133	-91,200,038,860
76	Telecommunications Equipment	-94,719,237,441	-89,710,300,912	-94,722,408,748	-95,602,660,382	-99,434,646,040	-106,354,389,314
78	Motor Vehicles	-83,775,506,254	-83,664,482,985	-108,129,674,056	-114,871,190,822	-125,526,837,530	-152,061,314,833

Table B-15. U.S. Exports of Total Merchandise by North American Industry Classification System (NAICS), 2010–2015

NAICS	Product	2010	2011	2012	2013	2014	2015
	TOTAL................	1,278,494,525,839	1,482,507,755,226	1,545,820,839,892	1,578,516,879,950	1,621,171,618,259	1,502,572,229,518
111	AGRICULTURAL PRODUCTS	60,246,115,997	71,811,892,719	71,077,654,776	68,935,141,909	72,928,649,705	62,916,966,292
112	OTHER ANIMALS................	1,577,937,669	1,950,506,085	2,371,776,854	2,441,584,330	2,257,947,965	2,090,662,796
113	FORESTRY PRODUCTS; NESOI	2,285,165,486	2,731,791,453	2,410,686,520	2,876,112,569	2,954,125,855	2,457,935,435
114	FISH; FRESH/CHILLED/FROZEN & OTHER MARINE PRODUCTS.......	4,240,128,806	5,368,534,971	5,264,255,239	5,484,471,190	5,717,074,867	5,530,717,069
211	OIL & GAS	9,643,007,423	12,295,824,042	11,403,814,171	17,595,592,630	29,552,071,433	20,332,957,866
212	MINERALS & ORES	17,245,865,797	25,631,210,520	23,878,357,256	20,518,414,803	18,998,822,335	14,496,326,494
311	FOOD MANUFACTURES	51,888,511,605	60,072,904,398	64,927,324,876	68,774,669,428	70,676,700,175	63,193,858,295
312	BEVERAGES & TOBACCO PRODUCTS................	5,765,053,072	6,795,158,560	7,438,987,391	8,843,526,321	8,960,008,356	9,487,269,175
313	TEXTILES & FABRICS	8,160,499,502	9,754,746,745	9,310,537,950	9,647,353,363	10,024,573,015	9,729,985,938
314	TEXTILE MILLS PRODUCTS	2,903,453,924	3,027,745,359	3,168,308,333	3,251,890,120	3,294,547,284	3,243,328,224
315	APPAREL MANUFACTURING PRODUCTS................	4,496,737,403	4,824,585,701	5,164,548,718	5,439,285,238	5,694,876,120	5,698,810,045
316	LEATHER & ALLIED PRODUCTS................	3,401,873,484	3,974,369,158	4,178,663,838	4,760,407,518	5,028,718,369	4,725,314,949
321	WOOD PRODUCTS	5,345,377,663	5,866,974,338	6,226,215,215	6,771,099,651	7,502,659,870	7,068,097,915
322	PAPER................	23,652,070,951	24,808,027,725	24,430,829,260	24,788,708,931	24,911,608,870	24,208,711,516
323	PRINTED MATTER AND RELATED PRODUCTS; NESOI................	6,426,951,885	6,533,111,439	6,476,065,480	6,404,743,185	6,041,827,469	5,696,739,418
324	PETROLEUM & COAL PRODUCTS................	61,438,246,495	101,932,699,766	111,149,840,010	119,521,377,095	117,382,042,850	77,999,922,314
325	CHEMICALS................	179,502,159,029	197,473,465,840	197,529,227,481	199,501,664,479	200,360,379,351	194,077,068,982
326	PLASTICS & RUBBER PRODUCTS	25,915,393,825	29,991,880,241	31,775,573,778	32,479,103,245	33,872,778,365	33,128,925,890
327	NONMETALLIC MINERAL PRODUCTS................	9,815,378,555	10,849,292,341	10,920,374,867	11,230,215,480	11,859,170,682	11,563,594,232
331	PRIMARY METAL MFG	53,539,504,478	76,612,958,883	78,403,600,792	73,406,514,178	64,076,740,259	55,720,563,341
332	FABRICATED METAL PRODUCTS; NESOI	35,765,029,740	40,260,465,704	43,721,702,376	46,364,164,773	49,251,486,571	47,049,739,171
333	MACHINERY; EXCEPT ELECTRICAL................	137,799,646,370	150,917,264,305	159,547,805,816	150,139,075,021	152,494,690,218	139,006,641,429
334	COMPUTER AND ELECTRONIC PRODUCTS	190,435,293,476	198,035,399,978	203,163,718,673	204,639,733,911	209,121,507,197	204,686,071,698
335	ELECTRICAL EQUIPMENT; APPLIANCES & COMPONENTS............	37,584,652,893	49,774,113,315	54,295,716,961	57,143,184,314	60,605,638,550	60,258,975,242
336	TRANSPORTATION EQUIPMENT................	190,886,685,380	210,276,806,860	241,336,911,762	258,286,017,093	273,838,878,770	275,636,039,768
337	FURNITURE & FIXTURES................	4,586,798,258	5,170,864,039	5,751,210,858	5,925,319,152	6,199,088,139	5,899,187,319
339	MISCELLANEOUS MANUFACTURED COMMODITIES	61,084,904,755	70,134,115,661	72,481,076,759	77,851,951,023	81,912,990,734	78,251,834,989
511	NEWSPAPERS; BOOKS & OTHER PUBLISHED MATTER; NESOI.......	961,498,686	908,879,337	0	0	0	0
910	WASTE AND SCRAP	29,571,981,985	32,786,002,955	27,837,261,470	23,794,514,712	21,132,685,966	17,683,660,237
920	USED OR SECOND-HAND MERCHANDISE	8,259,186,599	0	0	0	0	0
930	USED OR SECOND-HAND MERCHANDISE	0	19,842,457,085	19,106,789,258	19,070,363,962	20,581,464,308	18,807,440,608
980	GOODS RET TO CA (EXP); US GOODS RET & REIMPS (IMP)	169,813,253	188,623,352	174,244,353	107,935,621	118,267,848	86,838,239
990	SPECIAL CLASSIFICATION PROVISIONS; NESOI	43,899,601,395	41,905,082,351	40,897,758,801	42,522,744,705	43,819,596,763	41,838,044,632

Table B-16. U.S. Imports of Total Merchandise by North American Industry Classification System (NAICS), 2010–2015

NAICS	Product	2010	2011	2012	2013	2014	2015
	TOTAL............	1,913,856,594,014	2,207,954,346,316	2,276,267,147,199	2,267,986,733,622	2,356,365,502,725	2,248,232,395,233
111	AGRICULTURAL PRODUCTS	23,998,382,182	28,843,819,691	29,330,716,739	31,769,496,173	33,629,142,419	33,422,835,478
112	OTHER ANIMALS...........	4,115,991,476	4,250,886,258	4,682,266,152	5,219,033,839	6,392,456,097	6,124,449,791
113	FORESTRY PRODUCTS; NESOI	3,356,697,232	5,402,753,378	4,117,386,359	3,392,446,501	2,760,677,550	2,380,581,843
114	FISH; FRESH/CHILLED/FROZEN & OTHER MARINE PRODUCTS............	11,204,716,970	12,904,631,789	12,519,608,417	13,594,432,274	15,669,919,064	14,408,435,789
211	OIL & GAS............	280,195,200,317	353,111,286,911	326,727,170,532	286,286,120,737	263,230,135,916	135,184,749,639
212	MINERALS & ORES............	5,717,990,085	7,014,028,303	6,226,552,147	5,480,474,108	6,201,807,734	5,551,097,482
311	FOOD MANUFACTURES............	41,107,585,745	50,185,040,689	54,347,353,169	52,823,252,406	57,193,797,649	58,508,264,707
312	BEVERAGES & TOBACCO PRODUCTS............	16,078,795,756	17,697,660,286	18,832,798,345	19,976,557,477	20,936,652,296	21,958,950,158
313	TEXTILES & FABRICS............	6,535,865,605	7,501,445,532	7,775,018,127	8,041,069,947	8,460,234,693	8,652,830,657
314	TEXTILE MILLS PRODUCTS............	15,883,281,595	17,547,239,934	17,936,515,009	18,865,640,887	19,676,579,109	20,833,961,642
315	APPAREL MANUFACTURING PRODUCTS............	75,644,307,356	82,079,791,757	81,259,191,398	84,386,292,686	86,609,421,412	89,893,484,193
316	LEATHER & ALLIED PRODUCTS............	31,161,311,206	33,467,296,499	35,662,892,604	37,103,217,614	38,953,931,585	41,092,065,417
321	WOOD PRODUCTS	11,371,058,956	11,330,336,406	13,025,438,893	15,325,108,714	16,645,479,916	17,120,789,185
322	PAPER............	21,041,424,497	20,229,403,099	19,346,237,995	20,006,894,406	20,928,916,374	20,334,158,711
323	PRINTED MATTER AND RELATED PRODUCTS; NESOI.........	5,327,805,904	5,269,690,563	5,288,101,950	5,253,683,315	5,328,331,390	5,574,393,683
324	PETROLEUM & COAL PRODUCTS............	70,417,241,164	95,844,721,864	94,064,097,278	91,081,412,332	81,982,619,005	52,770,895,047
325	CHEMICALS............	176,331,095,769	201,853,880,847	197,899,882,644	195,425,075,245	205,742,036,317	213,774,641,872
326	PLASTICS & RUBBER PRODUCTS	34,717,709,004	42,146,776,414	45,932,510,435	47,295,039,055	49,657,200,455	50,357,754,520
327	NONMETALLIC MINERAL PRODUCTS	16,101,712,577	17,478,160,982	18,122,793,308	19,068,107,129	21,062,740,327	21,883,496,651
331	PRIMARY METAL MFG	79,639,958,238	104,037,247,772	101,463,650,111	92,282,548,917	101,225,705,008	84,938,947,432
332	FABRICATED METAL PRODUCTS; NESOI	47,147,568,390	54,660,161,516	61,161,640,117	62,106,346,503	66,579,144,232	68,480,667,833
333	MACHINERY; EXCEPT ELECTRICAL............	105,558,420,903	138,364,493,797	151,253,335,416	146,853,208,147	161,240,319,952	158,372,437,079
334	COMPUTER AND ELECTRONIC PRODUCTS	325,049,823,362	335,502,073,471	347,793,970,853	351,378,786,417	366,566,672,573	375,989,168,415
335	ELECTRICAL EQUIPMENT; APPLIANCES & COMPONENTS....	69,276,317,000	82,767,282,724	89,260,612,232	93,964,594,679	100,231,292,266	104,336,122,273
336	TRANSPORTATION EQUIPMENT............	241,172,221,933	271,307,801,905	318,036,223,326	334,175,814,688	356,729,843,429	379,162,996,227
337	FURNITURE & FIXTURES............	25,725,215,046	26,589,349,144	28,797,675,027	30,801,295,069	33,316,944,373	36,872,619,154
339	MISCELLANEOUS MANUFACTURED COMMODITIES	97,752,004,677	103,983,778,934	101,840,343,508	107,769,634,476	111,635,898,861	115,387,463,703
511	NEWSPAPERS; BOOKS & OTHER PUBLISHED MATTER; NESOI	34,692,938	42,154,684	0	0	0	0
910	WASTE AND SCRAP	5,254,454,964	6,665,426,033	7,283,423,030	6,448,290,760	6,748,676,603	5,059,716,773
920	USED OR SECOND-HAND MERCHANDISE	6,401,861,883	0	0	0	0	0
930	USED OR SECOND-HAND MERCHANDISE	0	7,423,522,119	8,512,956,935	9,841,046,864	10,246,560,536	13,214,954,511
980	GOODS RET TO CA (EXP); US GOODS RET & REIMPS (IMP)	40,911,120,487	44,647,183,374	51,977,682,154	55,252,721,243	59,932,904,050	65,642,717,085
990	SPECIAL CLASSIFICATION PROVISIONS; NESOI	19,624,760,797	17,805,019,641	15,789,102,989	16,719,091,014	20,849,461,534	20,946,748,283

Table B-17. U.S. Balance of Payments with World by North American Industry Classification System (NAICS), 2005–2015

NAICS	Product	2005	2006	2007	2008	2009
	TOTAL..	-772,372,707,994	-827,970,977,907	-808,763,121,157	-816,198,714,214	-503,581,850,449
111	AGRICULTURAL PRODUCTS	16,016,526,330	18,878,223,978	28,458,306,056	40,468,887,553	29,322,790,319
112	OTHER ANIMALS	-2,126,967,195	-2,792,793,732	-3,278,081,523	-2,868,821,327	-2,172,723,970
113	FORESTRY PRODUCTS; NESOI	-508,662,212	-976,193,699	-751,034,876	-1,442,018,529	-72,189,906
114	FISH; FRESH/CHILLED/FROZEN & OTHER MARINE PRODUCTS..	-5,590,323,968	-6,435,654,840	-6,541,378,418	-6,749,608,045	-6,234,760,476
211	OIL & GAS	-217,903,384,299	-253,873,909,372	-276,009,617,540	-384,215,266,919	-206,231,999,680
212	MINERALS & ORES	3,129,142,198	4,416,836,712	5,651,859,451	8,220,076,397	5,632,982,972
311	FOOD MANUFACTURES	-232,515,104	924,849,533	4,603,953,510	9,268,289,861	8,451,422,522
312	BEVERAGES & TOBACCO PRODUCTS	-9,655,219,661	-11,107,866,623	-12,106,977,359	-11,340,356,815	-10,130,048,644
313	TEXTILES & FABRICS	1,287,930,508	1,384,909,382	1,013,862,686	1,508,315,518	1,393,398,867
314	TEXTILE MILLS PRODUCTS	-10,965,068,475	-11,909,857,654	-12,538,318,763	-12,137,000,461	-10,702,328,124
315	APPAREL MANUFACTURING PRODUCTS	-69,671,437,798	-72,313,709,551	-74,833,638,304	-71,994,206,557	-62,864,658,946
316	LEATHER & ALLIED PRODUCTS	-23,664,062,268	-25,406,487,485	-26,289,359,799	-26,480,341,546	-22,767,423,379
321	WOOD PRODUCTS	-18,930,725,331	-17,571,617,527	-13,304,120,994	-8,814,583,825	-5,546,728,023
322	PAPER..	-4,807,299,163	-4,813,608,251	-2,973,931,013	-1,569,005,583	1,178,021,703
323	PRINTED MATTER AND RELATED PRODUCTS; NESOI..........	239,730,910	310,185,206	300,762,132	675,755,869	1,200,701,124
324	PETROLEUM & COAL PRODUCTS	-43,918,826,786	-43,333,615,151	-46,000,874,526	-31,634,946,886	-13,089,718,232
325	CHEMICALS	-4,943,413,746	-3,440,394,331	-2,072,373,820	-8,888,633,679	-3,057,601,182
326	PLASTICS & RUBBER PRODUCTS	-8,347,163,827	-9,077,316,183	-9,090,566,817	-8,547,081,285	-6,339,690,263
327	NONMETALLIC MINERAL PRODUCTS	-11,432,243,141	-12,375,144,633	-10,922,311,950	-8,675,926,320	-5,151,475,921
331	PRIMARY METAL MFG	-34,855,666,790	-47,771,259,538	-40,908,116,809	-41,228,191,007	-14,922,189,137
332	FABRICATED METAL PRODUCTS; NESOI	-15,696,187,999	-16,845,098,555	-18,069,817,986	-16,881,524,183	-9,907,654,679
333	MACHINERY; EXCEPT ELECTRICAL........................	-5,458,865,726	-4,077,610,320	10,470,919,417	20,528,756,495	25,591,318,295
334	COMPUTER AND ELECTRONIC PRODUCTS	-102,024,163,720	-110,013,388,845	-118,707,304,381	-109,832,041,697	-105,984,506,807
335	ELECTRICAL EQUIPMENT; APPLIANCES & COMPONENTS....	-25,473,574,979	-27,499,136,541	-30,886,246,818	-30,078,582,042	-24,642,288,144
336	TRANSPORTATION EQUIPMENT............................	-91,557,131,671	-88,710,133,400	-73,670,777,236	-49,350,075,983	-14,837,319,678
337	FURNITURE & FIXTURES................................	-21,957,054,349	-23,576,526,326	-23,819,452,238	-21,870,137,417	-17,537,850,171
339	MISCELLANEOUS MANUFACTURED COMMODITIES	-40,180,924,746	-40,958,021,530	-43,188,862,145	-38,698,382,590	-29,603,576,509
511	NEWSPAPERS; BOOKS & OTHER PUBLISHED MATTER; NESOI..	870,777,428	886,917,149	907,294,704	811,087,751	804,142,798
910	WASTE AND SCRAP	7,395,469,524	11,217,980,549	17,449,347,194	23,678,669,926	18,403,303,585
920	USED OR SECOND-HAND MERCHANDISE	-928,967,929	-485,848,340	-502,786,545	2,279,217,337	2,784,479,316
930	USED OR SECOND-HAND MERCHANDISE	0	0	0	0	0
980	GOODS RET TO CA (EXP); US GOODS RET & REIMPS (IMP)	-35,526,137,355	-37,000,341,854	-37,998,541,719	-39,283,491,309	-36,785,432,888
990	SPECIAL CLASSIFICATION PROVISIONS; NESOI	5,043,703,346	6,374,653,865	6,845,065,272	8,942,453,084	10,237,752,809

Table B-17.   U.S Balance of Payments with World by NAICS, 2005–2015—*Continued*

NAICS	Product	2010	2011	2012	2013	2014	2015
	TOTAL..	-635,362,068,175	-725,446,591,090	-730,446,307,307	-689,469,853,672	-735,193,884,466	-745,660,165,715
111	AGRICULTURAL PRODUCTS	36,247,733,815	42,968,073,028	41,746,938,037	37,165,645,736	39,299,507,286	29,494,130,814
112	OTHER ANIMALS	-2,538,053,807	-2,300,380,173	-2,310,489,298	-2,777,449,509	-4,134,508,132	-4,033,786,995
113	FORESTRY PRODUCTS; NESOI	-1,071,531,746	-2,670,961,925	-1,706,699,839	-516,333,932	193,448,305	77,353,592
114	FISH; FRESH/CHILLED/FROZEN & OTHER MARINE PRODUCTS	-6,964,588,164	-7,536,096,818	-7,255,353,178	-8,109,961,084	-9,952,844,197	-8,877,718,720
211	OIL & GAS	-270,552,192,894	-340,815,462,869	-315,323,356,361	-268,690,528,107	-233,678,064,483	-114,851,791,773
212	MINERALS & ORES	11,527,875,712	18,617,182,217	17,651,805,109	15,037,940,695	12,797,014,601	8,945,229,012
311	FOOD MANUFACTURES	10,780,925,860	9,887,863,709	10,579,971,707	15,951,417,022	13,482,902,526	4,685,593,588
312	BEVERAGES & TOBACCO PRODUCTS	-10,313,742,684	-10,902,501,726	-11,393,810,954	-11,133,031,156	-11,976,643,940	-12,471,680,983
313	TEXTILES & FABRICS	1,624,633,897	2,253,301,213	1,535,519,823	1,606,283,416	1,564,338,322	1,077,155,281
314	TEXTILE MILLS PRODUCTS	-12,979,827,671	-14,519,494,575	-14,768,206,676	-15,613,750,767	-16,382,031,825	-17,590,633,418
315	APPAREL MANUFACTURING PRODUCTS.............	-71,147,569,953	-77,255,206,056	-76,094,642,680	-78,947,007,448	-80,914,545,292	-84,194,674,148
316	LEATHER & ALLIED PRODUCTS...........................	-27,759,437,722	-29,492,927,341	-31,484,228,766	-32,342,810,096	-33,925,213,216	-36,366,750,468
321	WOOD PRODUCTS	-6,025,681,293	-5,463,362,068	-6,799,223,678	-8,554,009,063	-9,142,820,046	-10,052,691,270
322	PAPER	2,610,646,454	4,578,624,626	5,084,591,265	4,781,814,525	3,982,692,496	3,874,552,805
323	PRINTED MATTER AND RELATED PRODUCTS; NESOI..........	1,099,145,981	1,263,420,876	1,187,963,530	1,151,059,870	713,496,079	122,345,735
324	PETROLEUM & COAL PRODUCTS........................	-8,978,994,669	6,087,977,902	17,085,742,732	28,439,964,763	35,399,423,845	25,229,027,267
325	CHEMICALS...	3,171,063,260	-4,380,415,007	-370,655,163	4,076,589,234	-5,381,656,966	-19,697,572,890
326	PLASTICS & RUBBER PRODUCTS........................	-8,802,315,179	-12,154,896,173	-14,156,936,657	-14,815,935,810	-15,784,422,090	-17,228,828,630
327	NONMETALLIC MINERAL PRODUCTS...................	-6,286,334,022	-6,628,868,641	-7,202,418,441	-7,837,891,649	-9,203,569,645	-10,319,902,419
331	PRIMARY METAL MFG	-26,100,453,760	-27,424,288,889	-23,060,049,319	-18,876,034,739	-37,148,964,749	-29,218,384,091
332	FABRICATED METAL PRODUCTS; NESOI	-11,382,538,650	-14,399,695,812	-17,439,937,741	-15,742,181,730	-17,327,657,661	-21,430,928,662
333	MACHINERY; EXCEPT ELECTRICAL....................	32,241,225,467	12,552,770,508	8,294,470,400	3,285,866,874	-8,745,629,734	-19,365,795,650
334	COMPUTER AND ELECTRONIC PRODUCTS.........	-134,614,529,886	-137,466,673,493	-144,630,252,180	-146,739,052,506	-157,445,165,376	-171,303,096,717
335	ELECTRICAL EQUIPMENT; APPLIANCES & COMPONENTS....	-31,691,664,107	-32,993,169,409	-34,964,895,271	-36,821,410,365	-39,625,653,716	-44,077,147,031
336	TRANSPORTATION EQUIPMENT...........................	-50,285,536,553	-61,030,995,045	-76,699,311,564	-75,889,797,595	-82,890,964,659	-103,526,956,459
337	FURNITURE & FIXTURES.....................................	-21,138,416,788	-21,418,485,105	-23,046,464,169	-24,875,975,917	-27,117,856,234	-30,973,431,835
339	MISCELLANEOUS MANUFACTURED COMMODITIES	-36,667,099,922	-33,849,663,273	-29,359,266,749	-29,917,683,453	-29,722,908,127	-37,135,628,714
511	NEWSPAPERS; BOOKS & OTHER PUBLISHED MATTER; NESOI	926,805,748	866,724,653	0	0	0	0
910	WASTE AND SCRAP	24,317,527,021	26,120,576,922	20,553,838,440	17,346,223,952	14,384,009,363	12,623,943,464
920	USED OR SECOND-HAND MERCHANDISE	1,857,324,716	0	0	0	0	0
930	USED OR SECOND-HAND MERCHANDISE	0	12,418,934,966	10,593,832,323	9,229,317,098	10,334,903,772	5,592,486,097
980	GOODS RET TO CA (EXP); US GOODS RET & REIMPS (IMP)	-40,741,307,234	-44,458,560,022	-51,803,437,801	-55,144,785,622	-59,814,636,202	-65,555,878,846
990	SPECIAL CLASSIFICATION PROVISIONS; NESOI	24,274,840,598	24,100,062,710	25,108,655,812	25,803,653,691	22,970,135,229	20,891,296,349

Table B-18. Top 10 Imports, Exports, Deficit, and Surplus by North American Industry Classification System (NAICS), 2010–2105

TOP TEN IMPORTS		2010	2011	2012	2013	2014	2015
NAICS							
	TOTAL...	1,913,856,594,014	2,207,954,346,316	2,276,267,147,199	2,267,986,733,622	2,356,365,502,725	2,248,232,395,233
336	TRANSPORTATION EQUIPMENT..................	241,172,221,933	271,307,801,905	318,036,223,326	334,175,814,688	356,729,843,429	379,162,996,227
334	COMPUTER AND ELECTRONIC PRODUCTS	325,049,823,362	335,502,073,471	347,793,970,853	351,378,786,417	366,566,672,573	375,989,168,415
325	CHEMICALS....................................	176,331,095,769	201,853,880,847	197,899,882,644	195,425,075,245	205,742,036,317	213,774,641,872
333	MACHINERY; EXCEPT ELECTRICAL..............	105,558,420,903	138,364,493,797	151,253,335,416	146,853,208,147	161,240,319,952	158,372,437,079
211	OIL & GAS....................................	280,195,200,317	353,111,286,911	326,727,170,532	286,286,120,737	263,230,135,916	135,184,749,639
339	MISCELLANEOUS MANUFACTURED COMMODITIES	97,752,004,677	103,983,778,934	101,840,343,508	107,769,634,476	111,635,898,861	115,387,463,703
335	ELECTRICAL EQUIPMENT; APPLIANCES & COMPONENTS....	69,276,317,000	82,767,282,724	89,260,612,232	93,964,594,679	100,231,292,266	104,336,122,273
315	APPAREL MANUFACTURING PRODUCTS...........	75,644,307,356	82,079,791,757	81,259,191,398	84,386,292,686	86,609,421,412	89,893,484,193
331	PRIMARY METAL MFG............................	79,639,958,238	104,037,247,772	101,463,650,111	92,282,548,917	101,225,705,008	84,938,947,432
332	FABRICATED METAL PRODUCTS; NESOI	47,147,568,390	54,660,161,516	61,161,640,117	62,106,346,503	66,579,144,232	68,480,667,833

TOP 10 EXPORTS		2010	2011	2012	2013	2014	2015
NAICS							
	TOTAL...	1,278,494,525,839	1,482,507,755,226	1,545,820,839,892	1,578,516,879,950	1,621,171,618,259	1,502,572,229,518
336	TRANSPORTATION EQUIPMENT..................	190,886,685,380	210,276,806,860	241,336,911,762	258,286,017,093	273,838,878,770	275,636,039,768
334	COMPUTER AND ELECTRONIC PRODUCTS	190,435,293,476	198,035,399,978	203,163,718,673	209,140,076,759	209,121,507,197	204,686,071,698
325	CHEMICALS....................................	179,502,159,029	197,473,465,840	197,529,227,481	199,501,664,479	200,360,379,351	194,077,068,982
333	MACHINERY; EXCEPT ELECTRICAL..............	137,799,646,370	150,917,264,305	159,547,805,816	150,139,075,021	152,494,690,218	139,006,641,429
339	MISCELLANEOUS MANUFACTURED COMMODITIES	61,084,904,755	70,134,115,661	72,481,076,759	77,851,951,023	78,251,834,989	78,251,834,989
324	PETROLEUM & COAL PRODUCTS..................	61,438,246,495	101,932,699,766	111,149,840,010	119,521,377,095	117,382,042,850	77,999,922,314
311	FOOD MANUFACTURES.........................	51,888,511,605	60,072,904,398	64,927,324,876	68,774,669,428	70,676,700,175	63,193,858,295
111	AGRICULTURAL PRODUCTS.......................	60,246,115,997	71,811,892,719	71,077,654,776	68,935,141,909	72,928,649,705	62,916,966,292
335	ELECTRICAL EQUIPMENT; APPLIANCES & COMPONENTS....	37,584,652,893	49,774,113,315	54,295,716,961	57,143,184,314	60,605,638,550	60,258,975,242
331	PRIMARY METAL MFG............................	53,539,504,478	76,612,958,883	78,403,600,792	73,406,514,178	64,076,740,259	55,720,563,341

TOP 10 SURPLUS		2010	2011	2012	2013	2014	2015
NAICS							
	TOTAL...	-635,362,068,175	-725,446,591,090	-730,446,307,307	-689,469,853,672	-735,193,884,466	-745,660,165,715
111	AGRICULTURAL PRODUCTS.......................	36,247,733,815	42,968,073,028	41,746,938,037	37,165,645,736	39,299,507,286	29,494,130,814
324	PETROLEUM & COAL PRODUCTS..................	-8,978,994,669	6,087,977,902	17,085,742,732	28,439,964,763	35,399,423,845	25,229,027,267
990	SPECIAL CLASSIFICATION PROVISIONS; NESOI	24,274,840,598	24,100,062,710	25,108,655,812	25,803,653,691	22,970,135,229	20,891,296,349
910	WASTE AND SCRAP.............................	24,317,527,021	26,120,576,922	20,553,838,440	17,346,223,952	14,384,009,363	12,623,943,464
212	MINERALS & ORES.............................	11,527,875,712	18,617,182,217	17,651,805,109	15,037,940,695	12,797,014,601	8,945,229,012
930	USED OR SECOND-HAND MERCHANDISE	0	12,418,934,966	10,593,832,323	9,229,317,098	10,334,903,772	5,592,486,097
311	FOOD MANUFACTURES.........................	10,780,925,860	9,887,863,709	10,579,971,707	15,951,417,022	13,482,902,526	4,685,593,588
322	PAPER.......................................	2,610,646,454	4,578,624,626	5,084,591,265	4,781,814,525	3,982,692,496	3,874,552,805
313	TEXTILES & FABRICS..........................	1,624,633,897	2,253,301,213	1,535,519,823	1,606,283,416	1,564,338,322	1,077,155,281
323	PRINTED MATTER AND RELATED PRODUCTS; NESOI..........	1,099,145,981	1,263,420,876	1,187,963,530	1,151,059,870	713,496,079	122,345,735

TOP 10 DEFICIT		2010	2011	2012	2013	2014	2015
NAICS							
331	PRIMARY METAL MFG............................	-26,100,453,760	-27,424,288,889	-23,060,049,319	-18,876,034,739	-37,148,964,749	-29,218,384,091
337	FURNITURE & FIXTURES........................	-21,138,416,788	-21,418,485,105	-23,046,464,169	-24,875,975,917	-27,117,856,234	-30,973,431,835
316	LEATHER & ALLIED PRODUCTS....................	-27,759,437,722	-29,492,927,341	-31,484,228,766	-32,342,810,096	-33,925,213,216	-36,366,750,468
339	MISCELLANEOUS MANUFACTURED COMMODITIES	-36,667,099,922	-33,849,663,273	-29,359,266,749	-29,917,683,453	-29,722,908,127	-37,135,628,714
335	ELECTRICAL EQUIPMENT; APPLIANCES & COMPONENTS....	-31,691,664,107	-32,993,169,409	-34,964,895,271	-36,821,410,365	-39,625,653,716	-44,077,147,031
980	GOODS RET TO CA (EXP); US GOODS RET & REIMPS (IMP)	-40,741,307,234	-44,458,560,022	-51,803,437,801	-55,144,785,622	-59,814,636,202	-65,555,878,846
315	APPAREL MANUFACTURING PRODUCTS...........	-71,147,569,953	-77,255,206,056	-76,094,642,680	-78,947,007,448	-80,914,545,292	-84,194,674,148
336	TRANSPORTATION EQUIPMENT..................	-50,285,536,553	-61,030,995,045	-76,699,311,564	-75,889,797,595	-82,890,964,659	-103,526,956,459
211	OIL & GAS....................................	-270,552,192,894	-340,815,462,869	-315,323,356,361	-268,690,528,107	-233,678,064,483	-114,851,791,773
334	COMPUTER AND ELECTRONIC PRODUCTS	-134,614,529,886	-137,466,673,493	-144,630,252,180	-146,739,052,506	-157,445,165,376	-171,303,096,717

Table B-19.   Real Exports of Goods by Principal End-Use Category, 1995–2015

(Millions of dollars. Chained 2009 dollars.)

Year	Total Census Basis[1]	Foods, Feeds, & Beverages	End-Use Commodity Category					
			Industrial Supplies[2]	Capital Goods	Automotive Vehicles, etc.	Consumer Goods	Other Goods	Residual[3]
1995..........................	607,142	77,484	189,341	184,118	68,500	72,850	35,523	-20,673
1996..........................	671,491	75,007	200,959	218,553	71,293	78,193	41,472	-13,986
1997..........................	761,134	74,797	217,460	267,745	80,441	85,873	41,187	-6,368
1998..........................	779,103	74,332	216,636	279,581	78,511	89,222	44,604	-3,782
1999..........................	804,151	76,880	218,207	294,711	81,301	89,849	44,567	-1,363
2000..........................	892,787	81,160	240,086	341,042	85,974	98,624	42,899	3,002
2001..........................	837,603	83,314	229,278	307,589	80,379	97,520	42,142	-2,620
2002..........................	799,010	81,427	225,527	280,733	83,776	93,435	40,580	-6,468
2003..........................	822,698	82,794	235,436	288,752	85,141	98,541	39,086	-7,052
2004..........................	894,614	76,447	251,328	324,204	93,522	112,180	39,636	-2,704
2005..........................	957,748	79,974	258,792	353,829	102,087	123,614	40,788	-1,336
2006..........................	1,054,348	85,718	278,585	398,121	110,104	135,921	45,999	-99
2007..........................	1,138,006	91,109	297,495	428,775	123,191	149,935	47,504	-4
2008..........................	1,219,450	96,379	333,476	455,746	122,025	162,157	48,099	1,568
2009..........................	1,056,043	93,908	296,508	391,242	81,715	149,455	43,215	0
2010..........................	1,213,964	103,022	339,987	447,207	111,508	161,641	51,239	-639
2011..........................	1,307,424	101,013	370,108	494,777	130,436	168,230	45,820	-2,959
2012..........................	1,359,250	101,085	374,734	528,633	141,118	172,505	48,727	-7,552
2013..........................	1,396,258	100,839	391,200	533,311	146,625	181,140	50,436	-7,293
2014..........................	1,445,177	107,871	398,584	547,140	152,648	193,297	54,183	-8,546
2015..........................	1,433,669	110,353	397,168	535,020	145,256	196,751	55,960	-6,838

[1]Detailed data are presented on a Census basis. The information needed to convert to a BOP basis is not available.
[2]Includes petroleum and petroleum products.
[3]The "residual" represents the difference between total Census Basis exports or imports and the sum of the components.

Table B-20.   Real Imports of Goods by Principal End-Use Category, 1995–2015

(Millions of dollars. Chained (2009) dollars.)

Year	Total Census Basis[1]	Foods, Feeds, & Beverages	End-Use Commodity Category					
			Industrial Supplies[2]	Capital Goods	Automotive Vehicles, etc.	Consumer Goods	Other Goods	Residual[3]
1995	780,916	41,333	361,341	126,518	137,245	161,147	25,721	-72,388
1996	862,394	45,760	383,356	152,612	141,928	172,588	28,707	-62,557
1997	982,148	50,152	409,785	191,101	153,443	196,495	32,477	-51,304
1998	1,097,870	53,964	449,164	219,196	163,030	222,756	40,024	-50,265
1999	1,230,037	58,933	456,328	251,422	194,716	250,124	48,839	-30,325
2000	1,393,190	62,755	484,785	301,690	211,687	294,213	54,016	-15,956
2001	1,346,996	65,189	482,402	266,292	205,186	299,058	54,532	-25,664
2002	1,395,870	69,489	484,447	261,649	219,645	326,761	56,272	-22,394
2003	1,472,991	75,910	503,926	279,490	225,318	354,902	53,723	-20,277
2004	1,646,367	80,586	566,272	329,081	240,951	393,621	54,979	-19,124
2005	1,762,482	83,571	595,138	365,977	250,332	425,735	58,938	-17,210
2006	1,867,720	88,425	597,419	408,893	267,066	459,939	61,623	-15,644
2007	1,904,336	89,183	579,325	435,521	264,431	485,818	65,325	-15,267
2008	1,848,827	87,195	552,021	445,243	232,703	480,183	65,650	-14,168
2009	1,559,625	81,615	462,380	370,480	157,652	427,332	60,165	0
2010	1,790,737	84,714	488,948	453,764	223,753	482,774	59,525	-2,742
2011	1,900,890	87,252	497,191	514,569	246,095	505,467	60,394	-10,079
2012	1,948,072	90,098	479,322	554,626	282,460	500,853	66,455	-25,742
2013	1,968,585	93,137	463,623	567,430	293,823	516,037	69,918	-35,384
2014	2,053,544	97,529	464,396	607,060	314,324	538,389	77,321	-45,474
2015	2,145,200	100,871	465,881	623,939	340,376	578,854	84,746	-49,467

[1]Detailed data are presented on a Census basis. The information needed to convert to a BOP basis is not available.
[2]Includes petroleum and petroleum products.
[3]The "residual" represents the difference between total Census Basis exports or imports and the sum of the components. For additional information, see www.census.gov/foreign-trade/aip/priceadj.html

PART III: U.S. TRADE WITH COUNTRIES AND REGIONS

Table B-21. U.S. Exports of Total Merchandise to Individual Countries by Harmonized System, 2005–2015

Region	2005	2006	2007	2008	2009	2010
WORLD	901,081,812,545	1,025,967,497,363	1,148,198,722,191	1,287,441,996,730	1,056,042,963,028	1,278,494,525,839
Afghanistan............................	262,153,213	417,393,793	495,283,664	481,633,366	1,508,592,966	2,151,400,794
Albania..................................	18,513,925	27,631,235	33,965,115	40,031,060	48,018,565	46,432,350
Algeria...................................	1,106,190,448	1,101,903,341	1,652,434,839	1,243,228,549	1,107,826,652	1,194,325,446
Andorra..................................	10,549,473	8,988,508	14,463,888	15,723,474	9,426,362	7,682,080
Angola...................................	929,046,776	1,388,849,572	1,242,031,263	2,019,179,085	1,423,050,894	1,293,490,947
Anguilla..................................	32,186,758	43,139,388	92,544,430	81,032,495	52,914,578	35,575,958
Antigua and Barbuda................	190,447,421	193,606,251	240,400,286	182,521,043	156,889,923	158,339,672
Argentina	4,121,861,182	4,775,927,712	5,855,853,074	7,536,315,425	5,568,885,625	7,392,136,090
Armenia	65,483,218	80,368,168	110,609,110	151,418,421	77,094,568	113,450,618
Aruba	558,924,451	510,530,936	528,763,861	680,253,631	445,673,618	540,475,447
Australia................................	15,588,519,677	17,545,739,796	19,178,197,903	22,218,649,074	19,599,303,927	21,804,647,444
Austria	2,544,481,273	2,961,458,498	3,109,855,557	2,649,130,446	2,536,845,631	2,428,561,443
Azerbaijan	132,462,798	231,094,350	177,607,684	239,100,656	185,236,612	252,516,882
Bahamas................................	1,786,740,047	2,282,366,185	2,468,442,608	2,759,541,038	2,504,043,054	3,177,987,377
Bahrain..................................	350,784,510	474,459,291	591,325,145	829,534,521	667,407,395	1,235,144,570
Bangladesh............................	319,769,758	332,951,338	455,985,590	468,054,418	434,568,444	575,698,015
Barbados...............................	394,920,090	442,486,478	456,986,883	497,390,029	404,773,424	397,391,831
Belarus..................................	34,942,759	74,504,642	101,544,112	134,460,264	137,247,760	133,148,863
Belgium..................................	18,690,606,570	21,339,991,410	25,258,518,805	28,903,481,869	21,607,727,193	25,457,982,517
Belize....................................	217,562,773	238,752,478	234,216,134	352,655,245	252,698,520	289,388,047
Benin.....................................	72,278,749	115,490,858	289,417,071	846,307,384	397,376,762	462,534,820
Bermuda................................	490,497,944	634,413,551	660,014,871	821,682,240	807,392,576	636,569,462
Bhutan...................................	3,052,180	3,216,134	4,050,496	3,960,013	2,742,299	3,504,719
Bolivia...................................	219,479,092	215,237,769	277,677,271	389,305,755	431,413,764	507,981,144
Bosnia and Herzegovina...........	17,573,793	51,553,635	20,153,042	34,113,666	21,290,698	26,349,510
Botswana...............................	67,272,144	26,878,406	53,844,794	62,177,868	93,244,580	48,496,947
Brazil.....................................	15,371,717,849	18,887,031,477	24,172,315,213	32,298,654,561	26,095,455,340	35,417,674,011
British Indian Ocean Territory	806,112	1,301,705	978,717	1,345,244	1,774,962	1,479,708
British Virgin Islands................	124,856,685	215,003,633	176,177,065	309,884,797	232,953,888	145,778,454
Brunei....................................	49,614,155	47,964,160	139,629,502	111,514,845	100,205,408	124,168,019
Bulgaria.................................	267,934,420	292,957,323	306,140,544	509,444,129	224,157,518	170,881,502
Burkina Faso	25,110,810	18,104,296	33,139,512	24,492,570	25,823,754	46,587,532
Burma (Myanmar).....................	5,464,172	7,541,563	8,709,851	10,755,671	6,906,838	9,650,957
Burundi..................................	8,121,178	5,901,104	6,930,327	7,278,372	8,688,287	14,386,303
Cote d'Ivoire...........................	124,242,832	147,461,219	161,604,087	254,110,055	206,048,254	162,845,207
Cambodia...............................	69,652,929	74,498,253	138,840,903	154,175,269	127,090,376	153,825,031
Cameroon	117,313,887	120,048,004	132,920,223	125,067,070	153,522,465	132,270,395
Canada..................................	211,898,689,378	230,656,013,599	248,888,144,575	261,149,833,516	204,657,955,218	249,256,459,292
Cape Verde.............................	9,871,825	13,619,116	5,571,564	12,247,224	6,387,428	9,975,829
Cayman Islands.......................	680,670,387	631,688,819	640,184,709	745,896,003	643,342,674	581,661,967
Central African Republic............	14,781,003	25,088,871	19,747,922	23,302,776	31,485,494	10,339,636
Chad......................................	53,752,155	61,309,347	66,242,263	62,515,460	62,689,577	89,670,008
Chile......................................	5,133,523,351	6,585,849,415	8,148,107,198	11,857,443,806	9,345,620,179	10,906,674,806
China.....................................	41,192,010,123	53,673,008,343	62,936,891,576	69,732,837,543	69,496,678,611	91,911,080,944
Christmas Island	2,005,920	1,076,229	2,544,078	12,981,567	925,955	1,750,269
Cocos (Keeling) Islands	1,048,051	757,982	1,231,015	966,209	1,440,652	728,118
Colombia................................	5,462,357,164	6,708,603,972	8,557,677,097	11,437,270,464	9,451,459,411	12,067,665,283
Comoros.................................	295,219	108,899	367,032	411,481	1,631,394	1,259,238
Congo....................................	104,056,096	138,004,892	140,034,863	184,589,852	276,930,001	254,428,015
Cook Islands	1,372,809	3,027,954	2,393,727	2,790,773	1,963,686	3,858,635
Costa Rica..............................	3,598,560,177	4,132,381,499	4,580,459,896	5,679,825,053	4,699,532,055	5,178,268,088
Croatia...................................	158,621,993	146,545,016	247,039,191	466,762,837	201,742,862	311,801,078
Cuba......................................	369,034,678	340,470,678	447,061,040	711,500,939	532,777,218	363,112,464
Curacao..................................	0	0	0	0	0	0
Cyprus...................................	84,179,247	198,526,441	169,018,830	217,395,819	179,127,346	134,395,198
Czech Republic	1,053,557,481	1,122,604,496	1,262,342,930	1,378,420,100	969,635,528	1,410,841,262
Democratic Republic of Congo	64,968,131	70,719,051	112,907,113	130,318,867	79,486,985	93,267,329
Denmark.................................	1,918,423,705	2,268,482,228	2,889,652,859	2,711,049,826	2,056,087,203	2,132,446,964
Djibouti..................................	47,571,125	47,628,575	58,934,056	140,825,944	196,482,984	122,793,059
Dominica................................	61,540,001	67,998,163	83,832,387	105,399,066	76,601,184	72,843,630
Dominican Republic..................	4,718,733,392	5,350,539,554	6,084,052,712	6,594,369,844	5,268,819,948	6,579,238,536
East Timor..............................	8,685,474	11,579,082	10,930,555	5,042,480	2,350,110	4,325,772
Ecuador.................................	1,963,825,872	2,727,195,787	2,935,648,657	3,450,017,348	3,937,889,182	5,409,439,121
Egypt.....................................	3,159,259,288	4,028,986,029	5,259,281,033	6,002,196,132	5,253,082,399	6,832,542,194
El Salvador.............................	1,854,286,657	2,152,092,495	2,313,065,522	2,461,953,266	2,018,691,710	2,433,816,689
Equatorial Guinea....................	281,472,431	551,498,185	236,399,700	184,514,829	305,594,459	272,137,422
Eritrea...................................	31,058,711	8,847,564	6,112,826	14,872,461	6,735,077	2,384,567
Estonia..................................	145,425,805	221,419,402	242,279,007	225,553,251	189,474,502	187,880,428
Ethiopia.................................	455,635,812	137,266,509	167,478,262	301,580,906	266,866,655	773,159,838

Table B-21.   U.S. Exports of Total Merchandise to Individual Countries by Harmonized System, 2005–2015—*Continued*

Region	2011	2012	2013	2014	2015
WORLD	1,482,507,755,226	1,545,820,839,892	1,578,516,879,950	1,621,171,618,259	1,502,572,229,518
Afghanistan...................................	2,921,861,778	1,521,555,394	1,410,116,220	812,933,509	478,851,271
Albania..	47,562,162	54,082,290	74,364,825	51,256,821	30,952,665
Algeria...	1,596,975,135	1,363,163,393	1,848,703,921	2,616,922,429	1,875,734,479
Andorra..	5,161,272	2,238,367	5,796,907	3,789,433	3,336,817
Angola..	1,503,222,549	1,490,579,464	1,443,395,524	2,039,267,110	1,166,161,667
Anguilla..	31,193,536	27,409,044	31,037,512	58,385,175	47,602,633
Antigua and Barbuda......................	154,792,008	204,627,966	145,103,078	216,599,924	677,657,633
Argentina..	9,898,793,593	10,258,063,599	10,351,132,910	10,828,595,127	9,341,210,651
Armenia..	94,316,257	64,299,297	91,221,471	60,410,659	50,246,170
Aruba..	713,268,343	710,275,291	1,099,787,667	1,300,191,178	1,167,632,524
Australia...	27,626,182,324	31,161,378,813	26,123,737,344	26,682,046,260	25,035,790,152
Austria..	2,893,301,793	3,419,658,018	3,519,942,333	3,824,805,936	4,024,435,888
Azerbaijan......................................	337,884,996	492,623,482	380,998,744	950,256,109	477,316,108
Bahamas...	3,441,983,410	3,479,076,670	3,447,977,493	3,321,397,620	2,386,461,864
Bahrain...	1,214,407,158	1,176,914,298	1,026,301,420	1,060,071,969	1,270,662,445
Bangladesh.....................................	1,144,148,134	508,180,705	708,777,580	1,113,233,373	942,540,067
Barbados..	439,876,711	458,567,570	453,339,832	539,878,271	595,966,307
Belarus...	156,543,879	102,025,447	95,141,886	93,385,923	59,235,752
Belgium...	29,990,463,874	29,438,360,969	31,840,185,737	34,780,527,517	34,159,979,659
Belize..	355,682,393	265,606,023	240,629,948	236,689,797	285,240,264
Benin..	617,574,838	572,964,557	605,242,564	780,910,542	631,462,518
Bermuda...	611,441,769	622,432,927	537,422,110	646,715,539	600,945,255
Bhutan..	3,838,631	2,488,897	2,351,165	2,422,028	2,641,040
Bolivia..	667,847,026	763,010,279	1,051,415,463	1,008,607,293	931,431,709
Bosnia and Herzegovina.................	21,331,785	15,869,518	38,481,079	46,080,139	27,586,061
Botswana..	44,273,591	47,983,957	82,090,829	52,861,554	39,041,970
Brazil..	43,018,838,986	43,771,278,235	44,105,506,964	42,434,432,023	31,650,623,867
British Indian Ocean Territory	2,212,415	2,725,208	762,058	2,099,098	581,016
British Virgin Islands.......................	151,474,267	171,759,131	312,726,797	387,943,852	259,758,571
Brunei...	184,371,635	157,609,639	558,297,839	549,201,703	133,449,998
Bulgaria..	258,589,821	248,545,279	307,323,074	358,776,890	289,092,010
Burkina Faso...................................	33,260,220	47,276,772	78,571,883	73,991,538	53,875,343
Burma (Myanmar)...........................	48,949,883	65,765,942	145,830,603	92,856,414	227,140,755
Burundi...	32,788,844	19,939,674	16,711,425	5,569,408	5,650,192
Cote d'Ivoire...................................	131,405,294	188,087,985	167,433,243	239,077,767	266,335,569
Cambodia..	186,568,289	226,404,530	241,220,345	328,091,257	391,045,876
Cameroon..	220,567,654	253,043,417	335,737,087	301,072,860	224,961,698
Canada..	281,291,530,822	292,650,534,087	300,754,868,974	312,816,950,458	280,609,005,568
Cape Verde.....................................	11,462,670	7,765,222	9,134,281	7,283,602	7,321,660
Cayman Islands...............................	616,500,045	667,727,178	680,366,150	814,147,726	684,947,958
Central African Republic..................	12,335,446	8,515,840	4,103,350	32,322,366	34,309,874
Chad...	35,450,336	36,551,674	41,460,707	66,491,850	56,591,528
Chile...	15,993,031,002	18,773,140,514	17,515,894,876	16,541,530,653	15,445,137,965
China..	104,121,523,635	110,516,615,672	121,746,188,637	123,620,711,012	116,071,769,560
Christmas Island.............................	1,486,081	4,053,949	466,894	168,931	1,551,179
Cocos (Keeling) Islands	957,218	932,610	22,169,095	6,040,796	557,620
Colombia...	14,335,692,038	16,356,802,727	18,371,032,417	20,067,798,317	16,286,779,898
Comoros..	1,095,278	954,373	3,491,014	3,452,794	1,507,078
Congo..	227,293,001	237,200,621	222,397,877	321,644,003	249,220,232
Cook Islands	4,604,318	5,504,221	4,869,141	5,325,025	4,249,826
Costa Rica.......................................	6,099,250,515	7,236,638,312	7,223,384,099	6,962,104,221	6,079,415,736
Croatia..	511,383,383	310,054,427	308,852,551	339,595,076	331,976,272
Cuba...	363,316,479	464,458,419	359,609,641	299,064,037	180,215,206
Curacao...	484,200,988	691,942,132	687,514,148	611,613,765	522,079,698
Cyprus...	97,699,749	166,867,197	143,223,588	151,620,404	101,831,614
Czech Republic	1,684,705,096	1,832,279,706	1,943,358,124	2,302,481,825	1,976,037,865
Democratic Republic of Congo	165,925,390	199,549,248	169,825,711	181,865,401	136,189,374
Denmark..	2,247,948,078	2,224,454,815	2,231,067,390	2,360,660,519	2,202,093,582
Djibouti...	129,175,500	118,841,640	164,483,264	110,910,147	144,711,021
Dominica...	73,675,432	78,934,015	77,679,144	64,186,171	67,312,046
Dominican Republic.........................	7,325,686,377	6,967,401,065	7,158,187,556	7,928,448,983	7,113,829,302
East Timor.......................................	8,146,198	1,143,436	1,365,128	1,286,987	2,690,584
Ecuador...	6,078,061,107	6,692,731,994	7,678,971,679	8,131,244,311	5,794,812,688
Egypt...	6,228,228,507	5,498,319,529	5,175,215,624	6,478,374,126	4,752,983,685
El Salvador......................................	3,371,560,160	3,095,701,213	3,250,238,283	3,305,267,255	3,240,284,878
Equatorial Guinea............................	285,394,250	233,161,535	756,139,906	574,773,691	161,964,373
Eritrea...	4,308,872	5,863,859	13,476,312	5,327,596	3,497,538
Estonia..	309,602,800	235,986,120	293,183,114	308,541,604	288,143,789
Ethiopia...	689,890,633	1,274,672,068	688,507,736	1,668,912,927	1,555,249,376

Table B-21.   U.S. Exports of Total Merchandise to Individual Countries by Harmonized System, 2005–2015—*Continued*

Region	2005	2006	2007	2008	2009	2010
Falkland Islands (Malvinas)	9,049,418	1,637,590	973,369	805,502	2,356,305	2,718,134
Faroe Islands	2,528,152	3,968,862	2,800,199	14,339,798	9,870,000	2,129,580
Fiji	28,177,593	32,548,798	29,942,761	55,020,240	31,172,353	43,972,153
Finland	2,254,052,992	2,647,790,945	3,133,422,316	3,760,847,433	1,661,981,706	2,179,532,042
France	22,258,628,050	23,511,819,725	26,675,969,747	28,840,096,938	26,493,009,350	26,969,951,939
French Guiana	26,993,942	33,142,561	31,342,950	18,032,587	16,758,205	35,703,949
French Polynesia	111,838,384	108,158,633	124,414,483	130,331,165	112,758,869	121,590,707
French Southern Territories	273,678	129,968	392,357	4,238,293	963,568	588,625
Gabon	99,105,857	135,294,305	477,645,795	283,989,863	170,755,956	242,998,852
Gambia	30,604,418	21,202,373	20,000,988	28,878,320	33,648,113	29,253,787
Gaza Strip	231,120	266,920	4,634,860	61,183	22,823	1,830,513
Georgia	213,886,826	263,531,198	364,236,656	586,464,121	363,773,252	300,877,770
Germany	34,183,656,274	41,159,115,809	49,419,703,142	54,505,255,730	43,306,258,441	48,155,263,220
Ghana	337,389,713	289,476,368	416,384,899	608,412,179	715,935,461	989,339,154
Gibraltar	163,257,568	286,191,706	593,945,617	2,640,683,545	1,086,961,229	1,494,144,556
Greece	1,192,248,494	1,554,720,496	2,110,206,007	1,931,570,736	2,487,064,064	1,106,453,110
Greenland	5,085,009	2,972,467	4,418,684	34,892,248	7,072,819	8,577,516
Grenada	82,440,305	74,178,148	83,264,328	84,437,130	59,211,758	71,243,438
Guadeloupe	54,512,655	64,986,251	139,085,169	383,935,772	205,820,935	364,529,841
Guatemala	2,835,380,390	3,511,420,817	4,065,051,130	4,718,262,816	3,874,527,192	4,476,851,241
Guinea	93,597,060	64,750,375	73,531,245	101,802,826	94,793,067	85,061,952
Guinea Bissau	2,100,355	5,708,642	6,615,356	2,076,775	1,511,184	3,401,580
Guyana	176,704,601	179,440,313	187,879,827	288,518,675	260,367,286	290,703,439
Haiti	709,620,597	817,367,312	680,188,060	943,991,127	790,406,627	1,208,576,616
Heard Island and Mcdonald Islands	160,607	595,097	1,721,670	308,427	7,113,037	3,654,960
Honduras	3,253,813,808	3,687,064,970	4,461,359,257	4,846,217,272	3,367,600,743	4,606,443,933
Hong Kong	16,351,028,611	17,742,174,911	19,901,654,480	21,498,619,389	21,050,525,179	26,570,450,803
Hungary	1,023,258,213	1,187,640,766	1,291,867,910	1,430,952,895	1,232,876,763	1,290,393,339
Iceland	512,019,513	365,791,294	629,632,708	469,500,222	349,502,029	324,882,989
India	7,918,602,428	9,673,570,797	14,968,845,536	17,682,084,740	16,441,395,486	19,248,886,968
Indonesia	3,053,913,961	3,078,476,384	3,969,656,878	5,644,478,295	5,106,983,972	6,947,852,910
Iran	95,773,068	85,865,218	144,697,312	683,175,698	280,371,712	211,398,345
Iraq	1,373,986,265	1,490,615,192	1,560,201,195	2,069,789,108	1,772,408,085	1,643,064,073
Ireland	8,446,771,993	7,621,461,208	7,776,969,775	7,610,825,492	7,465,002,762	7,275,841,853
Israel	9,737,340,849	10,964,817,506	12,887,477,039	14,486,863,157	9,559,356,487	11,295,020,595
Italy	11,524,325,287	12,546,042,512	14,149,624,058	15,460,835,761	12,268,011,950	14,219,893,087
Jamaica	1,700,769,277	2,035,665,603	2,315,958,604	2,643,366,812	1,440,576,002	1,661,396,570
Japan	54,680,579,847	58,458,978,071	61,159,582,766	65,141,753,124	51,134,184,201	60,471,852,133
Jordan	644,195,347	650,333,336	856,173,325	940,321,131	1,191,811,231	1,172,174,641
Kazakhstan	538,286,932	646,175,651	752,764,327	985,519,036	603,491,712	730,293,302
Kenya	573,365,497	430,745,344	520,374,633	442,372,404	653,631,512	375,348,785
Kiribati	2,411,608	1,392,300	1,149,509	7,347,540	824,672	3,977,797
Kosovo	0	0	0	0	5,002,266	11,183,045
Kuwait	1,974,875,551	2,086,910,362	2,484,016,406	2,719,345,826	1,951,143,424	2,774,766,577
Kyrgyzstan	31,140,901	71,250,326	48,651,043	44,287,417	56,761,574	79,407,764
Lao People's Democratic Republic	9,807,849	6,958,897	5,464,940	18,346,685	20,321,593	12,644,576
Latvia	177,537,085	245,468,729	381,391,440	393,968,241	288,594,228	344,952,057
Lebanon	465,688,546	930,689,826	825,888,292	1,463,832,577	1,852,147,275	2,009,038,480
Lesotho	4,015,033	4,028,604	7,525,706	1,339,723	16,630,440	11,330,245
Liberia	69,320,320	67,840,342	75,769,497	156,687,752	94,745,252	191,351,777
Libyan Arab Jamahiriya	83,841,985	383,744,472	510,834,249	720,871,828	665,507,651	665,533,976
Liechtenstein	19,716,500	15,835,002	16,183,424	29,259,009	23,482,968	29,267,415
Lithuania	390,027,824	566,639,841	720,302,048	831,259,516	398,538,386	628,120,466
Luxembourg	711,292,070	581,322,055	925,549,780	988,035,453	1,292,061,259	1,439,673,708
Macau; SAR of China	101,575,899	200,225,783	226,447,445	306,742,843	209,196,460	225,189,155
Macedonia	31,556,267	22,426,182	33,561,327	36,114,737	34,837,071	33,332,833
Madagascar	28,205,237	44,737,462	32,129,605	70,754,620	105,868,563	115,994,454
Malawi	28,049,237	45,741,929	51,499,475	44,943,925	40,423,565	37,001,180
Malaysia	10,460,833,167	12,443,999,494	11,680,201,598	12,949,454,144	10,403,284,106	14,079,484,478
Maldives	9,255,550	17,647,304	19,321,264	20,294,509	17,424,044	28,284,498
Mali	32,421,928	43,130,545	31,901,355	30,908,863	36,747,987	37,274,320
Malta	193,709,217	162,538,078	207,214,338	253,437,906	208,459,569	457,387,915
Marshall Islands	75,484,350	15,487,320	22,887,016	25,148,907	77,579,432	91,184,680
Martinique	34,959,990	32,425,501	193,908,207	288,848,377	263,426,197	296,799,785
Mauritania	86,135,221	90,146,958	102,657,391	106,603,830	56,280,371	84,343,006
Mauritius	30,860,179	35,584,108	49,793,601	51,280,301	70,031,102	40,027,845
Mayotte	0	11,724	243,119	57,814	1,168,097	6,282,489
Mexico	120,247,580,142	133,721,712,754	135,918,138,711	151,220,056,463	128,892,137,645	163,664,645,537
Micronesia (Federated States of)	25,349,268	29,584,985	37,824,810	54,502,889	51,947,959	42,389,761
Moldova; Republic of	40,069,837	30,093,862	52,668,339	66,237,298	26,644,083	37,813,517

Table B-21.   U.S. Exports of Total Merchandise to Individual Countries by Harmonized System, 2005–2015—_Continued_

Region	2011	2012	2013	2014	2015
Falkland Islands (Malvinas)	3,957,498	4,347,073	1,241,492	7,845,600	2,917,708
Faroe Islands	3,560,628	1,627,283	2,453,563	2,360,974	2,336,863
Fiji	42,628,530	55,608,118	66,885,504	79,511,460	56,904,585
Finland	3,158,720,581	2,566,206,117	2,349,052,218	2,150,302,524	1,558,146,898
France	27,856,813,717	30,812,883,841	31,743,718,451	31,306,569,953	30,103,521,196
French Guiana	56,718,244	209,231,252	631,200,449	281,020,776	1,073,642,767
French Polynesia	126,618,809	129,855,209	126,189,637	129,553,300	120,047,865
French Southern Territories	1,425,658	1,239,070	1,749,592	8,251,616	8,026,602
Gabon	205,151,050	319,048,462	307,983,525	417,347,288	203,872,443
Gambia	29,366,112	27,458,509	34,135,359	41,538,614	37,899,622
Gaza Strip	47,297	105,165	178,138	169,040	183,934
Georgia	580,009,236	541,253,019	601,244,307	627,551,843	340,502,111
Germany	49,294,189,419	48,802,968,878	47,363,465,586	49,370,318,203	49,970,804,114
Ghana	1,199,086,566	1,322,494,666	981,388,029	1,186,269,188	949,913,963
Gibraltar	3,148,591,117	5,109,058,460	3,576,397,600	2,530,894,164	1,972,992,610
Greece	1,130,969,963	804,136,728	739,038,829	773,223,119	725,699,147
Greenland	7,302,165	15,856,790	19,148,034	12,692,465	8,076,839
Grenada	81,834,405	72,112,543	95,251,167	83,983,195	90,420,149
Guadeloupe	430,951,509	502,522,818	642,437,801	426,604,654	100,959,536
Guatemala	6,151,169,676	5,748,945,279	5,554,588,951	5,961,744,697	5,806,713,895
Guinea	256,160,269	154,622,237	79,462,980	65,185,635	135,350,114
Guinea Bissau	11,838,657	21,095,196	6,643,733	2,904,280	2,135,320
Guyana	363,441,299	359,571,070	318,863,043	369,986,060	368,129,666
Haiti	1,058,948,781	1,050,229,529	1,227,113,799	1,275,942,616	1,140,574,185
Heard Island and Mcdonald Islands	365,259	499,782	504,268	1,180,334	913,419
Honduras	6,166,370,382	5,714,670,349	5,420,255,599	5,961,437,622	5,214,668,234
Hong Kong	36,398,784,628	37,471,809,096	42,332,232,943	40,910,891,340	37,167,022,950
Hungary	1,479,338,284	1,566,156,776	1,726,956,134	1,843,893,619	1,715,278,037
Iceland	628,054,455	370,820,354	513,396,894	374,921,407	415,457,850
India	21,542,184,381	22,105,737,858	21,810,447,551	21,501,366,140	21,451,879,922
Indonesia	7,421,405,814	7,997,976,489	9,106,545,145	8,282,827,845	7,120,940,688
Iran	233,183,160	251,122,746	308,142,294	186,563,145	281,512,074
Iraq	2,400,364,843	2,053,842,278	2,003,374,954	2,105,504,854	1,971,478,767
Ireland	7,657,624,847	7,392,737,072	6,632,235,721	7,806,548,592	8,930,773,509
Israel	13,961,616,095	14,273,498,432	13,743,691,038	15,065,274,819	13,538,694,820
Italy	16,037,489,503	16,097,123,281	16,757,095,740	16,966,344,158	16,204,226,088
Jamaica	1,934,143,237	1,989,288,661	1,979,623,696	2,180,254,034	1,716,030,814
Japan	65,799,736,713	69,975,786,856	65,237,414,094	66,876,246,454	62,442,646,462
Jordan	1,449,688,144	1,766,366,354	2,085,026,459	2,050,402,326	1,358,977,191
Kazakhstan	827,138,922	883,647,324	1,150,177,842	1,007,874,954	510,479,071
Kenya	461,441,784	568,583,714	635,695,507	1,640,682,222	943,436,657
Kiribati	17,667,015	4,605,948	6,983,607	3,293,815	7,320,835
Kosovo	15,572,116	20,832,234	14,544,129	16,343,893	19,743,318
Kuwait	2,749,651,553	2,681,906,798	2,597,538,635	3,648,727,071	2,739,289,578
Kyrgyzstan	101,878,738	145,493,810	106,251,152	71,725,049	32,003,481
Lao People's Democratic Republic	26,084,818	33,494,345	24,400,348	28,488,310	24,584,007
Latvia	585,962,167	514,791,562	494,564,967	428,187,574	294,787,977
Lebanon	1,807,311,627	1,039,943,000	1,034,263,176	1,268,021,906	1,272,487,166
Lesotho	13,181,171	16,514,237	571,144	2,449,565	881,897
Liberia	195,207,824	241,089,095	173,207,630	184,502,715	135,807,551
Libyan Arab Jamahiriya	307,238,676	549,022,033	864,473,039	531,855,792	242,951,645
Liechtenstein	62,346,285	21,972,859	22,055,946	31,102,552	35,930,552
Lithuania	1,141,936,078	756,983,833	854,235,543	681,234,694	527,677,630
Luxembourg	1,585,845,119	1,903,143,233	1,848,801,276	1,516,224,621	1,394,174,730
Macau; SAR of China	291,499,829	345,460,636	351,203,334	433,401,819	542,354,584
Macedonia	29,456,706	21,117,500	54,778,259	33,850,337	30,678,977
Madagascar	56,283,902	64,275,029	64,007,569	46,811,501	54,553,731
Malawi	56,973,282	63,951,198	54,498,745	50,669,581	37,201,602
Malaysia	14,264,019,831	12,817,723,181	13,015,887,589	13,068,804,018	12,277,226,142
Maldives	44,835,389	30,051,856	28,778,952	28,985,734	35,143,208
Mali	55,077,612	59,745,089	49,893,003	38,462,373	72,426,079
Malta	752,427,011	390,983,065	563,593,854	917,598,314	490,660,579
Marshall Islands	143,791,762	142,133,251	65,478,036	94,570,567	53,912,135
Martinique	339,595,962	370,668,017	381,786,515	290,611,709	119,577,165
Mauritania	243,310,966	291,593,870	244,685,427	148,823,898	126,280,667
Mauritius	46,369,941	95,986,858	42,095,310	35,525,527	58,435,311
Mayotte	4,572,023	11,610,143	8,520,110	12,087,472	5,697,333
Mexico	198,288,737,278	215,875,115,867	225,954,367,783	240,331,176,824	235,745,137,477
Micronesia (Federated States of)	44,072,040	51,491,652	41,566,161	41,523,205	40,032,614
Moldova; Republic of	39,569,462	38,267,976	45,602,639	35,188,566	16,163,682

Table B-21.   U.S. Exports of Total Merchandise to Individual Countries by Harmonized System, 2005–2015—*Continued*

Region	2005	2006	2007	2008	2009	2010
Monaco	16,776,668	33,485,803	42,757,654	62,734,955	17,968,911	49,192,767
Mongolia	21,879,286	23,058,259	26,032,828	57,248,374	40,514,385	115,518,352
Montenegro	0	0	45,306,063	53,185,501	34,787,868	14,554,803
Montserrat	4,848,606	14,377,481	4,774,256	8,564,674	5,883,151	4,746,579
Morocco	480,792,527	837,929,033	1,294,157,002	1,435,863,486	1,630,259,886	1,947,613,644
Mozambique	62,825,299	64,369,218	114,979,532	213,387,796	189,612,914	224,019,682
Namibia	112,249,178	126,928,878	127,834,398	280,324,325	202,339,839	110,184,585
Nauru	1,624,750	3,782,469	8,140,371	11,240,397	3,687,213	2,492,127
Nepal	24,704,668	16,641,805	28,966,464	28,543,659	31,006,805	28,269,192
Netherlands	26,467,744,578	30,959,583,096	32,836,958,949	39,719,476,892	32,241,517,656	34,740,302,131
Netherlands Antilles	1,137,633,614	1,485,065,922	2,082,020,131	2,951,625,832	2,055,809,980	2,943,154,831
New Caledonia	38,403,106	43,607,213	57,785,454	89,120,063	77,859,989	108,035,793
New Zealand	2,592,076,963	2,806,165,775	2,717,562,746	2,533,906,801	2,158,504,659	2,820,164,709
Nicaragua	625,460,463	751,563,512	889,963,276	1,094,246,692	715,129,472	981,363,718
Niger	78,511,944	129,173,968	69,308,772	50,007,174	58,240,607	48,886,203
Nigeria	1,619,788,459	2,233,465,992	2,777,942,084	4,102,387,055	3,687,083,853	4,060,548,125
Niue	607,643	2,540,329	1,662,323	509,662	1,209,612	1,570,975
Norfolk Island	391,532	1,939,424	1,527,492	3,952,840	864,840	661,175
North Korea	5,757,048	0	1,728,160	52,151,230	856,793	2,867,073
Norway	1,941,882,004	2,393,968,843	3,040,287,529	3,292,198,210	2,789,788,721	3,099,984,444
Oman	570,725,120	828,660,320	1,059,179,720	1,381,973,854	1,126,324,482	1,105,209,532
Other Countries	216,283,336	124,385,407	441,208,607	182,997,431	233,738,869	375,897,966
Pakistan	1,251,631,940	1,722,633,113	1,943,577,099	1,897,845,402	1,617,950,218	1,901,071,676
Palau	12,225,240	10,755,456	13,803,500	14,065,965	14,796,127	14,157,003
Panama	2,162,020,485	2,660,135,037	3,669,201,342	4,887,253,843	4,292,943,517	6,065,898,991
Papua New Guinea	55,347,872	43,761,533	65,888,833	70,047,324	217,804,185	186,079,364
Paraguay	895,819,607	910,768,324	1,236,732,017	1,609,936,531	1,355,033,256	1,810,053,906
Peru	2,309,446,378	2,926,839,982	4,119,773,437	6,182,968,633	4,918,842,351	6,749,545,624
Philippines	6,895,406,023	7,616,937,667	7,712,299,275	8,294,867,172	5,766,367,618	7,376,713,359
Pitcairn Islands	456,290	1,365,209	1,894,797	0	568,212	3,683
Poland	1,267,748,385	1,960,750,731	3,123,428,696	4,130,606,117	2,301,516,671	2,982,925,333
Portugal	1,131,865,366	1,470,513,405	2,478,481,445	2,645,976,274	1,084,847,582	1,057,882,127
Qatar	986,642,413	1,278,589,136	2,523,625,528	2,715,854,933	2,713,238,087	3,159,769,790
Reunion	3,785,910	4,378,145	4,753,124	8,446,395	9,448,244	8,214,437
Romania	608,858,767	554,007,617	676,587,084	1,048,179,130	672,003,377	729,792,681
Russian Federation	3,962,270,261	4,700,325,257	7,283,267,667	9,334,581,764	5,332,081,493	5,993,665,458
Rwanda	10,534,162	11,684,654	16,050,053	20,449,259	34,145,955	30,608,174
Saint Helena	2,732,629	1,754,323	3,279,597	2,034,633	2,893,506	692,094
Saint Kitts and Nevis	94,069,439	127,215,672	110,676,625	123,894,416	108,056,908	131,030,912
Saint Lucia	135,389,135	149,061,140	165,252,471	241,025,030	136,219,773	401,530,949
Saint Pierre and Miquelon	980,031	446,610	221,553	400,795	135,133	14,691
Saint Vincent and the Grenadines	45,411,401	58,326,805	68,952,798	82,692,856	74,851,479	85,970,257
Samoa	14,538,961	18,293,393	16,716,327	13,306,266	18,683,664	19,124,418
San Marino	4,676,009	8,965,182	13,890,976	9,328,760	8,132,793	3,990,083
Sao Tome and Principe	10,153,283	3,709,233	8,414,824	3,268,944	4,018,129	1,358,738
Saudi Arabia	6,805,402,418	7,639,533,026	10,395,890,781	12,484,248,431	10,792,157,268	11,506,200,861
Senegal	141,499,953	96,865,399	150,414,680	137,103,698	175,723,538	218,782,926
Serbia	0	0	109,583,090	207,357,458	112,594,021	104,469,213
Serbia and Montenegro	132,496,330	147,142,660	0	0	0	0
Seychelles	17,912,292	9,525,964	9,473,317	24,967,766	34,068,446	10,681,706
Sierra Leone	37,829,353	39,246,151	55,420,539	59,360,501	42,537,601	61,057,483
Singapore	20,466,073,458	23,825,546,496	25,618,565,860	27,853,610,178	22,231,821,976	29,008,615,357
Sint Maarten	0	0	0	0	0	0
Slovakia	149,800,634	422,470,054	500,061,702	617,612,296	209,588,452	255,851,944
Slovenia	233,830,317	239,128,814	296,840,744	309,595,949	243,645,097	328,108,783
Solomon Islands	2,297,431	5,680,255	5,438,181	5,246,192	6,020,700	4,953,653
Somalia	8,831,504	19,945,456	20,693,618	64,345,393	4,099,468	1,457,879
South Africa	3,906,946,741	4,461,696,778	5,521,396,823	6,490,469,811	4,452,643,478	5,631,664,767
South Korea	27,571,605,977	32,219,124,163	34,401,709,969	34,668,671,020	28,611,928,167	38,820,637,297
South Sudan	0	0	0	0	0	0
Spain	6,839,116,578	7,401,168,666	9,766,108,527	12,189,817,902	8,716,930,087	10,355,445,923
Sri Lanka	197,631,294	236,645,925	227,147,226	283,253,936	229,571,323	178,740,142
Sudan	108,105,454	76,924,039	79,129,315	143,305,018	78,414,774	115,617,732
Suriname	245,701,079	258,783,296	303,625,324	406,402,258	380,392,824	362,090,799
Svalbard and Jan Mayen Island	5,677,609	5,729,024	926,112	2,204,770	868,604	7,674,628
Swaziland	11,856,893	12,091,430	29,002,898	12,120,383	14,552,515	23,582,688
Sweden	3,715,368,620	4,125,937,735	4,472,726,015	5,018,258,734	4,560,785,212	4,739,888,118
Switzerland	10,717,528,064	14,375,043,637	17,039,261,465	22,023,645,856	17,504,409,869	20,703,849,321
Syrian Arab Republic	155,049,379	224,314,878	361,420,332	408,864,143	303,870,805	503,311,144
Taiwan	21,614,496,927	22,709,360,952	25,828,669,191	24,926,275,971	18,485,640,877	26,050,037,333

Table B-21.   U.S. Exports of Total Merchandise to Individual Countries by Harmonized System, 2005–2015—*Continued*

Region	2011	2012	2013	2014	2015
Monaco	20,664,012	24,306,080	465,907,393	127,638,099	71,128,048
Mongolia	315,176,816	664,955,251	279,573,362	167,478,862	69,161,103
Montenegro	17,673,009	12,397,402	21,683,955	18,179,413	11,133,957
Montserrat	6,903,084	8,566,354	8,616,652	9,181,522	6,640,011
Morocco	2,823,307,066	2,170,396,557	2,483,726,772	2,101,792,019	1,625,204,959
Mozambique	459,242,488	351,608,971	303,016,499	375,163,570	264,203,995
Namibia	136,564,152	184,614,633	235,244,409	342,741,711	127,603,603
Nauru	499,196	2,208,920	758,585	812,299	1,733,650
Nepal	40,354,262	37,013,899	32,513,730	36,338,986	36,405,446
Netherlands	42,227,119,015	40,618,286,512	42,577,045,423	43,130,780,553	40,196,156,288
Netherlands Antilles	1,187,093,257	0	0	0	0
New Caledonia	115,339,950	75,103,196	72,868,672	121,389,089	88,651,277
New Zealand	3,581,197,846	3,228,539,259	3,225,401,631	4,257,495,396	3,631,061,903
Nicaragua	1,058,585,304	1,128,213,231	1,059,306,367	1,008,588,813	1,267,532,561
Niger	48,152,287	37,367,471	46,194,680	58,530,382	71,493,157
Nigeria	4,904,789,052	5,029,335,221	6,388,352,516	5,965,921,938	3,437,952,784
Niue	716,169	771,748	249,064	111,564	71,371
Norfolk Island	1,043,984	1,228,303	1,730,958	829,925	350,312
North Korea	9,405,834	11,952,220	6,582,817	24,028,661	4,751,721
Norway	3,629,656,458	3,501,159,741	4,616,023,641	4,421,280,695	3,570,633,150
Oman	1,436,672,881	1,746,916,573	1,570,964,193	2,015,048,219	2,355,271,013
Other Countries	225,387,686	175,000,278	179,871,109	101,833	0
Pakistan	1,988,785,840	1,530,065,196	1,645,795,477	1,511,946,351	1,837,506,933
Palau	16,831,030	16,755,532	18,237,634	20,521,307	25,693,198
Panama	8,251,646,494	9,828,759,247	10,564,548,080	10,470,366,130	7,663,548,283
Papua New Guinea	304,028,723	391,381,919	166,733,845	143,251,616	207,793,894
Paraguay	1,977,345,845	1,743,208,491	1,932,782,887	2,115,586,680	1,514,300,292
Peru	8,341,864,469	9,348,621,449	10,120,124,634	10,055,740,779	8,725,607,473
Philippines	7,727,870,939	8,087,361,107	8,403,390,567	8,507,327,093	7,907,893,167
Pitcairn Islands	15,696	40,527	0	55,591	17,405
Poland	3,143,110,865	3,346,364,002	3,778,311,068	3,660,192,491	3,715,441,301
Portugal	1,315,990,308	1,097,095,847	844,350,936	1,120,670,649	942,466,275
Qatar	2,806,681,719	3,577,715,161	4,957,973,407	5,172,353,195	4,222,426,394
Reunion	154,882,932	7,566,899	8,774,205	11,072,320	6,905,271
Romania	918,551,681	832,745,398	746,508,997	977,525,577	753,718,827
Russian Federation	8,318,439,250	10,695,291,383	11,144,747,483	10,751,940,455	7,087,111,574
Rwanda	119,651,782	30,489,992	25,191,269	21,219,489	14,287,710
Saint Helena	1,901,890	4,847,886	2,866,797	489,827	3,720,487
Saint Kitts and Nevis	115,840,644	106,150,374	142,958,744	180,006,632	149,707,108
Saint Lucia	315,651,418	376,957,631	594,301,914	693,823,181	510,811,024
Saint Pierre and Miquelon	118,559	179,852	261,629	4,364	227,459
Saint Vincent and the Grenadines	80,602,721	98,707,927	93,180,570	103,619,626	84,722,498
Samoa	23,786,831	24,702,919	28,394,642	22,948,737	22,719,660
San Marino	2,009,836	1,347,152	1,873,295	5,977,212	5,011,879
Sao Tome and Principe	6,123,966	870,234	1,998,050	1,088,495	853,963
Saudi Arabia	13,923,664,673	17,961,238,469	18,962,914,928	18,717,871,045	19,738,984,586
Senegal	265,150,828	149,125,719	229,108,446	172,699,813	196,428,411
Serbia	126,632,272	127,658,133	141,973,440	135,035,904	126,251,420
Serbia and Montenegro	0	0	0	0	0
Seychelles	13,056,829	14,968,779	12,189,931	12,687,753	18,542,809
Sierra Leone	102,791,973	100,735,979	82,411,287	87,931,206	77,325,724
Singapore	31,282,363,017	30,523,214,544	30,665,030,257	30,072,470,745	28,472,070,979
Sint Maarten	397,678,059	702,440,846	828,898,068	777,576,071	741,201,231
Slovakia	302,411,668	335,549,229	295,818,376	445,176,240	379,469,169
Slovenia	668,166,646	307,877,888	269,491,341	301,210,859	346,040,192
Solomon Islands	6,056,589	7,254,847	8,933,554	6,599,026	5,861,309
Somalia	6,081,543	16,734,553	15,959,166	35,653,738	45,026,584
South Africa	7,271,282,389	7,552,773,511	7,293,400,316	6,375,332,650	5,458,293,620
South Korea	43,461,636,035	42,282,565,212	41,648,727,506	44,625,106,925	43,445,547,484
South Sudan	7,361,905	32,540,784	13,417,224	46,148,430	19,613,532
Spain	11,031,589,790	9,551,906,914	10,244,036,471	10,199,733,019	10,310,270,517
Sri Lanka	303,547,816	223,950,414	311,911,749	350,623,186	361,920,786
Sudan	74,694,129	55,491,290	88,268,450	77,168,737	59,514,997
Suriname	433,918,837	499,266,829	449,846,279	518,996,406	443,643,313
Svalbard and Jan Mayen Island	2,052,453	125,458	1,633,247	3,394,498	380,164
Swaziland	20,075,203	40,226,860	22,681,861	25,679,849	28,521,751
Sweden	5,265,007,755	5,247,930,905	4,318,640,022	4,337,135,311	3,940,810,500
Switzerland	24,486,242,385	26,406,154,155	26,558,942,638	22,169,440,428	22,185,279,914
Syrian Arab Republic	230,164,836	19,471,324	21,644,824	6,841,771	3,072,304
Taiwan	25,932,497,638	24,337,097,719	25,522,769,412	26,667,368,300	25,860,086,344

Table B-21.   U.S. Exports of Total Merchandise to Individual Countries by Harmonized System, 2005–2015—*Continued*

Region	2005	2006	2007	2008	2009	2010
Tajikistan	28,786,700	43,090,408	52,685,573	51,428,157	41,171,507	57,013,199
Tanzania; United Republic of	96,443,910	160,673,885	173,961,966	169,325,571	157,948,337	163,499,769
Thailand	7,256,616,259	7,915,383,466	8,336,419,189	9,066,556,735	6,918,398,273	8,976,381,744
Togo	27,928,388	108,427,734	287,594,314	117,125,699	124,798,314	157,620,745
Tokelau Islands	79,822,527	44,750,446	55,422,404	39,335,534	12,926,185	3,938,459
Tonga	9,685,131	10,537,182	13,233,104	13,730,360	12,942,138	20,678,902
Trinidad and Tobago	1,416,748,479	1,614,598,036	1,779,841,581	2,250,213,184	1,988,348,722	1,924,931,875
Tunisia	261,166,520	362,970,070	402,999,020	502,430,863	501,332,614	572,780,850
Turkey	4,238,966,194	5,291,178,158	6,498,756,060	9,958,671,254	7,094,632,437	10,538,481,925
Turkmenistan	215,170,092	112,840,364	127,290,102	59,705,800	293,658,852	39,965,764
Turks and Caicos Islands	237,752,693	365,682,812	395,783,826	434,413,482	247,865,657	189,434,305
Tuvalu	42,460	64,290	51,512	130,423	151,784	620,945
Uganda	62,573,652	50,551,989	80,348,803	88,525,002	119,061,119	93,513,814
Ukraine	532,954,308	756,245,355	1,342,099,159	1,868,037,332	886,859,797	1,348,816,161
United Arab Emirates	8,119,527,357	10,277,016,479	10,786,648,688	14,417,398,443	12,210,863,357	11,662,455,901
United Kingdom	38,568,083,046	45,410,106,533	49,981,491,297	53,599,069,711	45,703,598,254	48,410,311,047
Uruguay	356,676,188	482,235,804	640,772,589	893,056,253	745,087,443	975,277,447
Uzbekistan	73,826,609	53,894,688	88,754,314	300,659,063	97,536,884	101,148,237
Vanuatu	9,138,578	9,059,099	23,948,479	63,755,418	3,903,181	18,940,232
Vatican City	24,181,227	12,037,913	18,266,111	9,275,122	7,351,678	3,193,465
Venezuela	6,420,897,723	9,002,343,708	10,200,506,826	12,610,041,006	9,315,456,954	10,644,795,910
Vietnam	1,193,152,202	1,100,283,809	1,903,057,411	2,789,448,762	3,097,194,382	3,705,548,752
Wallis and Futuna	408,737	178,050	212,545	706,910	535,497	778,132
West Bank	3,720,993	2,272,497	13,009,291	290,252	620,793	714,402
Western Sahara	28,656	16,063	344,442	91,132	158,569	53,902
Yemen	219,048,520	254,925,318	642,086,903	401,463,803	381,131,640	397,765,730
Zambia	29,113,109	51,633,652	69,394,927	78,704,324	57,273,292	56,415,126
Zimbabwe	45,540,976	47,583,947	105,250,099	92,874,918	85,459,651	67,565,121

Table B-21.   U.S. Exports of Total Merchandise to Individual Countries by Harmonized System, 2005–2015—*Continued*

Region	2011	2012	2013	2014	2015
Tajikistan	178,246,296	54,186,972	51,874,112	24,503,388	18,985,373
Tanzania; United Republic of	260,183,381	245,389,981	411,953,494	302,121,378	172,803,054
Thailand	10,929,873,027	10,887,802,586	11,797,010,707	11,817,244,742	11,230,569,735
Togo	209,689,039	370,550,165	1,007,500,845	1,024,635,368	311,819,809
Tokelau Islands	4,886,393	13,422,094	828,055	1,387,753	341,222
Tonga	19,269,574	26,892,624	19,238,838	20,031,820	13,817,538
Trinidad and Tobago	2,185,137,885	2,477,825,749	2,408,396,126	2,411,333,836	2,511,195,111
Tunisia	597,007,683	614,865,677	907,186,423	831,395,799	602,412,017
Turkey	14,695,214,372	12,474,727,209	12,078,652,726	11,650,864,328	9,502,498,123
Turkmenistan	70,967,048	92,019,532	261,778,552	455,524,961	80,839,805
Turks and Caicos Islands	204,953,122	209,629,786	225,789,558	281,886,815	279,728,597
Tuvalu	724,161	612,146	560,260	591,900	625,636
Uganda	94,038,056	100,125,293	122,740,389	78,262,341	88,315,069
Ukraine	2,138,824,978	1,936,270,509	1,924,811,744	1,239,060,772	862,088,348
United Arab Emirates	15,921,629,417	22,559,108,724	24,476,064,517	22,111,102,161	23,003,595,617
United Kingdom	56,033,108,347	54,860,484,359	47,361,236,230	53,848,331,596	56,114,618,863
Uruguay	1,258,319,413	1,359,476,870	1,754,607,247	1,606,543,390	1,295,148,749
Uzbekistan	102,560,932	284,611,052	356,435,025	212,945,403	137,962,928
Vanuatu	5,152,275	99,515,739	34,439,495	21,196,729	5,867,876
Vatican City	2,291,281	4,803,261	2,467,299	2,573,365	2,226,547
Venezuela	12,383,426,246	17,516,968,263	13,200,529,914	11,178,357,542	8,345,880,233
Vietnam	4,315,220,420	4,622,882,579	5,036,763,709	5,732,857,578	7,087,524,038
Wallis and Futuna	338,897	602,240	637,535	350,213	376,841
West Bank	1,145,816	1,521,509	894,527	1,755,072	903,282
Western Sahara	31,131	58,850	156,076	276,987	32,113
Yemen	389,745,032	469,466,337	518,251,949	368,876,623	158,039,977
Zambia	129,784,635	146,788,830	141,148,845	114,121,914	84,170,835
Zimbabwe	61,598,378	53,478,276	60,513,567	48,706,474	37,834,783

Table B-22.   U.S. Imports of Total Merchandise from Individual Countries by Harmonized System, 2005–2015

Region	2005	2006	2007	2008	2009	2010
WORLD	1,673,454,520,539	1,853,938,475,270	1,956,961,843,348	2,103,640,710,944	1,559,624,813,477	1,913,856,594,014
Afghanistan............................	67,310,191	45,293,754	74,368,065	84,666,855	116,092,967	85,253,641
Albania.................................	37,188,750	23,945,633	9,523,939	11,777,887	15,000,411	30,338,282
Algeria.................................	10,446,437,854	15,455,929,235	17,816,053,966	19,354,781,015	10,717,809,142	14,517,955,926
Andorra................................	673,148	2,724,343	438,421	871,819	528,376	475,977
Angola.................................	8,484,361,601	11,719,163,853	12,507,550,363	18,911,308,184	9,338,889,049	11,939,571,874
Anguilla...............................	3,754,737	4,188,938	4,589,017	4,336,094	5,745,072	2,546,333
Antigua and Barbuda................	4,414,365	5,770,840	8,735,511	4,867,521	9,333,195	5,491,328
Argentina	4,583,613,305	3,978,988,520	4,486,947,482	5,822,064,180	3,890,111,947	3,802,754,172
Armenia	46,191,425	46,488,110	33,060,289	42,676,252	77,590,356	75,477,021
Aruba	2,919,735,672	2,845,053,832	2,995,192,708	3,179,303,327	1,278,245,242	19,460,603
Australia..............................	7,342,178,950	8,204,002,398	8,615,018,556	10,588,812,772	8,011,502,299	8,582,910,903
Austria................................	6,102,944,725	8,304,346,256	10,668,880,036	8,457,019,639	6,378,561,635	6,835,322,637
Azerbaijan............................	45,361,225	716,145,853	1,887,358,487	4,360,907,679	1,972,636,461	1,988,547,744
Bahamas..............................	699,936,003	452,601,512	503,859,964	604,428,019	819,113,140	814,579,673
Bahrain................................	431,611,920	632,424,578	624,570,829	538,890,134	463,484,140	420,269,926
Bangladesh...........................	2,693,035,035	3,271,396,005	3,432,080,304	3,748,440,438	3,698,952,442	4,293,920,187
Barbados..............................	31,903,789	33,858,237	38,224,494	40,431,470	32,755,594	42,813,787
Belarus................................	345,161,433	539,135,748	1,033,063,515	1,069,859,689	573,882,418	174,532,251
Belgium...............................	13,022,902,740	14,405,413,443	15,281,179,930	17,308,063,970	13,825,678,762	15,551,880,550
Belize	98,265,102	146,896,012	105,015,575	153,998,548	99,551,376	120,183,702
Benin..................................	513,184	555,323	5,076,221	31,009,581	441,150	275,757
Bermuda..............................	87,276,753	16,130,711	23,713,200	140,059,938	13,004,671	22,450,895
Bhutan................................	615,516	1,067,423	817,401	421,120	207,222	390,840
Bolivia................................	293,216,045	362,382,227	362,586,543	510,958,430	504,460,133	680,157,819
Bosnia and Herzegovina.............	70,462,111	25,677,328	25,137,125	24,685,922	24,902,511	25,578,376
Botswana.............................	178,164,424	252,107,311	187,452,919	218,844,659	131,917,315	169,719,159
Brazil..................................	24,435,519,379	26,366,725,360	25,644,187,123	30,452,944,177	20,069,606,594	23,958,063,867
British Indian Ocean Territory	432,984	812,486	40,046	2,094,822	386,483	1,445,793
British Virgin Islands.................	33,579,607	25,885,608	43,059,852	10,754,411	6,041,920	19,032,108
Brunei.................................	562,742,346	550,147,536	404,567,281	114,252,920	41,579,781	11,874,902
Bulgaria...............................	454,262,612	458,198,843	426,091,585	390,755,028	228,005,426	259,660,260
Burkina Faso	2,084,203	1,019,743	1,466,370	584,724	2,116,452	2,378,915
Burma (Myanmar).....................	61,500	9,023	0	0	85,916	0
Burundi................................	4,423,229	1,865,823	1,111,160	2,842,780	4,082,268	3,351,556
Cote d'Ivoire..........................	1,197,975,160	701,643,464	600,126,497	1,091,621,084	744,787,235	1,176,742,074
Cambodia.............................	1,766,956,953	2,188,371,822	2,463,411,371	2,411,519,446	1,924,195,847	2,300,843,207
Cameroon.............................	158,161,864	273,306,894	297,256,563	614,041,521	249,733,020	297,061,683
Canada................................	290,384,293,155	302,437,859,257	317,056,762,618	339,491,425,363	226,248,448,986	277,636,732,987
Cape Verde	2,624,250	964,765	2,154,559	396,525	805,514	1,417,882
Cayman Islands.......................	53,497,875	14,870,360	21,402,499	14,011,520	13,576,016	11,119,266
Central African Republic..............	5,696,947	4,295,135	2,875,393	8,586,942	3,387,792	5,715,349
Chad...................................	1,498,086,294	1,917,967,195	2,145,358,641	3,334,330,745	1,984,050,440	2,044,099,705
Chile...................................	6,664,333,836	9,565,127,122	8,998,792,694	8,195,971,599	5,949,252,719	7,017,465,154
China..................................	243,470,104,795	287,774,352,612	321,442,866,934	337,772,627,823	296,373,883,488	364,952,633,595
Christmas Island......................	417,613	449,912	4,254,781	2,114,328	759,873	575,321
Cocos (Keeling) Islands	484,315	1,459,999	880,872	1,164,273	784,771	2,146,102
Colombia..............................	8,849,380,048	9,265,683,816	9,433,589,380	13,093,204,502	11,323,117,375	15,659,297,836
Comoros...............................	1,447,044	1,525,685	543,278	934,367	1,079,254	1,674,306
Congo..................................	1,622,901,540	3,097,196,829	3,070,660,832	5,073,722,883	3,104,966,371	3,316,007,911
Cook Islands	1,744,825	2,097,762	1,714,838	1,122,284	939,877	1,802,376
Costa Rica.............................	3,415,279,262	3,844,142,053	3,941,540,359	3,938,067,781	5,611,644,252	8,697,340,843
Croatia	364,277,603	353,190,168	331,779,414	270,743,003	250,740,454	335,880,075
Cuba...................................	0,070	143,654	262,151	39,126	20,534	347,081
Curacao...............................	0	0	0	0	0	0
Cyprus.................................	30,536,194	51,417,565	16,731,899	13,821,202	53,048,698	11,127,856
Czech Republic	2,192,863,031	2,349,148,106	2,430,571,465	2,568,678,718	1,933,356,631	2,450,064,527
Democratic Republic of Congo	263,558,216	85,110,567	206,450,730	266,185,350	330,509,461	527,634,392
Denmark...............................	5,144,201,650	5,540,100,620	6,064,385,266	6,446,407,831	5,510,513,708	6,011,905,061
Djibouti................................	1,101,206	3,295,217	4,484,550	7,037,833	2,902,314	2,993,096
Dominica..............................	3,344,243	3,148,318	1,757,969	2,356,831	2,754,139	1,595,534
Dominican Republic...................	4,603,684,143	4,532,378,534	4,215,643,656	3,977,827,623	3,329,451,899	3,671,724,506
East Germany..........................	0	0	0	0	0	0
East Timor.............................	84,963	11,996	322,548	23,548	66,821	0
Ecuador...............................	5,758,679,346	7,093,850,766	6,134,999,496	9,048,410,960	5,272,566,301	7,451,049,426
Egypt..................................	2,091,236,887	2,395,831,868	2,376,708,563	2,370,437,872	2,057,713,620	2,238,217,595
El Salvador............................	1,988,765,718	1,856,821,932	2,043,503,686	2,227,975,732	1,821,807,070	2,205,710,607
Equatorial Guinea.....................	1,561,137,497	1,732,968,500	1,776,930,965	3,367,281,138	2,489,126,608	2,213,646,595
Eritrea.................................	1,269,401	857,625	431,242	128,803	525,325	102,265
Estonia................................	511,379,949	526,251,180	296,183,003	392,082,830	162,214,764	697,510,943

Table B-22. U.S. Imports of Total Merchandise from Individual Countries by Harmonized System, 2005–2015—*Continued*

Region	2011	2012	2013	2014	2015
WORLD	2,207,954,346,316	2,276,267,147,199	2,267,986,733,622	2,356,365,502,725	2,248,232,395,233
Afghanistan..............................	26,139,389	36,765,072	45,514,058	74,496,178	23,454,045
Albania....................................	26,413,904	18,856,919	22,776,586	69,128,617	160,081,219
Algeria....................................	14,609,285,365	9,993,334,569	4,830,871,545	4,628,902,129	3,371,552,526
Andorra...................................	616,323	428,818	1,428,673	1,277,355	4,863,157
Angola....................................	13,597,473,429	9,823,874,266	8,742,942,417	5,719,811,538	2,806,494,883
Anguilla...................................	4,831,620	3,574,428	4,033,764	5,371,372	5,583,883
Antigua and Barbuda.................	6,581,579	9,640,118	9,606,755	7,922,209	6,856,395
Argentina................................	4,502,877,176	4,350,419,991	4,642,343,655	4,246,388,507	3,950,849,545
Armenia...................................	92,578,996	88,627,517	101,310,071	96,351,624	62,463,490
Aruba......................................	3,261,601,728	826,772,869	41,861,658	60,400,731	54,901,850
Australia..................................	10,242,853,389	9,566,806,259	9,272,561,327	10,697,338,973	10,894,021,864
Austria....................................	9,482,732,806	9,449,154,334	9,780,427,617	10,828,084,724	11,311,975,057
Azerbaijan...............................	2,424,516,997	1,094,919,275	1,136,157,099	1,011,918,275	507,148,173
Bahamas.................................	764,809,491	563,095,391	598,974,355	532,365,055	452,744,256
Bahrain....................................	518,411,567	701,016,392	635,587,426	965,337,016	902,425,581
Bangladesh..............................	4,877,104,938	4,915,569,502	5,351,935,923	5,277,214,429	5,991,251,839
Barbados.................................	46,467,359	54,133,580	55,394,266	51,380,076	68,174,291
Belarus....................................	362,531,886	153,440,844	104,894,811	131,685,319	158,249,733
Belgium...................................	17,431,303,419	17,367,885,511	19,010,319,465	20,962,039,751	19,482,272,633
Belize......................................	190,538,867	161,832,100	127,133,488	96,894,017	75,287,339
Benin......................................	1,970,887	2,673,580	3,128,498	5,424,728	4,944,880
Bermuda..................................	59,942,887	83,778,187	60,841,182	37,045,792	108,704,684
Bhutan....................................	518,691	568,747	538,582	311,899	3,398,158
Bolivia.....................................	901,535,776	1,682,336,183	1,251,602,202	1,934,935,040	1,006,481,438
Bosnia and Herzegovina............	49,691,067	51,579,899	57,733,704	84,087,459	78,282,267
Botswana.................................	293,169,506	221,039,055	277,714,441	317,998,575	211,913,954
Brazil......................................	31,736,521,991	32,123,378,693	27,541,199,001	30,021,032,794	27,468,230,316
British Indian Ocean Territory ...	5,912,974	19,452,854	17,739,892	13,986,140	15,818,366
British Virgin Islands.................	6,334,475	13,451,702	6,364,423	10,901,347	16,491,398
Brunei.....................................	23,414,888	86,299,780	17,184,938	31,874,542	19,402,766
Bulgaria...................................	415,736,901	509,430,226	513,729,166	608,220,555	597,694,693
Burkina Faso	3,605,288	2,303,644	6,108,975	6,229,952	3,592,979
Burma (Myanmar).....................	0	38,000	29,909,357	92,909,292	143,796,881
Burundi...................................	9,558,071	4,809,555	4,297,467	4,376,909	8,427,001
Cote d'Ivoire............................	1,270,636,148	1,099,495,980	1,013,449,247	1,192,531,008	1,027,885,570
Cambodia.................................	2,712,425,319	2,691,552,267	2,771,118,393	2,847,843,090	3,025,433,126
Cameroon................................	330,391,692	308,251,590	366,962,437	186,395,221	132,053,379
Canada....................................	315,324,753,291	324,263,012,583	332,503,645,324	349,277,843,644	296,155,598,992
Cape Verde..............................	1,467,584	3,966,021	2,356,117	1,730,090	2,219,050
Cayman Islands........................	18,506,138	15,050,708	32,472,988	24,337,353	97,496,341
Central African Republic............	5,998,567	4,070,088	2,787,401	1,364,570	3,124,670
Chad.......................................	3,174,028,680	2,660,336,285	2,459,150,663	2,328,580,839	1,303,322,183
Chile.......................................	9,076,034,955	9,366,566,426	10,384,687,850	9,479,430,152	8,772,414,027
China......................................	399,371,232,631	425,619,082,637	440,430,019,592	468,483,943,748	483,244,701,922
Christmas Island......................	1,481,051	492,828	1,037,150	2,334,007	2,120,840
Cocos (Keeling) Islands	1,511,838	975,730	1,027,873	3,177,044	3,809,085
Colombia.................................	23,114,211,762	24,621,667,665	21,626,226,647	18,315,926,813	14,074,816,613
Comoros..................................	1,778,891	1,959,039	2,843,049	2,085,628	1,211,821
Congo	2,420,086,749	1,488,475,391	1,166,601,446	424,266,780	304,303,884
Cook Islands	743,930	1,384,083	410,214	749,781	847,880
Costa Rica...............................	10,115,304,799	12,046,097,770	11,914,159,665	9,516,341,445	4,488,341,429
Croatia....................................	437,959,216	444,051,930	425,098,141	463,537,275	576,891,578
Cuba.......................................	5,625	94,355	0	0	0
Curacao...................................	557,820,793	850,195,262	401,554,297	369,310,941	335,229,109
Cyprus....................................	20,777,398	29,358,126	43,516,731	64,227,005	31,988,220
Czech Republic	3,344,147,441	3,930,627,396	3,922,921,802	4,403,473,200	4,497,634,904
Democratic Republic of Congo ...	605,570,262	40,992,382	75,559,485	154,450,323	153,738,045
Denmark..................................	6,760,153,719	6,777,117,904	6,494,360,492	7,534,436,140	7,760,022,813
Djibouti...................................	4,053,092	11,849,636	3,948,158	11,884,284	35,463,684
Dominica.................................	1,873,524	1,744,607	2,622,948	1,543,334	1,683,203
Dominican Republic..................	4,198,735,888	4,370,378,862	4,261,021,154	4,528,320,497	4,665,266,745
East Germany..........................	0	0	0	0	0
East Timor...............................	26,502	97,608	116,241	186,888	3,302,038
Ecuador...................................	9,622,290,751	9,484,411,908	11,491,157,685	10,869,429,986	7,467,258,698
Egypt......................................	2,058,680,312	3,000,102,332	1,614,573,961	1,411,081,466	1,405,853,699
El Salvador..............................	2,484,612,208	2,587,563,480	2,437,350,911	2,397,754,497	2,531,699,424
Equatorial Guinea.....................	1,190,780,854	1,699,803,812	897,998,983	255,000,849	163,143,050
Eritrea	140,467	199,965	157,595	107,505	106,871
Estonia....................................	962,254,679	506,541,064	422,575,859	564,953,941	503,500,720

Table B-22. U.S. Imports of Total Merchandise from Individual Countries by Harmonized System, 2005–2015—*Continued*

Region	2005	2006	2007	2008	2009	2010
Ethiopia	61,802,253	81,120,441	88,235,597	152,242,646	112,911,249	127,946,985
Falkland Islands (Malvinas)	9,261,546	12,236,875	4,853,273	7,266,821	8,305,197	5,431,691
Faroe Islands	4,276,273	4,098,846	7,072,763	16,039,178	61,779,802	72,309,799
Fiji	169,460,711	145,801,077	152,828,046	161,812,713	144,110,991	179,101,070
Finland	4,341,679,942	4,973,872,821	5,266,161,796	5,903,287,905	3,985,288,638	3,883,667,052
France	33,842,057,513	37,039,631,721	41,552,711,122	44,049,335,702	34,236,042,957	38,355,493,121
French Guiana	121,285	618,231	411,063	134,761	68,802	133,666
French Polynesia	60,124,235	58,097,854	62,225,745	72,363,757	29,274,435	52,864,206
French Southern Territories	51,640	98,404	552,580	526,012	122,788	22,095
Gabon	2,815,602,273	1,361,208,300	2,181,807,539	2,278,515,032	1,230,680,274	2,211,988,341
Gambia	427,153	286,817	148,308	641,418	1,213,545	3,136,988
Gaza Strip	1,443,661	805,535	1,456,718	2,282,712	5,289,434	3,182,665
Georgia	194,384,289	105,311,524	211,585,252	207,770,072	69,629,625	197,764,440
Germany	84,750,871,375	89,082,049,315	94,164,095,641	97,496,573,724	71,498,154,314	82,450,411,862
Ghana	158,409,617	192,183,281	198,817,253	222,167,657	134,997,139	273,398,451
Gibraltar	4,637,081	859,141	3,165,841	1,418,323	899,971	670,853
Greece	883,730,160	965,663,603	1,191,929,880	998,938,070	840,548,792	797,874,265
Greenland	17,255,599	10,350,546	9,927,092	6,104,898	7,563,517	8,293,926
Grenada	5,852,881	4,467,434	8,206,011	7,272,382	5,753,262	7,703,868
Guadeloupe	2,128,806	2,506,335	4,884,629	7,026,454	1,821,270	2,331,647
Guatemala	3,137,382,263	3,102,282,088	3,026,095,015	3,462,740,635	3,147,541,215	3,522,648,526
Guinea	74,733,573	93,930,743	99,153,784	106,404,893	67,270,175	68,527,476
Guinea Bissau	120,677	338,085	37,610	164,029	43,305	884,909
Guyana	119,931,261	125,296,756	123,376,969	145,829,091	173,205,470	298,628,416
Haiti	447,217,315	496,110,980	487,767,116	450,082,545	552,090,736	550,910,491
Heard Island and Mcdonald Islands	16,396	38,217	24,916	9,899	0	4,269
Honduras	3,749,243,099	3,717,498,062	3,912,104,025	4,041,228,449	3,319,283,433	3,932,993,035
Hong Kong	8,891,705,575	7,946,676,159	7,025,987,746	6,483,377,493	3,570,904,821	4,296,396,722
Hungary	2,561,172,978	2,584,325,846	2,827,524,521	3,102,759,935	2,223,435,499	2,491,186,229
Iceland	268,975,080	227,534,467	205,735,006	240,697,731	179,146,449	201,249,833
India	18,804,169,654	21,830,821,397	24,073,264,282	25,704,382,575	21,165,965,968	29,532,939,005
Indonesia	12,014,344,185	13,424,717,182	14,301,257,157	15,799,137,766	12,938,589,076	16,478,339,564
Iran	174,457,417	157,240,649	173,133,194	104,144,319	64,646,665	94,506,447
Iraq	9,053,695,686	11,545,825,685	11,395,568,898	22,079,805,295	9,263,280,814	12,143,262,688
Ireland	28,733,080,261	28,525,854,060	30,445,040,335	31,346,482,641	28,100,577,524	33,848,028,367
Israel	16,830,466,084	19,166,757,799	20,794,413,214	22,335,834,788	18,744,356,591	20,984,760,291
Italy	31,009,260,076	32,655,070,514	35,027,629,526	36,134,975,141	26,429,788,240	28,513,642,243
Jamaica	375,572,360	528,131,242	720,445,231	728,687,455	467,581,232	327,666,670
Japan	138,003,696,155	148,180,775,579	145,463,342,556	139,262,197,032	95,803,683,368	120,552,145,178
Jordan	1,266,849,860	1,422,068,471	1,328,914,662	1,137,458,858	924,088,226	974,122,585
Kazakhstan	1,101,145,431	960,627,787	1,251,503,224	1,603,386,006	1,543,537,843	1,872,411,829
Kenya	348,019,269	353,721,039	325,447,863	343,540,589	280,609,385	311,136,246
Kiribati	1,104,581	1,345,733	1,233,086	946,915	1,144,010	1,023,175
Kosovo	0	0	0	0	395,928	88,658
Kuwait	4,334,781,445	3,980,900,848	4,118,456,968	7,092,985,034	3,782,559,318	5,382,010,083
Kyrgyzstan	4,618,689	4,248,627	1,721,981	2,466,402	5,971,943	3,895,147
Lao People's Democratic Republic	4,166,156	8,697,185	19,997,151	42,446,674	43,401,655	59,099,362
Latvia	362,159,252	298,883,391	334,023,954	228,344,241	141,548,432	193,058,351
Lebanon	86,370,988	89,107,629	103,950,267	99,079,277	77,000,214	83,904,473
Lesotho	403,608,048	408,447,438	443,057,819	374,135,753	304,155,340	298,925,947
Liberia	90,827,263	139,934,121	115,201,403	143,461,589	80,390,237	180,010,405
Libyan Arab Jamahiriya	1,590,341,099	2,472,203,907	3,385,227,538	4,178,646,777	1,918,502,226	2,116,835,644
Liechtenstein	295,705,721	324,308,659	284,248,520	244,930,126	179,598,084	212,606,128
Lithuania	000,010,040	570,100,607	455,654,511	750,038,947	589,906,213	637,292,834
Luxembourg	388,834,493	534,089,083	526,213,489	536,134,661	442,865,412	450,693,951
Macau; SAR of China	1,249,022,120	1,229,876,811	1,095,104,484	915,398,213	237,151,881	141,095,010
Macedonia	48,149,502	42,228,712	72,644,690	77,725,385	44,320,386	37,037,254
Madagascar	323,631,165	281,134,442	337,938,081	324,334,881	253,404,445	108,403,236
Malawi	115,501,920	59,452,071	59,232,709	64,942,475	63,312,308	71,659,198
Malaysia	33,685,159,566	36,533,140,829	32,628,505,447	30,736,075,258	23,282,618,764	25,900,949,586
Maldives	5,496,456	1,498,697	2,022,387	3,591,362	2,885,616	1,597,413
Mali	3,649,953	8,039,348	9,461,812	5,128,880	3,736,022	6,305,215
Malta	282,653,662	370,722,942	328,664,457	278,647,712	218,525,377	261,826,487
Marshall Islands	17,205,126	14,440,107	11,707,788	19,254,641	13,648,213	11,819,682
Martinique	22,236,488	41,498,728	7,437,223	7,683,545	5,015,880	23,104,906
Mauritania	825,319	51,165,461	722,494	46,285,098	34,742,280	52,863,815
Mauritius	221,850,710	218,859,513	187,327,814	176,373,383	168,876,583	196,352,208
Mayotte	0	13,909	306,667	15,832	49,784	60,899
Mexico	170,108,614,084	198,253,159,036	210,713,966,788	215,941,618,934	176,654,372,581	229,985,623,006
Micronesia (Federated States of)	1,557,731	885,433	4,069,289	3,552,450	2,918,034	4,217,798

Table B-22. U.S. Imports of Total Merchandise from Individual Countries by Harmonized System, 2005–2015—Continued

Region	2011	2012	2013	2014	2015
Ethiopia	144,417,834	183,126,469	193,566,884	207,209,040	310,269,077
Falkland Islands (Malvinas)	6,895,485	11,210,967	13,623,943	19,667,827	14,273,948
Faroe Islands	105,951,574	72,626,589	126,272,024	138,082,047	97,897,991
Fiji	131,547,088	188,656,541	174,044,279	183,816,833	202,639,037
Finland	4,435,635,510	5,109,658,449	4,653,190,718	5,035,354,531	4,506,071,121
France	40,049,048,317	41,646,128,474	45,706,316,280	47,105,506,372	47,815,322,855
French Guiana	4,009,505	564,759	536,102	449,257	42,924
French Polynesia	54,031,076	59,411,496	36,492,874	40,363,119	43,030,557
French Southern Territories	36,544	28,659	186,269	519,437	13,953
Gabon	4,566,651,306	1,885,875,183	1,112,280,961	798,012,548	337,024,529
Gambia	82,442	351,843	1,686,367	311,792	896,754
Gaza Strip	2,917,763	315,468	450,493	196,409	12,534
Georgia	176,050,965	226,106,387	174,956,473	409,245,333	181,150,349
Germany	98,684,337,899	109,225,772,833	114,341,899,964	124,178,880,135	124,820,469,226
Ghana	779,001,271	291,433,200	365,840,155	271,956,983	309,367,660
Gibraltar	1,095,259	581,807	230,263	234,714	1,824,420
Greece	865,444,211	986,934,224	954,238,447	1,050,046,647	1,356,447,796
Greenland	7,486,174	6,753,866	9,440,170	5,470,118	3,800,273
Grenada	6,725,081	8,389,248	9,477,049	9,838,143	9,215,032
Guadeloupe	1,495,386	12,079,850	6,020,554	3,035,805	4,123,528
Guatemala	4,713,979,911	4,491,426,314	4,171,493,471	4,217,985,390	4,120,351,959
Guinea	80,662,565	103,058,967	98,965,928	86,298,531	79,616,516
Guinea Bissau	261,369	80,618	3,221,196	63,906	51,840
Guyana	424,540,486	522,973,550	466,372,129	501,387,960	431,099,884
Haiti	742,179,942	774,736,792	847,053,529	908,360,961	950,091,535
Heard Island and Mcdonald Islands	3,623	38,993	125	35,052	6,734
Honduras	4,500,958,709	4,647,809,134	4,543,138,877	4,645,946,578	4,755,934,545
Hong Kong	4,409,573,508	5,455,567,220	5,654,088,352	5,897,204,232	6,795,630,644
Hungary	2,948,676,937	3,201,285,721	3,767,870,817	5,331,552,627	5,721,266,311
Iceland	215,744,480	283,735,298	291,301,637	300,304,111	316,534,176
India	36,154,495,638	40,512,644,038	41,809,988,752	45,354,940,572	44,791,644,051
Indonesia	19,110,896,131	18,002,185,532	18,871,609,478	19,390,119,974	19,601,548,138
Iran	1,005,187	2,113,550	2,208,518	0	10,766,314
Iraq	16,959,778,626	19,265,352,919	13,305,738,476	13,827,118,618	4,353,472,677
Ireland	39,370,514,699	33,372,378,546	31,496,458,639	33,987,627,387	39,336,180,666
Israel	23,046,606,761	22,131,110,384	22,783,313,674	23,006,982,519	24,477,021,606
Italy	33,973,740,824	36,964,764,394	38,708,799,040	42,376,832,909	44,159,011,544
Jamaica	566,089,945	507,205,331	414,493,158	285,559,719	305,978,402
Japan	128,927,889,476	146,431,693,012	138,575,341,868	134,504,798,252	131,364,147,642
Jordan	1,060,516,505	1,155,531,816	1,197,255,973	1,401,342,767	1,491,618,691
Kazakhstan	1,679,301,906	1,564,968,259	1,421,402,621	1,410,792,766	816,099,815
Kenya	381,554,799	389,495,963	452,257,030	591,328,595	573,095,415
Kiribati	645,508	596,252	1,020,432	2,624,652	2,728,752
Kosovo	314,289	258,815	482,251	586,419	2,382,980
Kuwait	7,808,733,355	13,020,902,287	12,636,911,189	11,437,050,349	4,684,750,276
Kyrgyzstan	2,661,048	9,250,595	3,524,577	2,389,568	15,803,561
Lao People's Democratic Republic	58,852,777	25,043,011	30,513,983	32,996,472	45,189,001
Latvia	362,570,780	246,245,171	272,668,880	275,708,381	302,969,587
Lebanon	79,331,843	81,186,790	91,831,158	72,392,482	93,219,618
Lesotho	384,351,086	310,571,285	351,402,897	361,096,067	331,955,607
Liberia	158,180,247	144,013,452	96,532,769	83,394,462	44,940,717
Libyan Arab Jamahiriya	645,010,462	2,493,042,856	2,558,215,497	224,791,106	155,103,895
Liechtenstein	250,459,224	310,233,206	296,907,020	301,587,784	310,294,941
Lithuania	1,044,429,765	1,176,204,744	1,554,352,566	1,095,561,652	1,059,366,349
Luxembourg	495,112,965	553,224,144	641,150,152	757,172,367	639,038,795
Macau; SAR of China	113,087,899	94,934,494	94,596,746	74,703,801	121,919,528
Macedonia	52,489,815	86,760,394	62,030,010	167,315,162	203,357,353
Madagascar	87,130,577	109,876,814	179,763,551	215,955,747	319,783,011
Malawi	64,923,258	65,958,496	73,103,263	66,590,802	61,395,881
Malaysia	25,776,851,224	25,934,755,355	27,288,735,020	30,563,909,147	33,970,678,717
Maldives	2,880,675	17,616,884	20,313,347	23,190,355	21,737,873
Mali	4,078,609	3,643,750	3,680,149	4,841,000	4,504,283
Malta	244,060,459	255,004,291	212,093,419	174,241,773	241,219,869
Marshall Islands	14,938,789	18,947,235	16,965,963	14,479,142	29,067,047
Martinique	8,016,881	26,271,600	42,697,632	82,244,086	37,462,780
Mauritania	965,142	694,097	130,690,363	101,407,714	1,173,847
Mauritius	251,707,228	260,205,159	338,728,474	401,743,054	395,664,813
Mayotte	19,440	23,726	16,629	29,482	95,927
Mexico	262,873,595,958	277,593,639,546	280,556,040,242	295,739,481,074	296,407,901,065
Micronesia (Federated States of)	1,601,894	903,581	1,786,725	411,788	717,108

Table B-22. **U.S. Imports of Total Merchandise from Individual Countries by Harmonized System, 2005–2015**—*Continued*

Region	2005	2006	2007	2008	2009	2010
Moldova; Republic of	50,224,656	37,239,885	23,152,774	12,231,382	8,158,191	12,454,182
Monaco	37,485,881	31,613,736	21,409,669	22,262,090	38,711,264	24,491,047
Mongolia	143,645,404	113,862,404	83,494,478	52,783,141	14,809,669	11,555,218
Montenegro	0	0	5,364,015	467,110	16,634,009	3,947,306
Montserrat	953,906	792,966	553,644	229,826	869,051	514,359
Morocco	445,793,996	521,362,592	609,943,212	878,729,037	468,006,756	685,506,959
Mozambique	11,905,754	15,552,128	5,356,081	16,800,054	38,828,980	64,703,630
Namibia	129,590,672	115,802,611	219,690,700	301,248,671	328,590,093	195,144,043
Nauru	148,786	274,006	586,353	744,456	122,125	219,538
Nepal	111,212,077	99,427,883	89,943,562	84,900,738	54,722,162	60,515,370
Netherlands	14,862,041,511	17,342,261,801	18,403,138,184	21,122,912,325	16,098,460,471	19,055,457,711
Netherlands Antilles	922,413,941	1,119,301,627	781,853,927	809,311,163	475,840,675	1,026,183,628
New Caledonia	27,174,251	50,625,314	79,374,872	50,197,152	26,974,705	70,572,190
New Zealand	3,155,239,797	3,116,449,805	3,113,359,020	3,170,814,654	2,557,737,340	2,763,541,420
Nicaragua	1,180,787,602	1,526,005,860	1,603,506,406	1,703,594,149	1,612,420,986	2,007,563,561
Niger	65,513,390	123,747,286	9,557,150	44,331,439	106,262,402	26,516,420
Nigeria	24,239,356,731	27,863,119,324	32,770,232,230	38,068,007,014	19,128,179,390	30,515,949,850
Niue	138,878	73,373	397,357	75,716	21,638	31,904
Norfolk Island	173,150	139,729	391,107	34,049	543,227	9,925
North Korea	3,252	0	0	0	0	8,363
Norway	6,776,308,920	7,085,306,498	7,317,730,173	7,315,139,310	5,688,164,538	6,950,265,655
Oman	555,043,525	908,656,031	1,040,928,311	851,859,901	907,419,777	773,329,575
Other Countries	0	0	0	0	0	0
Pakistan	3,253,181,975	3,672,222,686	3,577,641,329	3,591,062,421	3,162,815,294	3,509,067,320
Palau	484,544	605,190	386,279	1,138,245	79,590	148,035
Panama	327,060,069	378,687,851	365,172,576	379,057,193	302,296,683	380,982,072
Papua New Guinea	58,451,246	83,700,225	108,515,622	105,578,627	102,931,047	96,678,304
Paraguay	51,645,596	58,038,901	67,969,086	78,403,962	56,405,447	62,138,779
Peru	5,119,155,770	5,880,385,320	5,271,605,833	5,812,452,843	4,223,312,297	5,243,307,323
Philippines	9,250,433,389	9,694,336,645	9,408,192,993	8,713,326,770	6,794,098,806	7,982,003,448
Pitcairn Islands	1,040,512	105,307	88,716	8,160	25,973	4,083
Poland	1,948,586,250	2,252,580,826	2,226,011,699	2,586,896,169	2,038,060,569	2,963,740,384
Portugal	2,328,674,933	3,060,090,808	3,049,347,631	2,451,436,100	1,577,117,726	2,141,532,920
Qatar	447,861,094	261,781,556	477,129,376	484,253,815	505,763,117	466,353,652
Reunion	5,835,528	7,005,406	3,393,874	3,323,432	8,465,902	9,274,545
Romania	1,207,584,718	1,118,958,893	1,054,374,999	1,106,678,028	751,593,550	1,007,798,236
Russian Federation	15,306,673,835	19,828,297,722	19,314,219,970	26,782,985,455	18,199,650,572	25,691,105,453
Rwanda	6,301,468	8,853,505	12,675,215	13,703,785	19,158,660	21,491,398
Saint Helena	3,269,267	1,580,295	5,322,626	10,244,513	6,125,880	7,210,590
Saint Kitts and Nevis	49,718,541	50,069,677	53,553,766	54,385,127	48,412,880	50,610,721
Saint Lucia	32,396,909	30,093,659	33,389,382	25,977,693	17,536,856	17,839,919
Saint Pierre and Miquelon	1,094,378	1,156,967	1,579,257	1,039,646	795,629	1,844,709
Saint Vincent and the Grenadines	15,650,342	2,023,811	1,246,611	952,953	1,179,723	1,779,259
Samoa	7,937,575	4,258,242	5,422,000	4,705,638	4,809,986	3,331,698
San Marino	1,389,972	3,076,542	1,445,506	803,502	660,200	3,807,070
Sao Tome and Principe	216,017	202,775	393,065	147,617	213,578	313,597
Saudi Arabia	27,192,642,038	31,689,028,037	35,625,986,830	54,747,448,525	22,053,149,818	31,412,822,978
Senegal	3,662,962	20,735,639	18,531,679	17,948,975	6,902,523	5,115,350
Serbia	0	0	58,272,494	71,646,409	61,958,600	164,275,702
Serbia and Montenegro	54,632,827	67,688,341	0	0	0	0
Seychelles	5,883,749	10,120,820	10,331,906	5,389,229	6,323,385	6,471,720
Sierra Leone	9,312,822	36,133,793	48,166,794	47,712,613	24,315,031	29,023,924
Singapore	15,110,089,622	17,768,095,532	18,393,659,432	15,884,931,018	15,704,899,318	17,427,588,477
Sint Maarten	0	0	0	0	0	0
Slovakia	960,730,063	1,405,044,637	1,504,800,578	1,301,052,164	627,789,439	1,073,148,169
Slovenia	413,019,469	483,157,986	488,353,109	466,522,694	387,715,222	465,114,510
Solomon Islands	1,351,564	2,192,606	1,116,542	1,233,173	767,107	990,748
Somalia	307,638	387,562	175,137	205,983	252,820	139,532
South Africa	5,885,639,948	7,500,754,236	9,054,116,703	9,948,021,279	5,878,856,481	8,220,181,819
South Korea	43,781,441,056	45,803,586,952	47,562,311,363	48,069,078,711	39,215,588,565	48,875,170,948
South Sudan	0	0	0	0	0	0
Spain	8,614,642,140	9,778,321,333	10,498,117,006	11,093,896,785	7,856,650,625	8,553,600,677
Sri Lanka	2,082,938,898	2,145,528,325	2,065,061,227	1,961,936,499	1,592,744,989	1,748,123,096
Sudan	13,574,271	6,208,722	7,477,239	5,011,426	9,882,346	8,067,712
Suriname	165,346,376	164,554,838	129,550,537	126,544,505	138,985,870	191,377,702
Svalbard and Jan Mayen Island	39,576	17,675	229,221	26,939	0	25,044
Swaziland	198,886,296	155,874,757	145,340,989	133,870,852	109,603,423	120,987,493
Sweden	13,820,977,243	13,870,398,860	13,023,904,257	12,498,322,694	8,185,507,543	10,497,387,347
Switzerland	12,999,881,084	14,229,862,998	14,760,206,008	17,781,886,332	16,052,924,450	19,136,758,378
Syrian Arab Republic	323,599,119	213,789,858	110,532,896	352,097,022	303,079,465	429,339,789

Table B-22. U.S. Imports of Total Merchandise from Individual Countries by Harmonized System, 2005–2015—Continued

Region	2011	2012	2013	2014	2015
Moldova; Republic of	16,194,614	25,344,634	35,264,959	35,463,324	43,920,552
Monaco	30,416,646	102,405,393	65,862,917	32,397,321	58,818,337
Mongolia	11,003,863	42,104,073	19,654,470	14,851,807	17,222,375
Montenegro	4,386,631	3,665,724	1,696,887	2,735,404	2,108,687
Montserrat	608,342	1,809,196	2,673,698	709,498	2,271,534
Morocco	995,660,068	932,130,007	976,123,625	994,810,432	1,011,856,360
Mozambique	34,966,794	38,531,780	76,072,912	100,002,374	96,026,702
Namibia	436,230,221	231,111,858	262,312,815	256,228,666	85,353,831
Nauru	319,977	473,434	600,011	595,453	520,870
Nepal	77,444,344	83,519,705	77,758,435	87,239,052	86,959,805
Netherlands	23,454,922,504	22,259,597,393	19,234,449,656	20,899,140,755	16,835,614,857
Netherlands Antilles	866,152,760	0	0	0	0
New Caledonia	91,128,908	57,574,834	69,561,109	84,763,467	47,038,156
New Zealand	3,167,658,057	3,436,819,255	3,486,824,819	3,984,536,630	4,292,770,709
Nicaragua	2,603,134,501	2,748,023,280	2,806,158,416	3,105,228,844	3,188,301,535
Niger	288,675,966	81,719,779	2,331,191	4,640,642	4,184,625
Nigeria	33,854,186,372	19,014,224,369	11,723,857,816	3,839,515,295	1,915,800,160
Niue	52,795	150,352	233,123	265,356	531,806
Norfolk Island	270,353	50,581	9,790	18,487	1,217,241
North Korea	0	0	0	0	0
Norway	8,304,891,628	6,566,005,881	5,510,574,445	5,385,870,993	4,760,200,206
Oman	2,208,302,314	1,354,422,658	1,022,621,882	978,192,950	906,993,161
Other Countries	0	0	0	0	0
Pakistan	3,832,115,894	3,627,553,133	3,688,503,361	3,675,523,024	3,701,018,609
Palau	210,252	455,246	349,785	555,471	544,832
Panama	389,380,075	540,342,228	448,745,053	431,685,691	408,293,396
Papua New Guinea	141,685,790	118,008,125	129,093,372	100,176,929	90,809,528
Paraguay	109,957,418	196,931,657	276,967,267	196,478,312	162,023,098
Peru	6,605,022,259	6,418,281,945	8,126,732,397	6,079,275,930	5,053,337,195
Philippines	9,144,859,310	9,580,451,380	9,268,689,135	10,189,867,612	10,233,690,672
Pitcairn Islands	2,772	4,511	3,439	130,416	12,162
Poland	4,378,519,315	4,621,448,472	4,885,379,184	5,198,273,476	5,637,927,607
Portugal	2,582,511,678	2,609,550,991	2,831,107,431	3,225,970,679	3,271,009,123
Qatar	1,199,704,662	1,011,454,913	1,300,913,475	1,742,377,351	1,354,237,789
Reunion	11,883,634	9,496,467	10,669,497	16,321,732	16,967,288
Romania	1,435,060,858	1,620,365,188	1,716,149,362	2,133,425,220	2,148,841,567
Russian Federation	34,619,049,348	29,364,796,545	27,085,690,703	23,659,576,570	16,366,161,581
Rwanda	30,857,888	33,286,667	24,422,296	40,697,812	45,643,909
Saint Helena	8,482,781	6,575,281	7,804,252	9,082,561	15,340,188
Saint Kitts and Nevis	54,708,710	56,825,770	54,301,053	56,819,007	56,753,359
Saint Lucia	17,981,919	15,187,839	16,535,511	18,555,538	29,004,460
Saint Pierre and Miquelon	208,618	2,878	56,971	6,582	185,620
Saint Vincent and the Grenadines	1,939,029	2,330,278	2,888,473	1,409,369	1,768,076
Samoa	2,971,100	2,389,292	4,493,443	5,218,063	4,220,542
San Marino	4,843,909	4,883,684	6,123,053	6,539,943	8,517,198
Sao Tome and Principe	981,624	553,482	253,002	1,015,300	773,369
Saudi Arabia	47,476,336,256	55,666,950,840	51,806,698,721	47,041,338,853	22,080,784,821
Senegal	6,766,267	16,771,627	16,981,303	25,490,641	71,965,108
Serbia	133,708,741	145,547,986	524,421,207	280,035,471	272,617,662
Serbia and Montenegro	0	0	0	0	0
Seychelles	6,265,409	4,645,786	5,761,388	4,122,516	5,838,990
Sierra Leone	26,550,327	17,845,303	41,550,945	28,874,375	39,589,210
Singapore	19,115,895,767	20,231,867,784	17,842,859,828	16,501,554,834	18,267,484,943
Sint Maarten	23,803,009	54,968,225	60,003,951	49,633,062	51,873,445
Slovakia	1,407,638,321	1,779,499,290	1,763,494,151	2,117,607,712	2,299,822,999
Slovenia	544,536,589	561,619,541	574,978,394	706,576,569	678,110,689
Solomon Islands	1,313,184	1,572,329	8,841,794	8,712,724	3,521,953
Somalia	1,105,295	975,637	1,193,888	547,902	896,112
South Africa	9,486,919,792	8,672,332,572	8,465,226,229	8,325,573,295	7,314,612,701
South Korea	56,661,359,461	58,898,926,491	62,370,452,198	69,679,824,288	71,758,696,721
South Sudan	17,202	9,869	201,285	67,609	192,583
Spain	11,017,979,491	11,767,974,982	11,667,754,249	14,459,154,005	14,129,841,512
Sri Lanka	2,085,760,230	2,257,259,152	2,451,358,887	2,678,397,636	2,889,922,190
Sudan	10,353,364	6,524,197	10,368,547	11,943,107	8,973,253
Suriname	301,585,222	288,524,031	303,122,465	452,710,013	146,224,404
Svalbard and Jan Mayen Island	3,484	8,417	20,635	3,628	28,231
Swaziland	89,284,003	66,637,548	58,940,474	81,649,559	21,498,430
Sweden	11,489,582,168	10,221,780,983	9,173,837,772	10,360,546,474	9,878,966,413
Switzerland	24,362,463,267	25,672,465,676	28,275,333,645	31,323,034,477	31,396,660,405
Syrian Arab Republic	393,238,838	19,456,989	19,213,370	12,370,136	6,544,106

Table B-22.   U.S. Imports of Total Merchandise from Individual Countries by Harmonized System, 2005–2015—*Continued*

Region	2005	2006	2007	2008	2009	2010
Taiwan	34,825,828,822	38,211,854,849	38,277,594,395	36,326,075,377	28,362,148,998	35,846,836,197
Tajikistan	241,029,155	60,688,032	308,476	8,214,575	8,514,252	1,504,909
Tanzania; United Republic of	33,695,475	34,577,005	46,210,928	55,799,797	49,436,379	42,814,550
Thailand	19,889,755,777	22,466,332,985	22,754,659,878	23,538,275,396	19,082,487,689	22,693,580,280
Togo	6,439,273	3,554,436	5,038,651	11,126,987	6,640,022	9,120,443
Tokelau Islands	10,800,762	5,034,914	7,234,663	5,358,994	16,973,913	3,530,465
Tonga	5,350,431	7,259,582	5,469,812	4,474,480	3,362,127	1,833,205
Trinidad and Tobago	7,890,883,780	8,362,389,038	8,789,605,945	9,030,310,974	5,180,155,507	6,613,277,597
Tunisia	263,768,113	470,269,514	457,626,409	644,062,681	325,785,611	405,457,480
Turkey	5,182,052,179	5,359,037,652	4,600,564,845	4,641,877,863	3,661,586,710	4,207,151,173
Turkmenistan	135,325,351	76,214,739	218,825,067	139,948,105	93,034,292	48,398,797
Turks and Caicos Islands	9,434,412	12,069,010	12,878,882	10,312,889	10,643,166	11,702,487
Tuvalu	56,868	22,515	27,609	88,237	89,205	20,559
Uganda	25,769,069	21,786,892	26,706,633	52,716,226	30,924,655	57,669,174
Ukraine	1,098,029,235	1,639,986,252	1,220,108,508	2,339,939,641	494,769,706	1,077,657,690
United Arab Emirates	1,468,316,627	1,385,377,995	1,337,494,857	1,286,233,771	1,497,950,835	1,145,388,271
United Kingdom	51,032,621,105	53,513,018,484	56,857,542,425	58,587,383,031	47,479,890,559	49,805,396,025
Uruguay	732,311,644	512,307,227	491,922,168	244,310,589	239,225,590	235,379,696
Uzbekistan	95,627,811	151,472,364	164,541,307	292,227,577	89,498,128	68,078,316
Vanuatu	2,489,141	2,259,094	884,784	1,290,513	1,790,895	1,585,396
Vatican City	282,286	1,486,574	148,497	295,465	184,453	2,012,056
Venezuela	33,978,134,805	37,133,806,400	39,909,629,330	51,423,628,380	28,059,033,911	32,707,387,180
Vietnam	6,631,158,734	8,566,663,500	10,632,819,531	12,901,097,887	12,287,816,472	14,867,855,640
Wallis and Futuna	22,469	45,300	33,153	3,850	34,085	15,622
West Bank	1,604,198	3,141,382	2,086,125	2,614,952	1,783,847	3,225,653
Western Sahara	0	0	47,690	4,200	0	19
Yemen	278,635,079	447,367,276	291,942,015	8,262,148	7,422,330	181,360,929
Zambia	31,702,890	28,448,224	48,779,933	51,456,184	8,517,140	29,567,049
Zimbabwe	94,328,983	103,297,522	72,529,444	111,994,040	22,096,319	58,900,871

Table B-22. U.S. Imports of Total Merchandise from Individual Countries by Harmonized System, 2005–2015—*Continued*

Region	2011	2012	2013	2014	2015
Taiwan	41,405,172,281	38,860,607,154	37,938,760,683	40,839,404,448	40,907,593,598
Tajikistan	12,287,776	26,838,677	671,817	3,615,929	31,123,801
Tanzania; United Republic of	58,954,228	114,862,791	70,326,213	86,235,902	104,935,180
Thailand	24,831,572,526	26,066,841,763	26,169,602,629	27,224,643,953	28,631,932,805
Togo	30,536,625	51,910,954	7,719,687	9,140,977	14,211,452
Tokelau Islands	6,699,608	5,242,736	1,621,208	851,718	1,848,379
Tonga	1,662,145	2,247,827	1,719,744	2,706,130	2,442,895
Trinidad and Tobago	8,112,990,551	8,158,370,115	6,493,927,516	5,995,752,563	4,314,344,265
Tunisia	352,049,887	737,859,325	748,909,039	524,319,403	546,271,256
Turkey	5,220,844,682	6,294,133,798	6,669,565,173	7,414,907,903	7,880,913,860
Turkmenistan	43,430,094	90,367,265	31,114,952	20,238,106	55,976,778
Turks and Caicos Islands	9,334,460	9,470,333	10,557,772	8,383,512	14,710,225
Tuvalu	2,031	40,005	34,138	83,070	228,118
Uganda	45,881,727	34,478,933	47,086,632	46,092,193	64,123,855
Ukraine	1,457,063,515	1,349,697,993	1,036,296,065	935,229,096	850,788,858
United Arab Emirates	2,439,791,392	2,252,977,531	2,291,216,863	2,819,605,214	2,468,033,306
United Kingdom	51,262,501,564	55,005,810,676	52,741,231,492	54,692,931,986	57,962,251,307
Uruguay	291,454,584	357,532,717	423,082,838	456,707,819	604,746,068
Uzbekistan	51,163,447	25,939,962	26,586,261	14,362,264	9,715,446
Vanuatu	1,860,207	2,596,805	4,192,881	7,134,359	3,671,320
Vatican City	513,337	278,011	236,591	841,325	1,218,395
Venezuela	43,256,522,079	38,723,837,591	31,997,529,566	30,220,133,632	15,564,232,752
Vietnam	17,487,840,228	20,267,676,965	24,651,035,884	30,615,564,081	38,019,696,227
Wallis and Futuna	5,742	19	296,015	34,768	93,303
West Bank	4,834,474	4,780,459	4,854,019	4,370,693	5,435,229
Western Sahara	17,651	114,438	710,261	125,008	44,063
Yemen	561,709,854	87,107,413	65,593,850	40,915,509	48,270,876
Zambia	47,321,448	63,020,002	37,700,326	55,669,752	47,114,386
Zimbabwe	51,421,685	52,453,255	13,887,943	64,644,521	*67,166,669*

Table B-23.   U.S. Imports of Goods from Regions and Individual Countries, Selected Years, 2000–2015

Country/Region	2000	2010	2011	2012	2013	2014	2015	Value Change, 2000–2015
WORLD	1,239,449	1,942,678	2,246,932	2,316,774	2,305,348	2,389,293	2,271,117	1,031,668
Europe	256,180	377,629	444,122	452,707	457,818	488,236	488,917	232,738
European Union (EU-28)	227,751	319,600	368,902	382,199	387,643	418,201	426,006	198,255
Austria	3,227	6,835	9,483	9,449	9,780	10,769	11,268	8,041
Belgium	9,929	15,552	17,431	17,368	19,012	20,885	19,513	9,584
Bulgaria	236	260	416	509	514	604	594	359
Croatia	141	336	438	444	425	463	575	434
Cyprus	23	11	21	29	44	64	32	8
Czech Republic	1,070	2,450	3,344	3,931	3,923	4,345	4,462	3,392
Denmark	2,965	6,012	6,760	6,777	6,494	7,504	7,727	4,762
Estonia	573	698	962	507	423	563	501	-72
Finland	3,251	3,884	4,436	5,110	4,668	5,016	4,499	1,248
France	29,800	38,355	40,049	41,646	45,706	46,874	47,644	17,844
Germany	58,513	82,450	98,684	109,226	114,349	123,260	124,139	65,626
Greece	592	798	865	987	954	1,048	1,355	763
Hungary	2,715	2,491	2,949	3,201	3,768	5,284	5,692	2,977
Ireland	16,463	33,848	39,371	33,372	31,496	33,956	39,355	22,892
Italy	25,043	28,514	33,974	36,965	38,709	42,115	44,005	18,962
Latvia	288	193	363	246	273	275	302	14
Lithuania	135	637	1,044	1,176	1,554	1,094	1,058	923
Luxembourg	332	451	495	553	641	755	637	306
Malta	482	262	244	255	212	173	240	-242
Netherlands	9,671	19,055	23,455	22,260	19,235	20,818	16,752	7,081
Poland	1,041	2,964	4,379	4,621	4,885	5,152	5,581	4,539
Portugal	1,579	2,142	2,583	2,610	2,831	3,209	3,257	1,678
Romania	473	1,008	1,435	1,620	1,716	2,103	2,136	1,663
Slovakia	241	1,073	1,408	1,779	1,763	2,100	2,280	2,039
Slovenia	313	465	545	562	575	699	672	359
Spain	5,713	8,554	11,018	11,768	11,668	14,416	14,090	8,376
Sweden	9,597	10,497	11,490	10,222	9,174	10,266	9,835	238
United Kingdom	43,345	49,805	51,263	55,006	52,850	54,392	57,805	14,460
Non-EU	28,429	58,029	75,220	70,508	70,175	70,036	62,912	34,483
Albania	8	30	26	19	23	69	160	152
Andorra	0	0	1	0	1	1	6	5
Belarus	104	175	363	153	105	131	158	54
Bosnia and Herzegovina	18	26	50	52	58	83	78	60
Faroe Islands	31	72	106	73	126	138	98	66
Gibraltar	2	1	1	1	0	0	2	0
Iceland	260	201	216	284	291	298	315	55
Kosovo		0	0	0	0	1	2	2
Liechtenstein	278	213	250	310	297	293	303	25
Macedonia	152	37	52	87	62	167	203	51
Moldova	106	12	16	25	35	35	44	-62
Monaco	23	24	30	102	66	32	59	36
Montenegro		4	4	4	2	3	2	2
Norway	5,706	6,950	8,305	6,566	5,511	5,357	4,736	-971
Russia	7,659	25,691	34,619	29,365	27,086	23,658	16,562	8,903
San Marino	7	4	5	5	6	6	8	1
Serbia		164	134	146	524	279	271	271
Svalbard, Jan Mayen Island	0	0	0	0	0	0	0	-0
Switzerland	10,160	19,137	24,362	25,672	28,275	31,191	31,230	21,070
Turkey	3,042	4,207	5,221	6,294	6,669	7,357	7,828	4,786
Ukraine	872	1,078	1,457	1,350	1,036	934	848	-24
Vatican City	2	2	1	0	0	1	1	-1
WESTERN HEMISPHERE	461,901	672,144	795,968	817,298	811,524	837,144	736,952	275,051
NAFTA	207,047	286,131	326,551	343,832	349,102	355,877	421,603	214,556
Canada	123,052	145,426	162,734	175,241	177,681	174,362	247,021	123,969
Mexico	83,995	140,705	163,817	168,591	171,421	181,515	174,582	90,587
Non-NAFTA	159,719	221,492	251,647	258,025	264,011	293,148	168,328	8,609
Canada	107,787	132,211	152,591	149,022	154,876	173,436	48,169	-59,618
Mexico	51,932	89,281	99,056	109,003	109,135	119,712	120,159	68,227
Caribbean	9,568	12,196	18,413	16,336	13,374	12,999	11,479	1,911
Anguilla	2	3	5	4	4	5	6	4
Antigua and Barbuda	2	5	7	10	10	8	7	5
Aruba	1,536	19	3,262	827	42	60	55	-1,481
Bahamas	275	815	765	563	599	532	453	178
Barbados	39	43	46	54	55	51	68	29
British Virgin Islands	31	19	6	13	6	11	16	-14
Cayman Islands	7	11	19	15	32	24	97	91

Table B-23.   U.S. Imports of Goods from Regions and Individual Countries, Selected Years, 2000–2015—*Continued*

Country/Region	2000	2010	2011	2012	2013	2014	2015	Value Change, 2000–2015
Cuba	0	0	0	0	0	0	0	-0
Curacao			558	850	402	369	335	335
Dominica	7	2	2	2	3	2	2	-5
Dominican Republic	4,383	3,672	4,199	4,370	4,261	4,520	4,660	277
Grenada	27	8	7	8	9	10	9	-18
Guadeloupe	10	2	1	12	6	3	4	-6
Haiti	297	551	742	775	847	908	950	653
Jamaica	648	328	566	507	414	285	304	-344
Martinique	2	23	8	26	43	82	37	36
Montserrat	0	1	1	2	3	1	2	2
Sint Maarten	0	0	24	55	60	50	52	52
St Kitts and Nevis	37	51	55	57	54	56	56	19
St Lucia	22	18	18	15	17	18	29	6
St Vincent and the Grenadines	9	2	2	2	3	1	2	-7
Trinidad and Tobago	2,229	6,613	8,113	8,158	6,494	5,995	4,321	2,092
Turks and Caicos Islands	6	12	9	9	11	8	15	9
Central America	12,158	20,867	24,998	27,223	26,448	24,387	19,557	7,399
Belize	94	120	191	162	127	97	75	-18
Costa Rica	3,539	8,697	10,115	12,046	11,914	9,500	4,469	930
El Salvador	1,933	2,206	2,485	2,588	2,437	2,396	2,540	607
Guatemala	2,608	3,523	4,714	4,491	4,171	4,217	4,120	1,513
Honduras	3,090	3,933	4,501	4,648	4,543	4,643	4,759	1,669
Nicaragua	588	2,008	2,603	2,748	2,806	3,104	3,186	2,598
Panama	307	381	389	540	449	431	408	101
South America	73,348	131,425	174,291	171,791	158,518	150,691	115,872	42,525
Argentina	3,100	3,803	4,503	4,350	4,642	4,243	3,948	849
Bolivia	185	680	902	1,682	1,252	1,935	1,007	822
Brazil	13,853	23,958	31,737	32,123	27,631	30,537	27,405	13,553
Chile	3,269	7,017	9,076	9,367	10,385	9,476	8,880	5,611
Colombia	6,968	15,659	23,114	24,622	21,626	18,300	14,057	7,089
Ecuador	2,238	7,451	9,622	9,484	11,491	10,856	7,439	5,201
Falkland Islands (Islas Malvin)	3	5	7	11	14	20	14	11
French Guiana	2	0	4	1	1	0	0	-2
Guyana	140	299	425	523	466	501	431	291
Paraguay	41	62	110	197	277	196	162	121
Peru	1,995	5,243	6,605	6,418	8,127	6,077	5,069	3,074
Suriname	135	191	302	289	303	453	146	11
Uruguay	313	235	291	358	423	456	606	293
Venezuela	18,623	32,707	43,257	38,724	31,997	30,219	15,564	-3,060
Other Western Hemisphere	61	33	68	91	70	42	113	51
Bermuda	39	22	60	84	61	37	109	70
Greenland	16	8	7	7	9	5	4	-12
St Pierre and Miquelon	6	2	0	0	0	0	0	-6
Asia	484,896	796,128	899,980	966,496	972,743	1,014,230	1,004,290	519,394
China	100,018	364,953	399,371	425,619	440,434	466,754	481,881	381,863
Hong Kong	11,449	4,296	4,410	5,456	5,689	5,869	6,703	-4,746
Japan	146,479	120,552	128,928	146,432	138,574	134,004	131,120	-15,360
Korea, South	40,308	48,875	56,661	58,899	62,433	69,518	71,827	31,520
Macau	1,266	141	113	95	95	74	122	-1,144
Taiwan	40,503	35,847	41,405	38,861	37,939	40,581	40,708	206
ASEAN-10	87,945	107,722	118,263	122,887	126,946	137,067	151,662	63,717
Brunei	384	12	23	86	17	32	19	-364
Burma	471	0	0	0	30	93	144	-327
Cambodia	826	2,301	2,712	2,692	2,771	2,847	3,023	2,198
East Timor	0	0	0	0	0	0	3	3
Indonesia	10,367	16,478	19,111	18,002	18,874	19,361	19,575	9,208
Laos	10	59	59	25	31	33	45	36
Malaysia	25,568	25,901	25,777	25,935	27,289	30,420	33,828	8,260
Philippines	13,935	7,982	9,145	9,580	9,269	10,144	10,200	-3,734
Singapore	19,178	17,428	19,116	20,232	17,843	16,426	18,235	-943
Thailand	16,385	22,694	24,832	26,067	26,169	27,123	28,595	12,209
Vietnam	821	14,868	17,488	20,268	24,654	30,589	37,993	37,172
Middle East	38,629	74,078	103,243	116,054	106,531	102,330	61,903	23,274
Bahrain	338	420	518	701	636	965	902	565
Gaza Strip admin. by Israel	0	3	3	0	0	0	0	-0
Iran	169	95	1	2	2	0	11	-158
Iraq	6,066	12,143	16,960	19,265	13,306	13,827	4,353	-1,713
Israel	12,964	20,985	23,047	22,131	22,783	22,962	24,452	11,488
Jordan	73	974	1,061	1,156	1,197	1,401	1,493	1,420
Kuwait	2,781	5,382	7,809	13,021	12,637	11,437	4,685	1,903

Table B-23.　U.S. Imports of Goods from Regions and Individual Countries, Selected Years, 2000–2015—*Continued*

Country/Region	2000	2010	2011	2012	2013	2014	2015	Value Change, 2000–2015
Lebanon	77	84	79	81	92	72	93	16
Oman	257	773	2,208	1,354	1,023	976	906	648
Qatar	486	466	1,200	1,011	1,301	1,742	1,306	821
Republic of Yemen	256	181	562	87	66	41	48	-207
Saudi Arabia	14,365	31,413	47,476	55,667	51,807	47,041	22,081	7,716
Syria	159	429	393	19	19	12	7	-152
United Arab Emirates	972	1,145	2,440	2,253	2,293	2,814	2,463	1,491
West Bank admin. by Israel	5	3	5	5	5	4	6	1
Central Asia	509	1,994	1,789	1,717	1,483	1,451	911	402
Kazakhstan	429	1,872	1,679	1,565	1,421	1,411	798	369
Kyrgyzstan	2	4	3	9	4	2	16	14
Tajikistan	9	2	12	27	1	4	31	22
Turkmenistan	28	48	43	90	31	20	56	28
Uzbekistan	41	68	51	26	27	14	10	-31
Other Asia	17,790	41,505	49,761	52,903	54,878	58,566	58,224	40,434
Afghanistan	1	85	26	37	46	72	22	21
Armenia	23	75	93	89	101	96	63	40
Azerbaijan	21	1,989	2,425	1,095	1,136	1,012	507	486
Bangladesh	2,418	4,294	4,877	4,916	5,353	5,278	5,985	3,568
Bhutan	1	0	1	1	1	0	3	3
Georgia	32	198	176	226	175	392	193	161
India	10,687	29,533	36,154	40,513	41,809	45,244	44,741	34,055
Maldives	94	2	3	18	20	23	22	-72
Mongolia	117	12	11	42	20	15	17	-100
Nepal	230	61	77	84	78	87	87	-143
Pakistan	2,167	3,509	3,832	3,628	3,688	3,672	3,696	1,529
Sri Lanka	2,002	1,748	2,086	2,257	2,451	2,676	2,888	886
Australia and Oceania	8,831	11,779	13,865	13,466	13,213	15,109	15,584	6,753
Australia	6,438	8,583	10,243	9,567	9,273	10,672	10,862	4,424
Christmas Island	1	1	1	0	1	2	2	2
Cocos (Keeling) Islands	0	2	2	1	1	3	4	3
Cook Islands	2	2	1	1	0	1	1	-1
Fiji	147	179	132	189	174	184	202	56
French Polynesia	44	53	54	59	36	40	43	-1
French Southern and Antarctic	0	0	0	0	0	1	0	0
Heard and McDonald Islands	0	0	0	0	0	0	0	-0
Kiribati	2	1	1	1	1	3	3	1
Marshall Islands	5	12	15	19	17	14	29	24
Micronesia	14	4	2	1	2	0	1	-13
New Caledonia	31	71	91	58	70	85	47	16
New Zealand	2,080	2,764	3,168	3,437	3,487	3,979	4,282	2,202
Niue	0	0	0	0	0	0	1	1
Norfolk Island	1	0	0	0	0	0	1	1
Palau	14	0	0	0	0	1	1	-13
Papua New Guinea	35	97	142	118	129	100	91	56
Pitcairn Islands	0	0	0	0	0	0	0	-0
Reunion	1	9	12	9	11	16	17	16
Samoa	6	3	3	2	4	5	4	-1
Solomon Islands	0	1	1	2	9	9	4	3
Tokelau	6	4	7	5	2	1	1	-5
Tonga	5	2	2	2	2	3	2	-2
Tuvalu	0	0	0	0	0	0	0	0
Vanuatu	1	2	2	3	4	7	4	3
Wallis and Futuna	0	0	0	0	0	0	0	0
Africa	27,642	84,999	92,997	66,807	50,050	34,573	25,375	-2,267
Algeria	2,724	14,518	14,609	9,993	4,831	4,629	3,372	647
Angola	3,555	11,940	13,597	9,824	8,743	5,720	2,808	-748
Benin	3	0	2	3	3	5	5	2
Botswana	41	170	293	221	278	318	212	171
British Indian Ocean Terr.	3	1	6	19	18	14	16	13
Burkina Faso	2	2	4	2	6	6	4	1
Burundi	8	3	10	5	4	4	8	0
Cabo Verde	4	1	1	4	2	2	2	-2
Cameroon	155	297	330	308	367	186	133	-22
Central African Republic	3	6	6	4	3	1	3	0
Chad	5	2,044	3,174	2,660	2,459	2,329	1,303	1,299
Comoros	3	2	2	2	3	2	1	-2
Congo (Brazzaville)	532	3,316	2,420	1,488	1,167	424	304	-228
Congo (Kinshasa)	215	528	606	41	76	154	154	-61

Table B-23. U.S. Imports of Goods from Regions and Individual Countries, Selected Years, 2000–2015—Continued

Country/Region	2000	2010	2011	2012	2013	2014	2015	Value Change, 2000–2015
Cote d'Ivoire	384	1,177	1,271	1,099	1,013	1,193	1,030	646
Djibouti	0	3	4	12	4	12	35	35
Egypt	888	2,238	2,059	3,000	1,615	1,410	1,406	518
Equatorial Guinea	155	2,214	1,191	1,700	898	255	163	8
Eritrea	0	0	0	0	0	0	0	0
Ethiopia	29	128	144	183	194	207	310	281
Gabon	2,197	2,212	4,567	1,886	1,112	798	337	-1,859
Gambia	0	3	0	0	2	0	1	1
Ghana	205	273	779	291	366	272	309	105
Guinea	88	69	81	103	99	86	80	-9
Guinea-Bissau	1	1	0	0	3	0	0	-0
Kenya	110	311	382	389	452	591	565	455
Lesotho	140	299	384	311	351	361	332	192
Liberia	46	180	158	144	97	83	45	-1
Libya	0	2,117	645	2,493	2,558	225	155	155
Madagascar	158	108	87	110	180	216	320	162
Malawi	55	72	65	66	73	67	61	6
Mali	10	6	4	4	4	5	4	-5
Mauritania	0	53	1	1	131	101	1	1
Mauritius	286	196	252	260	339	401	395	110
Mayotte		0	0	0	0	0	0	0
Morocco	441	686	996	932	976	992	1,011	570
Mozambique	24	65	35	39	76	100	96	72
Namibia	45	195	436	231	262	256	85	40
Nauru	1	0	0	0	1	1	1	-1
Niger	7	27	289	82	2	5	4	-3
Nigeria	10,538	30,516	33,854	19,014	11,724	3,839	1,916	-8,622
Rwanda	5	21	31	33	24	41	46	41
Sao Tome and Principe	1	0	1	1	0	1	1	0
Senegal	4	5	7	17	17	25	72	67
Seychelles	8	6	6	5	6	4	6	-2
Sierra Leone	4	29	27	18	42	29	39	36
Somalia	0	0	1	1	1	1	1	1
South Africa	4,210	8,220	9,487	8,672	8,465	8,318	7,335	3,125
South Sudan			0	0	0	0	0	0
St Helena	3	7	8	7	8	9	15	12
Sudan	2	8	10	7	10	12	9	7
Swaziland	53	121	89	67	59	82	21	-31
Tanzania	32	43	59	115	70	86	105	72
Togo	6	9	31	52	8	9	14	8
Tunisia	94	405	352	738	749	521	544	450
Uganda	29	58	46	34	47	46	64	35
Western Sahara	0	0	0	0	1	0	0	0
Zambia	18	30	47	63	38	56	47	29
Zimbabwe	113	59	51	52	14	65	67	-45

Table B-24.   U.S. Total Exports of Goods to Regions and Individual Countries, Selected Years, 2000–2015

Region	2000	2010	2011	2012	2013	2014	2015	Value Change, 2000–2015
WORLD	781,918	1,278,493	1,482,507	1,545,821	1,578,439	1,620,532	1,504,914	722,996
Europe	186,673	283,917	327,178	326,625	323,484	329,880	318,913	132,239
European Union (EU-28)	168,619	239,903	269,580	265,683	262,086	276,142	272,688	104,069
Austria	2,592	2,429	2,893	3,420	3,520	3,825	4,026	1,434
Belgium	13,926	25,458	29,990	29,438	31,928	34,790	34,115	20,189
Bulgaria	114	171	259	249	307	359	289	175
Croatia	90	312	511	310	309	340	332	242
Cyprus	190	134	98	167	143	152	102	-88
Czech Republic	736	1,411	1,685	1,832	1,943	2,302	1,978	1,243
Denmark	1,507	2,132	2,248	2,224	2,231	2,361	2,224	717
Estonia	88	188	310	236	293	308	289	201
Finland	1,571	2,180	3,159	2,566	2,349	2,150	1,572	1
France	20,362	26,970	27,857	30,813	31,735	31,301	30,077	9,716
Germany	29,448	48,155	49,294	48,803	47,362	49,363	49,947	20,498
Greece	1,222	1,106	1,131	804	739	773	730	-492
Hungary	569	1,290	1,479	1,566	1,727	1,843	1,714	1,145
Ireland	7,713	7,276	7,658	7,393	6,632	7,806	8,946	1,232
Italy	11,060	14,220	16,037	16,097	16,754	16,968	16,249	5,189
Latvia	134	345	586	515	495	428	295	161
Lithuania	60	628	1,142	757	854	681	528	469
Luxembourg	398	1,440	1,586	1,903	1,849	1,516	1,403	1,005
Malta	335	457	752	391	564	918	471	137
Netherlands	21,836	34,740	42,227	40,618	42,507	43,075	40,706	18,870
Poland	757	2,983	3,143	3,346	3,778	3,660	3,718	2,961
Portugal	984	1,058	1,316	1,097	844	1,136	940	-44
Romania	233	730	919	833	747	977	754	522
Slovakia	110	256	302	336	296	445	381	271
Slovenia	139	328	668	308	270	301	367	229
Spain	6,322	10,355	11,032	9,552	10,244	10,200	10,249	3,926
Sweden	4,554	4,740	5,265	5,248	4,318	4,340	3,932	-622
United Kingdom	41,571	48,410	56,033	54,860	47,348	53,823	56,353	14,782
Non-EU	18,054	44,014	57,597	60,942	61,397	53,737	46,225	28,171
Albania	21	46	48	54	74	51	31	10
Andorra	10	8	5	2	6	4	3	-7
Belarus	31	133	157	102	95	93	59	28
Bosnia and Herzegovina	44	26	21	16	38	46	28	-17
Faroe Islands	1	2	4	2	2	2	2	1
Gibraltar	15	1,494	3,149	5,109	3,576	2,531	2,005	1,990
Iceland	256	325	628	371	513	364	389	133
Kosovo		11	16	21	15	16	20	20
Liechtenstein	14	29	62	22	22	31	36	22
Macedonia	69	33	29	21	55	34	31	-38
Moldova	28	38	40	38	46	35	16	-11
Monaco	28	49	21	24	466	128	71	43
Montenegro	10	15	18	12	22	18	11	1
Norway	1,547	3,100	3,630	3,501	4,617	4,422	3,598	2,051
Russia	2,093	5,994	8,318	10,695	11,145	10,753	7,087	4,994
San Marino	1	4	2	1	2	6	5	4
Serbia	20	104	127	128	142	135	126	106
Svalbard, Jan Mayen Island	0	8	2	0	2	3	0	0
Switzerland	9,954	20,704	24,486	26,406	26,559	22,176	22,287	12,334
Turkey	3,720	10,538	14,695	12,475	12,073	11,645	9,556	5,836
Ukraine	191	1,349	2,139	1,936	1,925	1,240	860	669
Vatican City	2	3	2	5	2	3	2	0
WESTERN HEMISPHERE	348,902	548,563	647,413	691,726	711,204	736,701	670,020	321,118
NAFTA	169,195	248,792	290,587	314,154	327,683	343,800	328,460	159,266
Canada	57,846	85,128	92,299	98,279	101,613	103,552	92,083	34,237
Mexico	111,349	163,665	198,289	215,875	226,070	240,249	236,377	125,028
Non-NAFTA	121,095	164,129	188,993	194,371	199,142	208,869	188,244	67,149
Canada	121,095	164,129	188,993	194,371	199,142	208,869	188,244	67,149
Mexico	0	0	0	0	0	0	0	0
Caribbean	10,313	18,393	20,948	21,887	23,081	24,326	21,103	10,790
Anguilla	30	36	31	27	31	63	48	18
Antigua and Barbuda	138	158	155	205	145	217	670	532
Aruba	291	540	713	710	1,100	1,358	1,155	863
Bahamas	1,069	3,178	3,442	3,479	3,450	3,324	2,389	1,320
Barbados	307	397	440	459	452	540	592	285

Table B-24.   U.S. Total Exports of Goods to Regions and Individual Countries, Selected Years, 2000–2015—*Continued*

Region	2000	2010	2011	2012	2013	2014	2015	Value Change, 2000–2015
British Virgin Islands	63	146	151	172	313	387	260	196
Cayman Islands	354	582	617	668	680	814	685	330
Cuba	7	363	363	464	360	299	180	173
Curacao			484	692	688	612	503	503
Dominica	37	73	74	79	78	64	67	30
Dominican Republic	4,473	6,579	7,326	6,967	7,156	7,922	7,134	2,661
Grenada	80	71	82	72	95	84	90	11
Guadeloupe	86	365	431	503	642	427	102	16
Haiti	577	1,209	1,059	1,050	1,227	1,277	1,144	567
Jamaica	1,376	1,661	1,934	1,989	1,980	2,182	1,706	330
Martinique	22	297	340	371	382	291	119	97
Montserrat	11	5	7	9	9	9	7	-4
St Kitts and Nevis	58	131	116	106	143	185	150	91
St Lucia	108	402	316	377	594	694	496	388
St Vincent and the Grenadines	38	86	81	99	93	104	85	47
Sint Maarten			398	702	833	782	732	732
Trinidad and Tobago	1,100	1,925	2,185	2,478	2,404	2,411	2,512	1,412
Turks and Caicos Islands	89	189	205	210	226	282	280	191
Central America	10,926	24,032	31,454	33,019	33,288	33,905	29,888	18,962
Belize	208	289	356	266	241	237	285	76
Costa Rica	2,460	5,178	6,099	7,237	7,223	6,964	6,150	3,690
El Salvador	1,780	2,434	3,372	3,096	3,274	3,304	3,258	1,478
Guatemala	1,901	4,477	6,151	5,749	5,553	5,964	5,864	3,963
Honduras	2,584	4,606	6,166	5,715	5,373	5,961	5,238	2,654
Nicaragua	380	981	1,059	1,128	1,060	1,009	1,257	876
Panama	1,612	6,066	8,252	9,829	10,565	10,467	7,836	6,224
South America	36,942	92,572	114,811	127,656	127,453	125,141	101,715	64,773
Argentina	4,696	7,392	9,899	10,258	10,348	10,826	9,336	4,640
Bolivia	253	508	668	763	1,051	1,010	910	657
Brazil	15,321	35,418	43,019	43,771	44,093	42,429	31,666	16,345
Chile	3,461	10,907	15,993	18,773	17,518	16,515	15,587	12,127
Colombia	3,672	12,068	14,336	16,357	18,369	20,107	16,503	12,832
Ecuador	1,038	5,409	6,078	6,693	7,666	8,164	5,892	4,854
Falkland Islands (Islas Malvin)	0	3	4	4	1	8	3	3
French Guiana	17	36	57	209	631	281	1,073	1,056
Guyana	159	291	363	360	318	370	367	208
Paraguay	446	1,810	1,977	1,743	1,933	2,116	1,503	1,058
Peru	1,660	6,750	8,342	9,349	10,119	10,054	8,811	7,152
Suriname	134	362	434	499	450	519	444	310
Uruguay	537	975	1,258	1,359	1,755	1,606	1,302	765
Venezuela	5,550	10,645	12,383	17,517	13,201	11,138	8,317	2,767
Other Western Hemisphere	431	645	619	638	557	659	611	179
Bermuda	429	637	611	622	537	646	601	172
Greenland	1	9	7	16	19	13	9	8
St Pierre and Miquelon	2	0	0	0	0	0	0	-1
Asia	219,562	362,984	415,600	434,785	452,819	457,641	433,819	214,257
China	16,185	91,911	104,122	110,517	121,721	123,676	116,186	100,001
Hong Kong	14,582	26,570	36,399	37,472	42,340	40,858	37,174	22,592
Japan	64,924	60,472	65,800	69,976	65,216	66,827	62,472	-2,453
Korea, South	27,830	38,821	43,462	42,283	41,687	44,471	43,499	15,669
Macau	71	225	291	345	351	433	542	472
Taiwan	24,406	26,050	25,932	24,337	25,470	26,670	25,929	1,523
ASEAN - 10	47,138	70,399	76,395	75,421	78,978	78,587	75,080	27,942
Brunei	156	124	184	158	558	549	133	-23
Cambodia	32	154	187	226	241	328	392	361
Indonesia	2,402	6,948	7,421	7,998	9,097	8,284	7,123	4,721
East Timor	0	4	8	1	1	1	3	3
Laos	4	13	26	33	24	28	25	20
Malaysia	10,937	14,079	14,264	12,818	13,007	13,068	12,293	1,355
Myanmar (ex-Burma)	17	10	49	66	146	93	227	210
Philippines	8,799	7,377	7,728	8,087	8,404	8,453	7,909	-890
Singapore	17,806	29,009	31,282	30,523	30,667	30,237	28,657	10,850
Thailand	6,617	8,976	10,930	10,888	11,797	11,810	11,247	4,630
Vietnam	368	3,706	4,315	4,623	5,036	5,734	7,072	6,704
Middle East	19,006	48,677	58,525	69,578	73,288	73,742	71,890	52,884
Bahrain	449	1,235	1,214	1,177	1,018	1,060	1,274	825
Gaza Strip admin. by Israel	0	2	0	0	0	0	0	-0
Iran	17	211	233	251	308	187	282	265
Iraq	10	1,643	2,400	2,054	2,022	2,106	1,970	1,959
Israel	7,746	11,295	13,962	14,273	13,742	15,083	13,562	5,816

Table B-24.   U.S. Total Exports of Goods to Regions and Individual Countries, Selected Years, 2000–2015—*Continued*

Region	2000	2010	2011	2012	2013	2014	2015	Value Change, 2000–2015
Jordan	317	1,172	1,450	1,766	2,084	2,050	1,368	1,051
Kuwait	787	2,775	2,750	2,682	2,598	3,649	2,751	1,964
Lebanon	355	2,009	1,807	1,040	1,034	1,269	1,256	902
Oman	200	1,105	1,437	1,747	1,571	2,016	2,364	2,164
Qatar	191	3,160	2,807	3,578	4,958	5,173	4,232	4,041
Republic of Yemen	190	398	390	469	518	369	159	-31
Saudi Arabia	6,234	11,506	13,924	17,961	18,960	18,705	19,690	13,456
Syria	226	503	230	19	22	7	3	-223
United Arab Emirates	2,285	11,662	15,922	22,559	24,452	22,069	22,979	20,694
West Bank admin. by Israel	9	1	1	2	1	2	1	-8
Central Asia	401	1,008	1,281	1,460	1,926	1,774	778	377
Kazakhstan	124	730	827	884	1,150	1,009	509	385
Kyrgyzstan	23	79	102	145	106	72	32	9
Tajikistan	12	57	178	54	52	25	19	7
Turkmenistan	84	40	71	92	262	456	81	-4
Uzbekistan	158	101	103	285	356	213	138	-19
Other Asia	5,018	24,901	29,326	27,734	27,311	27,273	26,198	21,179
Afghanistan	8	2,151	2,922	1,522	1,410	792	500	492
Armenia	56	113	94	64	91	60	50	-5
Azerbaijan	210	253	338	493	381	950	470	260
Bangladesh	239	576	1,144	508	709	1,113	948	709
Bhutan	1	4	4	2	2	2	3	2
Georgia	110	301	580	541	601	628	342	232
India	3,667	19,249	21,542	22,106	21,811	21,608	21,530	17,862
Korea, North	3	3	9	12	7	24	5	2
Maldives	6	28	45	30	29	29	35	29
Mongolia	18	116	315	665	280	167	69	52
Nepal	35	28	40	37	33	36	36	1
Pakistan	462	1,901	1,989	1,530	1,646	1,512	1,838	1,376
Sri Lanka	205	179	304	224	312	350	372	168
Australia and Oceania	15,501	28,269	33,431	35,452	30,047	31,579	29,372	13,871
Australia	12,482	21,805	27,626	31,161	26,123	26,582	25,038	12,555
Christmas Island	1	2	1	4	0	0	2	0
Cocos (Keeling) Islands	1	1	1	1	22	6	1	-0
Cook Islands	1	4	5	6	5	5	4	3
Fiji	23	44	43	56	67	80	57	35
French Polynesia	94	122	127	130	126	130	120	26
French Southern and Antarctic	2	1	1	1	2	8	8	6
Heard and McDonald Islands	0	4	0	0	1	1	1	1
Kiribati	5	4	18	5	7	3	7	3
Marshall Islands	60	91	144	142	65	95	81	21
Micronesia	29	42	44	51	42	42	40	11
Netherlands Antilles	674	2,943	1,187					-674
New Caledonia	19	108	115	75	73	121	89	69
New Zealand	1,970	2,820	3,581	3,229	3,226	4,258	3,634	1,664
Niue	0	2	1	1	0	0	0	-0
Norfolk Island	1	1	1	1	2	1	0	-1
Palau	18	14	17	17	18	21	26	7
Papua New Guinea	23	186	304	391	167	143	207	185
Pitcairn Islands	3	0	0	0	0	0	0	-3
Reunion	3	8	155	8	9	11	7	3
Samoa	64	19	24	25	28	23	23	-41
Solomon Islands	6	5	6	7	9	7	6	-0
Tokelau	11	4	5	13	1	1	0	-10
Tonga	8	21	19	27	19	20	14	6
Tuvalu	0	1	1	1	1	1	1	1
Vanuatu	1	19	5	100	34	21	6	4
Wallis and Futuna	0	1	0	1	1	0	0	0
Africa	10,965	28,334	32,727	32,720	35,235	38,058	26,855	15,890
Algeria	862	1,194	1,597	1,363	1,849	2,617	1,876	1,015
Angola	225	1,293	1,503	1,491	1,443	2,039	1,164	938
Benin	26	463	618	573	605	781	632	606
Botswana	32	48	44	48	82	53	39	8
British Indian Ocean Terr.	1	1	2	3	1	2	1	-0
Burkina Faso	16	47	33	47	78	72	54	38
Burundi	2	14	33	20	17	6	6	4
Cameroon	59	132	221	253	336	301	221	161
Cabo Verde	7	10	11	8	9	7	7	0

Table B-24. U.S. Total Exports of Goods to Regions and Individual Countries, Selected Years, 2000–2015—*Continued*

Region	2000	2010	2011	2012	2013	2014	2015	Value Change, 2000–2015
Central African Republic	2	10	12	9	4	32	34	32
Chad	11	90	35	37	41	66	57	46
Comoros	1	1	1	1	3	3	2	1
Congo (Brazzaville)	82	254	227	237	222	321	249	167
Congo (Kinshasa)	10	93	166	200	170	182	136	126
Cote d'Ivoire	95	163	131	188	168	239	264	169
Djibouti	17	123	129	119	164	111	153	136
Egypt	3,334	6,833	6,228	5,498	5,175	6,473	4,748	1,414
Equatorial Guinea	96	272	285	233	756	575	159	63
Eritrea	17	2	4	6	13	5	3	-13
Ethiopia	165	773	690	1,275	689	1,669	1,555	1,389
Gabon	64	243	205	319	308	417	204	140
Gambia	9	29	29	27	34	42	38	29
Ghana	191	989	1,199	1,322	982	1,186	887	696
Guinea	68	85	256	155	79	65	135	67
Guinea-Bissau	0	3	12	21	7	3	2	2
Kenya	238	375	461	569	636	1,641	937	699
Lesotho	1	11	13	17	1	2	1	0
Liberia	43	191	195	241	173	184	136	93
Libya	18	666	307	549	865	532	218	200
Madagascar	16	116	56	64	64	47	55	39
Malawi	14	37	57	64	54	51	36	22
Mali	32	37	55	60	50	38	72	40
Mauritania	16	84	243	292	245	149	127	111
Mauritius	24	40	46	96	42	35	58	34
Mayotte		6	5	12	9	12	6	6
Morocco	523	1,948	2,823	2,170	2,484	2,102	1,608	1,085
Mozambique	57	224	459	352	303	375	265	208
Namibia	80	110	137	185	235	343	128	48
Nauru	4	2	0	2	1	1	2	-2
Niger	36	49	48	37	46	59	72	35
Nigeria	722	4,061	4,905	5,029	6,389	5,968	3,410	2,688
Rwanda	19	31	120	30	25	21	14	-5
Sao Tome and Principe	1	1	6	1	2	1	1	-0
Senegal	82	219	265	149	229	173	197	115
Seychelles	7	11	13	15	12	13	19	12
Sierra Leone	19	61	103	101	82	88	78	59
Somalia	5	1	6	17	16	36	46	41
South Africa	3,089	5,632	7,271	7,553	7,293	6,370	5,459	2,370
St Helena	0	1	2	5	3	0	4	3
South Sudan			7	33	13	47	19	19
Sudan	17	116	75	55	88	77	60	43
Swaziland	67	24	20	40	23	26	29	-38
Tanzania	45	163	260	245	412	302	171	127
Togo	11	158	210	371	1,008	1,025	234	223
Tunisia	289	573	597	615	870	831	560	271
Uganda	28	94	94	100	123	78	90	61
Zambia	19	56	130	147	141	114	84	65
Zimbabwe	52	68	62	53	61	49	36	-16

Table B-25.   U.S. Total Balance of Payments of Goods by Region and Individual Country, Selected Years, 2000–2015

Region	2000	2010	2011	2012	2013	2014	2015	Value Change (2000–2015)
WORLD	-457,531	-664,185	-764,425	-770,953	-726,908	-768,761	-3,776,031	-3,318,499
Europe	-69,507	-93,712	-411,404	-126,082	-134,335	-158,357	-807,830	-738,323
European Union (EU-28)	-59,131	-79,697	-99,322	-116,517	-125,557	-142,058	-698,693	-639,562
Austria	-635	-4,407	-6,589	-6,029	-6,261	-6,944	-15,294	-14,659
Belgium	3,996	9,906	12,559	12,070	12,916	13,904	-53,628	-57,624
Bulgaria	-121	-89	-157	-261	-206	-246	-884	-762
Croatia	-51	-24	73	-134	-116	-123	-907	-856
Cyprus	167	123	77	138	100	88	-134	-300
Czech Republic	-334	-1,039	-1,659	-2,098	-1,980	-2,042	-6,441	-6,106
Denmark	-1,458	-3,879	-4,512	-4,553	-4,263	-5,143	-9,952	-8,494
Estonia	-485	-510	-653	-271	-130	-254	-790	-305
Finland	-1,680	-1,704	-1,277	-2,543	-2,319	-2,865	-6,071	-4,391
France	-9,439	-11,386	-12,192	-10,833	-13,971	-15,573	-77,721	-68,283
Germany	-29,065	-34,295	-49,390	-60,423	-66,987	-73,896	-174,086	-145,021
Greece	630	309	266	-183	-215	-275	-2,084	-2,714
Hungary	-2,146	-1,201	-1,469	-1,635	-2,041	-3,441	-7,406	-5,260
Ireland	-8,750	-26,572	-31,713	-25,980	-24,864	-26,149	-48,301	-39,551
Italy	-13,982	-14,294	-17,936	-20,868	-21,955	-25,147	-60,254	-46,272
Latvia	-154	152	223	269	222	154	-597	-443
Lithuania	-76	-9	98	-419	-700	-413	-1,586	-1,510
Luxembourg	66	989	1,091	1,350	1,208	761	-2,040	-2,106
Malta	-148	196	508	136	352	744	-712	-564
Netherlands	12,165	15,685	18,772	18,359	23,272	22,257	-57,458	-69,624
Poland	-284	19	-1,235	-1,275	-1,107	-1,492	-9,299	-9,015
Portugal	-594	-1,084	-1,267	-1,512	-1,987	-2,073	-4,196	-3,602
Romania	-240	-278	-517	-788	-970	-1,125	-2,890	-2,650
Slovakia	-131	-817	-1,105	-1,444	-1,468	-1,655	-2,661	-2,530
Slovenia	-175	-137	124	-254	-305	-398	-1,039	-865
Spain	609	1,802	14	-2,216	-1,424	-4,216	-24,338	-24,948
Sweden	-5,043	-5,757	-6,225	-4,974	-4,855	-5,926	-13,767	-8,724
United Kingdom	-1,775	-1,395	4,771	-145	-5,502	-569	-114,158	-112,384
Non-EU	-10,376	-14,015	-3,176	-9,566	-8,778	-16,298	-109,136	-98,761
Albania	13	16	21	35	52	-18	-191	-204
Andorra	10	7	5	2	4	3	-9	-19
Belarus	-73	-41	-206	-51	-10	-38	-217	-144
Bosnia and Herzegovina	26	1	-28	-36	-19	-37	-105	-131
Faroe Islands	-30	-70	-102	-71	-124	-136	-100	-70
Gibraltar	14	1,493	3,147	5,108	3,576	2,531	-2,007	-2,021
Iceland	-4	124	412	87	222	66	-703	-699
Kosovo	0	11	15	21	14	16	-22	-22
Liechtenstein	-265	-183	-188	-288	-275	-262	-339	-75
Macedonia	-84	-4	-23	-66	-7	-133	-233	-150
Moldova	-78	25	23	13	10	-0	-60	18
Monaco	5	25	-10	-78	400	96	-130	-135
Montenegro	10	11	13	9	20	15	-13	-23
Norway	-4,159	-3,850	-4,675	-3,065	-894	-936	-8,334	-4,175
Russia	-5,566	-19,697	-26,301	-18,670	-15,941	-12,905	-23,648	-18,082
San Marino	-6	0	-3	-4	-4	-1	-13	-7
Serbia	20	-60	-7	-18	-382	-144	-397	-417
Svalbard, Jan Mayen Island	0	8	2	0	2	3	-0	-1
Switzerland	-206	1,567	124	734	-1,716	-9,015	-53,517	-53,311
Turkey	678	6,331	9,474	6,181	5,404	4,288	-17,384	-18,062
Ukraine	681	271	682	587	889	306	-1,708	-1,027
Vatican City	0	1	2	5	2	2	-3	-3
WESTERN HEMISPHERE	-112,999	-123,581	-148,555	-125,572	-100,320	-100,444	-1,406,971	-1,293,972
NAFTA	-37,853	-37,339	-35,964	-29,678	-21,419	-12,077	-750,063	-712,211
Canada	-65,207	-60,298	-70,435	-76,962	-76,068	-70,810	-339,104	-273,897
Mexico	27,354	22,960	34,472	47,284	54,649	58,734	-410,959	-438,313
Non-NAFTA	-38,624	-57,363	-62,654	-63,654	-64,869	-84,279	-356,572	-317,948
Canada	13,308	31,918	36,402	45,349	44,266	35,433	-236,413	-249,721
Mexico	-51,932	-89,281	-99,056	-109,003	-109,135	-119,712	-120,159	-68,227
Caribbean	745	6,196	2,535	5,552	9,706	11,327	-32,582	-33,327
Anguilla	28	33	26	24	27	58	-53	-82
Antigua and Barbuda	136	153	148	195	136	209	-677	-813
Aruba	-1,244	521	-2,548	-116	1,058	1,298	-1,210	35
Bahamas	794	2,363	2,677	2,916	2,851	2,793	-2,842	-3,636
Barbados	268	355	393	404	397	489	-660	-927

Table B-25. U.S. Total Balance of Payments of Goods by Region and Individual Country, Selected Years, 2000–2015—*Continued*

Region	2000	2010	2011	2012	2013	2014	2015	Value Change (2000–2015)
British Virgin Islands	33	127	145	158	306	376	-276	-309
Cayman Islands	348	571	598	653	648	790	-782	-1,130
Cuba	7	363	363	464	360	299	-180	-187
Curacao	0	0	-74	-158	286	243	-838	-838
Dominica	31	71	72	77	75	63	-69	-100
Dominican Republic	89	2,908	3,127	2,597	2,895	3,402	-11,794	-11,884
Grenada	53	64	75	64	86	74	-99	-152
Guadeloupe	76	362	429	490	636	424	-106	-182
Haiti	280	658	317	275	380	369	-2,094	-2,374
Jamaica	728	1,334	1,368	1,482	1,565	1,897	-2,010	-2,737
Martinique	20	274	332	344	339	208	-156	-176
Montserrat	11	4	6	7	6	9	-9	-19
St Kitts and Nevis	22	80	61	49	89	129	-206	-228
St Lucia	85	384	298	362	578	676	-524	-609
St Vincent and the Grenadines	29	84	79	96	90	102	-87	-116
Sint Maarten	0	0	374	647	773	733	-784	-784
Trinidad and Tobago	-1,130	-4,688	-5,928	-5,681	-4,090	-3,584	-6,832	-5,703
Turks and Caicos Islands	83	178	196	200	215	274	-294	-377
Central America	-1,232	3,165	6,456	5,795	6,840	9,518	-49,445	-48,212
Belize	115	169	165	104	114	140	-360	-475
Costa Rica	-1,078	-3,519	-4,016	-4,809	-4,691	-2,536	-10,619	-9,540
El Salvador	-153	228	887	508	837	909	-5,799	-5,646
Guatemala	-707	954	1,437	1,258	1,381	1,747	-9,984	-9,277
Honduras	-506	673	1,665	1,067	830	1,317	-9,997	-9,491
Nicaragua	-208	-1,026	-1,545	-1,620	-1,747	-2,095	-4,443	-4,234
Panama	1,305	5,685	7,862	9,288	10,116	10,036	-8,244	-9,550
								0
South America	-36,406	-38,852	-59,480	-44,136	-31,065	-25,550	-217,587	-181,182
Argentina	1,596	3,589	5,396	5,908	5,706	6,583	-13,284	-14,880
Bolivia	68	-172	-234	-919	-201	-925	-1,917	-1,985
Brazil	1,468	11,460	11,282	11,648	16,462	11,893	-59,071	-60,539
Chile	192	3,889	6,917	9,407	7,133	7,039	-24,467	-24,658
Colombia	-3,296	-3,592	-8,779	-8,265	-3,257	1,807	-30,560	-27,264
Ecuador	-1,200	-2,042	-3,544	-2,792	-3,826	-2,692	-13,330	-12,130
Falkland Islands (Islas Malvin)	-3	-3	-3	-7	-12	-12	-17	-14
French Guiana	15	36	53	209	631	281	-1,073	-1,088
Guyana	19	-8	-61	-163	-148	-131	-798	-818
Paraguay	405	1,748	1,867	1,546	1,656	1,919	-1,666	-2,071
Peru	-335	1,506	1,737	2,930	1,992	3,977	-13,880	-13,545
Suriname		171	132	211	147	66	-590	-589
Uruguay	224	740	967	1,002	1,332	1,150	-1,908	-2,132
Venezuela	-13,073	-22,063	-30,873	-21,207	-18,796	-19,081	-23,881	-10,807
								0
Other Western Hemisphere	370	613	551	548	486	617	-723	-1,093
Bermuda	390	614	551	539	477	610	-709	-1,099
Greenland	-15	0	-0	9	10	7	-13	1
St Pierre and Miquelon	-5	-2	-0	0	0	-0	-0	4
								0
Asia	-265,334	-433,143	-484,380	-531,711	-519,924	-556,589	-1,438,109	-1,172,774
China	-83,833	-273,042	-295,250	-315,102	-318,713	-343,079	-598,067	-514,234
Hong Kong	3,133	22,274	31,989	32,016	36,651	34,989	-43,877	-47,010
Japan	-81,555	-60,080	-63,128	-76,456	-73,358	-67,176	-193,592	-112,037
Korea, South	-12,478	-10,055	-13,200	-16,616	-20,747	-25,047	-115,326	-102,848
Macau	-1,196	84	178	251	257	359	-665	531
Taiwan	-16,097	-9,797	-15,473	-14,524	-12,469	-13,911	-66,637	-50,540
								0
ASEAN - 10	-40,806	-37,323	-41,868	-47,465	-47,968	-58,480	-226,742	-185,936
Brunei	-228	112	161	71	541	517	-153	75
Cambodia	-439	154	187	226	211	235	-536	-97
Indonesia	1,576	4,647	4,709	5,306	6,326	5,437	-10,146	-11,722
East Timor	0	4	8	1	1	1	-6	-6
Laos	-10,363	-16,466	-19,085	-17,969	-18,849	-19,332	-19,600	-9,237
Malaysia	10,928	14,020	14,205	12,793	12,976	13,035	-12,338	-23,265
Myanmar (ex-Burma)	-25,551	-25,891	-25,728	-25,869	-27,144	-30,328	-34,056	-8,504
Philippines	-5,136	-605	-1,417	-1,493	-865	-1,691	-18,109	-12,974
Singapore	-1,372	11,581	12,166	10,291	12,824	13,811	-46,892	-45,520
Thailand	-9,768	-13,717	-13,902	-15,179	-14,372	-15,313	-39,842	-30,074
Vietnam	-454	-11,162	-13,173	-15,645	-19,618	-24,854	-45,065	-44,611
								0
Middle East	-19,623	-25,400	-44,718	-46,476	-33,243	-28,588	-133,793	-114,170
Bahrain	111	815	696	476	382	94	-2,176	-2,288
Gaza Strip admin. by Israel	0	-1	-3	-0	-0	-0	-0	-0
Iran	-152	117	232	249	306	187	-293	-141
Iraq	-6,055	-10,500	-14,559	-17,212	-11,284	-11,721	-6,322	-267
Israel	-5,219	-9,690	-9,085	-7,858	-9,041	-7,879	-38,014	-32,795

Table B-25.   U.S. Total Balance of Payments of Goods by Region and Individual Country, Selected Years, 2000–2015—*Continued*

Region	2000	2010	2011	2012	2013	2014	2015	Value Change (2000–2015)
Jordan..................................	244	198	389	611	887	650	-2,861	-3,105
Kuwait.................................	-1,994	-2,607	-5,059	-10,339	-10,039	-7,788	-7,435	-5,441
Lebanon...............................	278	1,925	1,728	959	942	1,196	-1,349	-1,627
Oman...................................	-58	332	-772	392	549	1,040	-3,270	-3,212
Qatar..................................	-294	2,693	1,607	2,566	3,657	3,431	-5,538	-5,244
Republic of Yemen................	-66	216	-172	382	453	328	-207	-141
Saudi Arabia........................	-8,131	-19,907	-33,553	-37,706	-32,847	-28,336	-41,771	-33,640
Syria...................................	67	74	-163	0	2	-6	-10	-77
United Arab Emirates............	1,313	10,517	13,482	20,306	22,159	19,255	-25,442	-26,755
West Bank admin. by Israel......	4	-3	-4	-3	-4	-3	-6	-11
								0
Central Asia......................	-108	-986	-508	-257	443	322	-1,689	-1,581
Kazakhstan..........................	-305	-1,142	-852	-681	-271	-402	-1,307	-1,002
Kyrgyzstan...........................	21	76	99	136	103	69	-47	-68
Tajikistan............................	3	56	166	27	51	21	-50	-53
Turkmenistan.......................	56	-8	28	2	231	435	-137	-193
Uzbekistan...........................	116	33	51	259	330	199	-148	-264
								0
Other Asia..........................	-12,772	-16,604	-20,434	-25,169	-27,567	-31,293	-84,422	-71,650
Afghanistan.........................	7	2,066	2,896	1,485	1,364	720	-521	-529
Armenia...............................	33	38	2	-24	-10	-36	-113	-145
Azerbaijan...........................	189	-1,736	-2,087	-602	-755	-62	-977	-1,166
Bangladesh..........................	-2,179	-3,718	-3,733	-4,407	-4,645	-4,164	-6,934	-4,755
Bhutan................................	0	3	3	2	2	2	-6	-6
Georgia...............................	78	103	404	315	426	236	-535	-613
India...................................	-7,019	-10,284	-14,612	-18,407	-19,997	-23,637	-66,271	-59,252
Korea, North........................	3	3	9	12	7	24	-5	-7
Maldives..............................	-88	27	42	12	8	6	-57	31
Mongolia.............................	-99	104	304	623	260	153	-87	13
Nepal..................................	-194	-32	-37	-47	-45	-50	-123	71
Pakistan..............................	-1,705	-1,608	-1,843	-2,097	-2,042	-2,160	-5,534	-3,829
Sri Lanka.............................	-1,797	-1,569	-1,782	-2,033	-2,139	-2,326	-3,260	-1,463
								0
Australia and Oceania............	6,670	16,490	19,566	21,986	16,834	16,470	-44,956	-51,625
Australia..............................	6,044	13,222	17,383	21,595	16,850	15,910	-35,900	-41,944
Christmas Island...................	1	1	0	4	-1	-2	-4	-5
Cocos (Keeling) Islands..........	1	-1	-1	-0	21	3	-4	-5
Cook Islands........................	-1	2	4	4	4	5	-5	-4
Fiji.....................................	-124	-135	-89	-133	-107	-104	-260	-136
French Polynesia...................	50	69	73	70	90	89	-163	-212
French Southern and Antarctic...	2	1	1	1	2	8	-8	-10
Heard and McDonald Islands.....	0	4	0	0	1	1	-1	-1
Kiribati...............................	3	3	17	4	6	1	-10	-13
Marshall Islands....................	55	79	129	123	49	80	-110	-165
Micronesia...........................	16	38	42	51	40	41	-41	-56
Netherlands Antilles...............	-45	1,917	321	0	0	0	0	45
New Caledonia......................	-12	37	24	18	3	36	-136	-124
New Zealand.........................	-110	57	414	-208	-261	279	-7,916	-7,806
Niue...................................	0	2	1	1	0	-0	-1	-1
Norfolk Island......................	1	1	1	1	2	1	-2	-2
Palau..................................	5	14	17	16	18	20	-26	-31
Papua New Guinea.................	-12	89	162	273	38	43	-298	-287
Pitcairn Islands....................	2	-0	0	0	-0	-0	-0	-2
Reunion...............................	3	-1	143	-2	-2	-5	-24	-27
Samoa.................................	58	16	21	22	24	18	-27	-85
Solomon Islands....................	0	1	5	6	0	-2	-9	-15
Tokelau...............................	5	0	-2	8	-1	1	-1	-6
Tonga.................................	3	19	18	25	18	17	-16	-19
Tuvalu................................	0	1	1	1	1	1	-1	-1
Vanuatu..............................	1	17	3	97	30	14	-10	-10
Wallis and Futuna..................	0	1	0	1	0	0	-0	-0
								0
Africa	-16,677	-56,665	-60,270	-34,088	-14,814	3,485	-52,229	-35,552
Algeria................................	-1,862	-13,324	-13,012	-8,630	-2,982	-2,012	-5,248	-3,386
Angola................................	-3,330	-10,646	-12,094	-8,333	-7,300	-3,681	-3,971	-641
Benin..................................	24	462	616	570	602	776	-637	-661
Botswana.............................	-10	-121	-249	-173	-196	-265	-251	-241
British Indian Ocean Terr..........	-2	0	-4	-17	-17	-12	-16	-14
Burkina Faso.........................	14	44	30	45	71	66	-58	-72
Burundi...............................	-6	11	23	15	12	1	-14	-8
Cameroon............................	-96	-165	-110	-55	-31	115	-354	-259
Cabo Verde..........................	3	9	10	4	7	6	-10	-13
Central African Republic..........	-1	5	6	4	1	31	-37	-36

Table B-25.   U.S. Total Balance of Payments of Goods by Region and Individual Country, Selected Years, 2000–2015—*Continued*

Region	2000	2010	2011	2012	2013	2014	2015	Value Change (2000–2015)
Chad	6	-1,954	-3,139	-2,624	-2,418	-2,262	-1,360	-1,366
Comoros	-3	-0	-1	-1	1	1	-3	-0
Congo (Brazzaville)	-450	-3,062	-2,193	-1,251	-944	-103	-553	-103
Congo (Kinshasa)	-205	-434	-440	159	94	27	-290	-85
Cote d'Ivoire	-289	-1,014	-1,139	-911	-846	-953	-1,294	-1,005
Djibouti	17	120	125	107	161	99	-188	-205
Egypt	2,446	4,594	4,170	2,498	3,561	5,062	-6,154	-8,601
Equatorial Guinea	-59	-1,942	-905	-1,467	-142	320	-322	-263
Eritrea	17	2	4	6	13	5	-4	-20
Ethiopia	137	645	545	1,092	495	1,462	-1,865	-2,001
Gabon	-2,133	-1,969	-4,362	-1,567	-804	-381	-541	1,592
Gambia	9	26	29	27	32	41	-39	-47
Ghana	-13	716	420	1,031	617	915	-1,197	-1,183
Guinea	-20	17	175	52	-20	-21	-214	-194
Guinea-Bissau	-0	3	12	21	3	3	-2	-2
Kenya	127	64	80	179	183	1,050	-1,502	-1,629
Lesotho	-140	-288	-371	-294	-351	-359	-333	-193
Liberia	-3	11	37	97	77	101	-181	-178
Libya	18	-1,451	-338	-1,944	-1,694	307	-373	-391
Madagascar	-142	8	-31	-46	-116	-169	-374	-232
Malawi	-42	-35	-8	-2	-19	-16	-97	-55
Mali	22	31	51	56	46	34	-77	-99
Mauritania	16	31	242	291	115	48	-128	-144
Mauritius	-262	-156	-205	-164	-297	-366	-454	-192
Mayotte	0	6	5	12	9	12	-6	-6
Morocco	82	1,262	1,828	1,238	1,508	1,110	-2,619	-2,701
Mozambique	32	159	424	313	227	275	-361	-393
Namibia	35	-85	-300	-46	-27	87	-213	-248
Nauru	3	2	0	2	0	0	-2	-5
Niger	29	22	-241	-44	44	54	-76	-105
Nigeria	-9,816	-26,455	-28,949	-13,985	-5,335	2,129	-5,326	4,490
Rwanda	14	9	89	-3	1	-19	-60	-74
Sao Tome and Principe	1	1	5	0	2	0	-2	-2
Senegal	78	214	258	132	212	147	-269	-346
Seychelles	-1	4	7	10	6	9	-24	-23
Sierra Leone	15	32	76	83	41	59	-117	-132
Somalia	4	1	5	16	15	35	-47	-51
South Africa	-1,121	-2,589	-2,216	-1,120	-1,172	-1,948	-12,794	-11,673
St Helena	0	1	2	5	3	0	-4	-4
South Sudan	-3	-7	-1	26	6	38	-34	-31
Sudan	16	108	64	49	78	65	-69	-85
Swaziland	14	-97	-69	-26	-36	-56	-50	-65
Tanzania	12	121	201	131	342	216	-276	-288
Togo	5	149	179	319	1,000	1,016	-248	-253
Tunisia	195	167	245	-123	121	311	-1,104	-1,299
Uganda	-1	36	48	66	76	32	-154	-153
Zambia	1	27	82	84	103	58	-131	-132
Zimbabwe	-60	9	10	1	47	-16	-104	-44

Table B-26.   U.S. Exports of North American Industry Classification System (NAICS) Manufactures by Region and Individual Country, 2010–2015

Country	2010	2011	2012	2013	2014	2015
WORLD	1,101,355,721,429	1,267,995,829,693	1,341,398,241,194	1,375,098,372,831	1,402,286,037,527	1,316,790,481,467
Canada.............................	222,542,348,628	250,383,300,358	264,101,438,614	268,073,045,873	271,596,948,931	246,297,695,549
Mexico..............................	147,599,397,419	176,966,109,772	194,661,807,080	204,206,802,739	215,720,437,077	214,183,866,570
China................................	64,198,153,197	70,629,069,987	73,235,584,770	86,709,009,967	91,175,566,147	89,132,276,917
Japan...............................	48,527,652,215	52,154,403,524	58,033,132,057	54,437,770,597	54,645,004,958	52,136,185,220
United Kingdom	41,777,300,805	48,861,159,542	47,424,337,510	39,672,583,742	45,215,950,070	48,616,903,471
Germany	43,303,165,994	43,781,386,091	43,141,484,833	41,666,307,176	43,803,509,537	44,646,890,626
South Korea	31,616,217,139	34,384,473,552	34,798,673,716	35,422,231,445	37,362,802,748	37,296,296,957
Netherlands.......................	31,577,729,136	37,394,099,403	36,563,445,565	37,947,981,193	37,995,653,634	36,404,152,329
Hong Kong	23,469,749,723	32,478,969,489	33,572,438,706	38,307,167,055	36,681,109,374	32,910,573,550
Belgium.............................	23,054,883,059	27,881,781,323	27,509,586,777	30,190,717,971	32,843,572,094	32,130,859,276
Brazil................................	32,692,415,219	39,325,473,104	41,021,331,113	40,084,193,775	38,707,411,336	29,610,769,972
France...............................	24,113,455,304	25,107,698,256	28,118,963,108	28,936,629,627	28,512,478,896	27,513,573,109
Singapore..........................	27,241,818,679	29,768,927,323	29,191,468,391	29,307,824,976	28,595,813,236	27,098,517,013
Australia............................	19,992,277,474	25,287,061,833	28,781,091,539	24,244,203,248	24,467,427,356	23,287,012,961
Taiwan..............................	21,647,517,030	20,721,464,280	19,842,340,225	21,619,865,886	22,505,126,978	22,605,405,991
United Arab Emirates	10,647,464,378	14,139,870,751	20,620,078,893	22,304,406,061	20,056,100,208	21,008,792,489
India.................................	16,997,288,252	18,348,874,441	18,952,045,100	19,462,891,912	18,978,741,484	18,617,233,292
Saudi Arabia......................	10,848,715,467	12,365,991,403	16,363,751,917	17,706,715,403	17,253,542,924	18,335,232,131
Switzerland........................	12,850,136,801	20,972,140,260	22,438,625,296	23,343,321,375	18,448,274,835	17,607,776,648
Colombia...........................	11,061,241,963	13,202,807,602	15,410,840,226	17,223,394,517	18,095,988,071	14,710,173,681
Chile.................................	9,944,188,535	14,442,592,901	17,309,779,441	15,926,132,775	15,008,667,459	14,586,337,698
Italy..................................	11,805,397,738	12,858,307,928	13,054,980,871	13,993,389,941	14,168,117,026	13,676,272,100
Israel................................	10,522,171,783	12,977,110,849	13,516,099,946	12,954,481,593	14,319,168,766	12,961,498,306
Malaysia............................	12,917,161,047	12,922,336,783	11,790,449,975	12,062,935,934	12,165,118,867	11,570,937,692
Thailand............................	7,711,928,452	9,298,319,821	9,474,545,017	10,691,512,366	10,556,205,900	10,050,619,799
Argentina	6,974,172,785	9,426,825,434	9,780,728,041	9,915,776,117	10,331,894,786	8,944,230,825
Ireland..............................	6,904,205,592	7,384,801,216	7,158,129,830	6,380,643,030	7,473,079,620	8,572,209,356
Peru..................................	5,909,111,707	7,344,576,040	8,670,512,143	9,212,871,002	8,815,606,003	7,813,714,654
Spain................................	8,298,907,883	8,864,440,287	7,494,715,567	7,938,468,532	7,593,354,761	7,770,217,362
Venezuela..........................	9,766,732,032	11,392,073,878	16,113,837,879	11,867,378,790	10,127,399,308	7,765,377,720
Panama.............................	5,580,985,846	7,586,955,614	9,174,204,092	9,626,863,055	9,137,179,003	7,001,290,430
Philippines	6,540,881,882	6,549,419,826	7,070,869,023	7,292,421,996	7,222,335,250	6,970,624,331
Turkey...............................	6,745,027,666	9,347,106,834	7,431,818,268	7,796,411,817	7,941,557,273	6,939,527,969
Russian Federation	5,629,848,821	7,682,697,015	9,822,982,781	10,201,359,075	10,165,998,942	6,711,113,971
Dominican Republic............	5,444,168,944	5,799,299,217	5,688,491,073	5,688,227,330	6,356,244,768	5,801,253,420
Indonesia	5,129,368,126	5,144,820,967	5,922,395,716	6,967,145,795	6,039,357,145	5,499,009,718
Costa Rica.........................	4,543,328,783	5,288,570,241	6,408,767,786	6,646,248,986	6,305,665,742	5,470,836,948
Ecuador.............................	4,775,142,767	5,528,146,746	6,133,102,660	7,049,885,882	7,480,007,688	5,315,513,113
Vietnam.............................	2,830,597,109	3,079,674,623	3,328,710,887	3,460,087,603	3,958,233,619	5,199,813,760
South Africa	5,110,571,507	6,592,555,392	6,953,429,478	6,767,020,037	5,864,870,905	5,048,130,311
Guatemala..........................	3,674,505,202	4,893,028,310	4,819,865,335	4,460,475,265	4,848,826,486	4,669,246,583
Honduras...........................	3,867,666,562	5,134,433,003	4,726,161,940	4,477,632,656	4,961,822,728	4,343,552,348
Qatar................................	3,054,393,291	2,647,082,957	3,440,562,783	4,794,741,831	5,003,482,904	4,043,868,448
Egypt.................................	4,570,460,248	3,602,550,065	4,058,203,154	3,824,009,913	4,893,814,198	4,014,272,735
Austria..............................	2,103,504,380	2,552,177,521	2,870,409,017	3,120,305,958	3,472,079,352	3,641,372,531
Poland...............................	2,417,953,611	2,580,857,854	3,007,760,926	3,462,980,693	3,315,456,811	3,415,795,152
Sweden.............................	4,098,968,038	4,525,821,784	4,596,674,151	3,790,012,699	3,771,868,825	3,414,970,982
Norway	2,807,679,091	3,314,126,714	3,207,707,768	4,254,597,024	4,013,070,544	3,251,767,788
New Zealand	2,464,372,024	3,179,587,446	2,844,857,686	2,826,166,001	3,790,193,970	3,188,845,411
El Salvador........................	1,951,441,151	2,668,658,166	2,433,379,014	2,694,338,970	2,740,604,410	2,662,005,402
Kuwait...............................	2,646,912,778	2,529,621,477	2,475,757,942	2,399,683,055	3,307,901,112	2,548,850,040
Nigeria..............................	3,155,822,275	2,892,291,775	3,115,895,809	4,406,372,648	4,448,530,696	2,448,061,531
Oman................................	1,001,061,721	1,314,773,437	1,637,214,281	1,474,194,677	1,908,759,980	2,249,856,642
Trinidad and Tobago...........	1,682,318,558	1,923,510,432	2,203,342,823	2,092,233,699	2,107,956,394	2,199,443,320
Bahamas...........................	2,787,962,294	3,001,720,649	3,027,485,661	2,916,427,013	2,870,927,008	2,064,257,052
Denmark............................	1,902,880,486	1,998,781,269	2,004,016,344	1,996,796,443	2,077,170,568	1,907,685,474
Czech Republic	1,304,127,709	1,571,616,929	1,718,269,461	1,819,305,219	2,171,015,341	1,856,366,395
Iraq..................................	1,478,224,045	1,797,637,996	1,921,548,450	1,952,257,256	1,970,251,230	1,807,792,955
Algeria..............................	1,094,433,332	1,515,723,060	1,199,565,240	1,702,386,354	2,456,360,095	1,753,459,627
Hungary............................	1,202,254,744	1,399,818,875	1,490,621,294	1,639,451,606	1,735,719,701	1,617,947,128
Paraguay...........................	1,742,525,946	1,930,172,234	1,708,085,624	1,897,906,351	2,073,428,747	1,476,942,391
Gibraltar............................	991,393,562	2,279,015,155	3,648,844,835	2,512,074,984	1,825,906,728	1,472,659,719
Ethiopia.............................	591,454,284	581,114,626	1,190,646,545	605,252,852	1,577,498,828	1,442,698,925
Jamaica.............................	1,314,445,367	1,587,147,629	1,635,181,178	1,583,498,516	1,784,806,068	1,381,826,961
Morocco............................	1,548,970,056	2,266,890,660	1,629,539,027	1,991,615,890	1,451,716,591	1,312,617,274
Finland..............................	1,755,183,884	2,360,029,489	2,049,287,204	1,904,496,490	1,739,294,215	1,284,048,981
Pakistan............................	1,499,006,298	1,395,604,153	1,007,795,690	1,079,138,202	1,018,856,151	1,271,314,164
Uruguay............................	905,676,424	1,178,722,128	1,282,048,194	1,660,470,817	1,520,447,546	1,232,151,136
Luxembourg.......................	1,233,420,622	1,393,507,266	1,747,593,381	1,653,663,701	1,255,145,765	1,167,010,259

Table B-26.   U.S. Exports of North American Industry Classification System (NAICS) Manufactures by Region and Individual Country, 2010–2015—*Continued*

Country	2010	2011	2012	2013	2014	2015
Angola................................	1,237,690,688	1,435,448,367	1,403,385,772	1,368,987,217	1,965,821,611	1,121,293,995
French Guiana......................	28,890,901	51,178,246	206,377,941	627,827,863	277,717,478	1,070,712,303
Nicaragua............................	619,165,581	716,535,796	847,669,724	850,375,135	814,330,823	1,007,071,397
Lebanon..............................	1,857,725,069	1,376,469,207	738,785,754	748,364,036	981,946,757	993,201,688
Jordan.................................	1,020,249,445	899,887,525	1,260,898,642	1,399,294,876	1,598,601,514	945,466,251
Bahrain................................	1,080,180,527	1,005,722,633	929,884,640	797,911,161	811,567,963	899,575,793
Bolivia................................	485,613,907	611,654,140	719,848,761	980,599,880	935,949,782	869,165,061
Kenya.................................	305,751,966	350,951,180	455,554,160	537,033,336	1,537,708,081	843,303,184
Aruba..................................	495,723,117	647,330,973	653,156,743	898,607,499	856,468,657	838,481,151
Sint Maarten.......................	0	369,390,896	652,180,444	779,452,977	727,764,452	678,674,121
Ghana.................................	920,164,420	958,779,793	1,021,905,317	700,235,162	925,355,163	676,936,479
Haiti....................................	786,190,216	721,185,599	674,451,523	730,774,563	815,580,764	651,780,531
Romania..............................	525,112,772	672,546,094	694,720,587	590,819,434	887,085,407	651,419,454
Portugal..............................	832,845,916	884,099,787	743,646,304	611,236,685	669,501,181	645,383,226
Greece................................	892,153,194	964,683,137	668,586,768	626,712,713	639,924,308	597,032,686
Antigua and Barbuda............	133,264,489	128,356,558	167,832,632	121,889,717	184,741,937	570,053,826
Bermuda..............................	528,862,517	501,561,536	526,541,192	444,276,596	541,443,310	518,286,940
Cayman Islands....................	424,613,619	444,362,856	477,172,853	488,079,754	622,877,810	501,307,522
Barbados.............................	327,382,447	356,652,484	379,105,134	365,744,546	441,257,107	492,166,796
Kazakhstan..........................	714,276,629	677,510,871	847,548,412	1,106,563,085	976,726,374	489,702,150
Bangladesh..........................	311,239,970	737,831,165	356,896,451	497,515,290	808,313,832	488,036,926
Afghanistan..........................	2,049,679,670	2,829,463,853	1,455,317,796	1,382,062,216	769,957,217	479,837,366
Ukraine...............................	820,921,540	1,005,523,295	1,267,293,440	1,284,908,074	732,104,927	479,588,438
Azerbaijan...........................	244,695,498	332,677,056	476,334,999	377,643,331	942,993,058	463,067,208
Curacao...............................	0	452,997,753	642,131,154	643,233,527	567,322,823	461,600,490
Malta..................................	447,920,069	735,762,968	356,315,014	550,655,723	898,104,439	460,705,524
Tunisia................................	334,129,286	395,684,944	441,418,867	697,701,503	662,390,778	442,679,621
Saint Lucia..........................	341,533,225	270,013,065	320,082,488	505,149,242	598,332,827	425,833,135
Suriname.............................	327,182,054	386,990,379	448,538,638	405,108,439	469,095,915	401,255,137
Macau; SAR of China............	182,550,032	223,583,830	260,699,925	272,132,162	335,513,821	400,256,159
Lithuania.............................	585,651,118	512,843,083	439,825,270	476,208,612	382,688,582	380,458,831
Slovenia..............................	246,342,259	490,209,916	218,287,727	222,404,484	263,008,541	328,259,025
Benin..................................	446,373,081	209,164,899	215,879,743	276,246,326	387,513,379	318,004,252
Sri Lanka.............................	147,330,909	219,338,063	192,935,535	231,877,184	285,379,655	308,775,921
Slovakia..............................	194,852,611	221,286,216	222,830,201	222,117,711	347,804,066	299,337,859
Latvia..................................	317,100,086	381,309,109	382,348,657	427,072,738	381,145,717	281,295,692
Iceland................................	233,997,632	469,237,687	279,738,667	416,815,288	266,224,658	277,593,891
Guyana................................	205,958,526	261,626,791	267,901,196	237,119,533	277,918,499	276,646,671
Bulgaria...............................	152,407,306	228,891,882	218,066,472	272,272,896	310,729,523	268,560,623
Estonia................................	172,787,754	290,498,048	219,147,274	271,872,790	279,051,983	267,121,095
Georgia...............................	279,299,634	385,188,335	375,274,472	353,334,808	404,908,802	262,192,413
Mozambique.........................	177,282,411	360,067,279	298,360,279	276,959,101	322,787,297	252,281,799
Congo.................................	237,869,229	190,745,674	214,587,831	196,030,604	300,059,949	238,676,354
Belize.................................	247,731,286	302,135,073	223,497,997	198,057,915	197,218,251	237,350,580
Cote d'Ivoire........................	159,119,888	107,191,832	172,138,095	150,774,011	220,963,997	236,341,386
British Virgin Islands.............	123,997,238	121,371,203	128,389,896	281,879,710	352,229,784	226,184,073
Burma (Myanmar)..................	8,578,889	34,373,593	54,132,965	126,618,117	75,122,475	211,326,958
Iran....................................	138,376,674	184,759,282	137,599,794	233,050,543	152,548,618	208,330,508
Togo...................................	151,045,077	155,587,225	315,973,569	957,818,753	972,023,023	205,103,239
Papua New Guinea................	167,789,433	282,795,546	370,626,514	156,705,207	135,507,284	197,219,245
Gabon.................................	236,700,298	193,505,864	298,985,055	294,551,486	404,757,132	196,811,369
Cameroon............................	120,610,215	180,156,156	227,954,503	293,222,500	273,850,374	195,574,411
Libyan Arab Jamahiriya..........	592,729,893	241,087,894	335,065,152	611,999,563	440,426,799	171,142,121
Senegal...............................	203,079,548	235,773,515	118,048,681	193,372,800	133,272,622	167,320,295
Croatia................................	158,032,212	190,614,632	181,313,510	154,202,756	133,591,131	165,205,949
Cuba...................................	206,759,124	162,807,141	256,966,889	257,217,999	233,308,934	160,413,517
Equatorial Guinea.................	266,055,529	271,383,396	224,225,381	734,315,129	564,135,225	153,844,099
Turks and Caicos Islands	105,950,156	111,418,878	114,050,706	121,708,603	154,752,874	153,392,069
Cambodia............................	139,429,050	61,727,036	80,695,023	102,485,029	120,710,546	131,684,200
Tanzania; United Republic of...	119,964,259	163,905,254	196,460,526	355,498,734	247,866,465	129,233,666
Saint Kitts and Nevis	111,083,689	97,905,413	90,484,278	123,209,940	159,131,732	125,831,908
Brunei.................................	111,236,854	167,389,089	142,564,741	539,667,085	534,632,929	122,654,361
Mauritania...........................	77,155,227	236,694,034	283,133,454	227,416,476	142,510,432	119,685,387
Democratic Republic of Congo	71,730,464	136,853,927	159,173,157	142,366,926	147,855,794	116,940,982
Djibouti...............................	99,737,312	83,167,579	65,524,597	107,940,090	82,944,673	112,292,213
Guinea................................	67,904,717	206,911,632	115,618,328	52,871,081	43,982,866	109,060,897
Martinique...........................	260,380,092	300,769,592	330,546,539	343,885,339	265,668,971	104,911,215
French Polynesia..................	104,845,588	109,338,202	113,041,582	110,056,006	111,089,636	101,806,692
Serbia.................................	80,010,587	94,476,617	100,594,718	110,394,550	114,905,721	98,092,583
Cyprus................................	121,321,569	85,064,527	152,802,678	130,089,993	137,810,159	91,467,462

Table B-26.   U.S. Exports of North American Industry Classification System (NAICS) Manufactures by Region and Individual Country, 2010–2015—*Continued*

Country	2010	2011	2012	2013	2014	2015
Liberia	166,875,454	141,405,709	185,198,585	134,753,580	148,444,055	91,344,419
Namibia	90,139,471	87,364,195	123,804,665	177,410,689	270,265,726	89,949,437
Uzbekistan	74,249,419	67,124,735	252,786,708	338,653,671	164,876,997	80,932,046
Guadeloupe	293,360,263	355,287,768	421,461,900	539,836,156	360,460,360	80,551,855
Uganda	79,381,962	76,766,096	87,915,143	116,389,524	71,572,346	78,991,394
Turkmenistan	38,752,593	70,325,754	91,183,802	259,778,069	452,600,861	78,761,551
Zambia	50,153,372	115,171,749	129,554,321	126,017,456	102,221,474	76,385,403
Marshall Islands	82,391,114	129,827,201	124,413,913	57,806,843	89,490,792	71,378,525
Mali	34,297,212	48,348,088	54,347,577	45,372,942	33,331,018	66,005,091
Mongolia	113,241,102	243,292,068	594,838,957	249,279,587	156,074,522	65,575,186
Niger	42,106,725	27,633,623	27,515,339	39,635,889	43,552,271	64,002,156
Grenada	49,069,263	54,216,079	49,392,181	67,864,360	62,757,773	61,943,434
Saint Vincent and the Grenadines	60,742,381	60,439,170	66,281,733	64,958,505	72,432,336	61,316,028
Belarus	126,428,921	107,557,009	93,493,958	85,430,129	87,668,427	57,831,651
New Caledonia	83,519,079	75,763,972	57,569,804	54,301,984	97,583,792	57,357,853
Sierra Leone	49,939,196	74,123,475	80,388,248	61,161,421	68,094,391	53,179,308
Chad	82,777,432	23,657,687	23,747,992	39,264,268	58,758,910	51,824,601
Dominica	59,329,719	59,298,159	57,380,800	47,313,036	51,171,726	51,723,675
Burkina Faso	42,500,820	30,911,923	43,100,514	70,300,078	63,599,208	49,076,034
Fiji	28,901,316	31,385,195	35,865,657	49,955,476	56,482,775	44,764,037
Armenia	48,522,668	60,977,742	45,893,463	59,820,410	43,689,125	41,487,089
Somalia	1,214,826	2,043,155	11,877,831	13,899,218	30,076,473	39,363,148
Madagascar	112,683,983	51,180,115	58,262,363	59,883,440	42,395,525	39,141,503
Anguilla	29,159,669	25,590,952	22,111,912	24,490,152	52,249,784	38,794,487
Yemen	287,815,834	135,091,347	201,516,237	209,129,337	143,260,487	37,284,681
Liechtenstein	15,986,901	19,723,533	19,318,465	21,055,721	27,801,660	34,114,003
Maldives	26,065,131	42,923,775	27,857,137	25,935,515	26,735,971	34,043,018
Micronesia (Federated States of)	35,787,002	37,339,269	43,132,351	34,851,002	34,252,943	33,049,688
Gambia	28,550,299	25,291,556	23,307,939	27,462,490	36,004,792	32,506,551
Zimbabwe	62,743,148	42,028,645	48,389,304	45,079,634	40,305,487	31,079,001
Central African Republic	8,668,017	9,682,705	6,979,613	3,479,482	28,546,906	30,471,649
Mauritius	36,361,957	40,057,336	90,035,318	35,075,970	31,505,573	29,603,264
Monaco	24,029,707	7,866,424	11,924,443	454,080,516	76,553,132	28,644,341
Macedonia	24,439,477	18,156,091	13,664,881	41,682,471	18,138,411	28,313,426
Albania	43,998,665	39,781,083	49,717,684	66,831,097	46,993,393	27,901,722
Kyrgyzstan	68,152,078	39,825,556	93,283,482	63,945,185	39,104,496	27,783,059
Malawi	21,719,735	32,099,607	45,610,778	38,251,791	30,085,344	27,249,201
Lao People's Democratic Republic	11,827,298	21,269,258	30,338,494	22,796,098	26,026,449	23,225,996
Nepal	24,751,706	35,097,827	32,881,306	28,122,098	30,277,646	22,911,050
Botswana	25,448,505	22,197,453	27,176,017	42,221,879	26,288,986	21,578,566
Samoa	17,068,671	21,220,213	22,112,330	25,252,062	20,919,895	20,734,054
Palau	11,447,538	13,532,343	13,443,520	14,487,647	15,866,930	20,434,019
Swaziland	17,251,968	14,585,964	33,423,954	17,076,588	22,264,887	19,203,484
Bosnia and Herzegovina	17,961,280	17,566,073	13,384,615	32,142,991	19,364,698	18,592,491
Tajikistan	12,959,694	118,478,145	14,448,883	23,302,204	15,315,615	18,442,695
Seychelles	10,023,052	12,543,690	14,548,891	11,764,750	12,130,973	17,148,598
Moldova; Republic of	25,431,728	34,237,165	33,728,419	40,496,473	31,093,267	15,097,132
Sudan	33,220,808	21,777,786	18,735,275	43,208,102	37,208,157	13,974,556
South Sudan	0	3,467,139	27,782,613	10,092,819	14,235,603	13,270,227
Tonga	16,723,746	15,701,841	22,979,171	15,574,873	16,220,970	11,228,212
Kosovo	9,707,341	12,541,984	17,135,910	12,957,089	11,508,147	10,879,856
Rwanda	27,842,909	116,704,684	28,679,785	23,361,656	19,306,740	10,802,816
Greenland	8,098,147	6,714,062	14,797,247	17,832,877	12,066,861	8,926,042
Montenegro	11,920,749	11,352,143	8,814,256	17,467,677	13,169,436	8,073,692
French Southern Territories	564,652	1,269,790	1,160,311	1,675,735	7,998,481	7,745,242
Reunion	7,896,490	154,468,356	6,464,056	7,650,174	9,929,214	5,784,429
Cape Verde	7,429,067	8,346,718	5,839,291	7,003,842	4,943,711	5,518,969
Montserrat	3,788,774	5,240,509	6,697,359	6,831,893	7,022,394	5,078,445
Burundi	11,610,971	26,976,143	16,911,640	14,010,350	4,664,192	5,076,447
Mayotte	3,447,929	4,246,012	4,861,700	7,829,760	11,076,958	5,073,021
San Marino	2,896,265	1,829,066	1,083,074	1,232,326	4,271,868	4,895,472
Kiribati	823,822	2,279,596	3,290,296	5,830,323	2,162,877	4,824,544
Cook Islands	3,403,941	3,967,783	4,801,380	4,124,848	4,847,407	3,725,194
Vanuatu	11,956,821	2,946,446	57,521,894	19,873,135	12,455,907	3,706,576
Saint Helena	651,828	1,799,318	4,822,543	2,799,875	443,222	3,404,900
Solomon Islands	3,558,997	3,332,156	3,868,162	5,041,944	3,879,071	3,318,952
Eritrea	2,005,016	3,056,182	5,381,349	12,832,981	4,624,878	3,270,950
Andorra	7,543,771	5,064,633	2,141,360	5,105,281	3,134,045	3,249,155
Falkland Islands (Malvinas)	2,317,648	3,601,226	3,793,783	1,073,425	7,675,275	2,667,443
East Timor	3,305,526	7,601,210	1,111,744	1,230,126	1,183,239	2,654,018

Table B-26. U.S. Exports of North American Industry Classification System (NAICS) Manufactures by Region and Individual Country, 2010–2015—*Continued*

Country	2010	2011	2012	2013	2014	2015
Bhutan	3,201,540	3,013,440	2,446,509	2,300,973	2,373,310	2,600,541
Faroe Islands	1,631,774	2,590,052	1,531,351	1,884,232	2,243,683	2,225,319
Guinea Bissau	3,217,220	10,444,551	18,914,440	4,833,968	2,698,842	2,052,983
Vatican City	2,831,841	1,994,754	4,267,960	1,384,889	1,649,218	1,561,903
Christmas Island	858,066	628,541	3,709,939	276,130	129,243	1,469,723
Comoros	1,075,731	1,030,127	921,568	3,457,221	3,422,976	1,442,707
Nauru	1,215,509	467,747	2,108,621	715,764	769,105	1,299,861
West Bank	704,985	1,055,816	1,362,233	756,407	1,647,574	874,657
Heard Island and Mcdonald Islands	3,241,324	347,204	437,979	470,416	103,588	855,540
Sao Tome and Principe	1,274,426	5,929,334	783,460	1,923,043	1,025,054	817,856
North Korea	0	489,112	497,686	453,950	408,004	804,206
Syrian Arab Republic	59,313,920	38,261,903	13,863,638	18,510,521	1,869,605	789,869
Tuvalu	589,631	670,634	581,326	532,361	560,427	587,828
British Indian Ocean Territory	1,188,516	1,414,245	2,573,488	731,475	2,053,694	560,356
Lesotho	591,193	6,058,413	2,370,004	432,747	2,269,879	536,165
Cocos (Keeling) Islands	550,330	821,989	865,856	20,961,899	1,473,642	525,290
Svalbard and Jan Mayen Island	7,249,092	1,889,406	122,159	1,346,205	3,212,037	370,937
Norfolk Island	344,334	918,052	1,115,803	1,576,720	754,999	318,872
Wallis and Futuna	693,953	227,991	321,780	590,454	328,533	287,444
Gaza Strip	1,799,808	47,297	93,117	178,138	169,040	155,734
Tokelau Islands	3,281,043	3,638,451	12,747,400	306,373	773,208	148,475
Saint Pierre and Miquelon	13,729	109,213	137,361	234,826	3,995	144,490
Niue	1,160,835	400,112	712,737	202,029	98,588	67,227
Western Sahara	52,983	31,006	58,759	153,960	273,774	31,457
Pitcairn Islands	0	2,530	0	0	33,317	6,311
East Germany	0	0	0	0	0	0
Netherlands Antilles	2,740,836,007	1,102,652,248	0	0	0	0
Other Countries	0	0	0	0	0	0
Serbia and Montenegro	0	0	0	0	0	0

Table B-27.   U.S. Imports of North American Industry Classification System (NAICS) Manufactures by Region and Individual Countries, 2005–2015

Region	2005	2006	2007	2008	2009	2010
WORLD	1,346,674,074,592	1,481,720,382,737	1,550,859,513,926	1,577,505,662,957	1,236,411,260,042	1,513,075,417,621
Europe	317,889,533,480	346,759,472,033	366,612,704,740	388,982,846,673	291,788,352,232	336,881,131,094
European Union (EU-28)	284,713,748,603	306,432,115,836	325,988,116,595	338,078,318,107	255,688,375,488	290,648,409,712
Austria	5,822,328,635	7,892,614,214	10,253,769,638	8,119,052,897	6,095,380,858	6,612,575,207
Belgium	12,026,375,548	13,285,545,082	14,100,817,816	15,952,305,156	12,660,456,661	14,469,382,688
Bulgaria	401,578,782	411,698,663	366,319,297	329,444,098	178,827,030	216,399,874
Croatia	351,818,530	343,035,061	321,358,810	263,478,848	243,451,387	329,087,293
Cyprus	16,525,015	38,593,265	8,870,793	8,084,577	7,682,791	6,840,842
Czech Republic	2,091,697,400	2,255,444,764	2,326,755,527	2,466,520,002	1,848,130,468	2,345,183,340
Denmark	4,866,493,881	5,266,227,359	5,792,744,574	6,095,586,287	5,235,309,109	5,862,956,150
Estonia	475,481,041	512,670,817	288,900,482	381,407,603	144,483,161	684,489,113
Finland	4,217,159,256	4,875,783,404	5,157,265,098	5,787,095,610	3,872,173,341	3,785,288,277
France	30,565,926,501	33,329,402,253	37,059,406,879	39,804,325,771	30,536,041,133	33,844,884,988
Germany	80,632,044,716	84,186,419,983	88,937,045,841	92,365,989,829	67,492,571,197	78,537,814,536
Greece	702,698,662	854,914,152	1,061,727,052	884,454,120	608,155,677	645,343,429
Hungary	2,471,594,268	2,484,429,413	2,701,537,206	2,936,305,754	2,083,332,752	2,301,421,825
Ireland	27,921,798,025	27,678,359,879	29,581,054,353	30,317,751,016	26,953,183,869	32,348,147,014
Italy	29,516,972,632	31,026,721,459	33,140,692,872	34,371,552,253	24,885,868,003	26,997,012,877
Latvia	346,762,776	283,859,128	316,681,810	211,600,227	129,146,696	180,824,143
Lithuania	621,949,050	557,264,171	447,654,521	738,522,148	578,828,045	631,532,971
Luxembourg	368,127,929	507,235,852	460,421,939	463,333,806	254,468,008	368,947,067
Malta	276,904,712	342,232,835	315,061,932	267,451,684	211,017,401	256,981,939
Netherlands	12,349,910,921	14,895,217,556	15,084,039,326	16,564,249,075	11,476,915,684	13,489,781,335
Poland	1,868,798,550	2,154,842,484	2,152,498,537	2,466,217,386	1,912,787,130	2,825,059,845
Portugal	2,229,387,043	2,942,634,870	2,931,912,405	2,325,311,739	1,507,457,582	2,049,202,548
Romania	1,189,668,215	1,100,564,599	1,037,021,700	1,083,864,281	724,833,957	980,519,207
Slovakia	951,243,262	1,390,287,135	1,487,281,327	1,283,203,067	616,375,247	1,006,575,127
Slovenia	404,018,731	474,096,798	477,994,185	444,326,111	361,352,100	434,113,775
Spain	7,680,874,860	8,787,318,278	9,552,237,594	10,085,208,439	6,953,158,515	7,623,978,416
Sweden	13,177,086,987	13,299,575,600	12,462,641,405	11,948,566,608	7,815,100,288	10,096,675,463
United Kingdom	41,168,522,675	45,255,126,762	48,164,403,676	50,113,109,715	40,301,887,398	41,717,390,423
Non-EU	33,175,784,877	40,327,356,197	40,624,588,145	50,904,528,566	36,099,976,744	46,232,721,382
Albania	5,685,378	8,147,551	5,095,944	5,768,478	7,448,852	24,635,403
Belarus	342,756,907	470,865,612	1,025,652,983	1,061,325,527	569,288,610	173,703,741
Faroe Islands	105,854	242,949	315,357	388,483	66,235	282,834
Gibraltar	965,806	698,580	389,119	124,314	800,880	643,520
Iceland	78,362,431	82,666,619	80,056,486	108,534,413	76,537,737	99,347,089
Kosovo	0	0	0	0	380,088	69,884
Liechtenstein	292,408,088	279,832,486	281,599,596	242,270,402	178,363,100	208,755,250
Macedonia	39,271,555	32,744,686	53,567,840	57,715,332	14,058,092	18,804,111
Moldova	49,831,405	36,739,292	22,733,681	11,993,088	7,945,170	12,025,504
Monaco	24,404,066	17,400,539	17,209,003	18,001,985	14,273,764	18,864,806
Montenegro	0	0	4,635,457	354,234	16,350,909	3,702,291
Norway	2,809,746,762	3,850,837,894	4,954,578,050	5,247,476,521	3,830,541,785	5,158,476,814
Russia	12,048,333,105	16,139,431,685	15,455,073,540	21,163,399,835	12,881,953,992	17,777,711,103
San Marino	1,278,606	2,718,593	1,430,022	791,786	642,802	3,711,887
Serbia	53,562,881	65,295,840	55,869,410	68,867,244	60,627,069	118,696,015
Svalbard, Jan Mayen Island	39,218	17,675	0	26,939	0	24,240
Switzerland	11,528,847,993	12,709,883,900	13,247,134,832	16,326,152,172	14,807,644,832	17,680,470,375
Turkey	4,823,845,444	5,037,171,194	4,232,441,074	4,295,646,641	3,280,662,615	3,906,207,542
Ukraine	1,076,119,571	1,591,366,944	1,186,720,313	2,295,520,308	352,212,530	1,024,895,730
Vatican City	219,807	1,294,158	85,438	170,864	177,682	1,693,243
WESTERN HEMISPHERE						
NAFTA	342,285,174,143	369,931,486,204	385,919,689,267	373,718,652,110	290,754,548,803	372,151,078,469
Canada	207,812,979,579	215,769,699,013	220,922,864,180	210,323,517,688	150,316,039,480	187,652,776,355
Mexico	134,472,194,564	154,161,787,191	164,996,825,087	163,395,134,422	140,438,509,323	184,498,302,114
Caribbean	11,683,410,036	11,756,835,746	12,402,144,183	13,512,698,414	8,569,087,023	9,153,100,014
Anguilla	2,220,050	3,820,657	4,236,528	4,025,205	5,166,520	1,853,935
Antigua and Barbuda	892,402	748,316	1,189,672	1,149,245	1,643,519	663,407
Aruba	2,903,017,753	2,783,032,431	2,979,107,277	3,141,051,877	1,259,597,502	6,484,520
Bahamas	436,494,999	227,501,228	319,727,723	268,260,265	621,191,464	577,537,873
Barbados	22,313,414	24,429,481	29,584,613	32,093,930	24,968,468	36,010,340
British Virgin Islands	7,410,446	21,898,098	32,895,266	5,450,699	2,338,962	3,257,132
Cayman Islands	4,556,704	4,535,714	3,264,770	2,309,833	3,453,053	2,412,350
Cuba	9,709	0	0	0	0	5,625
Curacao	0	0	0	0	0	535,987,979
Dominica	1,831,704	2,045,978	1,048,069	1,490,815	979,017	856,693
Dominican Republic	4,261,660,395	4,113,650,526	3,785,794,617	3,548,479,290	2,833,180,587	3,135,288,877

Table B-27.   U.S. Imports of North American Industry Classification System (NAICS) Manufactures by Region and Individual Countries, 2005–2015—*Continued*

Region	2011	2012	2013	2014	2015	Value Change, 2005–2015	2005–2015 Annual Average percent Change
WORLD	1,719,885,788,819	1,809,100,281,745	1,834,000,726,399	1,927,026,129,824	1,943,752,829,400	597,078,754,808	4
Europe	400,196,161,665	413,227,643,184	417,333,280,523	447,290,414,914	443,415,838,120	125,526,304,640	3
European Union (EU-28)	340,155,734,840	352,616,313,723	356,101,525,728	385,840,180,955	389,424,710,067	104,710,961,464	3
Austria..	9,157,333,251	9,203,000,982	9,523,771,281	10,467,884,238	10,738,554,218	4,916,225,583	6
Belgium...	16,026,126,707	15,674,633,670	17,151,989,279	18,465,918,571	17,149,729,549	5,123,354,001	4
Bulgaria...	371,229,978	455,733,026	444,964,135	538,047,436	520,490,259	118,911,477	3
Croatia..	428,176,002	438,100,690	418,388,649	451,985,696	541,382,363	189,563,833	4
Cyprus...	10,844,699	13,741,609	26,822,229	46,054,742	18,630,411	2,105,396	1
Czech Republic	3,218,141,164	3,779,331,985	3,759,153,512	4,164,481,997	4,293,355,031	2,201,657,631	7
Denmark...	6,548,181,039	6,589,838,977	6,275,874,437	7,258,930,317	7,437,816,799	2,571,322,918	4
Estonia..	927,829,346	471,946,331	404,755,310	537,600,027	476,870,115	1,389,074	0
Finland...	4,324,555,526	4,972,369,779	4,558,291,682	4,902,379,848	4,325,439,111	108,279,855	0
France...	35,764,110,582	37,111,443,172	39,545,838,540	41,014,215,851	40,423,441,246	9,857,514,745	3
Germany...	94,197,478,099	104,035,135,122	108,902,086,937	117,315,460,416	117,447,149,781	36,815,105,065	4
Greece...	735,027,067	863,756,178	843,615,638	878,186,020	1,163,979,833	461,281,171	5
Hungary...	2,749,011,971	3,003,479,877	3,544,904,620	5,057,828,783	5,486,148,842	3,014,554,574	8
Ireland...	38,218,558,351	32,250,844,658	30,339,563,320	32,624,135,278	37,269,026,684	9,347,228,659	3
Italy..	32,462,766,529	35,060,535,381	36,516,186,121	39,799,946,656	41,373,453,147	11,856,480,515	3
Latvia..	350,479,841	236,016,036	260,625,226	259,787,131	280,837,790	-65,924,986	-2
Lithuania..	1,039,968,881	1,156,694,565	1,546,265,984	1,079,451,004	1,031,722,523	409,773,473	5
Luxembourg....................................	385,551,455	378,388,917	411,706,825	486,268,027	463,753,785	95,625,856	2
Malta...	237,902,476	242,785,783	206,257,700	166,345,307	160,820,187	-116,084,525	-5
Netherlands....................................	17,311,739,785	17,858,773,126	15,889,771,508	17,845,268,907	14,489,505,187	2,139,594,266	2
Poland...	4,241,818,655	4,420,316,410	4,671,367,310	4,826,802,921	5,220,820,500	3,352,021,950	11
Portugal...	2,437,266,277	2,473,209,646	2,651,651,617	3,051,076,199	3,081,941,111	852,554,068	3
Romania...	1,389,504,186	1,580,414,773	1,665,541,724	2,023,758,839	1,960,602,663	770,934,448	5
Slovakia...	1,376,460,334	1,749,172,561	1,727,443,116	2,063,164,215	2,231,732,481	1,280,489,219	9
Slovenia...	526,313,863	546,741,373	555,928,661	678,356,309	640,389,475	236,370,744	5
Spain..	10,216,722,711	10,702,924,923	10,626,301,020	13,250,031,298	12,686,112,990	5,005,238,130	5
Sweden..	11,039,291,727	9,871,840,478	8,816,122,903	9,830,138,869	9,342,513,419	-3,834,573,568	-3
United Kingdom	44,463,344,338	47,475,143,695	44,816,336,444	46,756,676,053	49,168,490,567	7,999,967,892	2
						0	0
Non-EU	60,040,426,825	60,611,329,461	61,231,754,795	61,450,233,959	53,991,128,053	20,815,343,176	5
Albania..	19,077,381	11,329,411	9,864,890	12,504,482	17,497,869	11,812,491	12
Belarus..	361,706,092	151,818,665	103,104,407	128,986,682	154,459,031	-188,297,876	-8
Faroe Islands..................................	669,723	637,136	575,879	757,924	6,408,078	6,302,224	51
Gibraltar..	176,761	177,329	57,444	111,076	222,488	-743,318	-14
Iceland..	113,987,155	127,384,493	101,505,965	124,995,012	127,652,169	49,289,738	5
Kosovo..	304,321	196,873	320,806	501,288	1,917,352	1,917,352	0
Liechtenstein..................................	245,432,897	306,374,042	292,576,699	290,542,985	300,192,843	7,784,755	0
Macedonia......................................	24,624,520	45,306,436	25,953,631	137,824,952	176,310,641	137,039,086	16
Moldova...	15,794,638	24,717,170	34,225,034	34,156,080	37,054,891	-12,776,514	-3
Monaco..	26,022,670	24,098,118	24,258,877	24,956,421	16,695,845	-7,708,221	-4
Montenegro	4,197,249	2,356,474	1,576,607	2,609,626	1,213,538	1,213,538	0
Norway..	5,134,293,996	5,036,175,699	4,331,791,946	4,087,736,690	3,791,656,223	981,909,461	3
Russia...	25,562,645,217	24,919,390,150	24,653,576,634	22,267,505,741	14,763,744,327	2,715,411,222	2
San Marino	4,700,047	4,548,274	5,819,712	6,086,867	8,055,993	6,777,387	20
Serbia..	128,373,754	140,098,840	512,518,516	258,510,636	264,137,691	210,574,810	17
Svalbard, Jan Mayen Island	2,462	8,080	19,267	0	26,587	-12,631	-4
Switzerland	22,298,770,583	22,734,103,796	24,108,888,441	26,678,174,790	26,514,945,198	14,986,097,205	9
Turkey...	4,681,393,822	5,797,536,493	6,065,840,058	6,594,567,425	7,107,690,218	2,283,844,774	4
Ukraine..	1,417,833,001	1,284,926,499	959,168,180	799,084,708	700,192,228	-375,927,343	-4
Vatican City	420,536	145,483	111,802	620,574	1,054,843	835,036	17
WESTERN HEMISPHERE						0	0
						0	0
NAFTA..	413,519,998,043	438,014,375,745	446,390,361,539	463,971,455,429	469,275,931,778	126,990,757,635	3
Canada..	207,270,031,117	215,133,559,039	216,059,325,538	218,305,446,154	208,464,908,152	651,928,573	0
Mexico..	206,249,966,926	222,880,816,706	230,331,036,001	245,666,009,275	260,811,023,626	126,338,829,062	7
						0	0
Caribbean	15,283,272,325	12,273,850,686	10,575,019,116	10,489,669,225	8,882,502,814	-2,800,907,222	-3
Anguilla...	3,864,248	2,774,301	2,866,162	4,500,147	4,834,595	2,614,545	8
Antigua and Barbuda........................	1,120,898	701,874	2,237,128	697,855	539,967	-352,435	-5
Aruba..	3,234,439,525	783,902,403	13,604,347	5,383,351	29,403,350	-2,873,614,403	-37
Bahamas..	556,536,901	231,865,687	258,744,507	245,570,034	117,935,448	-318,559,551	-12
Barbados..	39,886,386	40,903,408	42,177,242	40,970,239	57,028,993	34,715,579	10
British Virgin Islands........................	3,374,681	5,521,061	4,140,724	2,389,864	5,036,144	-2,374,302	-4
Cayman Islands...............................	1,516,406	1,350,071	5,195,442	9,753,003	82,041,692	77,484,988	34
Cuba...	0	0	0	0	0	-9,709	-100
Curacao...	769,661,852	358,928,262	321,962,530	314,487,758	0	0	0
Dominica..	737,222	526,278	713,650	670,919	851,239	-980,465	-7
Dominican Republic..........................	3,547,829,693	3,679,734,539	3,682,839,228	3,968,023,945	4,229,074,620	-32,585,775	-0

Table B-27. **U.S. Imports of North American Industry Classification System (NAICS) Manufactures by Region and Individual Countries, 2005–2015**—*Continued*

Region	2005	2006	2007	2008	2009	2010
Grenada	2,503,528	932,167	1,057,554	1,626,304	949,376	1,644,817
Guadeloupe	1,688,847	1,956,024	2,835,417	1,939,516	920,762	1,617,815
Haiti	430,220,857	466,321,242	467,817,361	427,550,526	525,877,051	532,395,602
Jamaica	234,190,076	355,972,339	538,128,640	542,057,742	322,018,636	201,026,263
Martinique	18,981,887	40,653,672	5,243,706	3,817,851	4,621,748	22,316,168
Montserrat	893,560	506,313	409,883	179,476	301,702	287,220
St Kitts and Nevis	46,152,481	46,119,419	45,524,778	49,171,098	40,988,907	41,542,720
St Lucia	26,616,100	26,238,695	30,531,720	14,509,509	13,410,371	14,279,931
St Vincent and the Grenadines	14,666,043	1,313,409	401,308	521,276	463,623	269,038
Sint Maarten	0	0	0	0	0	0
Trinidad and Tobago	3,266,629,205	3,634,995,825	4,152,833,093	5,466,918,501	2,905,371,262	4,036,667,484
Turks and Caicos Islands	459,876	164,212	512,188	95,456	1,644,493	694,225
Central America	10,870,866,139	11,093,131,300	11,247,902,374	11,546,657,360	11,966,306,379	16,358,965,101
Belize	49,214,167	52,904,198	41,476,713	33,038,031	24,400,493	19,840,938
Costa Rica	2,400,857,540	2,582,179,086	2,650,575,861	2,656,558,640	4,430,571,188	7,286,139,257
El Salvador	1,850,268,318	1,694,731,396	1,849,640,063	1,986,108,336	1,585,679,517	1,938,969,246
Guatemala	2,201,237,838	2,102,010,393	1,890,353,611	2,001,884,113	1,796,770,316	2,144,927,573
Honduras	3,260,085,257	3,244,293,787	3,324,368,221	3,336,776,002	2,683,547,812	3,205,023,845
Nicaragua	1,012,959,379	1,309,733,733	1,383,724,519	1,412,451,803	1,354,051,259	1,676,669,825
Panama	96,243,640	107,278,707	107,763,386	119,840,435	91,285,794	87,394,417
South America	44,869,616,992	47,965,592,656	44,425,014,280	46,122,487,666	28,266,829,923	33,497,972,140
Argentina	3,059,538,369	2,803,046,430	3,160,653,846	4,410,875,588	2,452,164,788	2,498,855,544
Bolivia	209,927,427	252,907,402	248,119,621	370,752,198	330,851,702	382,489,095
Brazil	20,646,168,098	21,206,344,458	19,671,793,654	19,974,584,737	11,812,022,102	13,836,967,108
Chile	4,281,548,682	6,939,560,213	5,859,677,628	5,350,731,696	3,465,180,464	4,503,167,741
Colombia	2,896,412,024	2,618,137,250	2,647,784,889	3,392,170,347	2,961,384,818	3,964,845,837
Ecuador	503,574,979	573,568,048	574,400,516	642,936,931	435,420,958	431,306,886
Falkland Islands (Islas Malvin)	114,240	27,250	54,348	138,778	3,670	13,441
French Guiana	91,852	246,363	125,806	22,175	58,342	69,789
Guyana	29,920,248	34,461,000	27,850,838	46,490,197	108,470,854	234,698,262
Paraguay	49,021,451	54,010,489	62,030,075	75,599,615	53,054,179	60,730,270
Peru	4,527,214,194	5,149,787,529	4,384,886,910	4,635,652,881	3,164,796,301	3,757,214,271
Suriname	143,008,567	140,710,827	104,178,352	96,274,003	100,676,301	155,538,331
Uruguay	684,767,091	467,800,575	439,123,992	186,782,461	184,257,495	178,654,947
Venezuela	7,838,309,770	7,724,984,822	7,244,333,805	6,939,476,059	3,198,487,949	3,493,420,618
Other Western Hemisphere	3,815,422	3,480,198	7,551,037	2,558,501	2,215,135	2,441,279
Bermuda	3,665,432	3,167,480	7,300,608	2,505,587	2,206,598	2,421,468
Greenland	90,497	280,929	26,892	52,914	8,537	19,811
St Pierre and Miquelon	59,493	31,789	223,537	0	0	0
Asia	595,307,992,188	667,327,627,420	701,465,829,520	710,166,812,833	582,539,889,623	716,668,871,849
China	237,689,353,920	280,763,146,603	313,574,409,211	328,859,589,938	289,089,916,662	356,943,509,404
Hong Kong	7,971,500,848	7,157,228,661	6,111,607,465	5,311,406,762	2,797,153,587	3,232,585,322
Japan	133,259,967,332	142,794,891,137	139,628,275,739	134,266,342,700	91,838,896,665	116,498,951,624
Korea, South	42,736,492,065	44,754,683,143	46,385,756,622	46,556,813,736	38,107,196,063	47,455,056,397
Saudi Arabia	2,107,354,029	1,224,430,740	1,460,348,575	1,418,955,594	932,769,582	1,183,137,767
Taiwan	33,424,630,065	36,589,318,467	36,042,752,424	34,398,159,211	26,995,080,861	33,641,056,615
ASEAN - 10	89,787,476,035	99,795,422,785	99,807,888,999	97,294,343,215	82,296,025,887	94,685,281,327
Brunei	167,614,658	121,216,759	112,539,424	73,240,828	39,896,154	8,463,346
Myanmar (ex-Burma)	0	0	0	0	85,916	0
Cambodia	1,736,154,733	2,162,736,164	2,447,305,057	2,400,210,156	1,911,408,293	2,288,820,656
East Timor	0	0	0	0	0	0
Indonesia	9,589,794,795	10,601,174,476	11,311,976,628	11,953,723,614	10,371,448,324	12,288,100,855
Laos	3,051,423	8,402,414	11,663,227	38,600,355	40,291,549	57,674,656
Malaysia	32,511,225,695	35,356,736,043	31,555,479,308	29,568,309,060	22,371,319,174	24,516,785,851
Philippines	8,825,957,213	9,210,050,977	8,996,596,397	8,327,588,128	6,436,850,317	7,588,789,347
Singapore	13,867,908,996	16,033,006,307	16,793,900,005	14,140,244,596	14,244,382,399	15,490,220,528
Thailand	18,014,139,535	19,794,632,351	19,954,608,717	20,350,399,120	16,392,591,256	19,615,028,250
Vietnam	5,071,628,987	6,507,467,294	8,623,820,236	10,442,027,358	10,487,752,505	12,831,397,838
Middle East	20,200,302,700	22,113,944,743	23,720,523,207	25,548,611,620	20,741,516,215	23,796,683,054
Andorra	150,774	2,618,530	206,784	561,674	335,704	323,133
Bahrain	342,762,630	435,536,529	439,927,468	458,658,058	351,033,118	369,046,725
Bosnia and Herzegovina	13,686,587	25,192,733	23,782,627	22,175,871	24,655,626	24,933,419
Gaza Strip admin. by Israel	1,429,636	797,727	1,454,624	2,280,808	5,286,150	3,180,336
Iran	155,208,493	142,738,723	153,109,537	87,434,827	56,772,958	86,715,893
Iraq	52,565,915	1,427,836	8,343,826	8,229,179	11,528,210	11,528,464
Israel	16,077,448,590	18,428,102,344	20,094,805,014	21,723,000,788	18,187,341,792	20,411,770,079
Jordan	1,226,015,757	1,392,545,108	1,282,098,571	1,081,312,610	878,949,366	925,955,492
Kuwait	480,643,878	202,408,852	335,986,073	425,498,219	110,727,661	187,349,197

Table B-27. U.S. Imports of North American Industry Classification System (NAICS) Manufactures by Region and Individual Countries, 2005–2015—*Continued*

Region	2011	2012	2013	2014	2015	Value Change, 2005–2015	2005–2015 Annual Average percent Change
Grenada	1,161,626	1,289,557	1,483,087	1,291,702	2,370,840	-132,688	-1
Guadeloupe	970,830	880,871	572,995	1,081,562	2,087,136	398,289	2
Haiti	718,607,292	748,763,146	823,972,332	878,945,625	921,010,612	490,789,755	8
Jamaica	368,295,797	297,118,209	191,492,315	86,113,638	97,443,380	-136,746,696	-8
Martinique	7,515,132	18,634,437	35,136,393	77,830,756	30,300,747	11,318,860	5
Montserrat	326,480	911,508	655,292	513,385	697,016	-196,544	-2
St Kitts and Nevis	45,249,437	49,299,335	44,467,060	45,699,257	42,576,569	-3,575,912	-1
St Lucia	14,789,771	12,042,586	11,927,917	11,149,474	12,732,871	-13,883,229	-7
St Vincent and the Grenadines	994,786	1,235,949	911,992	647,167	692,973	-13,973,070	-26
Sint Maarten	784,786	921,799	1,968,263	1,003,044	821,441	821,441	0
Trinidad and Tobago	5,965,424,352	6,036,386,119	5,127,670,416	4,792,699,818	3,244,368,952	-22,260,253	-0
Turks and Caicos Islands	184,224	159,286	280,094	246,682	654,229	194,353	4
						0	0
Central America	19,176,112,333	21,136,957,065	20,827,149,037	19,092,204,563	14,390,551,154	3,519,685,015	3
Belize	31,312,328	26,331,112	21,089,279	33,416,166	42,554,176	-6,659,991	-1
Costa Rica	8,476,368,254	10,246,394,859	10,114,356,188	7,931,817,278	2,964,521,319	563,663,779	2
El Salvador	2,071,894,366	2,295,487,419	2,193,453,294	2,247,766,709	2,309,093,068	458,824,750	2
Guatemala	2,667,888,684	2,398,357,067	2,196,561,769	2,281,738,032	2,297,585,529	96,347,691	0
Honduras	3,601,295,352	3,695,063,661	3,717,498,557	3,806,946,604	3,887,911,771	627,826,514	2
Nicaragua	2,212,216,317	2,332,661,847	2,428,014,058	2,681,157,644	2,770,865,713	1,757,906,334	11
Panama	115,137,032	142,661,100	156,175,892	109,362,130	118,019,578	21,775,938	2
						0	0
South America	44,751,009,637	47,367,794,770	46,411,687,610	44,688,451,134	38,640,451,930	-6,229,165,062	-1
Argentina	2,840,068,828	2,706,390,938	2,884,214,033	2,375,024,808	2,659,191,572	-400,346,797	-1
Bolivia	552,347,994	948,733,734	840,360,857	1,643,708,208	819,947,480	610,020,053	15
Brazil	18,203,013,649	20,130,915,045	18,810,002,155	19,598,723,460	18,628,622,656	-2,017,545,442	-1
Chile	6,206,764,551	6,350,773,666	6,651,369,341	5,448,950,035	5,159,137,104	877,588,422	2
Colombia	5,339,292,659	6,112,329,832	4,876,748,119	4,828,358,085	3,715,841,274	819,429,250	3
Ecuador	562,282,444	926,612,978	965,500,620	1,490,601,980	1,241,438,691	737,863,712	9
Falkland Islands (Islas Malvin)	6,151	5,628	15,049	35,436	52,823	-61,417	-7
French Guiana	234,073	15,418	508,843	152,958	24,947	-66,905	-12
Guyana	363,202,039	422,457,515	360,546,857	375,760,133	342,405,470	312,485,222	28
Paraguay	104,720,957	181,077,124	139,887,796	104,014,889	117,789,007	68,767,556	9
Peru	4,534,449,632	4,731,363,356	6,283,073,983	3,971,269,786	3,177,703,250	-1,349,510,944	-3
Suriname	264,614,532	248,306,264	237,691,145	392,812,740	103,999,152	-39,009,415	-3
Uruguay	210,906,658	264,712,791	314,995,382	366,087,512	479,880,714	-204,886,377	-3
Venezuela	5,569,105,470	4,344,100,481	4,046,773,430	4,092,951,104	2,194,417,790	-5,643,891,980	-12
						0	0
Other Western Hemisphere	2,944,663	2,452,907	2,525,145	2,647,795	2,897,842	-917,580	-3
Bermuda	2,740,475	2,428,784	2,467,663	2,630,565	2,852,153	-813,279	-2
Greenland	204,188	23,579	53,594	17,230	30,180	-60,317	-10
St Pierre and Miquelon	0	544	3,888	0	15,509	-43,984	-13
						0	0
Asia	791,992,045,871	845,563,238,805	861,435,246,749	909,103,125,241	939,580,052,428	344,272,060,240	5
China	391,614,202,404	417,416,187,193	432,105,109,933	458,420,312,097	473,335,408,893	235,646,054,973	7
Hong Kong	3,006,160,379	3,162,429,349	2,962,828,554	3,175,201,421	4,478,152,183	-3,493,348,665	-6
Japan	125,269,752,234	142,086,197,940	134,344,386,700	129,747,572,288	126,684,113,379	-6,575,853,953	-1
Korea, South	55,492,504,271	57,688,961,445	60,898,411,541	68,168,967,389	70,087,700,306	27,351,208,241	5
Saudi Arabia	1,458,615,299	1,360,355,358	1,224,132,470	1,966,396,697	1,144,515,814	-962,838,215	-6
Taiwan	39,459,804,194	37,397,740,895	36,350,966,408	39,012,957,841	39,011,654,639	5,587,024,574	2
						0	0
ASEAN - 10	102,367,954,245	108,360,371,959	113,202,978,814	123,969,585,479	139,493,416,658	49,705,940,623	5
Brunei	12,641,553	8,425,340	11,461,999	21,073,189	12,148,476	-155,466,182	-23
Myanmar (ex-Burma)	0	0	9,993,315	39,479,464	98,108,924	98,108,924	0
Cambodia	2,706,103,942	2,682,853,460	2,763,877,463	2,827,694,056	3,014,540,644	1,278,385,911	6
East Timor	0	3,608	94,909	172,373	223,457	223,457	0
Indonesia	13,972,560,873	14,036,883,515	14,747,386,073	15,183,249,088	15,837,348,582	6,247,553,787	5
Laos	50,691,902	21,682,014	27,862,798	29,358,131	40,531,315	37,479,892	30
Malaysia	24,363,274,903	24,797,817,465	26,357,707,629	29,579,971,965	33,060,624,074	549,398,379	0
Philippines	8,694,111,799	9,084,371,765	8,824,406,058	9,647,235,798	9,843,096,608	1,017,139,395	1
Singapore	16,849,180,766	17,264,364,164	14,946,261,824	14,294,966,708	15,485,689,531	1,617,780,535	1
Thailand	20,725,332,043	22,657,774,156	23,808,723,914	25,030,751,523	26,867,329,423	8,853,189,888	4
Vietnam	14,994,056,464	17,806,196,472	21,705,202,832	27,315,633,184	35,233,775,624	30,162,146,637	21
						0	0
Middle East	26,837,848,386	27,102,205,135	27,863,859,154	28,772,854,436	29,842,592,979	9,642,290,279	4
Andorra	466,088	287,717	1,295,296	593,398	5,232,890	5,082,116	43
Bahrain	487,532,546	664,497,790	601,438,925	895,500,469	842,617,109	499,854,479	9
Bosnia and Herzegovina	48,476,385	50,530,924	56,187,629	81,746,010	75,484,147	61,797,560	19
Gaza Strip admin. by Israel	2,916,663	315,360	450,493	191,845	11,863	-1,417,773	-38
Iran	175,984	567,753	27,582	0	0	-155,208,493	-100
Iraq	12,332,707	21,122,665	2,976,997	138,957,832	11,286,559	-41,279,356	-14
Israel	22,267,752,180	21,467,047,003	22,083,707,910	22,153,844,679	23,413,871,056	7,336,422,466	4
Jordan	1,014,128,276	1,120,107,899	1,187,435,894	1,303,483,931	1,443,439,235	217,423,478	2
Kuwait	193,646,579	311,426,085	275,251,359	238,169,702	173,461,924	-307,181,954	-10

Table B-27. **U.S. Imports of North American Industry Classification System (NAICS) Manufactures by Region and Individual Countries, 2005–2015**—*Continued*

Region	2005	2006	2007	2008	2009	2010
Lebanon	72,868,713	79,053,132	92,716,361	80,740,649	64,049,055	73,232,957
Oman	139,290,864	100,301,765	129,501,693	213,181,740	128,792,315	385,503,854
Qatar	338,941,939	153,381,148	212,759,968	282,582,187	131,198,203	156,238,561
Syria	313,296,057	121,535,116	98,600,524	333,734,082	277,994,996	418,087,956
United Arab Emirates	959,383,016	1,009,061,855	825,456,862	826,408,829	511,690,304	741,482,968
West Bank admin. by Israel	1,592,593	3,132,360	2,066,261	2,516,731	1,061,012	1,135,722
Republic of Yemen	25,017,258	16,110,985	19,707,014	295,368	99,745	198,298
Central Asia	984,230,451	1,148,290,972	1,381,483,032	1,635,213,085	935,711,276	1,184,195,271
Kazakhstan	520,434,774	859,966,962	1,002,613,819	1,199,884,138	748,304,091	1,069,254,645
Kyrgyzstan	4,523,348	4,076,600	1,665,159	1,700,213	2,553,889	2,753,998
Tajikistan	240,214,684	60,496,845	208,342	7,649,603	8,435,396	1,464,220
Turkmenistan	132,085,066	74,265,658	215,414,479	136,673,524	89,967,398	46,659,000
Uzbekistan	86,972,579	149,484,907	161,581,233	289,305,607	86,450,502	64,063,408
Other Asia	27,146,684,743	30,986,270,169	33,352,784,246	34,877,376,972	28,805,622,825	38,058,415,068
Afghanistan	23,921,681	8,294,508	5,319,689	11,205,478	5,095,549	12,964,278
Armenia	43,251,421	41,390,674	27,827,861	33,150,162	73,437,957	74,528,996
Azerbaijan	40,678,933	20,337,562	123,894,339	54,311,239	1,211,903	2,196,740
Bangladesh	2,546,791,263	3,066,630,068	3,259,400,991	3,602,506,411	3,583,753,084	4,173,567,698
Bhutan	595,201	767,045	269,961	336,026	184,829	343,369
Georgia	99,358,619	103,147,281	205,209,156	203,249,144	65,297,709	180,241,637
India	17,661,337,397	20,613,952,579	22,963,467,034	24,496,761,681	20,139,217,282	28,281,116,511
Korea, North	3,252	0	0	0	0	0
Macau	1,240,975,104	1,218,996,443	1,087,047,146	906,189,248	222,552,787	135,553,401
Maldives	5,163,549	183,848	25,398	1,153,846	772,074	60,337
Mongolia	135,551,908	104,917,649	72,839,455	46,624,839	3,885,790	4,176,992
Nepal	106,774,633	97,019,828	86,040,821	79,049,850	49,573,765	54,217,218
Pakistan	3,202,279,688	3,620,547,626	3,515,764,234	3,540,909,709	3,118,499,190	3,442,517,244
Sri Lanka	2,040,002,094	2,090,085,058	2,005,678,161	1,901,929,339	1,542,140,906	1,696,930,647
Australia and Oceania	9,866,743,152	10,929,685,646	10,988,133,747	11,699,582,480	9,165,710,640	10,789,649,156
Australia	6,132,867,381	7,077,822,574	7,392,075,006	8,138,682,667	6,438,342,224	7,202,394,655
Christmas Island	249,133	284,436	2,976,793	541,547	665,919	560,480
Cocos (Keeling) Islands	468,953	1,410,880	774,098	1,114,278	720,491	2,092,197
Cook Islands	487,077	680,152	1,207,067	644,769	344,646	1,342,177
Fiji	148,502,881	125,324,668	126,742,345	134,214,342	118,818,472	140,951,141
French Polynesia	51,560,993	48,638,127	44,706,369	59,001,658	23,765,464	42,734,872
French Southern and Antarctic	51,640	97,752	500,627	34,925	30,451	16,236
Heard and McDonald Islands	1,251	38,217	24,916	9,899	0	0
Kiribati	2,231	189,625	27,000	56,309	197,560	356,355
Marshall Islands	3,549,336	1,260,278	4,841,903	3,686,249	4,104,741	6,272,425
Micronesia	1,354,955	153,640	17,406	201,282	213,392	279,823
Netherlands Antilles	736,508,801	914,756,262	604,517,042	621,811,595	373,129,691	924,118,956
New Caledonia	25,349,428	42,864,996	77,039,671	46,199,523	25,793,600	69,130,498
New Zealand	2,745,398,705	2,675,180,608	2,700,565,115	2,661,688,042	2,152,393,278	2,375,861,775
Niue	136,825	72,918	68,126	55,402	21,638	17,407
Norfolk Island	69,306	43,596	353,100	24,559	370,162	5,481
Palau	7,270	25,376	30,000	7,474	5,584	8,298
Papua New Guinea	8,648,166	32,678,220	21,164,027	23,617,156	20,394,306	16,616,446
Pitcairn Islands	1,032,364	101,672	77,442	8,160	4,182	0
Reunion	130,181	383,438	407,943	306,124	175,393	321,277
Samoa	4,246,317	1,867,994	2,596,662	2,097,408	2,230,132	2,897,882
Solomon Islands	363,982	207,590	208,023	177,826	54,971	134,883
Tokelau	5,394,482	4,658,912	6,683,610	4,950,430	3,503,305	3,171,703
Tonga	51,202	401,914	66,478	96,767	61,490	29,869
Tuvalu	50,465	22,515	27,609	84,043	88,456	9,204
Vanuatu	234,168	507,586	402,517	266,196	247,007	310,300
Wallis and Futuna	22,469	11,700	32,852	3,850	34,085	14,816
Africa	13,896,923,670	15,953,071,534	17,790,544,778	21,753,366,920	13,358,320,284	18,108,202,123
Algeria	1,697,462,943	2,014,090,615	2,005,090,909	3,282,471,254	2,444,623,312	3,269,059,972
Angola	273,210,729	302,681,551	364,185,208	359,856,542	320,470,607	425,431,726
Benin	101,215	158,312	509,359	15,155,604	126,854	61,146
Botswana	177,004,771	251,004,377	186,272,891	217,584,851	131,236,686	166,916,499
British Indian Ocean Terr.	430,249	647,040	40,046	370,428	321,238	1,044,347
Burkina Faso	370,908	229,616	778,647	311,171	784,661	2,047,027
Burundi	21,606	58,043	66,453	81,590	5,569	0
Capo Verde	2,603,050	912,462	1,900,774	334,848	680,730	1,061,677
Cameroon	112,551,885	161,437,123	175,635,836	224,492,779	152,699,362	176,547,065
Central African Republic	5,474,491	4,081,738	2,767,190	8,292,355	3,283,194	5,416,946
Chad	404,425,392	95,025,319	26,258,809	132,169,897	125,086,183	258,585,333
Comoros	559,177	839,146	497,127	606,293	719,561	1,403,511

Table B-27.   U.S. Imports of North American Industry Classification System (NAICS) Manufactures by Region and Individual Countries, 2005–2015—*Continued*

Region	2011	2012	2013	2014	2015	Value Change, 2005–2015	2005–2015 Annual Average percent Change
Lebanon	67,232,504	63,264,174	81,552,559	63,437,904	74,209,774	1,341,061	0
Oman	548,983,523	976,267,501	914,970,280	955,626,797	887,647,646	748,356,782	20
Qatar	412,392,162	876,442,902	1,052,858,485	1,431,046,005	1,199,277,680	860,335,741	13
Syria	285,091,724	14,378,330	7,911,270	6,850,183	5,673,160	-307,622,897	-33
United Arab Emirates	1,473,827,243	1,533,534,973	1,595,696,770	1,501,369,650	1,707,030,016	747,647,000	6
West Bank admin. by Israel	1,845,590	2,161,687	1,763,692	1,809,452	3,075,342	1,482,749	7
Republic of Yemen	21,048,232	252,372	334,013	226,579	274,578	-24,742,680	-36
						0	0
Central Asia	1,135,227,601	1,609,827,062	1,403,625,400	1,317,470,653	780,900,793	-203,329,658	-2
Kazakhstan	1,029,846,625	1,473,591,972	1,361,315,852	1,296,230,359	672,826,006	152,391,232	3
Kyrgyzstan	2,385,666	2,523,125	1,221,862	1,444,385	15,345,075	10,821,727	13
Tajikistan	12,260,141	26,195,003	151,653	2,207,710	30,728,103	-209,486,581	-19
Turkmenistan	41,201,357	84,227,012	18,853,282	13,516,726	55,101,557	-76,983,509	-8
Uzbekistan	49,533,812	23,289,950	22,082,751	4,071,473	6,900,052	-80,072,527	-22
						0	0
Other Asia	45,349,976,858	49,378,962,469	51,078,947,775	54,551,806,940	54,721,596,784	27,574,912,041	7
Afghanistan	5,166,286	4,479,790	5,903,311	6,515,883	13,792,202	-10,129,479	-5
Armenia	92,024,684	87,530,139	97,078,518	91,916,646	59,510,711	16,259,290	3
Azerbaijan	6,249,058	29,079,382	49,535,299	55,708,227	48,128,045	7,449,112	2
Bangladesh	4,787,330,779	4,757,858,075	5,264,153,580	5,217,408,561	5,899,597,561	3,352,806,298	9
Bhutan	504,524	560,407	420,161	229,866	3,113,191	2,517,990	18
Georgia	174,198,727	223,477,791	173,934,801	388,619,259	188,787,798	89,429,179	7
India	34,309,471,839	38,380,732,125	39,355,961,211	42,478,188,127	41,925,184,426	24,263,847,029	9
Korea, North	0	0	0	0	0	-3,252	-100
Macau	103,269,027	87,037,781	66,939,574	58,502,688	93,073,206	-1,147,901,898	-23
Maldives	22,515	264,043	94,706	226,657	591,738	-4,571,811	-19
Mongolia	1,780,907	1,164,548	2,112,459	1,564,532	3,771,212	-131,780,696	-30
Nepal	71,575,680	72,100,384	69,366,033	78,401,712	77,403,472	-29,371,161	-3
Pakistan	3,776,189,183	3,551,623,491	3,623,982,817	3,587,687,462	3,609,890,278	407,610,590	1
Sri Lanka	2,022,193,649	2,183,054,513	2,369,465,305	2,586,837,320	2,798,752,944	758,750,850	3
						0	0
Australia and Oceania	12,280,902,310	11,056,284,910	11,011,537,572	12,802,250,697	13,194,134,073	3,327,390,921	3
Australia	8,383,628,902	7,696,016,613	7,715,057,444	9,056,270,795	9,115,195,686	2,982,328,305	4
Christmas Island	523,716	417,447	1,015,468	1,105,196	1,824,735	1,575,602	22
Cocos (Keeling) Islands	1,503,993	959,139	996,917	3,159,095	3,573,735	3,104,782	23
Cook Islands	332,447	773,443	280,272	612,923	625,030	137,953	3
Fiji	111,924,542	166,295,144	152,713,683	166,181,098	182,862,178	34,359,297	2
French Polynesia	38,754,277	34,406,258	21,270,940	22,208,322	18,181,992	-33,379,001	-10
French Southern and Antarctic	16,503	10,591	153,970	518,047	0	-51,640	-100
Heard and McDonald Islands	3,538	38,716	0	26,941	5,200	3,949	15
Kiribati	3,370	46,335	2,965	11,227	16,009	13,778	22
Marshall Islands	6,979,585	5,983,104	6,499,679	4,410,870	1,346,920	-2,202,416	-9
Micronesia	229,540	301,237	274,852	191,459	354,171	-1,000,784	-13
Netherlands Antilles	803,888,780	0	0	0	0	-736,508,801	-100
New Caledonia	89,010,735	55,820,868	67,610,479	82,207,236	41,558,826	16,209,398	5
New Zealand	2,797,095,581	3,065,707,594	3,021,225,773	3,442,317,832	3,812,847,633	1,067,448,928	3
Niue	28,832	112,798	167,552	225,683	324,377	187,552	9
Norfolk Island	159,143	49,339	2,557	14,468	1,166,271	1,096,965	33
Palau	2,904	16,050	221,833	150,159	286,046	278,776	44
Papua New Guinea	39,540,887	20,424,837	10,552,158	5,415,303	6,449,322	-2,198,844	-3
Pitcairn Islands	0	2,918	0	120,486	0	-1,032,364	-100
Reunion	232,346	203,544	834,999	3,899,131	394,396	264,215	12
Samoa	2,160,022	1,877,478	4,341,592	5,076,065	3,327,597	-918,720	-2
Solomon Islands	109,666	952,915	7,005,779	6,889,356	2,715,068	2,351,086	22
Tokelau	4,355,280	4,355,114	597,244	624,667	421,276	-4,973,206	-23
Tonga	107,609	79,503	175,948	111,887	322,607	268,215	19
Tuvalu	282	37,544	17,068	61,902	131,521	81,056	10
Vanuatu	304,713	1,396,381	224,269	408,723	111,293	-122,875	-7
Wallis and Futuna	5,117	0	294,131	31,826	92,184	69,715	15
						0	0
Africa	22,917,010,220	20,046,950,083	19,976,953,376	19,578,436,054	16,055,981,503	2,159,057,833	1
Algeria	5,095,956,821	4,130,066,632	3,447,675,959	4,302,204,846	3,274,105,593	1,576,642,650	7
Angola	666,047,055	546,881,511	605,566,148	545,563,078	292,574,073	19,363,344	1
Benin	1,368,793	109,265	135,713	297,981	325,279	224,064	12
Botswana	290,502,372	219,689,550	275,428,659	317,247,253	210,340,234	33,335,463	2
British Indian Ocean Terr.	5,424,969	19,413,874	17,699,889	13,703,947	14,931,210	14,500,961	43
Burkina Faso	2,276,962	219,161	1,041,525	2,140,209	993,014	622,106	10
Burundi	127,625	441,414	1,195,141	24,379	2,765,534	2,743,928	62
Capo Verde	1,361,444	3,806,234	2,243,341	1,639,681	1,758,316	-844,734	-4
Cameroon	286,150,076	211,550,355	236,946,495	156,923,721	105,678,417	-6,873,468	-1
Central African Republic	5,593,597	4,020,998	2,766,206	1,310,268	1,558,326	-3,916,165	-12
Chad	86,417,749	408,499,391	3,554,845	58,703,308	30,575,858	-373,849,534	-23
Comoros	1,755,133	1,946,329	1,924,421	1,328,453	511,006	-48,171	-1

Table B-27.   U.S. Imports of North American Industry Classification System (NAICS) Manufactures by Region and Individual Countries, 2005–2015—*Continued*

Region	2005	2006	2007	2008	2009	2010
Congo (Brazzaville)	181,986,047	236,619,143	170,687,740	116,339,572	127,215,311	178,008,850
Congo (Kinshasa)	129,172,891	78,455,962	157,123,291	196,456,455	10,624,190	63,345,574
Cote d'Ivoire	211,195,810	173,574,360	125,507,079	439,210,224	189,110,173	254,821,201
Djibouti	315,031	24,179	209,846	273,417	1,253,076	1,143,167
Egypt	1,148,372,932	1,474,314,199	1,489,729,701	1,508,016,190	1,148,195,548	1,513,310,135
Equatorial Guinea	144,670,986	87,734,826	208,394,629	184,874,348	66,400,678	137,940,276
Eritrea	295,355	377,007	112,586	89,824	480,398	96,786
Ethiopia	7,267,472	8,743,799	9,977,289	18,808,698	13,214,864	13,013,774
Gambia	7,097,592	6,459,207	37,822,801	32,405,775	19,038,085	4,801,885
Gabon	400,767	264,673	67,451	431,162	732,937	284,410
Ghana	125,114,330	121,324,758	151,598,986	186,833,020	59,209,403	157,098,384
Guinea	13,079,284	19,699,684	9,320,094	11,509,636	3,241,084	3,674,562
Guinea-Bissau	6,778	283,506	17,586	154,973	43,305	858,681
Kenya	298,482,571	302,311,568	278,938,300	285,466,785	228,135,858	239,129,466
Lesotho	401,774,517	407,509,445	436,213,680	370,534,781	300,789,265	298,797,737
Liberia	996,849	10,168,347	342,215	2,034,718	4,861,226	26,739,781
Libya	227,733,914	393,428,411	707,489,154	1,226,182,413	469,196,127	462,943,485
Madagascar	285,533,559	246,441,298	300,506,323	290,597,847	221,289,831	75,654,993
Malawi	29,166,566	25,397,541	26,988,087	23,121,106	18,321,550	20,463,040
Mali	1,355,324	3,231,911	6,613,807	2,967,653	1,628,151	4,234,391
Mauritania	286,985	87,906	368,160	1,340,956	66,202	233,792
Mauritius	207,192,371	200,058,568	171,356,154	156,363,851	156,179,915	181,436,052
Mayotte	0	8,489	304,507	15,832	49,784	60,634
Morocco	332,851,091	392,706,157	457,939,215	467,839,045	270,705,960	426,088,631
Mozambique	8,250,782	11,596,040	493,425	1,067,489	18,521,265	36,519,203
Namibia	118,768,657	108,021,643	52,690,407	45,226,749	44,561,176	54,730,219
Nauru	123,920	213,379	121,167	94,357	116,934	211,659
Niger	60,501,230	112,143,458	2,479,320	1,825,344	100,686,526	25,748,384
Nigeria	1,257,072,732	980,883,434	997,912,842	1,637,707,600	676,139,978	1,198,711,578
Rwanda	287,637	506,194	1,480,026	1,068,469	1,177,235	1,554,925
St Helena	1,000,513	543,199	547,823	394,798	241,528	976,109
Sao Tome and Principe	215,332	147,647	371,189	117,005	102,042	286,997
Senegal	2,029,834	16,735,874	5,880,115	12,196,381	3,162,067	2,509,161
Seychelles	5,085,894	8,752,618	7,590,139	4,541,166	5,095,647	6,091,835
Sierra Leone	7,879,588	8,163,616	8,569,126	13,590,675	8,099,650	9,467,848
Somalia	256,689	294,409	132,650	59,340	114,052	78,314
South Africa	5,483,007,993	7,070,871,143	8,466,073,849	9,417,734,295	5,565,031,541	7,828,800,053
South Sudan	0	0	0	0	0	0
Sudan	0	3,722	0	17,574	90,217	18,139
Swaziland	198,192,958	155,537,330	144,904,446	133,277,545	109,322,606	120,610,080
Tanzania	16,717,837	14,182,450	14,648,169	19,890,500	10,926,093	15,562,136
Togo	433,307	2,477,746	451,301	266,155	731,250	607,459
Tunisia	180,792,896	311,321,863	447,340,489	537,437,823	295,651,603	334,635,869
Uganda	7,429,595	5,493,430	9,872,672	3,770,667	2,510,067	12,774,511
Western Sahara	0	0	47,350	4,200	0	0
Zambia	30,785,791	27,947,975	47,609,094	50,616,414	7,646,099	29,111,147
Zimbabwe	89,525,047	96,844,078	69,697,249	108,866,481	18,371,830	57,441,561

Table B-27. U.S. Imports of North American Industry Classification System (NAICS) Manufactures by Region and Individual Countries, 2005–2015—*Continued*

Region	2011	2012	2013	2014	2015	Value Change, 2005–2015	2005–2015 Annual Average percent Change
Congo (Brazzaville)	343,764,199	138,217,996	364,351,447	271,230,308	73,913,428	-108,072,619	-9
Congo (Kinshasa)	63,376,876	34,440,347	61,865,814	111,020,328	134,027,450	4,854,559	0
Cote d'Ivoire	218,735,925	270,850,785	219,722,063	317,963,651	160,791,305	-50,404,505	-3
Djibouti	35,752	123,131	105,282	386,814	768,891	453,860	9
Egypt	1,628,728,553	1,548,125,448	1,337,645,309	1,312,109,758	1,293,961,085	145,588,153	1
Equatorial Guinea	123,571,633	102,764,195	124,531,957	121,372,896	82,529,643	-62,141,343	-5
Eritrea	99,622	164,659	122,385	69,557	62,833	-232,522	-14
Ethiopia	20,238,136	25,970,346	39,430,815	44,043,998	55,314,213	48,046,741	23
Gambia	11,963,748	96,918,848	45,122,445	87,612,765	67,974,801	60,877,209	25
Gabon	50,792	237,403	1,575,481	193,811	602,055	201,288	4
Ghana	181,565,134	128,768,829	62,604,107	85,854,520	69,706,647	-55,407,683	-6
Guinea	6,536,691	5,664,947	4,278,116	3,869,038	3,615,385	-9,463,899	-12
Guinea-Bissau	97,790	57,483	22,519	16,916	6,042	-736	-1
Kenya	295,539,166	289,651,994	366,249,057	420,604,219	426,751,494	128,268,923	4
Lesotho	384,254,004	310,509,486	351,169,562	360,856,504	331,652,248	-70,122,269	-2
Liberia	884,853	1,084,552	826,685	2,119,453	3,534,346	2,537,497	13
Libya	247,801,282	240,596,564	782,584,980	79,656,481	97,899,393	-129,834,521	-8
Madagascar	55,321,905	68,588,224	107,086,332	137,012,635	195,648,190	-89,885,369	-4
Malawi	24,902,011	16,953,270	20,337,780	21,496,174	23,201,092	-5,965,474	-2
Mali	1,790,567	1,395,788	1,501,864	2,269,922	2,418,630	1,063,306	6
Mauritania	647,088	437,868	801,113	802,834	395,206	108,221	3
Mauritius	238,009,567	246,040,797	328,651,416	385,454,770	380,128,753	172,936,382	6
Mayotte	3,360	9,791	9,338	18,312	70,020	70,020	0
Morocco	636,786,427	580,922,326	663,708,928	734,536,716	755,148,073	422,296,982	9
Mozambique	10,209,069	7,449,161	19,636,506	42,210,089	32,297,729	24,046,947	15
Namibia	234,470,681	120,887,867	107,793,175	105,499,835	43,432,194	-75,336,463	-10
Nauru	295,601	460,623	425,529	402,747	483,514	359,594	15
Niger	287,856,682	81,406,450	1,196,198	2,286,178	1,151,025	-59,350,205	-33
Nigeria	1,925,705,764	1,243,391,703	1,550,619,376	974,856,611	459,429,217	-797,643,515	-10
Rwanda	9,092,104	1,288,346	1,476,373	1,575,246	2,424,246	2,136,609	24
St Helena	623,723	728,499	618,426	222,542	746,981	-253,532	-3
Sao Tome and Principe	235,151	522,466	234,006	854,885	634,512	419,180	11
Senegal	3,053,510	11,498,812	11,408,770	16,748,118	46,329,258	44,299,424	37
Seychelles	5,145,601	3,008,429	4,505,081	3,394,377	3,918,745	-1,167,149	-3
Sierra Leone	15,614,677	9,231,929	12,941,698	11,651,372	11,126,201	3,246,613	4
Somalia	935,691	680,531	834,085	396,278	60,315	-196,374	-13
South Africa	8,954,047,614	7,961,153,599	7,917,525,882	7,773,385,117	6,672,672,182	1,189,664,189	2
South Sudan	0	300	52,181	54,048	40,559	40,559	0
Sudan	360	12,743	0	0	0	0	0
Swaziland	88,960,304	65,923,716	57,665,653	80,428,635	20,426,879	-177,766,079	-20
Tanzania	16,154,369	67,374,366	32,412,370	43,294,092	51,287,029	34,569,192	12
Togo	1,661,385	49,056,201	3,178,588	5,243,855	10,870,791	10,437,484	38
Tunisia	331,428,706	653,143,066	714,811,220	494,828,216	489,926,921	309,134,025	10
Uganda	10,186,389	5,256,180	11,100,533	8,348,333	9,921,549	2,491,954	3
Western Sahara	17,409	16,662	705,127	122,785	43,790	43,790	0
Zambia	45,271,958	60,753,816	37,071,092	54,515,775	46,179,225	15,393,434	4
Zimbabwe	48,355,795	48,564,827	10,258,370	56,457,416	56,340,558	-33,184,489	-5

Table B-28.   U.S. Balance of Payments of North American Industry Classification System (NAICS) Manufactures by Region and Individual Countries, 2005–2015

Region	2005	2006	2007	2008	2009	2010
WORLD	-541,373,106,434	-567,293,931,174	-542,086,258,509	-465,228,812,382	-318,466,052,530	-411,719,696,192
Europe						
European Union (EU-28)...............	-116,511,859,645	-114,267,869,273	-107,658,569,610	-97,125,941,223	-56,779,004,488	-79,148,543,861
Austria..............................	-3,494,040,628	-5,194,177,423	-7,412,826,615	-5,769,449,700	-3,777,374,264	-4,509,070,827
Belgium.............................	5,259,778,237	6,358,274,764	9,300,091,377	10,712,524,727	7,187,213,538	8,585,500,371
Bulgaria............................	-202,993,693	-200,725,028	-122,256,963	89,218,548	25,319,224	-63,992,568
Croatia.............................	-253,760,776	-243,499,279	-167,713,981	-37,839,816	-94,981,267	-171,055,081
Cyprus..............................	58,252,541	146,438,836	144,082,862	187,152,581	157,883,263	114,480,727
Czech Republic	-1,129,861,077	-1,218,068,937	-1,188,396,557	-1,228,887,563	-962,625,551	-1,041,055,631
Denmark............................	-3,187,017,890	-3,249,114,610	-3,203,077,878	-3,717,016,125	-3,393,890,472	-3,960,075,664
Estonia.............................	-344,717,410	-305,810,088	-59,739,873	-167,987,621	37,529,136	-511,701,359
Finland.............................	-2,320,560,813	-2,622,722,278	-2,518,479,501	-2,530,143,586	-2,476,073,231	-2,030,104,393
France..............................	-10,051,743,816	-11,719,719,046	-12,475,498,698	-14,153,186,347	-6,576,377,230	-9,731,429,684
Germany............................	-49,309,563,057	-46,668,998,626	-43,826,177,809	-42,993,375,855	-27,846,529,154	-35,234,648,542
Greece..............................	307,773,438	448,024,973	653,215,431	681,144,111	1,667,528,078	246,809,765
Hungary............................	-1,499,892,903	-1,378,392,226	-1,489,455,427	-1,583,201,042	-948,962,180	-1,099,167,081
Ireland..............................	-19,754,514,257	-20,357,278,650	-22,132,027,791	-23,073,371,145	-19,748,717,006	-25,443,941,422
Italy................................	-19,489,647,762	-20,089,541,546	-21,050,105,547	-20,973,753,700	-14,370,244,652	-15,191,615,139
Latvia..............................	-190,230,193	-54,900,330	37,176,618	130,027,982	144,034,600	136,275,943
Lithuania...........................	-298,410,747	-56,316,713	226,276,565	35,384,007	-218,709,144	-45,881,853
Luxembourg.........................	252,827,978	-446,867	328,267,752	390,827,915	913,528,019	864,473,555
Malta..............................	-93,215,387	-191,134,663	-120,756,992	-22,170,020	-13,696,569	190,938,130
Netherlands.........................	11,894,026,760	13,294,656,968	14,671,084,492	19,559,760,507	18,355,455,477	18,087,947,801
Poland..............................	-699,090,764	-344,203,353	717,492,646	1,130,151,647	92,864,497	-407,106,234
Portugal............................	-1,294,524,100	-1,691,368,793	-864,391,457	-112,264,236	-683,843,700	-1,216,356,632
Romania............................	-740,489,454	-697,589,569	-516,335,173	-319,030,758	-156,275,151	-455,406,435
Slovakia............................	-818,549,528	-993,926,212	-1,038,828,369	-964,534,887	-451,666,963	-811,722,516
Slovenia............................	-202,810,914	-272,401,419	-213,355,267	-166,913,321	-130,228,265	-187,771,516
Spain..............................	-2,077,032,715	-2,709,778,244	-1,860,544,658	-87,584,702	220,205,828	674,929,467
Sweden.............................	-9,896,543,709	-9,646,296,473	-8,489,855,176	-7,525,087,084	-3,747,612,578	-5,997,707,425
United Kingdom	-6,935,307,006	-4,608,854,441	-4,986,433,621	-4,616,335,740	17,241,229	59,910,382
Non-EU	-14,548,560,893	-16,532,422,891	-10,039,002,695	-9,941,218,826	-10,013,661,794	-15,770,022,584
Albania.............................	12,184,989	17,121,342	26,936,597	33,116,714	34,334,064	19,363,262
Andorra.............................	9,834,823	5,484,644	12,469,395	14,809,907	9,032,460	7,220,638
Belarus.............................	-319,409,229	-409,497,940	-932,075,426	-935,325,491	-436,069,640	-47,274,820
Faroe Islands........................	2,371,352	3,078,848	2,326,103	6,937,581	3,831,874	1,348,940
Gibraltar............................	115,803,715	235,280,353	494,164,703	2,413,232,458	826,071,676	990,750,042
Iceland.............................	327,214,229	193,464,821	415,744,542	229,414,458	172,285,546	134,650,543
Kosovo.............................	0	0	0	0	3,928,983	9,637,457
Liechtenstein........................	-273,859,503	-265,230,101	-266,902,184	-217,341,987	-160,866,905	-192,768,349
Macedonia..........................	-8,657,594	-11,271,761	-31,083,700	-28,322,234	12,908,570	5,635,366
Moldova............................	-15,723,539	-15,683,067	22,983,295	50,942,336	13,522,879	13,406,224
Monaco.............................	-10,612,886	6,037,196	10,578,375	27,277,863	-1,124,890	5,164,901
Montenegro	0	0	37,212,489	46,116,041	12,334,173	8,128,457
Norway.............................	-1,073,441,817	-1,679,540,584	-2,202,804,619	-2,263,686,124	-1,278,211,683	-2,350,797,723
Russia..............................	-8,301,616,025	-11,644,302,714	-8,588,800,311	-12,364,416,906	-7,842,326,417	-12,147,862,282
San Marino	2,300,467	2,750,668	9,223,928	5,717,881	6,825,140	-815,622
Serbia..............................	60,809,384	60,185,073	38,428,976	102,393,503	35,395,664	-38,685,428
Svalbard, Jan Mayen Island	5,339,716	5,657,920	834,262	1,939,091	772,101	7,224,852
Switzerland..........................	-2,553,758,605	-838,296,886	993,865,217	1,544,699,215	-3,313,842,265	-4,830,333,574
Turkey..............................	-1,928,934,056	-1,245,939,993	17,579,677	2,060,399,058	1,499,062,672	2,838,820,124
Ukraine.............................	-621,763,413	-961,513,775	-117,022,921	-677,360,225	384,217,124	-203,974,190
Vatican City	23,357,099	9,793,065	17,338,907	8,238,035	4,257,080	1,138,598
WESTERN HEMISPHERE	-42,854,719,129	-31,073,155,451	-13,509,617,293	38,571,720,702	54,388,695,506	60,398,374,510
NAFTA..............................	-39,408,806,617	-38,526,716,359	-38,868,747,263	-8,876,209,356	7,512,787,538	-2,009,332,422
Canada.............................	-15,391,744,720	-6,409,484,620	3,138,488,351	20,271,396,669	31,484,894,912	34,889,572,273
Mexico.............................	-24,017,061,897	-32,117,231,739	-42,007,235,614	-29,147,606,025	-23,972,107,374	-36,898,904,695
Caribbean	-252,759,950	1,283,508,337	1,905,980,082	3,034,647,273	4,230,341,089	6,424,116,234
Anguilla.............................	23,880,841	31,163,115	73,350,933	63,355,942	37,621,663	27,305,734
Antigua and Barbuda.................	156,028,844	162,264,785	194,469,709	147,972,703	126,947,405	132,601,082
Aruba..............................	-2,378,027,287	-2,310,944,768	-2,489,024,298	-2,508,802,597	-843,433,432	489,238,597
Bahamas...........................	1,122,895,315	1,770,368,733	1,834,223,930	2,125,895,061	1,579,045,616	2,210,424,421
Barbados...........................	312,358,160	353,313,354	354,777,697	377,103,043	303,362,212	291,372,107
British Virgin Islands.................	98,209,117	168,466,778	121,375,124	272,877,482	208,193,865	120,740,106
Cayman Islands......................	504,758,846	443,909,798	452,110,612	536,894,761	460,796,355	422,201,269
Cuba...............................	199,401,472	175,691,465	218,433,539	303,010,594	267,241,047	206,759,124
Curacao............................	0	0	0	0	0	0
Dominica...........................	48,494,485	57,096,440	73,001,220	83,585,242	65,866,953	58,473,026
Dominican Republic..................	-39,632,678	598,563,640	1,519,411,755	2,172,678,650	1,647,740,024	2,308,880,067
Grenada	50,667,246	45,867,863	49,867,208	52,456,024	40,686,166	47,424,446
Guadeloupe.........................	42,510,655	48,791,230	108,222,365	329,980,740	164,338,703	291,742,448

Table B-28. U.S. Balance of Payments of North American Industry Classification System (NAICS) Manufactures by Region and Individual Countries, 2005–2015—*Continued*

Region	2011	2012	2013	2014	2015	2005–2015 Value Change
WORLD	-451,889,959,126	-467,702,040,551	-458,902,353,568	-524,740,092,297	-626,962,347,933	-85,589,241,499
Europe						
European Union (EU-28)	-103,981,640,408	-118,168,147,422	-125,432,125,172	-143,366,269,702	-147,352,188,110	-30,840,328,465
Austria	-6,605,155,730	-6,332,591,965	-6,403,465,323	-6,995,804,886	-7,097,181,687	-3,603,141,059
Belgium	11,855,654,616	11,834,953,107	13,038,728,692	14,377,653,523	14,981,129,727	9,721,351,490
Bulgaria	-142,338,096	-237,666,554	-172,691,239	-227,317,913	-251,929,636	-48,935,943
Croatia	-237,561,370	-256,787,180	-264,185,893	-318,394,565	-376,176,414	-122,415,638
Cyprus	74,219,828	139,061,069	103,267,764	91,755,417	72,837,051	14,584,510
Czech Republic	-1,646,524,235	-2,061,062,524	-1,939,848,293	-1,993,466,656	-2,436,988,636	-1,307,127,559
Denmark	-4,549,399,770	-4,585,822,633	-4,279,077,994	-5,181,759,749	-5,530,131,325	-2,343,113,435
Estonia	-637,331,298	-252,799,057	-132,882,520	-258,548,044	-209,749,020	134,968,390
Finland	-1,964,526,037	-2,923,082,575	-2,653,795,192	-3,163,085,633	-3,041,390,130	-720,829,317
France	-10,656,412,326	-8,992,480,064	-10,609,208,913	-12,501,736,955	-12,909,868,137	-2,858,124,321
Germany	-50,416,092,008	-60,893,650,289	-67,235,779,761	-73,511,950,879	-72,800,259,155	-23,490,696,098
Greece	229,656,070	-195,169,410	-216,902,925	-238,261,712	-566,947,147	-874,720,585
Hungary	-1,349,193,096	-1,512,858,583	-1,905,453,014	-3,322,109,082	-3,868,201,714	-2,368,308,811
Ireland	-30,833,757,135	-25,092,714,828	-23,958,920,290	-25,151,055,658	-28,696,817,328	-8,942,303,071
Italy	-19,604,458,601	-22,005,554,510	-22,522,796,180	-25,631,829,630	-27,697,181,047	-8,207,533,285
Latvia	30,829,268	146,332,621	166,447,512	121,358,586	457,902	190,688,095
Lithuania	-527,125,798	-716,869,295	-1,070,057,372	-696,762,422	-651,263,692	-352,852,945
Luxembourg	1,007,955,811	1,369,204,464	1,241,956,876	768,877,738	703,256,474	450,428,496
Malta	497,860,492	113,529,231	344,398,023	731,759,132	299,885,337	393,100,724
Netherlands	20,082,359,618	18,704,672,439	22,058,209,685	20,150,384,727	21,914,647,142	10,020,620,382
Poland	-1,660,960,801	-1,412,555,484	-1,208,386,617	-1,511,346,110	-1,805,025,348	-1,105,934,584
Portugal	-1,553,166,490	-1,729,563,342	-2,040,414,932	-2,381,575,018	-2,436,557,885	-1,142,033,785
Romania	-716,958,092	-885,694,186	-1,074,722,290	-1,136,673,432	-1,309,183,209	-568,693,755
Slovakia	-1,155,174,118	-1,526,342,360	-1,505,325,405	-1,715,360,149	-1,932,944,622	-1,113,845,094
Slovenia	-36,103,947	-328,453,646	-333,524,177	-415,347,768	-312,130,450	-109,319,536
Spain	-1,352,282,424	-3,208,209,356	-2,687,832,488	-5,656,676,537	-4,915,895,628	-2,838,862,913
Sweden	-6,513,469,943	-5,275,166,327	-5,026,110,204	-6,058,270,044	-5,927,542,437	3,969,001,272
United Kingdom	4,397,815,204	-50,806,185	-5,143,752,702	-1,540,725,983	-551,587,096	6,383,719,910
Non-EU	-14,611,985,993	-12,157,067,485	-10,562,213,798	-17,615,347,005	-16,935,081,327	-2,386,520,434
Albania	20,703,702	38,388,273	56,966,207	34,488,911	10,403,853	-1,781,136
Andorra	4,598,545	1,853,643	3,809,985	2,540,647	-1,983,735	-11,818,558
Belarus	-254,149,083	-58,324,707	-17,674,278	-41,318,255	-96,627,380	222,781,849
Faroe Islands	1,920,329	894,215	1,308,353	1,485,759	-4,182,759	-6,554,111
Gibraltar	2,278,838,394	3,648,667,506	2,512,017,540	1,825,795,652	1,472,437,231	1,356,633,516
Iceland	355,250,532	152,354,174	315,309,323	141,229,646	149,941,722	-177,272,507
Kosovo	12,237,663	16,939,037	12,636,283	11,006,859	8,962,504	8,962,504
Liechtenstein	-225,709,364	-287,055,577	-271,520,978	-262,741,325	-266,078,840	7,780,663
Macedonia	-6,468,429	-31,641,555	15,728,840	-119,686,541	-147,997,215	-139,339,621
Moldova	18,442,527	9,011,249	6,271,439	-3,062,813	-21,957,759	-6,234,220
Monaco	-18,156,246	-12,173,675	429,821,639	51,596,711	11,948,496	22,561,382
Montenegro	7,154,894	6,457,782	15,891,070	10,559,810	6,860,154	6,860,154
Norway	-1,820,167,282	-1,828,467,931	-77,194,922	-74,666,146	-539,888,435	533,553,382
Russia	-17,879,948,202	-15,096,407,369	-14,452,217,559	-12,101,506,799	-8,052,630,356	248,985,669
San Marino	-2,870,981	-3,465,200	-4,587,386	-1,814,999	-3,160,521	-5,460,988
Serbia	-33,897,137	-39,504,122	-402,123,966	-143,604,915	-166,045,108	-226,854,492
Svalbard, Jan Mayen Island	1,886,944	114,079	1,326,938	3,212,037	344,350	-4,995,366
Switzerland	-1,326,630,323	-295,478,500	-765,567,066	-8,229,899,955	-8,907,168,550	-6,353,409,945
Turkey	4,665,713,012	1,634,281,775	1,730,571,759	1,346,989,848	-168,162,249	1,760,771,807
Ukraine	-412,309,706	-17,633,059	325,739,894	-66,979,781	-220,603,790	401,159,623
Vatican City	1,574,218	4,122,477	1,273,087	1,028,644	507,060	-22,850,039
						0
WESTERN HEMISPHERE	84,091,196,215	105,873,206,158	113,234,729,956	112,459,319,875	66,105,926,839	108,960,645,968
NAFTA	13,829,412,087	20,748,869,949	25,889,487,073	23,345,930,579	-8,794,369,659	30,614,436,958
Canada	43,113,269,241	48,967,879,575	52,013,720,335	53,291,502,777	37,832,787,397	53,224,532,117
Mexico	-29,283,857,154	-28,219,009,626	-26,124,233,262	-29,945,572,198	-46,627,157,056	-22,610,095,159
Caribbean	2,006,708,898	5,379,793,623	8,080,529,228	9,208,323,286	7,939,828,459	8,192,588,409
Anguilla	21,726,704	19,337,611	21,623,990	47,749,637	33,959,892	10,079,051
Antigua and Barbuda	127,235,660	167,130,758	119,652,589	184,044,082	569,513,859	413,485,015
Aruba	-2,587,108,552	-130,745,660	885,003,152	851,085,306	809,077,801	3,187,105,088
Bahamas	2,445,183,748	2,795,619,974	2,657,682,506	2,625,356,974	1,946,321,604	823,426,289
Barbados	316,766,098	338,201,726	323,567,304	400,286,868	435,137,803	122,779,643
British Virgin Islands	117,996,522	122,868,835	277,738,986	349,839,920	221,147,929	122,938,812
Cayman Islands	442,846,450	475,822,782	482,884,312	613,124,807	419,265,830	-85,493,016
Cuba	162,801,516	256,966,889	257,217,999	233,308,934	160,413,517	-38,987,955
Curacao	-82,990,226	-127,530,698	284,305,265	245,360,293	147,112,732	147,112,732
Dominica	58,560,937	56,854,522	46,599,386	50,500,807	50,872,436	2,377,951
Dominican Republic	2,251,469,524	2,008,756,534	2,005,388,102	2,388,220,823	1,572,178,800	1,611,811,478
Grenada	53,054,453	48,102,624	66,381,273	61,466,071	59,572,594	8,905,348
Guadeloupe	354,316,938	420,581,029	539,263,161	359,378,798	78,464,719	35,954,064

Table B-28.   U.S. Balance of Payments of North American Industry Classification System (NAICS) Manufactures by Region and Individual Countries, 2005–2015—*Continued*

Region	2005	2006	2007	2008	2009	2010
Haiti	129,917,525	194,856,550	33,077,462	172,112,266	-16,949,211	253,794,614
Jamaica	1,205,175,099	1,356,112,070	1,355,301,991	1,569,202,717	775,046,269	1,113,419,104
Martinique	10,638,819	-14,096,206	171,898,578	254,480,005	230,476,320	238,063,924
Montserrat	3,004,163	12,763,790	3,225,911	5,684,649	4,292,675	3,501,554
Sint Maarten	0	0	0	0	0	0
St Kitts and Nevis	34,981,523	63,272,474	47,437,192	56,610,155	50,625,604	69,540,969
St Lucia	87,388,447	98,162,171	109,367,589	201,213,567	102,325,477	327,253,294
St Vincent and the Grenadines	18,589,322	43,456,870	51,207,337	57,896,981	52,940,311	60,473,343
Trinidad and Tobago	-2,017,875,801	-2,220,228,487	-2,593,530,115	-3,482,099,414	-1,159,620,984	-2,354,348,926
Turks and Caicos Islands	133,875,937	204,656,672	217,774,343	242,538,702	132,798,051	105,255,931
Central America	1,655,164,528	3,626,443,485	6,030,780,126	8,678,661,776	4,193,389,364	4,125,859,310
Belize	137,662,204	150,372,418	156,097,614	268,923,503	190,991,378	227,890,348
Costa Rica	815,016,525	1,112,534,272	1,392,360,841	2,321,504,430	-281,889,034	-2,742,810,474
El Salvador	-324,702,557	117,684,057	85,626,895	-9,078,226	15,935,149	12,471,905
Guatemala	112,672,766	709,427,723	1,394,607,363	1,778,622,984	1,235,340,881	1,529,577,629
Honduras	-374,078,081	6,118,676	551,347,231	722,244,086	78,374,315	662,642,717
Nicaragua	-597,715,487	-810,114,062	-792,860,578	-716,709,191	-875,656,986	-1,057,504,244
Panama	1,886,309,158	2,340,420,401	3,243,600,760	4,313,154,190	3,830,293,661	5,493,591,429
South America	-5,233,289,614	2,002,647,902	16,858,930,686	34,993,166,651	37,749,692,286	51,323,198,274
Argentina	860,995,037	1,701,782,981	2,402,791,134	2,711,310,220	2,812,739,698	4,475,317,241
Bolivia	-4,014,071	-58,178,081	10,162,122	-5,323,069	80,084,829	103,124,812
Brazil	-6,155,375,061	-3,281,355,138	3,094,016,258	10,227,708,884	12,546,291,547	18,855,448,111
Chile	543,563,407	-822,126,817	1,557,772,208	5,565,907,160	5,137,639,109	5,441,020,794
Colombia	1,861,310,040	3,182,718,822	4,627,980,086	6,312,519,336	5,499,003,459	7,096,396,126
Ecuador	1,309,179,894	1,952,741,756	2,076,379,635	2,462,757,172	3,066,180,457	4,343,835,881
Falkland Islands (Islas Malvin)	8,534,454	1,211,562	812,791	571,024	2,294,114	2,304,207
French Guiana	24,413,943	30,059,660	28,718,823	15,909,111	14,877,191	28,821,112
Guyana	85,109,239	89,217,141	105,670,193	114,531,540	48,411,523	-28,739,736
Paraguay	831,663,980	837,696,680	1,131,287,855	1,429,143,297	1,210,463,865	1,681,795,676
Peru	-2,462,610,295	-2,472,731,317	-767,526,478	953,056,834	1,241,468,351	2,151,897,436
Suriname	78,941,076	91,994,940	170,272,734	272,344,768	246,236,394	171,643,723
Uruguay	-348,253,488	-15,061,654	164,362,251	644,479,593	504,699,736	727,021,477
Venezuela	-1,866,747,769	764,677,367	2,256,231,074	4,288,250,781	5,339,302,013	6,273,311,414
Other Western Hemisphere	384,972,524	540,961,184	563,439,076	741,454,358	702,485,229	534,533,114
Bermuda	380,293,831	538,409,807	559,343,219	708,502,723	695,788,350	526,441,049
Greenland	4,596,037	2,537,602	4,127,873	32,612,654	6,580,558	8,078,336
St Pierre and Miquelon	82,656	13,775	-32,016	338,981	116,321	13,729
Asia	-374,388,775,227	-414,136,957,970	-422,388,415,963	-411,638,509,753	-326,185,342,514	-397,041,002,659
China	-205,763,296,326	-239,873,622,704	-266,555,355,591	-278,833,540,484	-240,106,941,952	-292,745,356,207
Hong Kong	7,228,253,218	9,074,568,127	11,920,864,098	13,883,213,566	15,965,986,569	20,237,164,401
Japan	-87,610,097,773	-93,724,976,984	-89,100,932,558	-82,786,514,274	-50,526,027,287	-67,961,299,409
South Korea	-18,433,445,034	-16,498,845,110	-17,213,430,530	-19,228,482,892	-14,952,979,211	-15,838,839,258
Saudi Arabia	4,284,565,282	5,904,628,643	8,210,552,956	10,420,106,954	9,368,220,765	9,665,577,700
Taiwan	-14,267,717,945	-16,574,295,986	-14,197,750,922	-14,231,886,496	-11,967,573,156	-11,993,539,585
ASEAN - 10	-44,119,528,634	-47,880,760,695	-45,828,802,960	-37,615,558,136	-34,034,832,469	-32,039,148,415
Brunei	-122,910,323	-77,570,625	19,132,539	28,533,007	50,439,124	102,773,508
Cambodia	-1,680,461,161	-2,099,463,146	-2,321,653,842	-2,258,492,328	-1,794,640,877	-2,149,391,606
East Timor	4,009,531	4,326,733	3,646,258	4,705,230	2,215,910	3,305,526
Indonesia	-7,466,663,602	-8,531,676,978	-8,688,148,961	-8,263,319,558	-6,662,081,102	-7,158,732,729
Laos	6,371,584	-1,599,954	-6,852,931	-21,060,995	-20,587,744	-45,847,358
Malaysia	-22,617,418,237	-23,598,782,092	-20,824,953,195	-17,715,725,773	-12,790,236,132	-11,599,624,804
Myanmar (ex-Burma)	5,166,604	7,360,236	8,494,592	7,716,287	4,007,097	8,578,889
Philippines	2,611,007,868	-2,193,694,520	-1,941,704,238	-1,054,901,006	-1,296,257,195	-1,047,907,465
Singapore	5,791,776,896	6,862,755,122	7,783,372,774	12,587,867,905	7,001,100,063	11,751,598,151
Thailand	-11,532,988,090	-12,702,483,504	-12,781,467,495	-12,717,387,642	-10,476,690,247	-11,903,099,798
Vietnam	-3,994,503,968	-5,549,931,967	-7,078,668,461	-8,213,493,263	-8,052,101,366	-10,000,800,729
Middle East	2,702,006,692	5,202,541,349	7,631,762,370	12,499,192,972	10,511,130,365	10,041,785,630
Bahrain	-65,802,689	-58,012,121	38,494,341	226,166,753	193,322,907	711,133,802
Bosnia and Herzegovina	3,289,079	25,493,132	-4,566,241	6,827,531	-5,153,499	-6,972,139
Gaza Strip admin. by Israel	-1,198,516	-760,638	3,180,236	-2,219,625	-5,263,327	-1,380,528
Iran	-67,769,817	-63,980,157	-70,600,570	32,786,600	58,492,612	51,660,781
Iraq	1,071,068,011	1,155,227,440	1,096,414,075	1,216,391,271	1,692,051,922	1,466,695,581
Israel	-6,922,498,803	-8,174,103,734	-8,082,145,536	-8,294,470,458	-9,208,447,512	-9,889,598,296
Jordan	-654,395,430	-876,076,884	-535,664,618	-226,970,624	168,571,004	94,293,953
Kuwait	1,365,598,218	1,785,604,929	2,043,020,195	2,165,315,942	1,732,551,828	2,459,563,581
Lebanon	321,945,411	784,366,230	650,960,486	1,286,196,453	1,683,303,579	1,784,492,112
Oman	406,486,219	697,498,796	877,965,866	1,096,501,779	944,796,956	639,347,880
Qatar	605,153,618	1,068,366,280	1,985,350,409	2,283,191,754	2,443,458,655	2,898,154,730
Republic of Yemen	108,910,955	134,336,192	340,070,118	246,781,950	224,354,696	287,617,536

Table B-28. U.S. Balance of Payments of North American Industry Classification System (NAICS) Manufactures by Region and Individual Countries, 2005–2015—*Continued*

Region	2011	2012	2013	2014	2015	2005–2015 Value Change
Haiti	2,578,307	-74,311,623	-93,197,769	-63,364,861	-269,230,081	-399,147,606
Jamaica	1,218,851,832	1,338,062,969	1,392,006,201	1,698,692,430	1,284,383,581	79,208,482
Martinique	293,254,460	311,912,102	308,748,946	187,838,215	74,610,468	63,971,649
Montserrat	4,914,029	5,785,851	6,176,601	6,509,009	4,381,429	1,377,266
Sint Maarten	368,606,110	651,258,645	777,484,714	726,761,408	677,852,680	677,852,680
St Kitts and Nevis	52,655,976	41,184,943	78,742,880	113,432,475	83,255,339	48,273,816
St Lucia	255,223,294	308,039,902	493,221,325	587,183,353	413,100,264	325,711,817
St Vincent and the Grenadines	59,444,384	65,045,784	64,046,513	71,785,169	60,623,055	42,033,733
Trinidad and Tobago	-4,041,913,920	-3,833,043,296	-3,035,436,717	-2,684,743,424	-1,044,925,632	972,950,169
Turks and Caicos Islands	111,234,654	113,891,420	121,428,509	154,506,192	152,737,840	18,861,903
						0
Central America	7,414,203,870	7,496,588,823	8,126,842,945	9,913,442,880	11,000,802,534	9,345,638,006
Belize	270,822,745	197,166,885	176,968,636	163,802,085	194,796,404	57,134,200
Costa Rica	-3,187,798,013	-3,837,627,073	-3,468,107,202	-1,626,151,536	2,506,315,629	1,691,299,104
El Salvador	596,763,800	137,891,595	500,885,676	492,837,701	352,912,334	677,614,891
Guatemala	2,225,139,626	2,421,508,268	2,263,913,496	2,567,088,454	2,371,661,054	2,258,988,288
Honduras	1,533,137,651	1,031,098,279	760,134,099	1,154,876,124	455,640,577	829,718,658
Nicaragua	-1,495,680,521	-1,484,992,123	-1,577,638,923	-1,866,826,821	-1,763,794,316	-1,166,078,829
Panama	7,471,818,582	9,031,542,992	9,470,687,163	9,027,816,873	6,883,270,852	4,996,961,694
						0
South America	60,335,431,212	71,708,930,870	70,678,051,556	69,440,756,759	55,435,205,875	60,668,495,489
Argentina	6,586,756,606	7,074,337,103	7,031,562,084	7,956,869,978	6,285,039,253	5,424,044,216
Bolivia	59,306,146	-228,884,973	140,239,023	-707,758,426	49,217,581	53,231,652
Brazil	21,122,459,455	20,890,416,068	21,274,191,620	19,108,687,876	10,982,147,316	17,137,522,377
Chile	8,235,828,350	10,959,005,775	9,274,763,434	9,559,717,424	9,427,200,594	8,883,637,187
Colombia	7,863,514,943	9,298,510,394	12,346,646,398	13,267,629,986	10,994,332,407	9,133,022,367
Ecuador	4,965,864,302	5,206,489,682	6,084,385,262	5,989,405,708	4,074,074,422	2,764,894,528
Falkland Islands (Islas Malvin)	3,595,075	3,788,155	1,058,376	7,639,839	2,614,620	-5,919,834
French Guiana	50,944,173	206,362,523	627,319,020	277,564,520	1,070,687,356	1,046,273,413
Guyana	-101,575,248	-154,556,319	-123,427,324	-97,841,634	-65,758,799	-150,868,038
Paraguay	1,825,451,277	1,527,008,500	1,758,018,555	1,969,413,858	1,359,153,384	527,489,404
Peru	2,810,126,408	3,939,148,787	2,929,797,019	4,844,336,217	4,636,011,404	7,098,621,699
Suriname	122,375,847	200,232,374	167,417,294	76,283,175	297,255,985	218,314,909
Uruguay	967,815,470	1,017,335,403	1,345,475,435	1,154,360,034	752,270,422	1,100,523,910
Venezuela	5,822,968,408	11,769,737,398	7,820,605,360	6,034,448,204	5,570,959,930	7,437,707,699
						0
Other Western Hemisphere	505,440,148	539,022,893	459,819,154	550,866,371	524,459,630	139,487,106
Bermuda	498,821,061	524,112,408	441,808,933	538,812,745	515,434,787	135,140,956
Greenland	6,509,874	14,773,668	17,779,283	12,049,631	8,895,862	4,299,825
St Pierre and Miquelon	109,213	136,817	230,938	3,995	128,981	46,325
Asia	-437,304,769,548	-470,640,130,443	-461,522,613,640	-504,455,151,662	-549,399,094,334	-175,010,319,107
China	-320,985,132,417	-344,180,602,423	-345,396,099,966	-367,244,745,950	-384,203,131,976	-178,439,835,650
Hong Kong	29,472,809,110	30,410,009,357	35,344,338,501	33,505,907,953	28,432,421,367	21,204,168,149
Japan	-73,115,348,710	-84,053,065,883	-79,906,616,103	-75,102,567,330	-74,547,928,159	13,062,169,614
South Korea	-21,108,030,719	-22,890,287,729	-25,476,180,096	-30,806,164,641	-32,791,403,349	-14,357,958,315
Saudi Arabia	10,907,376,104	15,003,396,559	16,482,582,933	15,287,146,227	17,190,716,317	12,906,151,035
Taiwan	-18,738,339,914	-17,555,400,670	-14,731,100,522	-16,507,830,863	-16,406,248,648	-2,138,530,703
ASEAN - 10	-35,312,094,716	-41,273,089,983	-42,628,253,689	-54,674,845,824	-72,612,348,812	-28,492,820,178
Brunei	154,747,536	134,139,401	528,205,086	513,559,740	110,505,885	233,416,208
Cambodia	-2,644,376,906	-2,602,158,437	-2,661,392,434	-2,706,983,510	-2,882,856,444	-1,202,395,283
East Timor	7,601,210	1,108,136	1,135,217	1,010,866	2,430,561	-1,578,970
Indonesia	-8,827,739,906	-8,114,487,799	-7,780,240,278	-9,143,891,943	-10,338,338,864	-2,871,675,262
Laos	-29,422,644	8,656,480	-5,066,700	-3,331,682	-17,305,319	-23,676,903
Malaysia	-11,440,938,120	-13,007,367,490	-14,294,771,695	-17,414,853,098	-21,489,686,382	1,127,931,855
Myanmar (ex-Burma)	34,373,593	54,132,965	116,624,802	35,643,011	113,218,034	108,051,430
Philippines	-2,144,691,973	-2,013,502,742	-1,531,984,062	-2,424,900,548	-2,872,472,277	-360,564,409
Singapore	12,919,746,557	11,927,104,227	14,361,563,152	14,300,846,528	11,612,827,482	5,821,050,586
Thailand	-11,427,012,222	-13,183,229,139	-13,117,211,548	-14,474,545,623	-16,816,709,624	-5,283,721,534
Vietnam	-11,914,381,841	-14,477,485,585	-18,245,115,229	-23,357,399,565	-30,033,961,864	-26,039,457,896
						0
Middle East	12,227,576,252	19,806,733,547	21,456,538,625	21,504,379,418	17,887,570,463	15,185,563,771
Bahrain	518,190,087	265,386,850	196,472,236	-83,932,506	56,958,684	122,761,373
Bosnia and Herzegovina	-30,910,312	-37,146,309	-24,044,638	-62,381,312	-56,891,656	-60,180,735
Gaza Strip admin. by Israel	-2,869,366	-222,243	-272,355	-22,805	143,871	1,342,387
Iran	184,583,298	137,032,041	233,022,961	152,548,618	208,330,508	276,100,325
Iraq	1,785,305,289	1,900,425,785	1,949,280,259	1,831,293,398	1,796,506,396	725,438,385
Israel	-9,290,641,331	-7,950,947,057	-9,129,226,317	-7,834,675,913	-10,452,372,750	-3,529,873,947
Jordan	-114,240,751	140,790,743	211,858,982	295,117,583	-497,972,984	156,422,446
Kuwait	2,335,974,898	2,164,331,857	2,124,431,696	3,069,731,410	2,375,388,116	1,009,789,898
Lebanon	1,309,236,703	675,521,580	666,811,477	918,508,853	918,991,914	597,046,503
Oman	765,789,914	660,946,780	559,224,397	953,133,183	1,362,208,996	955,722,777
Qatar	2,234,690,795	2,564,119,881	3,741,883,346	3,572,436,899	2,844,590,768	2,239,437,150
Republic of Yemen	114,043,115	201,263,865	208,795,324	143,033,908	37,010,103	-71,900,852

Table B-28.   U.S. Balance of Payments of North American Industry Classification System (NAICS) Manufactures by Region and Individual Countries, 2005–2015—*Continued*

Region	2005	2006	2007	2008	2009	2010
Syria	-293,419,760	-105,688,059	-80,943,365	-289,943,526	-240,198,065	-358,774,036
United Arab Emirates	6,822,621,204	8,831,176,273	9,360,890,525	12,754,938,651	10,829,791,653	9,905,981,410
West Bank admin. by Israel	2,018,992	-906,330	9,336,449	-2,301,479	-503,044	-430,737
Central Asia	-212,895,999	-328,446,823	-410,513,021	-329,314,106	64,265,037	-275,804,858
Kazakhstan	-13,456,638	-243,843,215	-269,329,989	-239,425,615	-156,029,905	-354,978,016
Kyrgyzstan	9,384,804	51,683,333	26,193,045	31,177,407	46,887,916	65,398,080
Tajikistan	-227,804,431	-49,508,349	23,896,774	19,768,126	-216,239	11,495,474
Turkmenistan	60,692,207	33,282,818	-89,272,944	-77,864,814	203,390,786	-7,906,407
Uzbekistan	-41,711,941	-120,061,410	-101,999,907	-62,969,210	-29,767,521	10,186,011
Other Asia	-18,196,618,708	-19,437,747,787	-16,844,809,805	-15,415,726,857	-10,506,591,175	-16,131,542,658
Afghanistan	218,837,977	375,479,841	452,109,948	438,982,636	1,467,987,747	2,036,715,392
Armenia	-3,754,494	17,043,723	26,228,095	88,395,375	-28,588,333	-26,006,328
Azerbaijan	82,079,441	187,079,702	43,600,915	178,659,174	176,465,900	242,498,758
Bangladesh	-2,307,175,493	-2,834,122,039	-3,022,210,581	-3,349,973,286	-3,347,210,941	-3,862,327,728
Bhutan	2,394,701	1,759,274	3,614,610	2,295,348	2,490,143	2,858,171
Georgia	76,276,495	100,581,419	60,734,473	316,052,879	266,851,700	99,057,997
India	-10,808,682,027	-12,091,492,120	-9,560,557,221	-8,715,189,351	-5,719,865,200	-11,283,828,259
North Korea	96,992	0	0	3,763,018	0	0
Macau	-1,161,110,573	-1,054,529,084	-908,315,545	-655,672,343	-59,118,955	46,996,631
Maldives	3,612,661	16,320,140	17,608,457	17,146,226	15,101,337	26,004,794
Mongolia	-119,265,323	-83,958,114	-53,678,671	8,924,416	29,013,618	109,064,110
Nepal	-85,618,779	-82,705,609	-60,980,312	-53,816,944	-23,139,422	-29,465,512
Pakistan	-2,208,547,632	-2,121,695,418	-2,007,560,746	-2,031,207,030	-1,915,466,490	-1,943,510,946
Sri Lanka	-1,885,762,654	-1,867,509,502	-1,835,403,227	-1,664,086,975	-1,371,112,279	-1,549,599,738
Australia and Oceania	8,367,733,721	9,574,192,033	11,329,668,474	14,385,752,716	13,310,434,525	14,995,234,075
Australia	8,348,639,626	9,183,700,306	10,190,858,188	12,460,826,454	11,719,928,637	12,789,882,819
Christmas Island	1,673,043	711,431	-567,577	12,349,529	161,854	297,586
Cocos (Keeling) Islands	484,012	-786,583	394,305	-209,631	484,281	-1,541,867
Cook Islands	709,135	1,974,078	880,494	1,795,712	1,375,052	2,061,764
Fiji	-126,269,722	-100,640,651	-105,518,863	-96,128,876	-96,978,703	-112,049,825
French Polynesia	45,037,630	44,122,760	63,242,715	53,327,562	73,959,579	62,110,716
French Southern and Antarctic	210,653	26,068	-114,022	4,191,137	902,046	548,416
Heard and McDonald Islands	144,569	372,963	1,611,550	250,356	6,733,564	3,241,324
Kiribati	1,525,630	703,418	621,294	4,569,292	275,975	467,467
Marshall Islands	67,721,922	11,778,109	15,069,727	17,503,431	68,339,370	76,118,689
Micronesia	19,471,352	25,114,558	31,890,327	48,117,524	35,789,785	35,507,179
Netherlands Antilles	317,340,334	462,285,439	1,336,019,838	2,137,105,442	1,540,309,815	1,816,717,051
New Caledonia	4,150,330	-7,346,052	-30,920,896	18,151,252	33,347,825	14,388,581
New Zealand	-422,960,850	-125,590,725	-303,258,980	-451,102,005	-314,979,499	88,510,249
Niue	332,377	2,231,127	1,280,287	276,525	621,287	1,143,428
Norfolk Island	143,271	556,126	93,803	1,510,173	106,829	338,853
Palau	10,159,815	8,912,869	11,475,685	11,493,798	11,615,922	11,439,240
Papua New Guinea	42,962,135	7,959,704	38,498,351	41,465,895	181,655,818	151,172,987
Pitcairn Islands	-703,473	1,178,058	1,592,415	-8,160	557,821	0
Reunion	3,511,135	3,852,523	4,273,434	7,801,563	9,082,540	7,575,213
Samoa	8,199,755	13,985,858	11,544,374	9,941,470	13,867,910	14,170,789
Solomon Islands	1,242,104	2,704,749	1,645,107	1,333,988	2,211,041	3,424,114
Tokelau	30,951,983	23,636,590	28,817,098	27,672,092	7,705,598	109,340
Tonga	7,623,975	8,013,804	10,643,204	11,108,844	10,572,389	16,693,877
Tuvalu	-17,994	39,312	21,143	40,605	54,956	580,427
Vanuatu	5,115,735	4,636,837	19,556,927	62,161,110	2,396,025	11,646,521
Wallis and Futuna	335,239	59,357	18,546	207,634	336,808	679,137
Africa	1,426,046,575	-857,717,622	179,678,578	519,384,002	6,812,826,235	4,846,264,327
Algeria	-776,635,958	-1,149,867,201	-832,752,192	-2,311,955,207	-1,443,743,624	-2,174,626,640
Angola	619,942,296	1,051,818,937	831,168,062	1,579,452,168	1,053,467,006	812,258,962
Benin	64,885,594	106,465,131	269,621,946	812,521,559	384,006,991	446,311,935
Botswana	-145,940,752	-240,498,239	-157,029,138	-183,778,261	-66,508,703	-141,467,994
British Indian Ocean Terr.	359,383	-395,633	546,135	176,471	1,282,006	144,169
Burkina Faso	21,090,816	14,331,656	27,776,458	22,417,569	22,126,902	40,453,793
Burundi	5,703,635	2,296,216	4,459,100	4,867,672	6,280,033	11,610,971
Cameroon	-259,000	-48,543,840	-46,981,959	-108,395,877	-12,489,135	-55,936,850
Cabo Verde	3,897,627	8,861,457	1,207,075	8,185,762	3,233,598	6,367,390
Central African Republic	7,132,584	17,151,241	12,489,445	11,368,004	18,464,278	3,251,071
Chad	-355,406,530	-42,255,696	33,555,382	-78,686,750	-65,736,852	-175,807,901
Comoros	-371,165	-740,784	-143,212	-220,268	481,379	-327,780
Congo (Brazzaville)	-88,204,364	-111,749,809	-51,330,996	57,050,330	134,024,769	59,860,379
Congo (Kinshasa)	-82,580,682	-23,010,702	-84,477,445	-104,743,275	54,151,747	8,384,890
Cote d'Ivoire	-96,361,704	-32,550,908	26,418,604	-195,462,408	-3,779,422	-95,701,313
Djibouti	23,146,309	27,371,732	48,731,846	72,747,834	132,485,582	98,594,145
Egypt	1,132,137,888	1,236,110,200	1,720,897,710	1,927,597,751	2,731,442,068	3,057,150,113
Equatorial Guinea	131,358,371	453,148,497	22,125,164	-26,335,693	226,701,070	128,115,253

Table B-28.   U.S. Balance of Payments of North American Industry Classification System (NAICS) Manufactures by Region and Individual Countries, 2005–2015—*Continued*

Region	2011	2012	2013	2014	2015	2005–2015 Value Change
Syria....................	-246,829,821	-514,692	10,599,251	-4,980,578	-4,883,291	288,536,469
United Arab Emirates..................	12,666,043,508	19,086,543,920	20,708,709,291	18,554,730,558	19,301,762,473	12,479,141,269
West Bank admin. by Israel..................	-789,774	-799,454	-1,007,285	-161,878	-2,200,685	-4,219,677
						0
Central Asia......................	-161,962,540	-310,575,775	388,616,814	331,153,690	-85,279,292	127,616,707
Kazakhstan....................	-352,335,754	-626,043,560	-254,752,767	-319,503,985	-183,123,856	-169,667,218
Kyrgyzstan....................	37,439,890	90,760,357	62,723,323	37,660,111	12,437,984	3,053,180
Tajikistan....................	106,218,004	-11,746,120	23,150,551	13,107,905	-12,285,408	215,519,023
Turkmenistan....................	29,124,397	6,956,790	240,924,787	439,084,135	23,659,994	-37,032,213
Uzbekistan....................	17,590,923	229,496,758	316,570,920	160,805,524	74,031,994	115,743,935
						0
Other Asia......................	-20,491,621,998	-25,597,247,443	-27,056,440,137	-30,747,584,342	-32,263,462,245	-14,066,843,537
Afghanistan....................	2,824,297,567	1,450,838,006	1,376,158,905	763,441,334	466,045,164	247,207,187
Armenia....................	-31,046,942	-41,636,676	-37,258,108	-48,227,521	-18,023,622	-14,269,128
Azerbaijan....................	326,427,998	447,255,617	328,108,032	887,284,831	414,939,163	332,859,722
Bangladesh....................	-4,049,499,614	-4,400,961,624	-4,766,638,290	-4,409,094,729	-5,411,560,635	-3,104,385,142
Bhutan....................	2,508,916	1,886,102	1,880,812	2,143,444	-512,650	-2,907,351
Georgia....................	210,989,608	151,796,681	179,400,007	16,289,543	73,404,615	-2,871,880
India....................	-15,960,597,398	-19,428,687,025	-19,893,069,299	-23,499,446,643	-23,307,951,134	-12,499,269,107
North Korea....................	489,112	497,686	453,950	408,004	804,206	707,214
Macau....................	120,314,803	173,662,144	205,192,588	277,011,133	307,182,953	1,468,293,526
Maldives....................	42,901,260	27,593,094	25,840,809	26,509,314	33,451,280	29,838,619
Mongolia....................	241,511,161	593,674,409	247,167,128	154,509,990	61,803,974	181,069,297
Nepal....................	-36,477,853	-39,219,078	-41,243,935	-48,124,066	-54,492,422	31,126,357
Pakistan....................	-2,380,585,030	-2,543,827,801	-2,544,844,615	-2,568,831,311	-2,338,576,114	-130,028,482
Sri Lanka....................	-1,802,855,586	-1,990,118,978	-2,137,588,121	-2,301,457,665	-2,489,977,023	-604,214,369
						0
Australia and Oceania......................	18,181,222,630	21,470,448,076	16,646,935,318	16,078,314,148	13,873,068,271	5,505,334,550
Australia....................	16,903,432,931	21,085,074,926	16,529,145,804	15,411,156,561	14,171,817,275	5,823,177,649
Christmas Island....................	104,825	3,292,492	-739,338	-975,953	-355,012	-2,028,055
Cocos (Keeling) Islands....................	-682,004	-93,283	19,964,982	-1,685,453	-3,048,445	-3,532,457
Cook Islands....................	3,635,336	4,027,937	3,844,576	4,234,484	3,100,164	2,391,029
Fiji....................	-80,539,347	-130,429,487	-102,758,207	-109,698,323	-138,098,141	-11,828,419
French Polynesia....................	70,583,925	78,635,324	88,785,066	88,881,314	83,624,700	38,587,070
French Southern and Antarctic....................	1,253,287	1,149,720	1,521,765	7,480,434	7,745,242	7,534,589
Heard and McDonald Islands....................	343,666	399,263	470,416	76,647	850,340	705,771
Kiribati....................	2,276,226	3,243,961	5,827,358	2,151,650	4,808,535	3,282,905
Marshall Islands....................	122,847,616	118,430,809	51,307,164	85,079,922	70,031,605	2,309,683
Micronesia....................	37,109,729	42,831,114	34,576,150	34,061,484	32,695,517	13,224,165
Netherlands Antilles....................	298,763,468	0	0	0	0	-317,340,334
New Caledonia....................	-13,246,763	1,748,936	-13,308,495	15,376,556	15,799,027	11,648,697
New Zealand....................	382,491,865	-220,849,908	-195,059,772	347,876,138	-624,002,222	-201,041,372
Niue....................	371,280	599,939	34,477	-127,095	-257,150	-589,527
Norfolk Island....................	758,909	1,066,464	1,574,163	740,531	-847,399	-990,670
Palau....................	13,529,439	13,427,470	14,265,814	15,716,771	20,147,973	9,988,158
Papua New Guinea....................	243,254,659	350,201,677	146,153,049	130,091,981	190,769,923	147,807,788
Pitcairn Islands....................	2,530	-2,918	0	-87,169	6,311	709,784
Reunion....................	154,236,010	6,260,512	6,815,175	6,030,083	5,390,033	1,878,898
Samoa....................	19,060,191	20,234,852	20,910,470	15,843,830	17,406,457	9,206,702
Solomon Islands....................	3,222,490	2,915,247	-1,963,835	-3,010,285	603,884	-638,220
Tokelau....................	-716,829	8,392,286	-290,871	148,541	-272,801	-31,224,784
Tonga....................	15,594,232	22,899,668	15,398,925	16,109,083	10,905,605	3,281,630
Tuvalu....................	670,352	543,782	515,293	498,525	456,307	474,301
Vanuatu....................	2,641,733	56,125,513	19,648,866	12,047,184	3,595,283	-1,520,452
Wallis and Futuna....................	222,874	321,780	296,323	296,707	195,260	-139,979
						0
Africa......................	1,736,017,978	5,919,650,565	8,732,933,768	12,159,042,049	6,745,020,728	8,181,966,303
Algeria....................	-3,580,233,761	-2,930,501,392	-1,745,289,605	-1,845,844,751	-1,520,645,966	-744,010,008
Angola....................	769,401,312	856,504,261	763,421,069	1,420,258,533	828,719,922	208,777,626
Benin....................	207,796,106	215,770,478	276,110,613	387,215,398	317,678,973	252,793,379
Botswana....................	-268,304,919	-192,513,533	-233,206,780	-290,958,267	-188,761,668	-42,820,916
British Indian Ocean Terr....................	-4,010,724	-16,840,386	-16,968,414	-11,650,253	-14,370,854	-14,730,237
Burkina Faso....................	28,634,961	42,881,353	69,258,553	61,458,999	48,083,020	26,992,204
Burundi....................	26,848,518	16,470,226	12,815,209	4,639,813	2,310,913	-3,392,722
Cameroon....................	-105,993,920	16,404,148	56,276,005	116,926,653	89,895,994	90,154,994
Cabo Verde....................	6,985,274	2,033,057	4,760,501	3,304,030	3,760,653	-136,974
Central African Republic....................	4,089,108	2,958,615	713,276	27,236,638	28,913,323	21,780,739
Chad....................	-62,760,062	-384,751,399	35,709,423	55,602	21,248,743	376,655,273
Comoros....................	-725,006	-1,024,761	1,532,800	2,094,523	931,701	1,302,866
Congo (Brazzaville)....................	-153,018,525	76,369,835	-168,320,843	28,829,641	164,762,926	252,967,290
Congo (Kinshasa)....................	73,477,051	124,732,810	80,501,112	36,835,466	-17,086,468	65,494,214
Cote d'Ivoire....................	-111,544,093	-98,712,690	-68,948,052	-96,999,654	75,550,081	171,911,785
Djibouti....................	83,131,827	65,401,466	107,834,808	82,557,859	111,523,322	88,377,013
Egypt....................	1,973,821,512	2,510,077,706	2,486,364,604	3,581,704,440	2,720,311,650	1,588,173,762
Equatorial Guinea....................	147,811,763	121,461,186	609,783,172	442,762,329	71,314,456	-60,043,915

Table B-28. U.S. Balance of Payments of North American Industry Classification System (NAICS) Manufactures by Region and Individual Countries, 2005–2015—*Continued*

Region	2005	2006	2007	2008	2009	2010
Eritrea	15,791,017	3,311,960	5,662,657	8,519,159	1,846,159	1,908,230
Ethiopia	317,336,220	71,503,765	62,043,376	121,238,198	142,575,009	578,440,510
Gambia	17,802,071	17,854,156	18,796,688	27,385,676	27,979,441	28,265,889
Gabon	88,592,284	124,792,811	434,387,313	244,326,388	144,795,148	231,898,413
Ghana	174,056,368	138,747,387	225,059,943	384,728,818	619,675,265	763,066,036
Guinea	63,328,097	32,895,343	45,724,084	68,464,472	73,805,570	64,230,155
Guinea-Bissau	1,966,693	3,041,847	2,142,409	1,682,371	1,418,716	2,358,539
Kenya	215,283,556	29,544,736	164,071,557	82,992,292	280,117,342	66,622,500
Lesotho	-398,569,898	-404,024,443	-430,272,474	-369,693,665	-284,367,065	-298,206,544
Liberia	51,442,805	44,335,748	59,667,825	130,112,666	71,917,363	140,135,673
Libya	-148,169,156	-43,283,095	-253,743,384	-556,073,363	163,224,290	129,786,408
Madagascar	-265,622,179	-209,455,426	-274,065,619	-227,078,869	-118,712,126	37,028,990
Malawi	-11,656,553	2,609,915	2,354,675	1,461,750	1,494,800	1,256,695
Mali	26,759,405	30,053,733	16,632,947	25,048,830	31,968,156	30,062,821
Mauritania	76,460,920	87,604,507	96,759,806	97,395,104	52,388,581	76,921,435
Mauritius	-177,951,458	-166,442,267	-134,272,896	-118,276,037	-109,718,641	-145,074,095
Mayotte	0	3,043	-296,251	37,254	942,862	3,387,295
Morocco	-19,083,738	156,405,602	184,472,628	546,102,628	1,024,527,369	1,122,881,425
Mozambique	41,557,887	34,541,370	82,520,176	173,787,397	125,818,069	140,763,208
Namibia	-28,267,687	-4,100,454	44,181,694	200,402,784	128,987,922	35,409,252
Nauru	1,038,580	1,388,485	1,235,945	4,175,105	525,026	1,003,850
Niger	-11,455,269	-16,757,091	58,047,286	36,424,656	-65,625,450	16,358,341
Nigeria	-206,221,689	721,944,306	1,062,026,518	1,414,573,313	2,159,227,718	1,957,110,697
Rwanda	8,200,416	9,557,994	13,372,492	17,812,645	29,831,435	26,287,984
Sao Tome and Principe	9,826,797	3,429,735	7,772,087	3,045,940	3,867,285	987,429
Senegal	128,231,997	63,146,912	121,212,256	106,407,298	153,919,353	200,570,387
Seychelles	11,562,144	353,527	1,123,711	19,812,423	28,644,661	3,931,217
Sierra Leone	21,357,343	25,651,096	34,390,136	35,170,068	27,760,403	40,471,348
Somalia	4,186,980	5,606,955	8,117,356	23,547,010	1,080,347	1,136,512
South Africa	-1,856,999,379	-2,896,476,482	-3,455,611,559	-3,543,961,544	-1,491,578,093	-2,718,228,546
South Sudan	0	0	0	0	0	0
St Helena	1,654,083	1,145,903	2,655,533	1,572,137	2,533,574	-324,281
Sudan	26,404,582	14,725,706	21,623,266	65,996,698	25,404,739	33,202,669
Swaziland	-187,200,876	-144,506,741	-118,205,452	-123,354,735	-96,312,292	-103,358,112
Tanzania	60,181,793	92,827,961	112,075,589	95,250,087	109,245,899	104,402,123
Togo	25,219,219	102,597,591	280,880,436	108,309,435	110,356,482	150,437,618
Tunisia	47,341,246	-42,813,321	-217,533,696	-126,628,967	66,497,172	-506,583
Uganda	36,321,739	32,166,763	45,956,104	68,507,470	102,023,171	66,607,451
Western Sahara	28,189	15,801	291,468	85,516	81,033	52,983
Zambia	-12,817,627	10,780,641	7,913,936	15,626,472	43,984,730	21,042,225
Zimbabwe	-48,756,845	-60,385,856	14,226,027	-32,358,259	44,785,119	5,301,587

Table B-28. U.S. Balance of Payments of North American Industry Classification System (NAICS) Manufactures by Region and Individual Countries, 2005–2015—*Continued*

Region	2011	2012	2013	2014	2015	2005–2015 Value Change
Eritrea	2,956,560	5,216,690	12,710,596	4,555,321	3,208,117	-12,582,900
Ethiopia	560,876,490	1,164,676,199	565,822,037	1,533,454,830	1,387,384,712	1,070,048,492
Gambia	25,240,764	23,070,536	25,887,009	35,810,981	31,904,496	14,102,425
Gabon	181,542,116	202,066,207	249,429,041	317,144,367	128,836,568	40,244,284
Ghana	777,214,659	893,136,488	637,631,055	839,500,643	607,229,832	433,173,464
Guinea	200,374,941	109,953,381	48,592,965	40,113,828	105,445,512	42,117,415
Guinea-Bissau	10,346,761	18,856,957	4,811,449	2,681,926	2,046,941	80,248
Kenya	55,412,014	165,902,166	170,784,279	1,117,103,862	416,551,690	201,268,134
Lesotho	-378,195,591	-308,139,482	-350,736,815	-358,586,625	-331,116,083	67,453,815
Liberia	140,520,856	184,114,033	133,926,895	146,324,602	87,810,073	36,367,268
Libya	-6,713,388	94,468,588	-170,585,417	360,770,318	73,242,728	221,411,884
Madagascar	-4,141,790	-10,325,861	-47,202,892	-94,617,110	-156,506,687	109,115,492
Malawi	7,197,596	28,657,508	17,914,011	8,589,170	4,048,109	15,704,662
Mali	46,557,521	52,951,789	43,871,078	31,061,096	63,586,461	36,827,056
Mauritania	236,046,946	282,695,586	226,615,363	141,707,598	119,290,181	42,829,261
Mauritius	-197,952,231	-156,005,479	-293,575,446	-353,949,197	-350,525,489	-172,574,031
Mayotte	4,242,652	4,851,909	7,820,422	11,058,646	5,003,001	5,003,001
Morocco	1,630,104,233	1,048,616,701	1,327,906,962	717,179,875	557,469,201	576,552,939
Mozambique	349,858,210	290,911,118	257,322,595	280,577,208	219,984,070	178,426,183
Namibia	-147,106,486	2,916,798	69,617,514	164,765,891	46,517,243	74,784,930
Nauru	172,146	1,647,998	290,235	366,358	816,347	-222,233
Niger	-260,223,059	-53,891,111	38,439,691	41,266,093	62,851,131	74,306,400
Nigeria	966,586,011	1,872,504,106	2,855,753,272	3,473,674,085	1,988,632,314	2,194,854,003
Rwanda	107,612,580	27,391,439	21,885,283	17,731,494	8,378,570	178,154
Sao Tome and Principe	5,694,183	260,994	1,689,037	170,169	183,344	-9,643,453
Senegal	232,720,005	106,549,869	181,964,030	116,524,504	120,991,037	-7,240,960
Seychelles	7,398,089	11,540,462	7,259,669	8,736,596	13,229,853	1,667,709
Sierra Leone	58,508,798	71,156,319	48,219,723	56,443,019	42,053,107	20,695,764
Somalia	1,107,464	11,197,300	13,065,133	29,680,195	39,302,833	35,115,853
South Africa	-2,361,492,222	-1,007,724,121	-1,150,505,845	-1,908,514,212	-1,624,541,871	232,457,508
South Sudan	3,467,139	27,782,313	10,040,638	14,181,555	13,229,668	13,229,668
St Helena	1,175,595	4,094,044	2,181,449	220,680	2,657,919	1,003,836
Sudan	21,777,426	18,722,532	43,208,102	37,208,157	13,974,556	-12,430,026
Swaziland	-74,374,340	-32,499,762	-40,589,065	-58,163,748	-1,223,395	185,977,481
Tanzania	147,750,885	129,086,160	323,086,364	204,572,373	77,946,637	17,764,844
Togo	153,925,840	266,917,368	954,640,165	966,779,168	194,232,448	169,013,229
Tunisia	64,256,238	-211,724,199	-17,109,717	167,562,562	-47,247,300	-94,588,546
Uganda	66,579,707	82,658,963	105,288,991	63,224,013	69,069,845	32,748,106
Western Sahara	13,597	42,097	-551,167	150,989	-12,333	-40,522
Zambia	69,899,791	68,800,505	88,946,364	47,705,699	30,206,178	43,023,805
Zimbabwe	-6,327,150	-175,523	34,821,264	-16,151,929	-25,261,557	*23,495,288*

Table B-29.   U.S. Exports by North American Industry Classification System (NAICS) by Region and Country, 2005–2015

Region	Partner	2005	2006	2007	2008	2009
WORLD	World	38,656,772,281	43,276,332,247	55,549,680,766	70,497,463,364	57,647,255,656
Europe		6,229,952,872	6,484,070,635	8,416,627,084	9,015,267,056	6,672,980,985
European Union (EU-28)		5,086,616,853	5,288,443,094	6,644,268,180	7,239,722,747	4,937,944,808
Austria	Austria	34,999,216	38,659,737	61,459,794	78,005,842	27,538,549
Belgium	Belgium	344,594,363	318,298,676	351,685,031	300,452,226	260,288,164
Bulgaria	Bulgaria	10,990,523	8,867,280	8,616,790	11,570,051	10,483,684
Croatia	Croatia	6,964,213	4,937,035	5,118,211	8,375,027	5,749,538
Cyprus	Cyprus	4,836,270	7,209,609	8,532,040	11,243,415	6,571,352
Czech Republic	Czech Republic	29,128,094	20,034,539	32,470,467	18,419,830	18,231,282
Denmark	Denmark	89,982,691	100,707,956	133,919,318	134,340,267	74,078,721
Estonia	Estonia	7,821,030	8,929,098	10,267,674	6,944,502	4,353,327
Finland	Finland	15,777,622	11,327,958	13,065,094	15,643,501	15,287,143
France	France	426,185,025	440,740,564	482,398,297	495,700,821	369,173,312
Germany	Germany	1,034,172,595	1,001,287,447	1,260,481,652	1,639,542,364	1,134,389,636
Greece	Greece	118,483,674	98,026,030	133,058,046	108,463,175	82,131,313
Hungary	Hungary	10,678,004	13,018,744	14,711,022	9,919,445	19,443,085
Ireland	Ireland	76,205,296	81,713,452	116,310,034	135,400,678	75,402,777
Italy	Italy	485,925,144	411,189,963	576,729,662	612,885,335	488,048,715
Latvia	Latvia	17,490,467	12,704,226	22,548,530	45,209,483	12,035,853
Lithuania	Lithuania	61,781,522	59,374,207	34,680,862	47,153,026	32,285,788
Luxembourg	Luxembourg	24,133,897	21,284,203	31,607,307	35,025,760	29,182,003
Malta	Malta	5,068,360	5,900,830	8,318,544	4,373,062	7,578,041
Netherlands	Netherlands	724,204,506	1,156,318,659	1,019,067,868	1,116,847,011	707,998,051
Poland	Poland	33,659,454	45,182,743	66,154,791	81,593,693	57,579,214
Portugal	Portugal	148,257,916	146,005,925	320,812,844	317,690,164	112,380,650
Romania	Romania	37,973,175	32,342,812	52,678,722	53,751,114	47,242,805
Slovakia	Slovakia	247,717	1,863,054	652,888	18,703,218	368,815
Slovenia	Slovenia	1,426,395	1,393,032	6,071,163	6,049,733	1,632,299
Spain	Spain	681,771,685	645,144,728	1,168,584,021	1,280,680,058	772,222,948
Sweden	Sweden	64,329,529	57,598,851	57,695,377	56,638,126	51,337,924
United Kingdom	United Kingdom	589,528,470	538,381,736	646,572,131	589,101,820	514,929,819
Non-EU		1,143,336,019	1,195,627,541	1,772,358,904	1,775,544,309	1,735,036,177
Albania	Albania	71,839	148,193	1,164,798	255,613	923,696
Andorra	Andorra	423,720	790,000	1,666,289	138,859	0
Belarus	Belarus	398,850	153,013	193,203	594,653	671,274
Faroe Islands	Faroe Islands	0	484,122	78,150	392,120	111,710
Gibraltar	Gibraltar	8,500	0	0	8,100	0
Iceland	Iceland	6,017,419	5,908,977	6,735,375	9,283,120	5,439,245
Kosovo	Kosovo	0	0	0	0	2,906
Liechtenstein	Liechtenstein	63,000	49,000	10,340	84,084	13,000
Macedonia	Macedonia	97,210	30,316	49,053	133,758	52,733
Moldova	Moldova; Republic of	585,452	61,412	212,652	43,436	37,643
Monaco	Monaco	70,590	132,482	4,655,640	101,153	19,007
Montenegro	Montenegro	0	0	230,193	935,504	798,928
Norway	Norway	70,012,202	50,160,868	85,540,916	76,662,367	46,047,237
Russia	Russia	167,652,808	149,016,522	224,003,740	254,856,397	237,922,094
San Marino	San Marino	949,883	3,284,870	3,000,640	2,378,947	292,926
Serbia	Serbia	2,403,195	4,019,412	4,937,688	7,944,402	3,713,447
Svalbard, Jan Mayen Island	Svalbard and Jan Mayen Island	144,600	14,669	75,000	81,200	20,000
Switzerland	Switzerland	96,425,174	144,554,731	173,718,521	272,526,133	255,893,086
Turkey	Turkey	756,615,575	745,782,185	1,089,178,147	1,060,139,787	1,127,664,197
Ukraine	Ukraine	41,396,002	90,621,482	176,614,382	88,903,910	55,170,247
Vatican City	Vatican City	0	415,287	294,177	80,766	242,801
WESTERN HEMISPHERE		12,275,544,603	13,942,092,889	17,131,766,989	22,095,974,830	17,278,733,336
NAFTA		9,493,315,144	10,624,386,317	12,414,934,450	15,523,037,015	12,957,753,296
Canada	Canada	5,683,763,362	6,140,735,424	6,866,481,156	7,617,179,616	7,143,978,576
Mexico	Mexico	3,809,551,782	4,483,650,893	5,548,453,294	7,905,857,399	5,813,774,720
Caribbean		721,588,600	833,639,990	1,043,282,540	1,472,729,171	1,084,808,378
Anguilla	Anguilla	1,127,495	1,670,379	1,453,095	1,504,681	1,584,073
Antigua and Barbuda	Antigua and Barbuda	3,703,925	4,407,527	4,856,735	6,112,318	3,836,833
Aruba	Aruba	2,489,777	3,968,592	4,497,226	6,154,011	6,479,013
Bahamas	Bahamas	29,019,489	34,761,406	35,748,571	29,112,950	33,154,709
Barbados	Barbados	22,123,532	21,078,376	26,679,293	39,679,442	34,833,580
British Virgin Islands	British Virgin Islands	5,165,140	6,648,824	2,088,527	1,758,052	2,089,017
Cayman Islands	Cayman Islands	12,232,633	17,709,338	18,313,742	17,663,028	10,721,716
Cuba	Cuba	163,644,011	161,345,905	224,120,386	403,106,237	260,875,722
Curacao	Curacao	0	0	0	0	0
Dominica	Dominica	292,448	418,847	690,548	1,147,596	662,768

Table B-29.   U.S. Exports by North American Industry Classification System (NAICS) by Region and Country, 2005–2015—*Continued*

Region	Partner	2010	2011	2012	2013	2014	2015
WORLD	World	68,349,347,958	81,862,725,228	81,124,373,389	79,738,156,657	83,855,827,395	73,011,125,676
Europe		8,164,857,950	9,122,339,851	9,043,488,758	10,238,485,777	10,988,192,607	10,089,059,917
European Union (EU-28)		5,885,009,803	6,231,214,790	6,517,937,472	7,367,617,138	8,460,295,242	8,174,157,467
Austria	Austria	16,760,591	21,070,675	29,445,367	41,404,500	18,912,315	12,056,265
Belgium	Belgium	447,042,292	299,033,376	259,509,037	276,779,502	386,875,839	447,354,272
Bulgaria	Bulgaria	10,062,150	17,579,387	17,473,806	21,569,840	29,080,200	7,998,410
Croatia	Croatia	7,633,378	15,449,131	7,949,768	12,367,906	10,340,845	9,673,416
Cyprus	Cyprus	7,341,410	7,378,860	4,966,888	6,385,124	6,691,977	5,390,770
Czech Republic	Czech Republic	16,338,957	16,696,475	13,580,004	22,705,100	17,306,551	13,314,172
Denmark	Denmark	75,995,444	112,201,468	80,481,936	115,410,527	135,697,684	138,209,099
Estonia	Estonia	7,750,558	8,150,849	8,155,692	10,563,901	17,431,847	12,344,725
Finland	Finland	16,368,374	14,122,651	12,502,890	11,028,844	32,710,914	28,577,298
France	France	471,387,451	494,259,958	429,617,209	496,252,300	498,432,666	482,389,506
Germany	Germany	1,341,170,799	1,276,139,298	1,834,008,874	1,878,362,062	1,823,370,217	1,964,564,038
Greece	Greece	100,603,042	67,010,809	61,331,521	65,395,827	75,002,822	51,511,301
Hungary	Hungary	14,167,676	9,702,515	15,313,423	20,097,809	35,364,400	27,752,816
Ireland	Ireland	65,917,323	73,514,139	53,899,515	79,597,387	130,501,649	81,080,423
Italy	Italy	540,590,878	629,891,781	540,978,713	783,814,249	778,116,055	848,033,010
Latvia	Latvia	6,757,236	9,992,387	9,221,348	12,300,768	11,768,936	5,423,859
Lithuania	Lithuania	33,107,035	48,094,899	52,491,737	73,895,881	86,493,465	53,127,209
Luxembourg	Luxembourg	31,115,954	17,778,278	30,427,382	49,934,855	14,007,349	19,482,987
Malta	Malta	1,795,618	2,537,653	3,406,645	3,730,281	3,366,985	1,959,169
Netherlands	Netherlands	803,436,315	1,018,066,123	827,752,699	920,024,893	1,414,717,801	1,385,738,346
Poland	Poland	45,766,956	83,808,988	83,296,162	68,026,157	54,522,827	63,833,948
Portugal	Portugal	135,292,720	262,143,586	195,053,496	118,471,958	326,948,644	180,129,110
Romania	Romania	29,285,189	32,062,298	48,930,571	32,146,754	33,727,344	62,958,357
Slovakia	Slovakia	468,760	1,523,286	3,425,017	2,842,790	2,508,615	1,139,109
Slovenia	Slovenia	1,867,242	3,114,754	2,686,419	4,059,066	1,762,083	1,978,891
Spain	Spain	1,046,186,754	1,110,263,935	1,148,096,582	1,499,873,476	1,676,566,061	1,470,300,656
Sweden	Sweden	62,206,543	70,927,283	67,937,460	58,003,074	58,510,899	67,467,131
United Kingdom	United Kingdom	548,593,158	508,699,948	675,997,311	682,572,307	779,558,252	730,369,174
Non-EU		2,279,848,147	2,891,125,061	2,525,551,286	2,870,868,639	2,527,897,365	1,914,902,450
Albania	Albania	784,101	1,130,779	1,048,043	781,967	1,001,104	967,602
Andorra	Andorra	2,780	0	4,469	521,899	580,640	0
Belarus	Belarus	659,862	261,197	491,139	536,288	1,160,420	729,249
Faroe Islands	Faroe Islands	371,013	867,038	0	320,319	32,972	0
Gibraltar	Gibraltar	76,727	0	8,215	26,712	26,244	26,208
Iceland	Iceland	6,314,210	6,185,898	4,507,640	5,330,523	7,337,114	12,810,718
Kosovo	Kosovo	11,340	80,850	0	0	30,000	83,964
Liechtenstein	Liechtenstein	0	0	0	0	0	0
Macedonia	Macedonia	347,027	184,067	98,478	132,493	839,284	412,505
Moldova	Moldova; Republic of	6,927,017	432,504	944,104	765,145	1,157,353	316,806
Monaco	Monaco	55,039	139,142	0	3,927	0	336,736
Montenegro	Montenegro	770,048	1,077,826	549,141	1,035,038	1,779,783	920,438
Norway	Norway	73,681,717	56,173,554	53,112,156	58,994,507	64,441,449	79,925,001
Russia	Russia	274,702,770	380,621,716	596,072,326	706,221,513	434,536,756	279,079,804
San Marino	San Marino	959,067	79,400	172,028	519,670	1,557,399	76,787
Serbia	Serbia	2,318,091	2,849,216	5,038,610	9,825,246	7,573,576	12,442,179
Svalbard, Jan Mayen Island	Svalbard and Jan Mayen Island	110,000	0	0	369,713,656	0	0
Switzerland	Switzerland	175,055,456	249,054,308	219,731,371	369,713,656	269,581,788	327,711,069
Turkey	Turkey	1,664,435,684	2,078,014,311	1,507,425,003	1,522,480,819	1,617,105,819	1,139,695,399
Ukraine	Ukraine	72,004,405	113,973,255	136,030,405	192,814,712	118,430,341	58,818,357
Vatican City	Vatican City	261,793	0	318,158	844,205	725,323	549,628
WESTERN HEMISPHERE		19,179,805,221	23,385,160,498	22,007,375,636	22,759,956,632	24,376,956,320	21,521,300,038
NAFTA		14,441,822,115	17,366,952,389	17,318,964,001	16,649,099,369	17,427,125,750	16,247,733,037
Canada	Canada	7,896,979,348	8,656,109,897	8,741,196,252	9,287,770,863	9,685,515,426	9,173,484,265
Mexico	Mexico	6,544,842,767	8,710,842,492	8,577,767,749	7,361,328,506	7,741,610,324	7,074,248,772
Caribbean		1,012,841,707	1,233,680,198	1,060,346,739	992,517,106	1,023,488,949	885,351,183
Anguilla	Anguilla	972,659	620,148	742,327	1,462,776	1,373,649	1,484,842
Antigua and Barbuda	Antigua and Barbuda	2,539,807	2,592,571	2,937,763	3,040,367	3,125,897	4,427,766
Aruba	Aruba	8,096,562	9,988,366	7,382,528	8,396,867	10,803,909	10,119,816
Bahamas	Bahamas	35,013,416	39,045,897	39,209,460	38,935,841	45,073,149	41,675,817
Barbados	Barbados	31,366,999	40,793,349	35,670,777	43,473,926	48,343,671	42,293,507
British Virgin Islands	British Virgin Islands	2,472,774	7,719,165	4,733,630	3,700,913	3,868,542	4,181,327
Cayman Islands	Cayman Islands	8,350,303	7,314,467	9,615,038	10,463,299	12,815,774	13,405,364
Cuba	Cuba	152,913,670	196,989,355	200,371,255	96,523,261	59,138,201	15,459,357
Curacao	Curacao	0	1,944,583	2,110,838	2,858,830	3,541,591	5,214,670
Dominica	Dominica	473,645	608,659	8,162,823	858,293	520,488	1,758,726

Table B-29. U.S. Exports by North American Industry Classification System (NAICS) by Region and Country, 2005–2015—*Continued*

Region	Partner	2005	2006	2007	2008	2009
Dominican Republic	Dominican Republic	273,947,112	347,012,156	433,265,110	533,907,808	412,893,653
Grenada	Grenada	4,241,478	6,741,935	7,584,782	17,752,914	6,039,847
Guadeloupe	Guadeloupe	2,249,680	4,580,329	2,488,082	2,988,138	2,498,164
Haiti	Haiti	42,203,888	29,224,966	45,885,767	82,853,580	54,907,680
Jamaica	Jamaica	85,293,279	106,075,042	130,561,241	197,701,853	143,364,867
Martinique	Martinique	2,168,216	2,873,358	1,142,179	1,687,023	2,273,998
Montserrat	Montserrat	0	30,119	251,489	299,213	65,071
Sint Maarten	Sint Maarten	0	0	0	0	0
St Kitts and Nevis	St Kitts and Nevis	911,269	1,610,816	2,688,565	1,861,569	2,111,332
St Lucia	St Lucia	2,924,347	3,280,578	3,578,915	3,167,116	3,464,890
St Vincent and the Grenadines	St Vincent and the Grenadines	3,477,361	5,737,322	8,202,856	9,784,626	10,454,045
Trinidad and Tobago	Trinidad and Tobago	60,418,404	68,321,569	83,020,163	105,130,196	88,390,446
Turks and Caicos Islands	Turks and Caicos Islands	3,955,116	6,142,606	6,165,268	9,356,820	4,106,954
Central America		891,245,792	1,047,399,667	1,331,427,873	1,750,292,235	1,348,689,329
Belize	Belize	7,996,546	8,943,398	9,559,068	14,885,231	9,322,479
Costa Rica	Costa Rica	230,166,757	239,175,378	330,733,778	451,087,839	321,283,521
El Salvador	El Salvador	145,388,261	156,407,128	199,006,096	279,270,485	226,771,405
Guatemala	Guatemala	210,755,299	315,520,627	345,170,364	431,729,908	325,145,010
Honduras	Honduras	127,864,790	158,186,478	195,321,279	249,137,885	213,495,856
Nicaragua	Nicaragua	83,865,650	83,361,699	113,870,602	137,017,955	104,096,293
Panama	Panama	85,208,489	85,804,959	137,766,686	187,162,932	148,574,765
South America		1,152,635,603	1,418,911,825	2,323,793,033	3,331,569,793	1,867,232,903
Argentina	Argentina	26,259,136	35,057,741	35,208,003	49,442,004	45,265,690
Bolivia	Bolivia	4,463,994	1,547,859	1,442,736	4,999,409	1,632,168
Brazil	Brazil	70,371,851	129,011,988	221,134,975	412,833,433	143,512,303
Chile	Chile	49,312,631	144,093,807	244,812,929	252,822,621	118,206,588
Colombia	Colombia	485,847,600	626,790,616	921,762,871	1,181,455,414	611,021,172
Ecuador	Ecuador	86,307,696	102,831,205	161,447,538	136,549,059	131,424,656
Falkland Islands (Islas Malvin)	Falkland Islands (Malvinas)	0	0	0	0	0
French Guiana	French Guiana	505,041	412,844	349,490	829,696	554,035
Guyana	Guyana	8,799,195	10,382,441	9,081,622	16,338,282	11,686,997
Paraguay	Paraguay	582,167	440,975	694,045	634,238	996,025
Peru	Peru	154,856,186	126,362,681	344,887,509	294,656,490	293,897,380
Suriname	Suriname	4,160,936	4,673,211	5,223,728	5,843,297	6,385,483
Uruguay	Uruguay	3,638,785	4,699,670	6,685,268	8,718,686	11,109,252
Venezuela	Venezuela	257,530,385	232,606,787	371,062,319	966,447,164	491,541,154
Other Western Hemisphere		16,759,464	17,755,090	18,329,093	18,346,616	20,249,430
Bermuda	Bermuda	15,923,199	17,426,090	18,299,828	18,334,132	20,249,430
Greenland	Greenland	88,514	0	29,265	12,484	0
St Pierre and Miquelon	St Pierre and Miquelon	747,751	329,000	0	0	0
Asia		17,723,585,805	20,229,530,789	25,283,471,289	34,980,726,856	30,374,488,961
		14,280,043,926	16,138,475,998	19,327,339,900	27,101,061,058	24,580,096,702
China	China	4,526,745,914	5,586,948,119	6,694,666,993	10,172,123,932	11,597,834,005
Hong Kong	Hong Kong	422,783,172	503,544,530	613,606,798	705,154,904	1,036,913,349
Japan	Japan	6,020,419,669	6,287,662,436	7,325,446,039	9,704,526,691	7,149,393,213
South Korea	South Korea	1,654,646,237	2,096,959,661	2,448,418,720	3,957,319,530	2,659,374,309
Taiwan	Taiwan	1,655,448,934	1,663,361,252	2,245,201,350	2,561,936,001	2,136,581,826
ASEAN - 10		2,039,397,478	2,215,166,315	3,054,278,250	4,040,857,684	3,356,577,314
Saudi Arabia	Saudi Arabia	105,968,916	152,257,022	309,058,919	315,111,571	219,186,350
Brunei	Brunei	450,052	220,855	295,094	581,596	1,176,952
Cambodia	Cambodia	1,222,506	1,779,413	3,391,138	3,394,249	2,217,099
East Timor	East Timor	50,200	0	327,538	24,072	49,648
Indonesia	Indonesia	710,885,652	820,783,539	1,116,543,179	1,570,794,323	1,158,721,478
Laos	Lao People's Democratic Republic	106,406	27,825	308,605	339,101	6,688
Malaysia	Malaysia	222,512,690	213,990,176	290,918,520	255,103,629	367,735,225
Myanmar	Myanmar	0	0	3,500	324,475	0
Philippines	Philippines	412,718,386	417,966,650	447,134,634	825,491,453	481,947,901
Singapore	Singapore	68,447,193	64,623,440	83,121,528	104,796,491	109,721,074
Thailand	Thailand	436,580,004	442,901,001	567,507,048	591,927,183	649,499,093
Vietnam	Vietnam	80,455,473	100,616,394	235,668,547	372,969,541	366,315,806
Middle East		885,662,110	1,313,727,764	1,950,697,233	2,906,290,817	1,498,412,855
Bahrain	Bahrain	3,501,485	1,911,903	2,293,218	12,201,794	5,854,049
Gaza Strip admin. by Israel	Gaza Strip	0	0	0	0	0
Iran	Iran	8,254,693	6,924,461	62,145,195	562,954,271	165,106,142
Iraq	Iraq	210,314,108	297,741,939	416,018,482	791,007,151	1,992,536
Israel	Israel	176,835,631	293,335,966	401,111,119	575,642,037	234,493,280
Jordan	Jordan	37,040,111	102,583,734	66,336,013	33,059,589	78,020,841
Kuwait	Kuwait	13,017,093	24,913,488	28,032,475	29,402,359	32,306,507
Lebanon	Lebanon	48,451,606	42,465,696	60,212,198	58,748,685	57,617,987
Oman	Oman	3,308,667	4,229,014	9,593,304	21,369,995	8,994,847

Table B-29.   U.S. Exports by North American Industry Classification System (NAICS) by Region and Country, 2005–2015—*Continued*

Region	Partner	2010	2011	2012	2013	2014	2015
Dominican Republic	Dominican Republic	475,232,625	585,334,275	397,203,490	362,565,575	467,378,058	385,846,100
Grenada	Grenada	8,617,895	14,984,848	10,135,358	7,897,127	7,342,568	6,208,823
Guadeloupe	Guadeloupe	3,024,463	2,208,126	3,462,988	3,018,682	3,600,826	3,229,649
Haiti	Haiti	34,137,076	23,008,953	22,337,612	60,860,652	29,726,696	52,441,754
Jamaica	Jamaica	130,235,053	170,327,856	169,818,006	187,863,475	165,085,549	148,822,354
Martinique	Martinique	2,187,181	1,574,174	1,731,460	1,689,967	1,848,772	1,997,022
Montserrat	Montserrat	25,541	32,473	60,727	10,916	23,612	80,123
Sint Maarten	Sint Maarten	0	4,180,340	7,483,533	8,342,422	9,426,199	10,344,608
St Kitts and Nevis	St Kitts and Nevis	3,170,587	2,425,356	1,824,920	2,531,108	2,056,697	2,925,715
St Lucia	St Lucia	4,206,118	4,639,581	4,086,439	3,668,037	4,454,006	4,742,305
St Vincent and the Grenadines	St Vincent and the Grenadines	12,543,979	10,110,500	19,700,899	15,100,120	17,960,484	10,206,210
Trinidad and Tobago	Trinidad and Tobago	94,083,960	103,940,958	108,011,132	125,132,944	120,525,592	112,483,018
Turks and Caicos Islands	Turks and Caicos Islands	3,177,394	3,296,198	3,553,736	4,121,708	5,455,019	6,002,310
Central America		1,453,386,817	1,972,331,623	1,515,131,876	1,297,077,307	1,598,081,611	1,527,069,652
Belize	Belize	8,390,018	10,456,634	10,369,873	11,791,237	9,444,829	10,548,853
Costa Rica	Costa Rica	329,804,590	446,102,101	386,118,786	220,459,609	330,493,646	353,688,225
El Salvador	El Salvador	251,499,028	387,765,339	269,619,496	233,115,822	269,086,666	231,633,751
Guatemala	Guatemala	357,502,491	488,281,419	397,401,887	371,090,697	465,237,826	446,818,759
Honduras	Honduras	194,825,424	305,110,103	251,036,917	231,036,221	283,132,320	236,176,970
Nicaragua	Nicaragua	137,413,567	142,132,672	80,659,939	70,061,184	59,607,887	65,649,653
Panama	Panama	173,951,699	192,483,355	119,924,978	159,522,537	181,078,437	182,553,441
South America		2,249,695,495	2,789,372,010	2,097,445,450	3,804,776,347	4,309,642,831	2,841,128,629
Argentina	Argentina	61,246,876	62,663,536	58,892,969	47,379,003	50,343,499	46,919,408
Bolivia	Bolivia	3,449,596	1,711,170	2,999,210	7,751,291	6,736,755	4,282,486
Brazil	Brazil	250,362,045	474,732,062	143,858,083	1,407,202,213	923,814,290	244,995,880
Chile	Chile	183,774,583	185,790,310	153,926,333	291,013,304	199,480,778	149,610,407
Colombia	Colombia	527,921,636	648,179,319	470,685,034	626,795,797	1,425,933,432	1,292,297,317
Ecuador	Ecuador	115,386,626	155,580,978	117,012,288	131,621,969	146,575,091	118,403,436
Falkland Islands (Islas Malvin)	Falkland Islands (Malvinas)	0	0	163,052	0	6,935	7,546
French Guiana	French Guiana	657,697	441,008	281,130	471,154	415,749	599,195
Guyana	Guyana	15,914,402	21,570,440	20,176,769	22,512,804	26,887,785	32,167,674
Paraguay	Paraguay	1,907,233	1,803,087	1,712,732	1,998,038	2,049,621	2,257,542
Peru	Peru	489,831,117	609,737,413	260,259,164	470,387,117	858,265,396	617,136,013
Suriname	Suriname	6,269,680	8,024,893	7,065,083	6,781,606	6,338,043	6,684,808
Uruguay	Uruguay	8,947,879	9,065,867	12,032,051	13,214,641	11,823,666	11,177,133
Venezuela	Venezuela	584,026,125	610,071,927	848,381,552	777,647,410	650,971,791	314,589,784
Other Western Hemisphere		22,059,087	22,824,278	15,487,570	16,486,503	18,617,179	20,017,537
Bermuda	Bermuda	22,059,087	22,803,686	15,484,501	16,486,503	18,554,215	19,950,882
Greenland	Greenland	0	20,592	3,069	0	62,964	66,655
St Pierre and Miquelon	St Pierre and Miquelon	0	0	0	0	0	0
Asia		36,640,192,447	44,431,733,089	46,424,152,457	43,329,187,154	45,217,517,468	39,124,308,559
		29,758,568,331	34,613,949,480	38,679,028,730	35,048,901,396	36,072,054,842	30,296,776,981
China	China	15,481,164,153	17,219,047,075	22,984,689,497	21,562,541,491	20,957,704,776	17,084,251,963
Hong Kong	Hong Kong	1,201,301,221	1,492,290,227	1,951,112,394	2,066,723,820	1,628,461,856	1,502,929,617
Japan	Japan	7,645,932,955	9,094,734,821	8,174,040,027	6,879,088,824	7,574,228,379	6,717,966,272
South Korea	South Korea	3,344,599,220	4,300,703,402	3,471,319,797	2,767,708,380	3,768,983,552	3,166,264,964
Taiwan	Taiwan	2,085,570,782	2,507,173,955	2,097,867,015	1,772,838,881	2,142,676,279	1,825,364,165
ASEAN - 10		3,982,998,217	5,885,046,231	5,378,024,694	5,554,938,996	6,281,874,014	5,637,076,028
Saudi Arabia	Saudi Arabia	304,283,863	606,147,643	509,536,450	408,559,279	578,698,762	584,600,916
Brunei	Brunei	983,416	983,054	1,199,525	853,181	989,655	633,039
Cambodia	Cambodia	3,283,044	2,775,897	2,746,509	3,532,802	3,945,666	10,455,811
East Timor	East Timor	804,218	365,222	0	104,958	0	0
Indonesia	Indonesia	1,469,164,483	2,001,708,773	1,668,355,829	1,716,888,858	1,912,985,326	1,416,803,856
Laos	Lao People's Democratic Republic	164,409	444,094	247,580	362,937	362,484	55,912
Malaysia	Malaysia	343,930,979	555,023,965	408,121,389	432,441,565	459,680,689	415,918,102
Myanmar	Myanmar	885,960	11,590,473	2,712,449	7,560,256	6,699,698	6,651,893
Philippines	Philippines	549,198,090	880,702,912	770,496,046	812,642,333	917,299,776	716,334,051
Singapore	Singapore	104,108,358	136,171,831	142,584,131	146,637,559	150,641,018	134,256,138
Thailand	Thailand	702,392,920	905,479,713	948,850,059	756,643,167	771,402,226	810,001,684
Vietnam	Vietnam	503,798,477	783,652,654	923,174,727	1,268,712,101	1,479,168,714	1,541,364,626
Middle East		1,922,367,319	2,535,020,392	1,353,472,576	1,473,068,941	1,405,139,911	1,340,856,884
Bahrain	Bahrain	6,345,376	10,653,028	9,777,248	12,213,776	9,322,711	11,567,985
Gaza Strip admin. by Israel	Gaza Strip	0	0	0	0	0	28,200
Iran	Iran	73,007,116	48,265,921	113,509,492	75,091,751	34,000,943	73,842,300
Iraq	Iraq	116,292,762	531,323,422	59,319,089	4,435,893	19,838,411	64,689,387
Israel	Israel	374,588,223	538,525,539	275,037,115	272,726,004	374,209,240	201,873,531
Jordan	Jordan	80,972,103	236,225,413	54,865,688	83,771,295	68,786,569	75,077,721
Kuwait	Kuwait	33,139,688	36,414,145	36,664,389	48,003,317	41,651,086	42,370,164
Lebanon	Lebanon	91,633,480	101,528,597	46,633,950	49,093,366	55,822,753	48,627,717
Oman	Oman	24,467,741	55,975,822	26,427,453	7,396,076	5,589,605	11,176,128

Table B-29.   U.S. Exports by North American Industry Classification System (NAICS) by Region and Country, 2005–2015—*Continued*

Region	Partner	2005	2006	2007	2008	2009
Qatar	Qatar	734,842	3,731,411	1,798,502	2,840,469	6,810,893
Republic of Yemen	Republic of Yemen	83,322,037	102,299,502	278,872,785	150,937,082	153,440,452
Syria	Syrian Arab Republic	134,679,895	207,941,748	340,942,155	363,978,026	265,315,719
United Arab Emirates	United Arab Emirates	166,092,534	225,648,902	281,772,386	304,074,359	488,459,602
West Bank admin. by Israel	West Bank	109,408	0	1,569,401	75,000	0
Central Asia		9,133,932	14,868,127	10,375,639	6,565,730	3,663,276
Bosnia and Herzegovina	Bosnia and Herzegovina	211,363	113,034	261,860	735,883	1,261,685
Kazakhstan	Kazakhstan	8,224,755	13,710,766	9,510,581	4,230,281	1,249,013
Kyrgyzstan	Kyrgyzstan	0	4,637	5,280	40,200	15,950
Tajikistan	Tajikistan	604,259	950,708	171,087	675,789	38,443
Turkmenistan	Turkmenistan	0	23,512	0	0	0
Uzbekistan	Uzbekistan	93,555	65,470	426,831	883,577	1,098,185
Other Asia		509,348,359	547,292,585	940,780,267	925,951,567	935,738,814
Afghanistan	Afghanistan	11,844,495	20,596,528	26,101,449	18,739,652	4,375,710
Armenia	Armenia	337,308	817,550	6,990,751	1,111,697	1,206,505
Azerbaijan	Azerbaijan	294,886	236,127	97,200	146,253	538,077
Bangladesh	Bangladesh	55,801,251	58,852,434	158,314,494	151,421,539	143,897,183
Bhutan	Bhutan	12,274	0	57,654	33,431	0
Georgia	Georgia	7,984,736	13,928,646	5,687,299	9,961,662	5,488,512
India	India	222,050,281	282,116,702	377,486,160	397,199,840	470,155,519
Macau	Macau; SAR of China	505,537	279,545	1,447,079	767,113	206,799
Maldives	Maldives	265,850	835,187	1,237,755	793,931	1,282,662
Mongolia	Mongolia	4,030,432	85,643	5,279,693	54,500	5,056,845
Nepal	Nepal	632,096	360,876	1,160,124	559,887	1,582,017
North Korea	North Korea	5,656,804	0	1,728,160	48,120,143	0
Pakistan	Pakistan	185,745,589	159,715,848	304,308,313	258,174,245	249,391,557
Sri Lanka	Sri Lanka	14,186,820	9,467,499	50,884,136	38,867,674	52,557,428
Australia and Oceania		252,151,650	259,441,783	320,151,391	314,167,364	347,304,392
Australia	Australia	150,382,044	173,826,710	219,976,576	227,911,891	240,343,629
Christmas Island	Christmas Island	0	0	0	0	0
Cocos (Keeling) Islands	Cocos (Keeling) Islands	0	0	0	0	0
Cook Islands	Cook Islands	3,825	0	0	3,658	0
Fiji	Fiji	748,468	1,336,683	1,520,893	1,557,857	2,340,091
French Polynesia	French Polynesia	6,620,499	5,528,192	6,681,429	6,764,075	5,152,957
French Southern and Antarctic	French Southern Territories	0	0	0	0	16,689
Heard and McDonald Islands	Heard Island and Mcdonald Islands	0	159,180	0	0	0
Kiribati	Kiribati	3,500	0	0	0	0
Marshall Islands	Marshall Islands	195,121	274,918	428,628	532,846	494,968
Micronesia	Micronesia (Federated States of)	195,901	208,459	253,513	268,802	535,234
Netherlands Antilles	Netherlands Antilles	10,240,671	13,418,002	11,010,815	9,391,450	10,167,866
New Caledonia	New Caledonia	472,010	729,120	1,054,034	1,358,051	1,465,577
New Zealand	New Zealand	42,146,199	46,961,948	62,877,403	57,701,743	82,120,062
Niue	Niue	115,502	38,785	15,000	109,000	526,130
Norfolk Island	Norfolk Island	128,253	1,197,027	936,235	2,052,127	138,890
Palau	Palau	172,071	109,596	228,019	272,431	738,281
Papua New Guinea	Papua New Guinea	686,640	306,348	203,650	0	76,623
Pitcairn Islands	Pitcairn Islands	18,144	31,713	82,800	0	0
Reunion	Reunion	0	32,720	0	11,046	30,115
Samoa	Samoa	449,780	1,346,719	1,630,825	450,803	1,187,210
Solomon Islands	Solomon Islands	0	159,060	285,000	460,000	943,729
Tokelau	Tokelau Islands	39,545,815	13,552,409	12,650,914	4,796,969	837,584
Tonga	Tonga	0	124,194	113,500	43,203	48,757
Tuvalu	Tuvalu	0	0	0	0	0
Vanuatu	Vanuatu	0	0	53,172	16,412	0
Wallis and Futuna	Wallis and Futuna	27,207	100,000	148,985	465,000	140,000
Africa		1,959,274,329	2,236,810,744	3,956,455,406	3,908,329,827	2,740,009,113
Algeria	Algeria	145,549,962	190,684,415	409,945,757	194,447,893	78,536,708
Angola	Angola	10,673,285	8,943,937	10,824,489	18,804,481	2,477,369
Benin	Benin	166,571	330,015	517,823	40,000	248,350
Botswana	Botswana	13,000	28,062	102,762	23,189	230,400
British Indian Ocean Terr.	British Indian Ocean Territory	0	0	21,604	26,310	0
Burkina Faso	Burkina Faso	1,762,670	1,841,836	2,269,457	791,517	634,466
Burundi	Burundi	1,927,479	3,218,426	1,096,395	2,055,879	1,950,048
Cabo Verde	Cabo Verde	1,828,680	1,920,177	1,481,477	2,740	0
Cameroon	Cameroon	2,587,225	4,040,883	538,634	4,193,404	6,299,003
Central African Republic	Central African Republic	258,606	205,798	1,817,455	1,072,519	4,285,965
Chad	Chad	2,691,980	6,676,343	3,680,502	7,249,531	458,841
Comoros	Comoros	33,369	0	0	0	0
Congo (Brazzaville)	Congo (Brazzaville)	1,275,895	937,557	6,339,720	791,005	2,309,791
Congo (Kinshasa)	Congo (Kinshasa)	10,209,661	7,717,114	27,361,884	22,075,093	4,268,443

Table B-29.   U.S. Exports by North American Industry Classification System (NAICS) by Region and Country, 2005–2015—*Continued*

Region	Partner	2010	2011	2012	2013	2014	2015
Qatar	Qatar	5,556,693	8,791,485	9,158,797	9,287,617	10,305,031	11,885,259
Republic of Yemen	Republic of Yemen	106,836,833	184,778,697	135,868,167	144,248,872	93,117,385	98,270,894
Syria	Syrian Arab Republic	442,382,238	191,296,380	5,549,307	3,131,603	4,892,291	2,572,903
United Arab Emirates	United Arab Emirates	567,145,066	591,151,943	580,502,605	763,531,251	687,496,388	698,866,883
West Bank admin. by Israel	West Bank	0	90,000	159,276	138,120	107,498	7,812
Central Asia		8,996,222	18,773,436	11,836,168	13,768,819	13,249,691	6,553,888
Bosnia and Herzegovina	Bosnia and Herzegovina	1,332,923	909,725	2,256,980	2,400,310	1,183,637	1,359,250
Kazakhstan	Kazakhstan	5,445,510	17,166,868	8,565,650	7,520,836	10,031,068	2,697,987
Kyrgyzstan	Kyrgyzstan	17,450	32,597	41,784	1,335,023	117,489	77,881
Tajikistan	Tajikistan	1,548,771	8,460	51,635	67,452	4,442	51,746
Turkmenistan	Turkmenistan	0	44,124	15,617	34,339	104,281	57,319
Uzbekistan	Uzbekistan	651,568	611,662	904,502	2,410,859	1,808,774	2,309,705
Other Asia		967,262,358	1,378,943,550	1,001,790,289	1,238,509,002	1,445,199,010	1,843,044,778
Afghanistan	Afghanistan	12,234,609	13,629,597	6,285,648	1,197,617	6,446,842	7,768,199
Armenia	Armenia	905,424	944,571	1,276,313	3,929,565	1,523,789	321,484
Azerbaijan	Azerbaijan	944,945	671,029	463,611	233,355	253,814	289,430
Bangladesh	Bangladesh	224,024,651	368,118,898	123,853,441	172,189,060	286,382,446	409,665,957
Bhutan	Bhutan	0	0	0	16,650	11,350	0
Georgia	Georgia	4,959,657	6,662,020	3,217,370	5,334,924	8,598,730	6,350,471
India	India	485,930,823	589,099,327	650,574,910	725,685,412	924,937,866	1,045,968,598
Macau	Macau; SAR of China	308,531	773,972	655,165	584,245	1,800,909	3,953,562
Maldives	Maldives	1,138,790	1,373,776	1,442,457	745,123	1,206,977	392,695
Mongolia	Mongolia	60,854	29,361	4,529,461	228,731	1,499,010	615,314
Nepal	Nepal	780,482	905,667	239,993	888,401	1,499,869	744,150
North Korea	North Korea	1,762,973	0	0	0	0	0
Pakistan	Pakistan	209,346,349	327,415,359	192,939,577	261,321,305	160,454,672	316,722,163
Sri Lanka	Sri Lanka	24,864,270	69,319,973	16,312,343	66,154,614	50,582,736	50,252,755
Australia and Oceania		358,595,211	384,997,246	445,042,131	417,922,342	523,289,141	463,506,775
Australia	Australia	239,018,991	284,516,498	337,254,994	320,721,005	377,657,441	338,105,919
Christmas Island	Christmas Island	10,341	336,901	97,965	5,267	0	0
Cocos (Keeling) Islands	Cocos (Keeling) Islands	0	0	0	0	4,157,062	0
Cook Islands	Cook Islands	0	121,408	74,242	13,890	20,199	0
Fiji	Fiji	3,833,339	1,523,800	1,899,620	2,086,787	2,643,072	1,528,362
French Polynesia	French Polynesia	5,657,362	5,904,500	5,930,603	6,012,336	6,656,812	4,679,244
French Southern and Antarctic	French Southern Territories	13,108	8,014	17,873	0	29,496	20,195
Heard and McDonald Islands	Heard Island and Mcdonald Islands	0	0	0	0	0	0
Kiribati	Kiribati	0	177,166	0	0	32,318	0
Marshall Islands	Marshall Islands	349,934	331,519	419,996	360,644	606,054	402,423
Micronesia	Micronesia (Federated States of)	384,436	298,218	335,112	492,883	1,007,770	1,022,183
Netherlands Antilles	Netherlands Antilles	12,133,904	3,796,338	0	0	0	0
New Caledonia	New Caledonia	979,698	1,126,011	1,337,967	1,182,960	1,218,385	632,143
New Zealand	New Zealand	93,853,130	83,965,835	94,088,887	84,127,003	125,778,362	114,298,086
Niue	Niue	256,250	256,430	0	20,000	0	0
Norfolk Island	Norfolk Island	256,349	39,342	0	0	0	0
Palau	Palau	653,590	848,525	776,207	975,525	1,527,714	1,480,348
Papua New Guinea	Papua New Guinea	49,337	201,317	73,344	20,578	6,166	238,503
Pitcairn Islands	Pitcairn Islands	0	0	0	0	0	0
Reunion	Reunion	61,645	46,000	922,422	842,481	915,414	722,294
Samoa	Samoa	792,450	1,109,903	1,024,790	834,527	511,791	272,487
Solomon Islands	Solomon Islands	114,670	294,000	513,440	45,000	133,274	0
Tokelau	Tokelau Islands	31,623	0	25,542	0	300,433	0
Tonga	Tonga	90,054	0	0	165,873	83,578	101,438
Tuvalu	Tuvalu	0	0	0	0	0	0
Vanuatu	Vanuatu	0	0	0	0	3,800	3,150
Wallis and Futuna	Wallis and Futuna	55,000	95,521	249,127	15,583	0	0
Africa		3,629,999,163	4,313,106,858	3,029,314,129	2,812,733,643	2,749,770,026	1,812,950,387
Algeria	Algeria	90,306,103	65,054,304	146,999,194	130,366,320	141,366,141	113,029,716
Angola	Angola	7,929,525	6,776,713	19,078,202	11,953,233	10,920,532	4,846,423
Benin	Benin	1,332,866	119,315	500,150	1,137,145	1,935,854	6,274,453
Botswana	Botswana	28,327	16,315	22,534	124,605	205,100	8,820
British Indian Ocean Terr.	British Indian Ocean Territory	0	15,093	0	13,407	0	0
Burkina Faso	Burkina Faso	138,341	280,549	1,002,886	1,293,210	3,411,879	1,440,923
Burundi	Burundi	1,657,046	4,474,612	1,439,545	1,535,408	0	34,107
Cabo Verde	Cabo Verde	201,134	51,090	0	44,270	172,543	138,294
Cameroon	Cameroon	5,676,316	11,497,499	10,579,026	23,012,752	8,242,091	9,543,406
Central African Republic	Central African Republic	487,093	694,351	87,152	0	10,866	18,620
Chad	Chad	4,257,161	9,738,156	9,432,808	26,775	5,029,612	2,097,110
Comoros	Comoros	0	0	0	0	0	0
Congo (Brazzaville)	Congo (Brazzaville)	2,190,794	16,713,299	3,044,894	9,576,948	6,094,824	59,620
Congo (Kinshasa)	Congo (Kinshasa)	6,309,180	10,973,963	14,731,983	2,725,980	7,364,151	127,081

Table B-29.   U.S. Exports by North American Industry Classification System (NAICS) by Region and Country, 2005-2015—*Continued*

Region	Partner	2005	2006	2007	2008	2009
Cote d'Ivoire	Cote d'Ivoire	1,994,028	2,268,069	2,264,081	569,492	4,835,561
Djibouti	Djibouti	21,850,694	14,740,150	3,748,525	61,274,443	53,351,835
Egypt	Egypt	658,107,222	847,324,835	1,572,449,474	1,711,457,086	1,062,858,610
Equatorial Guinea	Equatorial Guinea	71,084	447,669	165,003	153,476	171,569
Eritrea	Eritrea	12,901,923	4,737,740	0	5,671,978	3,939,842
Ethiopia	Ethiopia	115,774,404	35,904,102	77,431,333	136,914,926	81,065,339
Gabon	Gabon	380,319	563,820	177,870	587,304	870,101
Gambia	Gambia	34,465	56,637	96,403	99,159	7,500
Ghana	Ghana	13,834,104	10,099,608	14,918,061	5,438,631	1,862,566
Guinea	Guinea	346,380	352,453	3,976,740	504,839	190,947
Guinea-Bissau	Guinea Bissau	0	155,795	0	0	0
Kenya	Kenya	18,870,792	41,075,822	26,701,024	36,127,166	100,931,584
Lesotho	Lesotho	557,729	435,213	1,397,097	18,377	0
Liberia	Liberia	2,453,772	1,171,223	1,577,800	607,116	2,022,096
Libya	Libyan Arab Jamahiriya	2,778,775	28,461,648	48,803,977	34,604,125	19,383,461
Madagascar	Madagascar	6,764,136	6,494,295	4,702,005	4,790,359	1,324,975
Malawi	Malawi	3,995,515	6,776,837	7,323,004	9,277,414	11,339,694
Mali	Mali	1,230,227	8,186,750	3,987,674	356,936	375,701
Mauritania	Mauritania	7,834,574	781,754	3,780,301	5,358,234	1,971,169
Mauritius	Mauritius	602,836	645,074	10,757,362	11,240,117	754,505
Mayotte	Mayotte	0	0	234,726	0	149,863
Morocco	Morocco	146,512,449	241,153,399	511,409,114	215,505,474	225,367,574
Mozambique	Mozambique	9,360,056	14,560,275	24,666,294	29,577,926	35,015,534
Namibia	Namibia	3,645,514	7,392,817	5,207,970	3,093,313	603,859
Nauru	Nauru	391,862	2,000,200	6,385,600	6,342,968	2,844,820
Niger	Niger	4,244,435	8,620,858	1,488,290	833,351	1,705,320
Nigeria	Nigeria	527,936,726	474,428,763	657,449,122	943,415,122	762,107,262
Rwanda	Rwanda	1,368,228	926,099	274,411	31,650	40,800
Sao Tome and Principe	Sao Tome and Principe	0	2,600	0	0	0
Senegal	Senegal	4,028,978	4,498,554	12,022,442	1,170,113	770,044
Seychelles	Seychelles	399,454	142,790	392,786	137,375	0
Sierra Leone	Sierra Leone	3,521,574	1,011,183	3,402,900	4,606,788	1,195,056
Somalia	Somalia	3,699,100	12,426,606	11,553,365	38,017,810	2,143,839
South Africa	South Africa	73,197,803	48,472,524	196,268,296	193,155,201	57,614,852
South Sudan	South Sudan	0	0	0	0	0
St Helena	St Helena	9,518	0	5,114	22,214	20,906
Sudan	Sudan	77,715,626	60,314,082	57,217,462	76,129,818	51,376,140
Swaziland	Swaziland	559,115	336,041	592,651	179,403	654,979
Tanzania	Tanzania; United Republic of	4,768,235	15,725,743	17,765,177	23,100,148	12,126,913
Togo	Togo	10,000	0	835,784	0	2,625
Tunisia	Tunisia	27,322,304	86,066,358	160,170,901	76,196,754	123,042,463
Uganda	Uganda	12,919,808	6,960,478	18,555,720	9,201,617	8,571,471
Western Sahara	Western Sahara	0	0	0	0	0
Zambia	Zambia	4,955,064	6,432,166	3,097,132	3,573,347	329,835
Zimbabwe	Zimbabwe	3,347,118	8,115,151	17,204,456	7,414,696	5,368,519

Table B-29. **U.S. Exports by North American Industry Classification System (NAICS) by Region and Country, 2005–2015**—*Continued*

Region	Partner	2010	2011	2012	2013	2014	2015
Cote d'Ivoire	Cote d'Ivoire	118,949	600,103	2,047,156	2,387,713	2,648,151	507,653
Djibouti	Djibouti	18,365,108	38,256,548	45,027,667	46,660,847	18,653,024	34,013,119
Egypt	Egypt	1,630,060,883	1,936,864,794	1,135,552,780	929,379,255	1,166,280,207	507,840,052
Equatorial Guinea	Equatorial Guinea	254,106	2,874,407	739,380	836,983	631,044	400,566
Eritrea	Eritrea	0	0	0	0	0	0
Ethiopia	Ethiopia	134,235,933	87,555,971	64,808,598	54,487,928	70,006,939	83,752,968
Gabon	Gabon	256,298	62,780	440,419	183,737	537,785	194,167
Gambia	Gambia	0	111,665	823,433	2,165,721	70,000	3,252
Ghana	Ghana	2,364,261	18,074,032	37,305,822	12,437,711	33,687,653	20,045,219
Guinea	Guinea	1,838,796	2,849,775	8,612	0	3,533	7,007
Guinea-Bissau	Guinea Bissau	98,988	722,109	1,523,668	1,480,893	0	12,000
Kenya	Kenya	30,834,544	39,511,202	44,533,710	48,621,321	34,161,896	43,894,617
Lesotho	Lesotho	3,230	6,753,358	13,614,722	0	0	0
Liberia	Liberia	3,992,543	6,528,321	6,605,347	6,399,778	4,737,260	10,511,989
Libya	Libyan Arab Jamahiriya	54,118,627	30,387,259	13,114,154	70,911,507	23,892,653	32,494,177
Madagascar	Madagascar	595,028	2,895,563	3,358,234	13,964	2,637	385,613
Malawi	Malawi	6,425,026	10,232,597	7,100,255	5,610,991	218,975	940,353
Mali	Mali	807,954	1,363,102	1,999,586	36,520	1,396,649	1,617,365
Mauritania	Mauritania	3,511,231	14,401	84,800	9,331,542	374,260	1,281,126
Mauritius	Mauritius	1,755,951	4,385,653	3,729,147	4,899,064	2,134,435	1,151,212
Mayotte	Mayotte	2,514,605	138,638	6,481,928	420,959	832,529	483,254
Morocco	Morocco	276,606,746	236,649,170	117,810,934	119,375,369	131,907,486	131,353,956
Mozambique	Mozambique	34,517,157	66,138,987	31,458,159	6,594,183	1,357,259	1,728,440
Namibia	Namibia	1,774,593	10,071,328	7,165,034	6,946,055	854,624	7,575,249
Nauru	Nauru	1,087,861	0	0	0	0	0
Niger	Niger	2,728,254	5,886,221	286,665	249,055	1,452,456	131,166
Nigeria	Nigeria	808,287,098	1,196,293,482	984,037,461	987,821,215	726,583,568	557,207,627
Rwanda	Rwanda	475,420	1,223,697	58,962	0	0	0
Sao Tome and Principe	Sao Tome and Principe	0	0	0	0	0	9,639
Senegal	Senegal	307,885	373,824	519,727	4,357,587	8,601,721	936,354
Seychelles	Seychelles	24,726	56,314	30,475	53,204	83,079	560,546
Sierra Leone	Sierra Leone	2,471,302	5,778,816	1,964,655	141,919	42,890	235,376
Somalia	Somalia	0	3,352,417	4,029,125	1,011,561	3,923,047	4,466,736
South Africa	South Africa	165,193,121	168,632,072	83,727,821	111,523,257	95,699,530	74,134,222
South Sudan	South Sudan	0	3,356,808	3,074,424	2,295,143	30,994,828	2,591,134
St Helena	St Helena	22,694	0	0	0	0	10,928
Sudan	Sudan	80,555,882	52,569,497	36,157,478	44,932,093	39,675,889	46,302,960
Swaziland	Swaziland	956,218	636,456	2,044,037	1,532,756	1,695,661	1,543,796
Tanzania	Tanzania; United Republic of	12,582,002	55,662,148	4,610,517	16,019,820	12,261,292	9,395,039
Togo	Togo	372,611	883,352	1,046,866	65,369	5,882,916	287,974
Tunisia	Tunisia	222,411,391	176,776,916	151,179,441	131,147,553	141,788,966	95,084,278
Uganda	Uganda	5,044,760	9,067,574	2,521,072	295,750	425,285	953,796
Western Sahara	Western Sahara	0	0	0	0	0	0
Zambia	Zambia	199,150	88,594	115,773	144,066	248,139	234,478
Zimbabwe	Zimbabwe	1,714,345	3,021,648	1,657,711	151,201	1,268,167	*1,052,411*

Table B-30.   U.S. Agricultural Imports by North American Industry Classification System (NAICS) from Regions and Individual Countries, 2005–2015

Region	2005	2006	2007	2008	2009	2010
WORLD	30,866,199,326	34,602,750,540	37,661,869,527	41,089,023,712	36,804,139,689	42,675,787,860
Europe	2,168,524,700	2,281,940,911	2,496,923,824	2,227,209,237	2,439,182,846	2,505,886,268
European Union (EU-28)	1,349,541,957	1,380,877,650	1,505,246,957	1,435,261,844	1,342,172,123	1,356,996,457
Austria	5,209,026	1,128,846	1,924,276	3,313,913	1,240,289	1,716,535
Belgium	28,917,728	31,217,752	22,994,211	28,151,587	28,815,461	33,602,619
Bulgaria	42,490,594	34,355,067	41,438,771	44,998,714	35,506,035	30,816,790
Croatia	5,303,122	4,217,518	3,401,790	3,187,113	2,685,657	2,458,705
Cyprus	1,495,303	990,754	844,893	756,461	809,538	198,514
Czech Republic	2,016,509	2,401,249	3,064,310	4,508,668	4,246,301	4,096,149
Denmark	32,446,446	23,274,816	23,597,212	17,331,098	41,059,507	37,419,092
Estonia	5,868,693	5,272,325	4,220,052	2,165,401	1,576,345	2,328,034
Finland	16,345,897	9,538,021	7,285,918	12,638,167	7,603,407	16,012,622
France	101,490,971	98,964,900	108,047,929	118,283,246	106,170,117	133,264,440
Germany	113,198,690	140,865,012	160,564,138	165,411,679	115,046,263	75,178,382
Greece	65,394,412	36,315,278	44,484,435	46,704,477	42,338,523	29,247,852
Hungary	4,928,018	5,674,544	5,340,740	4,264,413	2,090,791	2,952,073
Ireland	49,346,675	38,547,299	54,018,592	33,286,923	31,251,747	18,813,010
Italy	74,484,917	83,178,398	112,664,015	128,402,278	107,164,920	60,866,075
Latvia	1,029,472	279,558	234,606	132,720	206,228	399,581
Lithuania	1,105,290	2,107,715	2,614,001	1,026,810	392,813	1,641,795
Luxembourg	2,160	474	0	0	0	56,218
Malta	422,498	1,586,625	2,141,203	3,529,164	1,614,488	1,643,915
Netherlands	485,587,099	514,252,995	507,966,384	454,198,461	446,305,175	493,330,585
Poland	10,466,004	9,395,262	12,387,951	13,887,503	22,034,631	31,677,834
Portugal	6,594,226	6,750,998	6,104,621	5,301,675	5,298,254	5,888,486
Romania	1,251,700	3,759,817	230,232	733,232	717,776	1,379,043
Slovakia	719,466	754,669	993,199	1,063,719	660,466	469,317
Slovenia	105,343	478,834	1,810,203	7,767,593	4,210,793	3,535,680
Spain	159,918,042	195,365,368	204,728,971	163,956,378	144,402,499	188,533,072
Sweden	46,037,847	17,397,569	16,347,972	18,104,427	11,512,731	7,624,264
United Kingdom	87,365,809	112,805,987	155,796,332	152,156,024	177,211,368	171,845,775
Non-EU	818,982,743	901,063,261	991,676,867	791,947,393	1,097,010,723	1,148,889,811
Andorra	285,111	58,492	213,352	293,748	168,853	85,689
Bosnia and Herzegovina	19,185	50,546	76,679	10,043	12,748	10,340
Albania	4,592,105	3,419,429	3,787,133	5,671,299	5,384,726	5,201,362
Belarus	12,000	8,454	27,046	7,055	4,600	0
Faroe Islands	4,143,325	3,068,929	6,744,403	15,604,699	61,505,051	71,945,723
Gibraltar	0	3,461	0	0	0	0
Iceland	143,298,755	133,891,968	117,661,401	92,601,556	84,654,364	96,061,430
Kosovo	0	0	0	0	0	0
Liechtenstein	9,600	0	0	7,139	0	0
Macedonia	7,573,135	8,202,153	10,842,258	12,754,181	29,220,701	15,478,810
Moldova	4,799	79,450	145,749	145,189	67,682	179,013
Monaco	53,106	32,654	78,444	733,146	164,749	22,992
Montenegro	0	0	147,063	73,528	3,000	0
Norway	89,000,384	137,922,412	157,370,750	147,996,072	316,725,459	496,535,897
Russia	323,779,375	389,462,681	432,402,549	314,174,566	297,815,503	271,231,444
San Marino	0	0	0	0	0	0
Serbia	72,267	297,667	786,945	411,674	150,090	383,419
Svalbard, Jan Mayen Island	0	0	0	0	0	0
Switzerland	7,007,118	7,424,971	11,960,147	8,352,766	26,449,442	9,781,732
Turkey	232,493,855	208,277,622	240,089,330	183,123,109	266,515,414	175,074,540
Ukraine	6,638,623	8,862,372	9,343,618	9,987,623	8,168,341	6,897,420
Vatican City	0	0	0	0	0	0
WESTERN HEMISPHERE	19,014,415,929	21,350,913,643	23,905,938,297	25,951,572,253	23,643,645,663	26,401,417,342
NAFTA	10,601,106,048	11,898,685,938	13,721,913,060	15,037,155,810	13,044,703,527	14,798,305,925
Canada	5,709,646,507	6,715,982,634	7,778,596,720	9,014,779,093	6,782,347,198	7,347,472,058
Mexico	4,891,459,541	5,182,703,304	5,943,316,340	6,022,376,717	6,262,356,329	7,450,833,867
Caribbean	220,690,101	260,895,398	252,635,725	245,044,087	292,114,977	271,161,919
Anguilla	0	0	0	0	0	0
Antigua and Barbuda	55,364	175,934	0	0	138,678	0
Aruba	7,500	0	10,060	0	0	16,182
Bahamas	50,236,527	51,073,978	51,001,348	55,866,170	44,757,719	51,420,841
Barbados	1,607,288	1,246,174	1,085,284	757,551	626,720	681,212
British Virgin Islands	115,061	0	14,064	402,289	177,530	0
Cayman Islands	60,700	1,358,992	5,086	11,000	0	0
Dominica	106,979	67,224	35,072	154,651	104,925	29,124
Dominican Republic	92,165,541	110,213,413	111,249,008	110,074,259	170,512,820	139,124,122

Table B-30.   U.S. Agricultural Imports by North American Industry Classification System (NAICS) from Regions and Individual Countries, 2005–2015—*Continued*

Region	2011	2012	2013	2014	2015
WORLD	51,402,091,116	50,649,977,667	53,974,996,888	58,426,460,228	56,334,715,948
Europe	2,526,348,752	2,520,046,080	2,961,529,324	3,503,949,669	3,764,075,264
European Union (EU-28)	1,476,050,324	1,509,693,274	1,652,836,542	1,939,893,670	2,152,530,978
Austria..	1,500,048	3,885,876	2,362,871	2,582,605	5,001,449
Belgium..	46,478,070	45,904,191	39,244,704	28,468,647	28,524,567
Bulgaria..	33,143,936	38,807,220	41,129,404	48,653,059	45,153,517
Croatia	1,896,453	1,211,313	1,631,478	1,192,176	2,326,770
Cyprus	2,878,328	1,771,257	1,984,456	2,124,394	2,087,029
Czech Republic	2,569,365	3,265,291	4,555,028	5,214,619	4,126,391
Denmark	32,656,077	18,307,718	45,975,124	58,066,162	38,353,840
Estonia...	2,803,122	3,176,987	3,212,070	4,276,320	4,053,184
Finland...	10,091,585	10,730,714	14,532,639	24,077,525	15,969,027
France..	136,886,385	141,152,610	168,902,588	176,050,872	187,303,779
Germany...	105,553,169	152,144,702	217,199,905	253,456,785	347,876,784
Greece...	40,944,527	41,147,347	45,670,674	55,617,919	51,764,894
Hungary...	3,339,675	3,130,344	6,448,393	4,275,600	4,589,331
Ireland..	34,810,687	42,412,222	42,131,792	50,727,346	71,321,482
Italy...	71,996,756	96,512,716	98,756,464	125,287,714	138,111,514
Latvia	331,036	638,456	2,844,630	3,867,047	7,140,504
Lithuania..	317,503	477,275	762,654	6,055,706	14,151,906
Luxembourg..	58,435	0	351	86,284	1,037,175
Malta	983,172	466,946	489,985	191,818	752,024
Netherlands..	525,505,675	456,924,159	448,373,017	493,079,242	463,231,418
Poland..	18,899,554	19,388,840	36,556,800	58,208,529	22,658,869
Portugal...	12,557,463	10,938,620	11,491,236	15,773,953	24,969,086
Romania...	1,071,733	3,686,193	15,256,679	27,353,621	110,818,561
Slovakia...	523,889	643,185	977,028	1,546,924	2,557,647
Slovenia...	2,253,055	1,324,359	1,516,274	2,011,291	3,897,781
Spain...	174,477,467	187,939,051	198,249,296	233,153,747	335,960,179
Sweden..	9,437,198	15,393,894	21,496,335	46,729,121	33,858,243
United Kingdom	202,085,961	208,311,788	181,084,667	211,764,644	184,934,027
Non-EU	1,050,298,428	1,010,352,806	1,308,692,782	1,564,055,999	1,611,544,286
Andorra	94,714	100,477	37,423	0	0
Bosnia and Herzegovina.......................	112,275	143,638	158,688	306,515	97,590
Albania	5,971,082	6,926,875	11,854,158	12,981,386	12,033,663
Belarus..	7,037	54,701	34,206	12,887	24,242
Faroe Islands......................................	105,069,182	71,921,375	125,658,378	137,246,142	91,290,864
Gibraltar...	0	0	0	0	0
Iceland...	96,179,067	128,274,263	148,408,510	154,554,413	167,984,737
Kosovo...	3,032	0	55,370	20,014	27,833
Liechtenstein......................................	27,105	0	0	0	0
Macedonia	27,060,645	34,186,344	34,471,636	28,263,367	25,178,546
Moldova..	106,307	267,039	626,356	712,256	6,214,109
Monaco..	0	229,300	5,901	3,346	6,353
Montenegro	2,100	0	0	0	0
Norway...	323,894,348	250,600,559	312,695,328	422,118,107	484,356,516
Russia...	280,108,345	232,834,577	332,221,018	340,632,398	335,684,489
San Marino	0	0	0	0	0
Serbia..	329,074	669,848	7,839,484	198,055	198,436
Svalbard, Jan Mayen Island	0	0	0	0	0
Switzerland...	9,819,074	11,111,789	11,810,589	10,612,265	9,348,086
Turkey	196,351,759	263,636,387	306,119,382	401,549,834	358,980,032
Ukraine..	5,163,282	9,395,634	16,696,355	54,845,014	120,118,790
Vatican City	0	0	0	0	0
WESTERN HEMISPHERE	31,386,437,373	32,253,198,963	35,373,700,087	38,083,246,117	36,785,770,427
NAFTA..	16,515,066,114	17,695,011,638	19,476,301,499	21,174,328,921	20,956,023,126
Canada..	8,007,475,795	8,683,654,772	9,833,926,225	10,444,235,166	9,381,269,885
Mexico	8,507,590,319	9,011,356,866	9,642,375,274	10,730,093,755	11,574,753,241
Caribbean	286,385,217	324,928,381	309,358,194	326,736,223	332,579,613
Anguilla..	0	0	0	0	0
Antigua and Barbuda............................	6,960	1,160,000	67,500	94,604	0
Aruba...	0	0	18,775	19,388	0
Bahamas..	46,896,374	54,117,525	48,602,086	44,457,912	49,023,778
Barbados..	624,824	1,233,804	1,689,864	1,688,335	1,970,028
British Virgin Islands.............................	0	0	7,528	3,450	7,735
Cayman Islands...................................	0	0	17,100	0	539,813
Dominica..	161,396	133,724	161,940	57,052	97,274
Dominican Republic..............................	156,748,807	184,477,107	172,150,889	184,126,511	171,326,255

Table B-30.   U.S. Agricultural Imports by North American Industry Classification System (NAICS) from Regions and Individual Countries, 2005–2015—*Continued*

Region	2005	2006	2007	2008	2009	2010
Grenada	2,360,777	2,523,053	4,567,713	4,340,474	3,991,107	5,569,096
Guadeloupe	0	148,907	0	0	0	39,975
Haiti	10,503,847	13,358,107	13,873,766	16,908,578	17,096,173	12,750,725
Jamaica	26,789,766	25,951,297	24,705,765	27,137,566	26,544,287	26,431,818
Martinique	0	0	0	0	0	255,912
Montserrat	0	0	0	0	0	0
Sint Maarten	0	0	0	0	0	0
St Kitts and Nevis	114,125	132,300	463,854	341,008	460,661	168,300
St Lucia	27,498	19,061	25,783	58,076	79,252	47,972
St Vincent and the Grenadines	494,745	322,344	393,512	110,621	113,017	154,612
Trinidad and Tobago	27,606,273	46,388,387	37,849,456	23,235,196	22,851,754	30,587,653
Turks and Caicos Islands	8,438,110	7,916,227	7,355,954	5,646,648	4,660,334	3,884,375
Central America	2,365,895,545	2,584,239,362	2,851,434,028	3,131,328,623	2,952,284,485	3,218,892,025
Belize	44,475,125	43,202,414	29,120,196	28,568,253	24,364,271	28,081,692
Costa Rica	829,634,141	1,050,451,489	1,075,605,859	1,096,744,365	1,001,928,765	1,152,699,192
El Salvador	71,710,713	71,142,922	95,653,730	118,103,511	92,386,951	83,188,779
Guatemala	736,497,717	711,717,030	863,399,481	993,144,519	1,080,881,160	1,065,081,131
Honduras	396,861,541	379,812,788	457,687,939	504,553,083	434,612,794	490,432,468
Nicaragua	147,979,439	195,121,284	199,227,440	258,760,526	222,808,188	281,613,709
Panama	138,736,869	132,791,435	130,739,383	131,454,366	95,302,356	117,795,054
South America	5,809,402,969	6,596,017,683	7,068,766,471	7,529,998,751	7,345,708,149	8,103,056,571
Argentina	257,612,326	344,201,608	382,176,251	358,797,116	323,883,733	339,187,867
Bolivia	22,222,646	23,966,586	29,177,605	39,356,674	47,675,502	62,258,272
Brazil	1,002,621,251	1,142,116,678	1,277,787,101	1,411,538,984	1,396,279,618	1,744,858,171
Chile	1,833,625,501	2,203,212,323	2,297,521,361	2,357,706,898	2,133,114,263	2,185,315,473
Colombia	1,222,113,637	1,246,838,703	1,341,984,067	1,508,558,735	1,431,729,970	1,610,402,144
Ecuador	912,721,038	1,026,434,162	1,045,232,088	1,101,603,616	1,292,203,352	1,294,355,088
Falkland Islands (Islas Malvin)	9,065,260	12,169,647	4,758,607	7,080,381	8,272,572	5,415,399
French Guiana	0	0	0	0	0	0
Guyana	38,924,486	37,804,350	40,367,798	40,320,223	39,498,080	37,407,884
Paraguay	1,403,187	1,866,966	4,042,922	1,541,589	2,168,625	780,147
Peru	355,279,578	416,493,447	502,196,004	558,853,911	567,621,934	725,857,073
Suriname	20,282,243	21,445,888	23,203,909	26,660,269	30,829,061	28,870,331
Uruguay	28,703,938	23,770,130	21,960,057	18,414,116	14,142,174	21,514,346
Venezuela	104,827,878	95,697,195	98,358,701	99,566,239	58,289,265	46,834,376
Other Western Hemisphere	17,321,266	11,075,262	11,189,013	8,044,982	8,834,525	10,000,902
Bermuda	555,000	137,950	132,546	1,029,297	576,184	193,000
Greenland	15,734,185	9,815,438	9,704,671	5,983,942	7,464,935	7,965,273
St Pierre and Miquelon	1,032,081	1,121,874	1,351,796	1,031,743	793,406	1,842,629
Asia	7,942,763,210	9,388,966,347	9,650,111,800	11,024,951,827	9,029,293,177	11,736,572,236
China	1,624,228,915	2,147,690,514	2,250,815,064	2,418,301,452	2,255,056,911	2,622,150,980
Hong Kong	18,741,980	27,274,114	25,000,313	23,707,131	23,239,419	23,929,079
Japan	180,258,881	208,376,989	215,739,229	239,070,132	234,811,354	215,031,659
South Korea	81,441,390	81,892,377	89,692,606	102,202,285	106,861,332	117,098,861
Taiwan	162,867,785	152,474,062	166,626,700	196,817,973	175,314,181	177,309,284
ASEAN - 10	4,760,864,479	5,670,496,539	5,914,340,626	6,998,727,980	5,338,675,115	7,486,045,744
Brunei	1,530,555	4,343,363	3,126,442	2,395,043	212,477	55,200
Cambodia	27,412,322	21,350,709	6,534,710	6,936,849	9,104,123	7,246,125
East Timor	0	0	0	0	0	0
Indonesia	1,916,172,535	2,280,121,585	2,308,002,746	2,985,555,243	1,969,559,131	3,104,338,168
Laos	607,222	106,432	8,163,357	3,637,446	2,552,170	677,627
Malaysia	244,156,512	308,758,367	300,190,689	395,230,899	202,690,775	328,811,141
Myanmar	0	0	0	0	0	0
Philippines	124,166,215	138,479,538	135,843,903	127,485,609	117,585,137	125,423,406
Singapore	56,682,628	45,615,260	41,266,260	50,152,041	29,770,562	41,942,654
Thailand	1,485,446,005	1,905,168,104	1,946,426,594	2,147,971,552	1,846,706,226	2,310,671,914
Vietnam	904,690,385	966,553,181	1,164,785,925	1,279,363,298	1,160,494,514	1,566,879,509
Middle East	117,177,727	105,182,331	109,645,903	87,450,624	89,444,162	93,811,201
Bahrain	332,572	661,505	153,889	894,863	867,499	751,307
Gaza Strip admin. by Israel	0	0	0	0	0	0
Iran	2,781,232	2,454,074	2,933,791	2,502,390	2,359,512	2,260,385
Iraq	999,807	265,464	300,465	142,692	307,063	250,875
Israel	65,454,087	64,543,290	73,639,259	60,469,730	70,088,467	61,708,300
Jordan	179,984	154,091	384,836	131,157	142,616	158,422
Kuwait	0	0	13,640	0	45,900	30,680
Lebanon	360,201	440,455	483,422	622,819	943,442	1,600,020
Oman	4,037,228	1,987,852	2,021,856	1,396,914	541,766	323,161
Qatar	33,263	9,000	0	30,000	50,000	60,000
Republic of Yemen	4,379,654	4,511,140	4,491,093	5,161,464	1,995,497	3,346,860
Saudi Arabia	7,102,393	3,524,215	1,975,502	1,207,130	462,919	5,039,448

Table B-30. U.S. Agricultural Imports by North American Industry Classification System (NAICS) from Regions and Individual Countries, 2005–2015—*Continued*

Region	2011	2012	2013	2014	2015
Grenada	4,739,378	4,577,834	5,485,249	5,906,850	5,546,991
Guadeloupe	7,680	0	0	0	0
Haiti	17,558,557	19,587,252	17,625,572	20,198,438	19,578,142
Jamaica	27,247,826	29,041,498	32,522,258	30,898,179	36,087,566
Martinique	0	0	0	0	0
Montserrat	0	365,821	0	0	8,993
Sint Maarten	0	7,200	0	6,500	3,000
St Kitts and Nevis	339,380	421,393	412,550	488,250	380,285
St Lucia	81,802	123,621	36,875	228,209	425,318
St Vincent and the Grenadines	159,727	213,030	229,417	272,230	61,546
Trinidad and Tobago	28,006,021	26,686,519	27,245,532	34,448,130	43,690,799
Turks and Caicos Islands	3,806,485	2,782,053	3,085,059	3,842,185	3,832,090
Central America	4,268,817,406	4,359,593,849	4,140,114,394	4,238,171,853	4,199,053,349
Belize	26,617,489	25,664,791	31,377,483	28,181,203	25,088,624
Costa Rica	1,278,921,206	1,330,631,237	1,325,995,583	1,383,574,568	1,249,143,059
El Salvador	229,896,685	140,548,003	120,373,337	69,089,191	97,841,411
Guatemala	1,634,093,047	1,652,748,920	1,607,498,085	1,598,601,652	1,642,751,194
Honduras	661,317,842	728,131,681	644,514,258	683,022,727	698,681,881
Nicaragua	327,349,003	359,523,128	289,725,174	363,466,695	378,674,494
Panama	110,622,134	122,346,089	120,630,474	112,235,817	106,872,686
South America	10,308,991,331	9,867,398,332	11,438,910,059	12,338,558,040	11,295,436,123
Argentina	454,715,021	574,128,332	821,747,702	668,455,137	607,334,652
Bolivia	80,650,232	87,081,217	158,117,738	197,685,694	129,756,657
Brazil	2,518,730,704	2,146,137,843	2,153,098,005	2,374,947,556	1,867,550,674
Chile	2,439,848,083	2,595,492,999	3,358,839,782	3,471,026,500	3,171,579,848
Colombia	2,010,628,588	1,762,594,534	1,863,587,006	2,027,878,234	2,060,875,625
Ecuador	1,609,555,027	1,527,835,045	1,638,016,633	1,931,567,256	1,797,527,664
Falkland Islands (Islas Malvin)	6,881,016	11,200,983	13,554,305	19,482,475	12,888,327
French Guiana	0	0	0	0	0
Guyana	32,505,254	51,956,604	56,243,452	48,428,395	56,604,190
Paraguay	3,847,763	12,094,769	132,396,269	85,585,712	36,103,305
Peru	1,049,250,912	987,996,451	1,097,590,954	1,378,904,346	1,412,731,504
Suriname	22,977,482	25,788,162	31,882,615	33,429,689	29,772,020
Uruguay	39,991,860	49,873,784	65,924,262	45,506,942	66,315,257
Venezuela	39,409,389	35,217,609	47,911,336	55,660,104	46,396,400
Other Western Hemisphere	7,177,305	6,266,763	9,015,941	5,451,080	2,678,216
Bermuda	16,000	53,042	49,040	70,518	57,000
Greenland	6,953,403	6,213,721	8,914,045	5,380,562	2,455,174
St Pierre and Miquelon	207,902	0	52,856	0	166,042
Asia	14,921,413,282	13,614,934,582	13,294,236,275	14,213,956,575	13,077,345,585
China	2,905,133,609	2,948,443,236	3,045,122,359	3,157,830,113	3,000,046,524
Hong Kong	29,892,490	29,428,129	32,485,156	33,082,372	50,528,232
Japan	239,470,858	263,711,051	270,487,660	299,454,970	297,556,224
South Korea	135,737,502	138,157,875	142,200,420	143,330,243	163,788,334
Taiwan	214,794,983	210,007,246	198,281,644	216,423,789	221,700,342
ASEAN - 10	9,818,741,586	8,288,038,592	7,475,914,701	7,864,078,932	6,904,069,875
Brunei	0	18,478	1,758,862	1,690,142	315,282
Cambodia	2,972,772	4,866,316	3,369,999	5,524,381	1,643,272
East Timor	0	0	0	0	3,051,927
Indonesia	4,268,938,269	3,506,533,419	3,206,324,483	3,251,075,102	2,803,041,407
Laos	7,634,715	177,414	1,527,581	3,244,377	4,030,283
Malaysia	423,176,410	326,610,305	201,840,057	287,337,616	161,515,351
Myanmar	0	0	19,854,753	53,032,365	45,224,598
Philippines	148,127,186	225,850,877	179,335,448	164,520,220	140,160,048
Singapore	43,094,458	48,530,099	30,770,614	24,350,852	21,192,660
Thailand	2,964,685,829	2,150,362,997	1,549,136,512	1,381,692,110	1,308,796,533
Vietnam	1,960,111,947	2,025,088,687	2,281,996,392	2,691,611,767	2,415,098,514
Middle East	95,646,785	96,231,214	108,324,337	112,989,786	113,780,589
Bahrain	1,135,694	313,937	400,175	223,972	100,502
Gaza Strip admin. by Israel	0	0	0	0	0
Iran	15,750	0	0	0	0
Iraq	1,170,555	859,226	3,255,241	955,571	131,975
Israel	70,521,890	73,159,853	84,602,705	95,409,913	97,834,079
Jordan	701,723	1,027,180	1,501,547	1,165,571	1,412,161
Kuwait	15,470	30,940	60,781	57,291	72,691
Lebanon	880,984	1,405,516	1,019,742	797,068	1,409,048
Oman	86,532	132,186	125,188	463,531	46,000
Qatar	20,000	70,000	15,000	80,000	125,000
Republic of Yemen	424,011	1,709,376	1,235,925	1,373,848	1,340,985
Saudi Arabia	3,616,752	3,358,960	1,604,742	1,416,593	3,494,756

Table B-30.   U.S. Agricultural Imports by North American Industry Classification System (NAICS) from Regions and Individual Countries, 2005–2015—*Continued*

Region	2005	2006	2007	2008	2009	2010
Syria	595,457	163,655	160,159	33,780	129,475	45,746
United Arab Emirates	30,921,849	26,467,590	23,087,991	14,771,413	10,899,707	17,074,381
West Bank admin. by Israel	0	0	0	86,272	610,299	1,161,616
Central Asia	1,800,919	1,851,331	3,170,036	3,363,807	3,809,493	2,714,359
Kazakhstan	398,980	388,333	633,022	270,600	1,042,632	1,041,205
Kyrgyzstan	4,487	0	0	272,602	1,237,005	180,960
Tajikistan	12,000	0	6,432	0	0	0
Turkmenistan	432,855	155,728	1,253,019	1,504,566	879,394	1,236,204
Uzbekistan	952,597	1,307,270	1,277,563	1,316,039	650,462	255,990
Other Asia	995,381,134	993,728,090	875,081,323	955,310,443	802,081,210	998,481,069
Afghanistan	602	768,654	1,568,717	6,789,434	6,288,448	1,720,096
Armenia	238,300	162,100	43,830	16,870	98,131	129,814
Azerbaijan	1,859,493	1,320,980	1,919,108	1,473,611	2,271,325	1,375,586
Bangladesh	142,949,995	195,148,707	163,379,487	139,502,309	109,310,371	109,133,322
Bhutan	0	0	45,950	18,785	0	0
Georgia	229,263	41,875	3,894	12,989	5,453	934,542
India	810,087,941	741,512,784	653,144,160	755,165,054	646,161,730	837,968,678
Macau	491,057	49,156	61,317	599	11,889	3,466
Maldives	271,632	1,230,410	1,898,329	2,260,469	1,343,071	1,373,106
Mongolia	867,503	3,032,749	2,703,477	2,523,263	1,039,094	49,280
Nepal	278,221	204,842	264,650	582,666	343,976	112,055
Pakistan	10,168,697	10,175,772	10,727,168	8,186,789	8,625,370	8,236,151
Sri Lanka	27,938,430	40,080,061	39,321,236	38,777,605	26,582,352	37,444,973
Australia and Oceania	563,331,318	533,137,668	602,594,272	566,661,997	493,512,048	477,457,649
Australia	245,532,079	217,965,149	230,106,054	214,852,479	167,974,056	138,415,762
Christmas Island	15,497	9,085	0	0	0	0
Cocos (Keeling) Islands	0	0	0	0	59,680	0
Cook Islands	1,093,785	247,644	319,335	223,325	63,874	70,794
Fiji	10,073,897	10,087,379	15,389,327	16,913,932	14,036,828	13,509,526
French Polynesia	6,136,012	7,733,518	14,589,960	10,914,514	4,107,007	5,348,112
French Southern and Antarctic	0	0	0	0	91,536	0
Heard and McDonald Islands	0	0	0	0	0	0
Kiribati	978,139	784,657	900,140	801,819	645,495	525,851
Marshall Islands	8,129,019	6,758,540	4,619,665	7,662,480	6,067,619	4,749,602
Micronesia	152,903	453,708	3,929,019	3,066,347	2,429,390	3,106,096
Netherlands Antilles	274,257	326,087	91,666	0	6,000	0
New Caledonia	1,085,846	6,128,986	1,445,981	2,865,024	290,317	738,901
New Zealand	232,480,357	222,858,576	251,426,716	224,139,720	206,476,424	223,413,694
Niue	2,053	0	310,276	0	0	0
Norfolk Island	98,099	77,536	16,594	6,604	3,356	4,145
Palau	317,834	575,797	295,786	0	0	2,805
Papua New Guinea	46,083,436	46,749,906	71,066,926	77,710,331	79,029,880	75,175,284
Pitcairn Islands	0	0	0	0	13,916	0
Reunion	5,541,741	6,486,492	2,865,600	2,840,744	8,217,073	8,918,272
Samoa	820,983	835,855	913,129	605,141	655,512	342,610
Solomon Islands	926,907	1,057,968	842,759	856,402	626,792	765,427
Tokelau	8,693	202,929	54,005	11,693	75,002	24,154
Tonga	3,005,655	3,435,413	2,963,520	2,494,899	1,700,331	1,511,536
Tuvalu	0	0	0	0	0	0
Vanuatu	574,126	362,443	447,814	696,543	941,960	835,078
Africa	1,177,164,169					
Algeria	827,859	326,325	732,579	579,111	747,682	240,562
Angola	0	0	0	0	0	0
Benin	355,706	315,418	268,098	111,165	249,106	141,576
Botswana	0	0	0	1,500	0	0
British Indian Ocean Terr.	0	0	0	0	0	0
Burkina Faso	189,450	15,563	95,880	0	135,437	94,422
Burundi	4,346,962	1,798,315	1,039,234	2,749,629	4,060,314	3,328,787
Cabo Verde	0	0	235,622	32,651	0	316,273
Cameroon	12,011,900	10,898,318	13,867,868	18,521,315	11,774,867	26,736,362
Central African Republic	62,269	53,356	5,644	2,624	20,816	165,987
Chad	14,889,691	19,336,621	6,017,735	9,831,588	8,925,659	5,816,104
Comoros	850,337	682,528	42,618	325,764	353,977	264,370
Congo (Brazzaville)	307,935	555,793	113,574	376,459	98,488	154,053
Congo (Kinshasa)	631,482	890,193	1,197,477	945,181	331,591	1,895,654
Cote d'Ivoire	539,319,427	399,025,608	381,881,920	570,975,685	525,068,856	688,099,514
Djibouti	560,224	787,906	819,574	1,091,685	178,572	765,339
Egypt	16,761,999	17,149,762	10,373,077	8,300,976	9,729,149	11,536,600
Equatorial Guinea	52,153	49,579	28,017	27,795	27,042	21,111
Eritrea	762,000	144,000	147,186	14,110	21,615	0
Ethiopia	45,964,101	52,418,062	68,434,203	112,260,678	79,473,904	97,297,114

Table B-30.   U.S. Agricultural Imports by North American Industry Classification System (NAICS) from Regions and Individual Countries, 2005–2015—*Continued*

Region	2011	2012	2013	2014	2015
Syria	31,136	26,337	24,280	16,000	31,250
United Arab Emirates	15,895,444	12,994,180	12,994,802	10,043,151	7,049,911
West Bank admin. by Israel	1,130,844	1,143,523	1,484,209	987,277	732,231
Central Asia	3,191,321	9,292,942	17,398,958	24,034,007	12,119,557
Kazakhstan	1,737,832	2,377,765	5,564,411	12,429,791	10,273,615
Kyrgyzstan	105,171	29,673	166,035	0	13,623
Tajikistan	0	0	5,040	2,291	7,902
Turkmenistan	735,003	4,940,636	10,643,686	5,306,896	475,000
Uzbekistan	613,315	1,944,868	1,019,786	6,295,029	1,349,417
Other Asia	1,478,804,148	1,631,624,297	2,004,021,040	2,362,732,363	2,313,755,908
Afghanistan	2,112,427	5,498,800	3,668,929	2,541,560	1,500,136
Armenia	129,700	88,630	52,279	123,562	222,563
Azerbaijan	361,082	190,681	443,310	0	208,822
Bangladesh	77,486,333	58,008,546	72,427,135	42,186,627	53,461,125
Bhutan	0	0	0	0	0
Georgia	5,595	10,464	3,925	479,107	893,740
India	1,335,167,419	1,479,402,625	1,836,557,267	2,214,324,298	2,149,415,223
Macau	0	53,127	5,004	0	67,721
Maldives	2,647,356	14,598,218	19,796,802	21,848,134	20,518,611
Mongolia	0	0	838,124	1,771,842	1,318,028
Nepal	138,788	124,561	78,036	97,842	35,790
Pakistan	11,554,015	13,422,109	10,796,403	11,301,689	11,139,325
Sri Lanka	49,201,433	60,226,536	59,353,826	68,057,702	74,974,824
Australia and Oceania	491,915,319	519,292,667	558,377,243	654,323,356	625,335,389
Australia	132,544,543	156,508,658	210,822,983	241,411,886	210,304,225
Christmas Island	0	0	4,500	0	0
Cocos (Keeling) Islands	0	0	0	0	5,000
Cook Islands	94,429	463,823	58,550	0	14,682
Fiji	15,522,931	15,679,590	15,150,497	14,455,208	15,457,743
French Polynesia	9,673,506	18,057,635	9,840,422	13,030,722	14,227,372
French Southern and Antarctic	0	15,856	0	0	0
Heard and McDonald Islands	0	0	0	0	0
Kiribati	493,096	401,836	822,546	2,476,069	2,530,301
Marshall Islands	5,574,875	10,446,241	8,896,241	8,398,659	8,827,323
Micronesia	1,171,380	287,949	627,801	158,375	233,707
Netherlands Antilles	0	0	0	0	0
New Caledonia	1,208,660	708,652	548,018	609,867	295,569
New Zealand	215,163,891	209,942,601	230,124,214	269,517,716	275,867,767
Niue	0	0	0	0	0
Norfolk Island	0	0	0	0	0
Palau	15,992	15,986	38,918	113,653	99,008
Papua New Guinea	96,855,488	94,607,048	66,874,160	83,304,422	74,532,885
Pitcairn Islands	0	0	0	0	0
Reunion	9,561,380	9,216,951	9,796,667	12,337,199	16,498,593
Samoa	339,494	344,107	42,365	95,769	516,466
Solomon Islands	685,270	349,445	1,551,843	1,052,349	648,800
Tokelau	304,689	21,477	0	0	10,013
Tonga	1,320,634	1,206,384	1,274,079	1,267,661	1,824,796
Tuvalu	0	0	0	0	0
Vanuatu	1,385,061	1,018,428	1,903,439	6,093,801	3,441,139
Africa					
Algeria	759,158	451,190	466,370	538,254	2,309,752
Angola	0	0	0	0	0
Benin	221,674	1,111,846	2,818,001	3,602,427	3,997,985
Botswana	0	0	0	0	0
British Indian Ocean Terr.	0	0	0	0	0
Burkina Faso	781,572	1,199,302	2,757,894	2,985,115	65,619
Burundi	9,398,816	4,331,180	3,094,846	4,278,205	5,645,922
Cabo Verde	84,328	5,508	81,634	0	110,375
Cameroon	42,234,213	47,700,521	28,253,445	18,742,774	13,093,399
Central African Republic	331,340	0	5,942	32,137	41,004
Chad	6,751,670	8,727,384	11,870,077	10,241,860	10,478,809
Comoros	22,018	0	916,788	735,346	668,060
Congo (Brazzaville)	132,859	442,512	297,259	1,336,165	983,574
Congo (Kinshasa)	1,355,600	3,727,610	3,180,818	6,199,265	7,232,026
Cote d'Ivoire	893,024,559	697,250,291	784,582,031	862,191,805	858,878,322
Djibouti	874,398	1,529,793	354,746	1,061,543	1,477,594
Egypt	20,391,967	15,476,958	15,951,638	19,301,971	16,657,759
Equatorial Guinea	82,083	18,696	6,177	16,518	5,285
Eritrea	18,689	30,160	14,914	13,900	0
Ethiopia	111,695,645	93,478,291	101,318,042	110,135,819	146,388,905

Table B-30.   U.S. Agricultural Imports by North American Industry Classification System (NAICS) from Regions and Individual Countries, 2005–2015—*Continued*

Region	2005	2006	2007	2008	2009	2010
Gabon	296,482	1,337,192	1,481,624	2,908,486	1,518,849	5,699,397
Gambia	8,654	18,706	9,932	9,580	454,332	2,741,007
Ghana	24,672,836	62,447,065	45,529,955	27,910,859	65,754,982	107,516,762
Guinea	400,838	466,371	199,348	1,061,828	76,931	666,942
Guinea-Bissau	50,159	43,891	20,024	0	0	0
Kenya	41,516,365	43,760,045	38,804,962	45,891,492	41,484,344	54,826,538
Lesotho	0	0	0	0	0	0
Liberia	89,281,208	129,131,184	114,432,540	140,973,146	74,634,085	126,525,515
Libya	9,000	15,065	0	0	0	0
Madagascar	36,970,695	33,869,771	36,501,049	32,106,689	30,346,747	31,223,629
Malawi	82,047,857	34,007,871	32,185,472	41,756,404	44,884,032	51,173,524
Mali	93,531	150,976	127,944	133,850	78,951	36,993
Mauritania	273,920	158,041	220,741	192,543	210,475	289,635
Mauritius	13,373,299	17,308,231	13,985,246	16,020,483	11,408,780	12,681,362
Morocco	7,515,337	11,252,203	21,414,745	30,576,753	27,890,844	48,400,915
Mozambique	3,141,553	3,723,237	3,140,823	2,159,146	5,458,056	9,292,879
Namibia	5,811,040	5,247,202	7,499,124	4,273,325	883,177	1,223,593
Nauru	0	39,312	160,996	69,300	0	0
Niger	45,055	68,635	9,038	10,000	173,093	7,500
Nigeria	56,299,667	14,613,833	21,911,818	61,937,323	60,496,887	44,220,499
Rwanda	5,084,403	6,576,954	6,912,170	10,188,326	14,386,981	18,536,046
Sao Tome and Principe	0	28,037	2,030	0	68,953	0
Senegal	887,602	2,331,784	9,123,440	1,494,557	1,160,617	936,571
Seychelles	137,919	328,808	1,402,874	0	6,971	9,949
Sierra Leone	148,276	58,799	13,194	59,209	89,390	172,185
Somalia	50,328	63,846	35,635	134,173	52,902	46,590
South Africa	114,462,134	128,837,901	102,504,855	95,935,128	87,370,540	115,582,850
South Sudan	0	0	0	0	0	0
St Helena	1,912,027	972,442	4,699,842	9,669,896	5,821,305	6,087,654
Sudan	13,538,855	6,205,000	7,463,239	4,993,852	9,426,961	7,989,470
Swaziland	0	1,820	0	0	0	120,468
Tanzania	15,404,839	18,620,968	27,458,179	32,368,031	36,082,047	25,901,874
Togo	3,796,427	850,038	4,222,425	8,979,341	5,770,561	8,169,104
Tunisia	2,009,752	2,470,224	3,389,553	3,288,620	4,850,915	4,539,112
Uganda	18,170,636	15,144,463	14,140,223	15,676,119	25,389,702	32,150,071
Western Sahara	0	0	0	0	0	0
Zambia	564,527	360,282	1,028,564	664,741	625,577	202,951
Zimbabwe	1,295,453	2,834,427	969,424	1,037,282	45,0893	608,952

Table B-30.   U.S. Agricultural Imports by North American Industry Classification System (NAICS) from Regions and Individual Countries, 2005–2015—*Continued*

Region	2011	2012	2013	2014	2015
Gabon	10,818,691	385,440	2,441,205	1,963,843	3,232,765
Gambia	0	31,273	45,129	63,669	176,986
Ghana	248,897,922	153,818,330	173,403,989	177,106,841	213,170,641
Guinea	1,703,612	171,234	1,194,649	619,198	202,257
Guinea-Bissau	160,896	0	104,380		11,060
Kenya	74,360,276	85,326,803	67,319,010	90,502,766	95,346,080
Lesotho	31,250	0	0	0	0
Liberia	156,841,868	142,848,717	91,299,686	73,456,127	41,155,589
Libya	0	0	0	0	0
Madagascar	29,209,579	39,717,758	51,888,104	76,310,009	121,853,327
Malawi	39,818,379	48,712,653	52,667,208	44,855,804	37,717,785
Mali	96,010	50,704	38,843	52,537	420,448
Mauritania	118,732	215,984	194,400	309,311	332,453
Mauritius	11,967,128	11,963,604	8,581,827	13,567,990	13,769,214
Morocco	29,823,368	26,792,708	38,912,092	82,740,035	111,043,302
Mozambique	10,041,323	12,587,689	19,261,898	13,392,477	17,244,416
Namibia	4,361,757	5,966,756	6,997,432	5,454,874	303,805
Nauru	0	0	0	0	0
Niger	14,043	3,593	10,596	0	26,284
Nigeria	92,767,420	77,043,842	34,086,636	54,944,960	15,598,269
Rwanda	21,487,373	27,838,753	19,556,583	24,290,915	25,001,328
Sao Tome and Principe	0	0	0	0	0
Senegal	1,148,681	2,005,146	3,137,812	3,735,340	2,640,544
Seychelles	54,219	192,040	187,422	190,888	83,983
Sierra Leone	27,120	59,263	0	11,220	101,168
Somalia	53,941	143,402	107,152	128,162	745,803
South Africa	122,087,612	130,325,444	155,372,785	155,378,024	181,344,759
South Sudan	0	0	102,988	0	11,290
St Helena	7,712,753	5,825,902	7,140,578	8,793,165	14,353,268
Sudan	10,346,085	6,510,252	10,368,547	11,941,634	8,968,547
Swaziland	182,060	170,400	0	0	0
Tanzania	40,857,139	43,882,412	33,956,948	38,341,983	43,276,139
Togo	28,730,610	2,306,531	4,228,587	3,370,888	2,452,912
Tunisia	8,412,325	10,655,760	14,127,473	14,448,180	25,657,782
Uganda	33,412,620	28,126,555	31,577,168	28,466,607	29,473,458
Western Sahara	0	97,228	0	0	0
Zambia	380,699	2,799,375	2,496,893	4,594,499	8,060,978
Zimbabwe	1,890,310				

Table B-31.   U.S. Agricultural Balance of Payments by Regions and Individual Countries, 2005–2015

Region	2005	2006	2007	2008	2009	2010
WORLD	7,790,572,955	8,673,581,707	17,887,811,239	29,408,439,652	20,843,115,967	25,673,560,098
Europe	4,061,308,748	4,201,448,762	5,918,327,002	6,788,222,751	4,233,979,740	5,659,064,931
European Union (EU-28)	3,737,074,896	3,907,565,444	5,139,021,223	5,804,460,903	3,595,772,685	4,528,013,346
Austria	29,790,190	37,530,891	59,535,518	74,691,929	26,298,260	15,044,056
Belgium	315,676,635	287,080,924	328,690,820	272,300,639	231,472,703	413,439,673
Bulgaria	-31,500,071	-25,487,787	-32,821,981	-33,428,663	-25,022,351	-20,754,640
Croatia	1,661,091	719,517	1,716,421	5,187,914	3,063,881	5,174,673
Cyprus	3,340,967	6,218,855	7,687,147	10,486,954	5,761,814	7,142,896
Czech Republic	27,111,585	17,633,290	29,406,157	13,911,162	13,984,981	12,242,808
Denmark	57,536,245	77,433,140	110,322,106	117,009,169	33,019,214	38,576,352
Estonia	1,952,337	3,656,773	6,047,622	4,779,101	2,776,982	5,422,524
Finland	-568,275	1,789,937	5,779,176	3,005,334	7,683,736	355,752
France	324,694,054	341,775,664	374,350,368	377,417,575	263,003,195	338,123,011
Germany	920,973,905	860,422,435	1,099,917,514	1,474,130,685	1,019,343,373	1,265,992,417
Greece	53,089,262	61,710,752	88,573,611	61,758,698	39,792,790	71,355,190
Hungary	5,749,986	7,344,200	9,370,282	5,655,032	17,352,294	11,215,603
Ireland	26,858,621	43,166,153	62,291,442	102,113,755	44,151,030	47,104,313
Italy	411,440,227	328,011,565	464,065,647	484,483,057	380,883,795	479,724,803
Latvia	16,460,995	12,424,668	22,313,924	45,076,763	11,829,625	6,357,655
Lithuania	60,676,232	57,266,492	32,066,861	46,126,216	31,892,975	31,465,240
Luxembourg	24,131,737	21,283,729	31,607,307	35,025,760	29,182,003	31,059,736
Malta	4,645,862	4,314,205	6,177,341	843,898	5,963,553	151,703
Netherlands	238,617,407	642,065,664	511,101,484	662,648,550	261,692,876	310,105,730
Poland	23,193,450	35,787,481	53,766,840	67,706,190	35,544,583	14,089,122
Portugal	141,663,690	139,254,927	314,708,223	312,388,489	107,082,396	129,404,234
Romania	36,721,475	28,582,995	52,448,490	53,017,882	46,525,029	27,906,146
Slovakia	-471,749	1,108,385	-340,311	17,639,499	-291,651	-557
Slovenia	1,321,052	914,198	4,260,960	-1,717,860	-2,578,494	-1,668,438
Spain	521,853,643	449,779,360	963,855,050	1,116,723,680	627,820,449	857,653,682
Sweden	18,291,682	40,201,282	41,347,405	38,533,699	39,825,193	54,582,279
United Kingdom	502,162,661	425,575,749	490,775,799	436,945,796	337,718,451	376,747,383
Non-EU	324,233,852	293,883,318	779,305,779	983,761,848	638,207,055	1,131,051,585
Albania	-4,520,266	-3,271,236	-2,622,335	-5,415,686	-4,461,030	-4,417,261
Belarus	386,850	144,559	166,157	587,598	666,674	659,862
Faroe Islands	-4,143,325	-2,584,807	-6,666,253	-15,212,579	-61,393,341	-71,574,710
Gibraltar	8,500	-3,461	0	8,100	0	76,727
Iceland	-137,281,336	-127,982,991	-110,926,026	-83,318,436	-79,215,119	-89,747,220
Kosovo	0	0	0	0	2,906	11,340
Liechtenstein	53,400	49,000	10,340	76,945	13,000	0
Macedonia	-7,475,925	-8,171,837	-10,793,205	-12,620,423	-29,167,968	-15,131,783
Moldova	580,653	-18,038	66,903	-101,753	-30,039	6,748,004
Monaco	17,484	99,828	4,577,196	-631,993	-145,742	32,047
Montenegro	0	0	83,130	861,976	795,928	770,048
Norway	-18,988,182	-87,761,544	-71,829,834	-71,333,705	-270,678,222	-422,854,180
Russia	-156,126,567	-240,446,159	-208,398,809	-59,318,169	-59,893,409	3,471,326
San Marino	949,883	3,284,870	3,000,640	2,378,947	292,926	959,067
Serbia	2,330,928	3,721,745	4,150,743	7,532,728	3,563,357	1,934,672
Svalbard, Jan Mayen Island	144,600	14,669	75,000	81,200	20,000	110,000
Switzerland	89,418,056	137,129,760	161,758,374	264,173,367	229,443,644	165,273,724
Turkey	524,121,720	537,504,563	849,088,817	877,016,678	861,148,783	1,489,361,144
Ukraine	34,757,379	81,759,110	167,270,764	78,916,287	47,001,906	65,106,985
Vatican City	0	415,287	294,177	80,766	242,801	261,793
WESTERN HEMIOPIIERE	-6,738,871,326	-7,408,820,754	-6,774,171,308	-3,855,597,423	-6,364,912,327	-7,221,612,121
NAFTA	-1,107,790,904	-1,274,299,621	-1,306,978,610	485,881,205	-86,950,231	-356,483,810
Canada	-25,883,145	-575,247,210	-912,115,564	-1,397,599,477	361,631,378	549,507,290
Mexico	-1,081,907,759	-699,052,411	-394,863,046	1,883,480,682	-448,581,609	-905,991,100
Caribbean	500,898,499	572,744,592	790,646,815	1,227,685,084	792,693,401	741,679,788
Anguilla	1,127,495	1,670,379	1,453,095	1,504,681	1,584,073	972,659
Antigua and Barbuda	3,648,561	4,231,593	4,856,735	6,112,318	3,698,155	2,539,807
Aruba	2,482,277	3,968,592	4,487,166	6,154,011	6,479,013	8,080,380
Bahamas	-21,217,038	-16,312,572	-15,252,777	-26,753,220	-11,603,010	-16,407,425
Barbados	20,516,244	19,832,202	25,594,009	38,921,891	34,206,860	30,685,787
British Virgin Islands	5,050,079	6,648,824	2,074,463	1,355,763	1,911,487	2,472,774
Cayman Islands	12,171,933	16,350,346	18,308,656	17,652,028	10,721,716	8,350,303
Cuba	163,644,011	161,345,905	224,120,386	403,106,237	260,875,722	152,913,670
Curacao	0	0	0	0	0	0
Dominica	185,469	351,623	655,476	992,945	557,843	444,521

Table B-31.   U.S. Agricultural Balance of Payments by Regions and Individual Countries, 2005–2015—*Continued*

Region	2011	2012	2013	2014	2015	2005–2015 Value Change
WORLD	30,460,634,112	30,474,395,722	25,763,159,769	25,429,367,167	16,676,409,728	8,885,836,773
Europe	6,596,198,088	6,523,682,324	7,276,630,665	7,483,968,813	6,325,082,243	2,263,773,495
European Union (EU-28)	4,755,164,466	5,008,244,198	5,714,780,596	6,520,401,572	6,021,626,489	2,284,551,593
Austria	19,570,627	25,559,491	39,041,629	16,329,710	7,054,816	-22,735,374
Belgium	252,555,306	213,604,846	237,534,798	358,407,192	418,829,705	103,153,070
Bulgaria	-15,564,549	-21,333,414	-19,559,564	-19,572,859	-37,155,107	-5,655,036
Croatia	13,552,678	6,738,455	10,736,428	9,148,669	7,346,646	5,685,555
Cyprus	4,500,532	3,195,631	4,400,668	4,567,583	3,303,741	-37,226
Czech Republic	14,127,110	10,314,713	18,150,072	12,091,932	9,187,781	-17,923,804
Denmark	79,545,391	62,174,218	69,435,403	77,631,522	99,855,259	42,319,014
Estonia	5,347,727	4,978,705	7,351,831	13,155,527	8,291,541	6,339,204
Finland	4,031,066	1,772,176	-3,503,795	8,633,389	12,608,271	13,176,546
France	357,373,573	288,464,599	327,349,712	322,381,794	295,085,727	-29,608,327
Germany	1,170,586,129	1,681,864,172	1,661,162,157	1,569,913,432	1,616,687,254	695,713,349
Greece	26,066,282	20,184,174	19,725,153	19,384,903	-253,593	-53,342,855
Hungary	6,362,840	12,183,079	13,649,416	31,088,800	23,163,485	17,413,499
Ireland	38,703,452	11,487,293	37,465,595	79,774,303	9,758,941	-17,099,680
Italy	557,895,025	444,465,997	685,057,785	652,828,341	709,921,496	298,481,269
Latvia	9,661,351	8,582,892	9,456,138	7,901,889	-1,716,645	-18,177,640
Lithuania	47,777,396	52,014,462	73,133,227	80,437,759	38,975,303	-21,700,929
Luxembourg	17,719,843	30,427,382	49,934,504	13,921,065	18,445,812	-5,685,925
Malta	1,554,481	2,939,699	3,240,296	3,175,167	1,207,145	-3,438,717
Netherlands	492,560,448	370,828,540	471,651,876	921,638,559	922,506,928	683,889,521
Poland	64,909,434	63,907,322	31,469,357	-3,685,702	41,175,079	17,981,629
Portugal	249,586,123	184,114,876	106,980,722	311,174,691	155,160,024	13,496,334
Romania	30,990,565	45,244,378	16,890,075	6,373,723	-47,860,204	-84,581,679
Slovakia	999,397	2,781,832	1,865,762	961,691	-1,418,538	-946,789
Slovenia	861,699	1,362,060	2,542,792	-249,208	-1,918,890	-3,239,942
Spain	935,786,468	960,157,531	1,301,624,180	1,443,412,314	1,134,340,477	612,486,834
Sweden	61,490,085	52,543,566	36,506,739	11,781,778	33,608,888	15,317,206
United Kingdom	306,613,987	467,685,523	501,487,640	567,793,608	545,435,147	43,272,486
						0
Non-EU	1,841,033,622	1,515,438,126	1,561,850,069	963,567,241	303,455,754	-20,778,098
Albania	-4,840,303	-5,878,832	-11,072,191	-11,980,282	-11,066,061	-6,545,795
Belarus	254,160	436,438	502,082	1,147,533	705,007	318,157
Faroe Islands	-104,202,144	-71,921,375	-125,338,059	-137,213,170	-91,290,864	-87,147,539
Gibraltar	0	8,215	26,712	26,244	26,208	17,708
Iceland	-89,993,169	-123,766,623	-143,077,987	-147,217,299	-155,174,019	-17,892,683
Kosovo	77,818	0	-55,370	9,986	56,131	56,131
Liechtenstein	-27,105	0	0	0	0	-53,400
Macedonia	-26,876,578	-34,087,866	-34,339,143	-27,424,083	-24,766,041	-17,290,116
Moldova	326,197	677,065	138,789	445,097	-5,897,303	-6,477,956
Monaco	139,142	-229,300	-1,974	-3,346	330,383	312,899
Montenegro	1,075,726	549,141	1,035,038	1,779,783	920,438	920,438
Norway	-267,720,794	-197,488,403	-253,700,821	-357,676,658	-404,431,515	-385,443,333
Russia	100,513,371	363,237,749	374,000,495	93,904,358	-56,604,685	99,521,882
San Marino	79,400	172,028	519,670	1,557,399	76,787	-873,096
Serbia	2,520,142	4,368,762	1,985,762	7,375,521	12,243,743	9,912,815
Svalbard, Jan Mayen Island	0	0	0	0	0	-144,600
Switzerland	239,235,234	208,619,582	357,903,067	258,969,523	318,362,983	228,944,927
Turkey	1,881,662,552	1,243,788,616	1,216,361,437	1,215,555,985	780,715,367	256,593,647
Ukraine	108,809,973	126,634,771	176,118,357	63,585,327	-61,300,433	-96,057,812
Vatican City	0	318,158	844,205	725,323	549,628	549,628
						0
WESTERN HEMISPHERE	-8,001,276,875	-10,245,823,327	-12,613,743,455	-13,706,289,797	-15,264,470,389	-8,525,599,063
						0
NAFTA	851,886,275	-376,047,637	-2,827,202,130	-3,747,203,171	-4,708,290,089	-3,600,499,185
Canada	648,634,102	57,541,480	-546,155,362	-758,719,740	-207,785,620	-181,902,475
Mexico	203,252,173	-433,589,117	-2,281,046,768	-2,988,483,431	-4,500,504,469	-3,418,596,710
						0
Caribbean	947,294,981	735,418,358	683,158,912	696,752,726	552,771,570	51,873,071
Anguilla	620,148	742,327	1,462,776	1,373,649	1,484,842	357,347
Antigua and Barbuda	2,585,611	1,777,763	2,972,867	3,031,293	4,427,766	779,205
Aruba	9,988,366	7,382,528	8,378,092	10,784,521	10,119,816	7,637,539
Bahamas	-7,850,477	-14,908,065	-9,666,245	615,237	-7,347,961	13,869,077
Barbados	40,168,525	34,436,973	41,784,062	46,655,336	40,323,479	19,807,235
British Virgin Islands	7,719,165	4,733,630	3,693,385	3,865,092	4,173,592	-876,487
Cayman Islands	7,314,467	9,615,038	10,446,199	12,815,774	12,865,551	693,618
Cuba	196,989,355	200,371,255	96,523,261	59,138,201	15,459,357	-148,184,654
Curacao	1,944,583	2,110,838	2,858,830	3,541,591	5,214,670	5,214,670
Dominica	447,263	8,029,099	696,353	463,436	1,661,452	1,475,983

Table B-31. U.S. Agricultural Balance of Payments by Regions and Individual Countries, 2005–2015—*Continued*

Region	2005	2006	2007	2008	2009	2010
Dominican Republic	181,781,571	236,798,743	322,016,102	423,833,549	242,380,833	336,108,503
Grenada	1,880,701	4,218,882	3,017,069	13,412,440	2,048,740	3,048,799
Guadeloupe	2,249,680	4,431,422	2,488,082	2,988,138	2,498,164	2,984,488
Haiti	31,700,041	15,866,859	32,012,001	65,945,002	37,811,507	21,386,351
Jamaica	58,503,513	80,123,745	105,855,476	170,564,287	116,820,580	103,803,235
Martinique	2,168,216	2,873,358	1,142,179	1,687,023	2,273,998	1,931,269
Montserrat	0	30,119	251,489	299,213	65,071	25,541
Sint Maarten	0	0	0	0	0	0
St Kitts and Nevis	797,144	1,478,516	2,224,711	1,520,561	1,650,671	3,002,287
St Lucia	2,896,849	3,261,517	3,553,132	3,109,040	3,385,638	4,158,146
St Vincent and the Grenadines	2,982,616	5,414,978	7,809,344	9,674,005	10,341,028	12,389,367
Trinidad and Tobago	32,812,131	21,933,182	45,170,707	81,895,000	65,538,692	63,496,307
Turks and Caicos Islands	-4,482,994	-1,773,621	-1,190,686	3,710,172	-553,380	-706,981
Central America	-1,474,649,753	-1,536,839,695	-1,520,006,155	-1,381,036,388	-1,603,595,156	-1,765,505,208
Belize	-36,478,579	-34,259,016	-19,561,128	-13,683,022	-15,041,792	-19,691,674
Costa Rica	-599,467,384	-811,276,111	-744,872,081	-645,656,526	-680,645,244	-822,894,602
El Salvador	73,677,548	85,264,206	103,352,366	161,166,974	134,384,454	168,310,249
Guatemala	-525,742,418	-396,196,403	-518,229,117	-561,414,611	-755,736,150	-707,578,640
Honduras	-268,996,751	-221,626,310	-262,366,660	-255,415,198	-221,116,938	-295,607,044
Nicaragua	-64,113,789	-111,759,585	-85,356,838	-121,742,571	-118,711,895	-144,200,142
Panama	-53,528,380	-46,986,476	7,027,303	55,708,566	53,272,409	56,156,645
South America	-4,656,767,366	-5,177,105,858	-4,744,973,438	-4,198,428,958	-5,478,475,246	-5,853,361,076
Argentina	-231,353,190	-309,143,867	-346,968,248	-309,355,112	-278,618,043	-277,940,991
Bolivia	-17,758,652	-22,418,727	-27,734,869	-34,357,265	-46,043,334	-58,808,676
Brazil	-932,249,400	-1,013,104,690	-1,056,652,126	-998,705,551	-1,252,767,315	-1,494,496,126
Chile	-1,784,312,870	-2,059,118,516	-2,052,708,432	-2,104,884,277	-2,014,907,675	-2,001,540,890
Colombia	-736,266,037	-620,048,087	-420,221,196	-327,103,321	-820,708,798	-1,082,480,508
Ecuador	-826,413,342	-923,602,957	-883,784,550	-965,054,557	-1,160,778,696	-1,178,968,462
Falkland Islands (Islas Malvin)	-9,065,260	-12,169,647	-4,758,607	-7,080,381	-8,272,572	-5,415,399
French Guiana	505,041	412,844	349,490	829,696	554,035	657,697
Guyana	-30,125,291	-27,421,909	-31,286,176	-23,981,941	-27,811,083	-21,493,482
Paraguay	-821,020	-1,425,991	-3,348,877	-907,351	-1,172,600	1,127,086
Peru	-200,423,392	-290,130,766	-157,308,495	-264,197,421	-273,724,554	-236,025,956
Suriname	-16,121,307	-16,772,677	-17,980,181	-20,816,972	-24,443,578	-22,600,651
Uruguay	-25,065,153	-19,070,460	-15,274,789	-9,695,430	-3,032,922	-12,566,467
Venezuela	152,702,507	136,909,592	272,703,618	866,880,925	433,251,889	537,191,749
Other Western Hemisphere	-561,802	6,679,828	7,140,080	10,301,634	11,414,905	12,058,185
Bermuda	15,368,199	17,288,140	18,167,282	17,304,835	19,673,246	21,866,087
Greenland	-15,645,671	-9,815,438	-9,675,406	-5,971,458	-7,464,935	-7,965,273
St Pierre and Miquelon	-284,330	-792,874	-1,351,796	-1,031,743	-793,406	-1,842,629
Asia	9,780,942,019	10,841,245,404	15,634,735,747	23,955,610,097	21,345,014,183	24,903,526,962
China	2,902,516,999	3,439,257,605	4,443,851,929	7,753,822,480	9,342,777,094	12,859,013,173
Hong Kong	404,041,192	476,270,416	588,606,485	681,447,773	1,013,673,930	1,177,372,142
Japan	5,840,160,788	6,079,285,447	7,109,706,810	9,465,456,559	6,914,581,859	7,430,901,296
Saudi Arabia	98,866,523	148,732,807	307,083,417	313,904,441	218,723,431	299,244,415
South Korea	1,573,204,847	2,015,067,284	2,358,726,114	3,855,117,245	2,552,512,977	3,227,500,359
Taiwan	1,492,581,149	1,510,887,190	2,078,574,650	2,365,118,028	1,961,267,645	1,908,261,498
ASEAN - 10	-2,827,435,917	-3,607,587,246	-3,169,121,295	-3,272,981,867	-2,201,284,151	-3,807,331,390
Brunei	-1,080,503	-4,122,508	-2,831,348	-1,813,447	964,475	928,216
Cambodia	-26,189,816	-19,571,296	-3,143,572	-3,542,600	-6,887,024	-3,963,081
East Timor	50,200	0	327,538	24,072	49,648	804,218
Indonesia	-1,205,286,883	-1,459,338,046	-1,191,459,567	-1,414,760,920	-810,837,653	-1,635,173,685
Laos	-500,816	-78,607	-7,854,752	-3,298,345	-2,545,482	-513,218
Malaysia	-21,643,822	-94,768,191	-9,272,169	-140,127,270	165,044,450	15,119,838
Myanmar	0	0	3,500	324,475	0	885,960
Philippines	288,552,071	279,487,112	311,290,731	698,005,844	364,362,764	423,774,684
Singapore	11,764,565	19,008,180	41,855,268	54,644,450	79,950,512	62,165,704
Thailand	-1,048,866,001	-1,462,267,103	-1,378,919,546	-1,556,044,369	-1,197,207,133	-1,608,278,994
Vietnam	-824,234,912	-865,936,787	-929,117,378	-906,393,757	-794,178,708	-1,063,081,032
Middle East	775,917,563	1,212,863,644	1,844,664,950	2,820,618,274	1,410,511,696	1,834,835,240
Andorra	138,609	731,508	1,452,937	-154,889	-168,853	-82,909
Bahrain	3,168,913	1,250,398	2,139,329	11,306,931	4,986,550	5,594,069
Bosnia and Herzegovina	192,178	62,488	185,181	725,840	1,248,937	1,322,583
Gaza Strip admin. by Israel	0	0	0	0	0	0
Iran	5,473,461	4,470,387	59,211,404	560,451,881	162,746,630	70,746,731
Iraq	209,314,301	297,476,475	415,718,017	790,864,459	1,685,473	116,041,887
Israel	111,381,544	228,792,676	327,471,860	515,172,307	164,404,813	312,879,923
Jordan	36,860,127	102,429,643	65,951,177	32,928,432	77,878,225	80,813,681
Kuwait	13,017,093	24,913,488	28,018,835	29,402,359	32,260,607	33,109,008
Lebanon	48,091,405	42,025,241	59,728,776	58,125,866	56,674,545	90,033,460

Table B-31.   U.S. Agricultural Balance of Payments by Regions and Individual Countries, 2005–2015—*Continued*

Region	2011	2012	2013	2014	2015	2005–2015 Value Change
Dominican Republic....................	428,585,468	212,726,383	190,414,686	283,251,547	214,519,845	32,738,274
Grenada	10,245,470	5,557,524	2,411,878	1,435,718	661,832	-1,218,869
Guadeloupe.........................	2,200,446	3,462,988	3,018,682	3,600,826	3,229,649	979,969
Haiti................................	5,450,396	2,750,360	43,235,080	9,528,258	32,863,612	1,163,571
Jamaica.............................	143,080,030	140,776,508	155,341,217	134,187,370	112,734,788	54,231,275
Martinique..........................	1,574,174	1,731,460	1,689,967	1,848,772	1,997,022	-171,194
Montserrat..........................	32,473	-305,094	10,916	23,612	71,130	71,130
Sint Maarten	4,180,340	7,476,333	8,342,422	9,419,699	10,341,608	10,341,608
St Kitts and Nevis	2,085,976	1,403,527	2,118,558	1,568,447	2,545,430	1,748,286
St Lucia.............................	4,557,779	3,962,818	3,631,162	4,225,797	4,316,987	1,420,138
St Vincent and the Grenadines........	9,950,773	19,487,869	14,870,703	17,688,254	10,144,664	7,162,048
Trinidad and Tobago.................	75,934,937	81,324,613	97,887,412	86,077,462	68,792,219	35,980,088
Turks and Caicos Islands	-510,287	771,683	1,036,649	1,612,834	2,170,220	6,653,214
						0
Central America......................	-2,296,485,783	-2,844,461,973	-2,843,037,087	-2,640,090,242	-2,671,983,697	-1,197,333,944
Belize	-16,160,855	-15,294,918	-19,586,246	-18,736,374	-14,539,771	21,938,808
Costa Rica..........................	-832,819,105	-944,512,451	-1,105,535,974	-1,053,080,922	-895,454,834	-295,987,450
El Salvador..........................	157,868,654	129,071,493	112,742,485	199,997,475	133,792,340	60,114,792
Guatemala...........................	-1,145,811,628	-1,255,347,033	-1,236,407,388	-1,133,363,826	-1,195,932,435	-670,190,017
Honduras............................	-356,207,739	-477,094,764	-413,478,037	-399,890,407	-462,504,911	-193,508,160
Nicaragua...........................	-185,216,331	-278,863,189	-219,663,990	-303,858,808	-313,024,841	-248,911,052
Panama..............................	81,861,221	-2,421,111	38,892,063	68,842,620	75,680,755	129,209,135
						0
South America........................	-7,519,619,321	-7,769,952,882	-7,634,133,712	-8,028,915,209	-8,454,307,494	-3,797,540,128
Argentina...........................	-392,051,485	-515,235,363	-774,368,699	-618,111,638	-560,415,244	-329,062,054
Bolivia..............................	-78,939,062	-84,082,007	-150,366,447	-190,948,939	-125,474,171	-107,715,519
Brazil...............................	-2,043,998,642	-2,002,279,760	-745,895,792	-1,451,133,266	-1,622,554,794	-690,305,394
Chile................................	-2,254,057,773	-2,441,566,666	-3,067,826,478	-3,271,545,722	-3,021,969,441	-1,237,656,571
Colombia............................	-1,362,449,269	-1,291,909,500	-1,236,791,209	-601,944,802	-768,578,308	-32,312,271
Ecuador.............................	-1,453,974,049	-1,410,822,757	-1,506,394,664	-1,784,992,165	-1,679,124,228	-852,710,886
Falkland Islands (Islas Malvin)........	-6,881,016	-11,037,931	-13,554,305	-19,475,540	-12,880,781	-3,815,521
French Guiana	441,008	281,130	471,154	415,749	599,195	94,154
Guyana..............................	-10,934,814	-31,779,835	-33,730,648	-21,540,610	-24,436,516	5,688,775
Paraguay............................	-2,044,676	-10,382,037	-130,398,231	-83,536,091	-33,845,763	-33,024,743
Peru................................	-439,513,499	-727,737,287	-627,203,837	-520,638,950	-795,595,491	-595,172,099
Suriname	-14,952,589	-18,723,079	-25,101,009	-27,091,646	-23,087,212	-6,965,905
Uruguay.............................	-30,925,993	-37,841,733	-52,709,621	-33,683,276	-55,138,124	-30,072,971
Venezuela...........................	570,662,538	813,163,943	729,736,074	595,311,687	268,193,384	115,490,877
						0
Other Western Hemisphere	15,646,973	9,220,807	7,470,562	13,166,099	17,339,321	17,901,123
Bermuda	22,787,686	15,431,459	16,437,463	18,483,697	19,893,882	4,525,683
Greenland...........................	-6,932,811	-6,210,652	-8,914,045	-5,317,598	-2,388,519	13,257,152
St Pierre and Miquelon	-207,902	0	-52,856	0	-166,042	118,288
Asia	29,510,112,818	32,808,978,229	30,035,276,667	31,003,835,018	26,046,865,384	16,265,923,365
China...............................	14,313,913,466	20,036,246,261	18,517,419,132	17,799,874,663	14,084,205,439	11,181,688,440
Hong Kong..........................	1,462,397,737	1,921,684,265	2,034,238,664	1,595,379,484	1,452,401,385	1,048,360,193
Japan...............................	8,855,263,963	7,910,328,976	6,608,601,164	7,274,773,409	6,420,410,048	580,249,260
Saudi Arabia........................	602,530,891	506,177,490	406,954,537	577,282,169	581,106,160	482,239,637
South Korea	4,164,965,900	3,333,161,922	2,625,507,960	3,625,653,309	3,002,476,630	1,429,271,783
Taiwan..............................	2,292,378,972	1,887,859,769	1,574,557,237	1,926,252,490	1,603,663,823	111,082,674
						0
ASEAN - 10..........................	-4,539,842,998	-3,419,550,348	-2,329,534,984	-2,160,903,680	-1,851,594,763	975,841,154
Brunei	983,054	1,181,047	-905,681	-700,487	317,757	1,398,260
Cambodia............................	-196,875	-2,119,807	162,803	-1,578,715	8,812,539	35,002,355
East Timor...........................	365,222	0	104,958	0	-3,051,927	-3,102,127
Indonesia............................	-2,267,229,496	-1,838,177,590	-1,489,435,625	-1,338,089,776	-1,386,237,551	-180,950,668
Laos	-7,190,621	70,166	-1,164,644	-2,881,893	-3,974,371	-3,473,555
Malaysia............................	131,847,555	81,511,084	230,601,508	172,343,073	254,402,751	276,046,573
Myanmar............................	11,590,473	2,712,449	-12,294,497	-46,332,667	-38,572,705	-38,572,705
Philippines..........................	732,575,726	544,645,169	633,306,885	752,779,556	576,174,003	287,621,932
Singapore...........................	93,077,373	94,054,032	115,866,945	126,290,166	113,063,478	101,298,913
Thailand............................	-2,059,206,116	-1,201,512,938	-792,493,345	-610,289,884	-498,794,849	550,071,152
Vietnam.............................	-1,176,459,293	-1,101,913,960	-1,013,284,291	-1,212,443,053	-873,733,888	-49,498,976
						0
Middle East	2,443,693,095	1,262,617,656	1,369,075,444	1,295,024,480	1,231,832,711	455,915,148
Andorra.............................	-94,714	-96,008	484,476	580,640	0	-138,609
Bahrain..............................	9,517,334	9,463,311	11,813,601	9,098,739	11,467,483	8,298,570
Bosnia and Herzegovina...............	797,450	2,113,342	2,241,622	877,122	1,261,660	1,069,482
Gaza Strip admin. by Israel	0	0	0	0	28,200	28,200
Iran	48,250,171	113,509,492	75,091,751	34,000,943	73,842,300	68,368,839
Iraq	530,152,867	58,459,863	1,180,652	18,882,840	64,557,412	-144,756,889
Israel...............................	468,003,649	201,877,262	188,123,299	278,799,327	104,039,452	-7,342,092
Jordan..............................	235,523,690	53,838,508	82,269,748	67,620,998	73,665,560	36,805,433
Kuwait..............................	36,398,675	36,633,449	47,942,536	41,593,795	42,297,473	29,280,380
Lebanon.............................	100,647,613	45,228,434	48,073,624	55,025,685	47,218,669	-872,736

Table B-31. U.S. Agricultural Balance of Payments by Regions and Individual Countries, 2005–2015—*Continued*

Region	2005	2006	2007	2008	2009	2010
Oman	-728,561	2,241,162	7,571,448	19,973,081	8,453,081	24,144,580
Qatar	701,579	3,722,411	1,798,502	2,810,469	6,760,893	5,496,693
Republic of Yemen	78,942,383	97,788,362	274,381,692	145,775,618	151,444,955	103,489,973
Syria	134,084,438	207,778,093	340,781,996	363,944,246	265,186,244	442,336,492
United Arab Emirates	135,170,685	199,181,312	258,684,395	289,302,946	477,559,895	550,070,685
West Bank admin. by Israel	109,408	0	1,569,401	-11,272	-610,299	-1,161,616
Central Asia	7,121,650	12,903,762	6,943,743	2,466,040	-1,407,902	4,948,940
Kazakhstan	7,825,775	13,322,433	8,877,559	3,959,681	206,381	4,404,305
Kyrgyzstan	-4,487	4,637	5,280	-232,402	-1,221,055	-163,510
Tajikistan	592,259	950,708	164,655	675,789	38,443	1,548,771
Turkmenistan	-432,855	-132,216	-1,253,019	-1,504,566	-879,394	-1,236,204
Uzbekistan	-859,042	-1,241,800	-850,732	-432,462	447,723	395,578
Other Asia	-486,032,775	-446,435,505	65,698,944	-29,358,876	133,657,604	-31,218,711
Afghanistan	11,843,893	19,827,874	24,532,732	11,950,218	-1,912,738	10,514,513
Armenia	99,008	655,450	6,946,921	1,094,827	1,108,374	775,610
Azerbaijan	-1,564,607	-1,084,853	-1,821,908	-1,327,358	-1,733,248	-430,641
Bangladesh	-87,148,744	-136,296,273	-5,064,993	11,919,230	34,586,812	114,891,329
Bhutan	12,274	0	11,704	14,646	0	0
Georgia	7,755,473	13,886,771	5,683,405	9,948,673	5,483,059	4,025,115
India	-588,037,660	-459,396,082	-275,658,000	-357,965,214	-176,006,211	-352,037,855
Macau	14,480	230,389	1,385,762	766,514	194,910	305,065
Maldives	-5,782	-395,223	-660,574	-1,466,538	-60,409	-234,316
Mongolia	3,162,929	-2,947,106	2,576,216	-2,468,763	4,017,751	11,574
Nepal	353,875	156,034	895,474	-22,779	1,238,041	668,427
North Korea	5,656,804	0	1,728,160	48,120,143	0	1,762,973
Pakistan	175,576,892	149,540,076	293,581,145	249,987,456	240,766,187	201,110,198
Sri Lanka	-13,751,610	-30,612,562	11,562,900	90,069	25,975,076	-12,580,703
Australia and Oceania	-311,179,668	-273,695,885	-282,442,881	-252,494,633	-146,207,656	-118,862,438
Australia	-95,150,035	-44,138,439	-10,129,478	13,059,412	72,369,573	100,603,229
Christmas Island	-15,497	-9,085	0	0	0	10,341
Cocos (Keeling) Islands	0	0	0	0	-59,680	0
Cook Islands	-1,089,960	-247,644	-319,335	-219,667	-63,874	-70,794
Fiji	-9,325,429	-8,750,696	-13,868,434	-15,356,075	-11,696,737	-9,676,187
French Polynesia	484,487	-2,205,326	-7,908,531	-4,150,439	1,045,950	309,250
French Southern and Antarctic	0	0	0	0	-74,847	13,108
Heard and McDonald Islands	0	159,180	0	0	0	0
Kiribati	-974,639	-784,657	-900,140	-801,819	-645,495	-525,851
Marshall Islands	-7,933,898	-6,483,622	-4,191,037	-7,129,634	-5,572,651	-4,399,668
Micronesia	42,998	-245,249	-3,675,506	-2,797,545	-1,894,156	-2,721,660
Netherlands Antilles	9,966,414	13,091,915	10,919,149	9,391,450	10,161,866	12,133,904
New Caledonia	-613,836	-5,399,866	-391,947	-1,506,973	1,175,260	240,797
New Zealand	-190,334,158	-175,896,628	-188,549,313	-166,437,977	-124,356,362	-129,560,564
Niue	113,449	38,785	-295,276	109,000	526,130	256,250
Norfolk Island	30,154	1,119,491	919,641	2,045,523	135,534	252,204
Palau	-145,763	-466,201	-67,767	272,431	738,281	650,785
Papua New Guinea	-45,396,796	-46,443,558	-70,863,276	-77,710,331	-78,953,257	-75,125,947
Pitcairn Islands	18,144	31,713	82,800	0	-13,916	0
Reunion	-5,541,741	-6,453,772	-2,865,600	-2,829,698	-8,186,958	-8,856,627
Samoa	-371,203	510,864	717,696	-154,338	531,698	449,840
Solomon Islands	-926,907	-898,908	-557,759	-396,402	316,937	-650,757
Tokelau	39,537,122	13,349,480	12,596,909	4,785,276	762,582	7,469
Tonga	-3,005,655	-3,311,219	-2,850,020	-2,451,696	-1,651,574	-1,421,482
Tuvalu	0	0	0	0	0	0
Vanuatu	-574,126	-362,443	-394,642	-680,131	-941,960	-835,078
Wallis and Futuna	27,207	100,000	148,985	465,000	140,000	55,000
Africa	782,110,160	1,189,018,773	2,950,154,072	2,589,701,429	1,541,503,158	2,075,544,798
Algeria	144,722,103	190,358,090	409,213,178	193,868,782	77,789,026	90,065,541
Angola	10,673,285	8,943,937	10,824,489	18,804,481	2,477,369	7,929,525
Benin	-189,135	14,597	249,725	-71,165	-756	1,191,290
Botswana	13,000	28,062	102,762	21,689	230,400	28,327
British Indian Ocean Terr.	0	0	21,604	26,310	0	0
Burkina Faso	1,573,220	1,826,273	2,173,577	791,517	499,029	43,919
Burundi	-2,419,483	1,420,111	57,161	-693,750	-2,110,266	-1,671,741
Cabo Verde	1,828,680	1,920,177	1,245,855	-29,911	0	-115,139
Cameroon	-9,424,675	-6,857,435	-13,329,234	-14,327,911	-5,475,864	-21,060,046
Central African Republic	196,337	152,442	1,811,811	1,069,895	4,265,149	321,106
Chad	-12,197,711	-12,660,278	-2,337,233	-2,582,057	-8,466,818	-1,558,943
Comoros	-816,968	-682,528	-42,618	-325,764	-353,977	-264,370

Table B-31.   U.S. Agricultural Balance of Payments by Regions and Individual Countries, 2005–2015—*Continued*

Region	2011	2012	2013	2014	2015	2005–2015 Value Change
Oman	55,889,290	26,295,267	7,270,888	5,126,074	11,130,128	11,858,689
Qatar	8,771,485	9,088,797	9,272,617	10,225,031	11,760,259	11,058,680
Republic of Yemen	184,354,686	134,158,791	143,012,947	91,743,537	96,929,909	17,987,526
Syria	191,265,244	5,522,970	3,107,323	4,876,291	2,541,653	-131,542,785
United Arab Emirates	575,256,499	567,508,425	750,536,449	677,453,237	691,816,972	556,646,287
West Bank admin. by Israel	-1,040,844	-984,247	-1,346,089	-879,779	-724,419	-833,827
						0
Central Asia	14,672,390	286,246	-6,030,449	-11,967,953	-6,924,919	-14,046,569
Kazakhstan	15,429,036	6,187,885	1,956,425	-2,398,723	-7,575,628	-15,401,403
Kyrgyzstan	-72,574	12,111	1,168,988	117,489	64,258	68,745
Tajikistan	8,460	51,635	62,412	2,151	43,844	-548,415
Turkmenistan	-690,879	-4,925,019	-10,609,347	-5,202,615	-417,681	15,174
Uzbekistan	-1,653	-1,040,366	1,391,073	-4,486,255	960,288	1,819,330
						0
Other Asia	-99,860,598	-629,834,008	-765,512,038	-917,533,353	-470,711,130	15,321,645
Afghanistan	11,517,170	786,848	-2,471,312	3,905,282	6,268,063	-5,575,830
Armenia	814,871	1,187,683	3,877,286	1,400,227	98,921	-87
Azerbaijan	309,947	272,930	-209,955	253,814	80,608	1,645,215
Bangladesh	290,632,565	65,844,895	99,761,925	244,195,819	356,204,832	443,353,576
Bhutan	0	0	16,650	11,350	0	-12,274
Georgia	6,656,425	3,206,906	5,330,999	8,119,623	5,456,731	-2,298,742
India	-746,068,092	-828,827,715	-1,110,871,855	-1,289,386,432	-1,103,446,625	-515,408,965
Macau	773,972	602,038	579,241	1,800,909	3,885,841	3,871,361
Maldives	-1,273,580	-13,155,761	-19,051,679	-20,641,157	-20,125,916	-20,120,134
Mongolia	29,361	4,529,461	-609,393	-272,832	-702,714	-3,865,643
Nepal	766,879	115,432	810,365	1,402,027	708,360	354,485
North Korea	0	0	0	0	0	-5,656,804
Pakistan	315,861,344	179,517,468	250,524,902	149,152,983	305,582,838	130,005,946
Sri Lanka	20,118,540	-43,914,193	6,800,788	-17,474,966	-24,722,069	-10,970,459
						0
Australia and Oceania	-106,918,073	-74,250,536	-140,454,901	-131,034,215	-161,828,614	149,351,054
Australia	151,971,955	180,746,336	109,898,022	136,245,555	127,801,694	222,951,729
Christmas Island	336,901	97,965	767	0	0	15,497
Cocos (Keeling) Islands	0	0	0	4,157,062	-5,000	-5,000
Cook Islands	26,979	-389,581	-44,660	20,199	-14,682	1,075,278
Fiji	-13,999,131	-13,779,970	-13,063,710	-11,812,136	-13,929,381	-4,603,952
French Polynesia	-3,769,006	-12,127,032	-3,828,086	-6,373,910	-9,548,128	-10,032,615
French Southern and Antarctic	8,014	2,017	0	29,496	20,195	20,195
Heard and McDonald Islands	0	0	0	0	0	0
Kiribati	-315,930	-401,836	-822,546	-2,443,751	-2,530,301	-1,555,662
Marshall Islands	-5,243,356	-10,026,245	-8,535,597	-7,792,605	-8,424,900	-491,002
Micronesia	-873,162	47,163	-134,918	849,395	788,476	745,478
Netherlands Antilles	3,796,338	0	0	0	0	-9,966,414
New Caledonia	-82,649	629,315	634,942	608,518	336,574	950,410
New Zealand	-131,198,056	-115,853,714	-145,997,211	-143,739,354	-161,569,681	28,764,477
Niue	256,430	0	20,000	0	0	-113,449
Norfolk Island	39,342	0	0	0	0	-30,154
Palau	832,533	760,221	936,607	1,414,061	1,381,340	1,527,103
Papua New Guinea	-96,654,171	-94,533,704	-66,853,582	-83,298,256	-74,294,382	-28,897,586
Pitcairn Islands	0	0	0	0	0	-18,144
Reunion	-9,515,380	-8,294,529	-8,954,186	-11,421,785	-15,776,299	-10,234,558
Samoa	770,409	680,683	792,162	416,022	-243,979	127,224
Solomon Islands	-391,270	163,995	-1,506,843	-919,075	-648,800	278,107
Tokelau	-304,689	4,065	0	300,433	-10,013	-39,547,135
Tonga	-1,320,634	-1,206,384	-1,108,206	-1,184,083	-1,723,358	1,282,297
Tuvalu	0	0	0	0	0	0
Vanuatu	-1,385,061	-1,018,428	-1,903,439	-6,090,001	-3,437,989	-2,863,863
Wallis and Futuna	95,521	249,127	15,583	0	0	-27,207
						0
Africa	2,237,130,468	1,286,808,754	1,025,579,684	778,785,515	-269,238,896	-1,051,349,056
Algeria	64,295,146	146,548,004	129,899,950	140,827,887	110,719,964	-34,002,139
Angola	6,776,713	19,078,202	11,953,233	10,920,532	4,846,423	-5,826,862
Benin	-102,359	-611,696	-1,680,856	-1,666,573	2,276,468	2,465,603
Botswana	16,315	22,534	124,605	205,100	8,820	-4,180
British Indian Ocean Terr.	15,093	0	13,407	0	0	0
Burkina Faso	-501,023	-196,416	-1,464,684	426,764	1,375,304	-197,916
Burundi	-4,924,204	-2,891,635	-1,559,438	-4,278,205	-5,611,815	-3,192,332
Cabo Verde	-33,238	-5,508	-37,364	172,543	27,919	-1,800,761
Cameroon	-30,736,714	-37,121,495	-5,240,693	-10,500,683	-3,549,993	5,874,682
Central African Republic	363,011	87,152	-5,942	-21,271	-22,384	-218,721
Chad	2,986,486	705,424	-11,843,302	-5,212,248	-8,381,699	3,816,012
Comoros	-22,018	0	-916,788	-735,346	-668,060	148,908

Table B-31.   U.S. Agricultural Balance of Payments by Regions and Individual Countries, 2005–2015—*Continued*

Region	2005	2006	2007	2008	2009	2010
Congo (Brazzaville)	967,960	381,764	6,226,146	414,546	2,211,303	2,036,741
Congo (Kinshasa)	9,578,179	6,826,921	26,164,407	21,129,912	3,936,852	4,413,526
Cote d'Ivoire	-537,325,399	-396,757,539	-379,617,839	-570,406,193	-520,233,295	-687,980,565
Djibouti	21,290,470	13,952,244	2,928,951	60,182,758	53,173,263	17,599,769
Egypt	641,345,223	830,175,073	1,562,076,397	1,703,156,110	1,053,129,461	1,618,524,283
Equatorial Guinea	18,931	398,090	136,986	125,681	144,527	232,995
Eritrea	12,139,923	4,593,740	-147,186	5,657,868	3,918,227	0
Ethiopia	69,810,303	-16,513,960	8,997,130	24,654,248	1,591,435	36,938,819
Gabon	83,837	-773,372	-1,303,754	-2,321,182	-648,748	-5,443,099
Gambia	25,811	37,931	86,471	89,579	-446,832	-2,741,007
Ghana	-10,838,732	-52,347,457	-30,611,894	-22,472,228	-63,892,416	-105,152,501
Guinea	-54,458	-113,918	3,777,392	-556,989	114,016	1,171,854
Guinea-Bissau	-50,159	111,904	-20,024	0	0	98,988
Kenya	-22,645,573	-2,684,223	-12,103,938	-9,764,326	59,447,240	-23,991,994
Lesotho	557,729	435,213	1,397,097	18,377	0	3,230
Liberia	-86,827,436	-127,959,961	-112,854,740	-140,366,030	-72,611,989	-122,532,972
Libya	2,769,775	28,446,583	48,803,977	34,604,125	19,383,461	54,118,627
Madagascar	-30,206,559	-27,375,476	-31,799,044	-27,316,330	-29,021,772	-30,628,601
Malawi	-78,052,342	-27,231,034	-24,862,468	-32,478,990	-33,544,338	-44,748,498
Mali	1,136,696	8,035,774	3,859,730	223,086	296,750	770,961
Mauritania	7,560,654	623,713	3,559,560	5,165,691	1,760,694	3,221,596
Mauritius	-12,770,463	-16,663,157	-3,227,884	-4,780,366	-10,654,275	-10,925,411
Mayotte	0	0	234,726	0	149,863	2,514,605
Morocco	138,997,112	229,901,196	489,994,369	184,928,721	197,476,730	228,205,831
Mozambique	6,218,503	10,837,038	21,525,471	27,418,780	29,557,478	25,224,278
Namibia	-2,165,526	2,145,615	-2,291,154	-1,180,012	-279,318	551,000
Nauru	391,862	1,960,888	6,224,604	6,273,668	2,844,820	1,087,861
Niger	4,199,380	8,552,223	1,479,252	823,351	1,532,227	2,720,754
Nigeria	471,637,059	459,814,930	635,537,304	881,477,799	701,610,375	764,066,599
Rwanda	-3,716,175	-5,650,855	-6,637,759	-10,156,676	-14,346,181	-18,060,626
Sao Tome and Principe	0	-25,437	-2,030	0	-68,953	0
Senegal	3,141,376	2,166,770	2,899,002	-324,444	-390,573	-628,686
Seychelles	261,535	-186,018	-1,010,088	137,375	-6,971	14,777
Sierra Leone	3,373,298	952,384	3,389,706	4,547,579	1,105,666	2,299,117
Somalia	3,648,772	12,362,760	11,517,730	37,883,637	2,090,937	-46,590
South Africa	-41,264,331	-80,365,377	93,763,441	97,220,073	-29,755,688	49,610,271
South Sudan	0	0	0	0	0	0
St Helena	-1,902,509	-972,442	-4,694,728	-9,647,682	-5,800,399	-6,064,960
Sudan	64,176,771	54,109,082	49,754,223	71,135,966	41,949,179	72,566,412
Swaziland	559,115	334,221	592,651	179,403	654,979	835,750
Tanzania	-10,636,604	-2,895,225	-9,693,002	-9,267,883	-23,955,134	-13,319,872
Togo	-3,786,427	-850,038	-3,386,641	-8,979,341	-5,767,936	-7,796,493
Tunisia	25,312,552	83,596,134	156,781,348	72,908,134	118,191,548	217,872,279
Uganda	-5,250,828	-8,183,985	4,415,497	-6,474,502	-16,818,231	-27,105,311
Western Sahara	0	0	0	0	0	0
Zambia	4,390,537	6,071,884	2,068,568	2,908,606	-295,742	-3,801
Zimbabwe	2,051,665	5,280,724	16,235,032	6,377,414	4,917,626	1,105,393

Table B-31.   U.S. Agricultural Balance of Payments by Regions and Individual Countries, 2005–2015—*Continued*

Region	2011	2012	2013	2014	2015	2005–2015 Value Change
Congo (Brazzaville)	16,580,440	2,602,382	9,279,689	4,758,659	-923,954	-1,891,914
Congo (Kinshasa)	9,618,363	11,004,373	-454,838	1,164,886	-7,104,945	-16,683,124
Cote d'Ivoire	-892,424,456	-695,203,135	-782,194,318	-859,543,654	-858,370,669	-321,045,270
Djibouti	37,382,150	43,497,874	46,306,101	17,591,481	32,535,525	11,245,055
Egypt	1,916,472,827	1,120,075,822	913,427,617	1,146,978,236	491,182,293	-150,162,930
Equatorial Guinea	2,792,324	720,684	830,806	614,526	395,281	376,350
Eritrea	-18,689	-30,160	-14,914	-13,900	0	-12,139,923
Ethiopia	-24,139,674	-28,669,693	-46,830,114	-40,128,880	-62,635,937	-132,446,240
Gabon	-10,755,911	54,979	-2,257,468	-1,426,058	-3,038,598	-3,122,435
Gambia	111,665	792,160	2,120,592	6,331	-173,734	-199,545
Ghana	-230,823,890	-116,512,508	-160,966,278	-143,419,188	-193,125,422	-182,286,690
Guinea	1,146,163	-162,622	-1,194,649	-615,665	-195,250	-140,792
Guinea-Bissau	561,213	1,523,668	1,376,513	0	940	51,099
Kenya	-34,849,074	-40,793,093	-18,697,689	-56,340,870	-51,451,463	-28,805,890
Lesotho	6,722,108	13,614,722	0	0	0	-557,729
Liberia	-150,313,547	-136,243,370	-84,899,908	-68,718,867	-30,643,600	56,183,836
Libya	30,387,259	13,114,154	70,911,507	23,892,653	32,494,177	29,724,402
Madagascar	-26,314,016	-36,359,524	-51,874,140	-76,307,372	-121,467,714	-91,261,155
Malawi	-29,585,782	-41,612,398	-47,056,217	-44,636,829	-36,777,432	41,274,910
Mali	1,267,092	1,948,882	-2,323	1,344,112	1,196,917	60,221
Mauritania	-104,331	-131,184	9,137,142	64,949	948,673	-6,611,981
Mauritius	-7,581,475	-8,234,457	-3,682,763	-11,433,555	-12,618,002	152,461
Mayotte	138,638	6,481,928	420,959	832,529	483,254	483,254
Morocco	206,825,802	91,018,226	80,463,277	49,167,451	20,310,654	-118,686,458
Mozambique	56,097,664	18,870,470	-12,667,715	-12,035,218	-15,515,976	-21,734,479
Namibia	5,709,571	1,198,278	-51,377	-4,600,250	7,271,444	9,436,970
Nauru	0	0	0	0	0	-391,862
Niger	5,872,178	283,072	238,459	1,452,456	104,882	-4,094,498
Nigeria	1,103,526,062	906,993,619	953,734,579	671,638,608	541,609,358	69,972,299
Rwanda	-20,263,676	-27,779,791	-19,556,583	-24,290,915	-25,001,328	-21,285,153
Sao Tome and Principe	0	0	0	0	9,639	9,639
Senegal	-774,857	-1,485,419	1,219,775	4,866,381	-1,704,190	-4,845,566
Seychelles	2,095	-161,565	-134,218	-107,809	476,563	215,028
Sierra Leone	5,751,696	1,905,392	141,919	31,670	134,208	-3,239,090
Somalia	3,298,476	3,885,723	904,409	3,794,885	3,720,933	72,161
South Africa	46,544,460	-46,597,623	-43,849,528	-59,678,494	-107,210,537	-65,946,206
South Sudan	3,356,808	3,074,424	2,192,155	30,994,828	2,579,844	2,579,844
St Helena	-7,712,753	-5,825,902	-7,140,578	-8,793,165	-14,342,340	-12,439,831
Sudan	42,223,412	29,647,226	34,563,546	27,734,255	37,334,413	-26,842,358
Swaziland	454,396	1,873,637	1,532,756	1,695,661	1,543,796	984,681
Tanzania	14,805,009	-39,271,895	-17,937,128	-26,080,691	-33,881,100	-23,244,496
Togo	-27,847,258	-1,259,665	-4,163,218	2,512,028	-2,164,938	1,621,489
Tunisia	168,364,591	140,523,681	117,020,080	127,340,786	69,426,496	44,113,944
Uganda	-24,345,046	-25,605,483	-31,281,418	-28,041,322	-28,519,662	-23,268,834
Western Sahara	0	-97,228	0	0	0	0
Zambia	-292,105	-332,809	-231,251	-291,322	-143,775	-4,534,312
Zimbabwe	1,131,338	-1,141,664	-2,345,692	-3,326,332	-7,008,567	*-9,060,232*

Table B-32. Top 30 Purchasers and Suppliers of U.S. Agricultural Products by North American Industry Classification System (NAICS), 2005–2015

Country	2005	2006	2007	2008	2009
TOTAL OF TOP PURCHASERS (EXPORTS)........	33,540,871,765	37,472,578,771	46,396,359,496	59,600,162,761	50,726,406,084
China........................	4,526,745,914	5,586,948,119	6,694,666,993	10,172,123,932	11,597,834,005
Canada.......................	5,683,763,362	6,140,735,424	6,866,481,156	7,617,179,616	7,143,978,576
Mexico.......................	3,809,551,782	4,483,650,893	5,548,453,294	7,905,857,399	5,813,774,720
Japan........................	6,020,419,669	6,287,662,436	7,325,446,039	9,704,526,691	7,149,393,213
South Korea..................	1,654,646,237	2,096,959,661	2,448,418,720	3,957,319,530	2,659,374,309
Germany......................	1,034,172,595	1,001,287,447	1,260,481,652	1,639,542,364	1,134,389,636
Taiwan.......................	1,655,448,934	1,663,361,252	2,245,201,350	2,561,936,001	2,136,581,826
Vietnam......................	80,455,473	100,616,394	235,668,547	372,969,541	366,315,806
Hong Kong....................	422,783,172	503,544,530	613,606,798	705,154,904	1,036,913,349
Spain........................	681,771,685	645,144,728	1,168,584,021	1,280,680,058	772,222,948
Indonesia....................	710,885,652	820,783,539	1,116,543,179	1,570,794,323	1,158,721,478
Netherlands..................	724,204,506	1,156,318,659	1,019,067,868	1,116,847,011	707,998,051
Colombia.....................	485,847,600	626,790,616	921,762,871	1,181,455,414	611,021,172
Turkey.......................	756,615,575	745,782,185	1,089,178,147	1,060,139,787	1,127,664,197
India........................	222,050,281	282,116,702	377,486,160	397,199,840	470,155,519
Italy........................	485,925,144	411,189,963	576,729,662	612,885,335	488,048,715
Thailand.....................	436,580,004	442,901,001	567,507,048	591,927,183	649,499,093
United Kingdom...............	589,528,470	538,381,736	646,572,131	589,101,820	514,929,819
Philippines..................	412,718,386	417,966,650	447,134,634	825,491,453	481,947,901
United Arab Emirates.........	166,092,534	225,648,902	281,772,386	304,074,359	488,459,602
Peru.........................	154,856,186	126,362,681	344,887,509	294,656,490	293,897,380
Saudi Arabia.................	105,968,916	152,257,022	309,058,919	315,111,571	219,186,350
Nigeria......................	527,936,726	474,428,763	657,449,122	943,415,122	762,107,262
Egypt........................	658,107,222	847,324,835	1,572,449,474	1,711,457,086	1,062,858,610
France.......................	426,185,025	440,740,564	482,398,297	495,700,821	369,173,312
Belgium......................	344,594,363	318,298,676	351,685,031	300,452,226	260,288,164
Guatemala....................	210,755,299	315,520,627	345,170,364	431,729,908	325,145,010
Malaysia.....................	222,512,690	213,990,176	290,918,520	255,103,629	367,735,225
Bangladesh...................	55,801,251	58,852,434	158,314,494	151,421,539	143,897,183
Dominican Republic...........	273,947,112	347,012,156	433,265,110	533,907,808	412,893,653
TOTAL OF TOP SUPPLIERS (IMPORTS)...........	27,927,277,779	31,604,390,057	34,590,385,765	37,794,684,521	33,876,126,099
Mexico.......................	4,891,459,541	5,182,703,304	5,943,316,340	6,022,376,717	6,262,356,329
Canada.......................	5,709,646,507	6,715,982,634	7,778,596,720	9,014,779,093	6,782,347,198
Chile........................	1,833,625,501	2,203,212,323	2,297,521,361	2,357,706,898	2,133,114,263
China........................	1,624,228,915	2,147,690,514	2,250,815,064	2,418,301,452	2,255,056,911
Indonesia....................	1,916,172,535	2,280,121,585	2,308,002,746	2,985,555,243	1,969,559,131
Vietnam......................	904,690,385	966,553,181	1,164,785,925	1,279,363,298	1,160,494,514
India........................	810,087,941	741,512,784	653,144,160	755,165,054	646,161,730
Colombia.....................	1,222,113,637	1,246,838,703	1,341,984,067	1,508,558,735	1,431,729,970
Brazil.......................	1,002,621,251	1,142,116,678	1,277,787,101	1,411,538,984	1,396,279,618
Ecuador......................	912,721,038	1,026,434,162	1,045,232,088	1,101,603,616	1,292,203,352
Guatemala....................	736,497,717	711,717,030	863,399,481	993,144,519	1,080,881,160
Peru.........................	355,279,578	416,493,447	502,196,004	558,853,911	567,621,934
Thailand.....................	1,485,446,005	1,905,168,104	1,946,426,594	2,147,971,552	1,846,706,226
Costa Rica...................	829,634,141	1,050,451,489	1,075,605,859	1,096,744,365	1,001,928,765
Cote d'Ivoire................	539,319,427	399,025,608	381,881,920	570,975,685	525,068,856
Honduras.....................	396,861,541	379,812,788	457,687,939	504,553,083	434,612,794
Argentina....................	257,612,326	344,201,608	382,176,251	358,797,116	323,883,733
Norway.......................	89,000,384	137,922,412	157,370,750	147,996,072	316,725,459
Netherlands..................	485,587,099	514,252,995	507,966,384	454,198,461	446,305,175
Nicaragua....................	147,979,439	195,121,284	199,227,440	258,760,526	222,808,188
Turkey.......................	232,493,855	208,277,622	240,089,330	183,123,109	266,515,414
Germany......................	113,198,690	140,865,012	160,564,138	165,411,679	115,046,263
Spain........................	159,918,042	195,365,368	204,728,971	163,956,378	144,402,499
Russian Federation..........	323,779,375	389,462,681	432,402,549	314,174,566	297,815,503
Japan........................	180,258,881	208,376,989	215,739,229	239,070,132	234,811,354
New Zealand..................	232,480,357	222,858,576	251,426,716	224,139,720	206,674,424
Taiwan.......................	162,867,785	152,474,062	166,626,700	196,817,973	175,314,181
Ghana........................	24,672,836	62,447,065	45,529,955	27,910,859	65,754,982
Australia....................	245,532,079	217,965,149	230,106,054	214,852,479	167,974,056
France.......................	101,490,971	98,964,900	108,047,929	118,283,246	106,170,117

Table B-32. Top 30 Purchasers and Suppliers of U.S. Agricultural Products by North American Industry Classification System (NAICS), 2005–2015—*Continued*

Country	2010	2011	2012	2013	2014	2015
TOTAL OF TOP PURCHASERS (EXPORTS)........	60,501,938,979	72,141,047,129	73,449,983,431	70,563,493,055	75,601,653,982	66,459,624,960
China..........	15,481,164,153	17,219,047,075	22,984,689,497	21,562,541,491	20,957,704,776	17,084,251,963
Canada..........	7,896,979,348	8,656,109,897	8,741,196,252	9,287,770,863	9,685,515,426	9,173,484,265
Mexico..........	6,544,842,767	8,710,842,492	8,577,767,749	7,361,328,506	7,741,610,324	7,074,248,772
Japan..........	7,645,932,955	9,094,734,821	8,174,040,027	6,879,088,824	7,574,228,379	6,717,966,272
South Korea	3,344,599,220	4,300,703,402	3,471,319,797	2,767,708,380	3,768,983,552	3,166,264,964
Germany	1,341,170,799	1,276,139,298	1,834,008,874	1,878,362,062	1,823,370,217	1,964,564,038
Taiwan..........	2,085,570,782	2,507,173,955	2,097,867,015	1,772,838,881	2,142,676,279	1,825,364,165
Vietnam..........	503,798,477	783,652,654	923,174,727	1,268,712,101	1,479,168,714	1,541,364,626
Hong Kong	1,201,301,221	1,492,290,227	1,951,112,394	2,066,723,820	1,628,461,856	1,502,929,617
Spain..........	1,046,186,754	1,110,263,935	1,148,096,582	1,499,873,476	1,676,566,061	1,470,300,656
Indonesia	1,469,164,483	2,001,708,773	1,668,355,829	1,716,888,858	1,912,985,326	1,416,803,856
Netherlands	803,436,315	1,018,066,123	827,752,699	920,024,893	1,414,717,801	1,385,738,346
Colombia..........	527,921,636	648,179,319	470,685,034	626,795,797	1,425,933,432	1,292,297,317
Turkey	1,664,435,684	2,078,014,311	1,507,425,003	1,522,480,819	1,617,105,819	1,139,695,399
India..........	485,930,823	589,099,327	650,574,910	725,685,412	924,937,866	1,045,968,598
Italy..........	540,590,878	629,891,781	540,978,713	783,814,249	778,116,055	848,033,010
Thailand	702,392,920	905,479,713	948,850,059	756,643,167	771,402,226	810,001,684
United Kingdom	548,593,158	508,699,948	675,997,311	682,572,307	779,558,252	730,369,174
Philippines	549,198,090	880,702,912	770,496,046	812,642,333	917,299,776	716,334,051
United Arab Emirates	567,145,066	591,151,943	580,502,605	763,531,251	687,496,388	698,866,883
Peru	489,831,117	609,737,413	260,259,164	470,387,117	858,265,396	617,136,013
Saudi Arabia	304,283,863	606,147,643	509,536,450	408,559,279	578,698,762	584,600,916
Nigeria	808,287,098	1,196,293,482	984,037,461	987,821,215	726,583,568	557,207,627
Egypt..........	1,630,060,883	1,936,864,794	1,135,552,780	929,379,255	1,166,280,207	507,840,052
France	471,387,451	494,259,958	429,617,209	496,252,300	498,432,666	482,389,506
Belgium..........	447,042,292	299,033,376	259,509,037	276,779,502	386,875,839	447,354,272
Guatemala	357,502,491	488,281,419	397,401,887	371,090,697	465,237,826	446,818,759
Malaysia..........	343,930,979	555,023,965	408,121,389	432,441,565	459,680,689	415,918,102
Bangladesh	224,024,651	368,118,898	123,853,441	172,189,060	286,382,446	409,665,957
Dominican Republic..........	475,232,625	585,334,275	397,203,490	362,565,575	467,378,058	385,846,100
TOTAL OF TOP SUPPLIERS (IMPORTS)..........	39,513,052,525	47,620,186,524	46,846,532,994	50,047,514,749	54,138,454,974	52,110,142,640
Mexico..........	7,450,833,867	8,507,590,319	9,011,356,866	9,642,375,274	10,730,093,755	11,574,753,241
Canada..........	7,347,472,058	8,007,475,795	8,683,654,772	9,833,926,225	10,444,235,166	9,381,269,885
Chile..........	2,185,315,473	2,439,848,083	2,595,492,999	3,358,839,782	3,471,026,500	3,171,579,848
China..........	2,622,150,980	2,905,133,609	2,948,443,236	3,045,122,359	3,157,830,113	3,000,046,524
Indonesia	3,104,338,168	4,268,938,269	3,506,533,419	3,206,324,483	3,251,075,102	2,803,041,407
Vietnam..........	1,566,879,509	1,960,111,947	2,025,088,687	2,281,996,392	2,691,611,767	2,415,098,514
India..........	837,968,678	1,335,167,419	1,479,402,625	1,836,557,267	2,214,324,298	2,149,415,223
Colombia..........	1,610,402,144	2,010,628,588	1,762,594,534	1,863,587,006	2,027,878,234	2,060,875,625
Brazil..........	1,744,858,171	2,518,730,704	2,146,137,843	2,153,098,005	2,374,947,556	1,867,550,674
Ecuador	1,294,355,088	1,609,555,027	1,527,835,045	1,638,016,633	1,931,567,256	1,797,527,664
Guatemala	1,065,081,131	1,634,093,047	1,652,748,920	1,607,498,085	1,598,601,652	1,642,751,194
Peru	725,857,073	1,049,250,912	987,996,451	1,097,590,954	1,378,904,346	1,412,731,504
Thailand	2,310,671,914	2,964,685,829	2,150,362,997	1,549,136,512	1,381,692,110	1,308,796,533
Costa Rica	1,152,699,192	1,278,921,206	1,330,631,237	1,325,995,583	1,383,574,568	1,249,143,059
Cote d'Ivoire	688,099,514	893,024,559	697,250,291	784,582,031	862,191,805	858,878,322
Honduras	490,432,468	661,317,842	728,131,681	644,514,258	683,022,727	698,681,881
Argentina	339,187,867	454,715,021	574,128,332	821,747,702	668,455,137	607,334,652
Norway	496,535,897	323,894,348	250,600,559	312,695,328	422,118,107	484,356,516
Netherlands	493,330,585	525,505,675	456,924,159	448,373,017	493,079,242	463,231,418
Nicaragua	281,613,709	327,349,003	359,523,128	289,725,174	363,466,695	378,674,494
Turkey	175,074,540	196,351,759	263,636,387	306,119,382	401,549,834	358,980,032
Germany	75,178,382	105,553,169	152,144,702	217,199,905	253,456,785	347,876,784
Spain..........	188,533,072	174,477,467	187,939,051	198,249,296	233,153,747	335,960,179
Russian Federation	271,231,444	280,108,345	232,834,577	332,221,018	340,632,398	335,684,489
Japan..........	215,031,659	239,470,858	263,711,051	270,487,660	299,454,970	297,556,224
New Zealand	223,413,694	215,163,891	209,942,601	230,124,214	269,517,716	275,867,767
Taiwan..........	177,309,284	214,794,983	210,007,246	198,281,644	216,423,789	221,700,342
Ghana..........	107,516,762	248,897,922	153,818,330	173,403,989	177,106,841	213,170,641
Australia	138,415,762	132,544,543	156,508,658	210,822,983	241,411,886	210,304,225
France	133,264,440	136,886,385	141,152,610	168,902,588	176,050,872	187,303,779

Table B-33.   Top 30 Suppliers of U.S. Agricultural Products by North American Industry Classification System (NAICS), 2005–2015

Country	2005	2006	2007	2008	2009	2010
TOTAL OF TOP SUPPLIERS (IMPORTS)	27,927,277,779	31,604,390,057	34,590,385,765	37,794,684,521	33,876,126,099	39,513,052,525
Mexico	4,891,459,541	5,182,703,304	5,943,316,340	6,022,376,717	6,262,356,329	7,450,833,867
Canada	5,709,646,507	6,715,982,634	7,778,596,720	9,014,779,093	6,782,347,198	7,347,472,058
Chile	1,833,625,501	2,203,212,323	2,297,521,361	2,357,706,898	2,133,114,263	2,185,315,473
China	1,624,228,915	2,147,690,514	2,250,815,064	2,418,301,452	2,255,056,911	2,622,150,980
Indonesia	1,916,172,535	2,280,121,585	2,308,002,746	2,985,555,243	1,969,559,131	3,104,338,168
Vietnam	904,690,385	966,553,181	1,164,785,925	1,279,363,298	1,160,494,514	1,566,879,509
India	810,087,941	741,512,784	653,144,160	755,165,054	646,161,730	837,968,678
Colombia	1,222,113,637	1,246,838,703	1,341,984,067	1,508,558,735	1,431,729,970	1,610,402,144
Brazil	1,002,621,251	1,142,116,678	1,277,787,101	1,411,538,984	1,396,279,618	1,744,858,171
Ecuador	912,721,038	1,026,434,162	1,045,232,088	1,101,603,616	1,292,203,352	1,294,355,088
Guatemala	736,497,717	711,717,030	863,399,481	993,144,519	1,080,881,160	1,065,081,131
Peru	355,279,578	416,493,447	502,196,004	558,853,911	567,621,934	725,857,073
Thailand	1,485,446,005	1,905,168,104	1,946,426,594	2,147,971,552	1,846,706,226	2,310,671,914
Costa Rica	829,634,141	1,050,451,489	1,075,605,859	1,096,744,365	1,001,928,765	1,152,699,192
Cote d'Ivoire	539,319,427	399,025,608	381,881,920	570,975,685	525,068,856	688,099,514
Honduras	396,861,541	379,812,788	457,687,939	504,553,083	434,612,794	490,432,468
Argentina	257,612,326	344,201,608	382,176,251	358,797,116	323,883,733	339,187,867
Norway	89,000,384	137,922,412	157,370,750	147,996,072	316,725,459	496,535,897
Netherlands	485,587,099	514,252,995	507,966,384	454,198,461	446,305,175	493,330,585
Nicaragua	147,979,439	195,121,284	199,227,440	258,760,526	222,808,188	281,613,709
Turkey	232,493,855	208,277,622	240,089,330	183,123,109	266,515,414	175,074,540
Germany	113,198,690	140,865,012	160,564,138	165,411,679	115,046,263	75,178,382
Spain	159,918,042	195,365,368	204,728,971	163,956,378	144,402,499	188,533,072
Russian Federation	323,779,375	389,462,681	432,402,549	314,174,566	297,815,503	271,231,444
Japan	180,258,881	208,376,989	215,739,229	239,070,132	234,811,354	215,031,659
New Zealand	232,480,357	222,858,576	251,426,716	224,139,720	206,476,424	223,413,694
Taiwan	162,867,785	152,474,062	166,626,700	196,817,973	175,314,181	177,309,284
Ghana	24,672,836	62,447,065	45,529,955	27,910,859	65,754,982	107,516,762
Australia	245,532,079	217,965,149	230,106,054	214,852,479	167,974,056	138,415,762
France	101,490,971	98,964,900	108,047,929	118,283,246	106,170,117	133,264,440

Table B-33.   Top 30 Suppliers of U.S. Agricultural Products by North American Industry Classification System (NAICS), 2005–2015—*Continued*

Country	2011	2012	2013	2014	2015
TOTAL OF TOP SUPPLIERS (IMPORTS)............	47,620,186,524	46,846,532,994	50,047,514,749	54,138,454,974	52,110,142,640
Mexico...	8,507,590,319	9,011,356,866	9,642,375,274	10,730,093,755	11,574,753,241
Canada..	8,007,475,795	8,683,654,772	9,833,926,225	10,444,235,166	9,381,269,885
Chile...	2,439,848,083	2,595,492,999	3,358,839,782	3,471,026,500	3,171,579,848
China..	2,905,133,609	2,948,443,236	3,045,122,359	3,157,830,113	3,000,046,524
Indonesia...	4,268,938,269	3,506,533,419	3,206,324,483	3,251,075,102	2,803,041,407
Vietnam...	1,960,111,947	2,025,088,687	2,281,996,392	2,691,611,767	2,415,098,514
India..	1,335,167,419	1,479,402,625	1,836,557,267	2,214,324,298	2,149,415,223
Colombia..	2,010,628,588	1,762,594,534	1,863,587,006	2,027,878,234	2,060,875,625
Brazil...	2,518,730,704	2,146,137,843	2,153,098,005	2,374,947,556	1,867,550,674
Ecuador...	1,609,555,027	1,527,835,045	1,638,016,633	1,931,567,256	1,797,527,664
Guatemala...	1,634,093,047	1,652,748,920	1,607,498,085	1,598,601,652	1,642,751,194
Peru..	1,049,250,912	987,996,451	1,097,590,954	1,378,904,346	1,412,731,504
Thailand..	2,964,685,829	2,150,362,997	1,549,136,512	1,381,692,110	1,308,796,533
Costa Rica..	1,278,921,206	1,330,631,237	1,325,995,583	1,383,574,568	1,249,143,059
Cote d'Ivoire......................................	893,024,559	697,250,291	784,582,031	862,191,805	858,878,322
Honduras..	661,317,842	728,131,681	644,514,258	683,022,727	698,681,881
Argentina...	454,715,021	574,128,332	821,747,702	668,455,137	607,334,652
Norway..	323,894,348	250,600,559	312,695,328	422,118,107	484,356,516
Netherlands.......................................	525,505,675	456,924,159	448,373,017	493,079,242	463,231,418
Nicaragua...	327,349,003	359,523,128	289,725,174	363,466,695	378,674,494
Turkey..	196,351,759	263,636,387	306,119,382	401,549,834	358,980,032
Germany...	105,553,169	152,144,702	217,199,905	253,456,785	347,876,784
Spain...	174,477,467	187,939,051	198,249,296	233,153,747	335,960,179
Russian Federation	280,108,345	232,834,577	332,221,018	340,632,398	335,684,489
Japan...	239,470,858	263,711,051	270,487,660	299,454,970	297,556,224
New Zealand	215,163,891	209,942,601	230,124,214	269,517,716	275,867,767
Taiwan..	214,794,983	210,007,246	198,281,644	216,423,789	221,700,342
Ghana...	248,897,922	153,818,330	173,403,989	177,106,841	213,170,641
Australia..	132,544,543	156,508,658	210,822,983	241,411,886	210,304,225
France..	136,886,385	141,152,610	168,902,588	176,050,872	187,303,779

Table B-34.   U.S. Total Exports, Imports, and Balances by Area, 2000–2015

EXPORTS

Year	WORLD	NAFTA	Japan	China	European Union (EU-28)	Other Americas	ASEAN - 10	Rest of World
2000	781,918	322,065	64,924	16,185	168,619	179,707	47,138	135,833
2001	729,100	309,207	57,452	19,182	162,525	57,344	43,789	123,749
2002	693,104	318,538	51,449	22,128	147,049	50,814	41,924	121,070
2003	724,771	361,171	52,004	28,368	155,889	51,202	45,244	124,464
2004	814,875	403,339	53,569	34,428	172,057	60,560	47,614	145,646
2005	901,082	451,276	54,681	41,192	186,201	71,192	49,469	165,817
2006	1,025,969	489,509	58,459	53,673	212,880	86,898	56,129	193,255
2007	1,148,197	546,399	61,160	62,937	244,413	104,703	59,524	230,182
2008	1,287,441	441,050	65,142	69,733	272,277	134,029	66,898	266,781
2009	1,056,042	548,563	51,134	69,497	220,801	107,500	53,781	219,512
2010	1,278,493	647,413	60,472	91,911	239,903	299,771	70,399	266,870
2011	1,482,507	691,726	65,800	104,122	269,580	356,825	76,395	318,972
2012	1,545,821	711,204	69,976	110,517	265,683	377,571	75,421	332,322
2013	1,578,439	736,701	65,216	121,721	262,086	383,521	78,978	339,052
2014	1,620,532	670,020	66,827	123,676	276,142	392,900	78,587	338,596
2015	1,504,914	321,118	62,472	116,186	272,688	341,559	75,080	308,461

IMPORTS

Year	WORLD	NAFTA	Japan	China	European Union (EU-28)	Other Americas	ASEAN-10	Rest of World
2000	1,239,449	207,047	146,479	100,018	227,751	95,135	87,945	215,356
2001	813,221	1,943,417	126,473	102,278	227,564	87,781	76,385	192,860
2002	838,040	1,977,834	121,429	125,193	233,495	90,479	78,340	189,272
2003	920,777	2,071,668	118,037	152,436	254,394	102,845	81,853	211,506
2004	1,083,707	227,701,264	129,805	196,682	283,610	125,909	88,257	259,926
2005	1,242,228	2,534,574	138,004	243,470	310,802	154,081	98,915	298,388
2006	1,383,088	2,869,585	148,181	287,774	332,412	165,724	111,201	339,285
2007	1,458,392	2,930,568	145,463	321,443	354,741	167,800	111,007	361,081
2008	1,575,755	3,065,927	139,262	337,773	367,888	194,195	110,141	432,615
2009	1,180,569	220,044,679	95,804	296,374	282,052	135,823	92,100	281,814
2010	1,942,678	286,131	120,552	364,953	319,600	164,521	107,722	361,543
2011	2,246,932	326,551	128,928	399,371	368,902	217,770	118,263	439,464
2012	2,316,774	343,832	146,432	425,619	382,199	215,441	122,887	424,765
2013	2,305,348	349,102	138,574	440,434	387,643	198,411	126,946	402,485
2014	2,389,293	355,877	134,004	466,754	418,201	188,119	137,067	398,109
2015	2,271,117	421,603	131,120	481,881	426,006	147,021	151,662	344,269

BALANCES

Year	WORLD	NAFTA	Japan	China	European Union (EU-28)	Other Americas	ASEAN-10	Rest of World
2000	-457,531	115,018	-81,555	-83,833	-59,131	84,572	-40,806	-79,523
2001	-84,121	114,865	-69,022	-83,096	-65,039	-30,437	-32,596	-69,110
2002	-144,936	120,755	-69,979	-103,065	-86,446	-39,664	-36,416	-68,202
2003	-196,006	154,004	-66,032	-124,068	-98,505	-51,642	-36,609	-87,042
2004	-268,832	175,638	-76,237	-162,254	-111,553	-65,349	-40,643	-114,280
2005	-341,146	197,819	-83,323	-202,278	-124,600	-82,889	-49,446	-132,571
2006	-357,119	202,551	-89,722	-234,101	-119,532	-78,826	-55,071	-146,030
2007	-310,195	253,342	-84,304	-258,506	-110,328	-63,097	-51,484	-130,900
2008	-288,314	134,457	-74,120	-268,040	-95,611	-60,165	-43,243	-165,834
2009	-124,527	328,518	-44,669	-226,877	-61,250	-28,323	-38,319	-62,302
2010	-664,185	361,282	-60,080	-273,042	-79,697	135,250	-37,323	-94,674
2011	-764,425	365,175	-63,128	-295,250	-99,322	139,055	-41,868	-120,492
2012	-770,953	367,372	-70,450	-315,102	-116,517	162,131	-47,465	-92,443
2013	-726,909	387,599	-73,358	-318,713	-125,557	185,110	-47,968	-63,433
2014	-768,761	314,143	-67,176	-343,079	-142,058	204,781	-58,480	-59,513
2015	-766,204	-100,485	-68,648	-365,695	-153,318	194,539	-76,582	-35,808

Table B-35.   U.S. Trade in Services, by Type of Service and by Country or Affiliation, 2005–2015

(Millions of dollars.)

Country	Exports — Total services										
	2005	2006	2007	2008	2009	2010	2011	2012	2013	2014	2015
ALL COUNTRIES......................	373,006	416,738	488,396	532,817	512,722	563,333	627,781	656,411	701,455	743,257	750,860
Canada.............................	32,794	37,853	42,663	45,375	43,463	53,126	58,319	61,943	62,850	62,016	56,436
Europe..........................	151,748	168,549	204,532	227,640	207,429	214,164	238,487	243,330	249,242	268,636	274,318
Austria................................	n.a.	n.a.	n.a.	n.a.	n.a.	n.a.	n.a.	n.a.	1,469	1,571	1,563
Belgium[1]............................	4,712	5,650	6,590	7,300	7,534	8,001	10,514	11,441	5,442	5,799	6,149
Bulgaria..............................	n.a.	n.a.	n.a.	n.a.	n.a.	n.a.	n.a.	n.a.	353	442	445
Croatia...............................	n.a.	n.a.	n.a.	n.a.	n.a.	n.a.	n.a.	n.a.	230	363	363
Cyprus...............................	n.a.	n.a.	n.a.	n.a.	n.a.	n.a.	n.a.	n.a.	301	217	185
Czech Republic	n.a.	n.a.	n.a.	n.a.	n.a.	n.a.	n.a.	n.a.	1,217	1,200	1,196
Denmark.............................	n.a.	n.a.	n.a.	n.a.	n.a.	n.a.	n.a.	n.a.	4,002	3,954	4,284
Estonia...............................	n.a.	n.a.	n.a.	n.a.	n.a.	n.a.	n.a.	n.a.	111	134	131
Finland...............................	n.a.	n.a.	n.a.	n.a.	n.a.	n.a.	n.a.	n.a.	2,398	2,159	1,822
France...............................	12,892	13,044	15,098	17,232	16,369	16,761	18,721	17,631	18,558	19,212	19,669
Germany.............................	20,373	19,951	24,451	27,488	24,576	24,896	27,070	26,807	26,939	28,170	29,762
Greece...............................	n.a.	n.a.	n.a.	n.a.	n.a.	n.a.	n.a.	n.a.	943	1,023	952
Hungary..............................	n.a.	n.a.	n.a.	n.a.	n.a.	n.a.	n.a.	n.a.	906	907	991
Ireland...............................	n.a.	16,838	22,196	25,678	26,137	25,979	29,483	29,631	32,799	40,402	41,909
Italy...................................	7,100	7,465	9,160	9,554	8,513	8,452	9,199	8,679	8,567	9,056	9,091
Latvia................................	n.a.	n.a.	n.a.	n.a.	n.a.	n.a.	n.a.	n.a.	103	125	138
Lithuania............................	n.a.	n.a.	n.a.	n.a.	n.a.	n.a.	n.a.	n.a.	180	200	217
Luxembourg[1]......................	n.a.	n.a.	n.a.	n.a.	n.a.	n.a.	n.a.	n.a.	6,539	6,648	6,546
Malta.................................	n.a.	n.a.	n.a.	n.a.	n.a.	n.a.	n.a.	n.a.	199	178	169
Netherlands........................	8,581	9,324	11,775	15,504	13,269	12,990	15,461	15,476	15,648	17,067	16,312
Norway...............................	1,968	2,160	2,818	3,296	2,780	3,387	3,632	3,818	3,656	3,862	3,720
Poland...............................	n.a.	n.a.	n.a.	n.a.	n.a.	n.a.	n.a.	n.a.	2,328	2,414	2,436
Portugal.............................	n.a.	n.a.	n.a.	n.a.	n.a.	n.a.	n.a.	n.a.	1,087	1,205	1,118
Romania.............................	n.a.	n.a.	n.a.	n.a.	n.a.	n.a.	n.a.	n.a.	1,017	945	968
Russia...............................	n.a.	n.a.	n.a.	n.a.	n.a.	n.a.	n.a.	n.a.	6,137	6,661	4,682
Slovakia.............................	n.a.	n.a.	n.a.	n.a.	n.a.	n.a.	n.a.	n.a.	286	342	352
Slovenia.............................	n.a.	n.a.	n.a.	n.a.	n.a.	n.a.	n.a.	n.a.	183	191	201
Spain.................................	4,472	5,427	6,694	7,950	6,977	6,676	7,442	6,599	6,348	6,748	6,675
Sweden..............................	4,304	4,063	5,057	5,655	5,542	5,834	5,714	5,763	6,102	6,491	6,138
Switzerland.........................	11,567	13,558	17,141	20,132	19,585	21,719	23,736	27,467	27,462	29,128	31,112
Turkey...............................	n.a.	n.a.	n.a.	n.a.	n.a.	n.a.	n.a.	n.a.	2,952	2,839	3,118
United Kingdom	44,313	49,695	59,185	59,983	50,606	53,568	57,314	59,535	59,806	64,095	66,930
Other.................................	31,466	21,377	24,369	27,868	25,543	25,901	30,198	30,485	4,972	4,886	4,977
Latin America and Other Western Hemisphere......................	62,387	73,096	88,484	95,964	93,358	106,293	118,308	123,140	149,833	159,682	159,304
South and Central America	44,590	49,679	57,247	63,733	61,502	70,809	81,465	87,374	94,568	98,444	101,274
Argentina............................	1,853	2,272	2,805	3,433	3,735	4,820	5,813	6,284	7,109	7,261	8,070
Brazil.................................	5,887	7,439	10,058	12,788	13,572	18,405	23,270	25,093	26,808	28,746	28,146
Chile.................................	1,264	1,434	1,769	2,001	2,047	2,452	3,271	3,610	3,441	3,697	4,006
Colombia............................	n.a.	n.a.	n.a.	n.a.	n.a.	n.a.	n.a.	n.a.	6,240	6,701	6,470
Costa Rica..........................	n.a.	n.a.	n.a.	n.a.	n.a.	n.a.	n.a.	n.a.	1,704	1,750	1,771
El Salvador.........................	n.a.	n.a.	n.a.	n.a.	n.a.	n.a.	n.a.	n.a.	778	866	1,017
Guatemala..........................	n.a.	n.a.	n.a.	n.a.	n.a.	n.a.	n.a.	n.a.	1,378	1,498	1,487
Honduras............................	n.a.	n.a.	n.a.	n.a.	n.a.	n.a.	n.a.	n.a.	903	983	998
Mexico...............................	22,533	23,802	24,978	26,232	22,940	24,614	26,436	28,190	29,865	30,245	31,509
Nicaragua...........................	n.a.	n.a.	n.a.	n.a.	n.a.	n.a.	n.a.	n.a.	375	401	414
Panama..............................	n.a.	n.a.	n.a.	n.a.	n.a.	n.a.	n.a.	n.a.	1,497	1,590	1,640
Peru..................................	n.a.	n.a.	n.a.	n.a.	n.a.	n.a.	n.a.	n.a.	3,017	3,034	3,879
Venezuela...........................	2,629	3,152	4,085	4,811	5,278	5,141	5,674	6,445	7,371	6,868	6,839
Other.................................	10,424	11,579	13,550	14,470	13,930	15,376	17,002	17,752	4,083	4,804	5,027
Other Western Hemisphere..........	17,796	23,417	31,237	32,231	31,856	35,484	36,843	35,766	55,264	61,238	58,030
Bermuda.............................	4,923	6,327	8,228	9,591	10,831	11,263	11,169	9,737	10,640	11,165	11,841
Dominican Republic...............	n.a.	n.a.	n.a.	n.a.	n.a.	n.a.	n.a.	n.a.	1,468	1,544	1,553
United Kingdom Islands, Caribbean............................	n.a.	n.a.	n.a.	n.a.	n.a.	n.a.	n.a.	n.a.	36,627	41,623	37,373
Other.................................	12,874	17,090	23,009	22,641	21,024	24,221	25,673	26,028	6,529	6,906	7,263
Africa..............................	7,159	8,363	9,517	10,827	11,450	11,997	13,227	13,450	13,791	14,518	14,566
Morocco.............................	n.a.	n.a.	n.a.	n.a.	n.a.	n.a.	n.a.	n.a.	581	551	657
Nigeria...............................	n.a.	n.a.	n.a.	n.a.	n.a.	n.a.	n.a.	n.a.	2,302	2,633	2,750

° = Transactions are possible but are zero for a given period.
* = Transactions between zero and +/- $500,000.
D = Suppressed to avoid disclosure of individual companies.
n.a. = Transactions are possible, but data are not available.
..... = Not applicable
n.i.e. = Not included elsewhere
[1] For the years 1999–2012, data presented in the line for "Belgium" include both Belgium and Luxembourg.

Table B-35. U.S. Trade in Services, by Type of Service and by Country or Affiliation, 2005–2015—*Continued*

(Millions of dollars.)

Country	Imports — Total services										
	2005	2006	2007	2008	2009	2010	2011	2012	2013	2014	2015
ALL COUNTRIES......................	304,448	341,165	372,575	409,052	386,801	409,313	435,761	452,013	461,087	481,264	488,657
Canada............................	22,582	23,921	25,694	25,973	23,691	27,351	30,518	31,138	30,779	30,277	28,992
Europe..........................	134,228	153,197	168,728	184,044	167,096	172,108	185,316	189,335	194,678	203,444	205,710
Austria.......................	n.a.	n.a.	n.a.	n.a.	n.a.	n.a.	n.a.	n.a.	1,789	1,872	1,553
Belgium[1].....................	2,975	3,524	4,152	4,684	5,440	5,430	6,397	6,242	5,149	5,782	5,808
Bulgaria.......................	n.a.	n.a.	n.a.	n.a.	n.a.	n.a.	n.a.	n.a.	483	505	454
Croatia........................	n.a.	n.a.	n.a.	n.a.	n.a.	n.a.	n.a.	n.a.	192	225	232
Cyprus........................	n.a.	n.a.	n.a.	n.a.	n.a.	n.a.	n.a.	n.a.	132	165	159
Czech Republic..............	n.a.	n.a.	n.a.	n.a.	n.a.	n.a.	n.a.	n.a.	920	1,013	1,123
Denmark......................	n.a.	n.a.	n.a.	n.a.	n.a.	n.a.	n.a.	n.a.	2,105	2,259	2,681
Estonia........................	n.a.	n.a.	n.a.	n.a.	n.a.	n.a.	n.a.	n.a.	142	131	106
Finland........................	n.a.	n.a.	n.a.	n.a.	n.a.	n.a.	n.a.	n.a.	1,833	2,271	2,069
France.........................	12,957	15,257	16,396	15,148	15,548	15,820	17,571	16,543	14,995	16,455	16,372
Germany......................	23,818	26,911	29,881	33,372	28,668	28,397	30,028	31,290	32,491	32,494	31,668
Greece........................	n.a.	n.a.	n.a.	n.a.	n.a.	n.a.	n.a.	n.a.	2,325	2,443	2,726
Hungary.......................	n.a.	n.a.	n.a.	n.a.	n.a.	n.a.	n.a.	n.a.	686	760	809
Ireland........................	n.a.	8,868	13,474	13,822	12,716	12,071	12,539	13,037	13,637	14,260	15,882
Italy...........................	9,426	10,067	10,211	9,913	8,690	9,552	10,494	10,838	10,353	10,568	10,823
Latvia.........................	n.a.	n.a.	n.a.	n.a.	n.a.	n.a.	n.a.	n.a.	107	72	84
Lithuania.....................	n.a.	n.a.	n.a.	n.a.	n.a.	n.a.	n.a.	n.a.	449	449	485
Luxembourg[1]..............	n.a.	n.a.	n.a.	n.a.	n.a.	n.a.	n.a.	n.a.	1,646	1,647	1,796
Malta..........................	n.a.	n.a.	n.a.	n.a.	n.a.	n.a.	n.a.	n.a.	396	462	659
Netherlands.................	7,767	7,709	7,519	8,708	7,159	8,061	8,495	8,299	9,302	9,651	10,181
Norway........................	1,638	1,639	1,326	2,230	1,624	1,811	2,086	2,345	2,575	2,728	2,585
Poland.........................	n.a.	n.a.	n.a.	n.a.	n.a.	n.a.	n.a.	n.a.	1,913	1,737	1,795
Portugal.......................	n.a.	n.a.	n.a.	n.a.	n.a.	n.a.	n.a.	n.a.	1,487	1,618	1,517
Romania.......................	n.a.	n.a.	n.a.	n.a.	n.a.	n.a.	n.a.	n.a.	1,072	1,191	1,346
Russia.........................	n.a.	n.a.	n.a.	n.a.	n.a.	n.a.	n.a.	n.a.	2,725	2,586	2,400
Slovakia.......................	n.a.	n.a.	n.a.	n.a.	n.a.	n.a.	n.a.	n.a.	85	129	152
Slovenia.......................	n.a.	n.a.	n.a.	n.a.	n.a.	n.a.	n.a.	n.a.	89	91	82
Spain..........................	3,240	3,939	4,452	5,030	4,808	4,852	5,666	5,501	5,256	5,620	5,687
Sweden........................	2,325	2,879	3,133	3,662	3,623	3,098	2,945	2,935	2,790	3,237	3,298
Switzerland...................	12,560	14,811	16,991	19,274	19,307	19,892	19,699	21,740	22,210	22,034	21,323
Turkey.........................	n.a.	n.a.	n.a.	n.a.	n.a.	n.a.	n.a.	n.a.	2,115	2,107	2,080
United Kingdom..............	33,682	38,614	41,870	45,259	38,510	42,307	46,997	46,888	49,038	52,285	52,891
Other..........................	23,841	18,978	19,324	22,942	21,001	20,818	22,399	23,674	4,190	4,598	4,886
Latin America and Other Western Hemisphere......................	54,687	61,409	65,585	79,213	84,602	87,596	88,913	91,285	91,950	96,711	99,715
South and Central America.........	26,153	29,171	31,063	34,307	31,370	32,790	37,044	39,981	42,265	46,290	50,112
Argentina......................	785	905	1,026	1,259	1,186	1,432	1,714	1,898	1,746	1,669	2,068
Brazil..........................	1,817	3,012	3,499	4,514	4,703	5,143	6,959	7,498	7,679	8,275	7,833
Chile..........................	657	1,035	881	1,004	956	1,045	1,346	1,544	1,456	1,426	1,568
Colombia......................	n.a.	n.a.	n.a.	n.a.	n.a.	n.a.	n.a.	n.a.	2,286	2,878	3,216
Costa Rica.....................	n.a.	n.a.	n.a.	n.a.	n.a.	n.a.	n.a.	n.a.	2,264	2,301	2,591
El Salvador....................	n.a.	n.a.	n.a.	n.a.	n.a.	n.a.	n.a.	n.a.	1,112	751	770
Guatemala....................	n.a.	n.a.	n.a.	n.a.	n.a.	n.a.	n.a.	n.a.	923	1,022	999
Honduras......................	n.a.	n.a.	n.a.	n.a.	n.a.	n.a.	n.a.	n.a.	642	665	648
Mexico.........................	14,421	14,870	15,334	15,904	14,021	13,966	14,663	15,444	17,256	19,887	21,930
Nicaragua.....................	n.a.	n.a.	n.a.	n.a.	n.a.	n.a.	n.a.	n.a.	547	590	604
Panama........................	n.a.	n.a.	n.a.	n.a.	n.a.	n.a.	n.a.	n.a.	1,101	1,276	1,283
Peru...........................	n.a.	n.a.	n.a.	n.a.	n.a.	n.a.	n.a.	n.a.	2,092	2,137	2,000
Venezuela.....................	506	624	642	718	708	620	686	776	658	681	819
Other..........................	7,966	8,725	9,680	10,908	9,795	10,584	11,675	12,822	2,502	2,711	2,894
Other Western Hemisphere..........	28,534	32,237	34,522	44,906	53,232	54,807	51,869	51,304	49,685	50,422	49,603
Bermuda.......................	12,416	15,745	17,892	24,675	33,769	31,975	29,070	27,659	27,053	26,485	25,051
Dominican Republic...........	n.a.	n.a.	n.a.	n.a.	n.a.	n.a.	n.a.	n.a.	3,348	3,854	4,363
United Kingdom Islands, Caribbean........................	n.a.	n.a.	n.a.	n.a.	n.a.	n.a.	n.a.	n.a.	7,855	7,652	7,010
Other..........................	16,119	16,492	16,631	20,230	19,462	22,831	22,798	23,646	11,429	12,431	13,179
Africa..............................	4,640	5,147	6,057	7,683	8,011	7,934	9,029	8,903	8,445	8,373	8,239
Morocco.......................	n.a.	n.a.	n.a.	n.a.	n.a.	n.a.	n.a.	n.a.	444	553	585
Nigeria........................	n.a.	n.a.	n.a.	n.a.	n.a.	n.a.	n.a.	n.a.	524	485	468

Table B-35. U.S. Trade in Services, by Type of Service and by Country or Affiliation, 2005–2015—*Continued*

(Millions of dollars.)

Country	Exports Total services										
	2005	2006	2007	2008	2009	2010	2011	2012	2013	2014	2015
South Africa	1,596	1,888	2,191	2,253	2,489	2,488	2,875	2,898	2,902	3,062	3,184
Other	5,563	6,475	7,326	8,575	8,961	9,509	10,352	10,552	8,007	8,271	7,976
Middle East	16,276	19,839	20,290	21,515	22,856	21,148	23,195	24,633	26,390	27,835	29,218
Bahrain	n.a.	n.a.	n.a.	n.a.	n.a.	n.a.	n.a.	n.a.	399	347	321
Israel	2,559	2,929	3,185	3,549	3,624	3,609	4,106	4,090	4,521	4,812	4,772
Jordan	n.a.	n.a.	n.a.	n.a.	n.a.	n.a.	n.a.	n.a.	645	686	710
Oman	n.a.	n.a.	n.a.	n.a.	n.a.	n.a.	n.a.	n.a.	367	417	434
Saudi Arabia	2,564	3,209	4,489	5,019	6,176	5,883	6,465	8,236	9,335	9,352	9,943
Other	11,152	13,700	12,616	12,947	13,056	11,657	12,625	12,307	11,123	12,220	13,038
Asia and Pacific	97,344	106,766	120,675	129,114	131,694	154,029	173,711	187,366	196,572	207,919	214,468
Australia	7,789	9,084	11,208	13,078	13,857	15,690	18,530	18,983	20,096	21,444	22,264
Brunei	n.a.	n.a.	n.a.	n.a.	n.a.	n.a.	n.a.	n.a.	80	90	74
China	8,698	10,578	13,136	15,845	17,061	22,500	28,435	33,039	37,523	44,490	48,444
Hong Kong	3,872	4,708	5,570	5,861	5,986	5,775	6,439	6,488	8,901	9,945	9,848
India	5,218	6,546	8,653	10,043	9,977	10,322	11,780	12,308	13,318	15,180	18,107
Indonesia	1,343	1,403	1,547	1,680	1,592	1,760	1,913	2,190	2,209	2,458	2,516
Japan	39,539	39,208	37,948	39,751	38,042	43,259	43,830	46,662	45,684	46,800	44,315
Korea, Republic of	9,361	11,076	12,485	13,663	13,232	15,451	16,664	18,162	20,956	20,238	20,512
Malaysia	1,478	1,498	1,472	1,697	1,866	2,103	2,671	2,627	2,537	2,776	2,854
New Zealand	1,003	1,033	1,477	1,615	1,556	1,736	2,128	2,074	2,005	2,267	2,389
Philippines	1,665	1,590	1,936	2,296	1,923	2,039	2,117	2,527	2,418	2,361	2,510
Singapore	5,727	6,146	7,470	6,970	7,303	10,380	11,613	13,389	11,305	11,788	14,359
Taiwan	6,438	6,429	6,207	6,209	6,888	9,742	10,839	11,784	11,779	12,656	12,302
Thailand	1,549	1,441	1,674	1,830	1,788	1,998	2,200	2,557	2,682	2,876	2,704
Vietnam	n.a.	n.a.	n.a.	n.a.	n.a.	n.a.	n.a.	n.a.	1,725	1,885	2,043
Other	3,661	6,024	9,893	8,572	10,625	11,273	14,552	14,577	13,354	10,665	9,226
International organizations and unallocated	5,298	2,272	2,236	2,382	2,473	2,576	2,534	2,548	2,777	2,651	2,549
Addenda:											
European Union[2]	130,855	144,371	176,219	194,234	175,116	179,237	199,223	199,076	204,115	221,366	226,817
Euro area[2]	n.a.	n.a.	n.a.	n.a.	n.a.	n.a.	n.a.	n.a.	127,831	140,265	142,965
CAFTA-DR countries	n.a.	n.a.	n.a.	n.a.	n.a.	n.a.	n.a.	n.a.	6,606	7,041	7,242
NAFTA countries	55,327	61,655	67,641	71,607	66,403	77,740	84,755	90,133	92,715	92,261	87,945
By affiliation:											
Unaffiliated	276,814	307,679	355,347	391,478	371,432	411,427	454,757	474,636	499,752	525,491	531,421
Affiliated	96,193	109,058	133,049	141,340	141,289	151,905	173,025	181,775	201,703	217,766	219,439
U.S. parents' trade with their foreign affiliates	n.a.	85,622	107,350	112,514	110,858	120,438	138,647	144,259	161,957	179,050	177,694
U.S. affiliates' trade with their foreign parent groups	n.a.	23,435	25,699	28,826	30,431	31,467	34,377	37,516	39,746	38,716	41,745

⁰ = Transactions are possible but are zero for a given period.
* = Transactions between zero and +/- $500,000.
D = Suppressed to avoid disclosure of individual companies.
n.a. = Transactions are possible, but data are not available.
..... = Not applicable
n.i.e. = Not included elsewhere
[1]For the years 1999–2012, data presented in the line for "Belgium" include both Belgium and Luxembourg.
[2]For a small portion of transactions, data on individual European countries are not separately available. These transactions, as well as transactions with European regional organizations, are included as part of the "Other" category for Europe. Differences between the European Union and the Euro Area totals and the sum of the individual member countries may result from these transactions and from rounding.

Table B-35.   U.S. Trade in Services, by Type of Service and by Country or Affiliation, 2005–2015—*Continued*

(Millions of dollars.)

Country	Imports Total services										
	2005	2006	2007	2008	2009	2010	2011	2012	2013	2014	2015
South Africa	999	1,352	1,330	1,747	1,503	1,570	1,641	1,768	1,644	1,612	1,563
Other	3,642	3,795	4,727	5,936	6,508	6,364	7,388	7,135	5,833	5,723	5,623
Middle East	16,612	17,374	18,007	19,260	19,967	18,049	17,229	15,628	15,606	15,964	16,460
Bahrain	n.a.	n.a.	n.a.	n.a.	n.a.	n.a.	n.a.	n.a.	1,076	1,085	1,080
Israel	3,020	3,830	3,951	4,405	4,340	4,588	5,067	5,152	5,163	5,725	6,060
Jordan	n.a.	n.a.	n.a.	n.a.	n.a.	n.a.	n.a.	n.a.	625	583	574
Oman	n.a.	n.a.	n.a.	n.a.	n.a.	n.a.	n.a.	n.a.	351	337	328
Saudi Arabia	1,258	1,473	2,039	1,807	2,547	1,357	1,217	1,091	1,238	1,271	1,131
Other	12,333	12,071	12,018	13,049	13,080	12,104	10,946	9,384	7,152	6,963	7,287
Asia and Pacific	66,612	79,457	88,356	91,702	83,130	95,203	104,416	114,406	119,374	125,233	129,318
Australia	4,119	4,540	5,045	5,505	5,445	5,269	6,190	6,862	6,627	6,496	7,008
Brunei	n.a.	n.a.	n.a.	n.a.	n.a.	n.a.	n.a.	n.a.	9	14	9
China	6,857	10,140	11,800	10,924	9,560	10,609	11,781	13,040	13,908	13,974	15,108
Hong Kong	5,116	6,488	7,037	7,175	5,693	6,419	6,704	7,044	7,656	8,456	8,775
India	4,752	7,054	9,950	12,654	12,222	14,711	17,376	18,773	20,387	22,359	24,693
Indonesia	449	382	546	523	498	539	549	670	610	738	780
Japan	20,577	23,896	24,370	24,609	21,353	24,589	24,700	27,275	30,166	31,194	29,411
Korea, Republic of	6,911	8,257	8,920	8,079	7,857	9,334	9,735	10,641	10,643	10,708	11,127
Malaysia	639	1,012	1,084	1,289	1,066	1,276	1,306	1,451	1,417	1,707	1,810
New Zealand	915	1,056	1,120	1,154	1,052	1,230	1,411	1,394	1,773	1,789	1,946
Philippines	1,683	1,784	2,288	2,590	2,482	2,642	3,135	3,968	4,363	5,066	5,361
Singapore	3,242	3,164	3,379	4,069	4,068	4,279	5,224	5,558	5,578	6,109	6,770
Taiwan	6,311	6,798	7,313	6,236	4,758	5,865	6,499	7,234	7,171	7,406	7,650
Thailand	1,525	1,621	1,936	1,906	1,821	1,975	2,062	2,381	2,534	2,672	2,945
Vietnam	n.a.	n.a.	n.a.	n.a.	n.a.	n.a.	n.a.	n.a.	739	890	1,039
Other	3,515	3,262	3,569	4,989	5,252	6,468	7,742	8,113	5,791	5,656	4,887
International organizations and unallocated	5,086	662	148	1,177	304	1,071	341	1,318	255	1,262	223
Addenda:											
European Union[2]	114,742	130,902	144,529	155,681	138,334	143,615	156,132	157,056	161,185	169,792	172,784
Euro area[2]	n.a.	n.a.	n.a.	n.a.	n.a.	n.a.	n.a.	n.a.	101,172	105,796	107,842
CAFTA-DR countries	n.a.	n.a.	n.a.	n.a.	n.a.	n.a.	n.a.	n.a.	8,837	9,182	9,976
NAFTA countries	37,003	38,791	41,028	41,877	37,712	41,317	45,181	46,582	48,036	50,165	50,922
By affiliation:											
Unaffiliated	246,085	272,413	295,524	322,373	297,244	312,144	321,890	333,111	331,036	342,836	347,402
Affiliated	58,363	68,751	77,051	86,680	89,558	97,170	113,872	118,902	130,051	138,428	141,255
U.S. parents' trade with their foreign affiliates	n.a.	36,899	43,218	48,584	51,663	56,698	70,975	72,038	80,220	87,159	90,502
U.S. affiliates' trade with their foreign parent groups	n.a.	31,852	33,833	38,096	37,895	40,471	42,898	46,863	49,831	51,270	50,753

0 = Transactions are possible but are zero for a given period.
* = Transactions between zero and +/- $500,000.
D = Suppressed to avoid disclosure of individual companies.
n.a. = Transactions are possible, but data are not available.
..... = Not applicable
n.i.e. = Not included elsewhere
[1]For the years 1999–2012, data presented in the line for "Belgium" include both Belgium and Luxembourg.
[2]For a small portion of transactions, data on individual European countries are not separately available. These transactions, as well as transactions with European regional organizations, are included as part of the "Other" category for Europe. Differences between the European Union and the Euro Area totals and the sum of the individual member countries may result from these transactions and from rounding.

SECTION C

U.S. COMMODITY TRADE
BY GEOGRAPHIC AREA

SECTION C: U.S. COMMODITY TRADE BY GEOGRAPHIC AREA

HIGHLIGHTS

The largest trade deficit the U.S. experienced occurred in 2006 at $762 billion. As the Great Recession hit in December 2007, U.S. exports fell while imports rose, creating a growing imbalance. By 2009, the trade deficit fell 50 percent. The deficit continued fluctuating until 2015, settling at $752 billion, a mere 0.4 percent below the 2006 amount. The United States maintains a surplus with many of its trading partners but the largest surplus is only $30.5 billion with Hong Kong. The deficit with China, continues to grow, reaching -$365.7 billion in 2015. Germany and Japan follow China but at much smaller amounts, -$74.2 billion and -$68.6 billion respectively.

Canada purchases nearly 19 percent of all U.S. exports, followed by Mexico at 15 percent. These two countries plus the U.S. form the North American Free Trade Agreement (NAFTA). The goal of NAFTA was to eliminate barriers to trade and investment between the U.S., Canada, and Mexico. The implementation of NAFTA on January 1, 1994 brought the immediate elimination of tariffs on more than one-half of Mexico's exports to the U.S. and more than one-third of U.S. exports to Mexico.

The U.S. buys $482.9 billion from China which represents 21.5 percent of all imports, followed by Canada and Mexico at 13.2 percent each.

The United States' top export is nuclear reactors and parts which accounts for nearly 14 percent of all exports. Followed by electric machinery at 11.3 percent.

The top three imports accounts for 41.4 percent of all U.S. imports. The U.S. buys as well as sells electric machinery such as TV equipment. In addition, the U.S. buys and sells nuclear reactors and parts. Nuclear reactors represent 14.4 percent of all imports followed by vehicles and parts at 12.4 percent.

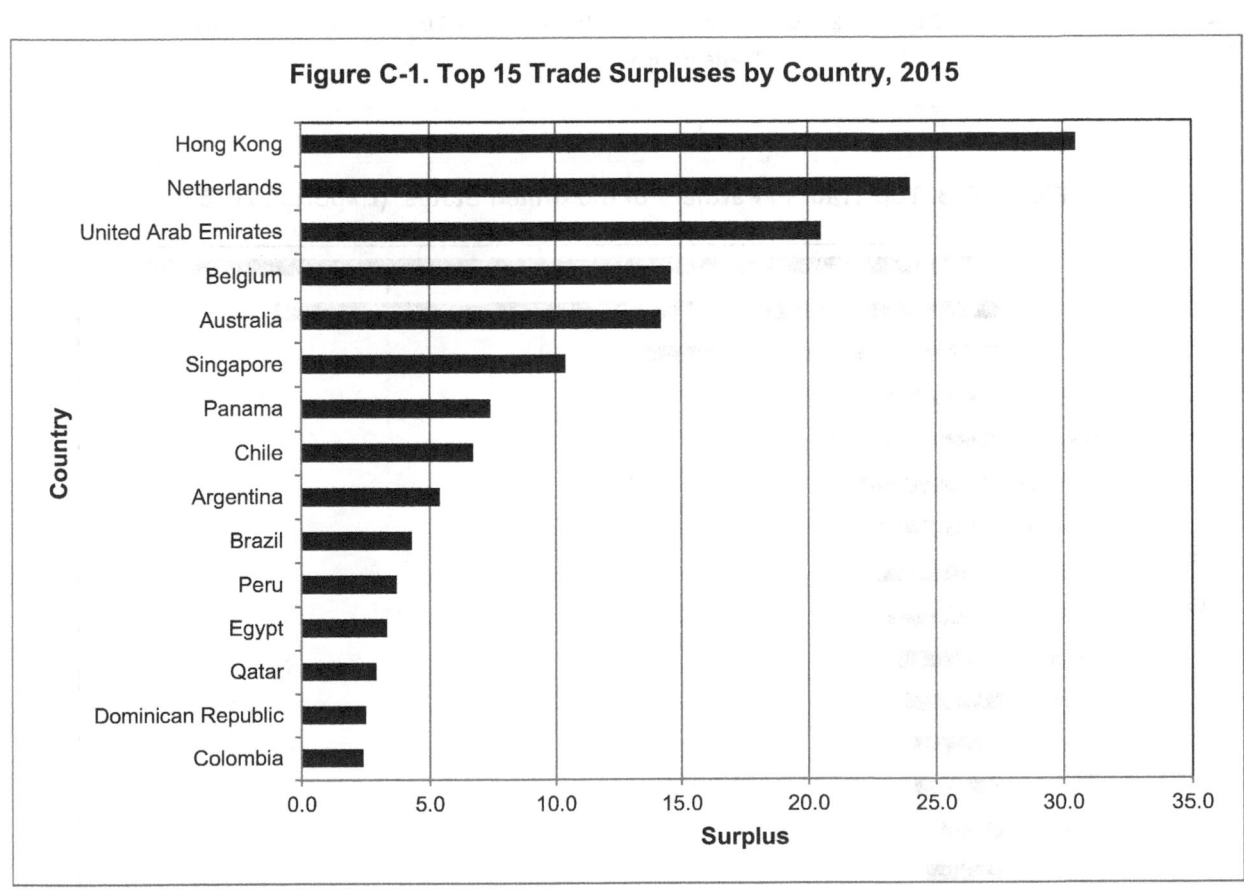

Figure C-1. Top 15 Trade Surpluses by Country, 2015

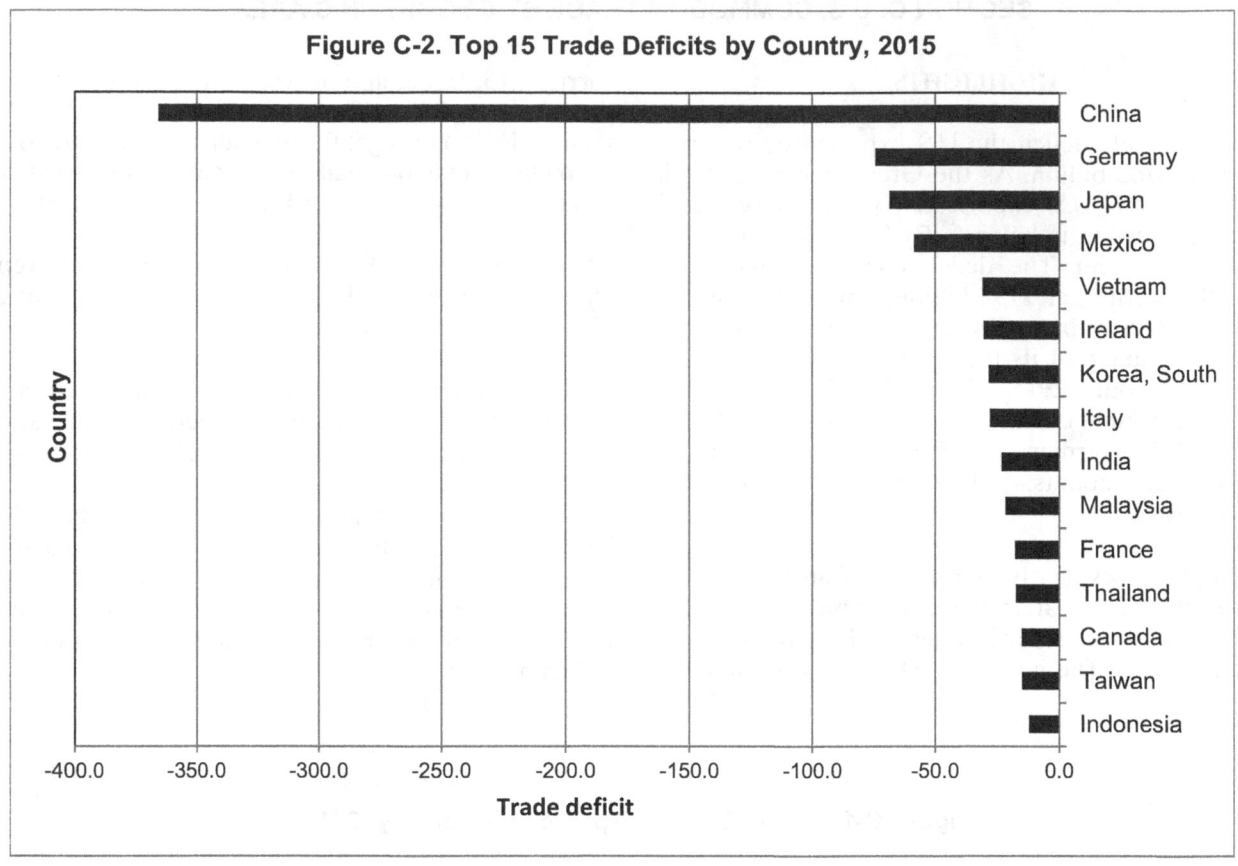

Figure C-2. Top 15 Trade Deficits by Country, 2015

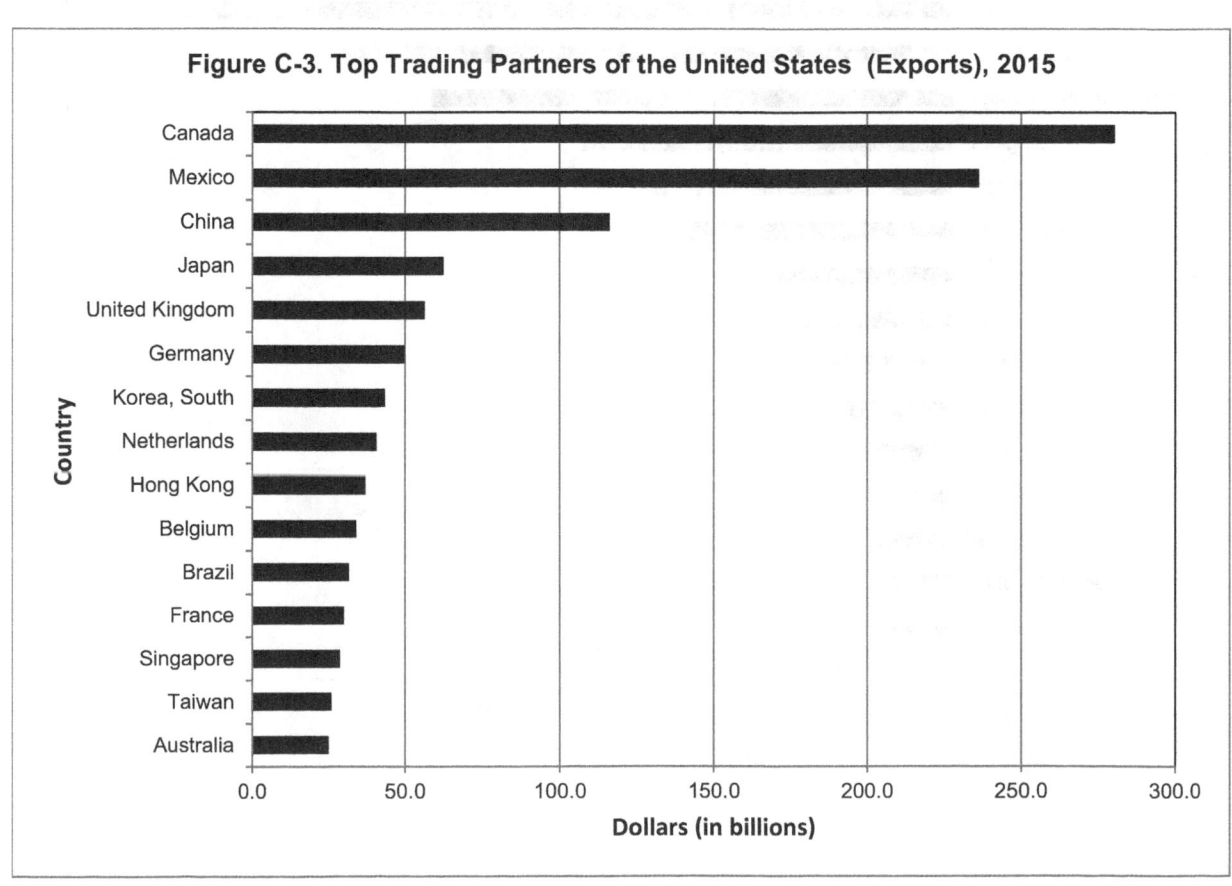

Figure C-3. Top Trading Partners of the United States (Exports), 2015

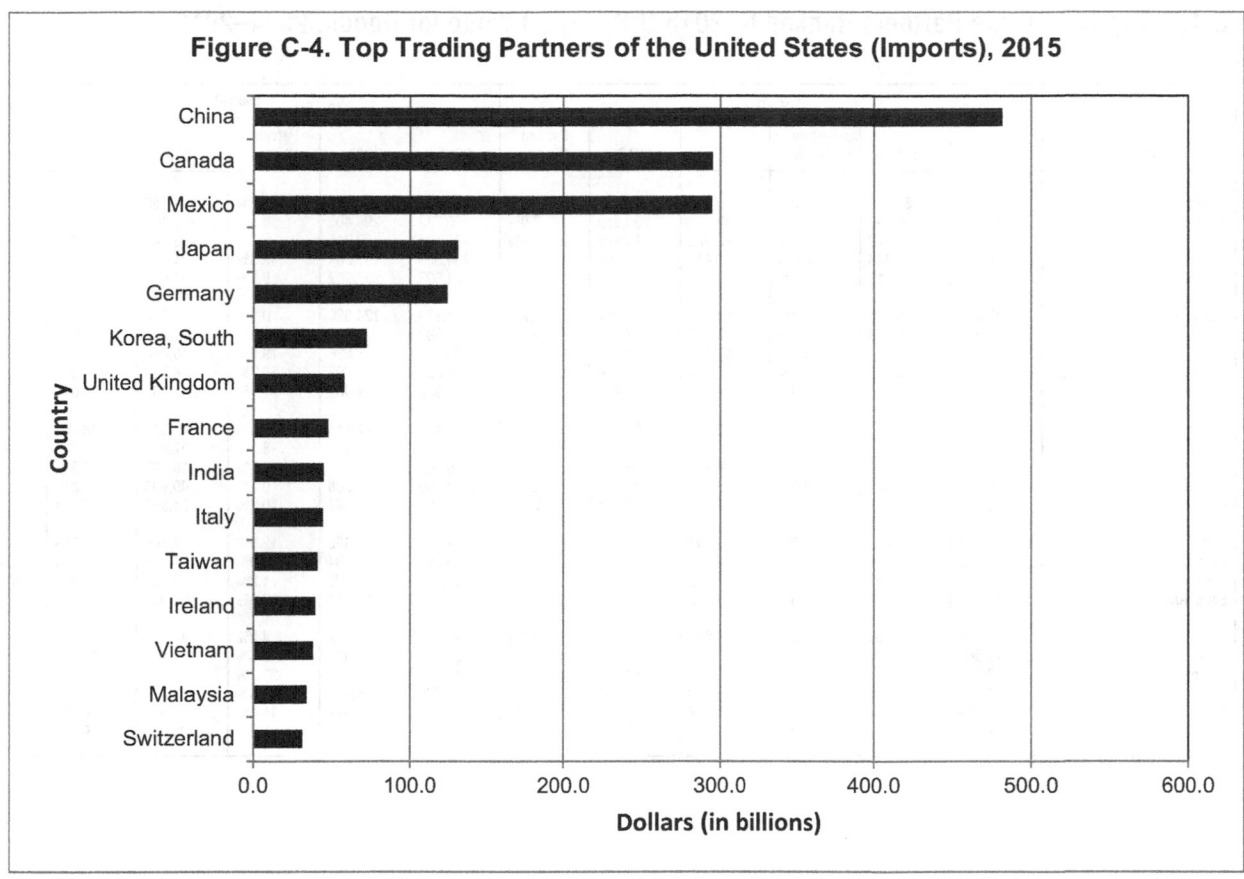

Figure C-4. Top Trading Partners of the United States (Imports), 2015

ABOUT THE DATA

The tables presented in Section C provide detailed pictures of U.S. commodity trade with individual countries. The tables in this section provide export and import data using 2-digit Harmonized System (HS) codes. These data are from three different bureaus within Department of Commerce: Census Bureau, Bureau of Economic Analysis (BEA), and International Trade Administration (ITA). The data are ranked according to 2015 exports value of goods.

Table C-1.   Top U.S. Trade Partners Ranked by 2015 U.S. Export Value for Goods, 2014–2016

(In millions of U.S. dollars.)

Rank	Country	EXPORTS						IMPORTS					
		2014	2015	Percent Change	2015	2016	Percent Change	2014	2015	Percent Change	2015	2016	Percent Change
1	Canada	312,817	280,609	-10.3%	280,609	266,827	-4.9%	349,278	296,156	-15.2%	296,156	278,067	-6.1%
2	Mexico	240,331	235,745	-1.9%	235,745	230,959	-2.0%	295,739	296,408	0.2%	296,408	294,151	-0.8%
3	China	123,621	116,072	-6.1%	116,072	115,775	-0.3%	468,484	483,245	3.2%	483,245	462,813	-4.2%
4	Japan	66,876	62,443	-6.6%	62,443	63,264	1.3%	134,505	131,364	-2.3%	131,364	132,202	0.6%
5	United Kingdom	53,848	56,115	4.2%	56,115	55,396	-1.3%	54,693	57,962	6.0%	57,962	54,326	-6.3%
6	Germany	49,370	49,971	1.2%	49,971	49,362	-1.2%	124,179	124,820	0.5%	124,820	114,227	-8.5%
7	Korea	44,625	43,446	-2.6%	43,446	42,266	-2.7%	69,680	71,759	3.0%	71,759	69,932	-2.5%
8	Netherlands	43,131	40,196	-6.8%	40,196	40,377	0.5%	20,899	16,836	-19.4%	16,836	16,152	-4.1%
9	Hong Kong	40,911	37,167	-9.2%	37,167	34,908	-6.1%	5,897	6,796	15.2%	6,796	7,386	8.7%
10	Belgium	34,781	34,160	-1.8%	34,160	32,271	-5.5%	20,962	19,482	-7.1%	19,482	17,020	-12.6%
11	France	31,307	30,104	-3.8%	30,104	30,941	2.8%	47,106	47,815	1.5%	47,815	46,765	-2.2%
12	Brazil	42,434	31,651	-25.4%	31,651	30,297	-4.3%	30,021	27,468	-8.5%	27,468	26,176	-4.7%
13	Singapore	30,072	28,472	-5.3%	28,472	26,868	-5.6%	16,502	18,267	10.7%	18,267	17,801	-2.6%
14	Taiwan	26,667	25,860	-3.0%	25,860	26,045	0.7%	40,839	40,908	0.2%	40,908	39,313	-3.9%
15	Switzerland	22,169	22,185	0.1%	22,185	22,701	2.3%	31,323	31,397	0.2%	31,397	36,374	15.9%
16	United Arab Emirates	22,111	23,004	4.0%	23,004	22,382	-2.7%	2,820	2,468	-12.5%	2,468	3,356	36.0%
17	Australia	26,682	25,036	-6.2%	25,036	22,225	-11.2%	10,697	10,894	1.8%	10,894	9,534	-12.5%
18	India	21,501	21,452	-0.2%	21,452	21,689	1.1%	45,355	44,792	-1.2%	44,792	45,998	2.7%
19	Saudi Arabia	18,718	19,739	5.5%	19,739	18,023	-8.7%	47,041	22,081	-53.1%	22,081	16,926	-23.3%
20	Italy	16,966	16,204	-4.5%	16,204	16,754	3.4%	42,377	44,159	4.2%	44,159	45,210	2.4%
21	Israel	15,065	13,539	-10.1%	13,539	13,197	-2.5%	23,007	24,477	6.4%	24,477	22,206	-9.3%
22	Colombia	20,068	16,287	-18.8%	16,287	13,099	-19.6%	18,316	14,075	-23.2%	14,075	13,796	-2.0%
23	Chile	16,542	15,445	-6.6%	15,445	12,941	-16.2%	9,479	8,772	-7.5%	8,772	8,799	0.3%
24	Malaysia	13,069	12,277	-6.1%	12,277	11,867	-3.3%	30,564	33,971	11.1%	33,971	36,687	8.0%
25	Thailand	11,817	11,231	-5.0%	11,231	10,573	-5.9%	27,225	28,632	5.2%	28,632	29,493	3.0%

Table C-2.   U.S. Trade by Commodity with Canada, 2010–2015

(In millions of U.S. dollars.)

Commodity and 2-digit Harmonized System (HS) code	2010	2011	2012	2013	2014	2015
EXPORTS						
Total..	249,256	281,292	292,651	300,755	312,817	280,609
87—VEHICLES; EXCEPT RAILWAY OR TRAMWAY; AND PARTS ETC	42,287	46,870	50,329	51,993	51,428	47,910
84—NUCLEAR REACTORS; BOILERS; MACHINERY ETC.; PARTS..............	38,741	44,210	47,201	45,552	46,790	43,133
85—ELECTRIC MACHINERY ETC; SOUND EQUIP; TV EQUIP; PTS	25,065	27,123	27,484	27,020	27,576	25,091
27—MINERAL FUEL; OIL ETC.; BITUMIN SUBST; MINERAL WAX..............	13,154	18,812	18,928	24,955	33,209	21,332
39—PLASTICS AND ARTICLES THEREOF......................................	11,374	12,614	13,050	13,183	13,790	12,642
90—OPTIC; PHOTO ETC; MEDIC OR SURGICAL INSTRMENTS ETC...........	7,959	8,855	9,683	9,478	9,217	8,586
73—ARTICLES OF IRON OR STEEL...	6,155	7,185	7,971	7,914	7,643	6,191
98—SPECIAL CLASSIFICATION PROVISIONS; NESOI	4,933	5,530	5,874	7,179	7,431	7,100
88—AIRCRAFT; SPACECRAFT; AND PARTS THEREOF	5,552	5,796	5,791	6,692	7,625	8,293
72—IRON AND STEEL..	6,123	6,886	6,646	6,036	6,274	4,678
94—FURNITURE; BEDDING ETC; LAMPS NESOI ETC; PREFAB BD	4,418	4,860	5,451	5,380	5,487	5,126
48—PAPER & PAPERBOARD & ARTICLES (INC PAPR PULP ARTL)	5,313	5,473	5,039	5,156	5,093	4,889
38—MISCELLANEOUS CHEMICAL PRODUCTS	3,537	4,117	4,420	4,858	4,568	4,054
40—RUBBER AND ARTICLES THEREOF	4,001	4,629	4,880	4,546	4,503	4,063
71—NAT ETC PEARLS; PREC ETC STONES; PR MET ETC; COIN	4,166	4,966	4,705	4,231	3,735	3,477
29—ORGANIC CHEMICALS..	3,997	4,188	3,942	4,208	4,455	3,950
30—PHARMACEUTICAL PRODUCTS	4,649	4,757	4,142	3,851	4,055	3,819
08—EDIBLE FRUIT & NUTS; CITRUS FRUIT OR MELON PEEL..................	2,991	3,316	3,502	3,679	3,697	3,472
76—ALUMINUM AND ARTICLES THEREOF	2,826	3,195	3,132	3,153	3,250	3,162
07—EDIBLE VEGETABLES & CERTAIN ROOTS & TUBERS	2,271	2,444	2,334	2,654	2,693	2,695
IMPORTS						
Total..	277,637	315,325	324,263	332,504	349,278	296,156
27—MINERAL FUEL; OIL ETC.; BITUMIN SUBST; MINERAL WAX..............	83,994	101,947	103,655	109,575	117,040	70,032
87—VEHICLES; EXCEPT RAILWAY OR TRAMWAY; AND PARTS ETC	46,121	49,804	57,590	55,704	56,193	55,561
84—NUCLEAR REACTORS; BOILERS; MACHINERY ETC.; PARTS..............	17,684	19,925	20,698	19,913	21,128	19,990
98—SPECIAL CLASSIFICATION PROVISIONS; NESOI	7,781	8,647	9,771	10,170	12,101	13,915
39—PLASTICS AND ARTICLES THEREOF......................................	9,070	10,333	10,215	10,630	11,283	10,711
88—AIRCRAFT; SPACECRAFT; AND PARTS THEREOF	4,548	5,310	5,849	6,646	7,964	8,410
44—WOOD AND ARTICLES OF WOOD; WOOD CHARCOAL......................	5,436	5,266	6,318	7,884	8,502	8,303
85—ELECTRIC MACHINERY ETC; SOUND EQUIP; TV EQUIP; PTS	7,920	8,202	8,256	7,888	7,913	7,515
76—ALUMINUM AND ARTICLES THEREOF	7,312	7,741	6,831	6,841	7,333	7,232
48—PAPER & PAPERBOARD & ARTICLES (INC PAPR PULP ARTL)	7,503	7,651	6,719	6,789	6,857	6,387
71—NAT ETC PEARLS; PREC ETC STONES; PR MET ETC; COIN	7,350	8,115	6,523	7,609	6,492	6,310
30—PHARMACEUTICAL PRODUCTS	4,116	3,778	3,927	3,633	4,396	5,253
72—IRON AND STEEL..	5,213	5,769	5,492	5,051	5,673	4,354
94—FURNITURE; BEDDING ETC; LAMPS NESOI ETC; PREFAB BD	3,503	3,800	3,906	3,874	4,088	4,345
73—ARTICLES OF IRON OR STEEL...	3,529	3,785	4,228	3,898	4,092	3,902
31—FERTILIZERS...	3,840	4,748	4,425	3,932	3,254	3,518
29—ORGANIC CHEMICALS..	3,969	4,621	4,107	4,488	4,603	3,052
90—OPTIC; PHOTO ETC; MEDIC OR SURGICAL INSTRMENTS ETC...........	2,559	2,816	2,942	2,823	2,794	2,998
99—SPECIAL IMPORT PROVISIONS; NESOI	2,083	2,021	1,777	2,092	2,765	2,827
19—PREP CEREAL; FLOUR; STARCH OR MILK; BAKERS WARES..............	2,163	2,328	2,402	2,532	2,652	2,799

Table C-3.   U.S. Trade by Commodity with Mexico, 2010–2015

(In millions of U.S. dollars.)

Commodity and 2-digit Harmonized System (HS) code	2010	2011	2012	2013	2014	2015
EXPORTS						
Total..	163,665	198,289	215,875	225,954	240,331	235,745
84—NUCLEAR REACTORS; BOILERS; MACHINERY ETC.; PARTS..............	24,742	31,397	35,995	38,525	43,179	42,070
85—ELECTRIC MACHINERY ETC; SOUND EQUIP; TV EQUIP; PTS.............	31,627	32,385	33,898	36,626	38,362	41,112
87—VEHICLES; EXCEPT RAILWAY OR TRAMWAY; AND PARTS ETC.........	14,535	17,894	20,278	21,607	21,252	22,406
27—MINERAL FUEL; OIL ETC.; BITUMIN SUBST; MINERAL WAX..............	14,258	23,630	23,658	23,084	23,683	18,037
39—PLASTICS AND ARTICLES THEREOF................................	11,444	12,673	13,914	15,281	16,442	16,509
98—SPECIAL CLASSIFICATION PROVISIONS; NESOI	5,219	6,130	6,615	6,892	7,394	7,134
90—OPTIC; PHOTO ETC; MEDIC OR SURGICAL INSTRMENTS ETC............	4,406	4,847	5,436	5,756	6,371	6,738
73—ARTICLES OF IRON OR STEEL....................................	3,083	3,634	4,590	4,945	5,477	5,233
29—ORGANIC CHEMICALS..	5,019	6,404	7,019	6,697	6,433	4,847
88—AIRCRAFT; SPACECRAFT; AND PARTS THEREOF	1,476	1,624	2,559	3,300	3,007	4,281
72—IRON AND STEEL...	2,718	3,737	4,170	4,038	4,395	4,133
48—PAPER & PAPERBOARD & ARTICLES (INC PAPR PULP ARTL)	3,296	3,453	3,655	3,819	3,871	3,938
76—ALUMINUM AND ARTICLES THEREOF	2,692	3,143	3,335	3,568	3,802	3,860
40—RUBBER AND ARTICLES THEREOF	2,081	2,594	3,058	3,139	3,558	3,469
10—CEREALS	2,932	4,753	4,503	3,438	3,580	3,418
02—MEAT AND EDIBLE MEAT OFFAL	2,304	2,698	2,770	3,047	3,700	3,063
38—MISCELLANEOUS CHEMICAL PRODUCTS	1,836	2,076	2,320	2,596	2,915	2,873
26—ORES; SLAG AND ASH..	317	1,082	1,261	1,887	2,551	2,660
94—FURNITURE; BEDDING ETC; LAMPS NESOI ETC; PREFAB BD	1,096	1,319	1,606	1,903	2,339	2,452
74—COPPER AND ARTICLES THEREOF.................................	1,791	2,019	2,121	2,272	2,209	2,211
IMPORTS						
Total..	229,986	262,874	277,594	280,556	295,739	296,408
87—VEHICLES; EXCEPT RAILWAY OR TRAMWAY; AND PARTS ETC.........	40,215	45,801	53,508	59,598	68,041	74,690
85—ELECTRIC MACHINERY ETC; SOUND EQUIP; TV EQUIP; PTS.............	53,868	54,309	56,816	57,393	58,684	63,156
84—NUCLEAR REACTORS; BOILERS; MACHINERY ETC.; PARTS..............	33,618	38,569	42,317	42,700	45,216	49,026
27—MINERAL FUEL; OIL ETC.; BITUMIN SUBST; MINERAL WAX..............	33,577	43,909	39,825	34,781	30,253	13,621
90—OPTIC; PHOTO ETC; MEDIC OR SURGICAL INSTRMENTS ETC............	8,794	9,736	10,355	10,713	11,600	12,232
94—FURNITURE; BEDDING ETC; LAMPS NESOI ETC; PREFAB BD	5,648	6,289	7,839	8,533	9,699	10,653
98—SPECIAL CLASSIFICATION PROVISIONS; NESOI	5,339	5,098	5,665	5,621	6,697	6,674
07—EDIBLE VEGETABLES & CERTAIN ROOTS & TUBERS	3,967	4,450	4,459	5,021	5,132	5,313
08—EDIBLE FRUIT & NUTS; CITRUS FRUIT OR MELON PEEL...............	2,705	2,921	3,322	3,695	4,481	5,159
71—NAT ETC PEARLS; PREC ETC STONES; PR MET ETC; COIN	6,604	9,773	9,634	7,107	5,741	5,084
39—PLASTICS AND ARTICLES THEREOF................................	3,041	3,506	3,774	4,070	4,613	4,712
22—BEVERAGES; SPIRITS AND VINEGAR	2,589	2,732	2,905	3,080	3,869	4,188
73—ARTICLES OF IRON OR STEEL....................................	2,680	3,306	3,801	3,640	4,315	4,188
62—APPAREL ARTICLES AND ACCESSORIES; NOT KNIT ETC.	2,326	2,542	2,528	2,490	2,509	2,403
99—SPECIAL IMPORT PROVISIONS; NESOI	1,652	1,663	1,610	1,787	2,194	2,307
40—RUBBER AND ARTICLES THEREOF	1,334	1,694	1,935	1,938	2,045	2,218
83—MISCELLANEOUS ARTICLES OF BASE METAL	1,165	1,278	1,418	1,622	1,664	1,794
72—IRON AND STEEL..	1,827	2,157	1,803	1,920	2,264	1,454
17—SUGARS AND SUGAR CONFECTIONARY	1,156	1,730	1,332	1,674	1,364	1,413
61—APPAREL ARTICLES AND ACCESSORIES; KNIT OR CROCHET	1,344	1,422	1,316	1,325	1,348	1,286

Table C-4. U.S. Trade by Commodity with China, 2010–2015

(In millions of U.S. dollars.)

Commodity and 2-digit Harmonized System (HS) code	2010	2011	2012	2013	2014	2015
EXPORTS						
Total..	91,911	104,122	110,517	121,746	123,621	116,072
88—AIRCRAFT; SPACECRAFT; AND PARTS THEREOF	5,763	6,398	8,366	12,587	13,928	15,441
85—ELECTRIC MACHINERY ETC; SOUND EQUIP; TV EQUIP; PTS	11,525	10,164	9,667	11,389	12,019	12,761
84—NUCLEAR REACTORS; BOILERS; MACHINERY ETC.; PARTS	11,220	12,247	11,554	12,207	12,489	12,248
12—OIL SEEDS ETC.; MISC GRAIN; SEED; FRUIT; PLANT ETC	11,037	10,714	15,147	13,699	14,937	11,091
87—VEHICLES; EXCEPT RAILWAY OR TRAMWAY; AND PARTS ETC	4,510	6,768	7,060	10,330	13,269	10,868
90—OPTIC; PHOTO ETC; MEDIC OR SURGICAL INSTRMENTS ETC............	5,204	5,758	7,035	7,667	7,527	7,923
39—PLASTICS AND ARTICLES THEREOF	4,842	5,123	4,698	4,755	5,078	4,910
47—WOOD PULP ETC; RECOVD (WASTE & SCRAP) PPR & PPRBD...........	3,052	3,995	3,820	3,602	3,364	3,414
10—CEREALS	336	1,012	1,535	2,373	1,767	2,466
29—ORGANIC CHEMICALS...	2,979	3,524	3,240	3,103	2,376	2,464
27—MINERAL FUEL; OIL ETC.; BITUMIN SUBST; MINERAL WAX..............	1,354	2,038	2,441	2,804	1,700	2,218
23—FOOD INDUSTRY RESIDUES & WASTE; PREP ANIMAL FEED............	831	645	953	1,783	1,705	2,079
44—WOOD AND ARTICLES OF WOOD; WOOD CHARCOAL	1,165	1,934	1,643	2,347	2,664	2,069
30—PHARMACEUTICAL PRODUCTS	617	982	1,067	1,220	1,609	1,938
38—MISCELLANEOUS CHEMICAL PRODUCTS	1,371	1,542	1,692	1,988	2,149	1,901
74—COPPER AND ARTICLES THEREOF..................................	2,886	3,774	3,941	3,470	2,910	1,837
76—ALUMINUM AND ARTICLES THEREOF	2,293	3,041	2,756	2,623	2,116	1,641
41—RAW HIDES AND SKINS (NO FURSKINS) AND LEATHER...................	1,040	1,300	1,470	1,770	1,813	1,440
03—FISH; CRUSTACEANS & AQUATIC INVERTEBRATES	732	1,131	1,114	1,095	1,151	1,008
26—ORES; SLAG AND ASH...	1,244	1,589	1,725	1,463	1,489	985
IMPORTS						
Total..	364,953	399,371	425,619	440,430	468,484	483,245
85—ELECTRIC MACHINERY ETC; SOUND EQUIP; TV EQUIP; PTS	90,819	98,703	110,713	117,535	127,333	133,163
84—NUCLEAR REACTORS; BOILERS; MACHINERY ETC.; PARTS	82,722	94,859	99,134	100,447	105,515	104,135
94—FURNITURE; BEDDING ETC; LAMPS NESOI ETC; PREFAB BD	19,956	20,493	22,443	24,133	25,481	28,100
95—TOYS; GAMES & SPORT EQUIPMENT; PARTS & ACCESSORIES	24,980	22,624	21,980	21,687	22,648	24,512
64—FOOTWEAR; GAITERS ETC. AND PARTS THEREOF	15,917	16,723	17,147	17,016	17,065	17,276
61—APPAREL ARTICLES AND ACCESSORIES; KNIT OR CROCHET	14,042	15,092	14,987	15,575	16,110	16,290
62—APPAREL ARTICLES AND ACCESSORIES; NOT KNIT ETC.	14,734	15,001	14,710	14,904	14,383	14,759
39—PLASTICS AND ARTICLES THEREOF	9,648	10,893	12,155	12,920	13,866	14,327
87—VEHICLES; EXCEPT RAILWAY OR TRAMWAY; AND PARTS ETC	6,997	8,183	9,379	9,825	11,492	13,028
90—OPTIC; PHOTO ETC; MEDIC OR SURGICAL INSTRMENTS ETC............	7,016	7,879	8,779	9,524	10,386	11,063
73—ARTICLES OF IRON OR STEEL..	7,337	8,645	9,369	8,928	9,851	10,471
42—LEATHER ART; SADDLERY ETC; HANDBAGS ETC; GUT ART	7,456	8,052	8,416	8,651	8,543	8,691
63—TEXTILE ART NESOI; NEEDLECRAFT SETS; WORN TEXT ART...........	5,878	6,212	6,366	6,798	7,096	7,704
29—ORGANIC CHEMICALS...	4,615	5,721	6,442	6,714	6,712	6,638
83—MISCELLANEOUS ARTICLES OF BASE METAL	3,321	3,583	3,837	4,202	4,352	4,771
40—RUBBER AND ARTICLES THEREOF	3,218	3,948	4,698	5,279	5,753	4,354
44—WOOD AND ARTICLES OF WOOD; WOOD CHARCOAL	2,769	2,800	3,166	3,319	3,712	3,991
82—TOOLS; CUTLERY ETC. OF BASE METAL & PARTS THEREOF	2,635	2,915	3,097	3,340	3,516	3,671
71—NAT ETC PEARLS; PREC ETC STONES; PR MET ETC; COIN	2,905	3,309	3,602	3,672	3,626	3,283

Table C-5. U.S. Trade by Commodity with Japan, 2010–2015

(In millions of U.S. dollars.)

Commodity and 2-digit Harmonized System (HS) code	2010	2011	2012	2013	2014	2015
EXPORTS						
Total..	60,472	65,800	69,976	65,237	66,876	62,443
88—AIRCRAFT; SPACECRAFT; AND PARTS THEREOF	5,109	4,870	8,286	7,066	7,299	7,119
90—OPTIC; PHOTO ETC; MEDIC OR SURGICAL INSTRMENTS ETC...........	7,227	7,736	8,156	7,976	7,406	7,098
84—NUCLEAR REACTORS; BOILERS; MACHINERY ETC.; PARTS..............	5,186	5,750	5,525	5,796	6,162	6,485
85—ELECTRIC MACHINERY ETC; SOUND EQUIP; TV EQUIP; PTS.............	4,333	4,998	5,507	4,918	5,155	5,217
30—PHARMACEUTICAL PRODUCTS	3,027	2,820	3,904	3,278	3,572	3,551
10—CEREALS	4,169	5,609	4,368	3,180	3,953	3,111
02—MEAT AND EDIBLE MEAT OFFAL	2,305	2,882	3,036	3,287	3,516	2,836
29—ORGANIC CHEMICALS	2,279	2,309	2,407	2,119	2,311	2,190
39—PLASTICS AND ARTICLES THEREOF	2,049	2,132	2,124	1,860	1,910	1,785
27—MINERAL FUEL; OIL ETC.; BITUMIN SUBST; MINERAL WAX............	1,820	2,499	2,659	2,710	2,714	1,754
12—OIL SEEDS ETC.; MISC GRAIN; SEED; FRUIT; PLANT ETC	1,767	1,682	1,909	1,753	1,701	1,680
71—NAT ETC PEARLS; PREC ETC STONES; PR MET ETC; COIN	1,277	1,565	1,419	1,488	1,560	1,369
38—MISCELLANEOUS CHEMICAL PRODUCTS	1,319	1,522	1,499	1,325	1,288	1,342
87—VEHICLES; EXCEPT RAILWAY OR TRAMWAY; AND PARTS ETC	1,271	1,547	1,917	1,585	1,448	1,324
98—SPECIAL CLASSIFICATION PROVISIONS; NESOI	1,840	1,139	1,022	1,012	1,223	1,155
28—INORG CHEM; PREC & RARE-EARTH MET & RADIOACT COMPD.......	2,033	2,066	1,753	1,533	1,364	1,146
08—EDIBLE FRUIT & NUTS; CITRUS FRUIT OR MELON PEEL................	746	792	879	879	890	911
03—FISH; CRUSTACEANS & AQUATIC INVERTEBRATES	736	787	747	690	740	823
44—WOOD AND ARTICLES OF WOOD; WOOD CHARCOAL......................	641	737	736	856	822	730
48—PAPER & PAPERBOARD & ARTICLES (INC PAPR PULP ARTL)	662	716	711	698	661	605
IMPORTS						
Total..	120,552	128,928	146,432	138,575	134,505	131,364
87—VEHICLES; EXCEPT RAILWAY OR TRAMWAY; AND PARTS ETC	41,572	41,023	51,336	49,762	45,264	46,083
84—NUCLEAR REACTORS; BOILERS; MACHINERY ETC.; PARTS..............	24,888	31,269	34,068	30,588	31,057	29,043
85—ELECTRIC MACHINERY ETC; SOUND EQUIP; TV EQUIP; PTS.............	18,353	18,288	20,059	18,405	17,311	16,494
90—OPTIC; PHOTO ETC; MEDIC OR SURGICAL INSTRMENTS ETC...........	6,124	6,900	6,855	6,650	6,651	6,512
88—AIRCRAFT; SPACECRAFT; AND PARTS THEREOF	2,092	2,580	3,269	3,848	4,887	4,766
98—SPECIAL CLASSIFICATION PROVISIONS; NESOI	2,103	1,829	2,588	2,306	2,370	2,479
40—RUBBER AND ARTICLES THEREOF	2,418	2,671	2,730	2,484	2,421	2,402
29—ORGANIC CHEMICALS	2,977	3,004	3,244	3,817	3,811	2,384
39—PLASTICS AND ARTICLES THEREOF	2,027	2,109	2,318	2,162	2,236	2,195
73—ARTICLES OF IRON OR STEEL	1,932	2,269	2,894	2,281	2,180	2,030
30—PHARMACEUTICAL PRODUCTS	1,990	1,464	1,186	1,127	1,020	1,570
72—IRON AND STEEL...	1,062	1,491	1,684	1,552	1,708	1,543
38—MISCELLANEOUS CHEMICAL PRODUCTS	1,520	1,807	1,711	1,456	1,465	1,472
99—SPECIAL IMPORT PROVISIONS; NESOI	1,231	1,181	1,135	1,189	1,445	1,297
91—CLOCKS AND WATCHES AND PARTS THEREOF...............................	753	927	926	1,095	1,043	976
37—PHOTOGRAPHIC OR CINEMATOGRAPHIC GOODS............................	819	895	893	866	890	950
82—TOOLS; CUTLERY ETC. OF BASE METAL & PARTS THEREOF	603	780	902	863	745	761
89—SHIPS; BOATS AND FLOATING STRUCTURES.................................	2	3	7	53	7	622
27—MINERAL FUEL; OIL ETC.; BITUMIN SUBST; MINERAL WAX............	639	589	617	675	510	621
68—ART OF STONE; PLASTER; CEMENT; ASBESTOS; MICA ETC.	255	318	343	327	370	429

Table C-6.   U.S. Trade by Commodity with United Kingdom, 2010–2015

(In millions of U.S. dollars.)

Commodity and 2-digit Harmonized System (HS) code	2010	2011	2012	2013	2014	2015
EXPORTS						
Total..................	48,410	56,033	54,860	47,361	53,848	56,115
88—AIRCRAFT; SPACECRAFT; AND PARTS THEREOF	5,767	6,775	6,595	8,375	9,135	9,684
84—NUCLEAR REACTORS; BOILERS; MACHINERY ETC.; PARTS	5,833	5,869	5,964	5,508	6,296	6,134
71—NAT ETC PEARLS; PREC ETC STONES; PR MET ETC; COIN	8,982	11,950	10,008	3,754	5,650	5,728
85—ELECTRIC MACHINERY ETC; SOUND EQUIP; TV EQUIP; PTS	3,384	3,709	3,704	3,386	3,789	3,834
30—PHARMACEUTICAL PRODUCTS	4,109	4,568	3,888	2,401	2,596	3,696
87—VEHICLES; EXCEPT RAILWAY OR TRAMWAY; AND PARTS ETC	1,678	2,126	2,081	2,094	2,687	3,063
90—OPTIC; PHOTO ETC; MEDIC OR SURGICAL INSTRMENTS ETC...........	2,721	2,812	2,769	2,732	2,868	2,835
97—WORKS OF ART; COLLECTORS' PIECES AND ANTIQUES....................	1,799	1,871	2,352	2,530	2,984	2,769
98—SPECIAL CLASSIFICATION PROVISIONS; NESOI	2,256	2,012	1,973	1,930	2,237	2,572
27—MINERAL FUEL; OIL ETC.; BITUMIN SUBST; MINERAL WAX..............	1,055	1,869	2,618	2,435	2,433	2,105
29—ORGANIC CHEMICALS..	824	965	1,420	1,168	1,094	1,427
39—PLASTICS AND ARTICLES THEREOF	1,025	1,144	1,160	1,186	1,308	1,296
33—ESSENTIAL OILS ETC; PERFUMERY; COSMETIC ETC PREPS	652	626	629	704	841	859
44—WOOD AND ARTICLES OF WOOD; WOOD CHARCOAL......................	231	225	314	439	648	851
38—MISCELLANEOUS CHEMICAL PRODUCTS	695	638	631	673	691	735
49—PRINTED BOOKS; NEWSPAPERS ETC; MANUSCRIPTS ETC...............	579	578	693	720	692	648
22—BEVERAGES; SPIRITS AND VINEGAR	437	739	579	461	430	549
73—ARTICLES OF IRON OR STEEL..	380	473	473	487	570	507
28—INORG CHEM; PREC & RARE-EARTH MET & RADIOACT COMPD.......	441	862	483	213	335	435
81—BASE METALS NESOI; CERMETS; ARTICLES THEREOF.....................	256	361	409	403	396	384
IMPORTS						
Total..................	49,805	51,263	55,006	52,741	54,693	57,962
84—NUCLEAR REACTORS; BOILERS; MACHINERY ETC.; PARTS..............	6,157	7,630	8,488	8,631	9,155	8,540
87—VEHICLES; EXCEPT RAILWAY OR TRAMWAY; AND PARTS ETC	4,198	4,667	5,760	6,210	6,573	8,026
29—ORGANIC CHEMICALS..	3,742	4,258	3,680	2,433	2,458	5,820
98—SPECIAL CLASSIFICATION PROVISIONS; NESOI	2,596	2,639	3,615	4,008	4,589	5,322
30—PHARMACEUTICAL PRODUCTS	5,675	3,959	3,533	3,286	3,849	5,188
27—MINERAL FUEL; OIL ETC.; BITUMIN SUBST; MINERAL WAX..............	7,987	7,571	7,627	7,182	5,744	3,572
90—OPTIC; PHOTO ETC; MEDIC OR SURGICAL INSTRMENTS ETC...........	2,738	3,124	3,263	3,195	3,225	3,295
85—ELECTRIC MACHINERY ETC; SOUND EQUIP; TV EQUIP; PTS	2,400	2,551	2,671	2,543	2,656	2,633
97—WORKS OF ART; COLLECTORS' PIECES AND ANTIQUES....................	1,176	1,391	1,797	1,676	1,678	2,078
22—BEVERAGES; SPIRITS AND VINEGAR	1,452	1,675	1,782	1,954	1,931	1,911
88—AIRCRAFT; SPACECRAFT; AND PARTS THEREOF	1,476	1,485	1,600	1,294	1,472	1,321
39—PLASTICS AND ARTICLES THEREOF	748	793	867	884	939	890
71—NAT ETC PEARLS; PREC ETC STONES; PR MET ETC; COIN	1,020	1,039	1,213	1,190	1,138	864
72—IRON AND STEEL...	639	746	720	627	1,190	780
38—MISCELLANEOUS CHEMICAL PRODUCTS	750	827	721	755	737	779
94—FURNITURE; BEDDING ETC; LAMPS NESOI ETC; PREFAB BD	365	467	540	528	772	732
33—ESSENTIAL OILS ETC; PERFUMERY; COSMETIC ETC PREPS	344	380	474	573	618	492
99—SPECIAL IMPORT PROVISIONS; NESOI	458	489	411	361	499	482
28—INORG CHEM; PREC & RARE-EARTH MET & RADIOACT COMPD.......	1,668	1,081	1,345	856	580	462
73—ARTICLES OF IRON OR STEEL..	338	407	707	547	446	461

Table C-7.   U.S. Trade by Commodity with Germany, 2010–2015

(In millions of U.S. dollars.)

Commodity and 2-digit Harmonized System (HS) code	2010	2011	2012	2013	2014	2015
EXPORTS						
Total..	48,155	49,294	48,803	47,363	49,370	49,971
87—VEHICLES; EXCEPT RAILWAY OR TRAMWAY; AND PARTS ETC	5,152	6,752	7,297	6,050	6,670	7,166
88—AIRCRAFT; SPACECRAFT; AND PARTS THEREOF	5,362	5,635	5,656	5,809	6,534	6,711
90—OPTIC; PHOTO ETC; MEDIC OR SURGICAL INSTRMENTS ETC............	5,483	5,854	5,857	5,996	6,140	6,134
84—NUCLEAR REACTORS; BOILERS; MACHINERY ETC.; PARTS..............	5,514	6,058	5,894	5,881	5,759	5,789
85—ELECTRIC MACHINERY ETC; SOUND EQUIP; TV EQUIP; PTS.............	4,472	4,460	4,174	4,262	4,590	4,667
30—PHARMACEUTICAL PRODUCTS	5,801	2,565	2,558	2,189	2,386	2,333
38—MISCELLANEOUS CHEMICAL PRODUCTS	1,303	1,491	1,461	1,582	1,674	1,652
98—SPECIAL CLASSIFICATION PROVISIONS; NESOI	1,905	1,449	1,391	1,363	1,448	1,535
29—ORGANIC CHEMICALS..	1,048	1,340	1,357	1,292	1,055	1,329
39—PLASTICS AND ARTICLES THEREOF	1,206	1,306	1,196	1,195	1,250	1,262
71—NAT ETC PEARLS; PREC ETC STONES; PR MET ETC; COIN	1,521	2,166	1,942	1,981	1,351	1,222
12—OIL SEEDS ETC.; MISC GRAIN; SEED; FRUIT; PLANT ETC	575	352	941	813	655	874
08—EDIBLE FRUIT & NUTS; CITRUS FRUIT OR MELON PEEL	380	434	467	649	750	719
70—GLASS AND GLASSWARE...	496	599	540	564	602	675
97—WORKS OF ART; COLLECTORS' PIECES AND ANTIQUES..............	256	370	364	359	527	564
28—INORG CHEM; PREC & RARE-EARTH MET & RADIOACT COMPD.......	584	569	418	342	556	515
27—MINERAL FUEL; OIL ETC.; BITUMIN SUBST; MINERAL WAX...........	930	1,417	1,075	796	668	511
33—ESSENTIAL OILS ETC; PERFUMERY; COSMETIC ETC PREPS	307	284	310	325	371	387
73—ARTICLES OF IRON OR STEEL...	335	347	343	334	422	348
68—ART OF STONE; PLASTER; CEMENT; ASBESTOS; MICA ETC.	152	169	155	187	269	302
IMPORTS						
Total..	82,450	98,684	109,226	114,342	124,179	124,820
87—VEHICLES; EXCEPT RAILWAY OR TRAMWAY; AND PARTS ETC	21,144	24,951	29,690	32,595	33,434	34,119
84—NUCLEAR REACTORS; BOILERS; MACHINERY ETC.; PARTS..............	16,466	20,246	22,117	21,868	23,870	24,033
30—PHARMACEUTICAL PRODUCTS	7,256	8,503	10,717	11,043	14,031	14,529
90—OPTIC; PHOTO ETC; MEDIC OR SURGICAL INSTRMENTS ETC............	7,282	8,732	8,808	8,908	9,266	9,030
85—ELECTRIC MACHINERY ETC; SOUND EQUIP; TV EQUIP; PTS.............	5,986	7,508	7,620	7,665	8,346	8,156
88—AIRCRAFT; SPACECRAFT; AND PARTS THEREOF	882	1,563	1,517	2,900	3,972	4,469
98—SPECIAL CLASSIFICATION PROVISIONS; NESOI	1,869	2,133	2,488	2,702	3,050	3,517
29—ORGANIC CHEMICALS..	2,503	2,831	3,070	3,357	3,319	2,846
39—PLASTICS AND ARTICLES THEREOF	1,986	2,198	2,393	2,523	2,873	2,779
73—ARTICLES OF IRON OR STEEL...	1,276	1,587	2,077	1,839	2,148	2,098
38—MISCELLANEOUS CHEMICAL PRODUCTS	1,127	1,266	1,418	1,645	1,611	1,450
99—SPECIAL IMPORT PROVISIONS; NESOI	944	1,061	983	966	1,404	1,402
72—IRON AND STEEL...	1,115	1,237	1,196	1,016	1,131	1,205
40—RUBBER AND ARTICLES THEREOF	816	1,085	1,157	1,154	1,203	1,176
97—WORKS OF ART; COLLECTORS' PIECES AND ANTIQUES..............	479	463	873	844	1,112	1,076
28—INORG CHEM; PREC & RARE-EARTH MET & RADIOACT COMPD.......	1,146	1,301	1,256	1,046	881	871
82—TOOLS; CUTLERY ETC. OF BASE METAL & PARTS THEREOF	571	635	724	803	894	850
48—PAPER & PAPERBOARD & ARTICLES (INC PAPR PULP ARTL)	816	877	862	783	743	818
94—FURNITURE; BEDDING ETC; LAMPS NESOI ETC; PREFAB BD	471	571	572	649	760	816
71—NAT ETC PEARLS; PREC ETC STONES; PR MET ETC; COIN	838	1,424	900	1,198	863	650

Table C-8.   U.S. Trade by Commodity with South Korea, 2010–2015

(In millions of U.S. dollars.)

Commodity and 2-digit Harmonized System (HS) code	2010	2011	2012	2013	2014	2015
EXPORTS						
Total...	388,206	434,616	422,826	416,487	446,251	434,455
84—NUCLEAR REACTORS; BOILERS; MACHINERY ETC.; PARTS..............	69,430	61,382	62,336	67,731	76,329	69,206
85—ELECTRIC MACHINERY ETC; SOUND EQUIP; TV EQUIP; PTS.............	50,737	60,775	62,053	61,076	59,231	61,242
88—AIRCRAFT; SPACECRAFT; AND PARTS THEREOF........................	24,310	25,912	34,170	32,956	28,755	44,382
90—OPTIC; PHOTO ETC; MEDIC OR SURGICAL INSTRMENTS ETC...........	26,616	28,763	29,608	27,570	28,675	30,273
87—VEHICLES; EXCEPT RAILWAY OR TRAMWAY; AND PARTS ETC	8,139	10,651	11,678	12,814	15,990	18,733
29—ORGANIC CHEMICALS..	21,482	22,695	20,153	18,521	18,691	16,140
39—PLASTICS AND ARTICLES THEREOF	12,361	13,737	13,448	15,454	15,654	14,318
02—MEAT AND EDIBLE MEAT OFFAL...............................	7,825	13,019	10,741	9,444	13,683	12,680
27—MINERAL FUEL; OIL ETC.; BITUMIN SUBST; MINERAL WAX..............	15,253	24,582	16,333	13,633	19,784	12,150
10—CEREALS	18,467	24,282	13,238	7,071	15,218	11,098
38—MISCELLANEOUS CHEMICAL PRODUCTS	8,094	8,182	9,618	10,139	10,282	10,232
30—PHARMACEUTICAL PRODUCTS	6,439	6,302	8,510	10,049	10,465	9,280
08—EDIBLE FRUIT & NUTS; CITRUS FRUIT OR MELON PEEL..................	3,708	4,945	6,802	6,925	7,503	7,438
28—INORG CHEM; PREC & RARE-EARTH MET & RADIOACT COMPD.......	7,386	8,416	8,339	5,992	6,407	6,633
98—SPECIAL CLASSIFICATION PROVISIONS; NESOI	10,250	7,242	5,808	5,711	6,865	6,570
76—ALUMINUM AND ARTICLES THEREOF	3,753	4,685	4,740	4,666	5,194	5,803
12—OIL SEEDS ETC.; MISC GRAIN; SEED; FRUIT; PLANT ETC	5,597	5,338	6,956	6,081	6,768	5,610
71—NAT ETC PEARLS; PREC ETC STONES; PR MET ETC; COIN	4,974	7,527	6,117	6,453	6,337	5,405
03—FISH; CRUSTACEANS & AQUATIC INVERTEBRATES	2,904	3,729	4,065	4,217	3,901	4,594
72—IRON AND STEEL...	11,314	15,749	13,117	10,784	7,672	4,415
IMPORTS						
Total...	48,875	56,661	58,899	62,370	69,680	71,759
87—VEHICLES; EXCEPT RAILWAY OR TRAMWAY; AND PARTS ETC	9,259	11,959	14,770	16,621	19,406	22,263
85—ELECTRIC MACHINERY ETC; SOUND EQUIP; TV EQUIP; PTS.............	15,267	16,080	12,770	14,695	15,476	14,670
84—NUCLEAR REACTORS; BOILERS; MACHINERY ETC.; PARTS..............	9,341	10,336	11,200	10,815	11,531	11,801
27—MINERAL FUEL; OIL ETC.; BITUMIN SUBST; MINERAL WAX..............	2,416	2,661	3,071	3,018	3,041	2,903
73—ARTICLES OF IRON OR STEEL.................................	1,544	2,145	2,753	2,577	3,320	2,460
72—IRON AND STEEL...	893	1,391	1,580	1,401	2,089	2,213
40—RUBBER AND ARTICLES THEREOF	1,573	1,989	2,156	1,823	1,828	1,945
39—PLASTICS AND ARTICLES THEREOF	1,065	1,266	1,466	1,661	1,830	1,869
29—ORGANIC CHEMICALS..	946	1,284	1,243	826	1,445	1,177
90—OPTIC; PHOTO ETC; MEDIC OR SURGICAL INSTRMENTS ETC...........	846	986	903	1,014	1,095	1,105
98—SPECIAL CLASSIFICATION PROVISIONS; NESOI	648	586	700	928	784	1,048
88—AIRCRAFT; SPACECRAFT; AND PARTS THEREOF........................	338	362	418	489	595	664
48—PAPER & PAPERBOARD & ARTICLES (INC PAPR PULP ARTL)	383	415	403	434	523	490
83—MISCELLANEOUS ARTICLES OF BASE METAL.....................	282	387	425	402	447	462
71—NAT ETC PEARLS; PREC ETC STONES; PR MET ETC; COIN	103	325	225	215	484	422
38—MISCELLANEOUS CHEMICAL PRODUCTS	186	261	241	269	240	401
82—TOOLS; CUTLERY ETC. OF BASE METAL & PARTS THEREOF	189	167	226	248	340	369
99—SPECIAL IMPORT PROVISIONS; NESOI	340	298	254	284	344	331
94—FURNITURE; BEDDING ETC; LAMPS NESOI ETC; PREFAB BD	182	211	250	331	365	308
74—COPPER AND ARTICLES THEREOF.............................	191	281	265	302	318	254

Table C-9.   U.S. Trade by Commodity with Netherlands, 2010–2015

(In millions of U.S. dollars.)

Commodity and 2-digit Harmonized System (HS) code	2010	2011	2012	2013	2014	2015
EXPORTS						
Total..	34,740	42,227	40,618	42,577	43,131	40,196
90—OPTIC; PHOTO ETC; MEDIC OR SURGICAL INSTRMENTS ETC...........	5,233	5,318	5,450	5,790	6,178	6,331
27—MINERAL FUEL; OIL ETC.; BITUMIN SUBST; MINERAL WAX..............	5,817	11,201	11,597	11,592	9,653	5,681
84—NUCLEAR REACTORS; BOILERS; MACHINERY ETC.; PARTS..............	4,049	4,102	4,237	4,093	4,292	4,486
85—ELECTRIC MACHINERY ETC; SOUND EQUIP; TV EQUIP; PTS..............	3,326	3,676	3,430	3,651	4,286	4,348
30—PHARMACEUTICAL PRODUCTS	3,930	3,037	2,920	3,381	4,096	4,230
88—AIRCRAFT; SPACECRAFT; AND PARTS THEREOF	1,499	1,877	1,433	1,525	1,442	2,084
29—ORGANIC CHEMICALS...	1,878	2,068	1,827	2,256	2,103	1,685
39—PLASTICS AND ARTICLES THEREOF..	1,054	1,172	1,085	1,144	1,234	1,278
87—VEHICLES; EXCEPT RAILWAY OR TRAMWAY; AND PARTS ETC	490	569	464	687	874	987
38—MISCELLANEOUS CHEMICAL PRODUCTS	751	874	846	742	835	835
98—SPECIAL CLASSIFICATION PROVISIONS; NESOI	962	720	698	724	760	715
12—OIL SEEDS ETC.; MISC GRAIN; SEED; FRUIT; PLANT ETC	186	291	178	264	593	620
28—INORG CHEM; PREC & RARE-EARTH MET & RADIOACT COMPD........	293	410	249	259	443	600
33—ESSENTIAL OILS ETC; PERFUMERY; COSMETIC ETC PREPS	341	389	399	430	474	516
08—EDIBLE FRUIT & NUTS; CITRUS FRUIT OR MELON PEEL...................	250	281	290	329	414	408
21—MISCELLANEOUS EDIBLE PREPARATIONS....................................	147	175	176	260	303	294
73—ARTICLES OF IRON OR STEEL...	125	151	131	241	179	280
26—ORES; SLAG AND ASH..	245	386	358	467	349	279
22—BEVERAGES; SPIRITS AND VINEGAR	268	538	347	203	260	265
20—PREP VEGETABLES; FRUIT; NUTS OR OTHER PLANT PARTS............	163	202	213	235	203	244
IMPORTS						
Total..	19,055	23,455	22,260	19,234	20,899	16,836
84—NUCLEAR REACTORS; BOILERS; MACHINERY ETC.; PARTS..............	2,305	3,843	3,245	2,606	4,519	3,245
27—MINERAL FUEL; OIL ETC.; BITUMIN SUBST; MINERAL WAX..............	3,202	4,734	4,830	3,588	3,248	1,559
30—PHARMACEUTICAL PRODUCTS	525	615	1,316	1,633	1,511	1,534
98—SPECIAL CLASSIFICATION PROVISIONS; NESOI	4,684	5,139	3,358	2,420	1,935	1,492
22—BEVERAGES; SPIRITS AND VINEGAR	1,221	1,147	1,163	1,151	1,092	1,154
29—ORGANIC CHEMICALS...	861	871	1,121	1,197	1,223	1,112
90—OPTIC; PHOTO ETC; MEDIC OR SURGICAL INSTRMENTS ETC...........	966	1,038	1,050	864	943	952
72—IRON AND STEEL..	444	489	549	532	791	575
85—ELECTRIC MACHINERY ETC; SOUND EQUIP; TV EQUIP; PTS..............	503	577	535	523	617	503
39—PLASTICS AND ARTICLES THEREOF..	371	430	452	458	502	486
28—INORG CHEM; PREC & RARE-EARTH MET & RADIOACT COMPD........	850	946	915	656	621	476
88—AIRCRAFT; SPACECRAFT; AND PARTS THEREOF	268	274	327	305	371	313
87—VEHICLES; EXCEPT RAILWAY OR TRAMWAY; AND PARTS ETC	69	76	85	88	154	220
38—MISCELLANEOUS CHEMICAL PRODUCTS	195	211	218	232	199	208
06—LIVE TREES; PLANTS; BULBS ETC.; CUT FLOWERS ETC.	197	208	188	189	192	182
97—WORKS OF ART; COLLECTORS' PIECES AND ANTIQUES..................	206	292	355	248	311	166
73—ARTICLES OF IRON OR STEEL...	71	77	96	135	111	160
18—COCOA AND COCOA PREPARATIONS..	250	297	267	202	168	144
99—SPECIAL IMPORT PROVISIONS; NESOI	94	103	88	82	123	128
35—ALBUMINOIDAL SUBST; MODIFIED STARCH; GLUE; ENZYMES	98	106	124	113	136	115

Table C-10.   U.S. Trade by Commodity with Hong Kong, 2010–2015

(In millions of U.S. dollars.)

Commodity and 2-digit Harmonized System (HS) code	2010	2011	2012	2013	2014	2015
EXPORTS						
Total..	26,570	36,399	37,472	42,332	40,911	37,167
71—NAT ETC PEARLS; PREC ETC STONES; PR MET ETC; COIN	4,938	11,388	12,911	16,264	13,790	11,457
85—ELECTRIC MACHINERY ETC; SOUND EQUIP; TV EQUIP; PTS	6,663	7,493	7,420	8,197	9,738	9,474
88—AIRCRAFT; SPACECRAFT; AND PARTS THEREOF	1,404	2,486	2,495	3,229	2,335	2,023
84—NUCLEAR REACTORS; BOILERS; MACHINERY ETC.; PARTS	2,246	2,451	2,587	2,342	2,228	1,918
97—WORKS OF ART; COLLECTORS' PIECES AND ANTIQUES...................	337	516	457	521	1,283	1,653
02—MEAT AND EDIBLE MEAT OFFAL	1,008	1,186	917	1,210	1,880	1,404
90—OPTIC; PHOTO ETC; MEDIC OR SURGICAL INSTRMENTS ETC...........	1,480	1,699	1,764	1,504	1,431	1,400
08—EDIBLE FRUIT & NUTS; CITRUS FRUIT OR MELON PEEL	929	1,154	1,541	1,540	1,262	1,153
39—PLASTICS AND ARTICLES THEREOF..................................	1,385	1,313	1,162	1,070	1,155	1,072
98—SPECIAL CLASSIFICATION PROVISIONS; NESOI	803	694	671	773	693	602
87—VEHICLES; EXCEPT RAILWAY OR TRAMWAY; AND PARTS ETC	536	766	534	394	519	451
33—ESSENTIAL OILS ETC; PERFUMERY; COSMETIC ETC PREPS	270	311	380	412	361	380
70—GLASS AND GLASSWARE	249	221	292	441	369	357
91—CLOCKS AND WATCHES AND PARTS THEREOF	145	202	183	194	216	216
30—PHARMACEUTICAL PRODUCTS	213	198	213	174	199	215
21—MISCELLANEOUS EDIBLE PREPARATIONS..............................	124	165	210	202	154	213
38—MISCELLANEOUS CHEMICAL PRODUCTS	269	421	185	261	196	182
03—FISH; CRUSTACEANS & AQUATIC INVERTEBRATES	93	130	161	193	135	149
22—BEVERAGES; SPIRITS AND VINEGAR	137	185	140	122	126	142
74—COPPER AND ARTICLES THEREOF...................................	326	259	216	245	183	141
IMPORTS						
Total..	4,296	4,410	5,456	5,654	5,897	6,796
98—SPECIAL CLASSIFICATION PROVISIONS; NESOI	936	1,294	2,165	2,594	2,599	2,175
71—NAT ETC PEARLS; PREC ETC STONES; PR MET ETC; COIN	565	683	785	749	806	1,757
85—ELECTRIC MACHINERY ETC; SOUND EQUIP; TV EQUIP; PTS	1,078	713	877	697	780	879
84—NUCLEAR REACTORS; BOILERS; MACHINERY ETC.; PARTS	289	320	299	288	235	243
39—PLASTICS AND ARTICLES THEREOF..................................	118	116	108	109	117	144
95—TOYS; GAMES & SPORT EQUIPMENT; PARTS & ACCESSORIES	124	145	113	100	114	143
94—FURNITURE; BEDDING ETC; LAMPS NESOI ETC; PREFAB BD	52	53	56	62	79	124
90—OPTIC; PHOTO ETC; MEDIC OR SURGICAL INSTRUMENTS ETC...........	97	111	103	110	106	121
62—APPAREL ARTICLES AND ACCESSORIES; NOT KNIT ETC.	90	90	83	89	86	88
49—PRINTED BOOKS; NEWSPAPERS ETC; MANUSCRIPTS ETC	104	89	61	55	62	84
61—APPAREL ARTICLES AND ACCESSORIES; KNIT OR CROCHET	95	78	70	62	71	83
42—LEATHER ART; SADDLERY ETC; HANDBAGS ETC; GUT ART..............	64	81	60	66	72	78
33—ESSENTIAL OILS ETC; PERFUMERY; COSMETIC ETC PREPS	12	12	11	9	11	67
99—SPECIAL IMPORT PROVISIONS; NESOI	55	48	40	32	52	52
48—PAPER & PAPERBOARD & ARTICLES (INC PAPR PULP ARTL)	59	35	48	75	94	47
64—FOOTWEAR; GAITERS ETC. AND PARTS THEREOF	60	40	36	41	28	46
73—ARTICLES OF IRON OR STEEL.......................................	34	29	39	39	40	45
21—MISCELLANEOUS EDIBLE PREPARATIONS..............................	32	34	34	38	32	42
91—CLOCKS AND WATCHES AND PARTS THEREOF	28	38	41	32	31	37
96—MISCELLANEOUS MANUFACTURED ARTICLES	25	29	23	24	22	34

Table C-11.   U.S. Trade by Commodity with Belgium, 2010–2015

(In millions of U.S. dollars.)

Commodity and 2-digit Harmonized System (HS) code	2010	2011	2012	2013	2014	2015
EXPORTS						
Total...	25,458	29,990	29,438	31,840	34,781	34,160
30—PHARMACEUTICAL PRODUCTS	1,771	2,652	3,219	4,067	5,557	6,466
29—ORGANIC CHEMICALS......................................	4,397	4,458	4,498	4,559	4,428	4,852
90—OPTIC; PHOTO ETC; MEDIC OR SURGICAL INSTRMENTS ETC...........	2,542	3,131	3,509	4,019	4,510	4,335
71—NAT ETC PEARLS; PREC ETC STONES; PR MET ETC; COIN	2,231	2,918	2,814	2,952	3,905	3,105
84—NUCLEAR REACTORS; BOILERS; MACHINERY ETC.; PARTS	2,655	3,431	3,438	3,228	3,444	3,039
39—PLASTICS AND ARTICLES THEREOF......................	2,042	2,176	2,096	2,365	2,395	2,160
27—MINERAL FUEL; OIL ETC.; BITUMIN SUBST; MINERAL WAX..............	851	1,715	1,124	2,075	1,343	1,277
87—VEHICLES; EXCEPT RAILWAY OR TRAMWAY; AND PARTS ETC	856	942	958	937	1,165	1,202
85—ELECTRIC MACHINERY ETC; SOUND EQUIP; TV EQUIP; PTS..............	974	1,030	1,005	969	1,006	1,135
38—MISCELLANEOUS CHEMICAL PRODUCTS	1,007	960	1,014	966	1,034	970
98—SPECIAL CLASSIFICATION PROVISIONS; NESOI	716	507	480	476	532	581
88—AIRCRAFT; SPACECRAFT; AND PARTS THEREOF	738	1,066	399	567	456	400
32—TANNING & DYE EXT ETC; DYE; PAINT; PUTTY ETC; INKS.................	421	608	534	459	481	393
40—RUBBER AND ARTICLES THEREOF........................	338	445	426	403	471	367
97—WORKS OF ART; COLLECTORS' PIECES AND ANTIQUES....................	161	93	94	138	239	287
08—EDIBLE FRUIT & NUTS; CITRUS FRUIT OR MELON PEEL...................	147	128	130	156	250	285
28—INORG CHEM; PREC & RARE-EARTH MET & RADIOACT COMPD.......	281	411	335	295	265	276
26—ORES; SLAG AND ASH.....................................	340	298	261	196	320	171
47—WOOD PULP ETC; RECOVD (WASTE & SCRAP) PPR & PPRBD..........	101	101	87	187	191	171
33—ESSENTIAL OILS ETC; PERFUMERY; COSMETIC ETC PREPS	226	238	252	168	164	169
IMPORTS						
Total...	15,552	17,431	17,368	19,010	20,962	19,482
71—NAT ETC PEARLS; PREC ETC STONES; PR MET ETC; COIN	3,211	3,990	3,739	4,206	4,085	3,790
30—PHARMACEUTICAL PRODUCTS	2,444	1,965	2,065	2,594	3,359	3,074
27—MINERAL FUEL; OIL ETC.; BITUMIN SUBST; MINERAL WAX..............	2,329	2,214	2,473	2,790	3,234	2,107
29—ORGANIC CHEMICALS......................................	1,910	1,855	841	1,446	1,879	1,985
98—SPECIAL CLASSIFICATION PROVISIONS; NESOI	790	1,022	1,365	1,563	2,079	1,969
87—VEHICLES; EXCEPT RAILWAY OR TRAMWAY; AND PARTS ETC	739	1,418	1,730	1,370	937	1,279
84—NUCLEAR REACTORS; BOILERS; MACHINERY ETC.; PARTS	1,040	1,324	1,538	1,381	1,344	1,279
39—PLASTICS AND ARTICLES THEREOF......................	308	351	358	371	498	556
85—ELECTRIC MACHINERY ETC; SOUND EQUIP; TV EQUIP; PTS..............	476	524	538	510	478	406
22—BEVERAGES; SPIRITS AND VINEGAR	170	219	243	250	324	394
97—WORKS OF ART; COLLECTORS' PIECES AND ANTIQUES....................	169	198	163	157	197	227
38—MISCELLANEOUS CHEMICAL PRODUCTS	100	118	150	179	144	194
72—IRON AND STEEL...	171	208	215	197	277	177
37—PHOTOGRAPHIC OR CINEMATOGRAPHIC GOODS.................	137	183	191	169	192	165
28—INORG CHEM; PREC & RARE-EARTH MET & RADIOACT COMPD.......	164	180	156	152	144	142
33—ESSENTIAL OILS ETC; PERFUMERY; COSMETIC ETC PREPS	89	105	107	99	119	130
18—COCOA AND COCOA PREPARATIONS........................	93	115	121	124	132	125
90—OPTIC; PHOTO ETC; MEDIC OR SURGICAL INSTRMENTS ETC...........	101	116	113	107	133	115
99—SPECIAL IMPORT PROVISIONS; NESOI	76	86	63	67	112	99
57—CARPETS AND OTHER TEXTILE FLOOR COVERINGS................	83	86	81	73	87	83

Table C-12.   U.S. Trade by Commodity with France, 2010–2015

(In millions of U.S. dollars.)

Commodity and 2-digit Harmonized System (HS) code	2010	2011	2012	2013	2014	2015
EXPORTS						
Total...	26,970	27,857	30,813	31,744	31,307	30,104
88—AIRCRAFT; SPACECRAFT; AND PARTS THEREOF	7,216	7,139	8,198	8,587	8,408	9,622
84—NUCLEAR REACTORS; BOILERS; MACHINERY ETC.; PARTS	2,680	2,780	2,759	2,676	2,784	2,748
27—MINERAL FUEL; OIL ETC.; BITUMIN SUBST; MINERAL WAX	1,173	2,359	3,741	4,892	4,594	2,669
85—ELECTRIC MACHINERY ETC; SOUND EQUIP; TV EQUIP; PTS	1,980	2,111	2,035	2,093	2,088	2,059
90—OPTIC; PHOTO ETC; MEDIC OR SURGICAL INSTRMENTS ETC............	2,356	2,322	2,206	2,236	2,060	1,889
29—ORGANIC CHEMICALS..	2,284	1,876	1,674	1,283	1,283	1,462
30—PHARMACEUTICAL PRODUCTS	1,566	1,221	1,930	1,601	1,574	1,409
98—SPECIAL CLASSIFICATION PROVISIONS; NESOI	1,192	942	1,028	1,137	1,035	974
71—NAT ETC PEARLS; PREC ETC STONES; PR MET ETC; COIN	462	506	887	653	957	891
38—MISCELLANEOUS CHEMICAL PRODUCTS	718	815	854	877	885	870
97—WORKS OF ART; COLLECTORS' PIECES AND ANTIQUES....................	631	570	521	632	754	804
39—PLASTICS AND ARTICLES THEREOF	548	576	574	527	521	492
87—VEHICLES; EXCEPT RAILWAY OR TRAMWAY; AND PARTS ETC	512	622	675	606	542	466
33—ESSENTIAL OILS ETC; PERFUMERY; COSMETIC ETC PREPS	194	178	189	259	286	327
81—BASE METALS NESOI; CERMETS; ARTICLES THEREOF	163	284	293	280	303	281
73—ARTICLES OF IRON OR STEEL...	207	234	254	277	246	254
76—ALUMINUM AND ARTICLES THEREOF	120	153	207	211	205	198
40—RUBBER AND ARTICLES THEREOF	212	270	257	182	176	189
75—NICKEL AND ARTICLES THEREOF	140	233	214	166	183	163
08—EDIBLE FRUIT & NUTS; CITRUS FRUIT OR MELON PEEL....................	119	136	133	126	138	151
IMPORTS						
Total...	38,355	40,049	41,646	45,706	47,106	47,815
84—NUCLEAR REACTORS; BOILERS; MACHINERY ETC.; PARTS	6,329	7,037	8,275	8,980	9,536	9,434
88—AIRCRAFT; SPACECRAFT; AND PARTS THEREOF	4,992	4,838	4,910	6,040	5,964	5,948
22—BEVERAGES; SPIRITS AND VINEGAR	2,697	3,145	3,397	3,531	3,674	3,777
97—WORKS OF ART; COLLECTORS' PIECES AND ANTIQUES....................	1,928	1,843	1,748	2,857	2,480	3,425
98—SPECIAL CLASSIFICATION PROVISIONS; NESOI	2,040	1,843	2,209	2,727	2,842	3,238
30—PHARMACEUTICAL PRODUCTS	4,791	3,521	3,026	2,648	2,470	2,797
90—OPTIC; PHOTO ETC; MEDIC OR SURGICAL INSTRMENTS ETC............	2,139	2,256	2,110	2,212	2,363	2,354
33—ESSENTIAL OILS ETC; PERFUMERY; COSMETIC ETC PREPS	1,484	1,705	1,763	1,901	2,160	2,196
85—ELECTRIC MACHINERY ETC; SOUND EQUIP; TV EQUIP; PTS	1,526	1,726	1,793	1,862	2,035	2,092
87—VEHICLES; EXCEPT RAILWAY OR TRAMWAY; AND PARTS ETC	913	1,070	941	872	1,108	1,046
71—NAT ETC PEARLS; PREC ETC STONES; PR MET ETC; COIN	468	537	643	776	923	955
27—MINERAL FUEL; OIL ETC.; BITUMIN SUBST; MINERAL WAX	1,249	1,810	1,793	1,957	1,512	918
29—ORGANIC CHEMICALS..	1,053	1,074	938	943	978	851
39—PLASTICS AND ARTICLES THEREOF	466	527	617	700	710	726
42—LEATHER ART; SADDLERY ETC; HANDBAGS ETC; GUT ART.............	380	443	554	564	619	650
38—MISCELLANEOUS CHEMICAL PRODUCTS	520	582	606	716	763	641
72—IRON AND STEEL...	344	453	421	417	533	553
40—RUBBER AND ARTICLES THEREOF	413	565	665	651	652	550
73—ARTICLES OF IRON OR STEEL...	349	463	488	416	467	414
99—SPECIAL IMPORT PROVISIONS; NESOI	333	350	310	311	409	409

Table C-13.   U.S. Trade by Commodity with Brazil, 2010–2015

(In millions of U.S. dollars.)

Commodity and 2-digit Harmonized System (HS) code	2010	2011	2012	2013	2014	2015
EXPORTS						
Total..	35,418	43,019	43,771	44,106	42,434	31,651
88—AIRCRAFT; SPACECRAFT; AND PARTS THEREOF	4,472	5,387	6,079	5,307	4,805	4,723
84—NUCLEAR REACTORS; BOILERS; MACHINERY ETC.; PARTS..............	7,155	7,934	7,744	7,284	6,530	4,660
27—MINERAL FUEL; OIL ETC.; BITUMIN SUBST; MINERAL WAX.............	4,194	6,398	7,300	6,587	7,405	3,821
85—ELECTRIC MACHINERY ETC; SOUND EQUIP; TV EQUIP; PTS............	4,283	4,645	4,771	5,214	4,386	3,255
90—OPTIC; PHOTO ETC; MEDIC OR SURGICAL INSTRMENTS ETC...........	1,877	2,054	2,206	2,290	2,281	1,937
39—PLASTICS AND ARTICLES THEREOF	1,835	2,096	1,995	2,264	2,065	1,800
29—ORGANIC CHEMICALS..	2,038	1,991	2,008	2,310	2,262	1,773
38—MISCELLANEOUS CHEMICAL PRODUCTS	866	1,050	1,245	1,510	1,632	1,192
87—VEHICLES; EXCEPT RAILWAY OR TRAMWAY; AND PARTS ETC	1,072	1,343	1,405	1,269	1,281	1,067
30—PHARMACEUTICAL PRODUCTS	1,207	992	1,097	1,156	1,380	1,044
31—FERTILIZERS..	672	1,172	992	1,026	950	847
28—INORG CHEM; PREC & RARE-EARTH MET & RADIOACT COMPD.......	550	779	832	784	734	739
98—SPECIAL CLASSIFICATION PROVISIONS; NESOI	768	808	791	774	779	615
40—RUBBER AND ARTICLES THEREOF	499	655	643	613	551	442
73—ARTICLES OF IRON OR STEEL	353	382	476	588	476	310
22—BEVERAGES; SPIRITS AND VINEGAR	51	1,141	250	134	282	264
32—TANNING & DYE EXT ETC; DYE; PAINT; PUTTY ETC; INKS.............	299	323	304	257	267	219
34—SOAP ETC; WAXES; POLISH ETC; CANDLES; DENTAL PREPS..........	157	195	201	236	249	208
86—RAILWAY OR TRAMWAY STOCK ETC; TRAFFIC SIGNAL EQUIP..........	160	220	304	221	117	187
33—ESSENTIAL OILS ETC; PERFUMERY; COSMETIC ETC PREPS...........	185	177	197	205	186	173
IMPORTS						
Total..	23,958	31,737	32,123	27,541	30,021	27,468
27—MINERAL FUEL; OIL ETC.; BITUMIN SUBST; MINERAL WAX.............	7,929	10,518	9,400	5,782	6,387	4,549
88—AIRCRAFT; SPACECRAFT; AND PARTS THEREOF	729	895	985	1,742	2,323	3,035
72—IRON AND STEEL	1,446	3,484	3,551	2,984	3,617	2,957
98—SPECIAL CLASSIFICATION PROVISIONS; NESOI	742	1,344	1,895	1,938	2,181	2,610
84—NUCLEAR REACTORS; BOILERS; MACHINERY ETC.; PARTS..............	1,747	2,342	2,658	1,862	1,957	1,664
09—COFFEE; TEA; MATE & SPICES	1,137	2,020	1,418	1,178	1,455	1,493
47—WOOD PULP ETC; RECOVD (WASTE & SCRAP) PPR & PPRBD..........	961	1,011	958	1,153	1,032	1,058
44—WOOD AND ARTICLES OF WOOD; WOOD CHARCOAL......................	608	543	626	742	844	894
68—ART OF STONE; PLASTER; CEMENT; ASBESTOS; MICA ETC.	570	585	643	817	851	848
29—ORGANIC CHEMICALS..	799	830	869	902	891	586
87—VEHICLES; EXCEPT RAILWAY OR TRAMWAY; AND PARTS ETC	422	558	589	423	562	546
22—BEVERAGES; SPIRITS AND VINEGAR	261	590	1,533	1,255	550	535
85—ELECTRIC MACHINERY ETC; SOUND EQUIP; TV EQUIP; PTS............	588	586	626	521	543	475
28—INORG CHEM; PREC & RARE-EARTH MET & RADIOACT COMPD.......	374	486	436	365	371	359
40—RUBBER AND ARTICLES THEREOF	488	582	566	373	392	340
20—PREP VEGETABLES; FRUIT; NUTS OR OTHER PLANT PARTS...........	335	362	328	277	404	329
71—NAT ETC PEARLS; PREC ETC STONES; PR MET ETC; COIN.............	290	316	245	242	326	314
16—EDIBLE PREPARATIONS OF MEAT; FISH; CRUSTACEANS ETC............	85	147	198	226	221	307
26—ORES; SLAG AND ASH..	211	164	210	228	387	303
39—PLASTICS AND ARTICLES THEREOF	185	193	190	193	190	257

Table C-14.   U.S. Trade by Commodity with Singapore, 2010–2015

(In millions of U.S. dollars.)

Commodity and 2-digit Harmonized System (HS) code	2010	2011	2012	2013	2014	2015
EXPORTS						
Total...	29,009	31,282	30,523	30,665	30,072	28,472
88—AIRCRAFT; SPACECRAFT; AND PARTS THEREOF	3,806	3,855	3,950	3,769	4,154	5,776
84—NUCLEAR REACTORS; BOILERS; MACHINERY ETC.; PARTS	5,599	5,864	5,507	5,243	5,292	4,881
85—ELECTRIC MACHINERY ETC; SOUND EQUIP; TV EQUIP; PTS	5,530	5,118	4,650	4,534	4,481	3,954
90—OPTIC; PHOTO ETC; MEDIC OR SURGICAL INSTRMENTS ETC...........	2,088	2,295	2,419	2,736	2,621	2,688
27—MINERAL FUEL; OIL ETC.; BITUMIN SUBST; MINERAL WAX	3,385	4,412	4,433	4,812	3,852	2,018
98—SPECIAL CLASSIFICATION PROVISIONS; NESOI	1,473	1,150	1,058	1,072	1,198	1,027
39—PLASTICS AND ARTICLES THEREOF	1,330	1,741	1,409	1,154	1,096	1,010
29—ORGANIC CHEMICALS..	880	830	862	1,217	1,010	984
38—MISCELLANEOUS CHEMICAL PRODUCTS	805	986	952	1,142	977	948
71—NAT ETC PEARLS; PREC ETC STONES; PR MET ETC; COIN	305	393	413	773	1,066	756
30—PHARMACEUTICAL PRODUCTS	163	183	237	348	388	411
40—RUBBER AND ARTICLES THEREOF	150	195	177	164	202	373
89—SHIPS; BOATS AND FLOATING STRUCTURES................................	34	62	535	78	55	311
33—ESSENTIAL OILS ETC; PERFUMERY; COSMETIC ETC PREPS	152	182	214	246	267	298
73—ARTICLES OF IRON OR STEEL..	349	374	387	361	347	275
87—VEHICLES; EXCEPT RAILWAY OR TRAMWAY; AND PARTS ETC	271	564	504	279	254	195
32—TANNING & DYE EXT ETC; DYE; PAINT; PUTTY ETC; INKS................	232	273	245	224	183	175
34—SOAP ETC; WAXES; POLISH ETC; CANDLES; DENTAL PREPS	165	158	151	167	181	169
28—INORG CHEM; PREC & RARE-EARTH MET & RADIOACT COMPD.......	269	330	226	146	130	160
21—MISCELLANEOUS EDIBLE PREPARATIONS.....................................	76	79	110	113	102	92
IMPORTS						
Total...	17,428	19,116	20,232	17,843	16,502	18,267
29—ORGANIC CHEMICALS..	2,608	4,457	4,956	3,669	3,784	3,541
84—NUCLEAR REACTORS; BOILERS; MACHINERY ETC.; PARTS	5,281	5,179	4,881	3,382	2,824	3,405
85—ELECTRIC MACHINERY ETC; SOUND EQUIP; TV EQUIP; PTS	2,752	2,948	2,811	2,661	2,460	2,562
90—OPTIC; PHOTO ETC; MEDIC OR SURGICAL INSTRMENTS ETC...........	1,243	1,662	1,994	2,074	2,358	2,530
98—SPECIAL CLASSIFICATION PROVISIONS; NESOI	1,592	1,821	2,543	2,652	1,862	2,433
30—PHARMACEUTICAL PRODUCTS	1,779	1,266	851	972	1,013	1,482
38—MISCELLANEOUS CHEMICAL PRODUCTS	124	175	211	275	604	814
71—NAT ETC PEARLS; PREC ETC STONES; PR MET ETC; COIN	63	184	161	165	326	327
39—PLASTICS AND ARTICLES THEREOF	214	208	248	291	304	258
27—MINERAL FUEL; OIL ETC.; BITUMIN SUBST; MINERAL WAX	129	142	82	772	171	134
99—SPECIAL IMPORT PROVISIONS; NESOI	268	298	296	165	148	132
88—AIRCRAFT; SPACECRAFT; AND PARTS THEREOF	104	107	95	210	90	98
49—PRINTED BOOKS; NEWSPAPERS ETC; MANUSCRIPTS ETC..............	123	108	74	55	53	43
87—VEHICLES; EXCEPT RAILWAY OR TRAMWAY; AND PARTS ETC	21	33	56	38	41	43
73—ARTICLES OF IRON OR STEEL..	24	32	26	30	40	37
94—FURNITURE; BEDDING ETC; LAMPS NESOI ETC; PREFAB BD	19	19	27	22	27	32
19—PREP CEREAL; FLOUR; STARCH OR MILK; BAKERS WARES..............	22	26	31	29	30	31
33—ESSENTIAL OILS ETC; PERFUMERY; COSMETIC ETC PREPS	32	30	32	26	23	28
70—GLASS AND GLASSWARE	2	2	4	6	13	27
32—TANNING & DYE EXT ETC; DYE; PAINT; PUTTY ETC; INKS................	62	63	54	43	30	26

Table C-15. U.S. Trade by Commodity with Taiwan, 2010–2015

(In millions of U.S. dollars.)

Commodity and 2-digit Harmonized System (HS) code	2010	2011	2012	2013	2014	2015
EXPORTS						
Total	26,050	25,932	24,337	25,523	26,667	25,860
84—NUCLEAR REACTORS; BOILERS; MACHINERY ETC.; PARTS	5,866	4,581	4,425	4,748	4,363	4,937
85—ELECTRIC MACHINERY ETC; SOUND EQUIP; TV EQUIP; PTS	4,645	5,046	4,466	4,041	4,222	4,500
88—AIRCRAFT; SPACECRAFT; AND PARTS THEREOF	1,299	812	846	1,752	2,860	2,890
90—OPTIC; PHOTO ETC; MEDIC OR SURGICAL INSTRMENTS ETC	2,017	1,849	1,788	1,633	1,838	1,815
93—ARMS AND AMMUNITION; PARTS AND ACCESSORIES THEREOF	220	41	28	573	535	1,529
29—ORGANIC CHEMICALS	1,145	1,447	1,323	1,138	1,269	930
39—PLASTICS AND ARTICLES THEREOF	837	969	861	851	884	810
10—CEREALS	910	1,217	716	603	801	674
12—OIL SEEDS ETC.; MISC GRAIN; SEED; FRUIT; PLANT ETC	694	753	825	652	782	633
02—MEAT AND EDIBLE MEAT OFFAL	379	367	340	455	467	515
72—IRON AND STEEL	1,264	1,873	1,595	1,243	1,040	491
28—INORG CHEM; PREC & RARE-EARTH MET & RADIOACT COMPD	702	752	656	583	660	442
38—MISCELLANEOUS CHEMICAL PRODUCTS	557	607	626	705	547	441
98—SPECIAL CLASSIFICATION PROVISIONS; NESOI	737	477	411	402	500	422
30—PHARMACEUTICAL PRODUCTS	344	300	343	394	391	371
87—VEHICLES; EXCEPT RAILWAY OR TRAMWAY; AND PARTS ETC	303	370	334	397	420	325
71—NAT ETC PEARLS; PREC ETC STONES; PR MET ETC; COIN	367	486	410	322	337	297
08—EDIBLE FRUIT & NUTS; CITRUS FRUIT OR MELON PEEL	206	247	289	290	310	291
27—MINERAL FUEL; OIL ETC.; BITUMIN SUBST; MINERAL WAX	142	105	467	1,127	784	229
48—PAPER & PAPERBOARD & ARTICLES (INC PAPR PULP ARTL)	211	233	218	214	222	216
IMPORTS						
Total	35,847	41,405	38,861	37,939	40,839	40,908
85—ELECTRIC MACHINERY ETC; SOUND EQUIP; TV EQUIP; PTS	15,661	18,121	14,656	13,897	14,721	14,178
84—NUCLEAR REACTORS; BOILERS; MACHINERY ETC.; PARTS	5,162	6,518	6,608	6,622	7,053	6,690
87—VEHICLES; EXCEPT RAILWAY OR TRAMWAY; AND PARTS ETC	1,870	2,151	2,379	2,366	2,447	2,696
73—ARTICLES OF IRON OR STEEL	1,848	2,234	2,346	2,295	2,471	2,536
39—PLASTICS AND ARTICLES THEREOF	1,342	1,493	1,585	1,681	1,755	1,858
90—OPTIC; PHOTO ETC; MEDIC OR SURGICAL INSTRMENTS ETC	889	1,010	1,094	1,094	1,265	1,224
94—FURNITURE; BEDDING ETC; LAMPS NESOI ETC; PREFAB BD	778	845	952	965	1,026	1,140
72—IRON AND STEEL	572	716	875	742	1,116	1,046
98—SPECIAL CLASSIFICATION PROVISIONS; NESOI	889	1,056	696	815	887	965
95—TOYS; GAMES & SPORT EQUIPMENT; PARTS & ACCESSORIES	752	768	840	807	865	935
40—RUBBER AND ARTICLES THEREOF	583	717	702	692	720	822
82—TOOLS; CUTLERY ETC. OF BASE METAL & PARTS THEREOF	538	647	678	678	682	750
83—MISCELLANEOUS ARTICLES OF BASE METAL	540	599	654	705	729	748
99—SPECIAL IMPORT PROVISIONS; NESOI	538	595	496	500	597	568
29—ORGANIC CHEMICALS	331	330	386	334	506	390
38—MISCELLANEOUS CHEMICAL PRODUCTS	127	164	183	252	263	269
70—GLASS AND GLASSWARE	175	207	214	223	231	253
61—APPAREL ARTICLES AND ACCESSORIES; KNIT OR CROCHET	360	337	297	263	262	243
27—MINERAL FUEL; OIL ETC.; BITUMIN SUBST; MINERAL WAX	397	156	315	40	67	241
89—SHIPS; BOATS AND FLOATING STRUCTURES	73	82	81	110	105	174

Table C-16.   U.S. Trade by Commodity with Switzerland, 2010–2015

(In millions of U.S. dollars.)

Commodity and 2-digit Harmonized System (HS) code	2010	2011	2012	2013	2014	2015
EXPORTS						
Total..	20,704	24,486	26,406	26,559	22,169	22,185
71—NAT ETC PEARLS; PREC ETC STONES; PR MET ETC; COIN	11,263	14,488	16,691	16,068	10,594	10,270
97—WORKS OF ART; COLLECTORS' PIECES AND ANTIQUES....................	1,847	1,902	1,992	1,810	2,271	2,703
30—PHARMACEUTICAL PRODUCTS...	2,106	2,371	1,688	2,075	2,277	2,094
90—OPTIC; PHOTO ETC; MEDIC OR SURGICAL INSTRMENTS ETC...........	1,189	1,213	1,197	1,338	1,327	1,355
88—AIRCRAFT; SPACECRAFT; AND PARTS THEREOF	691	498	746	871	1,022	895
84—NUCLEAR REACTORS; BOILERS; MACHINERY ETC.; PARTS..............	558	595	603	605	565	589
85—ELECTRIC MACHINERY ETC; SOUND EQUIP; TV EQUIP; PTS..............	507	507	469	555	590	579
98—SPECIAL CLASSIFICATION PROVISIONS; NESOI...............................	693	590	681	694	513	566
27—MINERAL FUEL; OIL ETC.; BITUMIN SUBST; MINERAL WAX..............	23	180	121	94	493	495
29—ORGANIC CHEMICALS...	305	316	296	320	397	423
87—VEHICLES; EXCEPT RAILWAY OR TRAMWAY; AND PARTS ETC	98	195	236	291	344	337
91—CLOCKS AND WATCHES AND PARTS THEREOF..............................	190	242	300	264	275	288
24—TOBACCO AND MANUFACTURED TOBACCO SUBSTITUTES	118	195	164	222	203	269
33—ESSENTIAL OILS ETC; PERFUMERY; COSMETIC ETC PREPS	139	145	157	160	175	189
32—TANNING & DYE EXT ETC; DYE; PAINT; PUTTY ETC; INKS..................	119	132	145	155	146	175
39—PLASTICS AND ARTICLES THEREOF..	101	109	110	104	113	141
73—ARTICLES OF IRON OR STEEL..	114	132	116	111	103	105
38—MISCELLANEOUS CHEMICAL PRODUCTS	90	79	72	72	80	81
81—BASE METALS NESOI; CERMETS; ARTICLES THEREOF....................	29	34	52	48	53	55
08—EDIBLE FRUIT & NUTS; CITRUS FRUIT OR MELON PEEL..................	33	40	45	49	49	42
IMPORTS						
Total..	19,137	24,362	25,672	28,275	31,323	31,397
30—PHARMACEUTICAL PRODUCTS...	5,021	6,659	7,386	8,309	9,581	9,421
98—SPECIAL CLASSIFICATION PROVISIONS; NESOI...............................	947	1,479	2,421	3,610	3,960	3,878
90—OPTIC; PHOTO ETC; MEDIC OR SURGICAL INSTRMENTS ETC...........	2,347	2,858	2,734	2,885	3,139	3,138
91—CLOCKS AND WATCHES AND PARTS THEREOF..............................	1,835	2,780	2,704	2,815	3,004	3,011
84—NUCLEAR REACTORS; BOILERS; MACHINERY ETC.; PARTS..............	1,884	2,395	2,391	2,406	2,654	2,676
71—NAT ETC PEARLS; PREC ETC STONES; PR MET ETC; COIN	1,377	2,039	1,585	1,664	2,047	1,809
29—ORGANIC CHEMICALS...	1,812	1,729	1,964	1,984	1,807	1,806
85—ELECTRIC MACHINERY ETC; SOUND EQUIP; TV EQUIP; PTS..............	947	1,079	1,088	1,090	1,200	1,262
22—BEVERAGES; SPIRITS AND VINEGAR..	383	447	547	676	769	938
97—WORKS OF ART; COLLECTORS' PIECES AND ANTIQUES....................	305	333	289	338	385	709
88—AIRCRAFT; SPACECRAFT; AND PARTS THEREOF	255	240	272	299	311	345
39—PLASTICS AND ARTICLES THEREOF..	221	246	255	245	265	266
99—SPECIAL IMPORT PROVISIONS; NESOI..	187	229	210	207	267	261
82—TOOLS; CUTLERY ETC. OF BASE METAL & PARTS THEREOF	158	191	202	194	219	225
33—ESSENTIAL OILS ETC; PERFUMERY; COSMETIC ETC PREPS	106	134	141	166	159	174
73—ARTICLES OF IRON OR STEEL..	107	130	135	118	147	125
09—COFFEE; TEA; MATE & SPICES	42	63	37	41	55	113
38—MISCELLANEOUS CHEMICAL PRODUCTS	82	76	87	81	93	99
04—DAIRY PRODS; BIRDS EGGS; HONEY; ED ANIMAL PR NESOI...........	63	61	66	83	83	89
32—TANNING & DYE EXT ETC; DYE; PAINT; PUTTY ETC; INKS..................	70	70	83	91	99	86

Table C-17.   U.S. Trade by Commodity with United Arab Emirates, 2010–2015

(In millions of U.S. dollars.)

Commodity and 2-digit Harmonized System (HS) code	2010	2011	2012	2013	2014	2015
EXPORTS						
Total..	11,662	15,922	22,559	24,476	22,111	23,004
88—AIRCRAFT; SPACECRAFT; AND PARTS THEREOF	1,780	3,632	7,132	5,592	4,873	5,826
85—ELECTRIC MACHINERY ETC; SOUND EQUIP; TV EQUIP; PTS........	1,198	1,353	2,231	3,414	3,090	3,330
87—VEHICLES; EXCEPT RAILWAY OR TRAMWAY; AND PARTS ETC	1,804	2,167	3,207	3,555	3,335	3,171
84—NUCLEAR REACTORS; BOILERS; MACHINERY ETC.; PARTS	2,108	2,559	2,890	2,963	3,255	3,162
71—NAT ETC PEARLS; PREC ETC STONES; PR MET ETC; COIN	632	1,258	1,756	2,412	1,567	1,600
90—OPTIC; PHOTO ETC; MEDIC OR SURGICAL INSTRMENTS ETC..........	560	560	600	554	644	620
98—SPECIAL CLASSIFICATION PROVISIONS; NESOI	337	350	449	518	512	566
08—EDIBLE FRUIT & NUTS; CITRUS FRUIT OR MELON PEEL..............	298	321	301	470	494	513
93—ARMS AND AMMUNITION; PARTS AND ACCESSORIES THEREOF......	290	380	729	1,056	328	329
73—ARTICLES OF IRON OR STEEL...................................	112	148	263	354	304	303
33—ESSENTIAL OILS ETC; PERFUMERY; COSMETIC ETC PREPS	194	240	210	245	273	262
39—PLASTICS AND ARTICLES THEREOF..............................	219	218	223	232	269	259
21—MISCELLANEOUS EDIBLE PREPARATIONS......................	70	84	102	125	169	193
38—MISCELLANEOUS CHEMICAL PRODUCTS	105	93	122	126	159	182
94—FURNITURE; BEDDING ETC; LAMPS NESOI ETC; PREFAB BD	107	106	122	132	177	149
30—PHARMACEUTICAL PRODUCTS	62	74	78	89	107	131
29—ORGANIC CHEMICALS...	117	147	143	146	111	127
02—MEAT AND EDIBLE MEAT OFFAL	77	121	147	142	142	119
12—OIL SEEDS ETC.; MISC GRAIN; SEED; FRUIT; PLANT ETC	176	178	204	220	121	102
95—TOYS; GAMES & SPORT EQUIPMENT; PARTS & ACCESSORIES	51	57	51	65	87	96
IMPORTS						
Total..	1,145	2,440	2,253	2,291	2,820	2,468
98—SPECIAL CLASSIFICATION PROVISIONS; NESOI	314	638	681	657	658	694
76—ALUMINUM AND ARTICLES THEREOF	195	665	606	589	626	667
31—FERTILIZERS...	26	0	35	129	253	249
73—ARTICLES OF IRON OR STEEL	148	198	117	101	121	165
71—NAT ETC PEARLS; PREC ETC STONES; PR MET ETC; COIN	68	157	223	126	81	131
84—NUCLEAR REACTORS; BOILERS; MACHINERY ETC.; PARTS	43	60	85	81	96	71
85—ELECTRIC MACHINERY ETC; SOUND EQUIP; TV EQUIP; PTS..............	15	23	32	45	53	68
27—MINERAL FUEL; OIL ETC.; BITUMIN SUBST; MINERAL WAX..............	79	394	182	173	640	60
54—MANMADE FILAMENTS; INCLUDING YARNS & WOVEN FABRICS.......	45	37	47	51	45	45
39—PLASTICS AND ARTICLES THEREOF..............................	45	70	63	49	31	34
72—IRON AND STEEL...	5	7	10	14	23	32
33—ESSENTIAL OILS ETC; PERFUMERY; COSMETIC ETC PREPS	13	12	8	10	20	25
94—FURNITURE; BEDDING ETC; LAMPS NESOI ETC; PREFAB BD	5	5	6	7	9	21
24—TOBACCO AND MANUFACTURED TOBACCO SUBSTITUTES	5	5	8	11	13	18
70—GLASS AND GLASSWARE	0	0	1	4	5	17
29—ORGANIC CHEMICALS...	7	6	7	3	1	13
99—SPECIAL IMPORT PROVISIONS; NESOI	8	9	10	7	10	12
88—AIRCRAFT; SPACECRAFT; AND PARTS THEREOF	0	2	1	1	5	11
68—ART OF STONE; PLASTER; CEMENT; ASBESTOS; MICA ETC.	2	3	3	5	6	11
52—COTTON; INCLUDING YARN AND WOVEN FABRIC THEREOF..............	8	9	8	10	8	10

Table C-18.   U.S. Trade by Commodity with Australia, 2010–2015

(In millions of U.S. dollars.)

Commodity and 2-digit Harmonized System (HS) code	2010	2011	2012	2013	2014	2015
EXPORTS						
Total..	21,805	27,626	31,161	26,124	26,682	25,036
84—NUCLEAR REACTORS; BOILERS; MACHINERY ETC.; PARTS..............	4,537	6,232	6,917	5,472	5,133	4,757
87—VEHICLES; EXCEPT RAILWAY OR TRAMWAY; AND PARTS ETC	2,411	3,967	5,850	3,484	3,647	3,364
88—AIRCRAFT; SPACECRAFT; AND PARTS THEREOF	1,625	1,985	2,199	1,876	2,361	2,889
85—ELECTRIC MACHINERY ETC; SOUND EQUIP; TV EQUIP; PTS..............	1,770	2,159	2,543	2,270	2,133	2,051
90—OPTIC; PHOTO ETC; MEDIC OR SURGICAL INSTRMENTS ETC............	1,936	2,217	2,369	2,152	2,148	2,042
98—SPECIAL CLASSIFICATION PROVISIONS; NESOI	1,207	1,425	1,599	1,258	1,338	1,199
30—PHARMACEUTICAL PRODUCTS	985	787	837	870	734	820
33—ESSENTIAL OILS ETC; PERFUMERY; COSMETIC ETC PREPS	354	420	473	532	541	570
39—PLASTICS AND ARTICLES THEREOF..................................	642	628	646	640	607	568
38—MISCELLANEOUS CHEMICAL PRODUCTS	423	473	481	477	464	457
40—RUBBER AND ARTICLES THEREOF	345	490	632	557	474	430
31—FERTILIZERS..	349	356	368	241	336	319
29—ORGANIC CHEMICALS...	358	482	433	363	354	289
71—NAT ETC PEARLS; PREC ETC STONES; PR MET ETC; COIN	817	874	377	584	756	273
73—ARTICLES OF IRON OR STEEL.....................................	209	255	319	308	341	265
08—EDIBLE FRUIT & NUTS; CITRUS FRUIT OR MELON PEEL..................	160	232	252	251	284	244
27—MINERAL FUEL; OIL ETC.; BITUMIN SUBST; MINERAL WAX.............	227	404	360	301	385	244
21—MISCELLANEOUS EDIBLE PREPARATIONS...........................	108	138	175	217	248	234
86—RAILWAY OR TRAMWAY STOCK ETC; TRAFFIC SIGNAL EQUIP..........	125	149	363	328	306	228
95—TOYS; GAMES & SPORT EQUIPMENT; PARTS & ACCESSORIES	176	191	223	240	253	215
IMPORTS						
Total..	8,583	10,243	9,567	9,273	10,697	10,894
02—MEAT AND EDIBLE MEAT OFFAL...................................	1,149	1,243	1,519	1,525	2,653	3,124
90—OPTIC; PHOTO ETC; MEDIC OR SURGICAL INSTRMENTS ETC............	764	804	704	695	733	722
98—SPECIAL CLASSIFICATION PROVISIONS; NESOI	472	612	667	567	686	693
71—NAT ETC PEARLS; PREC ETC STONES; PR MET ETC; COIN	1,068	1,254	801	938	872	693
26—ORES; SLAG AND ASH...	414	610	677	613	547	512
84—NUCLEAR REACTORS; BOILERS; MACHINERY ETC.; PARTS...............	411	492	535	495	514	487
88—AIRCRAFT; SPACECRAFT; AND PARTS THEREOF	158	324	350	454	508	461
22—BEVERAGES; SPIRITS AND VINEGAR	615	562	540	507	462	447
87—VEHICLES; EXCEPT RAILWAY OR TRAMWAY; AND PARTS ETC	137	199	254	303	346	319
28—INORG CHEM; PREC & RARE-EARTH MET & RADIOACT COMPD.......	221	307	283	312	286	304
30—PHARMACEUTICAL PRODUCTS	449	462	311	280	238	255
72—IRON AND STEEL...	340	588	221	174	274	252
85—ELECTRIC MACHINERY ETC; SOUND EQUIP; TV EQUIP; PTS	199	240	230	221	191	214
75—NICKEL AND ARTICLES THEREOF	386	505	388	247	343	204
27—MINERAL FUEL; OIL ETC.; BITUMIN SUBST; MINERAL WAX.............	269	396	251	82	64	189
11—MILLING PRODUCTS; MALT; STARCH; INULIN; WHT GLUTEN	161	143	132	194	199	166
48—PAPER & PAPERBOARD & ARTICLES (INC PAPR PULP ARTL)	71	70	94	105	148	135
29—ORGANIC CHEMICALS..	115	129	160	148	114	122
76—ALUMINUM AND ARTICLES THEREOF	87	112	83	80	102	109
79—ZINC AND ARTICLES THEREOF	13	12	54	1	100	98

Table C-19.   U.S. Trade by Commodity with India, 2010–2015

(In millions of U.S. dollars.)

Commodity and 2-digit Harmonized System (HS) code	2010	2011	2012	2013	2014	2015
EXPORTS						
Total..	19,249	21,542	22,106	21,810	21,501	21,452
71—NAT ETC PEARLS; PREC ETC STONES; PR MET ETC; COIN	4,207	4,621	5,836	5,764	5,250	6,594
84—NUCLEAR REACTORS; BOILERS; MACHINERY ETC.; PARTS	2,667	2,921	2,659	2,250	2,096	2,159
85—ELECTRIC MACHINERY ETC; SOUND EQUIP; TV EQUIP; PTS	1,363	1,538	1,399	1,312	1,394	1,346
90—OPTIC; PHOTO ETC; MEDIC OR SURGICAL INSTRMENTS ETC...........	1,084	1,185	1,241	1,287	1,263	1,296
88—AIRCRAFT; SPACECRAFT; AND PARTS THEREOF	1,277	773	1,374	2,953	2,943	1,294
27—MINERAL FUEL; OIL ETC.; BITUMIN SUBST; MINERAL WAX..............	1,080	1,751	1,628	1,246	1,235	1,093
29—ORGANIC CHEMICALS...	849	921	882	814	706	758
08—EDIBLE FRUIT & NUTS; CITRUS FRUIT OR MELON PEEL................	294	408	441	453	554	711
38—MISCELLANEOUS CHEMICAL PRODUCTS	454	622	542	550	576	698
39—PLASTICS AND ARTICLES THEREOF....................................	749	812	709	684	657	665
72—IRON AND STEEL..	557	732	675	367	344	499
47—WOOD PULP ETC; RECOVD (WASTE & SCRAP) PPR & PPRBD...........	348	452	420	423	608	462
98—SPECIAL CLASSIFICATION PROVISIONS; NESOI	360	363	392	320	326	382
30—PHARMACEUTICAL PRODUCTS	124	143	176	198	215	300
31—FERTILIZERS..	1,171	1,245	567	321	290	292
28—INORG CHEM; PREC & RARE-EARTH MET & RADIOACT COMPD.......	316	452	419	388	330	271
87—VEHICLES; EXCEPT RAILWAY OR TRAMWAY; AND PARTS ETC	192	261	272	167	170	200
48—PAPER & PAPERBOARD & ARTICLES (INC PAPR PULP ARTL)	233	319	260	246	189	160
73—ARTICLES OF IRON OR STEEL..	141	187	193	166	168	145
07—EDIBLE VEGETABLES & CERTAIN ROOTS & TUBERS	97	48	94	119	206	145
IMPORTS						
Total..	29,533	36,154	40,513	41,810	45,355	44,792
71—NAT ETC PEARLS; PREC ETC STONES; PR MET ETC; COIN	6,855	8,013	7,161	9,243	9,524	9,345
30—PHARMACEUTICAL PRODUCTS	2,390	3,213	4,223	4,486	4,812	5,922
27—MINERAL FUEL; OIL ETC.; BITUMIN SUBST; MINERAL WAX..............	2,324	3,187	3,261	3,935	4,600	2,664
84—NUCLEAR REACTORS; BOILERS; MACHINERY ETC.; PARTS	1,296	1,791	2,153	1,867	2,321	2,380
63—TEXTILE ART NESOI; NEEDLECRAFT SETS; WORN TEXT ART............	1,544	1,754	1,941	2,108	2,175	2,355
62—APPAREL ARTICLES AND ACCESSORIES; NOT KNIT ETC.	1,741	1,905	1,835	1,872	1,941	2,084
29—ORGANIC CHEMICALS..	1,716	1,982	2,178	2,188	2,250	2,017
61—APPAREL ARTICLES AND ACCESSORIES; KNIT OR CROCHET	1,417	1,465	1,255	1,383	1,505	1,621
87—VEHICLES; EXCEPT RAILWAY OR TRAMWAY; AND PARTS ETC	771	921	981	927	1,114	1,380
85—ELECTRIC MACHINERY ETC; SOUND EQUIP; TV EQUIP; PTS	1,446	1,476	1,472	1,271	1,343	1,276
73—ARTICLES OF IRON OR STEEL..	1,167	1,267	1,469	1,192	1,216	1,247
03—FISH; CRUSTACEANS & AQUATIC INVERTEBRATES	334	551	602	977	1,313	1,233
57—CARPETS AND OTHER TEXTILE FLOOR COVERINGS........................	523	562	597	664	795	854
13—LAC; GUMS; RESINS & OTHER VEGETABLE SAP & EXTRACT	296	1,036	3,522	1,782	1,352	735
94—FURNITURE; BEDDING ETC; LAMPS NESOI ETC; PREFAB BD	307	358	433	501	568	678
72—IRON AND STEEL..	398	503	551	472	801	601
42—LEATHER ART; SADDLERY ETC; HANDBAGS ETC; GUT ART..............	254	309	337	393	442	472
64—FOOTWEAR; GAITERS ETC. AND PARTS THEREOF	178	206	266	297	349	468
39—PLASTICS AND ARTICLES THEREOF....................................	335	394	410	412	459	449
68—ART OF STONE; PLASTER; CEMENT; ASBESTOS; MICA ETC.	256	272	298	330	356	397

Table C-20. U.S. Trade by Commodity with Saudi Arabia, 2010–2015

(In millions of U.S. dollars.)

Commodity and 2-digit Harmonized System (HS) code	2010	2011	2012	2013	2014	2015
EXPORTS						
Total...	11,506	13,924	17,961	18,963	18,718	19,739
87—VEHICLES; EXCEPT RAILWAY OR TRAMWAY; AND PARTS ETC	3,782	4,435	6,152	5,762	4,896	4,799
84—NUCLEAR REACTORS; BOILERS; MACHINERY ETC.; PARTS	2,274	3,055	3,538	3,633	3,601	3,923
88—AIRCRAFT; SPACECRAFT; AND PARTS THEREOF	866	558	1,580	2,121	2,019	3,640
85—ELECTRIC MACHINERY ETC; SOUND EQUIP; TV EQUIP; PTS	755	952	1,231	1,453	1,529	1,526
90—OPTIC; PHOTO ETC; MEDIC OR SURGICAL INSTRMENTS ETC...........	563	590	748	928	928	771
38—MISCELLANEOUS CHEMICAL PRODUCTS	313	308	488	395	462	428
98—SPECIAL CLASSIFICATION PROVISIONS; NESOI	284	336	313	398	414	413
30—PHARMACEUTICAL PRODUCTS	183	188	247	262	283	325
93—ARMS AND AMMUNITION; PARTS AND ACCESSORIES THEREOF.......	66	189	242	333	647	319
10—CEREALS	255	464	267	235	346	303
39—PLASTICS AND ARTICLES THEREOF..	219	215	269	308	303	297
73—ARTICLES OF IRON OR STEEL...	126	140	209	232	242	217
12—OIL SEEDS ETC.; MISC GRAIN; SEED; FRUIT; PLANT ETC	71	174	239	180	184	208
94—FURNITURE; BEDDING ETC; LAMPS NESOI ETC; PREFAB BD	183	172	191	222	225	192
29—ORGANIC CHEMICALS...	71	94	118	186	225	155
40—RUBBER AND ARTICLES THEREOF	62	69	107	121	140	148
08—EDIBLE FRUIT & NUTS; CITRUS FRUIT OR MELON PEEL....................	59	81	85	91	119	138
21—MISCELLANEOUS EDIBLE PREPARATIONS....................................	72	73	74	96	100	116
20—PREP VEGETABLES; FRUIT; NUTS OR OTHER PLANT PARTS	55	75	74	76	92	112
27—MINERAL FUEL; OIL ETC.; BITUMIN SUBST; MINERAL WAX..............	32	78	59	114	136	110
IMPORTS						
Total...	31,413	47,476	55,667	51,807	47,041	22,081
27—MINERAL FUEL; OIL ETC.; BITUMIN SUBST; MINERAL WAX..............	30,496	46,237	54,408	50,657	45,923	20,626
98—SPECIAL CLASSIFICATION PROVISIONS; NESOI	113	127	168	161	169	431
29—ORGANIC CHEMICALS..	388	509	458	432	329	319
31—FERTILIZERS...	169	265	194	164	213	183
76—ALUMINUM AND ARTICLES THEREOF	19	32	44	12	41	177
85—ELECTRIC MACHINERY ETC; SOUND EQUIP; TV EQUIP; PTS	1	1	11	52	69	70
73—ARTICLES OF IRON OR STEEL...	21	115	134	105	70	68
71—NAT ETC PEARLS; PREC ETC STONES; PR MET ETC; COIN	75	4	79	68	38	47
72—IRON AND STEEL..	6	9	4	3	25	41
54—MANMADE FILAMENTS; INCLUDING YARNS & WOVEN FABRICS.......	20	28	35	40	43	32
84—NUCLEAR REACTORS; BOILERS; MACHINERY ETC.; PARTS	20	19	18	24	19	18
55—MANMADE STAPLE FIBERS; INCL YARNS & WOVEN FABRICS	0	0	0	0	1	13
39—PLASTICS AND ARTICLES THEREOF..	23	40	18	6	10	11
56—WADDING; FELT ETC; SP YARN; TWINE; ROPES ETC.	4	2	1	1	2	7
28—INORG CHEM; PREC & RARE-EARTH MET & RADIOACT COMPD.......	0	39	46	51	60	5
99—SPECIAL IMPORT PROVISIONS; NESOI	2	2	1	2	3	4
68—ART OF STONE; PLASTER; CEMENT; ASBESTOS; MICA ETC.	8	10	9	9	5	3
38—MISCELLANEOUS CHEMICAL PRODUCTS	1	6	8	2	5	3
90—OPTIC; PHOTO ETC; MEDIC OR SURGICAL INSTRMENTS ETC...........	1	3	3	1	3	2
03—FISH; CRUSTACEANS & AQUATIC INVERTEBRATES	5	3	3	0	0	2

Table C-21.   U.S. Trade by Commodity with Italy, 2010–2015

(In millions of U.S. dollars.)

Commodity and 2-digit Harmonized System (HS) code	2010	2011	2012	2013	2014	2015
EXPORTS						
Total..	14,220	16,037	16,097	16,757	16,966	16,204
30—PHARMACEUTICAL PRODUCTS	1,405	1,679	1,826	1,787	1,818	2,532
84—NUCLEAR REACTORS; BOILERS; MACHINERY ETC.; PARTS..............	1,706	1,699	1,897	1,889	2,099	2,082
88—AIRCRAFT; SPACECRAFT; AND PARTS THEREOF	752	802	927	1,112	1,267	1,448
85—ELECTRIC MACHINERY ETC; SOUND EQUIP; TV EQUIP; PTS..............	1,169	1,062	926	914	1,315	1,056
90—OPTIC; PHOTO ETC; MEDIC OR SURGICAL INSTRMENTS ETC...........	1,282	1,224	1,074	999	1,095	1,049
71—NAT ETC PEARLS; PREC ETC STONES; PR MET ETC; COIN	1,145	1,219	1,100	963	1,311	946
27—MINERAL FUEL; OIL ETC.; BITUMIN SUBST; MINERAL WAX..............	1,059	1,826	1,615	1,325	1,312	897
87—VEHICLES; EXCEPT RAILWAY OR TRAMWAY; AND PARTS ETC	365	639	624	520	644	848
29—ORGANIC CHEMICALS..	593	868	1,516	2,209	857	459
98—SPECIAL CLASSIFICATION PROVISIONS; NESOI	533	449	428	433	427	436
38—MISCELLANEOUS CHEMICAL PRODUCTS	346	363	335	339	325	322
39—PLASTICS AND ARTICLES THEREOF..............................	291	343	278	289	288	318
08—EDIBLE FRUIT & NUTS; CITRUS FRUIT OR MELON PEEL..................	157	189	176	251	298	283
10—CEREALS..	150	182	137	262	224	261
97—WORKS OF ART; COLLECTORS' PIECES AND ANTIQUES...............	121	102	176	151	191	240
41—RAW HIDES AND SKINS (NO FURSKINS) AND LEATHER...................	207	305	220	264	298	239
47—WOOD PULP ETC; RECOVD (WASTE & SCRAP) PPR & PPRBD...........	438	408	352	336	249	236
48—PAPER & PAPERBOARD & ARTICLES (INC PAPR PULP ARTL)	254	308	251	255	235	229
44—WOOD AND ARTICLES OF WOOD; WOOD CHARCOAL.....................	189	162	114	161	170	153
68—ART OF STONE; PLASTER; CEMENT; ASBESTOS; MICA ETC............	72	92	98	126	191	149
IMPORTS						
Total..	28,514	33,974	36,965	38,709	42,377	44,159
84—NUCLEAR REACTORS; BOILERS; MACHINERY ETC.; PARTS..............	5,286	6,906	7,550	7,894	9,235	8,926
87—VEHICLES; EXCEPT RAILWAY OR TRAMWAY; AND PARTS ETC	1,477	1,779	2,219	2,754	3,555	5,135
30—PHARMACEUTICAL PRODUCTS	1,813	1,948	1,855	2,211	2,248	3,142
22—BEVERAGES; SPIRITS AND VINEGAR	1,666	1,924	1,943	2,115	2,229	2,250
85—ELECTRIC MACHINERY ETC; SOUND EQUIP; TV EQUIP; PTS..............	1,537	1,972	1,824	1,656	1,656	1,722
90—OPTIC; PHOTO ETC; MEDIC OR SURGICAL INSTRMENTS ETC...........	1,096	1,274	1,342	1,471	1,620	1,647
64—FOOTWEAR; GAITERS ETC. AND PARTS THEREOF	897	1,116	1,202	1,330	1,444	1,407
71—NAT ETC PEARLS; PREC ETC STONES; PR MET ETC; COIN	789	1,043	1,028	1,177	1,602	1,318
73—ARTICLES OF IRON OR STEEL....................................	731	683	1,037	1,095	1,098	1,116
94—FURNITURE; BEDDING ETC; LAMPS NESOI ETC; PREFAB BD	648	720	781	895	1,005	1,055
42—LEATHER ART; SADDLERY ETC; HANDBAGS ETC; GUT ART............	588	794	908	988	1,091	1,031
88—AIRCRAFT; SPACECRAFT; AND PARTS THEREOF	840	893	1,218	1,355	1,432	1,010
62—APPAREL ARTICLES AND ACCESSORIES; NOT KNIT ETC.	746	899	923	986	1,071	1,007
97—WORKS OF ART; COLLECTORS' PIECES AND ANTIQUES...............	599	606	805	913	827	982
29—ORGANIC CHEMICALS..	964	1,065	1,183	1,094	972	969
98—SPECIAL CLASSIFICATION PROVISIONS; NESOI	456	438	526	650	709	855
33—ESSENTIAL OILS ETC; PERFUMERY; COSMETIC ETC PREPS	409	455	457	510	637	670
39—PLASTICS AND ARTICLES THEREOF..............................	463	522	565	596	678	649
69—CERAMIC PRODUCTS..	431	429	460	543	594	640
68—ART OF STONE; PLASTER; CEMENT; ASBESTOS; MICA ETC............	351	374	419	536	568	595

Table C-22.   U.S. Trade by Commodity with Israel, 2010–2015

(In millions of U.S. dollars.)

Commodity and 2-digit Harmonized System (HS) code	2010	2011	2012	2013	2014	2015
EXPORTS						
Total..	11,295	13,962	14,273	13,744	15,065	13,539
71—NAT ETC PEARLS; PREC ETC STONES; PR MET ETC; COIN	4,543	5,997	5,396	5,769	6,817	5,442
85—ELECTRIC MACHINERY ETC; SOUND EQUIP; TV EQUIP; PTS	960	1,420	2,335	1,641	1,773	2,072
84—NUCLEAR REACTORS; BOILERS; MACHINERY ETC.; PARTS	864	1,268	1,225	1,016	1,063	1,055
88—AIRCRAFT; SPACECRAFT; AND PARTS THEREOF	818	677	729	822	988	820
90—OPTIC; PHOTO ETC; MEDIC OR SURGICAL INSTRMENTS ETC...........	558	667	566	667	564	586
87—VEHICLES; EXCEPT RAILWAY OR TRAMWAY; AND PARTS ETC	411	491	328	364	457	473
27—MINERAL FUEL; OIL ETC.; BITUMIN SUBST; MINERAL WAX................	341	374	500	420	465	367
98—SPECIAL CLASSIFICATION PROVISIONS; NESOI	318	349	371	331	316	340
93—ARMS AND AMMUNITION; PARTS AND ACCESSORIES THEREOF.......	160	106	120	93	237	310
39—PLASTICS AND ARTICLES THEREOF..	335	304	306	299	214	242
30—PHARMACEUTICAL PRODUCTS	120	126	217	286	182	188
08—EDIBLE FRUIT & NUTS; CITRUS FRUIT OR MELON PEEL....................	101	118	102	109	151	130
29—ORGANIC CHEMICALS..	140	155	163	151	177	120
38—MISCELLANEOUS CHEMICAL PRODUCTS	107	92	116	111	91	112
23—FOOD INDUSTRY RESIDUES & WASTE; PREP ANIMAL FEED.............	92	160	183	155	142	92
33—ESSENTIAL OILS ETC; PERFUMERY; COSMETIC ETC PREPS	37	43	44	52	59	73
48—PAPER & PAPERBOARD & ARTICLES (INC PAPR PULP ARTL)	93	94	82	75	78	67
73—ARTICLES OF IRON OR STEEL..	74	72	88	57	56	67
76—ALUMINUM AND ARTICLES THEREOF	53	63	54	69	62	59
10—CEREALS	207	352	99	80	164	58
IMPORTS						
Total..	20,985	23,047	22,131	22,783	23,007	24,477
71—NAT ETC PEARLS; PREC ETC STONES; PR MET ETC; COIN	7,884	9,346	8,375	8,970	9,444	8,501
30—PHARMACEUTICAL PRODUCTS	5,169	5,645	5,368	5,476	4,445	5,964
85—ELECTRIC MACHINERY ETC; SOUND EQUIP; TV EQUIP; PTS	1,546	1,428	1,542	1,406	1,510	2,395
84—NUCLEAR REACTORS; BOILERS; MACHINERY ETC.; PARTS	1,187	1,264	1,311	1,395	1,465	1,386
90—OPTIC; PHOTO ETC; MEDIC OR SURGICAL INSTRMENTS ETC...........	1,036	1,261	1,247	1,328	1,360	1,380
98—SPECIAL CLASSIFICATION PROVISIONS; NESOI	385	588	460	525	635	853
88—AIRCRAFT; SPACECRAFT; AND PARTS THEREOF	423	394	587	643	797	709
39—PLASTICS AND ARTICLES THEREOF..	329	366	383	404	485	513
29—ORGANIC CHEMICALS..	337	392	393	291	266	281
82—TOOLS; CUTLERY ETC. OF BASE METAL & PARTS THEREOF	153	194	218	218	261	245
31—FERTILIZERS...	89	243	175	139	265	170
28—INORG CHEM; PREC & RARE-EARTH MET & RADIOACT COMPD........	136	139	156	135	182	164
33—ESSENTIAL OILS ETC; PERFUMERY; COSMETIC ETC PREPS	91	101	109	135	127	133
68—ART OF STONE; PLASTER; CEMENT; ASBESTOS; MICA ETC.	53	59	75	80	122	129
93—ARMS AND AMMUNITION; PARTS AND ACCESSORIES THEREOF.......	82	74	105	166	117	105
38—MISCELLANEOUS CHEMICAL PRODUCTS	59	76	51	62	86	91
60—KNITTED OR CROCHETED FABRICS	59	59	83	60	91	85
73—ARTICLES OF IRON OR STEEL..	57	72	57	62	75	78
56—WADDING; FELT ETC; SP YARN; TWINE; ROPES ETC.	91	65	61	80	84	73
99—SPECIAL IMPORT PROVISIONS; NESOI	87	82	70	48	66	67

Table C-23.   U.S. Trade by Commodity with Columbia, 2010–2015

(In millions of U.S. dollars.)

Commodity and 2-digit Harmonized System (HS) code	2010	2011	2012	2013	2014	2015
EXPORTS						
Total..	12,068	14,336	16,357	18,371	20,068	16,287
27—MINERAL FUEL; OIL ETC.; BITUMIN SUBST; MINERAL WAX...........	2,249	2,728	3,462	5,283	6,069	4,426
84—NUCLEAR REACTORS; BOILERS; MACHINERY ETC.; PARTS..............	2,775	2,952	3,134	2,724	2,603	1,968
85—ELECTRIC MACHINERY ETC; SOUND EQUIP; TV EQUIP; PTS............	942	1,174	1,560	1,744	1,674	1,226
10—CEREALS	292	392	284	490	1,189	1,087
29—ORGANIC CHEMICALS..	816	969	901	979	922	795
39—PLASTICS AND ARTICLES THEREOF..............................	615	692	733	747	798	733
88—AIRCRAFT; SPACECRAFT; AND PARTS THEREOF....................	266	334	752	575	811	679
90—OPTIC; PHOTO ETC; MEDIC OR SURGICAL INSTRMENTS ETC...........	601	693	692	747	802	650
98—SPECIAL CLASSIFICATION PROVISIONS; NESOI	339	352	370	459	519	438
87—VEHICLES; EXCEPT RAILWAY OR TRAMWAY; AND PARTS ETC	488	654	602	752	622	426
23—FOOD INDUSTRY RESIDUES & WASTE; PREP ANIMAL FEED.............	78	138	176	284	278	412
38—MISCELLANEOUS CHEMICAL PRODUCTS	230	282	319	346	402	352
30—PHARMACEUTICAL PRODUCTS....................................	175	199	248	263	263	284
12—OIL SEEDS ETC.; MISC GRAIN; SEED; FRUIT; PLANT ETC	85	59	127	89	221	238
31—FERTILIZERS..	154	211	166	157	176	177
73—ARTICLES OF IRON OR STEEL....................................	179	320	553	278	234	143
21—MISCELLANEOUS EDIBLE PREPARATIONS..........................	56	69	90	119	148	138
48—PAPER & PAPERBOARD & ARTICLES (INC PAPR PULP ARTL)	160	165	150	168	148	137
02—MEAT AND EDIBLE MEAT OFFAL.................................	31	45	80	120	175	132
32—TANNING & DYE EXT ETC; DYE; PAINT; PUTTY ETC; INKS...............	88	116	102	95	108	102
IMPORTS						
Total..	15,659	23,114	24,622	21,626	18,316	14,075
27—MINERAL FUEL; OIL ETC.; BITUMIN SUBST; MINERAL WAX...........	10,486	16,846	17,667	15,386	11,964	8,147
71—NAT ETC PEARLS; PREC ETC STONES; PR MET ETC; COIN	1,647	2,249	3,180	2,479	2,105	1,701
09—COFFEE; TEA; MATE & SPICES	817	1,324	908	939	1,173	1,239
06—LIVE TREES; PLANTS; BULBS ETC.; CUT FLOWERS ETC.	562	578	646	669	664	624
99—SPECIAL IMPORT PROVISIONS; NESOI	212	195	175	234	267	290
98—SPECIAL CLASSIFICATION PROVISIONS; NESOI	88	102	149	159	185	215
08—EDIBLE FRUIT & NUTS; CITRUS FRUIT OR MELON PEEL	269	211	248	261	226	212
39—PLASTICS AND ARTICLES THEREOF..............................	155	171	154	135	147	141
62—APPAREL ARTICLES AND ACCESSORIES; NOT KNIT ETC.............	140	117	106	105	107	137
76—ALUMINUM AND ARTICLES THEREOF	45	41	53	71	95	123
61—APPAREL ARTICLES AND ACCESSORIES; KNIT OR CROCHET	120	107	104	113	93	91
17—SUGARS AND SUGAR CONFECTIONARY............................	60	72	90	67	102	87
21—MISCELLANEOUS EDIBLE PREPARATIONS..........................	126	139	111	103	86	85
70—GLASS AND GLASSWARE..	49	51	59	42	69	66
29—ORGANIC CHEMICALS..	41	43	49	49	64	66
84—NUCLEAR REACTORS; BOILERS; MACHINERY ETC.; PARTS..............	43	57	57	48	70	61
03—FISH; CRUSTACEANS & AQUATIC INVERTEBRATES	33	39	41	43	45	56
63—TEXTILE ART NESOI; NEEDLECRAFT SETS; WORN TEXT ART...........	24	30	27	38	38	44
73—ARTICLES OF IRON OR STEEL....................................	75	111	113	49	57	43
85—ELECTRIC MACHINERY ETC; SOUND EQUIP; TV EQUIP; PTS............	39	56	46	31	36	37

Table C-24.   U.S. Trade by Commodity with Chile, 2010–2015

(In millions of U.S. dollars.)

Commodity and 2-digit Harmonized System (HS) code	2010	2011	2012	2013	2014	2015
EXPORTS						
Total...	10,907	15,993	18,773	17,516	16,542	15,445
27—MINERAL FUEL; OIL ETC.; BITUMIN SUBST; MINERAL WAX..............	2,340	5,006	6,093	5,882	5,541	3,579
88—AIRCRAFT; SPACECRAFT; AND PARTS THEREOF.........................	357	512	1,203	831	1,632	2,969
84—NUCLEAR REACTORS; BOILERS; MACHINERY ETC.; PARTS..............	2,357	3,026	3,122	2,717	2,130	2,262
85—ELECTRIC MACHINERY ETC; SOUND EQUIP; TV EQUIP; PTS.............	877	1,098	1,237	1,071	976	1,007
87—VEHICLES; EXCEPT RAILWAY OR TRAMWAY; AND PARTS ETC	1,166	1,578	1,913	1,466	1,159	908
98—SPECIAL CLASSIFICATION PROVISIONS; NESOI	452	610	682	682	615	501
39—PLASTICS AND ARTICLES THEREOF....................................	473	491	535	537	517	481
90—OPTIC; PHOTO ETC; MEDIC OR SURGICAL INSTRMENTS ETC...........	331	382	427	459	425	435
29—ORGANIC CHEMICALS...	229	321	373	413	383	314
38—MISCELLANEOUS CHEMICAL PRODUCTS	162	188	208	217	222	220
40—RUBBER AND ARTICLES THEREOF	163	239	287	295	286	208
28—INORG CHEM; PREC & RARE-EARTH MET & RADIOACT COMPD........	147	194	217	232	207	192
48—PAPER & PAPERBOARD & ARTICLES (INC PAPR PULP ARTL)	154	165	161	168	152	163
30—PHARMACEUTICAL PRODUCTS	96	91	159	139	130	149
23—FOOD INDUSTRY RESIDUES & WASTE; PREP ANIMAL FEED.............	67	102	138	117	137	134
02—MEAT AND EDIBLE MEAT OFFAL	31	87	128	153	158	132
33—ESSENTIAL OILS ETC; PERFUMERY; COSMETIC ETC PREPS	94	108	122	142	145	132
95—TOYS; GAMES & SPORT EQUIPMENT; PARTS & ACCESSORIES	107	141	167	163	139	123
73—ARTICLES OF IRON OR STEEL..	117	111	101	138	107	115
21—MISCELLANEOUS EDIBLE PREPARATIONS..............................	44	51	63	70	78	86
IMPORTS						
Total...	7,017	9,076	9,367	10,385	9,479	8,772
74—COPPER AND ARTICLES THEREOF.....................................	2,239	3,270	3,175	3,507	2,200	1,917
08—EDIBLE FRUIT & NUTS; CITRUS FRUIT OR MELON PEEL................	1,515	1,510	1,410	1,754	1,754	1,871
03—FISH; CRUSTACEANS & AQUATIC INVERTEBRATES	559	866	988	1,326	1,590	1,315
44—WOOD AND ARTICLES OF WOOD; WOOD CHARCOAL.....................	518	573	564	701	742	812
40—RUBBER AND ARTICLES THEREOF	71	206	302	359	394	349
22—BEVERAGES; SPIRITS AND VINEGAR	279	300	349	325	302	291
28—INORG CHEM; PREC & RARE-EARTH MET & RADIOACT COMPD........	235	386	416	355	320	287
98—SPECIAL CLASSIFICATION PROVISIONS; NESOI	96	114	216	241	282	241
25—SALT; SULFUR; EARTH & STONE; LIME & CEMENT PLASTER...........	96	103	71	70	170	180
20—PREP VEGETABLES; FRUIT; NUTS OR OTHER PLANT PARTS.............	95	116	127	119	150	153
02—MEAT AND EDIBLE MEAT OFFAL	52	52	73	81	91	143
71—NAT ETC PEARLS; PREC ETC STONES; PR MET ETC; COIN	267	465	402	223	157	132
31—FERTILIZERS...	28	37	102	60	88	92
10—CEREALS	129	132	249	345	216	86
16—EDIBLE PREPARATIONS OF MEAT; FISH; CRUSTACEANS ETC...........	34	34	33	47	64	78
26—ORES; SLAG AND ASH...	115	161	101	27	58	78
12—OIL SEEDS ETC.; MISC GRAIN; SEED; FRUIT; PLANT ETC	88	110	107	106	78	77
84—NUCLEAR REACTORS; BOILERS; MACHINERY ETC.; PARTS..............	29	29	52	106	121	65
23—FOOD INDUSTRY RESIDUES & WASTE; PREP ANIMAL FEED.............	20	15	25	31	53	64
81—BASE METALS NESOI; CERMETS; ARTICLES THEREOF....................	51	52	56	47	41	56

Table C-25.   U.S. Trade by Commodity with Malyasia, 2010–2015

(In millions of U.S. dollars.)

Commodity and 2-digit Harmonized System (HS) code	2010	2011	2012	2013	2014	2015
EXPORTS						
Total...	14,079	14,264	12,818	13,016	13,069	12,277
85—ELECTRIC MACHINERY ETC; SOUND EQUIP; TV EQUIP; PTS............	7,054	6,759	5,819	5,421	6,168	6,001
84—NUCLEAR REACTORS; BOILERS; MACHINERY ETC.; PARTS...............	1,704	1,636	1,453	1,416	1,469	1,311
88—AIRCRAFT; SPACECRAFT; AND PARTS THEREOF..............................	903	1,029	1,185	1,624	1,165	993
90—OPTIC; PHOTO ETC; MEDIC OR SURGICAL INSTRMENTS ETC...........	676	687	774	765	802	781
39—PLASTICS AND ARTICLES THEREOF..	280	315	308	359	337	325
98—SPECIAL CLASSIFICATION PROVISIONS; NESOI	434	272	214	240	211	209
38—MISCELLANEOUS CHEMICAL PRODUCTS	156	186	188	318	151	201
27—MINERAL FUEL; OIL ETC.; BITUMIN SUBST; MINERAL WAX..............	278	262	76	45	34	156
28—INORG CHEM; PREC & RARE-EARTH MET & RADIOACT COMPD.......	83	158	177	167	176	146
12—OIL SEEDS ETC.; MISC GRAIN; SEED; FRUIT; PLANT ETC	142	165	182	170	173	139
21—MISCELLANEOUS EDIBLE PREPARATIONS......................................	82	90	128	150	144	136
04—DAIRY PRODS; BIRDS EGGS; HONEY; ED ANIMAL PR NESOI............	92	125	111	151	160	103
08—EDIBLE FRUIT & NUTS; CITRUS FRUIT OR MELON PEEL..................	87	105	112	127	115	102
29—ORGANIC CHEMICALS..	120	140	107	122	127	93
76—ALUMINUM AND ARTICLES THEREOF	51	54	53	62	64	92
30—PHARMACEUTICAL PRODUCTS	46	63	64	66	82	91
73—ARTICLES OF IRON OR STEEL..	69	76	106	111	110	86
32—TANNING & DYE EXT ETC; DYE; PAINT; PUTTY ETC; INKS..............	68	64	50	57	57	74
33—ESSENTIAL OILS ETC; PERFUMERY; COSMETIC ETC PREPS	48	40	50	55	61	70
70—GLASS AND GLASSWARE	149	187	109	91	84	67
IMPORTS						
Total...	25,901	25,777	25,935	27,289	30,564	33,971
85—ELECTRIC MACHINERY ETC; SOUND EQUIP; TV EQUIP; PTS............	11,581	12,473	13,340	14,821	17,959	21,399
84—NUCLEAR REACTORS; BOILERS; MACHINERY ETC.; PARTS...............	6,186	4,023	3,725	4,024	3,877	3,820
90—OPTIC; PHOTO ETC; MEDIC OR SURGICAL INSTRMENTS ETC...........	1,387	1,411	1,588	1,676	1,833	1,909
40—RUBBER AND ARTICLES THEREOF..	1,217	1,391	1,371	1,354	1,347	1,520
94—FURNITURE; BEDDING ETC; LAMPS NESOI ETC; PREFAB BD	787	739	808	742	796	866
15—ANIMAL OR VEGETABLE FATS; OILS ETC. & WAXES	1,066	1,678	1,340	1,070	882	656
98—SPECIAL CLASSIFICATION PROVISIONS; NESOI	436	513	527	511	413	465
38—MISCELLANEOUS CHEMICAL PRODUCTS	196	321	322	323	418	370
61—APPAREL ARTICLES AND ACCESSORIES; KNIT OR CROCHET	290	318	294	326	351	361
39—PLASTICS AND ARTICLES THEREOF..	182	198	217	224	230	277
73—ARTICLES OF IRON OR STEEL..	130	166	216	214	209	223
99—SPECIAL IMPORT PROVISIONS; NESOI	407	374	255	141	216	206
62—APPAREL ARTICLES AND ACCESSORIES; NOT KNIT ETC.	178	202	192	191	185	182
29—ORGANIC CHEMICALS..	143	173	146	158	218	179
80—TIN AND ARTICLES THEREOF..	91	106	96	94	135	168
44—WOOD AND ARTICLES OF WOOD; WOOD CHARCOAL........................	171	155	187	192	148	160
18—COCOA AND COCOA PREPARATIONS...	308	278	148	134	185	129
88—AIRCRAFT; SPACECRAFT; AND PARTS THEREOF..............................	41	54	65	83	95	111
95—TOYS; GAMES & SPORT EQUIPMENT; PARTS & ACCESSORIES	109	95	92	98	107	105
03—FISH; CRUSTACEANS & AQUATIC INVERTEBRATES	155	212	179	91	184	87

Table C-26.   U.S. Trade by Commodity with Thailand, 2010–2015

(In millions of U.S. dollars.)

Commodity and 2-digit Harmonized System (HS) code	2010	2011	2012	2013	2014	2015
EXPORTS						
Total..	8,976	10,930	10,888	11,797	11,817	11,231
85—ELECTRIC MACHINERY ETC; SOUND EQUIP; TV EQUIP; PTS.............	2,096	2,118	2,001	2,145	2,220	2,196
88—AIRCRAFT; SPACECRAFT; AND PARTS THEREOF............................	282	370	752	1,290	1,789	1,647
84—NUCLEAR REACTORS; BOILERS; MACHINERY ETC.; PARTS.............	1,439	1,334	1,503	1,394	1,313	1,223
71—NAT ETC PEARLS; PREC ETC STONES; PR MET ETC; COIN.............	364	1,465	826	1,588	951	619
90—OPTIC; PHOTO ETC; MEDIC OR SURGICAL INSTRMENTS ETC...........	565	571	623	603	540	610
39—PLASTICS AND ARTICLES THEREOF..	397	400	472	412	428	420
12—OIL SEEDS ETC.; MISC GRAIN; SEED; FRUIT; PLANT ETC.............	205	183	421	237	390	406
23—FOOD INDUSTRY RESIDUES & WASTE; PREP ANIMAL FEED.............	153	137	176	227	343	378
87—VEHICLES; EXCEPT RAILWAY OR TRAMWAY; AND PARTS ETC..........	119	143	262	319	299	327
29—ORGANIC CHEMICALS..	257	329	347	314	269	285
38—MISCELLANEOUS CHEMICAL PRODUCTS	166	202	227	207	220	236
10—CEREALS	125	163	186	172	161	217
98—SPECIAL CLASSIFICATION PROVISIONS; NESOI	257	238	220	215	203	200
52—COTTON; INCLUDING YARN AND WOVEN FABRIC THEREOF.............	256	403	174	185	190	174
30—PHARMACEUTICAL PRODUCTS	96	131	133	134	158	166
21—MISCELLANEOUS EDIBLE PREPARATIONS................................	67	68	131	146	140	151
27—MINERAL FUEL; OIL ETC.; BITUMIN SUBST; MINERAL WAX...........	190	344	301	166	151	128
72—IRON AND STEEL..	253	400	167	58	196	120
33—ESSENTIAL OILS ETC; PERFUMERY; COSMETIC ETC PREPS...........	101	108	117	123	119	110
32—TANNING & DYE EXT ETC; DYE; PAINT; PUTTY ETC; INKS................	86	109	103	69	76	106
IMPORTS						
Total..	22,694	24,832	26,067	26,170	27,225	28,632
84—NUCLEAR REACTORS; BOILERS; MACHINERY ETC.; PARTS...........	4,491	4,302	5,744	6,286	6,861	7,453
85—ELECTRIC MACHINERY ETC; SOUND EQUIP; TV EQUIP; PTS.............	5,762	6,306	6,330	6,304	6,788	7,410
40—RUBBER AND ARTICLES THEREOF	1,843	2,680	2,398	2,031	1,949	2,102
71—NAT ETC PEARLS; PREC ETC STONES; PR MET ETC; COIN.............	1,187	1,370	1,350	1,590	1,580	1,682
16—EDIBLE PREPARATIONS OF MEAT; FISH; CRUSTACEANS ETC...........	1,251	1,435	1,244	1,107	1,056	934
87—VEHICLES; EXCEPT RAILWAY OR TRAMWAY; AND PARTS ETC..........	310	329	553	601	695	847
90—OPTIC; PHOTO ETC; MEDIC OR SURGICAL INSTRMENTS ETC...........	530	534	529	661	780	794
61—APPAREL ARTICLES AND ACCESSORIES; KNIT OR CROCHET............	839	766	696	730	732	760
73—ARTICLES OF IRON OR STEEL..	253	312	418	397	422	527
20—PREP VEGETABLES; FRUIT; NUTS OR OTHER PLANT PARTS.............	377	419	411	442	444	503
39—PLASTICS AND ARTICLES THEREOF..	401	430	483	481	496	498
03—FISH; CRUSTACEANS & AQUATIC INVERTEBRATES	1,008	1,065	813	556	464	431
10—CEREALS	398	411	427	447	440	422
95—TOYS; GAMES & SPORT EQUIPMENT; PARTS & ACCESSORIES	224	215	241	303	280	295
62—APPAREL ARTICLES AND ACCESSORIES; NOT KNIT ETC.	495	453	412	352	325	294
98—SPECIAL CLASSIFICATION PROVISIONS; NESOI	258	294	283	339	315	278
94—FURNITURE; BEDDING ETC; LAMPS NESOI ETC; PREFAB BD	291	247	238	258	269	271
76—ALUMINUM AND ARTICLES THEREOF	195	194	233	265	229	270
21—MISCELLANEOUS EDIBLE PREPARATIONS................................	184	211	215	233	247	233
22—BEVERAGES; SPIRITS AND VINEGAR	57	99	128	133	175	204

SECTION D

U.S. COMMODITY TRADE HIGHLIGHTS

SECTION D: U.S. COMMODITY TRADE

HIGHLIGHTS

More detailed data of goods are presented in Section D. These include agriculture commodities, top ten exports and imports, crude oil, rare earth elements, and advanced technology products. Overall, of the top ten exports and imports, only seven are unique.

Agriculture

The United States is a major exporter and importer of agricultural products. However, several factors such as commodity prices, currency movement, demand for commodities, and the world economy have an impact on the amount of both imports and exports. Figure D-1 shows the total amounts of exports and imports in goods and services from 2005 through 2015 while Figure D-2 shows the imports and exports of agricultural products during the same period.

The U.S. does rely on imports of certain products, such as coffee and tea, sugar, wine, cocoa, cut flowers, and fresh fruit and vegetables. Likewise, the world relies on U.S. products for grains such as wheat, dairy products,

soybeans, poultry, and beef. The United States has a trade deficit in coffee, alcohol, cocoa, and sugar and a surplus in cereal, dairy, meat, and soybeans.

Since 2009, the major U.S. agriculture export destinations are China, Canada, and Mexico. Japan had been one of the top three up to 2008 but was replaced by China. All three countries have seen their share of exports increase. These countries account for over 40 percent of all exports.

As discussed in Section B, many of the products exported by the United States are also its imports. For example, electric machinery ranks as the largest U.S. import and the second largest export. Nuclear reactors are the opposite. The top 10 exports account for 68.6 percent of total exports and 67.6 percent of imports. Instead of using the mineral fuel category from the U.S. Census Bureau, crude oil data is provided by the U.S. Department of Interior, Energy Information Administration.

The U.S. has a trade deficit in seven of the ten unique traded products. The deficit ranges from $239.4 billion in nuclear reactors to $58 million in precious stones of

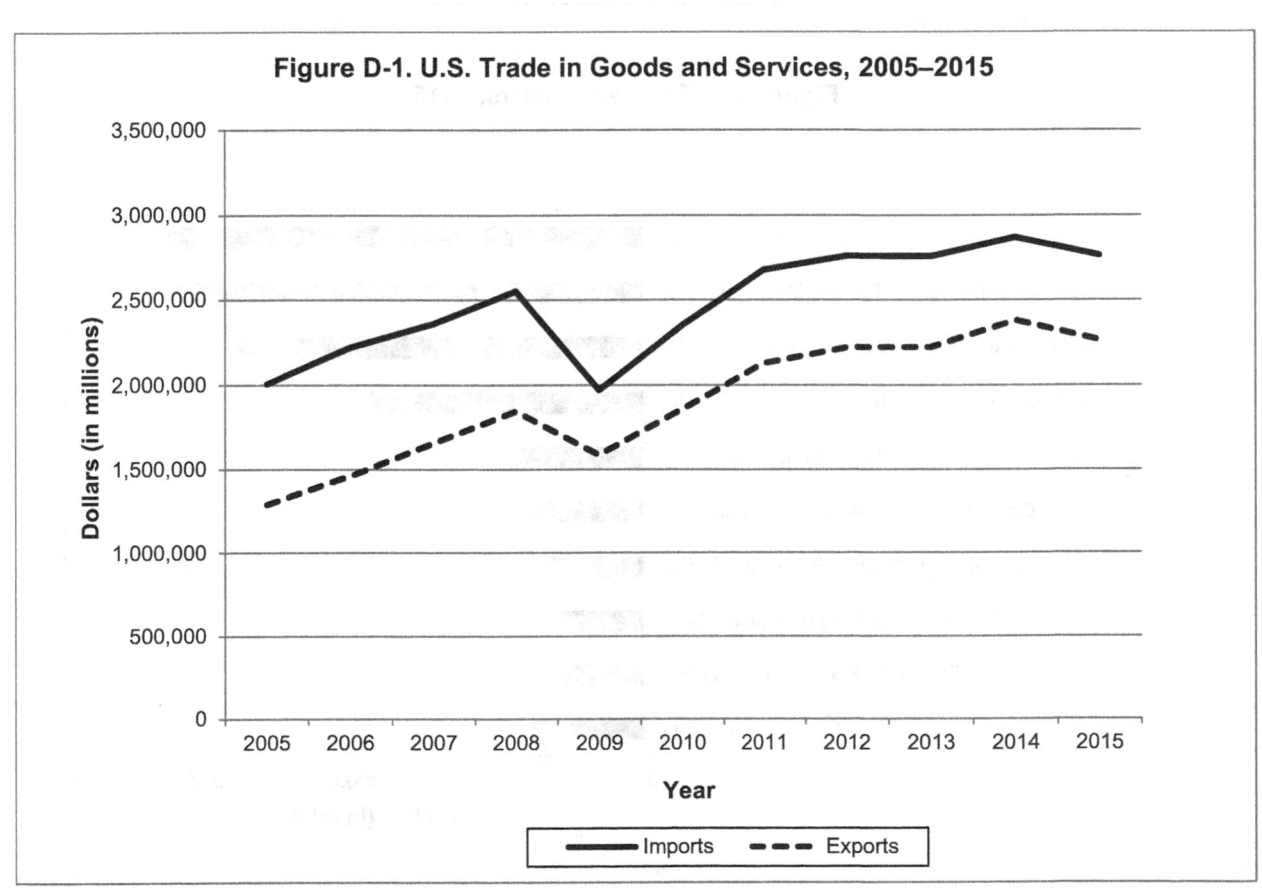

Figure D-1. U.S. Trade in Goods and Services, 2005–2015

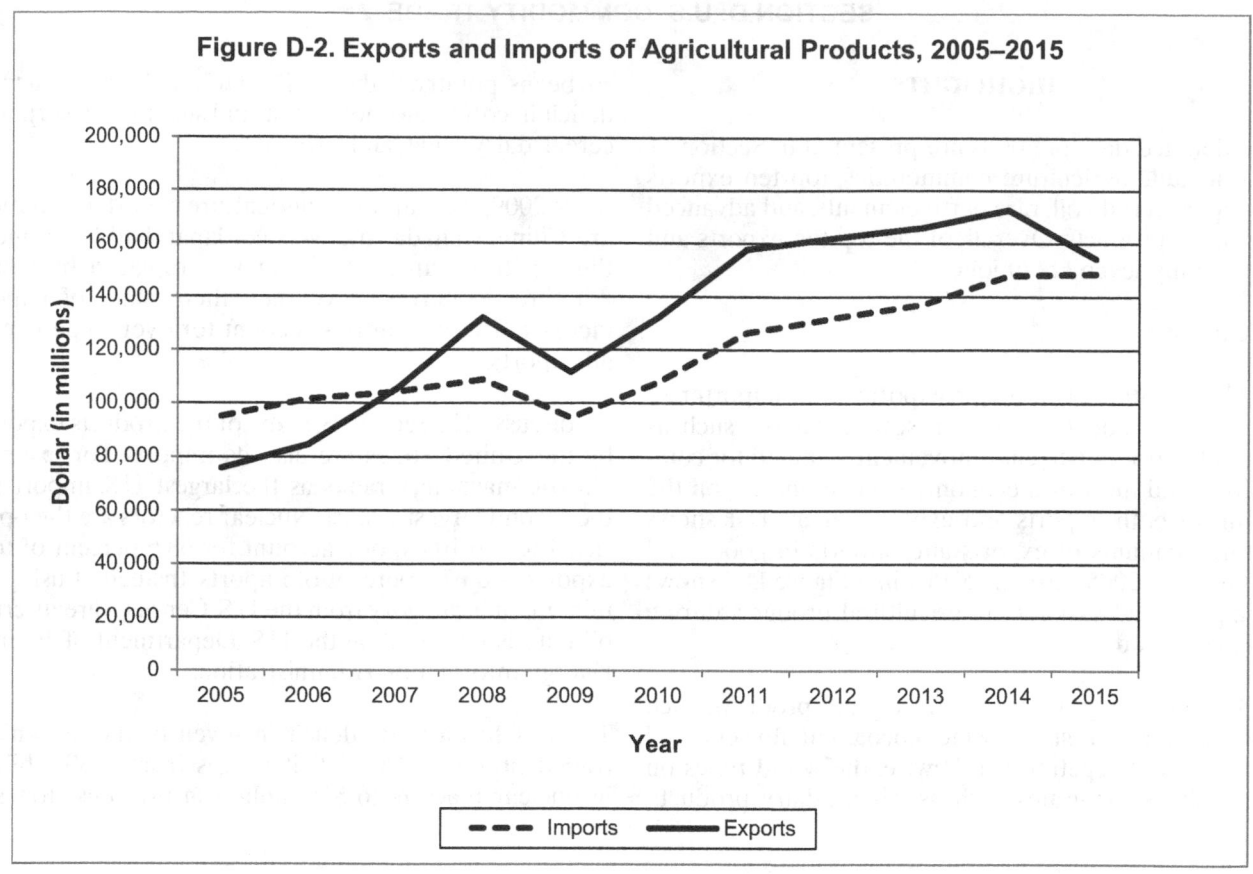

Figure D-2. Exports and Imports of Agricultural Products, 2005–2015

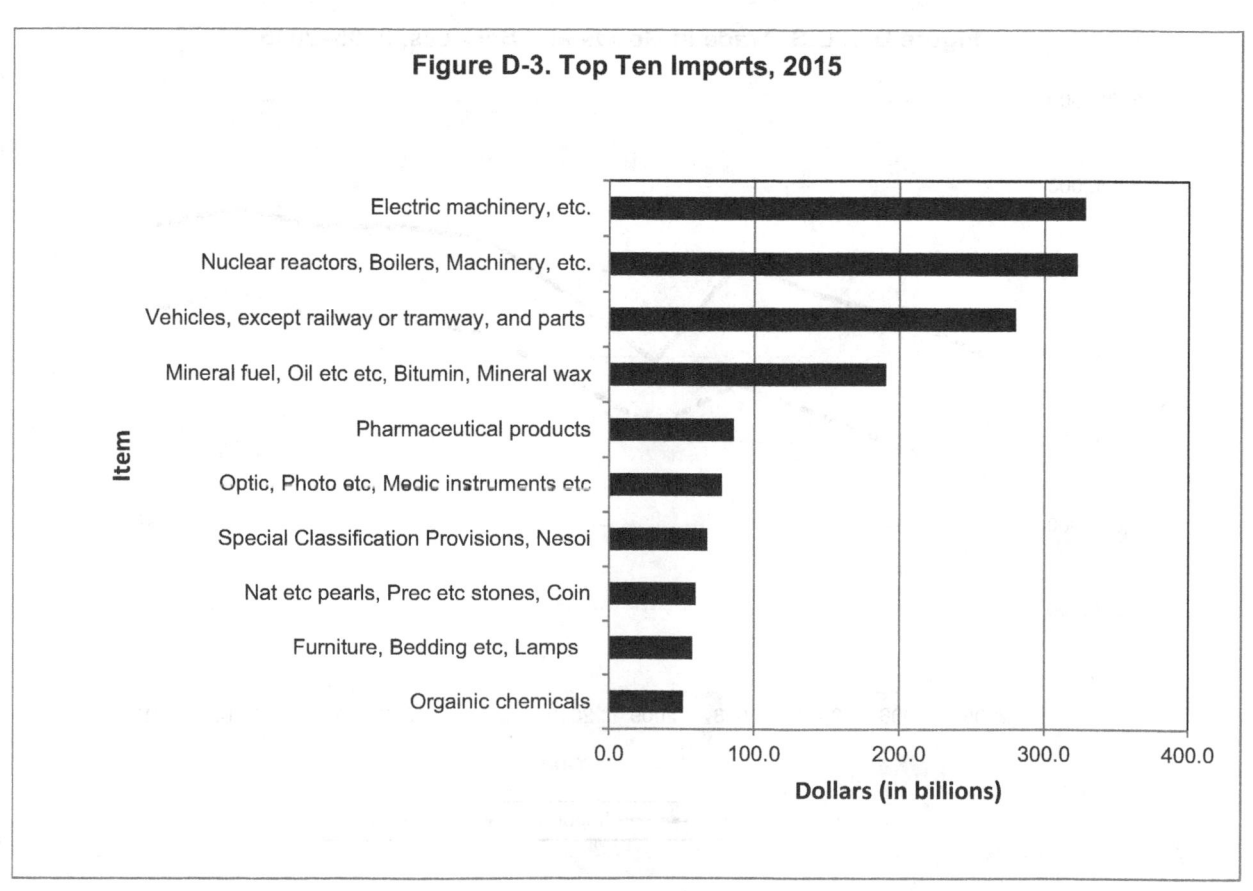

Figure D-3. Top Ten Imports, 2015

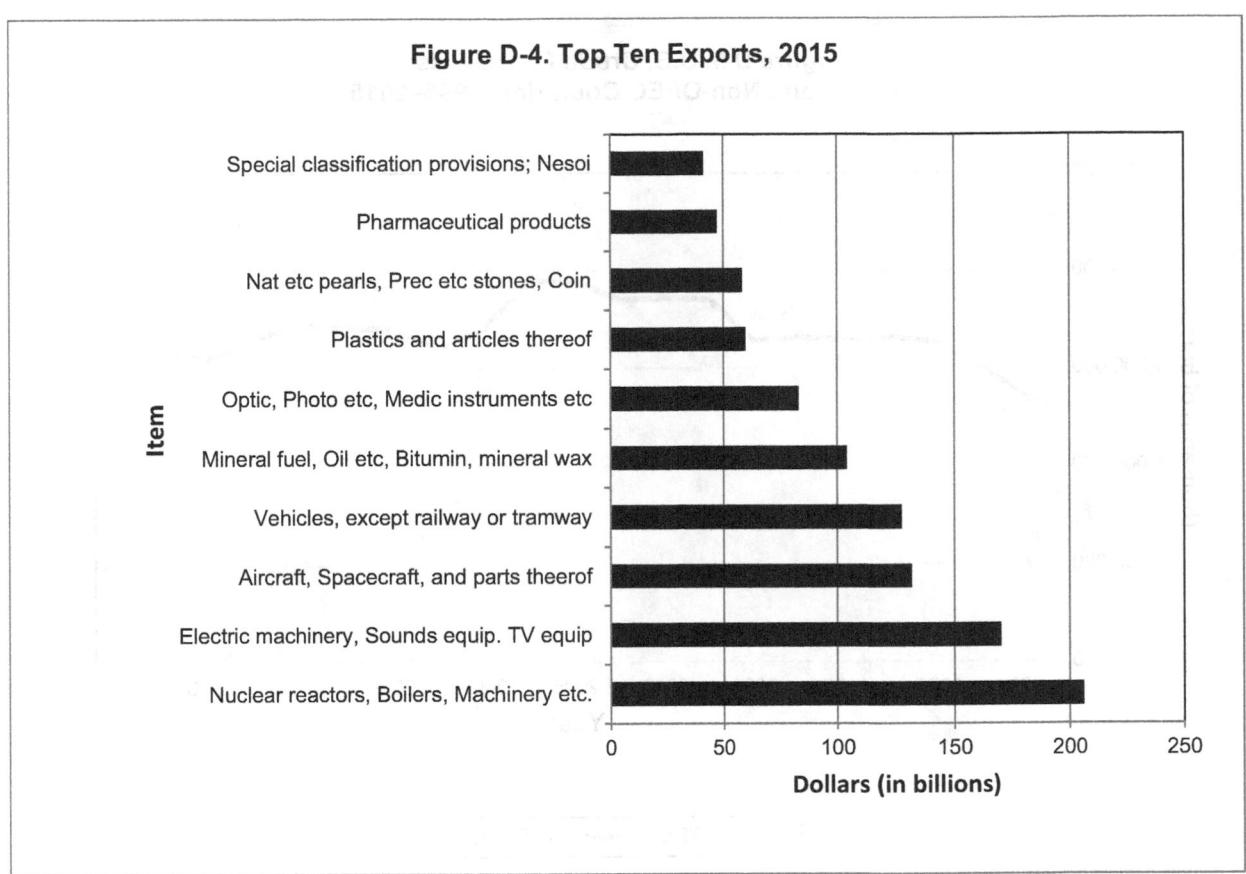

Figure D-4. Top Ten Exports, 2015

diamonds and gold. On the other hand, its surplus fluctuates between $96.50 billion in aircraft and spacecraft to $6.0 billion for optic instruments.

As with agricultural commodities, the U.S. trades with its NAFTA partners and China. Other countries include Belgium, Ireland, and Hong Kong. The U.S. ships organic chemicals, pharmaceutical products, and gold to them while India supplies the U.S. gold.

Crude Oil

Imports from OPEC[1] countries peaked in 2008 at 1.9 billion barrels, 55.3 percent of all U.S. imports. In 2015, that share fell to 36.3 percent while non-OPEC countries contributed 45.7 percent and 63.7 percent respectively. Non-OPEC countries overtook OPEC imports in 2002. Publication of U.S. import data are by the U.S. Department of Interior, Energy Information Administration. There are 55 non-OPEC countries.

The three largest OPEC suppliers of crude oil are Saudi Arab, Venezuela, and Nigeria, 34.8 percent, 27.4 percent and 19.6 percent respectively in 1993. By 2015, Saudi Arabia's share rose to 39.4 percent, Venezuela to 29.0 percent and Nigeria's share declined to just 2.0 percent.

Canada, the largest non-OPEC supplier of crude oil, represented 29.0 percent of oil imports in 1993. By 2015, that share jumped to 67.6 percent. Mexico, the other NAFTA partner to the U.S., supplied 27.8 percent in 1993 then fell to 14.7 percent in 2015.

U.S. crude oil exports reached an all time low of 3,296,000 barrels in 2002 then skyrocketed more than 50 fold by 2015. In the mid-2000s, oil reserves in the Bakken Formation, in mostly North Dakota, were estimated to be at 18 billion barrels. The application of new technologies such as hydraulic fracturing and horizontal drilling have contributed to a boom in Bakken oil production since 2000. In 2014 North Dakota became the second largest producer of oil, behind just Texas.

Rare Earth Elements

Rare earth elements (REE) are moderately abundant but rarely exist in pure form. They are the elements that have

---

[1] The members of the Organization of the Petroleum Exporting Countries (OPEC) are Algeria, Angola, Ecuador, Gabon, Iran, Iraq, Kuwait, Libya, Nigeria, Qatar, Saudi Arabia, United Arab Emirates and Venezuela.

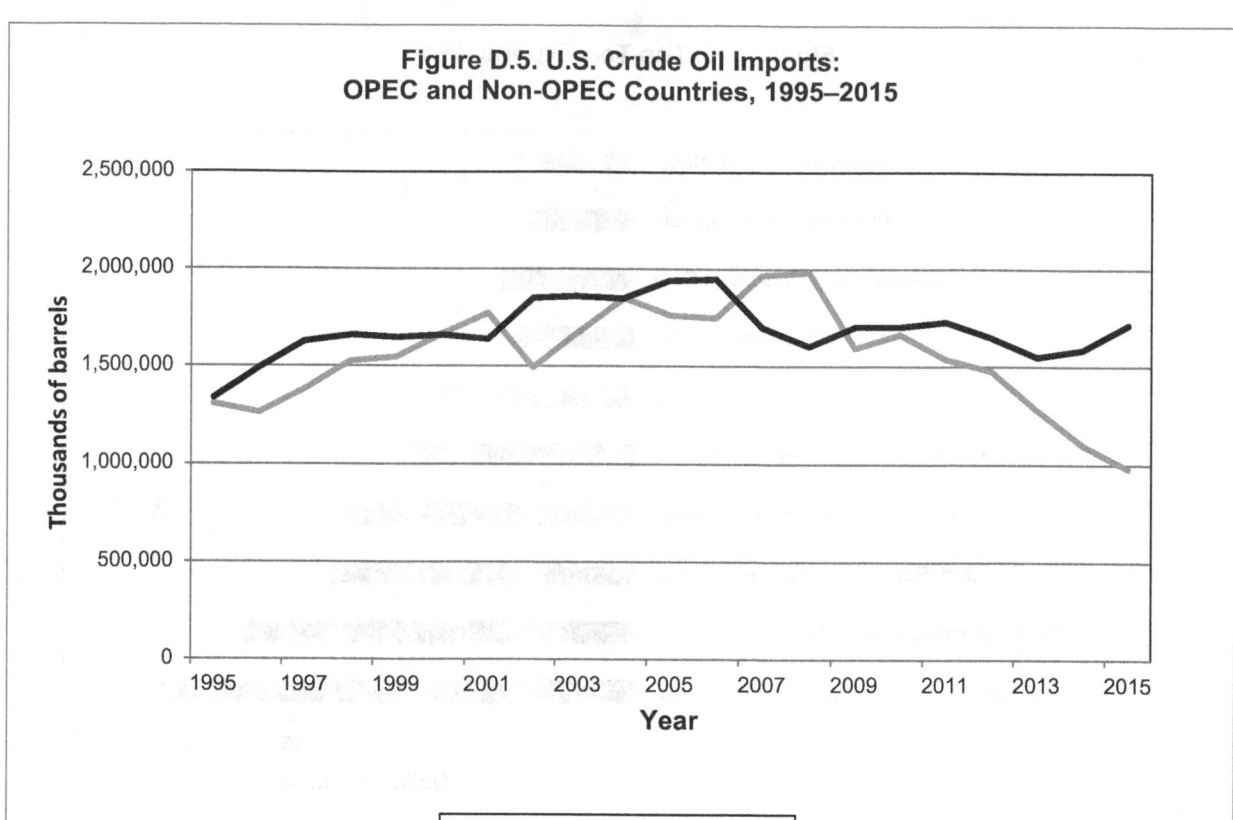

Figure D.5. U.S. Crude Oil Imports: OPEC and Non-OPEC Countries, 1995–2015

become irreplaceable to the world of technology owing to their unique magnetic, phosphorescent, and catalytic properties

The Japanese call these elements "the seeds of technology." The U.S. Department of Energy calls them "technology metals." They make possible the high tech world we live in today—everything from the miniaturization of electronics, to the enabling of green energy and medical technologies, to supporting a myriad of essential telecommunications and defense systems.

Rare earth metals and alloys that contain them are used in many devices that people use every day such as computer memory, DVDs, rechargeable batteries, cell phones, catalytic converters, magnets, fluorescent lighting and much more. Over 200 products now incorporate these elements, including batteries, catalysts, ceramic, medicine, and magnets. Rare earths are also used as catalysts, phosphors, and polishing compounds. These are used for air pollution control, illuminated screens on electronic devices, and the polishing of optical-quality glass. All of these products are expected to experience rising demand. China has become the world provider of the REEs, exporting over 70 percent, but the demand

for ATPs is inducing other countries to begin or restart production.

Advanced Technology Products

Advanced technology products (ATP) are considered cutting or leading edge in their field. ATP are not just laptops and smart phones but hybrid cars, robotics, aircraft, and military weapons. The U.S. Census Bureau classified 10 advanced technology products (ADP) into the following fields:

Biotechnology, Life Science, Opto-Electronics, Information & Communications, Electronics, Flexible Manufacturing, Advanced Materials, Aerospace, Weapons, Nuclear Technology. See the Appendix for the full definitions of each group.

Looking at the U.S. leading exports and imports, as discussed in Section D, Part 2, many similarities exist. Aircraft, spacecraft and parts are the third largest export. Vehicles and parts are the fourth largest export and the third largest import. Other top exports and imports that are classified as advanced technology products which need rare earth elements to function include:

- Electric machinery, sound and TV equipment, parts

- Pharmaceutical products

- Nuclear reactors, boilers, machinery, and parts

- Optic; photo, medical and surgical instruments.

United States' trade balance for ATP turned into a deficit of -$16.6 million in 2002 for the first time. It continued to decline until 2011, a new record for a deficit at -$98.7 million. Of the 10 categories, aerospace exported 37.3 percent of the $126 million. Opto-electronics was second with 28.1 percent of the ATP total.

Information and communications equipment, such as computers, disk drives and modems, accounted for over 54 percent of 2015 imports while aerospace was second at slightly less than 12 percent. Aerospace exports, such as new military helicopters, aircraft and flight simulators, accounted for 37.3 percent of 2015 exports. Information and communications equipment accounted for 28.1 percent of total.

As seen in many products in Section D, China, Canada, and Mexico are major trading partners in advanced technology products. According to the figures below, these three countries accounted for 52 percent of all exports while China supplied 46 percent of the U.S. ATP market, Mexico supplied 13 percent, and Japan 7 percent. Canada was tied with five other countries at five percent.

Trade deficits in ATP are not surprising, considering the overall trade deficit for the United States. The largest trade deficit is over $120 billion with China. Second is Ireland at $15 billion. Of the top 10 destinations for U.S. exports, only one, Canada, has a surplus of $13.3 billion. For U.S. purchases from the top 10 countries, Netherlands joins Canada at $7.0 billion.

ABOUT THE DATA

Section D provides another perspective on foreign trade by highlighting the top exported and imported commodities, ranked by 2015 values and including their HS – 6 digit groupings. Each commodity table includes details on the chief purchasers (exports) and suppliers (imports). Other

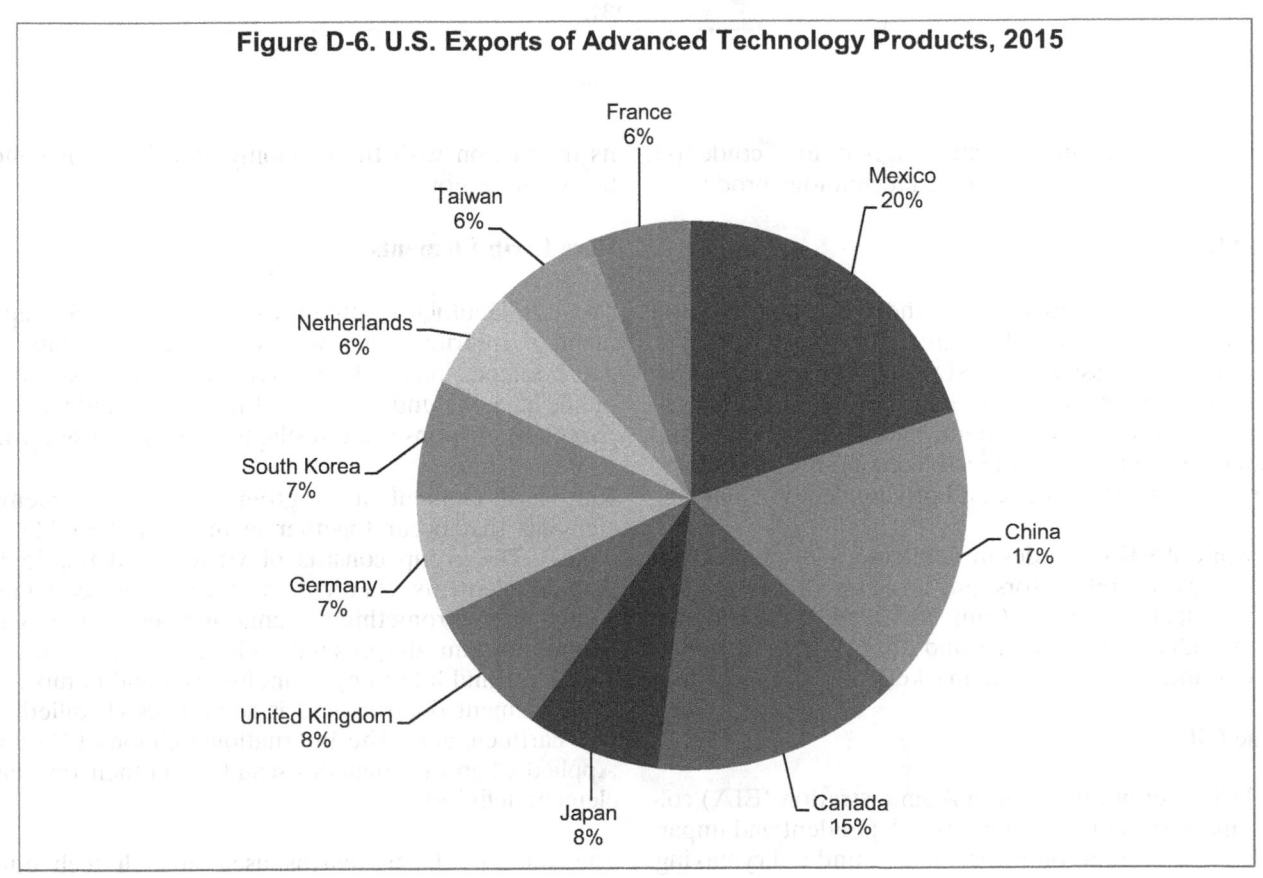

Figure D-6. U.S. Exports of Advanced Technology Products, 2015

- France 6%
- Mexico 20%
- Taiwan 6%
- China 17%
- Netherlands 6%
- South Korea 7%
- Germany 7%
- United Kingdom 8%
- Japan 8%
- Canada 15%

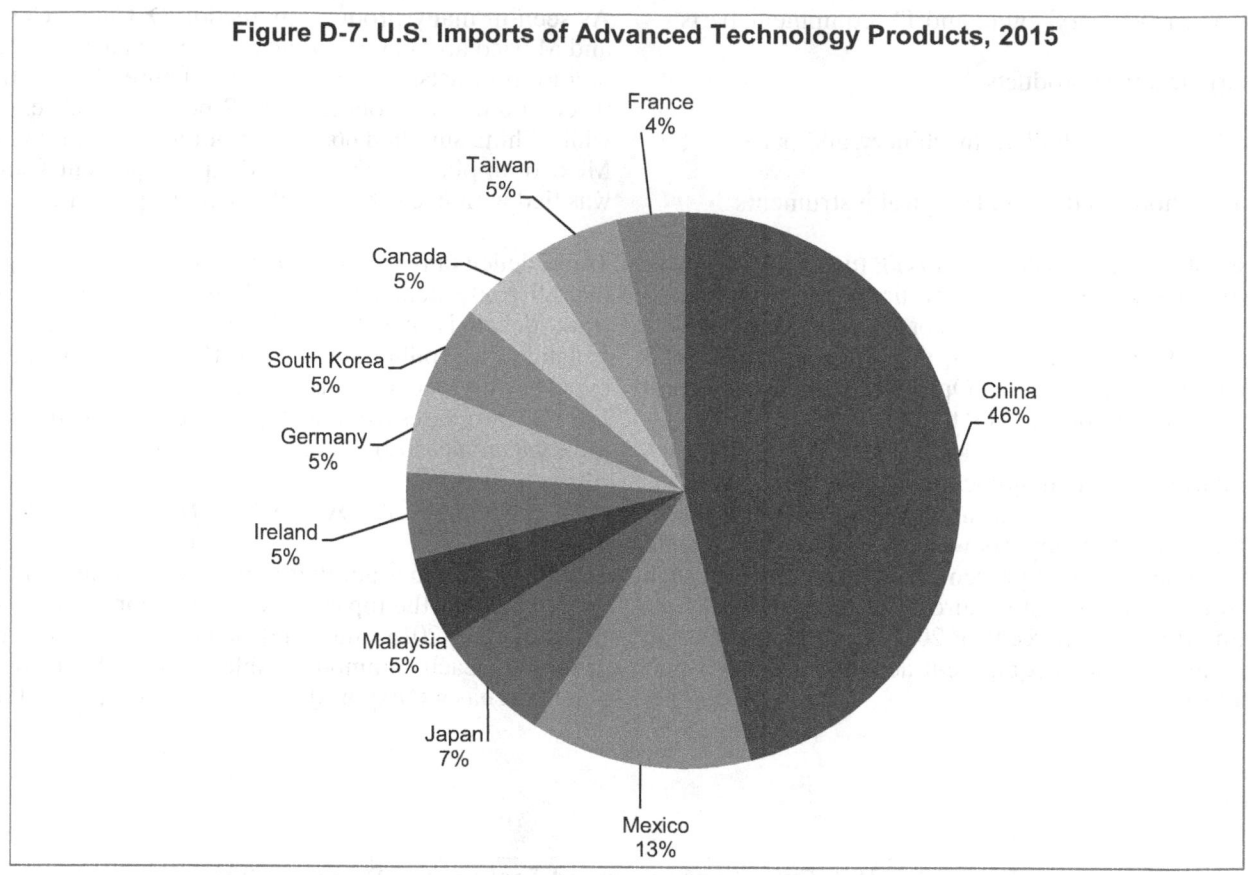

Figure D-7. U.S. Imports of Advanced Technology Products, 2015

commodities presented include agriculture, crude oil, rare earth elements and advanced technology products.

Agriculture

Agriculture data is provided by the U.S. Department of Agriculture, Economic Research Service at www.ers. usda.gov. The mission of USDA's Economic Research Service is to anticipate trends and emerging issues in agriculture, food, the environment, and rural America and to conduct high-quality, objective economic research to inform and enhance public and private decision making.

The work of ERS includes in-depth analyses of the economies, agricultural sectors, and policies of key trading partners such as Brazil, Canada, China, the European Union, India, Japan, Mexico, and South Korea as well as many countries in the global market.

Crude Oil

The U.S. Energy Information Administration (EIA) collects, analyzes, and disseminates independent and impartial energy information to promote sound policymaking, efficient markets, and public understanding of energy and

its interaction with the economy and the environment. See www.eia.gov.

Rare Earth Elements

The U.S. Geological Survey, as part of the U.S. Department of Interior, monitors, assesses, and conducts targeted science research so that policy makers and the public have the understanding they need to enhance preparedness, response, and resilience. See www.usgs.gov.

Rare earth elements are a group of seventeen chemical elements that occur together in the periodic table (see image). The group consists of yttrium and the 15 lanthanide elements (lanthanum, cerium, praseodymium, neodymium, promethium, samarium, europium, gadolinium, terbium, dysprosium, holmium, erbium, thulium, ytterbium, and lutetium). Scandium is found in most rare earth element deposits and is sometimes classified as a rare earth element. The International Union of Pure and Applied Chemistry includes scandium in their rare earth element definition.

The amount of rare earths used in high tech equipment is nominal but almost always critical to the unit's

General Advanced Technology Product Definitions	
Code	**Definition**
(01) Biotechnology	Focuses on medical and industrial applications of advanced scientific discoveries in genetics to the creation of new drugs, hormones, and other therapeutic items for both agricultural and human use.
(02) Life Science	Concentrates on the application of scientific advances (other than biological) to medical science. Recent advances, such as nuclear resonance imaging, echocardiography, and novel chemistry, coupled with new production techniques for the manufacture of drugs have led to many new products for the control or eradication of disease.
(03) Opto-Electronics	Encompasses electronic products and components that involve the emitting and/or detection of light. Examples of products included are optical scanners, optical disc players, solar cells, photo-sensitive semiconductors and laser printers.
(04) Information & Communications	Focuses on products that are able to process increased volumes of information in shorter periods of time. Includes central processing units, all computers and some peripheral units such as disk drive units and control units, along with modems, facsimile machines, and telephonic switching apparatus. Examples of other products included are radar apparatus and communication satellites.
(05) Electronics	Concentrates on recent design advances in electronic components (with the exception of opto-electronic components) that result in improved performance and capacity and in many cases reduced size. Products included are integrated circuits, multi-layer printed circuit boards and surface-mounted components such as capacitors and resistors.
(06) Flexible Manufacturing	Encompasses advances in robotics, numerically-controlled machine tools, and similar products involving industrial automation that allow for greater flexibility to the manufacturing process and reduce the amount of human intervention. Includes robots, numerically controlled machine tools and semiconductor production, and assembly machines.
(07) Advanced Materials	Encompasses recent advances in the development of materials that allow for further development and application of other advanced technologies. Examples are semiconductor materials, optical fiber cable, and video discs.
(08) Aerospace	Encompasses most new military and civil helicopters, airplanes and spacecraft (with the exception of communications satellites that are included under Information & Communications Technology). Other products included are turbojet aircraft engines, flight simulators, and automatic pilots.
(09) Weapons	Primarily encompasses products with military application. Includes such products as guided missiles and parts, bombs, torpedoes, mines, missiles, rocket launchers, and some firearms.
(10) Nuclear Technology	Encompasses nuclear power production apparatus. Includes nuclear reactors and parts, isotopic separation equipment and fuel cartridges. Excludes nuclear medical apparatus, which is included under Life Science Technology.

Source: U.S. Census Bureau http://www.census.gov/foreign-trade/reference/codes/atp/index.html

performance. For example, an iPhone uses eight rare earths—for everything from its colored screen, to its speakers, to the miniaturization of the phone's circuitry. While the amount of rare earths in each phone is very small, the quantity of phones sold each year is impressive

Advanced Technology Products

As expressed in the above section, many high-tech products incorporate rare earth elements properties. As such, special definitions have been developed to depict these new type of products. About 500 of some 22,000 commodity classification codes used in reporting U.S. merchandise trade are identified as "advanced technology" codes and they meet the following criteria:

- The code contains products whose technology is from a recognized high technology field (e.g.), biotechnology.

- These products represent leading edge technology in that field.

- Such products constitute a significant part of all items covered in the selected classification code.

Above are the categories and definitions provided by the U.S. Bureau. See https://www.census.gov/foreign-trade/statistics/country/index.html.

This product and commodity-based measure of advanced technology differs from broader North American Industry Classification System (NAICS) industry-based measures which include all goods produced by a particular industry group, regardless of the level of technology embodied in the goods. ATP classifications are assigned by the Foreign Trade Division of the U.S. Census Bureau.

Table D-1. U.S. Selected Agriculture Exports, 2005–2015

(Number in thousands.)

Item	2005	2006	2007	2008	2009	2010	2011	2012	2013	2014	2015
TOTAL	75,657	84,406	104,878	131,907	111,583	131,955	157,669	161,834	165,664	172,624	154,197
Soybeans	6,282	6,949	10,002	15,455	16,443	18,636	17,608	24,763	21,570	23,866	18,880
Prepared Foods	4,347	4,795	5,085	5,823	5,816	6,371	7,230	8,140	8,907	9,057	8,987
Forest Products	5,850	6,277	6,534	6,506	5,216	6,786	7,593	7,608	8,680	9,464	8,668
Corn	4,895	7,115	9,907	13,517	8,830	9,876	13,732	9,408	6,493	10,703	8,380
Tree Nuts	2,510	2,618	2,774	3,114	3,458	4,154	4,988	6,020	7,053	7,475	7,634
Beef & Beef Products	1,129	1,732	2,256	3,101	3,002	4,000	5,326	5,401	6,043	6,977	6,142
Wheat	4,410	4,205	8,375	11,294	5,380	6,771	11,145	8,166	10,442	7,701	5,625
Pork & Pork Products	2,493	2,697	2,976	4,521	4,056	4,561	5,906	6,124	5,833	6,452	5,365
Other Intermediate Products	2,617	2,961	3,566	3,609	3,552	3,779	4,186	4,540	4,803	5,091	4,837
Fish Products	3,837	3,974	4,007	3,979	3,725	4,188	5,234	4,889	4,797	5,011	4,816
Soybean meal	1,478	1,651	2,148	3,181	3,482	3,501	3,191	4,857	5,412	5,481	4,781
Dairy Products	1,386	1,593	2,718	3,436	1,936	3,380	4,426	4,737	6,236	6,581	4,689
Fresh Fruit	2,722	2,901	3,170	3,658	3,551	4,025	4,553	4,994	5,127	5,002	4,631
Cotton	3,929	4,514	4,589	4,812	3,365	5,890	8,466	6,253	5,629	4,411	3,902
Poultry Meat & Prods. (ex. eggs)	2,695	2,445	3,502	4,432	4,111	4,113	4,812	5,332	5,384	5,357	3,890
Biodiesel & Blends > B30	1,678	1,980	2,661	4,763	2,419	2,640	3,228	3,821	4,107	3,847	3,641
Distillers Grains	113	161	392	981	966	1,623	1,871	2,104	2,947	2,963	2,984
Processed Vegetables	1,341	1,450	1,631	2,032	1,957	2,032	2,369	2,581	2,772	2,935	2,908
Processed Fruit	1,040	1,184	1,344	1,650	1,562	1,723	2,065	2,236	2,409	2,522	2,765
Feeds & Fodders NESOI	1,428	1,547	1,748	2,140	1,762	2,103	2,403	2,669	3,057	3,048	2,706
Hides & Skins	1,777	2,045	2,166	2,064	1,465	2,284	2,663	2,784	3,134	2,925	2,435
Coarse Grains (ex. corn)	647	724	1,262	1,520	749	843	1,104	603	625	1,812	2,406
Fresh Vegetables	1,520	1,649	1,771	1,904	1,859	2,030	2,138	2,067	2,292	2,283	2,245
Wine & Beer	861	1,056	1,157	1,239	1,166	1,392	1,662	1,782	2,070	2,032	2,216
Rice	1,272	1,265	1,387	2,198	2,167	2,323	2,099	2,040	2,172	1,960	1,980
Ethanol	140	105	387	410	278	906	3,320	1,965	1,608	2,107	1,801
Essential Oils	1,005	1,051	1,187	1,270	1,264	1,372	1,499	1,609	1,705	1,742	1,792
Vegetable Oils NESOI	1,117	1,197	1,448	2,132	1,683	1,940	2,289	2,507	2,047	1,817	1,755
Chocolate & Cocoa Products	710	785	907	1,047	1,030	1,167	1,408	1,540	1,690	1,786	1,739
Condiments & Sauces	604	667	730	863	888	993	1,101	1,207	1,344	1,513	1,669
Distilled Spirits	726	844	984	1,049	1,007	1,125	1,286	1,419	1,454	1,524	1,521
Non-Alcoholic Bev. (ex. juices, coffee, tea)	416	453	510	707	792	786	912	1,061	1,184	1,265	1,352
Planting Seeds	706	684	794	1,039	894	951	1,110	1,236	1,313	1,400	1,289
Dog & Cat Food	807	965	1,039	1,176	1,132	1,128	1,256	1,309	1,351	1,301	1,281
Hay	472	504	572	648	807	898	1,004	1,250	1,326	1,169	1,280
Tobacco	990	1,141	1,208	1,238	1,159	1,168	1,149	1,101	1,138	1,086	1,109
Meat Products NESOI	785	877	993	802	823	904	980	1,020	1,106	1,117	1,088
Sugars & Sweeteners	423	590	771	747	689	1,102	1,340	1,493	1,358	1,184	1,081
Fruit & Vegetable Juices	690	779	864	947	910	999	1,149	1,115	1,117	1,043	958
Coffee, Roasted and Extracts	374	450	514	629	635	726	950	1,065	983	934	898
Snack Foods NESOI	444	456	496	598	605	614	692	776	829	868	852
Soybean Oil	292	360	725	1,374	1,043	1,569	1,267	1,153	910	811	803
Pulses	361	413	458	695	697	727	658	831	850	888	791
Live Animals	616	702	666	783	747	765	985	1,137	931	889	683
Eggs & Products	250	258	318	323	365	384	436	504	642	637	634
Peanuts	131	145	175	237	208	216	218	254	535	444	417
Animal Fats	453	483	814	948	674	999	1,213	812	635	581	414
Nursery Products & Cut Flowers	304	332	373	387	356	362	378	379	396	395	389
Oilseeds NESOI	241	278	342	371	328	389	340	342	413	365	358
Tea	73	106	143	175	177	214	254	279	312	312	276
Spices	52	57	62	71	75	78	86	100	99	109	115
Rapeseed	37	52	88	101	95	120	122	161	95	119	106
Oilseed Meal/Cake (ex. soybean)	89	76	62	83	107	155	89	112	118	110	86
Rubber & Allied Gums	53	61	65	67	64	112	115	106	87	89	80
Other Bulk Commodities	26	25	21	29	28	29	38	41	40	33	39
Palm Oil	9	17	34	29	20	23	25	25	39	21	18
Coffee, Unroasted	5	4	4	3	7	6	4	8	11	7	9
Cocoa Beans	-	-	0	0	-	4	0	0	-	-	2

Data Source: U.S. Census Bureau Trade Data.
Published by: United States Department of Agriculture, Foreign Agricultural Service.

Table D-2. U.S. Selected Agriculture Imports, 2005–2015

(Numbers in thousands.)

	2005	2006	2007	2008	2009	2010	2011	2012	2013	2014	2015
TOTAL	95,070,621	101,519,232	104,078,016	108,590,313	94,479,925	107,820,192	126,232,993	131,836,990	136,759,256	147,849,397	148,571,661
Other Consumer Oriented	4,529,345	5,473,992	6,175,306	6,747,366	6,524,173	7,424,711	8,359,652	9,074,201	9,469,599	10,080,207	10,801,860
Wine and Beer	6,876,483	7,742,155	8,257,604	8,301,708	7,363,756	7,797,242	8,451,969	8,834,407	9,039,559	9,601,588	10,091,669
Other Edible Fish & Seafood	5,281,148	5,893,417	6,321,775	6,502,500	6,140,711	6,711,012	7,599,906	8,260,915	8,675,063	9,425,940	9,149,845
Red Meats, FR/CH/FR	4,929,424	4,329,470	4,367,057	4,096,720	3,734,616	4,309,946	4,824,380	5,283,601	5,500,495	7,852,271	8,683,775
Other Fresh Fruit	3,221,510	3,607,461	4,251,543	4,320,118	4,589,782	5,159,402	5,320,591	5,602,649	6,449,848	7,420,891	8,202,685
Snack Foods	4,417,364	4,739,230	4,984,634	5,203,404	5,036,188	5,804,595	6,443,747	6,778,829	7,175,800	7,600,592	8,034,678
Processed Fruit & Vegetables	3,821,402	4,217,567	4,814,505	5,398,028	5,132,345	5,482,703	6,331,343	6,757,905	6,916,909	7,197,037	7,747,315
Fresh Vegetables	3,566,158	3,989,161	4,282,158	4,487,129	4,328,605	5,356,785	5,911,091	5,922,929	6,796,859	6,826,909	7,095,749
Other Intermediate Products	2,481,253	2,678,218	3,062,662	3,856,188	3,420,060	3,808,215	5,275,188	8,568,802	7,480,608	7,477,690	6,607,618
Other Value-Added Wood Prod	7,374,395	7,786,495	6,882,685	5,835,338	4,288,614	4,629,256	4,193,275	4,557,936	5,101,190	5,428,568	5,736,597
Shrimp	3,670,861	4,136,035	3,910,990	4,105,467	3,778,133	4,296,542	5,166,114	4,463,478	5,277,534	6,698,811	5,450,746
Coffee, Unroasted	2,501,975	2,829,397	3,236,773	3,804,443	3,375,153	4,054,975	6,906,364	5,807,719	4,669,939	5,228,618	5,118,631
Panel Products (Incl Plywood)	7,235,245	6,630,690	5,117,145	3,822,765	2,853,864	3,306,033	3,158,153	3,816,136	4,481,988	4,688,927	5,096,302
Softwood and Treated Lumber	8,267,667	7,623,575	5,845,319	3,858,280	2,359,960	3,042,149	2,988,179	3,531,742	4,585,687	5,213,779	4,916,422
Other Vegetable Oils	1,666,514	1,943,901	2,112,756	3,066,141	2,266,422	2,470,187	3,653,837	3,578,733	3,460,101	3,446,673	3,519,330
Essential Oils	2,444,934	2,491,012	2,476,190	2,692,655	2,299,383	2,462,045	2,571,305	2,564,385	2,838,620	3,064,218	3,448,704
Live Animals	1,960,047	2,461,264	2,952,445	2,603,315	1,864,009	2,220,446	2,175,636	2,479,077	2,503,255	3,380,341	3,133,638
Tree Nuts	1,081,460	1,054,906	1,121,701	1,261,989	1,215,964	1,397,325	1,767,167	1,750,212	1,871,665	2,250,335	2,650,462
Bananas and Plantains	1,129,500	1,195,575	1,218,954	1,366,834	1,569,710	1,778,999	1,970,968	2,069,456	2,146,252	2,179,105	2,218,802
Tropical Oils	613,137	737,112	1,113,795	1,946,878	1,298,145	1,637,815	2,650,529	2,092,973	2,011,792	2,136,896	1,950,614
Spices	600,735	640,531	787,241	967,340	855,096	1,002,400	1,257,254	1,333,811	1,441,920	1,615,082	1,852,691
Fruit & Vegetable Juices	1,005,027	1,150,218	1,741,335	1,922,196	1,357,965	1,407,147	1,941,516	1,846,902	1,855,299	1,898,689	1,833,834
Nursery Products	1,381,661	1,455,118	1,547,119	1,468,348	1,346,700	1,480,591	1,545,269	1,619,104	1,675,367	1,722,909	1,730,554
Other Dairy Products	1,337,910	1,305,681	1,406,871	1,581,036	1,159,923	1,199,588	1,400,551	1,601,597	1,502,361	1,718,772	1,728,510
Other Bulk Commodities	498,764	565,256	822,191	1,300,345	937,561	917,886	1,253,251	1,382,085	1,861,645	2,581,447	1,627,881
Rubber & Allied Products	1,562,163	2,042,875	2,135,630	2,874,737	1,286,985	2,834,545	4,790,651	3,404,709	2,578,570	1,971,134	1,512,444
Cocoa Beans	872,154	714,002	660,206	878,337	1,178,525	1,250,897	1,424,902	996,081	1,110,630	1,312,308	1,429,136
Lobster	1,058,403	1,083,143	1,054,589	1,056,911	786,835	1,030,364	1,077,358	1,109,066	1,127,303	1,294,286	1,424,476
Sugars, Sweeteners, Bev Bases	637,597	988,296	685,678	1,085,896	1,039,285	1,344,440	1,846,992	1,725,587	1,650,499	1,510,406	1,360,251
Cheese	1,006,657	1,029,438	1,107,273	1,168,217	1,004,352	967,031	1,072,952	1,093,017	1,145,001	1,274,747	1,290,772
Roasted & Instant Coffee	473,650	483,686	531,470	607,684	694,539	887,339	1,188,209	1,210,883	1,138,984	1,103,025	1,183,508
Tuna	916,331	937,671	1,047,935	1,200,157	1,152,983	1,306,892	1,377,326	1,431,723	1,427,300	1,318,775	1,172,329
Raw Beet & Cane Sugar	706,165	854,171	681,320	610,289	772,306	1,243,859	1,653,244	1,330,552	745,237	866,788	1,152,890
Cocoa Paste & Cocoa Butter	663,618	665,446	661,698	979,396	925,282	1,341,601	1,302,778	1,074,060	929,854	1,141,051	1,017,382
Planting Seeds	506,718	601,475	672,573	772,563	758,989	786,866	932,643	1,383,924	1,540,208	1,324,584	1,005,057
Coarse Grains	260,244	323,567	526,130	865,268	515,139	460,446	634,869	1,111,224	1,487,400	878,237	860,961
Feeds & Fodders	284,429	325,317	426,695	458,715	417,279	469,404	627,691	760,729	848,587	846,576	839,706
Red Meats, Prep/Pres	668,529	731,303	754,389	701,095	607,444	471,603	610,755	593,693	620,508	655,330	751,208
Salmon Whole or Eviscerated	365,753	494,071	522,832	515,385	562,357	651,552	632,846	627,457	712,311	699,326	750,109
Rice	224,927	326,735	395,473	563,004	608,315	593,674	651,894	679,188	757,403	788,255	740,919
Tobacco	665,082	743,041	834,072	806,717	897,179	722,321	738,069	884,858	952,616	865,559	740,233
Tea, Incl Herb	376,336	430,519	455,416	497,708	494,709	582,701	642,094	666,039	713,612	715,278	725,221
Wheat	172,197	309,606	500,385	1,069,224	690,770	560,859	641,737	829,456	1,059,827	997,293	704,486
Groundfish, Fillet/Steak	580,967	601,720	613,975	570,304	550,912	560,012	647,703	614,731	610,941	654,212	635,948
Hardwood Lumber	721,479	709,632	647,011	535,656	272,849	345,255	373,703	425,482	447,556	513,247	523,012
Hides & Skins	145,994	149,059	151,744	156,656	114,340	172,763	187,571	225,959	286,003	304,973	241,737
Logs and Chips	307,311	297,020	200,766	99,862	51,714	77,771	59,773	78,986	79,554	77,711	80,965

Data Source: U.S. Census Bureau Trade Data.
Published by: United States Department of Agriculture, Foreign Agricultural Service.

Table D-3.   Exports and Imports by Country: Beverages and Spirits, 2010–2015

EXPORTS

Area	2010	2011	2012	2013	2014	2015
World	4,712,806,821	7,814,659,221	6,887,352,486	6,952,722,650	7,624,827,163	7,562,243,238
Canada..	1,523,423,757	2,075,456,635	2,250,727,595	2,400,023,155	2,538,128,500	2,297,466,888
United Kingdom............................	436,674,327	738,837,159	579,048,520	461,499,355	430,498,212	548,840,829
Mexico..	355,428,496	490,761,522	556,953,297	557,724,582	524,772,389	503,697,873
Japan..	267,332,267	333,085,742	353,473,221	366,819,859	294,720,237	304,756,393
Netherlands.................................	267,632,496	538,025,161	346,940,435	202,959,220	260,474,021	264,900,172
Brazil..	50,609,866	1,140,813,992	250,217,150	133,533,955	281,793,503	264,137,519
Panama.......................................	48,641,267	75,438,508	95,644,345	93,239,109	178,061,160	242,732,925
China..	54,567,051	75,528,743	92,445,040	124,658,820	128,335,701	240,472,662
Germany......................................	180,601,092	181,146,951	184,863,613	260,111,178	208,466,699	228,686,213
Australia......................................	170,751,540	199,985,717	207,479,470	191,694,499	192,996,029	186,906,858

IMPORTS

Area	2010	2011	2012	2013	2014	2015
World	15,742,262,869	17,858,296,224	19,821,707,487	20,210,982,056	20,359,060,077	21,260,302,926
Mexico..	2,588,579,397	2,732,095,349	2,904,941,587	3,080,468,647	3,868,696,543	4,187,888,472
France..	2,696,789,575	3,145,284,801	3,396,648,456	3,531,330,074	3,673,869,935	3,776,572,396
Italy..	1,666,068,875	1,923,501,642	1,943,065,464	2,115,225,957	2,229,305,256	2,250,044,103
United Kingdom............................	1,451,643,503	1,675,373,953	1,781,763,787	1,953,849,392	1,930,836,034	1,910,943,335
Netherlands.................................	1,220,516,687	1,147,055,942	1,162,564,742	1,150,992,983	1,092,008,788	1,154,043,773
Switzerland..................................	382,925,811	446,899,117	547,475,988	676,033,271	769,136,092	937,580,994
Ireland..	463,858,376	541,740,801	582,529,798	630,767,429	619,458,286	740,516,668
Canada..	703,069,882	752,643,420	779,571,509	834,908,124	745,009,216	719,806,829
Austria..	406,338,662	479,345,965	548,954,631	530,107,602	515,294,118	626,625,780
Brazil..	261,103,954	590,189,589	1,532,867,953	1,255,044,839	550,477,477	535,292,011

Table D-4.   Exports and Imports by Country: Cereal and Grains, 2010–2015

EXPORTS

Area	2010	2011	2012	2013	2014	2015
World	20,036,820,271	28,347,941,016	20,616,227,140	20,301,036,516	22,825,948,714	18,799,966,274
Mexico	2,931,746,886	4,752,603,093	4,502,818,499	3,437,883,154	3,580,342,798	3,418,381,758
Japan	4,169,394,484	5,608,955,459	4,367,830,635	3,179,743,668	3,953,469,292	3,110,576,863
China..................................	336,005,223	1,012,389,250	1,534,976,967	2,372,628,606	1,766,923,160	2,466,361,238
South Korea..............................	1,846,700,000	2,428,154,895	1,323,808,673	707,103,781	1,521,758,888	1,109,812,502
Colombia..................................	291,709,526	391,999,191	283,581,614	490,082,905	1,188,586,040	1,086,625,017
Taiwan..................................	910,135,053	1,216,919,047	715,766,966	602,564,136	801,077,929	674,466,046
Canada..................................	539,888,417	558,947,054	528,616,309	516,897,994	644,724,181	574,154,488
Philippines	420,806,518	719,918,746	619,942,869	643,301,897	716,463,851	532,665,378
Nigeria..................................	832,445,380	1,170,455,311	977,219,249	960,716,598	706,302,472	525,035,605
Peru..................................	281,781,329	328,614,310	71,828,820	258,519,072	647,344,151	398,934,068

IMPORTS

Area	2010	2011	2012	2013	2014	2015
World	1,849,610,344	2,192,368,590	3,125,699,176	4,088,513,813	3,296,850,091	2,654,759,087
Canada..................................	1,012,357,297	1,296,621,972	1,669,832,834	2,097,438,127	1,788,241,644	1,347,027,952
Thailand	397,930,363	411,478,360	427,428,951	447,182,382	440,255,281	422,276,623
India..................................	109,162,955	124,503,802	139,926,916	167,189,776	179,069,815	168,582,135
Romania..................................	0	0	3,162,771	11,088,381	24,858,643	103,067,142
Chile..................................	129,492,973	132,335,374	249,009,305	344,727,039	216,406,549	86,423,408
Argentina	39,948,125	53,813,951	106,626,947	370,313,879	141,340,741	81,091,390
Peru..................................	3,118,916	6,054,667	14,966,712	30,856,176	73,739,238	63,646,819
Brazil..................................	51,500,864	33,281,751	255,996,636	289,558,075	14,479,332	59,023,837
Bolivia..................................	245,913	555,165	29,981,755	64,092,047	83,969,812	49,665,990
Turkey..................................	450,005	534,300	19,877,353	19,393,840	38,851,064	45,185,664

Table D-5.   Exports and Imports by Country: Cocoa, 2010–2015

EXPORTS

Area	2010	2011	2012	2013	2014	2015
World	1,385,233,144	1,592,859,889	1,717,000,953	1,870,791,003	2,118,581,220	1,949,866,177
Canada...............................	701,218,083	779,216,976	764,240,561	805,866,969	934,292,379	859,586,189
Mexico...............................	203,342,378	242,039,338	268,255,937	316,391,921	297,130,722	266,603,725
South Korea.......................	59,730,623	73,817,404	77,307,337	83,764,082	80,508,362	69,016,360
Japan.................................	43,174,328	47,217,817	58,710,838	56,645,063	55,055,712	56,561,618
Australia.............................	13,111,045	23,074,101	29,136,760	43,324,834	55,998,990	51,649,256
Philippines.........................	25,543,510	31,523,539	34,768,592	40,025,800	42,620,224	43,884,857
Hong Kong.........................	17,192,266	20,638,966	29,658,738	32,588,322	33,473,038	37,645,485
United Kingdom..................	9,825,070	14,168,083	18,739,044	23,288,439	27,363,010	35,932,480
China.................................	27,821,047	44,486,937	49,982,779	49,767,820	39,919,938	35,329,699
United Arab Emirates.........	15,262,361	16,047,359	18,711,158	21,567,197	29,444,310	32,663,983

IMPORTS

Area	2010	2011	2012	2013	2014	2015
World	4,299,538,823	4,686,269,266	4,102,624,842	4,164,281,075	4,734,473,290	4,865,669,172
Canada...............................	872,378,503	940,739,651	989,511,424	1,046,065,426	1,178,922,740	1,322,002,756
Cote d'Ivoire......................	770,216,674	870,536,893	731,539,646	806,705,774	933,433,087	913,505,246
Mexico...............................	454,217,243	532,885,085	514,979,618	499,374,658	479,174,659	501,604,754
Ecuador.............................	103,540,878	246,871,486	132,462,049	184,950,917	257,959,327	310,313,846
Indonesia...........................	447,086,838	209,061,356	158,389,501	176,892,036	252,540,358	276,766,044
Ghana.................................	181,908,291	269,364,144	175,999,025	178,191,859	190,463,922	218,151,304
Germany.............................	149,692,486	166,075,973	181,830,739	174,157,044	178,024,632	145,045,771
Netherlands........................	250,233,708	297,416,028	266,920,635	202,245,084	168,341,392	144,247,708
Malaysia.............................	307,624,775	278,390,628	148,165,409	133,820,260	185,150,499	128,804,220
Belgium..............................	93,016,997	115,193,940	120,601,552	123,622,803	131,729,300	125,209,813

Table D-6.   Exports and Imports by Selected Country: Coffee and Tea, 2010–2015

EXPORTS

Area	2010	2011	2012	2013	2014	2015
World	888,103,008	1,226,518,123	1,295,237,452	1,184,247,043	1,224,696,955	1,219,454,066
Canada..	598,867,677	850,096,701	930,279,753	824,450,713	864,790,934	812,845,078
Japan..	58,917,581	71,720,913	87,044,334	92,715,333	81,621,703	84,943,246
Mexico..	27,356,930	28,854,014	27,644,711	28,900,581	34,012,093	45,622,166
South Korea...................................	25,656,612	37,633,476	41,316,873	45,828,854	40,866,598	40,115,182
United Kingdom..............................	12,729,086	8,315,979	10,082,132	9,122,811	12,669,496	26,368,192
Taiwan..	7,132,836	11,130,048	12,522,973	11,642,526	16,580,301	22,576,474
China..	11,173,157	14,261,552	20,894,298	18,934,119	14,283,770	13,702,701
Germany..	16,208,503	60,324,848	25,416,122	14,932,648	16,054,095	13,002,236
Singapore......................................	14,183,846	16,054,526	20,805,828	21,423,849	15,793,747	11,946,317
Saudi Arabia..................................	5,223,841	7,176,539	8,275,777	7,195,211	8,862,031	10,681,645

IMPORTS

Area	2010	2011	2012	2013	2014	2015
World	5,741,806,507	9,117,179,534	8,066,032,970	6,978,424,824	7,686,909,615	7,967,179,631
Brazil..	1,137,442,477	2,019,698,109	1,418,091,235	1,178,462,688	1,455,498,655	1,493,229,381
Colombia..	817,229,965	1,324,312,367	907,609,054	939,183,128	1,172,730,932	1,238,605,877
Vietnam...	435,523,547	629,444,212	723,273,295	662,145,430	795,469,353	671,473,347
Indonesia.......................................	395,352,389	519,966,361	651,351,521	516,016,288	494,945,587	591,193,530
Canada..	311,528,037	444,844,007	448,337,655	427,554,259	423,125,901	468,578,777
Guatemala......................................	307,111,618	593,241,158	576,872,989	420,491,937	367,997,965	333,475,598
India...	174,787,027	248,965,725	274,306,621	247,273,147	252,462,917	324,643,414
Mexico..	287,789,221	550,132,269	524,209,330	398,278,819	343,699,728	306,914,210
China..	205,897,603	233,205,766	234,278,980	246,365,370	270,886,632	279,251,688
Peru...	260,678,214	433,466,959	302,094,421	222,798,974	268,744,027	240,713,430

Table D-7.   Exports and Imports by Country: Dairy Products, 2010–2015

EXPORTS

Area	2010	2011	2012	2013	2014	2015
World	3,223,273,009	4,113,779,080	4,252,529,967	5,769,222,235	6,160,374,243	4,447,901,155
Mexico..........	764,639,921	1,078,045,500	1,165,163,756	1,459,903,035	1,646,347,412	1,307,507,559
Canada..........	258,596,090	280,192,453	282,270,363	349,475,058	413,094,390	400,855,364
China..........	172,005,268	268,358,383	272,767,048	542,869,656	521,174,912	293,604,974
South Korea..........	118,402,740	202,447,244	202,751,874	276,442,304	385,805,433	280,435,340
Japan..........	193,782,752	285,090,456	246,388,022	270,705,552	374,147,705	261,232,652
Philippines..........	175,488,545	228,652,413	258,206,157	308,566,418	389,916,192	234,888,148
Indonesia..........	154,154,776	202,179,267	161,620,440	279,698,046	251,477,945	175,834,365
Vietnam..........	140,532,825	170,941,617	109,807,350	218,427,777	231,473,567	144,986,402
Malaysia..........	92,483,699	125,393,965	110,642,841	151,081,297	159,554,074	102,762,843
Australia..........	34,464,568	62,621,147	71,564,833	88,611,664	129,758,888	94,972,727

IMPORTS

Area	2010	2011	2012	2013	2014	2015
World	1,706,975,184	1,962,942,676	2,095,308,219	2,216,876,558	2,515,092,618	2,714,952,745
New Zealand..........	258,267,145	285,822,952	360,729,109	282,467,572	372,868,083	408,903,582
Italy..........	278,386,109	312,907,331	302,946,126	311,763,163	310,219,057	323,972,059
France..........	150,965,122	193,135,752	176,779,360	207,848,920	222,779,500	207,252,474
Canada..........	135,560,658	120,638,016	163,847,120	160,297,649	165,986,213	163,378,044
Spain..........	47,238,541	58,524,040	61,630,025	81,226,109	97,804,233	136,608,786
India..........	50,117,917	77,762,704	59,016,085	71,419,282	64,872,244	117,143,668
Argentina..........	72,842,215	124,590,225	140,658,317	152,573,841	159,562,802	113,720,564
Mexico..........	74,662,900	78,627,789	95,712,526	99,300,982	111,323,016	111,267,786
Netherlands..........	63,368,694	80,215,525	77,774,407	83,025,769	107,264,950	108,815,229
Vietnam..........	47,135,882	67,636,246	51,051,964	83,107,064	123,350,407	101,294,448

Table D-8.   Exports and Imports by Country: Fruits and Nuts, 2010–2015

EXPORTS

Area	2010	2011	2012	2013	2014	2015
World	10,142,478,585	11,767,712,352	13,263,744,191	14,532,740,414	14,856,806,331	14,459,437,122
Canada...	2,991,492,595	3,316,009,414	3,501,791,060	3,679,237,990	3,696,993,622	3,471,988,711
Hong Kong...	929,161,887	1,154,324,682	1,540,904,697	1,540,208,400	1,262,168,972	1,153,473,311
Japan...	745,629,938	792,426,018	878,703,718	878,770,932	889,906,518	910,700,445
Mexico..	523,546,485	611,149,020	783,157,626	838,754,163	817,778,375	842,007,538
Spain..	331,158,779	420,037,185	420,497,797	620,875,415	712,012,957	775,321,789
South Korea...	370,791,815	494,491,067	680,188,006	692,522,104	750,338,928	743,824,462
Germany..	380,497,390	433,879,551	466,506,512	649,112,062	749,817,768	718,987,653
India..	293,658,025	408,421,295	441,254,103	452,701,401	553,574,484	710,523,807
United Arab Emirates	297,685,940	320,824,233	301,260,586	470,096,120	493,966,998	512,794,628
Netherlands...	250,139,329	281,017,689	290,298,666	329,361,977	413,570,488	408,398,834

IMPORTS

Area	2,010	2,011	2,012	2,013	2,014	2,015
World	8,863,914,318	9,732,655,918	10,184,784,760	11,191,993,575	12,641,969,818	14,021,023,338
Mexico..	2,705,439,997	2,921,241,968	3,321,664,982	3,694,902,491	4,480,772,768	5,158,594,760
Chile..	1,514,500,275	1,509,847,543	1,409,577,650	1,753,868,902	1,753,892,894	1,870,716,321
Guatemala...	601,539,284	801,985,706	864,528,449	943,346,659	1,015,791,590	1,078,885,481
Costa Rica...	808,916,676	833,381,767	857,623,887	903,661,534	1,004,423,615	892,777,583
Vietnam..	344,706,974	406,073,665	394,745,746	515,513,908	615,941,512	801,772,599
Peru..	135,671,233	224,884,743	215,805,668	272,478,100	465,902,426	560,860,430
Ecuador..	474,857,159	510,794,296	461,519,382	456,420,232	448,195,007	494,161,544
Canada...	255,564,939	301,765,869	385,787,318	375,885,605	379,850,574	432,899,071
Honduras..	220,729,026	239,592,965	258,566,766	280,233,196	282,410,465	304,324,869
India..	189,980,313	312,489,276	275,799,023	276,551,739	227,019,828	238,578,118

Table D-9.   Exports and Imports by Country: Live Trees and Cut Flowers, 2010–2015

EXPORTS

Area	2010	2011	2012	2013	2014	2015
World	416,042,869	423,746,283	400,532,063	417,596,816	421,378,448	411,245,226
Canada..	256,032,337	242,234,904	219,682,410	229,131,989	224,553,695	215,176,620
Netherlands...	49,244,373	54,144,071	61,324,550	61,339,264	61,843,739	66,299,519
Mexico..	30,947,026	47,922,525	55,401,910	62,172,030	63,272,951	64,208,805
Peru...	642,208	467,701	1,166,928	1,826,345	6,068,176	7,659,824
China..	4,184,907	4,583,471	3,575,612	3,745,341	4,674,218	7,269,741
Spain..	3,011,067	3,395,785	5,202,821	4,321,794	6,515,061	5,145,904
Bahamas...	4,408,020	6,107,486	6,684,119	5,962,279	6,000,574	5,052,761
Japan	7,635,568	6,395,774	5,486,210	4,917,389	4,465,345	4,853,358
Belgium...	21,674,882	20,120,417	11,762,064	9,274,118	9,005,305	4,261,803

IMPORTS

Area	2,010	2,011	2,012	2,013	2,014	2,015
World	1,483,246,259	1,547,076,287	1,620,977,702	1,677,547,625	1,727,651,483	1,735,015,801
Colombia...	561,772,687	577,671,651	646,189,161	669,454,719	663,762,767	624,071,209
Canada..	284,110,603	288,264,544	282,824,866	292,654,416	320,915,573	332,100,711
Ecuador..	137,451,352	149,084,448	170,665,109	178,236,238	187,385,025	212,993,714
Netherlands...	196,748,321	208,072,029	187,595,386	188,932,294	191,895,939	182,163,611
Taiwan..	42,812,702	51,075,290	49,505,878	56,217,062	63,768,617	63,610,533
Costa Rica...	55,401,887	54,949,192	56,645,317	51,474,382	53,902,611	58,877,155
Mexico..	42,048,890	41,996,392	44,292,026	47,352,739	51,537,203	50,002,821
China..	23,254,846	28,593,636	29,396,297	31,695,029	37,355,593	40,573,435
Guatemala...	23,644,271	26,695,213	28,950,241	30,488,386	28,168,624	31,086,005
Thailand..	13,549,890	12,241,114	15,149,143	13,982,556	12,338,713	14,247,839

Table D-10.   Exports and Imports by Country: Meat, 2010–2015

EXPORTS

Area	2010	2011	2012	2013	2014	2015
World	12,051,903,134	15,357,261,104	16,096,226,509	16,274,745,442	17,665,168,093	14,278,381,054
Mexico	2,303,900,641	2,698,021,248	2,769,695,522	3,046,860,552	3,699,584,309	3,062,982,392
Japan	2,305,076,344	2,881,503,384	3,035,937,260	3,287,436,093	3,515,928,736	2,835,844,827
Canada	1,408,456,922	1,746,904,864	2,055,488,132	1,979,096,855	1,808,672,391	1,626,892,658
Hong Kong	1,008,290,118	1,185,520,781	916,830,414	1,209,736,293	1,880,447,103	1,403,954,305
South Korea	782,511,612	1,301,915,005	1,074,071,919	944,364,478	1,368,341,210	1,267,971,822
Taiwan	378,968,528	367,222,097	339,838,270	454,836,497	466,516,234	515,150,692
China	318,946,813	819,133,526	1,002,235,934	1,060,511,799	704,523,399	335,588,336
Netherlands	88,225,370	139,198,709	149,060,726	159,349,395	162,713,878	177,177,779
Philippines	156,771,787	163,692,986	177,448,690	196,888,148	194,962,990	155,932,893
Egypt	178,603,158	235,228,648	215,386,846	168,530,193	151,186,126	154,471,906

IMPORTS

Area	2010	2011	2012	2013	2014	2015
World	4,585,951,969	5,121,401,309	5,607,532,690	5,844,460,135	8,224,549,543	9,133,814,388
Australia	1,149,096,546	1,243,155,587	1,519,093,399	1,524,702,076	2,652,536,437	3,124,095,087
Canada	1,952,741,700	1,993,425,944	1,874,609,315	2,015,380,695	2,554,190,668	2,431,877,490
New Zealand	728,242,599	905,663,438	962,889,618	983,792,792	1,181,222,635	1,405,111,827
Mexico	227,655,484	345,975,644	547,663,232	583,179,044	836,453,714	1,070,992,502
Uruguay	73,954,963	75,350,037	119,068,771	140,770,516	172,084,968	262,119,658
Nicaragua	104,854,234	164,825,814	140,013,171	127,206,653	230,175,317	185,015,230
Chile	52,004,944	51,899,154	72,835,072	81,092,159	91,144,408	142,740,574
Denmark	135,108,863	140,509,805	143,520,301	127,229,986	146,735,662	128,774,204
Italy	48,955,502	56,564,165	67,598,232	72,550,539	76,988,874	77,287,612
Poland	8,435,375	6,563,883	7,624,415	19,501,002	69,267,684	74,164,282

Table D-11.   Exports and Imports by Country: Oilseeds and Soybeans, 2010–2015

EXPORTS

Area	2010	2011	2012	2013	2014	2015
World	21,959,179,277	21,231,783,916	29,688,506,908	26,955,408,692	28,876,576,254	23,619,245,783
China..................................	11,036,956,186	10,714,269,930	15,146,749,047	13,698,826,517	14,936,965,663	11,090,906,417
Mexico	2,055,498,345	2,245,587,909	2,603,010,528	2,329,225,877	2,419,647,971	1,935,971,632
Japan	1,767,070,529	1,681,589,315	1,908,810,998	1,752,604,405	1,701,464,279	1,679,670,202
Germany	575,008,229	352,210,671	940,511,815	812,524,356	655,245,240	874,474,165
Indonesia	826,500,566	868,790,629	1,030,595,765	1,004,941,050	1,072,222,461	796,515,129
Taiwan.................................	693,528,496	753,042,150	824,572,080	651,830,351	781,700,720	632,902,663
Netherlands..........................	186,020,367	291,408,795	177,969,434	263,755,838	593,165,721	620,438,337
South Korea	559,734,603	533,837,528	695,620,804	608,144,757	676,844,552	561,023,078
Canada	485,203,606	563,125,244	603,924,689	555,728,791	606,637,681	535,490,435
Spain...................................	401,166,226	256,832,742	376,236,418	598,871,627	585,608,664	470,164,596

IMPORTS

Area	2010	2011	2012	2013	2014	2015
World	1,650,274,918	2,054,018,052	2,325,827,557	2,955,427,187	3,606,373,372	2,568,847,191
Canada	666,066,162	898,176,870	879,883,378	1,026,837,065	1,130,800,521	816,109,811
China..................................	183,380,940	217,904,646	321,309,269	342,403,954	341,224,668	347,069,762
India	125,912,484	155,275,648	162,374,115	187,246,697	257,024,939	256,506,512
Netherlands..........................	74,029,530	66,198,145	79,652,789	80,840,297	141,344,245	96,019,194
Mexico	54,964,312	68,215,997	83,423,493	102,722,363	104,948,535	80,204,571
Chile...................................	87,767,353	110,075,556	106,891,320	106,461,694	78,172,753	77,347,931
Ukraine...............................	660,456	362,307	1,029,218	1,048,385	23,201,340	77,087,216
Argentina	23,383,716	36,440,211	101,255,515	53,819,439	60,348,700	68,259,622
Germany	36,247,762	43,951,352	40,846,311	51,940,575	48,847,675	55,613,123

Table D-12.   Exports and Imports by Country: Sugar, 2010–2015

EXPORTS

Area	2010	2011	2012	2013	2014	2015
World	1,741,252,237	2,166,356,133	2,560,099,709	2,476,526,283	2,267,383,043	1,970,833,844
Mexico	720,239,293	882,709,771	1,024,432,484	878,670,857	697,085,690	691,372,043
Canada	411,271,168	455,550,397	502,740,993	507,491,967	517,034,196	511,687,460
Japan	64,371,976	83,621,128	111,313,855	117,813,504	110,394,694	87,256,705
China	44,798,708	81,535,700	131,247,664	118,645,653	113,463,452	74,413,760
New Zealand	24,246,136	63,717,697	91,887,748	79,325,720	85,725,696	54,013,012
South Korea	28,290,469	41,777,996	42,915,359	46,880,017	57,168,648	49,116,091
Australia	21,931,563	29,321,985	42,487,554	54,274,103	45,860,912	44,064,671
United Kingdom	25,973,521	18,600,336	23,509,132	28,941,264	22,502,621	33,850,506
Singapore	16,970,547	25,292,075	38,342,198	39,380,094	36,263,317	32,062,011
Philippines	51,043,656	69,644,278	52,487,810	62,679,806	78,320,862	29,707,771

IMPORTS

Area	2010	2011	2012	2013	2014	2015
World	3,762,960,410	4,754,501,578	4,366,563,699	3,799,136,792	3,946,737,027	4,044,445,204
Mexico	1,156,239,594	1,730,105,245	1,332,432,859	1,674,430,170	1,363,894,448	1,413,148,101
Canada	652,795,104	722,433,371	758,083,695	777,569,107	793,461,957	790,706,973
Brazil	304,420,436	439,645,113	259,059,535	113,830,221	173,986,959	193,905,997
China	141,984,344	151,510,449	135,354,361	142,393,132	164,320,299	158,362,456
Guatemala	221,480,985	142,933,732	213,967,735	63,333,534	156,698,647	141,043,785
Dominican Republic	171,085,645	152,970,291	161,941,207	65,285,144	64,254,264	111,070,969
Germany	53,230,656	63,640,674	70,153,768	75,386,382	92,575,606	96,408,459
El Salvador	84,409,065	89,931,190	187,577,335	79,294,797	87,528,009	90,486,967
Colombia	60,412,856	71,818,988	90,256,060	66,875,180	102,057,739	86,558,056
Australia	91,394,606	101,557,374	126,652,962	44,516,395	61,944,333	69,390,278

Table D-13.   Exports and Imports by Country: Tobacco, 2010–2015

EXPORTS

Area	2010	2011	2012	2013	2014	2015
World	1,671,101,643	1,695,718,949	1,657,584,481	1,909,886,988	1,805,463,578	2,077,517,416
Canada	66,394,533	82,186,351	70,622,559	260,744,037	264,565,684	506,718,221
Switzerland	118,352,910	194,848,285	163,775,024	221,819,495	202,830,663	268,739,169
Japan	312,743,090	364,041,574	296,060,009	268,527,362	260,253,067	243,071,025
China	152,020,796	117,125,289	125,459,626	178,785,750	216,755,599	198,088,633
Dominican Republic	98,697,130	113,138,985	113,544,191	129,682,243	127,636,756	165,990,651
Mexico	126,318,809	163,432,802	135,228,671	113,319,359	96,644,840	93,200,875
Germany	70,284,594	86,677,239	73,441,933	83,517,211	57,221,115	62,601,472
Indonesia	45,482,074	49,449,370	52,460,734	75,295,895	77,889,939	62,564,926
Russian Federation	43,307,409	42,890,659	62,192,367	85,322,843	44,545,084	54,253,558

IMPORTS

Area	2010	2011	2012	2013	2014	2015
World	1,422,376,429	1,531,838,624	1,829,461,939	2,175,452,989	2,056,564,826	2,058,013,843
Dominican Republic	338,124,316	360,283,247	420,307,141	496,324,380	531,733,246	612,986,018
Brazil	276,846,696	279,718,323	376,870,759	413,927,377	271,980,625	254,681,984
Mexico	30,029,765	27,537,879	26,665,682	221,223,330	222,781,579	173,295,994
Turkey	111,142,555	142,133,445	181,701,615	170,499,040	196,700,105	165,461,428
Nicaragua	79,749,340	99,269,008	113,892,969	125,803,963	128,530,176	139,486,222
Canada	151,995,089	149,090,091	157,101,429	161,319,654	146,436,296	129,259,062
South Korea	27,105,629	33,521,565	34,362,215	51,179,520	58,814,978	89,695,068
Honduras	70,295,656	77,118,747	83,128,468	81,836,278	85,509,537	85,591,973
India	24,433,541	27,875,379	44,081,617	35,893,948	29,033,187	41,628,117
Indonesia	35,752,502	33,033,831	36,839,566	32,862,956	31,886,839	34,104,733

Table D-14.   Exports and Imports by Country: Vegetables, 2010–2015

EXPORTS

Area	2010	2011	2012	2013	2014	2015
World	3,784,499,541	3,939,248,155	4,044,613,580	4,404,427,386	4,511,818,098	4,363,056,510
Canada..	2,271,454,514	2,443,551,648	2,334,050,363	2,653,904,095	2,693,050,511	2,695,256,106
Mexico..	304,669,003	264,475,695	379,410,747	318,003,270	300,904,566	262,820,758
Japan..	277,544,184	296,203,167	308,627,394	268,014,094	268,446,373	222,655,560
India...	96,991,267	47,749,291	93,610,617	119,378,225	206,062,958	144,606,079
United Kingdom................................	86,786,177	85,137,649	110,742,834	118,056,640	120,043,982	127,629,798
Taiwan..	80,085,044	83,049,123	97,377,437	90,621,589	86,532,480	77,089,108
Netherlands......................................	33,477,410	41,248,547	37,556,615	45,937,866	62,861,424	52,423,392
China..	33,371,443	16,733,738	24,386,643	43,101,397	40,919,926	49,134,182
Dominican Republic..........................	29,686,871	34,626,664	37,803,519	28,961,858	28,140,814	46,506,960
Spain..	36,961,025	36,170,545	45,368,790	54,989,509	47,414,339	40,329,093

IMPORTS

Area	2010	2011	2012	2013	2014	2015
World	6,485,965,249	7,248,756,396	7,418,333,310	8,203,380,402	8,335,125,958	8,656,616,920
Mexico..	3,966,796,924	4,449,702,098	4,458,667,342	5,021,209,661	5,132,217,839	5,312,750,681
Canada..	1,191,037,631	1,307,445,242	1,297,225,154	1,498,083,351	1,528,719,932	1,520,596,839
China..	351,384,022	384,906,185	387,164,840	429,470,645	379,940,932	416,105,844
Peru...	272,222,275	280,533,849	327,251,226	376,308,133	360,243,336	382,870,331
Guatemala..	97,029,509	134,081,119	147,226,399	156,181,747	165,402,454	176,911,830
Costa Rica..	74,893,205	83,862,749	84,998,542	96,000,906	94,797,276	97,373,358
Netherlands......................................	69,053,717	88,320,512	74,085,486	65,550,900	67,085,557	84,422,068
India...	43,245,714	78,262,778	190,372,169	92,468,294	93,346,129	69,302,579
Spain..	45,758,624	16,907,789	13,355,550	16,301,364	25,296,598	60,351,902
Ecuador..	41,580,354	39,339,540	46,374,484	47,593,063	45,533,868	56,561,584

Table D-15.   Exports and Imports by Country: Aircraft, Spacecraft, and Parts, 2010–2015

EXPORTS

Area	2010	2011	2012	2013	2014	2015
World	79,617,922,992	87,757,246,448	104,440,079,691	114,886,824,530	125,291,175,809	131,627,865,014
China	5,762,796,389	6,398,398,620	8,366,104,861	12,587,374,948	13,927,951,108	15,440,943,511
United Kingdom	5,767,163,285	6,775,229,845	6,595,252,261	8,374,662,288	9,135,291,407	9,683,842,537
France	7,216,068,298	7,139,193,730	8,197,916,850	8,586,850,679	8,407,950,468	9,622,108,290
Canada	5,552,272,501	5,796,446,032	5,790,594,479	6,692,407,185	7,625,354,865	8,292,611,490
Japan	5,109,389,181	4,870,246,371	8,285,696,951	7,065,530,497	7,299,458,726	7,119,152,779
Germany	5,361,918,512	5,634,557,886	5,655,823,630	5,808,595,780	6,534,113,114	6,710,831,213
United Arab Emirates	1,780,318,362	3,631,866,236	7,132,474,365	5,591,524,567	4,873,129,091	5,825,565,444
Singapore	3,806,403,416	3,855,445,662	3,950,322,554	3,768,749,339	4,153,826,733	5,776,276,846
Brazil	4,472,008,126	5,387,266,500	6,078,658,061	5,306,966,341	4,805,361,069	4,722,679,788
South Korea	2,431,040,215	2,591,208,173	3,416,997,418	3,295,625,990	2,875,450,784	4,438,159,853

IMPORTS

Area	2010	2011	2012	2013	2014	2015
World	18,784,788,012	21,483,415,291	24,257,975,352	29,419,871,919	34,353,639,069	35,144,698,242
Canada	4,548,182,038	5,310,015,558	5,848,627,015	6,645,523,732	7,964,105,708	8,409,931,540
France	4,991,783,296	4,837,991,482	4,910,478,045	6,040,294,611	5,963,872,005	5,948,246,600
Japan	2,092,346,080	2,580,248,599	3,269,445,321	3,847,737,710	4,887,367,833	4,765,580,237
Germany	881,812,745	1,562,776,028	1,516,637,435	2,899,744,451	3,972,139,652	4,469,342,747
Brazil	728,847,153	894,547,647	984,514,773	1,742,032,721	2,323,267,867	3,035,479,344
United Kingdom	1,476,454,694	1,484,565,629	1,600,125,749	1,293,847,677	1,472,063,916	1,321,066,893
Mexico	283,287,924	454,025,038	785,819,837	842,711,407	1,173,062,121	1,143,396,058
Italy	839,993,307	893,067,602	1,218,415,833	1,355,044,695	1,431,647,066	1,009,803,455
Israel	422,610,788	393,749,028	587,214,487	643,209,823	796,925,487	708,735,396
South Korea	338,281,881	362,189,186	417,537,088	489,197,844	594,779,626	663,779,519

Table D-16. Exports and Imports by Country: Electric Machinery, 2010–2015

EXPORTS

Area	2010	2011	2012	2013	2014	2015
World	151,776,704,354	159,468,543,383	162,434,694,242	165,818,048,345	172,363,626,713	169,956,050,124
Mexico	31,627,373,800	32,385,289,582	33,897,578,165	36,626,018,631	38,361,523,119	41,111,591,393
Canada	25,064,855,683	27,123,249,594	27,483,604,826	27,020,052,670	27,576,274,968	25,090,973,947
China	11,524,897,695	10,164,158,455	9,667,167,407	11,388,647,532	12,019,482,124	12,760,674,037
Hong Kong	6,663,059,627	7,493,147,413	7,419,538,491	8,196,544,493	9,738,457,690	9,474,051,381
South Korea	5,073,732,095	6,077,546,691	6,205,327,101	6,107,613,105	5,923,104,446	6,124,207,276
Malaysia	7,054,434,892	6,759,214,936	5,818,800,433	5,421,127,502	6,167,837,455	6,001,488,985
Japan	4,332,771,519	4,998,182,557	5,506,627,282	4,918,442,336	5,154,631,159	5,216,790,058
Germany	4,472,184,689	4,459,956,535	4,173,724,935	4,262,207,388	4,590,147,301	4,666,862,585
Taiwan	4,644,570,447	5,045,614,973	4,466,349,849	4,041,412,285	4,222,032,084	4,500,481,897
Netherlands	3,326,118,631	3,675,630,193	3,430,004,567	3,651,495,802	4,285,786,836	4,348,000,343

IMPORTS

Area	2010	2011	2012	2013	2014	2015
World	258,235,732,124	278,578,502,864	291,562,129,068	298,482,465,393	315,812,496,521	328,286,273,785
China	90,819,304,050	98,702,750,576	110,712,693,453	117,534,663,660	127,333,490,956	133,163,487,206
Mexico	53,868,384,772	54,308,759,309	56,816,043,510	57,393,028,181	58,684,361,333	63,156,233,968
Malaysia	11,581,435,919	12,472,862,950	13,339,743,303	14,820,541,425	17,958,665,254	21,399,255,260
Japan	18,353,458,972	18,287,996,320	20,059,371,952	18,404,673,188	17,310,896,001	16,494,313,517
South Korea	15,266,918,806	16,080,490,571	12,770,460,315	14,695,083,636	15,476,202,210	14,670,074,324
Taiwan	15,661,187,364	18,121,360,365	14,655,707,494	13,897,348,934	14,721,464,589	14,178,365,123
Vietnam	807,771,760	997,923,065	1,438,165,094	1,957,305,866	3,749,929,673	8,302,982,326
Germany	5,986,256,838	7,507,597,258	7,619,709,434	7,665,341,111	8,345,566,844	8,155,651,396
Canada	7,920,418,486	8,201,695,474	8,255,656,051	7,887,656,902	7,912,779,334	7,514,816,314
Thailand	5,761,894,213	6,305,929,389	6,329,863,229	6,304,273,754	6,788,280,233	7,410,131,689

Table D-17.   Exports and Imports by Country: Furniture, 2010–2015

EXPORTS

Area	2010	2011	2012	2013	2014	2015
World	8,591,937,170	9,552,824,362	10,622,789,543	11,103,413,945	11,842,773,619	11,558,116,682
Canada	4,418,352,237	4,860,340,578	5,451,091,385	5,380,233,366	5,487,259,939	5,125,844,965
Mexico	1,096,283,882	1,319,008,344	1,605,551,895	1,902,502,664	2,338,537,262	2,451,524,821
China	191,957,010	221,868,067	218,956,209	234,000,792	298,505,216	314,639,121
United Kingdom	222,244,788	227,811,549	245,711,098	248,084,349	272,665,276	279,814,248
Japan	281,314,497	338,150,306	326,060,321	333,409,146	305,580,341	278,061,506
Saudi Arabia	183,369,330	171,586,972	191,385,565	222,394,823	224,842,002	192,148,684
Australia	103,944,033	132,334,872	148,617,978	172,186,064	163,383,444	179,671,404
United Arab Emirates	107,251,731	105,743,574	122,381,529	131,947,886	177,372,015	148,601,241
Germany	114,414,772	133,915,517	147,216,148	130,789,401	146,176,217	133,048,692
South Korea	56,750,999	73,472,627	67,155,558	104,328,741	116,377,920	127,864,077

IMPORTS

Area	2010	2011	2012	2013	2014	2015
World	37,821,166,238	39,790,724,984	44,365,466,241	47,661,903,375	51,938,811,977	56,924,568,716
China	19,955,925,871	20,493,091,043	22,442,985,811	24,133,281,078	25,480,878,909	28,100,192,571
Mexico	5,647,805,714	6,288,591,423	7,838,922,145	8,532,674,982	9,699,456,529	10,653,025,542
Canada	3,502,673,537	3,800,220,351	3,905,845,280	3,874,369,980	4,087,622,580	4,345,342,516
Vietnam	1,826,263,777	1,845,086,420	2,315,656,583	2,635,878,183	3,150,695,675	3,863,002,928
Taiwan	777,858,516	844,687,002	952,170,452	965,107,695	1,025,526,780	1,140,128,676
Italy	648,034,280	719,702,732	780,709,424	894,921,820	1,005,119,506	1,054,689,959
Malaysia	787,129,425	738,804,834	807,655,880	742,303,087	795,890,618	866,302,470
Germany	470,586,810	571,444,388	571,722,074	648,945,060	759,783,940	815,778,231
Indonesia	582,328,592	567,358,256	650,405,671	712,619,154	719,324,183	756,832,827
United Kingdom	365,163,786	467,388,508	539,904,978	527,949,277	771,531,367	731,722,249

Table D-18. Exports and Imports by Country: Nuclear Reactors, 2010–2015

EXPORTS

Area	2010	2011	2012	2013	2014	2015
World	73,960,066,842	79,383,778,894	83,367,062,357	84,344,595,248	84,976,899,318	83,444,556,553
Canada	7,959,446,915	8,855,165,605	9,683,314,675	9,478,255,852	9,217,285,818	8,585,597,939
China	5,204,003,380	5,757,912,929	7,034,587,311	7,667,147,188	7,527,379,877	7,922,584,119
Japan	7,227,318,145	7,736,136,943	8,155,940,569	7,975,852,015	7,406,346,106	7,098,054,155
Mexico	4,406,321,342	4,846,777,876	5,435,818,355	5,755,982,951	6,370,568,318	6,737,786,732
Netherlands	5,232,774,453	5,317,878,711	5,449,561,377	5,789,767,252	6,178,264,533	6,331,279,545
Germany	5,482,833,556	5,854,058,001	5,856,514,016	5,995,617,284	6,139,592,450	6,134,018,568
Belgium	2,542,401,253	3,131,098,676	3,509,434,233	4,019,329,691	4,510,134,792	4,335,418,711
South Korea	2,661,597,173	2,876,304,271	2,960,760,051	2,757,022,636	2,867,457,434	3,027,283,250
United Kingdom	2,720,570,033	2,811,804,524	2,769,092,222	2,732,236,222	2,868,338,060	2,834,658,090
Singapore	2,088,422,851	2,294,954,558	2,418,658,216	2,735,567,381	2,621,025,699	2,688,004,747

IMPORTS

Area	2010	2011	2012	2013	2014	2015
World	249,797,039,140	287,635,771,553	308,088,220,073	304,838,343,715	325,171,903,843	322,848,429,149
China	82,721,975,805	94,858,584,604	99,133,609,543	100,447,489,945	105,514,807,271	104,135,393,425
Mexico	33,618,329,458	38,569,359,899	42,317,330,882	42,699,866,904	45,215,689,763	49,026,215,314
Japan	24,887,695,689	31,269,161,413	34,067,688,651	30,588,252,477	31,057,110,256	29,042,602,898
Germany	16,465,972,925	20,246,477,682	22,117,079,167	21,867,990,604	23,870,081,114	24,032,682,494
Canada	17,684,316,720	19,924,904,679	20,697,961,119	19,912,963,105	21,128,121,250	19,990,062,888
South Korea	9,341,054,608	10,335,540,900	11,200,067,356	10,814,642,073	11,530,715,119	11,800,892,334
France	6,328,621,315	7,036,821,745	8,274,988,229	8,980,088,415	9,535,913,164	9,433,865,176
Italy	5,285,823,469	6,906,396,922	7,550,434,608	7,893,991,070	9,235,285,227	8,926,275,014
United Kingdom	6,156,827,028	7,630,351,859	8,488,440,478	8,630,706,688	9,155,407,617	8,540,138,325
Thailand	4,490,899,262	4,301,945,604	5,743,523,323	6,285,605,683	6,860,770,126	7,453,491,649

Table D-19.   Exports and Imports by Country: Optic-Photo, Medical or Surgical Instruments, 2010–2015

EXPORTS

Area	2010	2011	2012	2013	2014	2015
World	73,960,066,842	79,383,778,894	83,367,062,357	84,344,595,248	84,976,899,318	83,444,556,553
Canada	7,959,446,915	8,855,165,605	9,683,314,675	9,478,255,852	9,217,285,818	8,585,597,939
China	5,204,003,380	5,757,912,929	7,034,587,311	7,667,147,188	7,527,379,877	7,922,584,119
Japan	7,227,318,145	7,736,136,943	8,155,940,569	7,975,852,015	7,406,346,106	7,098,054,155
Mexico	4,406,321,342	4,846,777,876	5,435,818,355	5,755,982,951	6,370,568,318	6,737,786,732
Netherlands	5,232,774,453	5,317,878,711	5,449,561,377	5,789,767,252	6,178,264,533	6,331,279,545
Germany	5,482,833,556	5,854,058,001	5,856,514,016	5,995,617,284	6,139,592,450	6,134,018,568
Belgium	2,542,401,253	3,131,098,676	3,509,434,233	4,019,329,691	4,510,134,792	4,335,418,711
South Korea	2,661,597,173	2,876,304,271	2,960,760,051	2,757,022,636	2,867,457,434	3,027,283,250
United Kingdom	2,720,570,033	2,811,804,524	2,769,092,222	2,732,236,222	2,868,338,060	2,834,658,090
Singapore	2,088,422,851	2,294,954,558	2,418,658,216	2,735,567,381	2,621,025,699	2,688,004,747

IMPORTS

Area	2010	2011	2012	2013	2014	2015
World	58,876,075,643	66,081,084,213	68,810,632,221	71,136,644,228	75,440,937,299	77,441,367,524
Mexico	8,793,615,767	9,736,091,624	10,354,864,523	10,712,939,580	11,599,661,326	12,232,486,141
China	7,015,589,884	7,879,417,815	8,779,274,533	9,524,110,150	10,367,594,517	11,063,269,214
Germany	7,281,909,054	8,731,992,116	8,808,017,993	8,908,349,404	9,265,530,629	9,029,796,917
Japan	6,124,101,391	6,900,101,409	6,855,400,553	6,650,366,178	6,650,891,584	6,512,489,303
Ireland	5,070,451,247	5,177,952,283	5,285,010,050	5,762,897,720	5,766,149,636	5,755,471,667
United Kingdom	2,737,943,840	3,124,285,393	3,262,521,885	3,195,014,524	3,224,946,403	3,295,110,743
Switzerland	2,346,893,456	2,857,694,901	2,733,728,746	2,884,991,686	3,139,026,213	3,138,083,907
Canada	2,559,459,623	2,816,136,075	2,942,278,980	2,823,140,507	2,793,936,632	2,998,218,662
Singapore	1,243,221,650	1,662,220,061	1,994,427,365	2,074,452,033	2,358,498,879	2,529,524,578
France	2,139,226,860	2,255,686,388	2,109,823,708	2,211,919,590	2,362,794,637	2,353,916,693

Table D-20.   Exports and Imports by Country: Organic Chemicals, 2010–2015

EXPORTS

Area	2010	2011	2012	2013	2014	2015
World	40,928,206,521	45,682,439,840	46,079,294,886	46,599,579,308	42,326,082,876	38,755,176,681
Belgium..................................	4,396,710,160	4,457,930,250	4,498,217,888	4,559,304,151	4,428,110,659	4,852,066,724
Mexico	5,019,096,437	6,403,857,184	7,019,467,357	6,697,435,758	6,432,701,615	4,847,431,504
Canada..................................	3,996,827,963	4,188,042,620	3,942,361,920	4,207,737,711	4,455,035,012	3,949,594,336
China.....................................	2,979,165,562	3,524,176,837	3,239,506,263	3,102,616,716	2,375,758,562	2,463,771,537
Japan	2,278,696,700	2,308,885,209	2,407,240,798	2,118,899,592	2,311,279,316	2,189,625,960
Brazil	2,037,537,117	1,990,808,928	2,007,904,721	2,310,011,112	2,261,958,698	1,773,019,022
Netherlands...........................	1,878,151,713	2,067,907,287	1,826,777,101	2,255,635,394	2,102,969,512	1,685,109,163
South Korea	2,148,172,866	2,269,455,612	2,015,309,996	1,852,102,464	1,869,053,093	1,613,991,412
France	2,283,958,876	1,876,402,229	1,674,074,447	1,282,671,593	1,283,188,508	1,461,785,979

IMPORTS

Area	2010	2011	2012	2013	2014	2015
World	47,935,644,015	56,054,589,618	53,460,389,819	53,524,821,737	53,675,599,652	50,922,104,608
Ireland...................................	12,059,080,213	13,904,826,918	11,651,278,299	12,328,806,450	11,307,158,268	10,777,057,429
China.....................................	4,615,047,862	5,721,241,767	6,441,601,863	6,713,890,657	6,711,724,835	6,638,258,112
United Kingdom	3,742,470,710	4,257,625,542	3,679,907,645	2,432,588,906	2,458,269,131	5,819,613,665
Singapore..............................	2,607,637,945	4,457,419,156	4,955,973,448	3,669,006,351	3,784,078,711	3,541,130,769
Canada..................................	3,968,637,996	4,621,418,221	4,107,154,296	4,488,418,951	4,603,413,136	3,051,684,263
Germany	2,503,043,754	2,831,428,584	3,069,910,691	3,357,480,861	3,318,911,388	2,845,572,669
Japan	2,976,931,151	3,004,045,411	3,244,483,942	3,816,833,584	3,811,312,493	2,383,867,559
India	1,716,300,790	1,982,448,650	2,177,758,942	2,188,173,387	2,250,327,055	2,017,422,277
Belgium..................................	1,909,831,773	1,854,834,659	841,250,829	1,445,534,009	1,879,282,749	1,984,784,710
Switzerland	1,812,238,697	1,729,469,317	1,963,918,959	1,984,296,138	1,806,932,513	1,806,051,696

Table D-21. Exports and Imports by Country: Pharmaceutical Products, 2010–2015

EXPORTS

Area	2010	2011	2012	2013	2014	2015
World	40,788,229,885	38,341,460,576	40,129,282,726	39,707,839,099	43,983,359,926	47,293,310,441
Belgium	1,770,954,596	2,651,992,547	3,219,174,440	4,067,377,363	5,557,378,952	6,465,691,186
Netherlands	3,929,582,816	3,037,284,770	2,920,465,861	3,380,672,502	4,096,008,597	4,230,408,713
Canada	4,648,719,452	4,757,285,677	4,141,815,012	3,851,251,685	4,055,070,936	3,819,427,016
United Kingdom	4,108,748,500	4,567,755,969	3,888,410,416	2,400,963,171	2,596,041,935	3,696,032,501
Japan	3,026,506,529	2,820,296,626	3,903,673,304	3,278,463,102	3,572,130,321	3,551,409,457
Italy	1,405,465,225	1,678,697,790	1,826,447,606	1,787,308,257	1,818,221,382	2,531,725,330
Germany	5,800,946,122	2,564,503,474	2,558,079,746	2,189,200,223	2,385,950,743	2,333,450,964
Ireland	1,102,846,191	1,439,168,419	1,185,386,244	1,362,998,010	1,753,427,912	2,279,708,204
Spain	2,056,836,661	1,876,790,065	1,845,852,940	2,078,590,268	1,782,763,756	2,192,067,673
Switzerland	2,105,661,194	2,371,288,431	1,688,108,409	2,074,555,641	2,277,194,708	2,094,028,390

IMPORTS

Area	2010	2011	2012	2013	2014	2015
World	61,628,685,081	65,748,306,910	64,563,002,548	62,908,417,125	72,613,258,128	85,507,993,837
Ireland	11,178,641,640	15,026,431,484	11,007,610,424	7,423,218,881	10,345,399,057	15,163,847,177
Germany	7,255,559,497	8,502,660,294	10,716,705,991	11,042,819,236	14,030,549,290	14,529,014,703
Switzerland	5,020,976,201	6,658,789,921	7,386,313,107	8,308,845,512	9,581,154,534	9,420,883,308
Israel	5,168,936,255	5,645,314,381	5,368,041,987	5,476,132,618	4,445,463,622	5,964,382,938
India	2,389,810,455	3,212,773,464	4,223,414,025	4,485,992,979	4,812,100,181	5,922,258,980
Canada	4,115,989,942	3,778,188,333	3,926,724,925	3,633,485,568	4,395,918,390	5,253,356,566
United Kingdom	5,674,896,120	3,959,158,702	3,532,699,038	3,285,635,776	3,849,098,547	5,187,784,763
Denmark	1,622,776,138	1,981,241,334	2,512,138,662	2,617,319,507	3,072,119,748	3,355,822,425
Italy	1,812,600,414	1,947,570,051	1,854,609,937	2,211,358,403	2,248,462,887	3,142,485,138
Belgium	2,444,096,883	1,964,719,965	2,064,641,176	2,594,102,543	3,359,202,718	3,073,862,799

Table D-22. Exports and Imports by Country: Precious Stones, Diamonds, Etc. 2010–2015

EXPORTS

Area	2010	2011	2012	2013	2014	2015
World	52,137,973,983	72,611,396,268	72,995,044,704	72,487,187,993	64,895,567,418	58,733,878,893
Hong Kong	4,937,519,665	11,387,989,711	12,910,701,733	16,263,902,593	13,790,389,464	11,456,616,521
Switzerland	11,262,739,996	14,487,941,960	16,690,799,977	16,067,849,271	10,594,255,623	10,270,400,901
India	4,206,748,413	4,621,056,581	5,836,079,250	5,763,738,883	5,250,468,881	6,593,884,833
United Kingdom	8,981,821,526	11,950,280,038	10,007,683,406	3,754,486,090	5,650,115,999	5,727,613,250
Israel	4,542,602,946	5,997,421,056	5,395,599,677	5,768,502,323	6,816,791,215	5,441,553,293
Canada	4,165,591,208	4,966,050,409	4,705,423,035	4,230,870,614	3,735,093,280	3,477,152,943
Belgium	2,230,518,884	2,918,208,838	2,814,251,117	2,952,164,946	3,904,635,368	3,105,313,640
United Arab Emirates	632,230,550	1,257,869,733	1,755,869,672	2,412,380,885	1,566,821,921	1,599,750,861
Japan	1,276,716,249	1,565,242,389	1,418,833,128	1,488,258,660	1,560,048,226	1,368,852,491

IMPORTS

Area	2010	2011	2012	2013	2014	2015
World	54,219,642,145	69,178,026,504	64,374,267,835	66,526,207,513	64,880,065,213	59,309,039,710
India	6,855,156,122	8,012,699,836	7,161,161,049	9,243,390,898	9,523,817,009	9,345,202,233
Israel	7,883,818,020	9,346,085,537	8,375,090,760	8,969,993,876	9,443,590,670	8,500,533,538
Canada	7,349,592,425	8,115,046,284	6,522,808,960	7,608,988,441	6,492,147,645	6,309,895,004
Mexico	6,603,554,552	9,772,612,707	9,633,615,318	7,107,405,520	5,740,973,391	5,084,010,954
Belgium	3,211,396,920	3,989,588,138	3,738,853,194	4,205,784,801	4,084,913,611	3,790,426,749
China	2,905,309,340	3,309,383,283	3,601,942,127	3,672,305,152	3,626,022,218	3,282,659,370
South Africa	3,479,713,137	3,606,014,272	2,792,056,737	2,583,451,474	3,041,895,177	2,365,537,807
Switzerland	1,377,041,283	2,038,563,229	1,585,488,628	1,664,054,123	2,047,418,969	1,809,085,296
Hong Kong	565,398,098	682,671,760	785,455,816	749,158,958	806,108,264	1,757,175,036
Colombia	1,646,574,854	2,248,543,422	3,180,073,225	2,478,801,102	2,105,256,358	1,700,562,182
Thailand	1,186,678,723	1,369,614,306	1,350,408,950	1,590,023,628	1,579,870,018	1,681,507,078

Table D-23.   Exports and Imports by Country: Vehicles and Parts, 2010–2015

EXPORTS

Area	2010	2011	2012	2013	2014	2015
World	99,148,692,588	120,011,780,504	133,078,052,912	134,090,149,318	136,021,387,004	127,396,967,732
Canada	42,286,779,934	46,870,086,705	50,328,990,103	51,993,318,763	51,428,475,369	47,909,965,287
Mexico	14,535,425,253	17,893,829,807	20,278,049,793	21,607,458,132	21,251,595,090	22,405,971,645
China	4,510,486,489	6,767,790,242	7,059,856,154	10,330,140,689	13,268,973,639	10,868,228,935
Germany	5,152,274,322	6,752,064,465	7,297,111,992	6,050,401,551	6,670,475,258	7,165,817,092
Saudi Arabia	3,781,683,574	4,435,451,153	6,152,107,980	5,762,407,232	4,895,826,206	4,798,644,797
Australia	2,410,961,957	3,967,100,410	5,850,396,933	3,484,423,582	3,647,453,705	3,363,959,933
United Arab Emirates	1,803,699,617	2,167,484,821	3,207,228,999	3,555,033,710	3,334,571,497	3,170,774,104
United Kingdom	1,678,268,765	2,125,712,914	2,080,712,402	2,094,045,843	2,687,088,780	3,063,284,489
South Korea	813,908,000	1,065,078,230	1,167,848,409	1,281,395,976	1,598,977,899	1,873,253,920
Japan	1,270,697,722	1,546,949,113	1,916,652,909	1,585,432,586	1,447,838,861	1,323,797,364

IMPORTS

Area	2010	2011	2012	2013	2014	2015
World	182,789,210,416	202,618,529,448	240,003,940,732	249,017,542,957	261,650,574,600	279,899,687,298
Mexico	40,215,250,411	45,801,178,745	53,508,033,339	59,597,907,014	68,041,061,311	74,689,649,358
Canada	46,121,497,967	49,803,540,284	57,590,234,098	55,703,872,211	56,193,426,450	55,561,220,814
Japan	41,572,144,565	41,023,142,413	51,335,980,519	49,762,338,178	45,263,961,969	46,082,975,527
Germany	21,143,652,983	24,951,144,823	29,690,225,562	32,594,878,227	33,434,199,299	34,118,725,122
South Korea	9,258,880,119	11,959,018,561	14,769,911,543	16,620,669,092	19,406,435,242	22,263,076,382
China	6,997,237,261	8,182,836,097	9,378,714,833	9,825,133,130	11,492,332,856	13,027,624,208
United Kingdom	4,198,445,535	4,666,714,250	5,760,467,925	6,209,736,304	6,573,338,104	8,025,858,644
Italy	1,477,251,554	1,779,274,760	2,219,411,202	2,754,261,619	3,555,441,934	5,134,591,745
Taiwan	1,869,762,799	2,151,300,651	2,378,561,719	2,365,873,987	2,446,609,343	2,695,954,594
Hungary	164,316,733	193,851,709	230,318,915	524,772,326	1,737,406,908	2,281,205,185

Table D-24.   Crude Oil Imports by Country: 2010–2015

Area	2010	2011	2012	2013	2014	2015
TOTAL	3,362,856	3,261,422	3,120,755	2,821,480	2,680,626	2,687,409
Persian Gulf Countries	618,470	674,706	783,081	727,688	675,487	542,859
OPEC Countries	1,661,727	1,536,208	1,475,508	1,275,037	1,096,816	975,663
Algeria	119,579	64,816	43,791	10,461	2,091	1,060
Angola	139,736	122,210	81,206	73,445	50,883	45,103
Ecuador	76,484	74,230	64,618	84,717	77,799	82,302
Gabon	17,022	12,532	15,338	8,759	5,852	3,578
Indonesia	12,102	7,168	2,022	6,646	7,220	13,097
Iraq	151,619	167,652	174,080	124,402	134,642	83,726
Kuwait	71,275	69,542	110,892	118,821	112,913	74,460
Libya	15,608	3,328	20,358	15,864	1,753	1,078
Nigeria	358,924	280,079	148,482	87,403	21,242	19,856
Qatar		1,943				
Saudi Arabia	394,967	432,972	498,109	483,567	423,066	384,071
United Arab Emirates	609	2,597		898	4,866	602
Venezuela	332,926	316,839	333,972	275,459	267,561	283,405
Non-OPEC Countries	1,701,129	1,725,214	1,645,247	1,546,443	1,583,810	1,711,746
Albania					490	1,977
Argentina	10,636	10,188	7,700	4,921	10,438	6,644
Australia	3,706	3,333	2,210	523	578	3,635
Azerbaijan	20,216	13,052	8,699	10,414	8,397	4,821
Belize	841	1,078	958	669	202	360
Bolivia	2,598	2,171	1,258	294		
Brazil	92,905	84,754	69,193	40,071	52,892	69,388
Cameroon	18,397	13,118	11,296	10		
Canada	719,175	811,964	887,674	941,236	1,051,989	1,156,617
Chad	6,694	17,978	10,410	23,926	22,427	26,197
China	1,455	615	458	489		
Colombia	123,525	144,974	147,428	133,964	107,483	135,985
Congo (Brazzaville)	25,694	19,192	10,710	6,532	1,463	3,111
Congo (Kinshasa)	3,225	3,999	137	1		
Egypt	2,618	1,543	11,438	1,553		542
Equatorial Guinea	18,225	6,934	15,100	6,072	1,323	1,882
Ghana		2,954		993		
Guatemala	4,184	3,292	3,970	2,479	2,491	2,916
India						671
Italy			308			481
Ivory Coast (Cote d'Ivore)	3,130	1,303	1,394			
Kazakhstan	6,720	2,571				
Malaysia	959					182
Mauritania	670			1,245	690	
Mexico	420,567	402,052	356,715	310,402	284,966	251,102
Netherlands				503	256	
Norway	9,201	19,470	9,338	6,092	3,161	3,215
Oman	4,357	14,895	3,460	951		
Papua New Guinea						
Peru	4,962	4,078	3,078	4,135	3,446	2,015
Russia	98,122	81,512	37,034	15,387	6,674	13,990
Syria		1,076				
Thailand	4,576	6,327	7,363	3,119	2,352	
Trinidad and Tobago	16,303	12,115	9,901	2,775	1,798	2,537
Tunisia						
United Kingdom	43,873	13,316	6,445	7,696	3,479	4,154
Vietnam	4,471	3,583	3,594	4,586	3,743	3,320
Yemen		2,077				

Table D-25. Crude Oil Exports by Country: 2010–2015

(Thousands of barrels.)

Area	2010	2011	2012	2013	2014	2015
TOTAL	15,198	17,158	24,693	48,968	128,233	169,741
Brazil						641
Canada	15,198	16,824	24,688	48,702	120,871	156,034
China				267	288	420
Costa Rica		334				
France						624
Germany					117	
India						309
Italy					1,004	1,558
Korea					868	972
Mexico			5			
Netherlands						1,740
Singapore					796	
Spain					1,058	2,612
Switzerland					3,231	4,828

Table D-26. Sources of Rare Earth Elements Imports

(Percent of Total Imports.)

Time Period	China	France	Japan	Estonia	Russia	Other
1999–2002..........................	66	25	4	3		2
2003–2006..........................	84	6	4	0	2	4
2007–2010..........................	79	6	3	4	0	8
2011–2014..........................	71	6	6	7	0	10

Table D-27. Trade Balance: Advance Technology Products, 1990–2016

Year	Imports	Exports	Balance
1990	59,454	94,717	35,263
1991	63,252	101,641	38,389
1992	71,872	107,091	35,220
1993	81,233	108,357	27,123
1994	98,116	120,743	22,627
1995	124,787	138,481	13,694
1996	130,363	154,910	24,547
1997	147,285	179,539	32,254
1998	156,749	186,444	29,695
1999	181,179	200,277	19,098
2000	222,082	227,395	5,313
2001	195,177	199,628	4,451
2002	195,150	178,566	-16,584
2003	207,031	180,208	-26,823
2004	238,276	201,561	-36,715
2005	259,742	216,824	-42,918
2006	290,760	247,071	-43,689
2007	326,809	264,875	-61,934
2008	331,152	270,131	-61,021
2009	300,892	244,708	-56,184
2010	354,253	273,311	-80,942
2011	386,439	287,722	-98,717
2012	396,230	304,983	-91,246
2013	401,144	319,734	-81,410
2014	422,101	336,481	-85,619
2015	434,901	343,086	-91,815
2016	351,571	285,781	-65,790

Table D-28.   U.S. Trade in Advance Technology Products: Biotechnology, 2014 and 2015

(Millions of dollars.)

Item	2014				2015			
	Exports	Share	Imports	Share	Exports	Share	Imports	Share
TOTAL...	341,431		419,726		337,556		436,087	
Biotechnology	14,287	4.2%	13,601	3.2%	17,221	5.1%	17,213	3.9%
Life Science....................................	30,916	9.1%	44,654	10.6%	29,950	8.9%	48,541	11.1%
Opto-Electronics.............................	4,957	1.5%	24,871	5.9%	4,726	1.4%	26,858	6.2%
Information & Communications	95,424	27.9%	229,917	54.8%	94,813	28.1%	235,812	54.1%
Electronics	42,009	12.3%	35,624	8.5%	42,981	12.7%	36,540	8.4%
Flexible Manufacturing.....................	16,065	4.7%	12,250	2.9%	15,549	4.6%	14,416	3.3%
Advancd Materials............................	2,279	0.7%	2,521	0.6%	2,151	0.6%	2,198	0.5%
Aerospace	130,764	38.3%	52,528	12.5%	125,832	37.3%	51,318	11.8%
Weapons	3,672	1.1%	839	0.2%	3,214	1.0%	903	0.2%
Nuclear Technology..........................	1,058	0.3%	2,921	0.7%	1,119	0.3%	2,288	0.5%

Source: U.S. Census Bureau.

SECTION E

IMPORTS AND EXPORTS BY STATE

SECTION E: IMPORTS AND EXPORTS BY STATE

HIGHLIGHTS

Imports

The U.S. Census Bureau now compiles imports by state. Statistics for imported goods shipments are compiled from the records filed with Customs and Border Protection.[1]

Two states dominated the purchasing of goods from the world in 2015. California and Texas account for nearly half of the top 10 states' imports. The following ten states accounted for 66.0 percent of all imports. California alone accounted for 18.1 percent.

State	Amount (Billion)
California	$408.20
Texas	$251.50
New York	$133.00
Michigan	$124.10
Illinois	$121.20
New Jersey	$119.50
Georgia	$88.50
Pennsylvania	$80.00
Tennessee	$77.00
Florida	$73.40

China supplies the most goods followed by Canada and Mexico. The table below shows the top 10 states providing various products to the U.S. China provides the most imports for 22 U.S. states while the U.S.'s NAFTA partners supply 19 states. EU-28 countries include Belgium, Germany, Ireland, and the United Kingdom.[3] Asian countries were South Korea and Japan.

Exports

The leading exporting states are the same as the importing states except for two. Washington is the third largest exporter while New Jersey ranked sixth in imports.

State	Amount (Billion)
Texas	$251.10
California	165.4
Washington	86.3
New York	80.1
Illinois	64.4
Florida	53.8
Michigan	53.2
Ohio	50.7
Louisiana	50.4
Pennsylvania	49.2

States that rely on crude oil refining saw their imports decline as the price of crude oil fell. Louisiana's imports fell 59.4 percent and Texas 23.9 percent between 2014–2015. Hawaii's imports fell by 43.6 percent with Wyoming at 43.0 percent. The District of Colombia saw the largest increase of 104.1 percent. Maryland's imports increased at 25.6 percent.

The top three imports were electric machinery, nuclear reactors, and vehicles. California led in all three categories, while Texas was second in nuclear reactor and electric machinery. Michigan imported more than $30 billion in vehicles and parts. California imported the most passenger vehicles, Texas crude oil[2] and Michigan parts for passenger vehicles.

Hawaii increased its exports by 31 percent between 2014 and 2015 while the District of Colombia's exports rose 16.1 percent and Nevada 12.6 percent. On the other hand, as the price of crude oil plummeted, Wyoming, North Dakota, and Louisiana's exports declined 33.2 percent, 29.7 percent and 24.1 percent respectively. In fact, crude oil was North Dakota's largest export in 2015.

The top three exports were nuclear reactors and parts, electric machinery, and aircraft. Washington state exports nearly 40 percent of all civilian aircraft. Texas has the largest exports in electric machinery and nuclear reactors and parts, at 7.5 percent and 8.7 percent respectively. California was third largest in civilian aircraft, electric machinery, and nuclear reactors.

NAFTA neighbors Canada and Mexico account for one third of all U.S. exports. In third place is China, purchasing 8 percent of American products.

---

[1] The import statistics consist of goods valued at more than $2,000 per commodity shipped by individuals and organizations (including importers and customs brokers) into the U.S. from other countries. Estimates are made for low-value shipments by country of origin, based on previous bilateral trade patterns and periodically updated.
[2] See Section D Part 2 for crude oil imports.

---

[3] Britain citizens voted to discontinue its membership in the European in 2016.

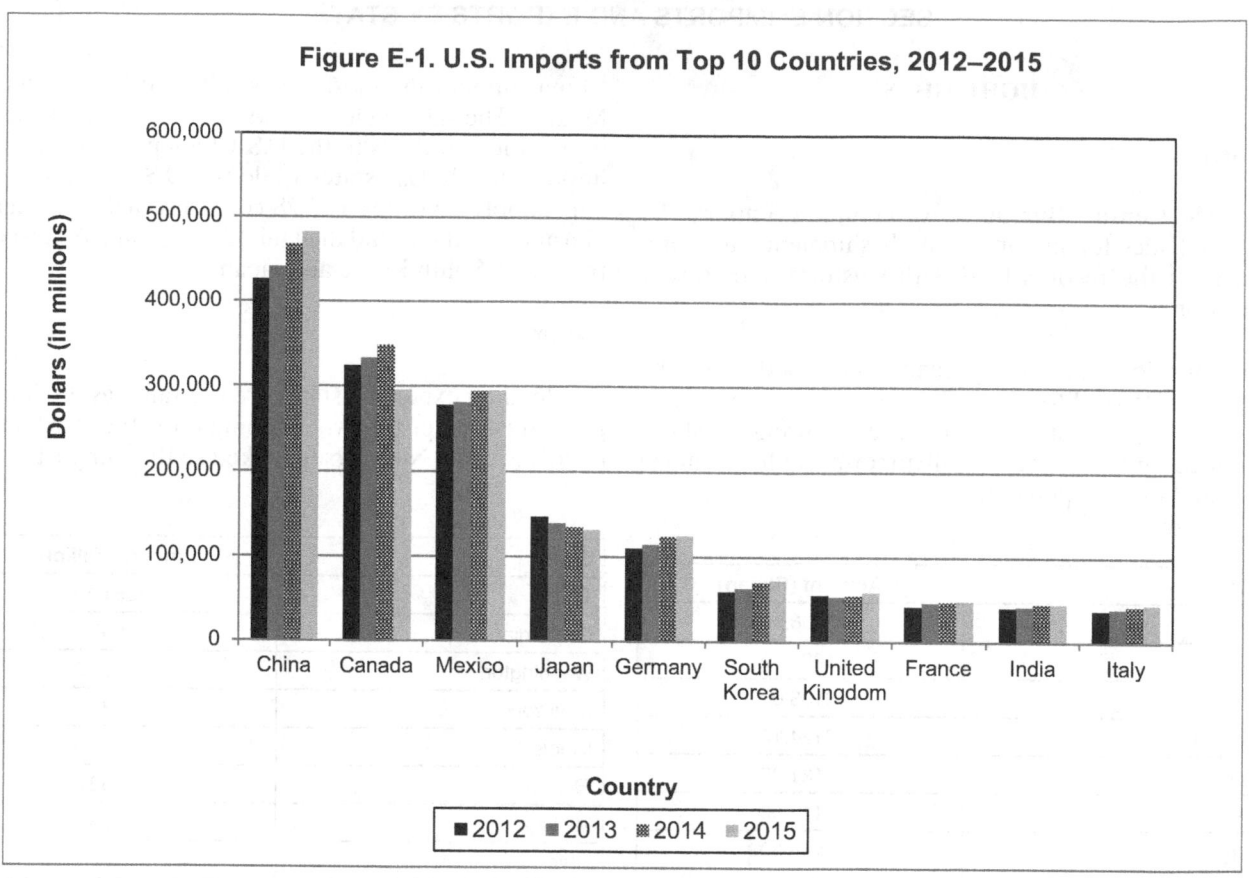

Figure E-1. U.S. Imports from Top 10 Countries, 2012–2015

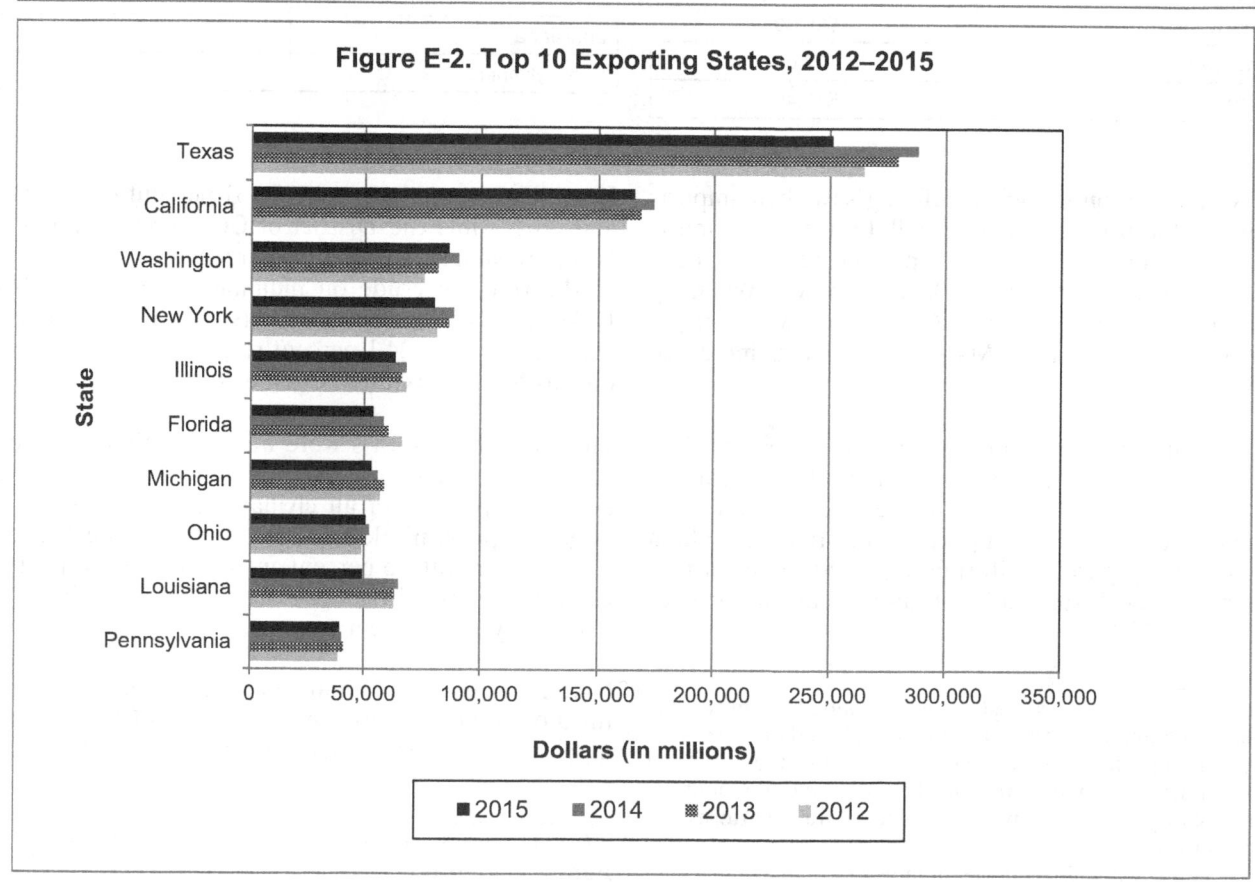

Figure E-2. Top 10 Exporting States, 2012–2015

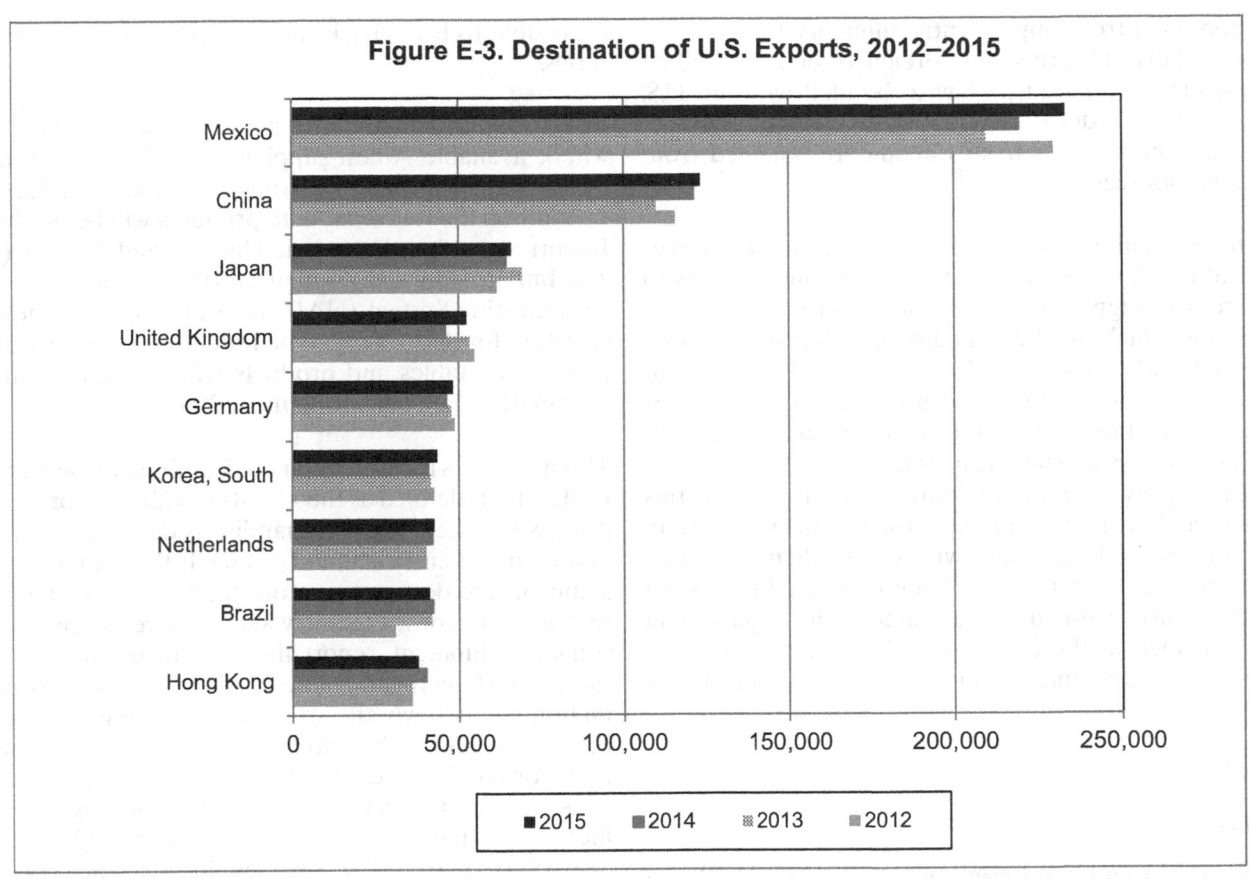

Figure E-3. Destination of U.S. Exports, 2012–2015

■ 2015   ■ 2014   ▦ 2013   ■ 2012

ABOUT THE DATA

This section presents a detailed export and import overview of each state. In Part 1, trade by country is presented for each state. The top 25 countries are listed for both imports and exports. Part 2 presents trade data by commodity.

Imports and exports by state are grouped by the 6-digit HS categories. More information can be found at http://www.census.gov/foreign-trade/statistics/state/index.html and https://www.census.gov/foreign-trade/aip/elom.html#authority.

Background

Exports

Data on U.S. exports of merchandise from the U.S. to all countries, except Canada, is compiled from the Electronic Export Information (EEI) filed by the US Principal Party in Interest (USPPI) or their agents through the Automated Export System (AES). The EEI is unique among Census Bureau data collection methods since it is not sent to respondents soliciting responses as in the case of surveys. Each EEI represents a shipment of one or more kinds of merchandise from one exporter to one foreign importer on a single carrier. Filing the EEI is mandatory under Chapter 9, Title 13, United States Code. Qualified exporters or their agents submit EEI data by automated means directly to the U.S. Census Bureau.

Since 1990, the United States has been substituting Canadian import statistics for U.S. exports to Canada in accordance with a 1987 Memorandum of Understanding signed by the Census Bureau, U.S. Customs and Border Protection, Canadian Customs, and Statistics Canada. Similarly, under this Memorandum of Understanding, Canada is substituting U.S. import statistics for Canadian exports to the United States. This data exchange includes only U.S. exports destined for Canada and does not include shipments destined for third countries by routes passing through Canada or shipments of certain grains and oilseeds to Canada for storage prior to exportation to a third country. These shipments are reported on and compiled from EEIs.

Imports

Published data on U.S. imports of merchandise is compiled primarily from automated data submitted through the U.S. Customs' Automated Commercial System and Automated Commercial Environment (ACE). Data are also compiled from import entry summary forms, warehouse withdrawal forms and Foreign Trade Zone (FTZ) documents as required by law to be filed with the U.S. Customs and Border Protection. Data on imports of electricity and natural gas from Canada are obtained from Canadian sources.

The import and export data measure the physical movement of merchandise in and out of the United States to and from foreign countries. Information on the export state from which the merchandise was shipped has been collected and made available since the 1980s. Beginning with January 2010 statistics, information on import state is available. To maintain confidentiality, the Census Bureau applies statistical procedures to protect the identity of any business or individual. The data in this release contain non-sampling error but do not contain sampling error. Data users who create their own estimates using data from USA Trade Online tables should cite the Census Bureau as the source of the original data only. Included at the end of this document is technical information, including definitions of terms and quality statements.

Data Series

Exports

Origin of Movement—Based on Origin State: In 1985, a new field indicating the state where the export journey begins was added to export reporting requirements. This field allowed the compilation of the State of Origin of Movement (OM) Series. The OM series based on origin state, that became available in 1987, provides export statistics based on the state from which the merchandise starts its journey to the port of export; that is, the data reflect the transportation origin of exports.

Origin of Movement—ZIP Code Based: In 2004 the ZIP Code of the USPPI, the party in the United States that receives the primary benefit monetary or otherwise from the shipment, was redefined to indicate the origin of movement of goods. Initially it did not necessarily represent the location of the USPPI. However, due to increased electronic reporting in the AES, the validity of the reported ZIP Code has improved significantly since 2004.

Imports

State of Destination (SD) Series: Also in the mid-1980s state data based on the import state of destination were added. However, in 1988, release of the data on import state of destination was discontinued due to quality concerns. Since then changes to the import reporting requirements along with growth of electronic reporting and a better understanding of the data's limitations has made it possible to bring back the import state of destination series.

Effective with January 2010 statistics, this new SD series will be available. A new supplement will be added to the FT900: U.S. International Trade in Goods and Services. In addition the following data products will be produced: Import state data by 6-digit Harmonized System (HS) and Import state data 4-digit North American Industry Classification System (NAICS). An example of the data structure for these files can be found on our website. Historical data tables and products will be made available for monthly data back to January 2008.

This new series is based upon the U.S. State of Destination Code. This is defined as the U.S. state, U.S. territory or U.S. possession where the merchandise is destined, as known at the time of entry summary filing. If the contents of the shipment are destined to more than one state, territory, or possession, or if the entry summary represents a consolidated shipment, report the state of destination with the greatest aggregate value. If in either case, this information is unknown, the state of the ultimate consignee, or the state where the entry is filed, in that order, should be reported. However, before either of these alternatives is used, a good faith effort should be made by the entry filer to ascertain the state where the imported merchandise will be delivered. In all cases, the state code reported should be derived from the standard postal two-letter state or territory abbreviation. For shipments into FTZ's, the import state represents the location of the zone.

Known Limitations in Uses of the Data

Exports

In certain cases, the export origin of movement does not reflect the transportation origin. Specifically whenever shipments are consolidated, the state will reflect the consolidation point rather than the origin of movement. This effect is particularly noticeable for agricultural shipments. For these shipments intermediaries located in inland states are shipping agricultural commodities down the Mississippi River for export from the port of New Orleans. In this case, the state reflects Louisiana, the state where the port of New Orleans is located, as the state of origin of movement. The states in which the commodities were grown and originally shipped are lost.

Another impact is on the states of distribution for non-manufactured exports. When goods are generally stored and then exported by central offices or intermediaries. The most visible result is to understate exports from the original production state and to overstate exports from the general office or consolidation point. For example, New York has ports that handle high-value shipments of non-manufactured products that may stand out.

Imports

In certain cases, the state of destination may not reflect the final location for which the imported goods are destined. Rather for these shipments, the state of destination, as known at the time the entry documentation is filed, may reflect an intermediary, storage, or distribution point. From there, these shipments may later be distributed to another location in another state as the ultimate destination. For example, a consolidated shipment of many automobiles may be shipped by the importing company to a distribution point in one state with the intent of later shipping the automobiles to numerous states for final sale.

PART I: STATE TRADE BY COUNTRY

Table E-1. State Trade by Country: Alabama, 2012–2015

(Top 25 countries based on 2015 dollar value. Value in millions of dollars.)

U.S. Exports by Origin State

Rank	Country	Value (Millions of dollars)				Percent of Share			
		2012	2013	2014	2015	2012	2013	2014	2015
	Total Alabama Exports and % Share of U.S. Total	19,577	19,293	19,440	19,370	1.3	1.2	1.2	1.3
	Total, Top 25 Countries and % Share of State Total	16,878	17,158	17,334	17,647	86.2	88.9	89.2	91.1
1	Canada	3,964	4,305	4,258	4,058	20.2	22.3	21.9	20.9
2	China	2,389	2,468	3,127	3,151	12.2	12.8	16.1	16.3
3	Mexico	2,030	2,221	2,334	2,889	10.4	11.5	12.0	14.9
4	Germany	2,547	2,233	2,162	2,478	13.0	11.6	11.1	12.8
5	United Kingdom	693	692	600	610	3.5	3.6	3.1	3.1
6	Japan	809	686	593	519	4.1	3.6	3.1	2.7
7	Korea, South	465	552	599	464	2.4	2.9	3.1	2.4
8	France	411	427	457	448	2.1	2.2	2.4	2.3
9	Brazil	640	631	475	338	3.3	3.3	2.4	1.7
10	United Arab Emirates	133	184	226	284	0.7	1.0	1.2	1.5
11	Australia	247	301	289	269	1.3	1.6	1.5	1.4
12	Netherlands	242	143	108	212	1.2	0.7	0.6	1.1
13	India	227	241	226	202	1.2	1.2	1.2	1.0
14	Belgium	254	222	234	199	1.3	1.2	1.2	1.0
15	Saudi Arabia	167	181	129	195	0.9	0.9	0.7	1.0
16	Colombia	189	204	215	187	1.0	1.1	1.1	1.0
17	South Africa	159	184	212	179	0.8	1.0	1.1	0.9
18	Singapore	196	218	143	143	1.0	1.1	0.7	0.7
19	Hong Kong	204	169	183	136	1.0	0.9	0.9	0.7
20	Italy	179	174	149	132	0.9	0.9	0.8	0.7
21	Honduras	220	211	198	129	1.1	1.1	1.0	0.7
22	Dominican Republic	109	136	103	128	0.6	0.7	0.5	0.7
23	Thailand	184	137	145	107	0.9	0.7	0.7	0.6
24	Chile	106	134	92	95	0.5	0.7	0.5	0.5
25	Spain	115	107	78	95	0.6	0.6	0.4	0.5

U.S. Imports by State of Final Destination

Rank	Country	Value (Millions of dollars)				Percent of Share			
		2012	2013	2014	2015	2012	2013	2014	2015
	Total Alabama Imports and % Share of U.S. Total	18,338	18,941	22,210	21,880	0.8	0.8	0.9	1.0
	Total, Top 25 Countries and % Share of State Total	16,963	17,642	20,524	20,203	92.5	93.1	92.4	92.3
1	South Korea	3,824	4,037	4,723	4,688	20.9	21.3	21.3	21.4
2	Germany	2,897	3,016	3,609	4,107	15.8	15.9	16.2	18.8
3	Mexico	1,186	1,406	3,540	2,869	6.5	7.4	15.9	13.1
4	China	1,958	1,973	2,034	2,174	10.7	10.4	9.2	9.9
5	Canada	1,618	2,026	2,217	2,047	8.8	10.7	10.0	9.4
6	Japan	1,182	1,320	1,311	1,015	6.4	7.0	5.9	4.6
7	Ecuador	4	2	4	258	0.0	0.0	0.0	1.2
8	Czech Republic	195	159	247	253	1.1	0.8	1.1	1.2
9	Vietnam	137	177	203	253	0.7	0.9	0.9	1.2
10	United Kingdom	177	199	191	242	1.0	1.1	0.9	1.1
11	Iraq	0	0	60	217	0.0	0.0	0.3	1.0
12	Taiwan	143	142	145	187	0.8	0.7	0.7	0.9
13	Colombia	307	188	230	176	1.7	1.0	1.0	0.8
14	Russia	96	148	63	175	0.5	0.8	0.3	0.8
15	Brazil	1,763	1,578	691	175	9.6	8.3	3.1	0.8
16	Honduras	246	219	170	170	1.3	1.2	0.8	0.8
17	Hungary	100	84	120	167	0.5	0.4	0.5	0.8
18	France	146	212	172	166	0.8	1.1	0.8	0.8
19	Italy	523	257	160	164	2.9	1.4	0.7	0.7
20	India	90	91	115	140	0.5	0.5	0.5	0.6
21	Australia	70	84	104	136	0.4	0.4	0.5	0.6
22	El Salvador	119	110	111	121	0.6	0.6	0.5	0.6
23	Spain	68	93	122	115	0.4	0.5	0.5	0.5
24	South Africa	45	55	103	95	0.2	0.3	0.5	0.4
25	Malaysia	72	64	79	91	0.4	0.3	0.4	0.4

'(Z)' indicates a percent change greater than 500.

Table E-2. State Trade by Country: Alaska, 2012–2015

(Top 25 countries based on 2015 dollar value. Value in millions of dollars.)

U.S. Exports by Origin State

Rank	Country	Value (Millions of dollars)				Percent of Share			
		2012	2013	2014	2015	2012	2013	2014	2015
	Total Alaska Exports and % Share of U.S. Total	4,543	4,528	5,111	4,675	0.3	0.3	0.3	0.3
	Total, Top 25 Countries and % Share of State Total	4,360	4,420	4,922	4,629	96.0	97.6	96.3	99.0
1	China	1,354	1,236	1,467	1,204	29.8	27.3	28.7	25.8
2	Japan	780	688	1,015	963	17.2	15.2	19.9	20.6
3	Korea, South	663	705	673	732	14.6	15.6	13.2	15.7
4	Canada	467	604	517	418	10.3	13.3	10.1	8.9
5	Germany	274	289	323	279	6.0	6.4	6.3	6.0
6	Spain	151	141	182	150	3.3	3.1	3.6	3.2
7	Netherlands	121	112	104	119	2.7	2.5	2.0	2.5
8	Malaysia	4	2	2	114	0.1	0.0	0.0	2.4
9	Taiwan	17	16	15	104	0.4	0.4	0.3	2.2
10	Australia	108	62	111	86	2.4	1.4	2.2	1.8
11	Singapore	124	217	100	72	2.7	4.8	2.0	1.5
12	Finland	45	43	65	57	1.0	0.9	1.3	1.2
13	Italy	14	8	69	57	0.3	0.2	1.4	1.2
14	Belgium	59	65	63	49	1.3	1.4	1.2	1.0
15	Thailand	12	41	41	49	0.3	0.9	0.8	1.0
16	France	37	50	51	47	0.8	1.1	1.0	1.0
17	United Kingdom	24	28	40	41	0.5	0.6	0.8	0.9
18	Lithuania	13	33	15	14	0.3	0.7	0.3	0.3
19	Portugal	32	15	15	14	0.7	0.3	0.3	0.3
20	Denmark	13	17	14	14	0.3	0.4	0.3	0.3
21	Philippines	12	5	1	12	0.3	0.1	0.0	0.3
22	Hong Kong	13	24	18	11	0.3	0.5	0.4	0.2
23	Indonesia	11	9	10	8	0.2	0.2	0.2	0.2
24	Mexico	9	7	10	8	0.2	0.2	0.2	0.2
25	United Arab Emirates	2	1	1	8	0.0	0.0	0.0	0.2

U.S. Imports by State of Final Destination

Rank	Country	Value (Millions of dollars)				Percent of Share			
		2012	2013	2014	2015	2012	2013	2014	2015
	Total Alaska Imports and % Share of U.S. Total	2,105	1,481	2,008	2,485	0.1	0.1	0.1	0.1
	Total, Top 25 Countries and % Share of State Total	2,023	1,451	1,975	2,457	96.1	98.0	98.4	98.9
1	China	201	181	333	655	9.5	12.2	16.6	26.4
2	Canada	646	548	644	612	30.7	37.0	32.1	24.6
3	Japan	281	66	86	528	13.3	4.5	4.3	21.2
4	Korea, South	444	439	357	328	21.1	29.6	17.8	13.2
5	Taiwan	9	12	15	68	0.4	0.8	0.7	2.7
6	Russia	172	18	321	47	8.2	1.2	16.0	1.9
7	Mexico	10	14	21	33	0.5	0.9	1.0	1.3
8	United Kingdom	124	21	36	30	5.9	1.4	1.8	1.2
9	Singapore	7	10	11	28	0.3	0.7	0.5	1.1
10	Thailand	1	1	15	17	0.0	0.1	0.7	0.7
11	Germany	20	17	24	16	1.0	1.1	1.2	0.6
12	France	38	42	49	14	1.8	2.8	2.4	0.6
13	Philippines	1	7	9	13	0.0	0.5	0.4	0.5
14	Italy	11	6	14	11	0.5	0.4	0.7	0.4
15	Malaysia	9	3	8	10	0.4	0.2	0.4	0.4
16	New Zealand	0	1	0	7	0.0	0.1	0.0	0.3
17	Netherlands	6	5	2	6	0.3	0.3	0.1	0.2
18	Denmark	2	5	8	6	0.1	0.3	0.4	0.2
19	Australia	9	4	4	5	0.4	0.3	0.2	0.2
20	Finland	2	21	3	5	0.1	1.4	0.1	0.2
21	Norway	5	4	3	5	0.2	0.3	0.1	0.2
22	Qatar	0	0	0	3	0.0	0.0	0.0	0.1
23	Sweden	15	5	4	3	0.7	0.3	0.2	0.1
24	Trinidad and Tobago	0	0	3	3	0.0	0.0	0.1	0.1
25	Switzerland	7	22	2	3	0.3	1.5	0.1	0.1

Table E-3. State Trade by Country: Arizona, 2012–2015

(Top 25 countries based on 2015 dollar value. Value in millions of dollars.)

U.S. Exports by Origin State

Rank	Country	Value (Millions of dollars)				Percent of Share			
		2012	2013	2014	2015	2012	2013	2014	2015
	Total Arizona Exports and % Share of U.S. Total	18,405	19,477	21,248	22,563	1.2	1.2	1.3	1.5
	Total, Top 25 Countries and % Share of State Total	16,986	17,954	19,696	21,155	92.3	92.2	92.7	93.8
1	Mexico	6,291	7,068	8,623	9,164	34.2	36.3	40.6	40.6
2	Canada	2,194	2,274	2,254	2,215	11.9	11.7	10.6	9.8
3	China	1,252	1,080	1,019	1,268	6.8	5.5	4.8	5.6
4	United Kingdom	915	875	1,101	1,066	5.0	4.5	5.2	4.7
5	Germany	678	740	753	833	3.7	3.8	3.5	3.7
6	Thailand	470	464	512	603	2.6	2.4	2.4	2.7
7	Japan	920	856	663	545	5.0	4.4	3.1	2.4
8	France	492	459	462	464	2.7	2.4	2.2	2.1
9	Brazil	373	363	352	435	2.0	1.9	1.7	1.9
10	Taiwan	320	392	482	431	1.7	2.0	2.3	1.9
11	Netherlands	350	368	330	424	1.9	1.9	1.6	1.9
12	Hong Kong	306	567	350	422	1.7	2.9	1.6	1.9
13	Singapore	493	433	488	406	2.7	2.2	2.3	1.8
14	Malaysia	406	400	349	388	2.2	2.1	1.6	1.7
15	Korea, South	254	227	308	364	1.4	1.2	1.4	1.6
16	Italy	198	176	159	343	1.1	0.9	0.7	1.5
17	Ireland	80	105	205	255	0.4	0.5	1.0	1.1
18	Israel	133	156	235	252	0.7	0.8	1.1	1.1
19	Saudi Arabia	115	113	246	235	0.6	0.6	1.2	1.0
20	Switzerland	191	211	224	234	1.0	1.1	1.1	1.0
21	Australia	274	226	248	225	1.5	1.2	1.2	1.0
22	United Arab Emirates	83	217	136	203	0.5	1.1	0.6	0.9
23	Belgium	115	77	118	166	0.6	0.4	0.6	0.7
24	Bolivia	2	2	5	110	0.0	0.0	0.0	0.5
25	India	81	103	73	103	0.4	0.5	0.3	0.5

U.S. Imports by State of Final Destination

Rank	Country	Value (Millions of dollars)				Percent of Share			
		2012	2013	2014	2015	2012	2013	2014	2015
	Total Arizona Imports and % Share of U.S. Total	18,948	19,024	19,716	19,679	0.8	0.8	0.8	0.9
	Total, Top 25 Countries and % Share of State Total	17,997	18,008	18,402	18,926	95.0	94.7	93.3	96.2
1	Mexico	6,753	7,037	7,305	7,596	35.6	37.0	37.1	38.6
2	China	2,737	2,478	2,708	2,643	14.4	13.0	13.7	13.4
3	Canada	1,534	1,515	1,561	1,505	8.1	8.0	7.9	7.6
4	Germany	679	570	640	773	3.6	3.0	3.2	3.9
5	Malaysia	1,286	1,199	898	753	6.8	6.3	4.6	3.8
6	Japan	1,216	1,377	1,025	749	6.4	7.2	5.2	3.8
7	United Kingdom	439	432	484	670	2.3	2.3	2.5	3.4
8	Brazil	59	131	601	500	0.3	0.7	3.0	2.5
9	Italy	155	229	324	489	0.8	1.2	1.6	2.5
10	Taiwan	533	503	494	488	2.8	2.6	2.5	2.5
11	Netherlands	300	280	352	443	1.6	1.5	1.8	2.3
12	France	303	284	357	436	1.6	1.5	1.8	2.2
13	Korea, South	325	294	278	307	1.7	1.5	1.4	1.6
14	India	167	176	193	225	0.9	0.9	1.0	1.1
15	Thailand	274	226	194	219	1.4	1.2	1.0	1.1
16	Singapore	422	398	218	211	2.2	2.1	1.1	1.1
17	Czech Republic	198	192	190	210	1.0	1.0	1.0	1.1
18	Vietnam	53	87	105	118	0.3	0.5	0.5	0.6
19	Philippines	123	112	81	91	0.6	0.6	0.4	0.5
20	Australia	76	75	81	91	0.4	0.4	0.4	0.5
21	Indonesia	83	70	96	86	0.4	0.4	0.5	0.4
22	Spain	63	38	44	85	0.3	0.2	0.2	0.4
23	Ireland	59	34	37	83	0.3	0.2	0.2	0.4
24	Hong Kong	67	105	41	78	0.4	0.6	0.2	0.4
25	Israel	93	169	96	77	0.5	0.9	0.5	0.4

Table E-4.   State Trade by Country: Arkansas, 2012–2015

(Top 25 countries based on 2015 dollar value. Value in millions of dollars.)

U.S. Exports by Origin State

Rank	Country	Value (Millions of dollars)				Percent of Share			
		2012	2013	2014	2015	2012	2013	2014	2015
	Total Arkansas Exports and % Share of U.S. Total	7,615	7,153	6,860	5,874	0.5	0.5	0.4	0.4
	Total, Top 25 Countries and % Share of State Total	6,177	5,976	5,329	5,135	81.1	83.5	77.7	87.4
1	Canada	1,653	1,571	1,423	1,206	21.7	22.0	20.7	20.5
2	Mexico	847	870	738	837	11.1	12.2	10.8	14.2
3	Japan	208	194	330	532	2.7	2.7	4.8	9.1
4	France	365	605	439	465	4.8	8.5	6.4	7.9
5	Singapore	179	133	191	251	2.4	1.9	2.8	4.3
6	China	719	683	437	201	9.4	9.5	6.4	3.4
7	United Kingdom	204	152	171	170	2.7	2.1	2.5	2.9
8	Korea, South	191	163	176	155	2.5	2.3	2.6	2.6
9	Belgium	198	174	162	135	2.6	2.4	2.4	2.3
10	Brazil	361	205	242	133	4.7	2.9	3.5	2.3
11	Netherlands	51	49	64	119	0.7	0.7	0.9	2.0
12	Germany	160	202	171	103	2.1	2.8	2.5	1.8
13	Hong Kong	192	274	117	100	2.5	3.8	1.7	1.7
14	Australia	160	161	91	90	2.1	2.3	1.3	1.5
15	Taiwan	95	78	74	78	1.2	1.1	1.1	1.3
16	Colombia	47	57	74	73	0.6	0.8	1.1	1.2
17	United Arab Emirates	69	45	41	73	0.9	0.6	0.6	1.2
18	Guatemala	56	60	68	67	0.7	0.8	1.0	1.1
19	Saudi Arabia	88	78	59	61	1.2	1.1	0.9	1.0
20	Chile	54	36	55	56	0.7	0.5	0.8	1.0
21	El Salvador	65	62	56	51	0.9	0.9	0.8	0.9
22	India	40	37	43	50	0.5	0.5	0.6	0.9
23	Italy	71	40	36	45	0.9	0.6	0.5	0.8
24	Haiti	52	44	42	45	0.7	0.6	0.6	0.8
25	Bermuda	51	1	31	42	0.7	0.0	0.5	0.7

U.S. Imports by State of Final Destination

Rank	Country	Value (Millions of dollars)				Percent of Share			
		2012	2013	2014	2015	2012	2013	2014	2015
	Total Arkansas Imports and % Share of U.S. Total	7,413	7,621	7,603	7,915	0.3	0.3	0.3	0.4
	Total, Top 25 Countries and % Share of State Total	7,054	7,286	7,296	7,576	95.2	95.6	96.0	95.7
1	China	2,100	2,263	2,530	2,583	28.3	29.7	33.3	32.6
2	France	1,565	1,910	1,608	1,682	21.1	25.1	21.1	21.3
3	Canada	918	1,008	910	797	12.4	13.2	12.0	10.1
4	Mexico	778	583	603	636	10.5	7.6	7.9	8.0
5	Germany	390	335	274	420	5.3	4.4	3.6	5.3
6	India	277	209	208	236	3.7	2.7	2.7	3.0
7	Taiwan	121	116	144	142	1.6	1.5	1.9	1.8
8	Korea, South	148	74	67	129	2.0	1.0	0.9	1.6
9	Italy	82	88	96	118	1.1	1.2	1.3	1.5
10	Japan	134	164	129	101	1.8	2.2	1.7	1.3
11	United Kingdom	75	74	97	92	1.0	1.0	1.3	1.2
12	Vietnam	37	41	76	92	0.5	0.5	1.0	1.2
13	Malaysia	11	26	50	67	0.1	0.3	0.7	0.8
14	Sweden	81	61	72	59	1.1	0.8	0.9	0.7
15	Brazil	24	15	23	53	0.3	0.2	0.3	0.7
16	Netherlands	38	58	59	44	0.5	0.8	0.8	0.6
17	Switzerland	17	5	20	43	0.2	0.1	0.3	0.5
18	Pakistan	37	39	39	41	0.5	0.5	0.5	0.5
19	Bangladesh	27	31	36	41	0.4	0.4	0.5	0.5
20	Thailand	65	76	53	38	0.9	1.0	0.7	0.5
21	Israel	45	30	68	35	0.6	0.4	0.9	0.4
22	Saudi Arabia	0	0	16	34	0.0	0.0	0.2	0.4
23	Indonesia	27	30	29	32	0.4	0.4	0.4	0.4
24	Spain	28	27	36	31	0.4	0.4	0.5	0.4
25	Australia	29	22	54	29	0.4	0.3	0.7	0.4

Table E-5. State Trade by Country: California, 2012–2015

(Top 25 countries based on 2015 dollar value. Value in millions of dollars.)

U.S. Exports by Origin State

Rank	Country	Value (Millions of dollars)				Percent of Share			
		2012	2013	2014	2015	2012	2013	2014	2015
	Total California Exports and % Share of U.S. Total	161,757	168,129	173,812	165,367	10.5	10.7	10.7	11
	Total, Top 25 Countries and % Share of State Total	143,696	149,077	152,709	146,837	88.8	88.7	87.9	88.8
1	Mexico	26,380	23,902	25,420	26,820	16.3	14.2	14.6	16.2
2	Canada	17,424	18,885	18,343	16,929	10.8	11.2	10.6	10.2
3	China	13,969	16,282	16,050	14,417	8.6	9.7	9.2	8.7
4	Japan	13,047	12,735	12,212	11,741	8.1	7.6	7.0	7.1
5	Hong Kong	7,827	7,792	8,487	8,766	4.8	4.6	4.9	5.3
6	Korea, South	8,246	8,362	8,594	8,698	5.1	5.0	4.9	5.3
7	Taiwan	6,315	7,521	7,464	7,821	3.9	4.5	4.3	4.7
8	Netherlands	4,339	4,806	5,353	5,633	2.7	2.9	3.1	3.4
9	Germany	4,980	5,591	5,429	5,345	3.1	3.3	3.1	3.2
10	United Kingdom	4,344	4,602	4,985	5,147	2.7	2.7	2.9	3.1
11	India	3,209	5,264	5,270	4,588	2.0	3.1	3.0	2.8
12	Singapore	4,011	4,162	4,444	3,931	2.5	2.5	2.6	2.4
13	Australia	4,062	3,671	3,794	3,433	2.5	2.2	2.2	2.1
14	Belgium	2,765	3,244	3,475	2,941	1.7	1.9	2.0	1.8
15	France	2,661	2,641	2,726	2,683	1.6	1.6	1.6	1.6
16	United Arab Emirates	1,812	1,652	1,912	2,431	1.1	1.0	1.1	1.5
17	Italy	1,856	1,992	2,102	2,013	1.1	1.2	1.2	1.2
18	Switzerland	1,741	1,954	2,515	2,003	1.1	1.2	1.4	1.2
19	Malaysia	2,398	2,352	2,277	1,831	1.5	1.4	1.3	1.1
20	Israel	2,658	2,321	2,319	1,801	1.6	1.4	1.3	1.1
21	Thailand	1,793	1,802	1,800	1,692	1.1	1.1	1.0	1.0
22	Spain	1,148	1,431	1,559	1,684	0.7	0.9	0.9	1.0
23	Chile	2,137	2,304	2,651	1,564	1.3	1.4	1.5	0.9
24	Brazil	3,009	2,108	1,953	1,548	1.9	1.3	1.1	0.9
25	Philippines	1,563	1,702	1,575	1,379	1.0	1.0	0.9	0.8

U.S. Imports by State of Final Destination

Rank	Country	Value (Millions of dollars)				Percent of Share			
		2012	2013	2014	2015	2012	2013	2014	2015
	Total California Imports and % Share of U.S. Total	376,487	381,065	403,369	408,180	16.5	16.8	17.2	18.2
	Total, Top 25 Countries and % Share of State Total	344,258	349,876	372,225	382,523	91.4	91.8	92.3	93.7
1	China	127,757	130,448	137,676	143,470	33.9	34.2	34.1	35.1
2	Mexico	36,059	36,257	41,261	45,069	9.6	9.5	10.2	11.0
3	Japan	41,473	38,384	38,285	38,503	11.0	10.1	9.5	9.4
4	Canada	25,842	26,382	27,893	27,854	6.9	6.9	6.9	6.8
5	Malaysia	9,811	11,352	14,030	16,797	2.6	3.0	3.5	4.1
6	Korea, South	12,270	13,044	14,915	15,533	3.3	3.4	3.7	3.8
7	Germany	12,045	12,993	12,053	12,706	3.2	3.4	3.0	3.1
8	Taiwan	11,198	10,931	12,059	12,526	3.0	2.9	3.0	3.1
9	Thailand	8,407	9,050	9,402	10,043	2.2	2.4	2.3	2.5
10	Vietnam	5,492	6,711	8,078	8,836	1.5	1.8	2.0	2.2
11	Saudi Arabia	8,469	8,805	10,687	6,161	2.2	2.3	2.6	1.5
12	Indonesia	4,614	4,920	4,943	4,681	1.2	1.3	1.2	1.1
13	United Kingdom	4,156	3,045	3,427	4,564	1.1	0.8	0.8	1.1
14	Singapore	3,513	3,919	3,841	4,180	0.9	1.0	1.0	1.0
15	India	2,880	3,365	4,393	3,855	0.8	0.9	1.1	0.9
16	Ecuador	6,400	7,355	5,505	3,727	1.7	1.9	1.4	0.9
17	Italy	2,881	3,041	3,220	3,654	0.8	0.8	0.8	0.9
18	France	2,504	2,959	3,471	3,631	0.7	0.8	0.9	0.9
19	Philippines	3,129	3,012	3,596	3,304	0.8	0.8	0.9	0.8
20	Colombia	4,132	2,865	2,987	2,608	1.1	0.8	0.7	0.6
21	Switzerland	1,989	2,109	2,196	2,464	0.5	0.6	0.5	0.6
22	Ireland	2,947	2,615	2,179	2,366	0.8	0.7	0.5	0.6
23	Brazil	2,410	2,484	2,181	2,121	0.6	0.7	0.5	0.5
24	Israel	1,906	1,872	1,898	1,996	0.5	0.5	0.5	0.5
25	Australia	1,974	1,959	2,051	1,874	0.5	0.5	0.5	0.5

Table E-6.   State Trade by Country: Colorado 2012–2015

(Top 25 countries based on 2015 dollar value. Value in millions of dollars.)

U.S. Exports by Origin State

Rank	Country	Value (Millions of dollars)				Percent of Share			
		2012	2013	2014	2015	2012	2013	2014	2015
	Total Colorado Exports and % Share of U.S. Total	8,170	8,546	8,337	7,978	0.5	0.5	0.5	0.5
	Total, Top 25 Countries and % Share of State Total	7,310	7,668	7,473	7,147	89.5	89.7	89.6	89.6
1	Canada	2,000	2,063	1,641	1,403	24.5	24.1	19.7	17.6
2	Mexico	849	917	1,068	1,079	10.4	10.7	12.8	13.5
3	China	676	659	655	662	8.3	7.7	7.9	8.3
4	Japan	426	441	509	467	5.2	5.2	6.1	5.9
5	Malaysia	224	274	337	356	2.7	3.2	4.0	4.5
6	Korea, South	266	341	335	350	3.3	4.0	4.0	4.4
7	Netherlands	280	304	341	290	3.4	3.6	4.1	3.6
8	Germany	282	240	254	262	3.5	2.8	3.0	3.3
9	United Kingdom	205	211	222	261	2.5	2.5	2.7	3.3
10	Switzerland	245	329	234	250	3.0	3.8	2.8	3.1
11	Hong Kong	233	251	259	238	2.9	2.9	3.1	3.0
12	Taiwan	144	182	191	205	1.8	2.1	2.3	2.6
13	Philippines	191	196	200	162	2.3	2.3	2.4	2.0
14	Belgium	137	171	208	162	1.7	2.0	2.5	2.0
15	Australia	172	181	167	157	2.1	2.1	2.0	2.0
16	United Arab Emirates	72	74	99	135	0.9	0.9	1.2	1.7
17	France	155	151	146	133	1.9	1.8	1.8	1.7
18	Brazil	172	185	167	98	2.1	2.2	2.0	1.2
19	India	119	112	88	93	1.5	1.3	1.1	1.2
20	Italy	85	62	64	83	1.0	0.7	0.8	1.0
21	Singapore	92	88	84	71	1.1	1.0	1.0	0.9
22	Ireland	87	40	27	67	1.1	0.5	0.3	0.8
23	Thailand	70	71	63	63	0.9	0.8	0.8	0.8
24	Chile	82	48	64	58	1.0	0.6	0.8	0.7
25	Saudi Arabia	45	75	49	42	0.6	0.9	0.6	0.5

U.S. Imports by State of Final Destination

Rank	Country	Value (Millions of dollars)				Percent of Share			
		2012	2013	2014	2015	2012	2013	2014	2015
	Total Colorado Imports and % Share of U.S. Total	12,649	12,821	14,237	13,487	0.6	0.6	0.6	0.6
	Total, Top 25 Countries and % Share of State Total	11,988	12,037	13,589	12,908	94.8	93.9	95.4	95.7
						0.0	0.0	0.0	0.0
1	Canada	4,450	4,034	4,315	3,207	35.2	31.5	30.3	23.8
2	China	1,865	1,925	2,267	2,424	14.7	15.0	15.9	18.0
3	Mexico	1,089	1,353	1,733	1,715	8.6	10.6	12.2	12.7
4	Germany	591	570	619	1,081	4.7	4.4	4.3	8.0
5	Switzerland	539	640	635	702	4.3	5.0	4.5	5.2
6	Australia	355	393	543	558	2.8	3.1	3.8	4.1
7	Korea, South	230	299	285	333	1.8	2.3	2.0	2.5
8	France	178	172	210	300	1.4	1.3	1.5	2.2
9	United Kingdom	249	276	307	260	2.0	2.2	2.2	1.9
10	Italy	354	225	265	244	2.8	1.8	1.9	1.8
11	Taiwan	205	197	194	218	1.6	1.5	1.4	1.6
12	India	378	376	311	214	3.0	2.9	2.2	1.6
13	Netherlands	143	156	237	199	1.1	1.2	1.7	1.5
14	Vietnam	144	174	171	197	1.1	1.4	1.2	1.5
15	Denmark	131	82	169	181	1.0	0.6	1.2	1.3
16	Austria	196	193	173	168	1.5	1.5	1.2	1.2
17	Japan	217	172	174	155	1.7	1.3	1.2	1.1
18	Spain	145	120	161	146	1.1	0.9	1.1	1.1
19	Slovenia	103	97	132	130	0.8	0.8	0.9	1.0
20	Norway	7	60	184	108	0.1	0.5	1.3	0.8
21	Malaysia	148	195	142	101	1.2	1.5	1.0	0.7
22	Sweden	108	105	95	89	0.9	0.8	0.7	0.7
23	Thailand	69	94	105	80	0.5	0.7	0.7	0.6
24	Philippines	60	62	75	56	0.5	0.5	0.5	0.4
25	New Zealand	31	66	87	44	0.2	0.5	0.6	0.3

Table E-7.   State Trade by Country: Connecticut, 2012–2015

(Top 25 countries based on 2015 dollar value. Value in millions of dollars.)

U.S. Exports by Origin State

Rank	Country	Value (Millions of dollars)				Percent of Share			
		2012	2013	2014	2015	2012	2013	2014	2015
	Total Connecticut Exports and % Share of U.S. Total	15,871	16,427	15,931	15,256	1.0	1.0	1.0	1.0
	Total, Top 25 Countries and % Share of State Total	13,979	14,456	14,086	13,752	88.1	88.0	88.4	90.1
1	France	1,907	2,425	2,211	1,932	12.0	14.8	13.9	12.7
2	Germany	1,486	1,397	1,712	1,653	9.4	8.5	10.7	10.8
3	Canada	1,915	1,910	1,914	1,623	12.1	11.6	12.0	10.6
4	United Arab Emirates	1,089	1,212	1,142	1,592	6.9	7.4	7.2	10.4
5	Mexico	1,142	1,213	1,281	1,320	7.2	7.4	8.0	8.7
6	China	1,009	911	907	1,030	6.4	5.5	5.7	6.8
7	United Kingdom	626	694	719	884	3.9	4.2	4.5	5.8
8	Japan	574	529	540	525	3.6	3.2	3.4	3.4
9	Netherlands	509	487	489	476	3.2	3.0	3.1	3.1
10	Korea, South	551	569	658	456	3.5	3.5	4.1	3.0
11	Belgium	294	238	235	285	1.9	1.4	1.5	1.9
12	Singapore	481	538	338	280	3.0	3.3	2.1	1.8
13	Brazil	321	318	309	244	2.0	1.9	1.9	1.6
14	Hong Kong	224	181	203	187	1.4	1.1	1.3	1.2
15	Switzerland	187	170	175	161	1.2	1.0	1.1	1.1
16	Dominican Republic	130	129	123	138	0.8	0.8	0.8	0.9
17	Israel	98	115	102	119	0.6	0.7	0.6	0.8
18	Taiwan	107	128	123	117	0.7	0.8	0.8	0.8
19	Malaysia	381	311	140	113	2.4	1.9	0.9	0.7
20	Italy	130	146	141	110	0.8	0.9	0.9	0.7
21	Turkey	319	229	122	104	2.0	1.4	0.8	0.7
22	Australia	148	161	104	104	0.9	1.0	0.7	0.7
23	Qatar	26	244	200	104	0.2	1.5	1.3	0.7
24	Saudi Arabia	196	86	85	101	1.2	0.5	0.5	0.7
25	India	131	114	113	93	0.8	0.7	0.7	0.6

U.S. Imports by State of Final Destination

Rank	Country	Value (Millions of dollars)				Percent of Share			
		2012	2013	2014	2015	2012	2013	2014	2015
	Total Connecticut Imports and % Share of U.S. Total	21,503	21,564	23,892	25,957	0.9	1	1	1.2
	Total, Top 25 Countries and % Share of State Total	19,304	19,479	21,454	23,749	89.8	90.3	89.8	91.5
1	United Kingdom	1,934	1,466	1,689	5,548	9.0	6.8	7.1	21.4
2	Canada	3,439	3,774	3,501	3,447	16.0	17.5	14.7	13.3
3	China	2,644	2,777	2,977	3,020	12.3	12.9	12.5	11.6
4	Mexico	1,693	1,016	2,576	2,468	7.9	4.7	10.8	9.5
5	Germany	1,620	1,519	1,856	1,935	7.5	7.0	7.8	7.5
6	Japan	994	1,069	1,091	948	4.6	5.0	4.6	3.7
7	France	717	911	765	660	3.3	4.2	3.2	2.5
8	Poland	503	545	532	585	2.3	2.5	2.2	2.3
9	Singapore	297	589	485	557	1.4	2.7	2.0	2.1
10	Italy	512	495	546	538	2.4	2.3	2.3	2.1
11	Netherlands	1,446	992	1,603	483	6.7	4.6	6.7	1.9
12	Switzerland	370	407	479	437	1.7	1.9	2.0	1.7
13	Chile	605	1,057	318	369	2.8	4.9	1.3	1.4
14	Taiwan	283	291	301	319	1.3	1.3	1.3	1.2
15	India	228	194	283	272	1.1	0.9	1.2	1.0
16	Ireland	93	600	124	260	0.4	2.8	0.5	1.0
17	Israel	247	288	290	258	1.1	1.3	1.2	1.0
18	Belgium	197	205	242	251	0.9	1.0	1.0	1.0
19	Brazil	391	270	343	247	1.8	1.3	1.4	1.0
20	Korea, South	188	158	206	244	0.9	0.7	0.9	0.9
21	Russia	210	155	520	234	1.0	0.7	2.2	0.9
22	Sweden	293	297	283	182	1.4	1.4	1.2	0.7
23	Vietnam	121	146	147	174	0.6	0.7	0.6	0.7
24	Australia	110	95	143	157	0.5	0.4	0.6	0.6
25	Spain	170	162	153	155	0.8	0.8	0.6	0.6

'(Z)' indicates a percent change greater than 500.

Table E-8.   State Trade by Country: Delaware, 2012–2015

(Top 25 countries based on 2015 dollar value. Value in millions of dollars.)

U.S. Exports by Origin State

Rank	Country	Value (Millions of dollars)				Percent of Share			
		2012	2013	2014	2015	2012	2013	2014	2015
	Total Delaware Exports and % Share of U.S. Total	5,114	5,338	5,267	5,403	0.3	0.3	0.3	0.4
	Total, Top 25 Countries and % Share of State Total	4,489	4,747	4,637	4,932	87.8	88.9	88.0	91.3
1	United Kingdom	755	495	488	882	14.8	9.3	9.3	16.3
2	Saudi Arabia	190	254	185	704	3.7	4.8	3.5	13.0
3	Canada	1,029	748	628	580	20.1	14.0	11.9	10.7
4	United Arab Emirates	76	241	292	387	1.5	4.5	5.5	7.2
5	China	413	449	456	387	8.1	8.4	8.7	7.2
6	Germany	303	242	390	263	5.9	4.5	7.4	4.9
7	Netherlands	271	264	184	225	5.3	4.9	3.5	4.2
8	Japan	345	226	177	191	6.7	4.2	3.4	3.5
9	Kuwait	35	52	49	160	0.7	1.0	0.9	3.0
10	Hong Kong	32	57	113	150	0.6	1.1	2.1	2.8
11	Mexico	145	127	106	146	2.8	2.4	2.0	2.7
12	Belgium	186	958	869	132	3.6	17.9	16.5	2.4
13	Singapore	122	105	143	107	2.4	2.0	2.7	2.0
14	Taiwan	96	95	112	96	1.9	1.8	2.1	1.8
15	Brazil	118	95	88	83	2.3	1.8	1.7	1.5
16	Costa Rica	57	56	70	63	1.1	1.0	1.3	1.2
17	Korea, South	113	115	101	61	2.2	2.2	1.9	1.1
18	Thailand	17	17	12	48	0.3	0.3	0.2	0.9
19	Oman	13	13	18	44	0.3	0.2	0.3	0.8
20	India	37	42	48	43	0.7	0.8	0.9	0.8
21	Qatar	18	17	16	41	0.4	0.3	0.3	0.8
22	Sweden	35	11	1	37	0.7	0.2	0.0	0.7
23	Colombia	26	28	30	35	0.5	0.5	0.6	0.6
24	Guatemala	43	20	32	33	0.8	0.4	0.6	0.6
25	Honduras	14	19	28	33	0.3	0.4	0.5	0.6

U.S. Imports by State of Final Destination

Rank	Country	Value (Millions of dollars)				Percent of Share			
		2012	2013	2014	2015	2012	2013	2014	2015
	Total Delaware Imports and % Share of U.S. Total	13,556	10,132	10,690	9,194	0.6	0.4	0.5	0.4
	Total, Top 25 Countries and % Share of State Total	10,069	8,647	8,944	8,529	74.3	85.3	83.7	92.8
1	Belgium	516	1,065	1,687	1,339	3.8	10.5	15.8	14.6
2	France	703	744	949	1,096	5.2	7.3	8.9	11.9
3	United Kingdom	2,768	1,013	687	979	20.4	10.0	6.4	10.6
4	Colombia	344	79	378	970	2.5	0.8	3.5	10.6
5	Canada	711	1,457	1,839	780	5.2	14.4	17.2	8.5
6	Mexico	233	244	336	555	1.7	2.4	3.1	6.0
7	China	474	474	504	382	3.5	4.7	4.7	4.2
8	Germany	288	301	416	338	2.1	3.0	3.9	3.7
9	Costa Rica	217	220	249	235	1.6	2.2	2.3	2.6
10	Sweden	144	62	113	218	1.1	0.6	1.1	2.4
11	Russia	1,746	1,481	203	188	12.9	14.6	1.9	2.0
12	Chile	201	198	247	180	1.5	2.0	2.3	2.0
13	Switzerland	88	56	67	165	0.6	0.6	0.6	1.8
14	Netherlands	439	289	187	146	3.2	2.9	1.7	1.6
15	Honduras	102	108	118	128	0.8	1.1	1.1	1.4
16	Japan	98	90	90	100	0.7	0.9	0.8	1.1
17	Spain	22	22	64	96	0.2	0.2	0.6	1.0
18	Guatemala	61	101	107	92	0.4	1.0	1.0	1.0
19	Taiwan	38	17	82	85	0.3	0.2	0.8	0.9
20	Nigeria	357	385	231	82	2.6	3.8	2.2	0.9
21	Italy	64	94	119	82	0.5	0.9	1.1	0.9
22	Brazil	357	48	150	78	2.6	0.5	1.4	0.8
23	Ireland	35	12	15	73	0.3	0.1	0.1	0.8
24	Malaysia	49	55	62	70	0.4	0.5	0.6	0.8
25	Austria	15	32	43	68	0.1	0.3	0.4	0.7

Table E-9. State Trade by Country: District of Columbia, 2012–2015

(Top 25 countries based on 2015 dollar value. Value in millions of dollars.)

U.S. Exports by Origin State

Rank	Description	Value (Millions of dollars)				Percent of Share			
		2012	2013	2014	2015	2012	2013	2014	2015
	Total District of Colombia Exports and % Share of U.S. Total	2,014	2,708	938	1,089	0.1	0.2	0.1	0.1
	Total, Top 25 Countries and % Share of State Total	1,935	2,645	874	1,058	96.1	97.7	93.2	97.2
1	United Arab Emirates	1,615	2,247	450	686	80.2	83.0	48.0	63.0
2	Oman	16	27	71	72	0.8	1.0	7.6	6.6
3	Morocco	104	114	37	47	5.2	4.2	3.9	4.3
4	Bahrain	27	6	10	41	1.3	0.2	1.1	3.8
5	Norway	2	0	1	26	0.1	0.0	0.1	2.4
6	Brazil	10	13	37	26	0.5	0.5	3.9	2.4
7	Kuwait	4	3	5	25	0.2	0.1	0.5	2.3
8	Argentina	1	7	8	19	0.0	0.3	0.9	1.7
9	Italy	28	69	51	17	1.4	2.5	5.4	1.6
10	United Kingdom	4	13	23	14	0.2	0.5	2.5	1.3
11	Chile	4	5	13	13	0.2	0.2	1.4	1.2
12	Canada	5	13	7	10	0.2	0.5	0.7	0.9
13	Switzerland	36	33	24	10	1.8	1.2	2.6	0.9
14	Denmark	19	50	78	8	0.9	1.8	8.3	0.7
15	Kazakhstan	0	0	17	8	0.0	0.0	1.8	0.7
16	Mexico	2	2	5	5	0.1	0.1	0.5	0.5
17	Germany	3	18	6	5	0.1	0.7	0.6	0.5
18	El Salvador	6	4	4	5	0.3	0.1	0.4	0.5
19	India	29	8	4	5	1.4	0.3	0.4	0.5
20	China	3	2	5	3	0.1	0.1	0.5	0.3
21	Tunisia	0	2	3	3	0.0	0.1	0.3	0.3
22	Colombia	11	3	2	2	0.5	0.1	0.2	0.2
23	France	2	3	11	2	0.1	0.1	1.2	0.2
24	Nigeria	3	3	1	2	0.1	0.1	0.1	0.2
25	Senegal	1	1	1	2	0.0	0.0	0.1	0.2

U.S. Imports by State of Final Destination

Rank	Country	Value (Millions of dollars)				Percent of Share			
		2012	2013	2014	2015	2012	2013	2014	2015
	Total District of Colombia Imports and % Share of U.S. Total	447	626	1,104	912	0	0	0	0
	Total, Top 25 Countries and % Share of State Total	395	584	992	864	88.4	93.3	89.9	94.7
1	Japan	42	42	117	164	9.4	6.7	10.6	18.0
2	India	11	34	237	140	2.5	5.4	21.5	15.4
3	United Kingdom	28	52	94	125	6.3	8.3	8.5	13.7
4	Germany	55	55	125	59	12.3	8.8	11.3	6.5
5	Canada	63	134	56	55	14.1	21.4	5.1	6.0
6	France	40	53	48	47	8.9	8.5	4.3	5.2
7	Italy	21	34	35	33	4.7	5.4	3.2	3.6
8	Qatar	3	48	73	29	0.7	7.7	6.6	3.2
9	China	20	21	29	27	4.5	3.4	2.6	3.0
10	Netherlands	5	10	25	26	1.1	1.6	2.3	2.9
11	Kuwait	3	1	26	24	0.7	0.2	2.4	2.6
12	Argentina	17	12	19	22	3.8	1.9	1.7	2.4
13	Djibouti	1	0	5	16	0.2	0.0	0.5	1.8
14	Korea, South	6	12	10	15	1.3	1.9	0.9	1.6
15	Australia	7	5	8	14	1.6	0.8	0.7	1.5
16	Ireland	5	14	19	10	1.1	2.2	1.7	1.1
17	Bahrain	0	0	25	10	0.0	0.0	2.3	1.1
18	Malaysia	5	7	5	10	1.1	1.1	0.5	1.1
19	Spain	12	6	5	9	2.7	1.0	0.5	1.0
20	Mexico	20	14	10	7	4.5	2.2	0.9	0.8
21	Sweden	3	4	4	6	0.7	0.6	0.4	0.7
22	Switzerland	4	6	14	5	0.9	1.0	1.3	0.5
23	Brazil	7	16	4	4	1.6	2.6	0.4	0.4
24	Austria	14	3	3	4	3.1	0.5	0.3	0.4
25	Portugal	3	0	0	4	0.7	0.0	0.0	0.4

Table E-10.   State Trade by Country: Florida, 2012–2015

(Top 25 countries based on 2015 dollar value. Value in millions of dollars.)

U.S. Exports by Origin State

Rank	Country	Value (Millions of dollars)				Percent of Share			
		2012	2013	2014	2015	2012	2013	2014	2015
	Total Florida Exports and % Share of U.S. Total	66,223	60,486	58,507	53,844	4.3	3.8	3.6	3.6
	Total, Top 25 Countries and % Share of State Total	51,113	45,705	41,957	39,144	77.2	75.6	71.7	72.7
1	Canada	3,846	4,547	4,029	3,875	5.8	7.5	6.9	7.2
2	Brazil	4,880	5,332	5,087	3,694	7.4	8.8	8.7	6.9
3	Mexico	2,228	2,191	2,226	2,714	3.4	3.6	3.8	5.0
4	Colombia	3,102	3,306	3,123	2,536	4.7	5.5	5.3	4.7
5	Venezuela	5,128	3,207	2,530	2,017	7.7	5.3	4.3	3.7
6	Germany	1,440	1,395	1,620	1,787	2.2	2.3	2.8	3.3
7	Dominican Republic	1,588	1,529	1,571	1,700	2.4	2.5	2.7	3.2
8	Peru	1,653	1,647	1,716	1,698	2.5	2.7	2.9	3.2
9	Chile	2,473	1,776	1,837	1,679	3.7	2.9	3.1	3.1
10	United Arab Emirates	1,685	2,212	1,764	1,538	2.5	3.7	3.0	2.9
11	Argentina	1,753	1,657	1,248	1,462	2.6	2.7	2.1	2.7
12	Switzerland	8,217	3,418	1,088	1,455	12.4	5.7	1.9	2.7
13	Panama	1,388	1,353	1,355	1,292	2.1	2.2	2.3	2.4
14	Costa Rica	1,083	1,125	1,153	1,260	1.6	1.9	2.0	2.3
15	United Kingdom	1,159	1,149	1,468	1,174	1.8	1.9	2.5	2.2
16	China	1,267	1,236	1,160	1,116	1.9	2.0	2.0	2.1
17	Paraguay	1,371	1,490	1,583	1,095	2.1	2.5	2.7	2.0
18	Bahamas	1,026	1,093	1,015	975	1.5	1.8	1.7	1.8
19	Ecuador	1,244	1,298	1,286	946	1.9	2.1	2.2	1.8
20	Saudi Arabia	530	558	680	937	0.8	0.9	1.2	1.7
21	Guatemala	901	920	905	921	1.4	1.5	1.5	1.7
22	Japan	1,046	1,055	1,099	904	1.6	1.7	1.9	1.7
23	Netherlands	896	905	997	853	1.4	1.5	1.7	1.6
24	Trinidad and Tobago	605	703	759	765	0.9	1.2	1.3	1.4
25	France	607	602	662	752	0.9	1.0	1.1	1.4

U.S. Imports by State of Final Destination

Rank	Country	Value (Millions of dollars)				Percent of Share			
		2012	2013	2014	2015	2012	2013	2014	2015
	Total Florida Imports and % Share of U.S. Total	71,222	72,258	71,782	73,437	3.1	3.2	3.1	3.3
	Total, Top 25 Countries and % Share of State Total	55,995	58,038	57,403	60,543	78.6	80.3	80.0	82.4
1	China	11,604	11,759	12,256	11,832	16.3	16.3	17.1	16.1
2	Mexico	5,621	4,846	4,556	5,552	7.9	6.7	6.3	7.6
3	Canada	4,056	4,251	3,872	4,199	5.7	5.9	5.4	5.7
4	Germany	1,918	2,108	2,122	3,976	2.7	2.9	3.0	5.4
5	France	3,126	2,902	3,365	3,585	4.4	4.0	4.7	4.9
6	Japan	4,230	3,798	2,931	3,274	5.9	5.3	4.1	4.5
7	Brazil	3,623	3,466	3,090	3,027	5.1	4.8	4.3	4.1
8	Vietnam	887	1,403	1,941	2,530	1.2	1.9	2.7	3.4
9	Colombia	3,984	3,031	2,309	2,311	5.6	4.2	3.2	3.1
10	Chile	1,342	2,360	2,846	2,113	1.9	3.3	4.0	2.9
11	United Kingdom	2,029	2,078	2,063	2,086	2.8	2.9	2.9	2.8
12	Italy	1,486	1,508	1,608	1,914	2.1	2.1	2.2	2.6
13	Korea, South	1,477	1,385	1,799	1,911	2.1	1.9	2.5	2.6
14	Switzerland	995	1,116	958	1,254	1.4	1.5	1.3	1.7
15	Ecuador	687	895	1,524	1,223	1.0	1.2	2.1	1.7
16	India	977	892	1,219	1,156	1.4	1.2	1.7	1.6
17	Dominican Republic	1,007	966	1,026	1,149	1.4	1.3	1.4	1.6
18	Venezuela	1,215	2,049	2,042	1,139	1.7	2.8	2.8	1.6
19	Peru	917	2,436	858	1,138	1.3	3.4	1.2	1.5
20	Taiwan	1,001	1,002	912	1,026	1.4	1.4	1.3	1.4
21	Spain	807	719	837	1,000	1.1	1.0	1.2	1.4
22	Honduras	601	770	982	967	0.8	1.1	1.4	1.3
23	Thailand	754	706	672	758	1.1	1.0	0.9	1.0
24	Trinidad and Tobago	1,127	990	899	717	1.6	1.4	1.3	1.0
25	Guatemala	523	603	716	709	0.7	0.8	1.0	1.0

Table E-11.   State Trade by Country: Georgia, 2012–2015

(Top 25 countries based on 2015 dollar value. Value in millions of dollars.)

U.S. Exports by Origin State

Rank	Country	Value (Millions of dollars)				Percent of Share			
		2012	2013	2014	2015	2012	2013	2014	2015
	Total Georgia Exports and % Share of U.S. Total	36,039	37,534	39,377	38,548	2.3	2.4	2.4	2.6
	Total, Top 25 Countries and % Share of State Total	27,829	28,742	30,139	30,277	77.2	76.6	76.5	78.5
1	Canada	6,727	6,337	6,507	6,406	18.7	16.9	16.5	16.6
2	Mexico	2,276	2,583	2,976	3,465	6.3	6.9	7.6	9
3	China	3,684	3,728	3,082	2,649	10.2	9.9	7.8	6.9
4	United Kingdom	1,130	1,516	1,640	1,808	3.1	4	4.2	4.7
5	Germany	1,017	1,095	1,333	1,482	2.8	2.9	3.4	3.8
6	Japan	1,300	1,483	1,379	1,366	3.6	4	3.5	3.5
7	Singapore	1,403	1,321	1,402	1,226	3.9	3.5	3.6	3.2
8	Brazil	980	1,165	1,394	1,204	2.7	3.1	3.5	3.1
9	Saudi Arabia	560	534	690	1,108	1.6	1.4	1.8	2.9
10	Australia	886	774	858	949	2.5	2.1	2.2	2.5
11	Hong Kong	747	653	790	914	2.1	1.7	2	2.4
12	Korea, South	837	807	1,243	856	2.3	2.2	3.2	2.2
13	Netherlands	654	755	849	809	1.8	2	2.2	2.1
14	Belgium	719	687	784	744	2	1.8	2	1.9
15	United Arab Emirates	638	791	703	744	1.8	2.1	1.8	1.9
16	Italy	482	560	528	661	1.3	1.5	1.3	1.7
17	France	507	487	520	544	1.4	1.3	1.3	1.4
18	Turkey	687	626	635	520	1.9	1.7	1.6	1.3
19	Taiwan	585	612	593	520	1.6	1.6	1.5	1.3
20	Poland	426	455	449	461	1.2	1.2	1.1	1.2
21	Chile	324	317	297	412	0.9	0.8	0.8	1.1
22	Vietnam	267	338	368	406	0.7	0.9	0.9	1.1
23	India	450	530	434	396	1.2	1.4	1.1	1
24	Thailand	207	249	330	318	0.6	0.7	0.8	0.8
25	Colombia	333	338	357	309	0.9	0.9	0.9	0.8

U.S. Imports by State of Final Destination

Rank	Country	Value (Millions of dollars)				Percent of Share			
		2012	2013	2014	2015	2012	2013	2014	2015
	Total Georgia Imports and % Share of U.S. Total	72,449	75,026	83,765	88,545	3.2	3.3	3.6	4
	Total, Top 25 Countries and % Share of State Total	63,896	67,501	75,839	80,706	88.2	90.0	90.5	91.1
1	China	15,816	17,624	18,651	19,734	21.8	23.5	22.3	22.3
2	Germany	12,028	13,343	17,239	16,365	16.6	17.8	20.6	18.5
3	Korea, South	6,258	6,175	6,221	7,348	8.6	8.2	7.4	8.3
4	Mexico	4,550	5,303	6,072	6,266	6.3	7.1	7.2	7.1
5	Japan	4,678	4,470	4,351	4,607	6.5	6.0	5.2	5.2
6	Canada	3,752	4,106	5,018	4,204	5.2	5.5	6.0	4.7
7	United Kingdom	1,947	1,897	2,107	3,543	2.7	2.5	2.5	4.0
8	India	1,245	1,608	1,844	2,102	1.7	2.1	2.2	2.4
9	France	1,635	1,543	1,620	1,855	2.3	2.1	1.9	2.1
10	Italy	1,192	1,258	1,504	1,570	1.6	1.7	1.8	1.8
11	Taiwan	911	1,104	1,237	1,444	1.3	1.5	1.5	1.6
12	Thailand	1,264	1,219	1,380	1,371	1.7	1.6	1.6	1.5
13	Vietnam	824	960	1,254	1,352	1.1	1.3	1.5	1.5
14	Indonesia	767	695	868	1,036	1.1	0.9	1.0	1.2
15	Chile	1,626	868	461	939	2.2	1.2	0.6	1.1
16	Belgium	432	401	568	897	0.6	0.5	0.7	1.0
17	Netherlands	838	796	901	814	1.2	1.1	1.1	0.9
18	Malaysia	821	781	744	812	1.1	1.0	0.9	0.9
19	Ireland	761	673	656	776	1.1	0.9	0.8	0.9
20	Austria	541	690	660	713	0.7	0.9	0.8	0.8
21	Brazil	834	618	743	688	1.2	0.8	0.9	0.8
22	Singapore	289	419	302	653	0.4	0.6	0.4	0.7
23	Bangladesh	422	381	525	619	0.6	0.5	0.6	0.7
24	Hungary	102	234	519	512	0.1	0.3	0.6	0.6
25	Pakistan	364	336	394	483	0.5	0.4	0.5	0.5

Table E-12.   State Trade by Country: Hawaii, 2012–2015

(Top 25 countries based on 2015 dollar value. Value in millions of dollars.)

U.S. Exports by Origin State

Rank	Country	Value (Millions of dollars)				Percent of Share			
		2012	2013	2014	2015	2012	2013	2014	2015
	Total Hawaii Exports and % Share of U.S. Total	732	598	1,447	1,896	0.0	0.0	0.1	0.1
	Total, Top 25 Countries and % Share of State Total	712	574	1,394	1,878	97.3	96.0	96.3	99.1
1	Australia	260	114	500	1,278	35.5	19.1	34.6	67.4
2	Singapore	35	103	132	119	4.8	17.2	9.1	6.3
3	Japan	127	86	184	80	17.3	14.4	12.7	4.2
4	China	71	89	221	78	9.7	14.9	15.3	4.1
5	Vietnam	3	4	6	74	0.4	0.7	0.4	3.9
6	Panama	1	11	106	62	0.1	1.8	7.3	3.3
7	Korea, South	45	41	93	40	6.1	6.9	6.4	2.1
8	Canada	30	21	27	30	4.1	3.5	1.9	1.6
9	Hong Kong	23	17	22	21	3.1	2.8	1.5	1.1
10	El Salvador	0	0	0	16	0.0	0.0	0.0	0.8
11	Taiwan	22	26	17	13	3.0	4.3	1.2	0.7
12	India	1	0	1	10	0.1	0.0	0.1	0.5
13	New Zealand	16	7	13	9	2.2	1.2	0.9	0.5
14	Switzerland	2	3	1	7	0.3	0.5	0.1	0.4
15	Philippines	4	4	4	7	0.5	0.7	0.3	0.4
16	Malaysia	11	1	10	6	1.5	0.2	0.7	0.3
17	United Kingdom	4	12	3	5	0.5	2.0	0.2	0.3
18	Malta	0	0	0	4	0.0	0.0	0.0	0.2
19	Guatemala	0	0	0	4	0.0	0.0	0.0	0.2
20	Indonesia	24	3	28	4	3.3	0.5	1.9	0.2
21	Thailand	5	2	3	3	0.7	0.3	0.2	0.2
22	Germany	5	4	16	2	0.7	0.7	1.1	0.1
23	Netherlands	17	20	3	2	2.3	3.3	0.2	0.1
24	France	2	3	3	2	0.3	0.5	0.2	0.1
25	Mexico	4	2	2	2	0.5	0.3	0.1	0.1

U.S. Imports by State of Final Destination

Rank	Country	Value (Millions of dollars)				Percent of Share			
		2012	2013	2014	2015	2012	2013	2014	2015
	Total Hawaii Imports and % Share of U.S. Total	6,662	6,097	5,330	3,760	0.3	0.3	0.2	0.2
	Total, Top 25 Countries and % Share of State Total	5,058	5,034	4,835	3,622	75.9	82.6	90.7	96.3
1	Indonesia	301	810	785	816	4.5	13.3	14.7	21.7
2	Russia	855	535	0	477	12.8	8.8	0.0	12.7
3	France	512	606	664	387	7.7	9.9	12.5	10.3
4	Japan	314	438	317	312	4.7	7.2	5.9	8.3
5	China	310	299	262	279	4.7	4.9	4.9	7.4
6	Canada	141	140	255	265	2.1	2.3	4.8	7.0
7	Korea, South	73	536	194	214	1.1	8.8	3.6	5.7
8	Vietnam	380	538	446	193	5.7	8.8	8.4	5.1
9	Argentina	542	265	531	132	8.1	4.3	10.0	3.5
10	Nigeria	0	0	80	111	0.0	0.0	1.5	3.0
11	Taiwan	33	45	46	51	0.5	0.7	0.9	1.4
12	Italy	38	43	43	38	0.6	0.7	0.8	1.0
13	Thailand	839	364	291	38	12.6	6.0	5.5	1.0
14	Ecuador	22	3	38	37	0.3	0.0	0.7	1.0
15	United Arab Emirates	0	0	634	34	0.0	0.0	11.9	0.9
16	United Kingdom	13	30	36	32	0.2	0.5	0.7	0.9
17	Germany	17	31	31	32	0.3	0.5	0.6	0.9
18	Australia	32	57	25	30	0.5	0.9	0.5	0.8
19	Philippines	24	29	27	28	0.4	0.5	0.5	0.7
20	New Zealand	31	32	31	27	0.5	0.5	0.6	0.7
21	Malaysia	6	37	15	19	0.1	0.6	0.3	0.5
22	Netherlands	12	25	19	19	0.2	0.4	0.4	0.5
23	Switzerland	47	35	33	19	0.7	0.6	0.6	0.5
24	Libya	509	105	0	17	7.6	1.7	0.0	0.5
25	Peru	5	32	33	15	0.1	0.5	0.6	0.4

Table E-13. State Trade by Country: Idaho, 2012–2015

(Top 25 countries based on 2015 dollar value. Value in millions of dollars.)

U.S. Exports by Origin State

Rank	Description	Value (Millions of dollars)				Percent of Share			
		2012	2013	2014	2015	2012	2013	2014	2015
	Total Idaho Exports and % Share of U.S. Total	6,120	5,783	5,137	4,296	0.4	0.4	0.3	0.3
	Total, Top 25 Countries and % Share of State Total	5,900	5,531	4,904	4,116	96.4	95.6	95.5	95.8
1	Canada	1,331	1,603	1,412	977	21.7	27.7	27.5	22.7
2	China	468	468	482	560	7.6	8.1	9.4	13.0
3	Taiwan	755	541	473	529	12.3	9.4	9.2	12.3
4	Singapore	963	431	386	414	15.7	7.5	7.5	9.6
5	Japan	302	209	280	289	4.9	3.6	5.5	6.7
6	Mexico	257	273	301	264	4.2	4.7	5.9	6.1
7	Korea, South	572	671	495	221	9.3	11.6	9.6	5.1
8	United Kingdom	78	100	125	125	1.3	1.7	2.4	2.9
9	Malaysia	176	242	194	123	2.9	4.2	3.8	2.9
10	Hong Kong	341	365	151	86	5.6	6.3	2.9	2.0
11	Netherlands	71	59	72	72	1.2	1.0	1.4	1.7
12	Philippines	65	80	96	65	1.1	1.4	1.9	1.5
13	Australia	108	78	101	64	1.8	1.3	2.0	1.5
14	Brazil	59	66	63	62	1.0	1.1	1.2	1.4
15	France	140	127	72	45	2.3	2.2	1.4	1.0
16	Germany	31	34	27	43	0.5	0.6	0.5	1.0
17	Indonesia	49	48	46	32	0.8	0.8	0.9	0.7
18	India	20	19	14	28	0.3	0.3	0.3	0.7
19	Thailand	24	26	20	24	0.4	0.4	0.4	0.6
20	Spain	24	17	21	22	0.4	0.3	0.4	0.5
21	Chile	15	23	24	20	0.2	0.4	0.5	0.5
22	Israel	17	16	15	17	0.3	0.3	0.3	0.4
23	Peru	15	15	17	13	0.2	0.3	0.3	0.3
24	New Zealand	14	15	11	12	0.2	0.3	0.2	0.3
25	Denmark	2	4	6	10	0.0	0.1	0.1	0.2

U.S. Imports by State of Final Destination

Rank	Country	Value (Millions of dollars)				Percent of Share			
		2012	2013	2014	2015	2012	2013	2014	2015
	Total Idaho Imports and % Share of U.S. Total	5,148	5,545	5,692	5,166	0.2	0.2	0.2	0.2
	Total, Top 25 Countries and % Share of State Total	5,025	5,405	5,541	5,065	97.6	97.5	97.3	98.0
1	China	702	1,100	1,499	1,583	13.6	19.8	26.3	30.6
2	Canada	952	1,019	879	914	18.5	18.4	15.4	17.7
3	Taiwan	554	953	1,034	842	10.8	17.2	18.2	16.3
4	Singapore	1,013	774	595	503	19.7	14.0	10.5	9.7
5	Japan	484	366	536	431	9.4	6.6	9.4	8.3
6	Korea, South	388	453	329	178	7.5	8.2	5.8	3.4
7	Mexico	181	74	97	137	3.5	1.3	1.7	2.7
8	Germany	59	98	64	63	1.1	1.8	1.1	1.2
9	France	20	24	18	43	0.4	0.4	0.3	0.8
10	Malaysia	16	13	17	43	0.3	0.2	0.3	0.8
11	Greece	55	71	60	42	1.1	1.3	1.1	0.8
12	Vietnam	25	22	29	32	0.5	0.4	0.5	0.6
13	Israel	39	47	56	31	0.8	0.8	1.0	0.6
14	New Zealand	41	54	36	29	0.8	1.0	0.6	0.6
15	Netherlands	12	18	16	28	0.2	0.3	0.3	0.5
16	United Kingdom	17	29	39	28	0.3	0.5	0.7	0.5
17	Italy	359	216	153	26	7.0	3.9	2.7	0.5
18	Austria	20	2	19	24	0.4	0.0	0.3	0.5
19	Thailand	5	6	9	16	0.1	0.1	0.2	0.3
20	Australia	24	25	6	15	0.5	0.5	0.1	0.3
21	India	18	10	19	14	0.3	0.2	0.3	0.3
22	Chile	8	7	12	13	0.2	0.1	0.2	0.3
23	Indonesia	16	17	7	11	0.3	0.3	0.1	0.2
24	Denmark	12	4	7	10	0.2	0.1	0.1	0.2
25	Hong Kong	7	3	3	9	0.1	0.1	0.1	0.2

Table E-14.   State Trade by Country: Illinois, 2012–2015

(Top 25 countries based on 2015 dollar value. Value in millions of dollars.)

U.S. Exports by Origin State

Rank	Country	Value (Millions of dollars)				Percent of Share			
		2012	2013	2014	2015	2012	2013	2014	2015
	Total Illinois Exports and % Share of U.S. Total	68,158	66,157	68,247	63,402	4.4	4.2	4.2	4.2
	Total, Top 25 Countries and % Share of State Total	60,137	58,698	60,906	56,744	88.2	88.7	89.2	89.5
1	Canada	19,415	20,305	22,082	17,421	28.5	30.7	32.4	27.5
2	Mexico	6,376	7,317	7,918	9,078	9.4	11.1	11.6	14.3
3	China	4,142	5,695	4,714	4,941	6.1	8.6	6.9	7.8
4	Germany	2,664	2,757	2,855	3,137	3.9	4.2	4.2	4.9
5	Australia	5,351	2,739	2,416	2,638	7.9	4.1	3.5	4.2
6	Japan	2,105	1,933	2,564	2,049	3.1	2.9	3.8	3.2
7	Netherlands	1,245	1,193	1,527	1,920	1.8	1.8	2.2	3.0
8	United Kingdom	2,047	1,581	1,610	1,747	3.0	2.4	2.4	2.8
9	Brazil	2,344	2,470	2,315	1,700	3.4	3.7	3.4	2.7
10	Belgium	1,882	1,576	1,634	1,612	2.8	2.4	2.4	2.5
11	Singapore	1,458	1,239	1,272	1,175	2.1	1.9	1.9	1.9
12	Hong Kong	652	756	981	1,160	1.0	1.1	1.4	1.8
13	Korea, South	960	912	956	1,102	1.4	1.4	1.4	1.7
14	Saudi Arabia	729	703	897	911	1.1	1.1	1.3	1.4
15	France	1,309	1,343	926	797	1.9	2.0	1.4	1.3
16	India	1,085	696	647	703	1.6	1.1	0.9	1.1
17	Chile	1,469	1,041	867	694	2.2	1.6	1.3	1.1
18	South Africa	1,277	948	1,044	672	1.9	1.4	1.5	1.1
19	Taiwan	949	919	926	634	1.4	1.4	1.4	1.0
20	United Arab Emirates	363	397	572	633	0.5	0.6	0.8	1.0
21	Switzerland	158	292	367	532	0.2	0.4	0.5	0.8
22	Colombia	403	448	505	443	0.6	0.7	0.7	0.7
23	Indonesia	531	486	516	355	0.8	0.7	0.8	0.6
24	Argentina	412	366	345	347	0.6	0.6	0.5	0.5
25	Russia	812	589	448	343	1.2	0.9	0.7	0.5

U.S. Imports by State of Final Destination

Rank	Country	Value (Millions of dollars)				Percent of Share			
		2012	2013	2014	2015	2012	2013	2014	2015
	Total Illinois Imports and % Share of U.S. Total	126,405	124,828	140,123	121,252	5.6	5.5	6	5.4
	Total, Top 25 Countries and % Share of State Total	119,305	117,904	132,723	114,597	94.4	94.5	94.7	94.5
1	China	27,799	25,784	29,464	31,178	22.0	20.7	21.0	25.7
2	Canada	39,305	39,880	45,458	29,745	31.1	31.9	32.4	24.5
3	Mexico	9,030	11,675	13,347	13,117	7.1	9.4	9.5	10.8
4	Japan	8,853	7,925	7,680	7,108	7.0	6.3	5.5	5.9
5	Germany	4,853	4,929	5,365	4,573	3.8	3.9	3.8	3.8
6	Korea, South	4,668	4,672	5,091	4,067	3.7	3.7	3.6	3.4
7	Vietnam	574	1,362	2,318	2,681	0.5	1.1	1.7	2.2
8	Taiwan	2,236	2,182	2,152	2,221	1.8	1.7	1.5	1.8
9	Ireland	1,316	610	1,802	1,985	1.0	0.5	1.3	1.6
10	United Kingdom	2,014	1,843	2,004	1,917	1.6	1.5	1.4	1.6
11	Italy	1,604	1,499	1,668	1,784	1.3	1.2	1.2	1.5
12	Brazil	685	743	1,816	1,782	0.5	0.6	1.3	1.5
13	Malaysia	1,853	1,721	1,724	1,646	1.5	1.4	1.2	1.4
14	India	1,158	1,193	1,364	1,410	0.9	1.0	1.0	1.2
15	France	1,582	1,343	1,343	1,302	1.3	1.1	1.0	1.1
16	Thailand	987	1,003	1,197	1,173	0.8	0.8	0.9	1.0
17	Switzerland	2,571	3,174	2,824	1,122	2.0	2.5	2.0	0.9
18	Australia	617	578	787	1,007	0.5	0.5	0.6	0.8
19	Netherlands	3,144	1,706	931	926	2.5	1.4	0.7	0.8
20	Singapore	901	868	870	829	0.7	0.7	0.6	0.7
21	Indonesia	617	729	930	822	0.5	0.6	0.7	0.7
22	Spain	889	770	714	617	0.7	0.6	0.5	0.5
23	New Zealand	565	460	541	582	0.4	0.4	0.4	0.5
24	Russia	709	682	790	523	0.6	0.5	0.6	0.4
25	Belgium	774	572	544	480	0.6	0.5	0.4	0.4

'(Z)' indicates a percent change greater than 500.

Table E-15.   State Trade by Country: Indiana, 2012–2015

(Top 25 countries based on 2015 dollar value. Value in millions of dollars.)

U.S. Exports by Origin State

Rank	Country	Value (Millions of dollars)				Percent of Share			
		2012	2013	2014	2015	2012	2013	2014	2015
	Total Indiana Exports and % Share of U.S. Total	34,399	34,155	35,467	33,652	2.2	2.2	2.2	2.2
	Total, Top 25 Countries and % Share of State Total	32,074	31,736	32,593	31,096	93.2	92.9	91.9	92.4
1	Canada	11,900	11,817	12,246	10,955	34.6	34.6	34.5	32.6
2	Mexico	3,907	4,001	5,022	4,804	11.4	11.7	14.2	14.3
3	Japan	1,752	1,805	1,644	1,691	5.1	5.3	4.6	5.0
4	France	1,767	1,387	1,354	1,481	5.1	4.1	3.8	4.4
5	Germany	2,156	1,928	1,624	1,438	6.3	5.6	4.6	4.3
6	China	1,309	1,346	1,436	1,269	3.8	3.9	4.0	3.8
7	United Kingdom	1,199	1,038	1,197	1,238	3.5	3.0	3.4	3.7
8	Italy	752	846	839	1,119	2.2	2.5	2.4	3.3
9	Netherlands	788	1,174	844	960	2.3	3.4	2.4	2.9
10	Ireland	547	546	604	916	1.6	1.6	1.7	2.7
11	Belgium	534	449	867	731	1.6	1.3	2.4	2.2
12	Korea, South	788	874	933	695	2.3	2.6	2.6	2.1
13	Brazil	818	1,027	807	574	2.4	3.0	2.3	1.7
14	Spain	826	519	300	526	2.4	1.5	0.8	1.6
15	Australia	647	564	618	514	1.9	1.7	1.7	1.5
16	Switzerland	127	159	170	309	0.4	0.5	0.5	0.9
17	India	267	223	255	284	0.8	0.7	0.7	0.8
18	Saudi Arabia	452	415	275	279	1.3	1.2	0.8	0.8
19	Hong Kong	447	483	500	233	1.3	1.4	1.4	0.7
20	Singapore	259	245	196	214	0.8	0.7	0.6	0.6
21	Colombia	152	169	196	213	0.4	0.5	0.6	0.6
22	United Arab Emirates	165	204	169	183	0.5	0.6	0.5	0.5
23	Taiwan	236	251	247	173	0.7	0.7	0.7	0.5
24	Argentina	140	135	139	160	0.4	0.4	0.4	0.5
25	Thailand	139	131	111	137	0.4	0.4	0.3	0.4

U.S. Imports by State of Final Destination

Rank	Country	Value (Millions of dollars)				Percent of Share			
		2012	2013	2014	2015	2012	2013	2014	2015
	Total Indiana Imports and % Share of U.S. Total	43,278	45,678	48,794	48,979	1.9	2	2.1	2.2
	Total, Top 25 Countries and % Share of State Total	41,753	44,146	47,282	47,559	96.5	96.6	96.9	97.1
1	China	6,067	6,796	7,721	8,319	14	14.9	15.8	17
2	Canada	7,679	7,789	8,121	7,864	17.7	17.1	16.6	16.1
3	Ireland	5,912	6,807	6,570	5,854	13.7	14.9	13.5	12
4	Mexico	3,567	3,967	5,130	5,255	8.2	8.7	10.5	10.7
5	Japan	5,223	4,972	4,945	4,370	12.1	10.9	10.1	8.9
6	Denmark	2,349	2,549	3,022	3,305	5.4	5.6	6.2	6.7
7	Germany	2,299	2,369	2,160	2,494	5.3	5.2	4.4	5.1
8	France	985	1,324	1,334	1,540	2.3	2.9	2.7	3.1
9	Switzerland	1,478	1,505	1,315	1,185	3.4	3.3	2.7	2.4
10	Brazil	284	693	835	1,022	0.7	1.5	1.7	2.1
11	United Kingdom	1,142	1,037	912	969	2.6	2.3	1.9	2
12	Taiwan	851	579	690	766	2	1.3	1.4	1.6
13	Vietnam	319	367	505	672	0.7	0.8	1	1.4
14	Italy	642	609	675	609	1.5	1.3	1.4	1.2
15	Thailand	564	527	604	507	1.3	1.2	1.2	1
16	Indonesia	191	168	362	463	0.4	0.4	0.7	0.9
17	India	434	393	427	404	1	0.9	0.9	0.8
18	Netherlands	402	453	477	402	0.9	1	1	0.8
19	Korea, South	344	323	319	335	0.8	0.7	0.7	0.7
20	Philippines	65	79	194	259	0.2	0.2	0.4	0.5
21	Russia	224	183	328	207	0.5	0.4	0.7	0.4
22	Austria	137	168	196	203	0.3	0.4	0.4	0.4
23	Honduras	184	190	167	198	0.4	0.4	0.3	0.4
24	Spain	66	97	109	188	0.2	0.2	0.2	0.4
25	Malaysia	345	202	162	168	0.8	0.4	0.3	0.3

Table E-16.   State Trade by Country: Iowa, 2012–2015

(Top 25 countries based on 2015 dollar value. Value in millions of dollars.)

U.S. Exports by Origin State

Rank	Country	Value (Millions of dollars)				Percent of Share			
		2012	2013	2014	2015	2012	2013	2014	2015
	Total Iowa Exports and % Share of U.S. Total	14,622	13,883	15,092	13,114	0.9	0.9	0.9	0.9
	Total, Top 25 Countries and % Share of State Total	12,615	12,167	13,481	11,880	86.3	87.6	89.3	90.6
1	Canada	4,371	4,432	4,618	3,835	29.9	31.9	30.6	29.2
2	Mexico	2,500	2,171	2,305	2,086	17.1	15.6	15.3	15.9
3	China	751	611	946	1,142	5.1	4.4	6.3	8.7
4	Japan	881	980	1,171	1,129	6.0	7.1	7.8	8.6
5	Germany	661	679	494	493	4.5	4.9	3.3	3.8
6	Korea, South	343	293	366	344	2.3	2.1	2.4	2.6
7	Australia	514	405	399	338	3.5	2.9	2.6	2.6
8	France	340	333	323	330	2.3	2.4	2.1	2.5
9	United Kingdom	374	291	384	289	2.6	2.1	2.5	2.2
10	Brazil	633	602	502	257	4.3	4.3	3.3	2.0
11	Netherlands	230	288	265	202	1.6	2.1	1.8	1.5
12	Hong Kong	109	151	240	194	0.7	1.1	1.6	1.5
13	Colombia	59	68	309	145	0.4	0.5	2.0	1.1
14	Taiwan	92	97	146	134	0.6	0.7	1.0	1.0
15	Ireland	19	58	99	120	0.1	0.4	0.7	0.9
16	Singapore	132	133	148	106	0.9	1.0	1.0	0.8
17	Italy	96	94	96	102	0.7	0.7	0.6	0.8
18	Saudi Arabia	81	80	102	93	0.6	0.6	0.7	0.7
19	Spain	61	79	119	90	0.4	0.6	0.8	0.7
20	Peru	45	36	125	87	0.3	0.3	0.8	0.7
21	Costa Rica	26	15	35	77	0.2	0.1	0.2	0.6
22	India	85	86	73	75	0.6	0.6	0.5	0.6
23	Philippines	52	65	70	73	0.4	0.5	0.5	0.6
24	New Zealand	51	51	78	70	0.3	0.4	0.5	0.5
25	Chile	109	69	68	67	0.7	0.5	0.5	0.5

U.S. Imports by State of Final Destination

Rank	Country	Value (Millions of dollars)				Percent of Share			
		2012	2013	2014	2015	2012	2013	2014	2015
	Total Iowa Imports and % Share of U.S. Total	9,432	9,571	10,081	9,444	0.4	0.4	0.4	0.4
	Total, Top 25 Countries and % Share of State Total	9,064	9,241	9,758	9,094	96.1	96.6	96.8	96.3
1	Canada	3,127	3,380	3,364	2,795	33.2	35.3	33.4	29.6
2	Mexico	1,430	1,471	1,726	1,610	15.2	15.4	17.1	17.0
3	China	1,293	1,354	1,412	1,548	13.7	14.1	14.0	16.4
4	Germany	680	681	756	595	7.2	7.1	7.5	6.3
5	Japan	498	290	278	383	5.3	3.0	2.8	4.1
6	Italy	299	306	327	286	3.2	3.2	3.2	3.0
7	France	221	178	171	191	2.3	1.9	1.7	2.0
8	Taiwan	183	179	176	184	1.9	1.9	1.7	1.9
9	Spain	111	93	157	168	1.2	1.0	1.6	1.8
10	India	193	134	157	166	2.0	1.4	1.6	1.8
11	United Kingdom	99	113	122	141	1.0	1.2	1.2	1.5
12	Korea, South	137	144	158	131	1.5	1.5	1.6	1.4
13	Brazil	136	125	131	120	1.4	1.3	1.3	1.3
14	Netherlands	66	81	92	101	0.7	0.8	0.9	1.1
15	Austria	69	101	89	96	0.7	1.1	0.9	1.0
16	Israel	73	67	94	91	0.8	0.7	0.9	1.0
17	Denmark	79	75	84	79	0.8	0.8	0.8	0.8
18	Vietnam	39	44	64	74	0.4	0.5	0.6	0.8
19	Poland	72	77	82	73	0.8	0.8	0.8	0.8
20	Switzerland	44	41	66	63	0.5	0.4	0.7	0.7
21	Thailand	36	50	58	45	0.4	0.5	0.6	0.5
22	Indonesia	11	19	29	42	0.1	0.2	0.3	0.4
23	Chile	99	141	97	40	1.0	1.5	1.0	0.4
24	Belgium	31	39	38	39	0.3	0.4	0.4	0.4
25	Argentina	37	57	30	34	0.4	0.6	0.3	0.4

Table E-17.   State Trade by Country: Kansas, 2012–2015

(Top 25 countries based on 2015 dollar value. Value in millions of dollars.)

U.S. Exports by Origin State

Rank	Country	Value (Millions of dollars)				Percent of Share			
		2012	2013	2014	2015	2012	2013	2014	2015
	Total Kansas Exports and % Share of U.S. Total	11,684	12,457	12,046	10,686	0.8	0.8	0.7	0.7
	Total, Top 25 Countries and % Share of State Total	9,980	10,610	10,251	9,361	85.4	85.2	85.1	87.6
1	Canada	2,745	2,606	2,561	2,387	23.5	20.9	21.3	22.3
2	Mexico	1,437	1,533	1,784	1,813	12.3	12.3	14.8	17.0
3	China	1,138	1,703	1,184	988	9.7	13.7	9.8	9.2
4	Japan	742	880	828	708	6.4	7.1	6.9	6.6
5	United Kingdom	524	477	523	432	4.5	3.8	4.3	4.0
6	Germany	366	323	335	308	3.1	2.6	2.8	2.9
7	Nigeria	575	326	289	296	4.9	2.6	2.4	2.8
8	Brazil	355	667	535	256	3.0	5.4	4.4	2.4
9	France	205	237	245	249	1.8	1.9	2.0	2.3
10	Korea, South	236	212	237	211	2.0	1.7	2.0	2.0
11	Australia	293	201	227	203	2.5	1.6	1.9	1.9
12	Singapore	184	143	160	193	1.6	1.1	1.3	1.8
13	Hong Kong	88	172	222	177	0.8	1.4	1.8	1.7
14	Taiwan	129	195	185	165	1.1	1.6	1.5	1.5
15	Netherlands	79	100	159	130	0.7	0.8	1.3	1.2
16	Italy	128	96	131	122	1.1	0.8	1.1	1.1
17	Philippines	63	74	104	112	0.5	0.6	0.9	1.0
18	Belgium	120	92	87	89	1.0	0.7	0.7	0.8
19	Switzerland	97	88	76	88	0.8	0.7	0.6	0.8
20	Vietnam	64	82	56	85	0.5	0.7	0.5	0.8
21	Israel	105	83	69	75	0.9	0.7	0.6	0.7
22	Colombia	90	98	74	73	0.8	0.8	0.6	0.7
23	India	82	60	65	69	0.7	0.5	0.5	0.6
24	South Africa	103	100	74	66	0.9	0.8	0.6	0.6
25	Thailand	32	62	40	66	0.3	0.5	0.3	0.6

U.S. Imports by State of Final Destination

Rank	Country	Value (Millions of dollars)				Percent of Share			
		2012	2013	2014	2015	2012	2013	2014	2015
	Total Kansas Imports and % Share of U.S. Total	10,873	10,756	11,806	11,666	0.5	0.5	0.5	0.5
	Total, Top 25 Countries and % Share of State Total	10,055	10,065	10,890	10,915	92.5	93.6	92.2	93.6
1	China	2,181	2,115	2,348	2,571	20.1	19.7	19.9	22.0
2	Canada	1,623	1,709	1,708	1,580	14.9	15.9	14.5	13.5
3	Taiwan	1,545	1,040	1,156	1,053	14.2	9.7	9.8	9.0
4	Mexico	1,008	962	963	1,013	9.3	8.9	8.2	8.7
5	Germany	775	758	745	914	7.1	7.0	6.3	7.8
6	United Kingdom	493	377	440	539	4.5	3.5	3.7	4.6
7	Japan	249	193	210	427	2.3	1.8	1.8	3.7
8	Vietnam	240	300	344	371	2.2	2.8	2.9	3.2
9	Korea, South	199	263	277	279	1.8	2.4	2.3	2.4
10	Australia	189	268	315	274	1.7	2.5	2.7	2.3
11	Brazil	175	194	223	233	1.6	1.8	1.9	2.0
12	France	185	206	243	226	1.7	1.9	2.1	1.9
13	Indonesia	115	143	146	165	1.1	1.3	1.2	1.4
14	Italy	116	512	610	164	1.1	4.8	5.2	1.4
15	Singapore	97	95	104	157	0.9	0.9	0.9	1.3
16	Trinidad and Tobago	161	196	172	130	1.5	1.8	1.5	1.1
17	Malaysia	111	118	131	123	1.0	1.1	1.1	1.1
18	Denmark	119	138	205	121	1.1	1.3	1.7	1.0
19	Turkey	90	92	96	111	0.8	0.9	0.8	1.0
20	Sweden	81	104	111	97	0.7	1.0	0.9	0.8
21	India	90	69	96	83	0.8	0.6	0.8	0.7
22	Israel	76	72	80	81	0.7	0.7	0.7	0.7
23	Philippines	30	25	30	71	0.3	0.2	0.3	0.6
24	Austria	32	51	72	69	0.3	0.5	0.6	0.6
25	Netherlands	76	63	69	62	0.7	0.6	0.6	0.5

Table E-18.   State Trade by Country: Kentucky, 2012–2015

(Top 25 countries based on 2015 dollar value. Value in millions of dollars.)

U.S. Exports by Origin State

Rank	Country	Value (Millions of dollars)				Percent of Share			
		2012	2013	2014	2015	2012	2013	2014	2015
	Total Kentucky Exports and % Share of U.S. Total	22,132	25,349	27,651	28,053	1.4	1.6	1.7	1.9
	Total, Top 25 Countries and % Share of State Total	20,347	23,562	25,946	26,481	91.9	93.0	93.8	94.4
1	Canada	7,339	7,774	7,688	7,234	33.2	30.7	27.8	25.8
2	United Kingdom	1,521	1,838	2,337	2,557	6.9	7.3	8.5	9.1
3	Mexico	1,714	1,865	2,309	2,236	7.7	7.4	8.4	8.0
4	China	1,055	1,351	1,654	1,925	4.8	5.3	6.0	6.9
5	France	433	1,020	1,973	1,756	2.0	4.0	7.1	6.3
6	Brazil	1,149	1,262	1,443	1,739	5.2	5.0	5.2	6.2
7	Japan	1,319	1,239	1,267	1,164	6.0	4.9	4.6	4.1
8	Belgium	481	499	599	973	2.2	2.0	2.2	3.5
9	Germany	650	906	935	945	2.9	3.6	3.4	3.4
10	Netherlands	587	688	855	943	2.7	2.7	3.1	3.4
11	Singapore	834	812	758	869	3.8	3.2	2.7	3.1
12	Hong Kong	582	793	774	684	2.6	3.1	2.8	2.4
13	Austria	388	489	361	577	1.8	1.9	1.3	2.1
14	Saudi Arabia	155	745	789	435	0.7	2.9	2.9	1.6
15	Korea, South	618	439	374	421	2.8	1.7	1.4	1.5
16	Australia	326	326	380	368	1.5	1.3	1.4	1.3
17	Malaysia	146	181	185	296	0.7	0.7	0.7	1.1
18	Russia	43	91	83	225	0.2	0.4	0.3	0.8
19	United Arab Emirates	138	261	313	213	0.6	1.0	1.1	0.8
20	Italy	207	177	181	209	0.9	0.7	0.7	0.7
21	India	125	136	121	160	0.6	0.5	0.4	0.6
22	Taiwan	271	297	220	148	1.2	1.2	0.8	0.5
23	Spain	100	153	143	145	0.5	0.6	0.5	0.5
24	Colombia	85	145	129	144	0.4	0.6	0.5	0.5
25	Argentina	80	75	76	116	0.4	0.3	0.3	0.4

U.S. Imports by State of Final Destination

Rank	Description	Value (Millions of dollars)				Percent of Share			
		2012	2013	2014	2015	2012	2013	2014	2015
	Total Kentucky Imports and % Share of U.S. Total	34,725	37,859	39,266	38,538	1.5	1.7	1.7	1.7
	Total, Top 25 Countries and % Share of State Total	32,048	35,056	36,489	36,580	92.3	92.6	92.9	94.9
1	Mexico	3,197	4,977	5,501	6,074	9.2	13.1	14.0	15.8
2	China	6,803	6,640	6,861	6,046	19.6	17.5	17.5	15.7
3	Japan	4,970	4,926	5,004	4,849	14.3	13.0	12.7	12.6
4	Canada	4,000	4,014	4,026	3,689	11.5	10.6	10.3	9.6
5	France	1,442	1,693	1,859	2,243	4.2	4.5	4.7	5.8
6	Germany	1,841	2,048	2,169	2,005	5.3	5.4	5.5	5.2
7	Italy	1,434	1,629	1,375	1,496	4.1	4.3	3.5	3.9
8	Switzerland	565	1,200	1,499	1,302	1.6	3.2	3.8	3.4
9	India	832	859	844	1,178	2.4	2.3	2.1	3.1
10	United Kingdom	1,066	1,134	1,172	1,158	3.1	3.0	3.0	3.0
11	Belgium	336	152	530	1,068	1.0	0.4	1.3	2.8
12	Korea, South	511	843	730	816	1.5	2.2	1.9	2.1
13	Taiwan	1,071	479	445	566	3.1	1.3	1.1	1.5
14	Vietnam	422	417	447	513	1.2	1.1	1.1	1.3
15	Ireland	307	532	548	477	0.9	1.4	1.4	1.2
16	Austria	199	257	332	432	0.6	0.7	0.8	1.1
17	Spain	407	469	497	432	1.2	1.2	1.3	1.1
18	Thailand	603	563	592	386	1.7	1.5	1.5	1.0
19	Philippines	339	491	408	329	1.0	1.3	1.0	0.9
20	Indonesia	388	398	336	300	1.1	1.1	0.9	0.8
21	Sweden	306	304	339	284	0.9	0.8	0.9	0.7
22	Netherlands	250	339	278	277	0.7	0.9	0.7	0.7
23	Brazil	329	291	275	246	0.9	0.8	0.7	0.6
24	Turkey	156	164	195	210	0.4	0.4	0.5	0.5
25	El Salvador	277	240	226	202	0.8	0.6	0.6	0.5

Table E-19. State Trade by Country: Louisiana, 2012–2015

(Top 25 countries based on 2015 dollar value. Value in millions of dollars.)

U.S. Exports by Origin State

Rank	Description	Value (Millions of dollars)				Percent of Share			
		2012	2013	2014	2015	2012	2013	2014	2015
	Total Louisiana Exports and % Share of U.S. Total	62,869	63,242	64,814	49,183	4.1	4	4	3.3
	Total, Top 25 Countries and % Share of State Total	50,001	48,968	51,760	39,524	79.5	77.4	79.9	80.4
1	China	9,311	7,949	8,439	6,623	14.8	12.6	13.0	13.5
2	Mexico	6,508	6,397	7,340	5,817	10.4	10.1	11.3	11.8
3	Canada	2,674	3,067	3,314	2,856	4.3	4.8	5.1	5.8
4	Netherlands	3,408	2,613	3,067	2,622	5.4	4.1	4.7	5.3
5	Japan	3,820	2,798	2,843	2,369	6.1	4.4	4.4	4.8
6	Colombia	1,415	1,865	2,842	2,077	2.3	2.9	4.4	4.2
7	Brazil	2,285	2,590	2,209	1,488	3.6	4.1	3.4	3.0
8	France	1,119	2,287	2,553	1,438	1.8	3.6	3.9	2.9
9	United Kingdom	1,200	1,300	1,250	1,418	1.9	2.1	1.9	2.9
10	Belgium	885	1,279	1,296	1,247	1.4	2.0	2.0	2.5
11	Germany	1,329	1,015	945	996	2.1	1.6	1.5	2.0
12	Singapore	2,270	2,777	1,552	995	3.6	4.4	2.4	2.0
13	Chile	1,679	822	980	939	2.7	1.3	1.5	1.9
14	Argentina	709	1,032	1,271	922	1.1	1.6	2.0	1.9
15	Spain	968	860	940	782	1.5	1.4	1.5	1.6
16	Korea, South	1,340	1,168	1,242	777	2.1	1.8	1.9	1.6
17	Dominican Republic	738	730	793	765	1.2	1.2	1.2	1.6
18	Guatemala	678	676	977	764	1.1	1.1	1.5	1.6
19	Venezuela	1,280	1,108	1,280	741	2.0	1.8	2.0	1.5
20	Gibraltar	1,639	1,233	730	718	2.6	1.9	1.1	1.5
21	Egypt	1,569	1,134	2,012	707	2.5	1.8	3.1	1.4
22	Ecuador	1,167	1,313	738	689	1.9	2.1	1.1	1.4
23	Peru	654	742	840	650	1.0	1.2	1.3	1.3
24	Saudi Arabia	533	482	611	572	0.8	0.8	0.9	1.2
25	Panama	826	1,730	1,695	552	1.3	2.7	2.6	1.1

U.S. Imports by State of Final Destination

Rank	Country	Value (Millions of dollars)				Percent of Share			
		2012	2013	2014	2015	2012	2013	2014	2015
	Total Louisiana Imports and % Share of U.S. Total	80,813	66,214	57,605	35,226	3.6	2.9	2.5	1.6
	Total, Top 25 Countries and % Share of State Total	70,151	59,512	52,234	30,910	86.8	89.9	90.7	87.7
1	Saudi Arabia	20,735	14,610	11,484	5,875	25.7	22.1	19.9	16.7
2	Venezuela	11,479	8,696	8,385	4,612	14.2	13.1	14.6	13.1
3	Russia	5,260	5,760	4,132	2,582	6.5	8.7	7.2	7.3
4	Algeria	1,304	1,641	1,834	1,916	1.6	2.5	3.2	5.4
5	Brazil	1,683	1,432	2,437	1,842	2.1	2.2	4.2	5.2
6	Canada	1,663	1,921	2,069	1,505	2.1	2.9	3.6	4.3
7	Mexico	5,132	4,702	3,291	1,475	6.4	7.1	5.7	4.2
8	China	1,149	1,024	1,310	1,294	1.4	1.5	2.3	3.7
9	Kuwait	7,798	5,238	4,207	1,292	9.6	7.9	7.3	3.7
10	Colombia	2,283	2,841	1,930	1,183	2.8	4.3	3.4	3.4
11	Iraq	2,396	2,375	1,878	1,049	3.0	3.6	3.3	3.0
12	Germany	553	744	796	674	0.7	1.1	1.4	1.9
13	Korea, South	521	467	686	666	0.6	0.7	1.2	1.9
14	Chad	804	1,126	750	646	1.0	1.7	1.3	1.8
15	United Kingdom	876	874	745	547	1.1	1.3	1.3	1.6
16	Trinidad and Tobago	822	571	682	515	1.0	0.9	1.2	1.5
17	France	363	437	478	447	0.4	0.7	0.8	1.3
18	Angola	1,836	1,095	774	436	2.3	1.7	1.3	1.2
19	Indonesia	443	534	550	417	0.5	0.8	1.0	1.2
20	Belgium	1,231	1,141	1,222	396	1.5	1.7	2.1	1.1
21	Italy	262	203	471	351	0.3	0.3	0.8	1.0
22	Malaysia	653	436	425	327	0.8	0.7	0.7	0.9
23	Japan	289	366	405	302	0.4	0.6	0.7	0.9
24	Ecuador	4	337	904	290	0.0	0.5	1.6	0.8
25	Norway	611	943	391	272	0.8	1.4	0.7	0.8

Table E-20.   State Trade by Country: Maine, 2012–2015

(Top 25 countries based on 2015 dollar value. Value in millions of dollars.)

U.S. Exports by Origin State

Rank	Country	Value (Millions of dollars)				Percent of Share			
		2012	2013	2014	2015	2012	2013	2014	2015
	Total Maine Exports and % Share of U.S. Total	3,048	2,687	2,712	2,724	0.2	0.2	0.2	0.2
	Total, Top 25 Countries and % Share of State Total	2,868	2,486	2,493	2,546	94.1	92.5	91.9	93.5
1	Canada	1,324	1,370	1,479	1,268	43.4	51.0	54.5	46.5
2	Malaysia	468	103	105	208	15.4	3.8	3.9	7.6
3	China	247	223	184	208	8.1	8.3	6.8	7.6
4	Germany	50	57	55	104	1.6	2.1	2.0	3.8
5	Japan	126	121	98	82	4.1	4.5	3.6	3.0
6	Korea, South	61	77	61	79	2.0	2.9	2.2	2.9
7	Italy	33	60	52	70	1.1	2.2	1.9	2.6
8	Mexico	35	43	54	60	1.1	1.6	2.0	2.2
9	United Kingdom	58	56	59	55	1.9	2.1	2.2	2.0
10	Netherlands	57	57	64	52	1.9	2.1	2.4	1.9
11	Taiwan	19	18	19	47	0.6	0.7	0.7	1.7
12	Belgium	65	47	41	47	2.1	1.7	1.5	1.7
13	Singapore	48	34	25	33	1.6	1.3	0.9	1.2
14	Australia	41	37	36	30	1.3	1.4	1.3	1.1
15	Hong Kong	27	34	38	29	0.9	1.3	1.4	1.1
16	United Arab Emirates	22	3	3	27	0.7	0.1	0.1	1.0
17	Philippines	1	3	3	23	0.0	0.1	0.1	0.8
18	France	18	14	10	20	0.6	0.5	0.4	0.7
19	Brazil	24	26	30	18	0.8	1.0	1.1	0.7
20	Ireland	31	14	13	16	1.0	0.5	0.5	0.6
21	Finland	19	17	21	16	0.6	0.6	0.8	0.6
22	Turkey	60	41	5	16	2.0	1.5	0.2	0.6
23	India	14	16	14	15	0.5	0.6	0.5	0.6
24	Colombia	8	6	14	12	0.3	0.2	0.5	0.4
25	Israel	12	10	10	12	0.4	0.4	0.4	0.4

U.S. Imports by State of Final Destination

Rank	Country	Value (Millions of dollars)				Percent of Share			
		2012	2013	2014	2015	2012	2013	2014	2015
	Total Maine Imports and % Share of U.S. Total	3,776	3,541	3,861	3,673	0.2	0.2	0.2	0.2
	Total, Top 25 Countries and % Share of State Total	3,487	3,353	3,570	3,446	92.3	94.7	92.5	93.8
1	Canada	1,921	2,197	2,060	1,939	50.9	62.0	53.4	52.8
2	China	331	353	357	465	8.8	10.0	9.2	12.7
3	United Kingdom	122	85	84	109	3.2	2.4	2.2	3.0
4	Germany	427	115	107	90	11.3	3.2	2.8	2.5
5	Vietnam	47	42	62	84	1.2	1.2	1.6	2.3
6	Denmark	7	6	46	76	0.2	0.2	1.2	2.1
7	Mexico	62	57	72	74	1.6	1.6	1.9	2.0
8	Netherlands	87	31	154	70	2.3	0.9	4.0	1.9
9	Japan	54	47	65	61	1.4	1.3	1.7	1.7
10	Italy	34	42	50	60	0.9	1.2	1.3	1.6
11	Bangladesh	35	22	40	46	0.9	0.6	1.0	1.3
12	Belgium	16	9	56	38	0.4	0.3	1.5	1.0
13	Philippines	40	40	22	37	1.1	1.1	0.6	1.0
14	Thailand	55	46	45	36	1.5	1.3	1.2	1.0
15	Russia	35	37	84	34	0.9	1.0	2.2	0.9
16	Malaysia	42	42	57	30	1.1	1.2	1.5	0.8
17	Switzerland	8	10	7	26	0.2	0.3	0.2	0.7
18	Taiwan	22	24	22	25	0.6	0.7	0.6	0.7
19	Peru	19	38	40	23	0.5	1.1	1.0	0.6
20	Brazil	5	7	22	22	0.1	0.2	0.6	0.6
21	Austria	15	11	12	22	0.4	0.3	0.3	0.6
22	Chile	11	13	20	21	0.3	0.4	0.5	0.6
23	Korea, South	21	19	21	20	0.6	0.5	0.5	0.5
24	India	20	25	30	19	0.5	0.7	0.8	0.5
25	France	52	36	34	19	1.4	1.0	0.9	0.5

Table E-21.   State Trade by Country: Maryland, 2012–2015

(Top 25 countries based on 2015 dollar value. Value in millions of dollars.)

U.S. Exports by Origin State

Rank	Description	Value (Millions of dollars)				Percent of Share			
		2012	2013	2014	2015	2012	2013	2014	2015
	Total Maryland Exports and % Share of U.S. Total	11,745	11,745	12,233	10,030	0.8	0.7	0.8	0.7
	Total, Top 25 Countries and % Share of State Total	8,943	8,806	9,480	8,272	76.1	75.0	77.5	82.5
1	Canada	1,792	1,859	1,884	1,535	15.3	15.8	15.4	15.3
2	Saudi Arabia	858	999	915	788	7.3	8.5	7.5	7.9
3	United Kingdom	574	498	486	567	4.9	4.2	4.0	5.7
4	China	559	563	732	487	4.8	4.8	6.0	4.9
5	Mexico	345	494	462	442	2.9	4.2	3.8	4.4
6	Netherlands	331	304	424	437	2.8	2.6	3.5	4.4
7	Japan	465	458	440	398	4.0	3.9	3.6	4.0
8	Egypt	390	356	622	380	3.3	3.0	5.1	3.8
9	Germany	299	279	337	378	2.5	2.4	2.8	3.8
10	Belgium	465	311	450	341	4.0	2.6	3.7	3.4
11	Australia	335	210	465	248	2.9	1.8	3.8	2.5
12	India	291	203	226	235	2.5	1.7	1.8	2.3
13	France	277	268	231	227	2.4	2.3	1.9	2.3
14	Algeria	7	23	83	202	0.1	0.2	0.7	2.0
15	Korea, South	292	237	191	201	2.5	2.0	1.6	2.0
16	Brazil	308	379	301	190	2.6	3.2	2.5	1.9
17	United Arab Emirates	195	271	216	174	1.7	2.3	1.8	1.7
18	Singapore	189	177	178	156	1.6	1.5	1.5	1.6
19	Israel	51	114	101	145	0.4	1.0	0.8	1.4
20	Italy	240	157	137	138	2.0	1.3	1.1	1.4
21	Colombia	82	58	76	132	0.7	0.5	0.6	1.3
22	Kuwait	229	220	176	119	1.9	1.9	1.4	1.2
23	Taiwan	126	120	115	118	1.1	1.0	0.9	1.2
24	Pakistan	101	99	105	117	0.9	0.8	0.9	1.2
25	Chile	142	148	127	117	1.2	1.3	1.0	1.2

U.S. Imports by State of Final Destination

Rank	Description	Value (Millions of dollars)				Percent of Share			
		2012	2013	2014	2015	2012	2013	2014	2015
	Total Maryland Imports and % Share of U.S. Total	25,082	26,578	30,072	31,501	1.1	1.2	1.3	1.4
	Total, Top 25 Countries and % Share of State Total	21,767	23,137	26,116	28,115	86.8	87.1	86.8	89.3
1	Germany	5,071	5,596	5,873	5,350	20.2	21.1	19.5	17.0
2	China	2,878	2,842	3,127	3,396	11.5	10.7	10.4	10.8
3	United Kingdom	1,300	1,021	1,318	2,962	5.2	3.8	4.4	9.4
4	Mexico	1,740	2,213	2,462	2,819	6.9	8.3	8.2	8.9
5	Japan	1,186	1,603	2,206	2,181	4.7	6.0	7.3	6.9
6	Canada	1,970	2,054	2,103	1,990	7.9	7.7	7.0	6.3
7	Thailand	683	912	911	1,004	2.7	3.4	3.0	3.2
8	Brazil	891	746	1,043	917	3.6	2.8	3.5	2.9
9	Sweden	447	342	499	833	1.8	1.3	1.7	2.6
10	Italy	585	737	709	700	2.3	2.8	2.4	2.2
11	Russia	559	418	498	570	2.2	1.6	1.7	1.8
12	India	559	416	712	538	2.2	1.6	2.4	1.7
13	South Africa	880	956	473	533	3.5	3.6	1.6	1.7
14	Belgium	246	223	229	507	1.0	0.8	0.8	1.6
15	France	472	554	595	485	1.9	2.1	2.0	1.5
16	Finland	259	325	412	482	1.0	1.2	1.4	1.5
17	Indonesia	374	399	506	451	1.5	1.5	1.7	1.4
18	Hungary	42	171	446	366	0.2	0.6	1.5	1.2
19	Malaysia	260	202	285	333	1.0	0.8	0.9	1.1
20	Austria	226	261	278	326	0.9	1.0	0.9	1.0
21	Vietnam	195	255	321	314	0.8	1.0	1.1	1.0
22	Turkey	158	207	286	291	0.6	0.8	1.0	0.9
23	Chile	360	300	360	283	1.4	1.1	1.2	0.9
24	Netherlands	250	225	282	241	1.0	0.8	0.9	0.8
25	Korea, South	176	161	182	241	0.7	0.6	0.6	0.8

Table E-22.   State Trade by Country: Massachusetts, 2012–2015

(Top 25 countries based on 2015 dollar value. Value in millions of dollars.)

U.S. Exports by Origin State

Rank	Country	Value (Millions of dollars)				Percent of Share			
		2012	2013	2014	2015	2012	2013	2014	2015
	Total Massachusetts Exports and % Share of U.S. Total	25,614	26,808	27,383	25,206	1.7	1.7	1.7	1.7
	Total, Top 25 Countries and % Share of State Total	22,927	24,053	24,629	22,871	89.5	89.7	89.9	90.7
1	Canada	3,474	3,734	3,699	3,090	13.6	13.9	13.5	12.3
2	Mexico	1,609	1,859	2,317	2,622	6.3	6.9	8.5	10.4
3	China	1,877	1,977	2,291	2,049	7.3	7.4	8.4	8.1
4	Germany	1,803	1,836	1,850	1,911	7.0	6.8	6.8	7.6
5	Japan	1,993	1,762	1,850	1,476	7.8	6.6	6.8	5.9
6	Netherlands	1,077	1,290	1,329	1,399	4.2	4.8	4.9	5.6
7	United Kingdom	2,589	1,408	2,349	1,183	10.1	5.3	8.6	4.7
8	Switzerland	434	1,281	804	1,023	1.7	4.8	2.9	4.1
9	Korea, South	1,029	902	991	1,005	4.0	3.4	3.6	4.0
10	Hong Kong	709	1,762	963	929	2.8	6.6	3.5	3.7
11	Ireland	509	638	794	843	2.0	2.4	2.9	3.3
12	Taiwan	918	824	654	687	3.6	3.1	2.4	2.7
13	Belgium	716	801	599	578	2.8	3.0	2.2	2.3
14	France	666	647	604	576	2.6	2.4	2.2	2.3
15	Singapore	538	502	564	564	2.1	1.9	2.1	2.2
16	Italy	488	461	506	455	1.9	1.7	1.8	1.8
17	Sweden	141	119	364	395	0.6	0.4	1.3	1.6
18	Australia	395	363	351	348	1.5	1.4	1.3	1.4
19	India	294	298	303	289	1.1	1.1	1.1	1.1
20	Brazil	442	392	332	288	1.7	1.5	1.2	1.1
21	Saudi Arabia	133	201	220	264	0.5	0.7	0.8	1.0
22	Malaysia	326	304	265	250	1.3	1.1	1.0	1.0
23	Spain	264	261	206	235	1.0	1.0	0.8	0.9
24	Philippines	284	218	227	216	1.1	0.8	0.8	0.9
25	Israel	219	212	198	197	0.9	0.8	0.7	0.8

U.S. Imports by State of Final Destination

Rank	Country	Value (Millions of dollars)				Percent of Share			
		2012	2013	2014	2015	2012	2013	2014	2015
	Total Massachusetts Imports and % Share of U.S. Total	32,958	34,361	34,436	33,493	1.4	1.5	1.5	1.5
	Total, Top 25 Countries and % Share of State Total	29,884	31,468	31,215	30,530	90.7	91.6	90.6	91.2
1	Canada	7,652	8,680	8,581	7,637	23.2	25.3	24.9	22.8
2	China	4,611	4,627	4,406	4,396	14.0	13.5	12.8	13.1
3	Mexico	3,267	3,379	3,595	3,900	9.9	9.8	10.4	11.6
4	Germany	1,677	1,737	1,852	1,821	5.1	5.1	5.4	5.4
5	Ireland	1,264	1,669	1,603	1,760	3.8	4.9	4.7	5.3
6	United Kingdom	2,550	2,411	2,052	1,507	7.7	7.0	6.0	4.5
7	Japan	926	863	935	1,231	2.8	2.5	2.7	3.7
8	France	823	958	882	858	2.5	2.8	2.6	2.6
9	Switzerland	739	780	824	852	2.2	2.3	2.4	2.5
10	Netherlands	774	878	942	782	2.3	2.6	2.7	2.3
11	Italy	631	647	680	691	1.9	1.9	2.0	2.1
12	Taiwan	584	594	620	659	1.8	1.7	1.8	2.0
13	Malaysia	496	458	491	510	1.5	1.3	1.4	1.5
14	Israel	245	292	338	424	0.7	0.8	1.0	1.3
15	Vietnam	262	238	268	390	0.8	0.7	0.8	1.2
16	Philippines	491	422	368	383	1.5	1.2	1.1	1.1
17	Singapore	341	291	335	380	1.0	0.8	1.0	1.1
18	Korea, South	333	365	413	376	1.0	1.1	1.2	1.1
19	Thailand	387	328	305	365	1.2	1.0	0.9	1.1
20	Colombia	746	760	563	354	2.3	2.2	1.6	1.1
21	Indonesia	285	258	288	344	0.9	0.8	0.8	1.0
22	India	257	279	303	297	0.8	0.8	0.9	0.9
23	Belgium	191	171	200	225	0.6	0.5	0.6	0.7
24	Norway	143	190	155	198	0.4	0.6	0.5	0.6
25	Sweden	210	192	219	192	0.6	0.6	0.6	0.6

Table E-23.   State Trade by Country: Michigan, 2012–2015

(Top 25 countries based on 2015 dollar value. Value in millions of dollars.)

U.S. Exports by Origin State

Rank	Country	Value (Millions of dollars)				Percent of Share			
		2012	2013	2014	2015	2012	2013	2014	2015
	Total Michigan Exports and % Share of U.S. Total	57,051	58,652	55,929	53,171	3.7	3.7	3.5	3.5
	Total, Top 25 Countries and % Share of State Total	52,703	55,169	52,718	50,433	92.4	94.1	94.3	94.9
1	Canada	25,486	26,175	25,674	23,356	44.7	44.6	45.9	43.9
2	Mexico	10,464	12,171	10,828	11,138	18.3	20.8	19.4	20.9
3	China	3,267	4,136	3,404	3,213	5.7	7.1	6.1	6
4	Germany	1,985	1,653	1,865	1,920	3.5	2.8	3.3	3.6
5	Japan	1,374	1,395	1,372	1,218	2.4	2.4	2.5	2.3
6	Korea, South	939	1,093	1,057	1,070	1.6	1.9	1.9	2
7	Italy	359	597	689	1,058	0.6	1	1.2	2
8	Australia	879	1,092	1,070	889	1.5	1.9	1.9	1.7
9	Brazil	693	776	715	822	1.2	1.3	1.3	1.5
10	United Kingdom	709	732	747	777	1.2	1.2	1.3	1.5
11	Belgium	712	811	664	687	1.2	1.4	1.2	1.3
12	United Arab Emirates	753	511	590	464	1.3	0.9	1.1	0.9
13	France	632	444	448	458	1.1	0.8	0.8	0.9
14	Thailand	301	377	350	392	0.5	0.6	0.6	0.7
15	Saudi Arabia	1,793	775	492	379	3.1	1.3	0.9	0.7
16	Netherlands	333	308	357	335	0.6	0.5	0.6	0.6
17	Spain	150	187	218	331	0.3	0.3	0.4	0.6
18	India	220	262	297	315	0.4	0.4	0.5	0.6
19	Argentina	135	265	382	280	0.2	0.5	0.7	0.5
20	South Africa	213	229	218	251	0.4	0.4	0.4	0.5
21	Taiwan	185	191	247	250	0.3	0.3	0.4	0.5
22	Chile	331	319	273	247	0.6	0.5	0.5	0.5
23	Switzerland	230	247	230	201	0.4	0.4	0.4	0.4
24	Hong Kong	229	232	317	200	0.4	0.4	0.6	0.4
25	Singapore	330	190	215	183	0.6	0.3	0.4	0.3

U.S. Imports by State of Final Destination

Rank	Country	Value (Millions of dollars)				Percent of Share			
		2012	2013	2014	2015	2012	2013	2014	2015
	Total Michigan Imports and % Share of U.S. Total	116,220	118,151	122,739	124,088	5.1	5.2	5.2	5.5
	Total, Top 25 Countries and % Share of State Total	113,628	115,069	119,835	121,226	97.8	97.4	97.6	97.7
1	Canada	49,527	48,696	49,025	45,703	42.6	41.2	39.9	36.8
2	Mexico	38,142	40,256	42,478	43,871	32.8	34.1	34.6	35.4
3	China	6,753	7,575	8,140	9,180	5.8	6.4	6.6	7.4
4	Germany	3,832	4,217	4,708	4,417	3.3	3.6	3.8	3.6
5	Italy	932	1,052	1,358	3,437	0.8	0.9	1.1	2.8
6	Japan	5,062	3,241	3,174	2,914	4.4	2.7	2.6	2.3
7	Korea, South	1,881	2,306	2,508	2,596	1.6	2	2	2.1
8	Spain	248	365	1,208	1,151	0.2	0.3	1	0.9
9	India	936	1,132	998	935	0.8	1	0.8	0.8
10	Taiwan	648	705	807	860	0.6	0.6	0.7	0.7
11	Thailand	664	571	749	743	0.6	0.5	0.6	0.6
12	United Kingdom	749	661	704	717	0.6	0.6	0.6	0.6
13	Malaysia	286	315	325	558	0.2	0.3	0.3	0.4
14	France	467	568	546	509	0.4	0.5	0.4	0.4
15	Brazil	661	552	561	492	0.6	0.5	0.5	0.4
16	Turkey	630	628	159	490	0.5	0.5	0.1	0.4
17	Sweden	402	356	345	393	0.3	0.3	0.3	0.3
18	Israel	405	379	346	377	0.3	0.3	0.3	0.3
19	Austria	366	311	338	368	0.3	0.3	0.3	0.3
20	Vietnam	103	144	205	351	0.1	0.1	0.2	0.3
21	Australia	189	185	258	288	0.2	0.2	0.2	0.2
22	Netherlands	203	227	243	230	0.2	0.2	0.2	0.2
23	Poland	129	131	195	216	0.1	0.1	0.2	0.2
24	Hungary	236	262	267	215	0.2	0.2	0.2	0.2
25	Switzerland	175	236	191	215	0.2	0.2	0.2	0.2

Table E-24.   State Trade by Country: Minnesota, 2012–2015

(Top 25 countries based on 2015 dollar value. Value in millions of dollars.)

U.S. Exports by Origin State

Rank	Country	Value (Millions of dollars)				Percent of Share			
		2012	2013	2014	2015	2012	2013	2014	2015
	Total Minnesota Exports and % Share of U.S. Total	20,827	20,760	21,408	19,988	1.3	1.3	1.3	1.3
	Total, Top 25 Countries and % Share of State Total	18,559	18,395	19,138	17,820	89.1	88.6	89.4	89.2
1	Canada	6,287	5,811	5,612	4,424	30.2	28.0	26.2	22.1
2	Mexico	1,296	1,473	2,240	2,381	6.2	7.1	10.5	11.9
3	China	2,028	1,964	1,801	1,804	9.7	9.5	8.4	9.0
4	Japan	1,180	1,081	1,217	1,116	5.7	5.2	5.7	5.6
5	Germany	728	761	746	837	3.5	3.7	3.5	4.2
6	Belgium	641	721	893	824	3.1	3.5	4.2	4.1
7	Korea, South	707	624	711	770	3.4	3.0	3.3	3.9
8	United Kingdom	511	529	529	534	2.5	2.5	2.5	2.7
9	Singapore	484	493	531	512	2.3	2.4	2.5	2.6
10	Philippines	496	552	571	472	2.4	2.7	2.7	2.4
11	Australia	479	457	466	456	2.3	2.2	2.2	2.3
12	Taiwan	489	406	406	420	2.3	2.0	1.9	2.1
13	Hong Kong	450	485	429	398	2.2	2.3	2.0	2.0
14	Ireland	336	351	411	390	1.6	1.7	1.9	2.0
15	Netherlands	444	518	322	343	2.1	2.5	1.5	1.7
16	France	353	393	354	337	1.7	1.9	1.7	1.7
17	Brazil	340	375	321	280	1.6	1.8	1.5	1.4
18	Thailand	273	272	259	256	1.3	1.3	1.2	1.3
19	India	204	189	322	215	1.0	0.9	1.5	1.1
20	Switzerland	159	215	204	210	0.8	1.0	1.0	1.1
21	Italy	243	253	228	206	1.2	1.2	1.1	1.0
22	Indonesia	84	135	171	169	0.4	0.7	0.8	0.8
23	Saudi Arabia	94	130	117	162	0.5	0.6	0.5	0.8
24	Malaysia	149	131	150	157	0.7	0.6	0.7	0.8
25	New Zealand	103	75	128	148	0.5	0.4	0.6	0.7

U.S. Imports by State of Final Destination

Rank	Country	Value (Millions of dollars)				Percent of Share			
		2012	2013	2014	2015	2012	2013	2014	2015
	Total Minnesota Imports and % Share of U.S. Total	32,871	33,022	34,693	28,576	1.4	1.5	1.5	1.3
	Total, Top 25 Countries and % Share of State Total	31,541	31,539	33,125	27,205	96.0	95.5	95.5	95.2
1	China	10,315	9,947	10,385	9,987	31.4	30.1	29.9	34.9
2	Canada	13,228	13,369	13,919	8,678	40.2	40.5	40.1	30.4
3	Mexico	2,119	1,963	2,138	2,002	6.4	5.9	6.2	7.0
4	Germany	851	953	1,076	946	2.6	2.9	3.1	3.3
5	Ireland	912	921	1,126	816	2.8	2.8	3.2	2.9
6	Taiwan	611	631	682	689	1.9	1.9	2.0	2.4
7	Brazil	353	204	114	635	1.1	0.6	0.3	2.2
8	Japan	505	471	447	397	1.5	1.4	1.3	1.4
9	Italy	384	423	468	391	1.2	1.3	1.3	1.4
10	United Kingdom	368	364	366	358	1.1	1.1	1.1	1.3
11	France	198	389	272	315	0.6	1.2	0.8	1.1
12	Malaysia	209	212	235	242	0.6	0.6	0.7	0.8
13	India	206	196	197	215	0.6	0.6	0.6	0.8
14	Korea, South	176	167	171	183	0.5	0.5	0.5	0.6
15	Switzerland	172	171	161	170	0.5	0.5	0.5	0.6
16	Costa Rica	65	151	127	155	0.2	0.5	0.4	0.5
17	Thailand	158	167	172	152	0.5	0.5	0.5	0.5
18	Vietnam	92	120	158	145	0.3	0.4	0.5	0.5
19	Denmark	87	104	131	126	0.3	0.3	0.4	0.4
20	Israel	126	155	195	110	0.4	0.5	0.6	0.4
21	Turkey	38	75	82	103	0.1	0.2	0.2	0.4
22	Sweden	166	149	149	100	0.5	0.5	0.4	0.3
23	Trinidad and Tobago	0	26	140	97	0.0	0.1	0.4	0.3
24	Peru	62	117	128	96	0.2	0.4	0.4	0.3
25	Netherlands	142	93	87	95	0.4	0.3	0.3	0.3

Table E-25.   State Trade by Country: Mississippi, 2012–2015

(Top 25 countries based on 2015 dollar value. Value in millions of dollars.)

U.S. Exports by Origin State

Rank	Country	Value (Millions of dollars)				Percent of Share			
		2012	2013	2014	2015	2012	2013	2014	2015
	Total Mississippi Exports and % Share of U.S. Total	11,794	12,398	11,450	10,786	0.8	0.8	0.7	0.7
	Total, Top 25 Countries and % Share of State Total	9,960	10,569	10,028	9,489	84.4	85.2	87.6	88.0
1	Canada	1,961	2,011	1,830	2,042	16.6	16.2	16.0	18.9
2	Mexico	1,166	1,301	1,225	1,129	9.9	10.5	10.7	10.5
3	Panama	2,159	2,050	1,479	1,107	18.3	16.5	12.9	10.3
4	Guatemala	307	219	360	538	2.6	1.8	3.1	5.0
5	China	863	670	644	517	7.3	5.4	5.6	4.8
6	Honduras	413	289	532	378	3.5	2.3	4.6	3.5
7	Belgium	333	344	330	335	2.8	2.8	2.9	3.1
8	Gibraltar	64	0	357	334	0.5	0.0	3.1	3.1
9	Japan	214	223	300	314	1.8	1.8	2.6	2.9
10	Netherlands	247	483	308	283	2.1	3.9	2.7	2.6
11	Germany	173	197	215	283	1.5	1.6	1.9	2.6
12	Peru	366	419	451	268	3.1	3.4	3.9	2.5
13	Colombia	277	313	200	227	2.3	2.5	1.7	2.1
14	United Arab Emirates	101	146	129	226	0.9	1.2	1.1	2.1
15	El Salvador	87	128	93	198	0.7	1.0	0.8	1.8
16	Brazil	348	481	445	183	3.0	3.9	3.9	1.7
17	United Kingdom	205	207	216	169	1.7	1.7	1.9	1.6
18	Trinidad and Tobago	7	8	9	152	0.1	0.1	0.1	1.4
19	Saudi Arabia	89	122	102	145	0.8	1.0	0.9	1.3
20	Korea, South	152	155	125	136	1.3	1.3	1.1	1.3
21	Australia	67	146	120	134	0.6	1.2	1.0	1.2
22	Singapore	137	348	127	123	1.2	2.8	1.1	1.1
23	Chile	92	99	202	106	0.8	0.8	1.8	1.0
24	India	44	58	69	85	0.4	0.5	0.6	0.8
25	Turkey	88	152	159	77	0.7	1.2	1.4	0.7

U.S. Imports by State of Final Destination

Rank	Country	Value (Millions of dollars)				Percent of Share			
		2012	2013	2014	2015	2012	2013	2014	2015
	Total Mississippi Imports and % Share of U.S. Total	20,666	20,003	17,254	14,063	0.9	0.9	0.7	0.6
	Total, Top 25 Countries and % Share of State Total	18,789	18,643	16,054	12,941	90.9	93.2	93.0	92.0
1	China	3,269	3,418	3,225	3,909	15.8	17.1	18.7	27.8
2	Mexico	4,530	4,874	2,792	1,411	21.9	24.4	16.2	10.0
3	Venezuela	2,596	2,300	2,170	1,220	12.6	11.5	12.6	8.7
4	Canada	906	1,159	1,336	1,079	4.4	5.8	7.7	7.7
5	Japan	752	895	922	834	3.6	4.5	5.3	5.9
6	Germany	564	550	644	662	2.7	2.7	3.7	4.7
7	Colombia	974	991	631	405	4.7	5.0	3.7	2.9
8	United Kingdom	819	903	616	359	4.0	4.5	3.6	2.6
9	Brazil	1,848	943	959	310	8.9	4.7	5.6	2.2
10	Vietnam	116	169	212	292	0.6	0.8	1.2	2.1
11	Malaysia	160	182	163	251	0.8	0.9	0.9	1.8
12	Taiwan	214	219	198	237	1.0	1.1	1.1	1.7
13	India	296	296	193	213	1.4	1.5	1.1	1.5
14	Russia	98	106	440	199	0.5	0.5	2.6	1.4
15	Italy	80	124	220	186	0.4	0.6	1.3	1.3
16	Bangladesh	84	135	144	186	0.4	0.7	0.8	1.3
17	Nigeria	676	653	236	168	3.3	3.3	1.4	1.2
18	Belgium	9	17	128	154	0.0	0.1	0.7	1.1
19	France	167	181	243	147	0.8	0.9	1.4	1.0
20	Honduras	116	136	143	142	0.6	0.7	0.8	1.0
21	Korea, South	106	114	122	139	0.5	0.6	0.7	1.0
22	Netherlands	154	105	117	133	0.7	0.5	0.7	0.9
23	Norway	11	24	10	125	0.1	0.1	0.1	0.9
24	Philippines	97	132	81	90	0.5	0.7	0.5	0.6
25	Australia	150	18	107	89	0.7	0.1	0.6	0.6

Table E-26.   State Trade by Country: Missouri, 2012–2015

(Top 25 countries based on 2015 dollar value. Value in millions of dollars.)

U.S. Exports by Origin State

Rank	Country	Value (Millions of dollars)				Percent of Share			
		2012	2013	2014	2015	2012	2013	2014	2015
	Total Missouri Exports and % Share of U.S. Total	13,903	12,930	14,141	13,617	0.9	0.8	0.9	0.9
	Total, Top 25 Countries and % Share of State Total	12,127	11,296	12,668	12,353	87.2	87.4	89.6	90.7
1	Canada	4,154	3,966	4,725	4,496	29.9	30.7	33.4	33.0
2	Mexico	1,822	2,005	2,347	2,475	13.1	15.5	16.6	18.2
3	China	1,141	850	872	870	8.2	6.6	6.2	6.4
4	Japan	651	610	611	508	4.7	4.7	4.3	3.7
5	Germany	257	328	406	485	1.8	2.5	2.9	3.6
6	Belgium	396	427	419	481	2.8	3.3	3.0	3.5
7	Korea, South	709	456	474	436	5.1	3.5	3.4	3.2
8	United Kingdom	351	322	357	364	2.5	2.5	2.5	2.7
9	Brazil	318	271	296	295	2.3	2.1	2.1	2.2
10	Australia	274	244	205	220	2.0	1.9	1.4	1.6
11	Ireland	52	58	163	203	0.4	0.4	1.2	1.5
12	Singapore	250	252	260	187	1.8	1.9	1.8	1.4
13	Saudi Arabia	289	234	219	158	2.1	1.8	1.5	1.2
14	France	225	196	171	142	1.6	1.5	1.2	1.0
15	Netherlands	306	180	187	137	2.2	1.4	1.3	1.0
16	Italy	212	172	131	123	1.5	1.3	0.9	0.9
17	India	132	157	165	122	0.9	1.2	1.2	0.9
18	Thailand	99	112	128	114	0.7	0.9	0.9	0.8
19	Taiwan	99	91	96	90	0.7	0.7	0.7	0.7
20	Switzerland	27	30	80	83	0.2	0.2	0.6	0.6
21	Hong Kong	152	115	115	80	1.1	0.9	0.8	0.6
22	United Arab Emirates	69	104	124	77	0.5	0.8	0.9	0.6
23	Egypt	19	19	22	75	0.1	0.1	0.2	0.6
24	Argentina	91	69	47	68	0.7	0.5	0.3	0.5
25	Vietnam	32	27	48	64	0.2	0.2	0.3	0.5

U.S. Imports by State of Final Destination

Rank	Country	Value (Millions of dollars)				Percent of Share			
		2012	2013	2014	2015	2012	2013	2014	2015
	Total Missouri Imports and % Share of U.S. Total	16,502	18,515	18,284	18,444	0.7	0.8	0.8	0.8
	Total, Top 25 Countries and % Share of State Total	15,533	17,537	17,242	17,464	94.1	94.7	94.3	94.7
1	China	4,086	4,532	4,554	4,796	24.8	24.5	24.9	26.0
2	Canada	3,198	4,066	3,312	3,389	19.4	22.0	18.1	18.4
3	Mexico	2,626	2,868	3,273	3,204	15.9	15.5	17.9	17.4
4	Germany	1,022	1,271	1,252	1,265	6.2	6.9	6.8	6.9
5	United Arab Emirates	461	554	619	603	2.8	3.0	3.4	3.3
6	Belgium	302	338	392	443	1.8	1.8	2.1	2.4
7	India	353	351	437	394	2.1	1.9	2.4	2.1
8	Taiwan	342	356	356	390	2.1	1.9	1.9	2.1
9	United Kingdom	354	411	355	338	2.1	2.2	1.9	1.8
10	Japan	350	366	376	287	2.1	2.0	2.1	1.6
11	France	388	239	232	277	2.4	1.3	1.3	1.5
12	Italy	237	250	280	258	1.4	1.4	1.5	1.4
13	Korea, South	199	205	214	228	1.2	1.1	1.2	1.2
14	Philippines	93	86	86	182	0.6	0.5	0.5	1.0
15	Chile	218	217	235	180	1.3	1.2	1.3	1.0
16	Netherlands	120	116	166	162	0.7	0.6	0.9	0.9
17	Israel	342	277	228	161	2.1	1.5	1.2	0.9
18	Switzerland	171	235	126	157	1.0	1.3	0.7	0.9
19	Finland	96	112	126	138	0.6	0.6	0.7	0.7
20	Vietnam	103	108	87	125	0.6	0.6	0.5	0.7
21	Turkey	49	66	90	116	0.3	0.4	0.5	0.6
22	Brazil	136	140	120	113	0.8	0.8	0.7	0.6
23	Thailand	111	99	79	100	0.7	0.5	0.4	0.5
24	Ireland	89	48	91	81	0.5	0.3	0.5	0.4
25	Spain	90	227	157	79	0.5	1.2	0.9	0.4

Table E-27.   State Trade by Country: Montana, 2012–2015

(Top 25 countries based on 2015 dollar value. Value in millions of dollars.)

U.S. Exports by Origin State

Rank	Country	Value (Millions of dollars)				Percent of Share			
		2012	2013	2014	2015	2012	2013	2014	2015
	Total Montana Exports and % Share of U.S. Total	1,576	1,506	1,545	1,386	0.1	0.1	0.1	0.1
	Total, Top 25 Countries and % Share of State Total	1,401	1,348	1,356	1,290	88.9	89.5	87.8	93.1
1	Canada	638	596	564	504	40.5	39.6	36.5	36.4
2	Korea, South	173	168	205	171	11.0	11.2	13.3	12.3
3	China	105	93	106	134	6.7	6.2	6.9	9.7
4	Japan	44	49	62	77	2.8	3.3	4.0	5.6
5	Belgium	83	65	44	41	5.3	4.3	2.8	3.0
6	Mexico	53	56	93	41	3.4	3.7	6.0	3.0
7	India	29	31	42	35	1.8	2.1	2.7	2.5
8	Taiwan	74	74	44	35	4.7	4.9	2.8	2.5
9	Germany	38	27	23	31	2.4	1.8	1.5	2.2
10	Netherlands	17	25	28	29	1.1	1.7	1.8	2.1
11	Singapore	11	20	21	26	0.7	1.3	1.4	1.9
12	United Kingdom	20	21	22	24	1.3	1.4	1.4	1.7
13	Italy	9	17	11	18	0.6	1.1	0.7	1.3
14	Malaysia	13	11	19	17	0.8	0.7	1.2	1.2
15	Philippines	29	11	8	14	1.8	0.7	0.5	1.0
16	France	5	7	7	14	0.3	0.5	0.5	1.0
17	Peru	4	15	7	13	0.3	1.0	0.5	0.9
18	Saudi Arabia	2	6	3	9	0.1	0.4	0.2	0.6
19	Ethiopia	0	0	0	9	0.0	0.0	0.0	0.6
20	United Arab Emirates	2	6	3	9	0.1	0.4	0.2	0.6
21	Hong Kong	4	5	7	8	0.3	0.3	0.5	0.6
22	Australia	21	16	12	8	1.3	1.1	0.8	0.6
23	Sweden	12	14	10	8	0.8	0.9	0.6	0.6
24	Colombia	3	4	5	8	0.2	0.3	0.3	0.6
25	Chile	11	9	9	7	0.7	0.6	0.6	0.5

U.S. Imports by State of Final Destination

Rank	Country	Value (Millions of dollars)				Percent of Share			
		2012	2013	2014	2015	2012	2013	2014	2015
	Total Montana Imports and % Share of U.S. Total	5,593	5,741	6,237	4,067	0.2	0.3	0.3	0.2
	Total, Top 25 Countries and % Share of State Total	5,534	5,729	6,223	4,054	98.9	99.8	99.8	99.7
1	Canada	5,168	5,216	5,556	3,511	92.4	90.9	89.1	86.3
2	Germany	125	178	196	152	2.2	3.1	3.1	3.7
3	Mexico	17	73	100	100	0.3	1.3	1.6	2.5
4	China	106	118	136	92	1.9	2.1	2.2	2.3
5	United Kingdom	21	31	33	51	0.4	0.5	0.5	1.3
6	Italy	11	10	60	29	0.2	0.2	1.0	0.7
7	Taiwan	10	14	15	23	0.2	0.2	0.2	0.6
8	India	8	9	67	22	0.1	0.2	1.1	0.5
9	France	13	29	13	13	0.2	0.5	0.2	0.3
10	Korea, South	16	17	7	12	0.3	0.3	0.1	0.3
11	Philippines	3	0	7	12	0.1	0.0	0.1	0.3
12	Japan	10	6	9	11	0.2	0.1	0.1	0.3
13	Colombia	0	0	0	5	0.0	0.0	0.0	0.1
14	Belgium	3	2	2	4	0.1	0.0	0.0	0.1
15	Netherlands	5	2	4	3	0.1	0.0	0.1	0.1
16	Australia	3	4	5	3	0.1	0.1	0.1	0.1
17	Vietnam	0	1	2	2	0.0	0.0	0.0	0.0
18	Lithuania	2	2	3	2	0.0	0.0	0.0	0.0
19	Finland	2	0	1	2	0.0	0.0	0.0	0.0
20	Thailand	2	1	2	2	0.0	0.0	0.0	0.0
21	Sweden	2	9	2	2	0.0	0.2	0.0	0.0
22	Switzerland	2	1	2	1	0.0	0.0	0.0	0.0
23	Austria	2	3	0	1	0.0	0.1	0.0	0.0
24	Israel	2	0	2	1	0.0	0.0	0.0	0.0
25	Norway	0	0	0	1	0.0	0.0	0.0	0.0

Table E-28.   State Trade by Country: Nebraska, 2012–2015

(Top 25 countries based on 2015 dollar value. Value in millions of dollars.)

U.S. Exports by Origin State

Rank	Country	Value (Millions of dollars)				Percent of Share			
		2012	2013	2014	2015	2012	2013	2014	2015
	Total Nebraska Exports and % Share of U.S. Total	7,455	7,390	7,863	6,556	0.5	0.5	0.5	0.4
	Total, Top 25 Countries and % Share of State Total	6,677	6,684	7,171	6,040	89.6	90.4	91.2	92.1
1	Canada	1,904	2,174	2,173	1,463	25.5	29.4	27.6	22.3
2	Mexico	1,806	1,154	1,349	1,257	24.2	15.6	17.2	19.2
3	Japan	469	566	733	792	6.3	7.7	9.3	12.1
4	China	487	588	610	493	6.5	8.0	7.8	7.5
5	Korea, South	320	295	357	350	4.3	4.0	4.5	5.3
6	Hong Kong	155	244	302	234	2.1	3.3	3.8	3.6
7	Netherlands	183	215	169	204	2.5	2.9	2.1	3.1
8	Australia	263	237	200	182	3.5	3.2	2.5	2.8
9	Germany	147	145	154	165	2.0	2.0	2.0	2.5
10	Belgium	97	99	101	93	1.3	1.3	1.3	1.4
11	Taiwan	95	102	120	87	1.3	1.4	1.5	1.3
12	Brazil	80	127	165	85	1.1	1.7	2.1	1.3
13	France	74	112	102	81	1.0	1.5	1.3	1.2
14	Italy	102	114	115	74	1.4	1.5	1.5	1.1
15	New Zealand	55	57	55	57	0.7	0.8	0.7	0.9
16	Singapore	37	51	76	55	0.5	0.7	1.0	0.8
17	Vietnam	55	60	58	54	0.7	0.8	0.7	0.8
18	South Africa	62	55	46	44	0.8	0.7	0.6	0.7
19	United Kingdom	62	52	42	43	0.8	0.7	0.5	0.7
20	Spain	45	53	61	42	0.6	0.7	0.8	0.6
21	Thailand	49	67	38	42	0.7	0.9	0.5	0.6
22	Portugal	2	8	42	39	0.0	0.1	0.5	0.6
23	Dominican Republic	22	21	33	37	0.3	0.3	0.4	0.6
24	Israel	34	33	28	36	0.5	0.4	0.4	0.5
25	Argentina	73	56	43	33	1.0	0.8	0.5	0.5

U.S. Imports by State of Final Destination

Rank	Country	Value (Millions of dollars)				Percent of Share			
		2012	2013	2014	2015	2012	2013	2014	2015
	Total Nebraska Imports and % Share of U.S. Total	3,576	3,703	4,050	4,130	0.2	0.2	0.2	0.2
	Total, Top 25 Countries and % Share of State Total	3,405	3,492	3,870	3,965	95.2	94.3	95.6	96.0
1	China	919	838	928	1,021	25.7	22.6	22.9	24.7
2	Canada	873	1,011	1,164	948	24.4	27.3	28.7	23.0
3	Germany	337	370	335	321	9.4	10.0	8.3	7.8
4	Mexico	182	197	274	295	5.1	5.3	6.8	7.1
5	Japan	247	249	263	288	6.9	6.7	6.5	7.0
6	United Kingdom	47	33	52	174	1.3	0.9	1.3	4.2
7	Austria	63	68	69	141	1.8	1.8	1.7	3.4
8	France	160	86	124	102	4.5	2.3	3.1	2.5
9	Brazil	42	21	113	86	1.2	0.6	2.8	2.1
10	Italy	113	186	110	84	3.2	5.0	2.7	2.0
11	Taiwan	61	68	65	74	1.7	1.8	1.6	1.8
12	Switzerland	11	10	8	66	0.3	0.3	0.2	1.6
13	Thailand	47	48	70	62	1.3	1.3	1.7	1.5
14	India	32	32	26	50	0.9	0.9	0.6	1.2
15	Korea, South	29	29	40	42	0.8	0.8	1.0	1.0
16	Vietnam	42	38	37	41	1.2	1.0	0.9	1.0
17	Ireland	70	59	53	39	2.0	1.6	1.3	0.9
18	Spain	11	11	8	20	0.3	0.3	0.2	0.5
19	Czech Republic	12	16	20	20	0.3	0.4	0.5	0.5
20	Sweden	31	34	32	19	0.9	0.9	0.8	0.5
21	Belgium	43	50	34	17	1.2	1.4	0.8	0.4
22	Philippines	8	8	8	16	0.2	0.2	0.2	0.4
23	Poland	12	12	10	14	0.3	0.3	0.2	0.3
24	Hungary	11	10	16	14	0.3	0.3	0.4	0.3
25	Indonesia	5	10	12	12	0.1	0.3	0.3	0.3

Table E-29.   State Trade by Country: Nevada, 2012–2015

(Top 25 countries based on 2015 dollar value. Value in millions of dollars.)

U.S. Exports by Origin State

Rank	Country	Value (Millions of dollars)				Percent of Share			
		2012	2013	2014	2015	2012	2013	2014	2015
	Total Nevada Exports and % Share of U.S. Total	10,261	8,701	7,692	8,658	0.7	0.6	0.5	0.6
	Total, Top 25 Countries and % Share of State Total	9,711	8,142	7,126	8,126	94.6	93.6	92.6	93.9
1	Switzerland	3,777	2,710	2,372	2,426	36.8	31.1	30.8	28.0
2	India	1,830	1,354	568	1,721	17.8	15.6	7.4	19.9
3	Canada	1,422	1,220	1,254	1,280	13.9	14.0	16.3	14.8
4	Mexico	336	389	405	447	3.3	4.5	5.3	5.2
5	China	561	593	584	425	5.5	6.8	7.6	4.9
6	Hong Kong	159	203	237	270	1.5	2.3	3.1	3.1
7	Japan	216	243	245	157	2.1	2.8	3.2	1.8
8	Israel	129	94	117	142	1.3	1.1	1.5	1.6
9	United Kingdom	162	139	171	111	1.6	1.6	2.2	1.3
10	Australia	159	179	122	104	1.5	2.1	1.6	1.2
11	Malaysia	61	62	75	104	0.6	0.7	1.0	1.2
12	Belgium	91	151	121	102	0.9	1.7	1.6	1.2
13	Germany	116	125	123	96	1.1	1.4	1.6	1.1
14	Korea, South	117	159	97	91	1.1	1.8	1.3	1.1
15	Singapore	95	78	87	85	0.9	0.9	1.1	1.0
16	Netherlands	71	53	77	84	0.7	0.6	1.0	1.0
17	Brazil	50	50	77	65	0.5	0.6	1.0	0.8
18	France	73	69	97	61	0.7	0.8	1.3	0.7
19	Philippines	15	39	62	57	0.1	0.4	0.8	0.7
20	Italy	53	59	52	55	0.5	0.7	0.7	0.6
21	Argentina	64	41	41	51	0.6	0.5	0.5	0.6
22	South Africa	83	70	71	49	0.8	0.8	0.9	0.6
23	Vietnam	6	6	9	49	0.1	0.1	0.1	0.6
24	Macau	23	10	16	49	0.2	0.1	0.2	0.6
25	Taiwan	42	45	47	43	0.4	0.5	0.6	0.5

U.S. Imports by State of Final Destination

Rank	Country	Value (Millions of dollars)				Percent of Share			
		2012	2013	2014	2015	2012	2013	2014	2015
	Total Nevada Imports and % Share of U.S. Total	8,331	8,582	7,850	9,590	0.4	0.4	0.3	0.4
	Total, Top 25 Countries and % Share of State Total	7,628	8,059	7,428	9,201	91.6	93.9	94.6	95.9
1	China	2,750	3,489	3,259	4,567	33.0	40.7	41.5	47.6
2	Canada	767	744	783	777	9.2	8.7	10.0	8.1
3	Malaysia	420	244	336	549	5.0	2.8	4.3	5.7
4	Mexico	358	358	393	475	4.3	4.2	5.0	5.0
5	Taiwan	302	339	373	383	3.6	4.0	4.8	4.0
6	Israel	144	305	155	325	1.7	3.6	2.0	3.4
7	Korea, South	1,465	1,182	678	223	17.6	13.8	8.6	2.3
8	United Kingdom	130	112	146	222	1.6	1.3	1.9	2.3
9	India	101	115	169	221	1.2	1.3	2.2	2.3
10	Philippines	191	205	149	213	2.3	2.4	1.9	2.2
11	France	120	113	111	197	1.4	1.3	1.4	2.1
12	Germany	134	168	156	144	1.6	2.0	2.0	1.5
13	Japan	94	95	94	119	1.1	1.1	1.2	1.2
14	Thailand	96	108	102	110	1.2	1.3	1.3	1.1
15	Vietnam	51	58	71	94	0.6	0.7	0.9	1.0
16	Belgium	66	24	83	93	0.8	0.3	1.1	1.0
17	Italy	62	66	80	84	0.7	0.8	1.0	0.9
18	Hong Kong	26	18	26	77	0.3	0.2	0.3	0.8
19	Switzerland	72	70	80	62	0.9	0.8	1.0	0.6
20	Indonesia	68	49	37	54	0.8	0.6	0.5	0.6
21	Cambodia	20	29	26	46	0.2	0.3	0.3	0.5
22	Australia	47	47	36	45	0.6	0.5	0.5	0.5
23	Bangladesh	17	19	26	44	0.2	0.2	0.3	0.5
24	Netherlands	30	36	33	38	0.4	0.4	0.4	0.4
25	Singapore	100	65	25	38	1.2	0.8	0.3	0.4

Table E-30.   State Trade by Country: New Hampshire, 2012–2015

(Top 25 countries based on 2015 dollar value. Value in millions of dollars.)

U.S. Exports by Origin State

Rank	Country	Value (Millions of dollars)				Percent of Share			
		2012	2013	2014	2015	2012	2013	2014	2015
	Total New Hampshire Exports and % Share of U.S. Total	3,488	3,511	4,227	4,007	0.2	0.2	0.3	0.3
	Total, Top 25 Countries and % Share of State Total	2,947	2,987	3,634	3,551	84.5	85.1	86.0	88.6
1	Canada	647	590	587	545	18.5	16.8	13.9	13.6
2	Mexico	474	409	449	503	13.6	11.6	10.6	12.6
3	China	273	266	299	282	7.8	7.6	7.1	7.0
4	United Arab Emirates	38	100	304	280	1.1	2.8	7.2	7.0
5	United Kingdom	143	144	201	265	4.1	4.1	4.8	6.6
6	Hong Kong	125	158	185	202	3.6	4.5	4.4	5.0
7	Germany	224	212	229	181	6.4	6.0	5.4	4.5
8	Netherlands	163	177	198	170	4.7	5.0	4.7	4.2
9	Ireland	14	19	50	148	0.4	0.5	1.2	3.7
10	France	102	108	123	122	2.9	3.1	2.9	3.0
11	Saudi Arabia	22	65	174	119	0.6	1.9	4.1	3.0
12	Japan	121	103	111	110	3.5	2.9	2.6	2.7
13	Italy	67	83	89	94	1.9	2.4	2.1	2.3
14	Australia	74	72	71	72	2.1	2.1	1.7	1.8
15	Singapore	55	69	66	68	1.6	2.0	1.6	1.7
16	Korea, South	71	56	68	61	2.0	1.6	1.6	1.5
17	Israel	30	37	44	48	0.9	1.1	1.0	1.2
18	Brazil	52	76	58	45	1.5	2.2	1.4	1.1
19	India	35	27	77	38	1.0	0.8	1.8	0.9
20	Spain	22	21	34	37	0.6	0.6	0.8	0.9
21	Malaysia	22	28	28	36	0.6	0.8	0.7	0.9
22	Norway	14	19	33	35	0.4	0.5	0.8	0.9
23	Sweden	33	34	26	32	0.9	1.0	0.6	0.8
24	Taiwan	35	35	43	30	1.0	1.0	1.0	0.7
25	Turkey	88	79	87	28	2.5	2.3	2.1	0.7

U.S. Imports by State of Final Destination

Rank	Country	Value (Millions of dollars)				Percent of Share			
		2012	2013	2014	2015	2012	2013	2014	2015
	Total New Hampshire Imports and % Share of U.S. Total	12,225	11,873	11,216	9,283	0.5	0.5	0.5	0.4
	Total, Top 25 Countries and % Share of State Total	11,718	11,518	10,743	8,766	95.9	97.0	95.8	94.4
1	Canada	8,047	7,950	6,919	4,898	65.8	67.0	61.7	52.8
2	China	888	932	1,106	1,143	7.3	7.8	9.9	12.3
3	Germany	458	523	516	524	3.7	4.4	4.6	5.6
4	Mexico	562	574	569	474	4.6	4.8	5.1	5.1
5	India	148	127	142	161	1.2	1.1	1.3	1.7
6	Ireland	114	143	123	147	0.9	1.2	1.1	1.6
7	Switzerland	143	126	117	128	1.2	1.1	1.0	1.4
8	Thailand	45	113	74	127	0.4	1.0	0.7	1.4
9	Japan	95	86	93	117	0.8	0.7	0.8	1.3
10	United Kingdom	184	150	136	104	1.5	1.3	1.2	1.1
11	Israel	83	91	70	100	0.7	0.8	0.6	1.1
12	Vietnam	37	47	96	99	0.3	0.4	0.9	1.1
13	Netherlands	258	67	70	99	2.1	0.6	0.6	1.1
14	Italy	77	80	131	89	0.6	0.7	1.2	1.0
15	Taiwan	218	126	90	86	1.8	1.1	0.8	0.9
16	France	115	103	97	71	0.9	0.9	0.9	0.8
17	Indonesia	49	49	52	60	0.4	0.4	0.5	0.6
18	Sweden	39	50	52	59	0.3	0.4	0.5	0.6
19	Russia	5	45	118	49	0.0	0.4	1.1	0.5
20	Belgium	15	8	9	49	0.1	0.1	0.1	0.5
21	Korea, South	48	52	52	48	0.4	0.4	0.5	0.5
22	Peru	13	22	19	35	0.1	0.2	0.2	0.4
23	Czech Republic	28	36	38	35	0.2	0.3	0.3	0.4
24	Portugal	46	15	23	33	0.4	0.1	0.2	0.4
25	Dominican Republic	4	3	30	31	0.0	0.0	0.3	0.3

Table E-31.   State Trade by Country: New Jersey, 2012–2015

(Top 25 countries based on 2015 dollar value. Value in millions of dollars.)

U.S. Exports by Origin State

Rank	Country	Value (Millions of dollars)				Percent of Share			
		2012	2013	2014	2015	2012	2013	2014	2015
	Total New Jersey Exports and % Share of U.S. Total	37,286	36,652	36,616	32,076	2.4	2.3	2.3	2.1
	Total, Top 25 Countries and % Share of State Total	29,297	30,313	30,803	27,680	78.6	82.7	84.1	86.3
1	Canada	6,935	6,793	6,961	6,564	18.6	18.5	19.0	20.5
2	Mexico	2,111	2,190	2,657	2,615	5.7	6.0	7.3	8.2
3	United Kingdom	1,849	2,089	2,061	2,129	5.0	5.7	5.6	6.6
4	China	1,424	1,580	1,425	1,546	3.8	4.3	3.9	4.8
5	Japan	1,622	1,604	1,696	1,365	4.4	4.4	4.6	4.3
6	Netherlands	2,088	2,098	1,881	1,324	5.6	5.7	5.1	4.1
7	Korea, South	1,076	1,149	1,432	1,221	2.9	3.1	3.9	3.8
8	Germany	1,325	1,233	1,211	1,099	3.6	3.4	3.3	3.4
9	France	740	867	1,140	1,056	2.0	2.4	3.1	3.3
10	Hong Kong	753	847	1,217	1,002	2.0	2.3	3.3	3.1
11	United Arab Emirates	728	929	1,016	875	2.0	2.5	2.8	2.7
12	Saudi Arabia	504	549	1,111	848	1.4	1.5	3.0	2.6
13	Israel	804	861	741	776	2.2	2.3	2.0	2.4
14	Belgium	1,165	1,191	851	772	3.1	3.2	2.3	2.4
15	India	504	452	540	630	1.4	1.2	1.5	2.0
16	Singapore	679	629	700	599	1.8	1.7	1.9	1.9
17	Brazil	1,388	732	649	514	3.7	2.0	1.8	1.6
18	Taiwan	537	520	476	491	1.4	1.4	1.3	1.5
19	Italy	567	638	793	490	1.5	1.7	2.2	1.5
20	Australia	447	527	520	458	1.2	1.4	1.4	1.4
21	Turkey	802	803	688	397	2.2	2.2	1.9	1.2
22	Switzerland	461	1,249	459	294	1.2	3.4	1.3	0.9
23	Venezuela	391	279	192	231	1.0	0.8	0.5	0.7
24	Ireland	160	198	174	200	0.4	0.5	0.5	0.6
25	Chile	239	305	212	181	0.6	0.8	0.6	0.6

U.S. Imports by State of Final Destination

Rank	Country	Value (Millions of dollars)				Percent of Share			
		2012	2013	2014	2015	2012	2013	2014	2015
	Total New Jersey Imports and % Share of U.S. Total	120,863	119,294	126,365	119,490	5.3	5.3	5.4	5.3
	Total, Top 25 Countries and % Share of State Total	94,445	96,990	103,684	100,676	78.1	81.3	82.1	84.3
1	China	16,617	16,773	18,112	18,579	13.7	14.1	14.3	15.5
2	Japan	9,285	10,314	9,722	10,527	7.7	8.6	7.7	8.8
3	Canada	9,444	9,073	9,805	7,798	7.8	7.6	7.8	6.5
4	Germany	7,083	7,086	7,536	7,197	5.9	5.9	6.0	6.0
5	Switzerland	5,341	4,730	5,520	7,188	4.4	4.0	4.4	6.0
6	India	5,111	5,705	6,426	6,292	4.2	4.8	5.1	5.3
7	Italy	4,863	5,719	6,628	5,890	4.0	4.8	5.2	4.9
8	Mexico	2,758	3,481	4,816	4,803	2.3	2.9	3.8	4.0
9	Korea, South	2,736	2,782	3,142	4,136	2.3	2.3	2.5	3.5
10	United Kingdom	5,751	7,274	6,642	3,756	4.8	6.1	5.3	3.1
11	France	3,670	3,494	3,494	3,433	3.0	2.9	2.8	2.9
12	Ireland	1,226	1,222	1,624	2,544	1.0	1.0	1.3	2.1
13	Spain	1,796	1,726	2,388	2,097	1.5	1.4	1.9	1.8
14	South Africa	1,828	1,873	2,055	1,886	1.5	1.6	1.6	1.6
15	Russia	1,923	1,458	2,034	1,704	1.6	1.2	1.6	1.4
16	Taiwan	1,586	1,621	1,715	1,608	1.3	1.4	1.4	1.3
17	Vietnam	808	1,010	1,275	1,590	0.7	0.8	1.0	1.3
18	Indonesia	1,073	1,279	1,437	1,529	0.9	1.1	1.1	1.3
19	Thailand	1,037	1,023	1,097	1,469	0.9	0.9	0.9	1.2
20	Brazil	975	746	939	1,205	0.8	0.6	0.7	1.0
21	Belgium	2,404	1,981	1,577	1,138	2.0	1.7	1.2	1.0
22	Saudi Arabia	3,212	3,504	2,459	1,123	2.7	2.9	1.9	0.9
23	Netherlands	2,281	1,361	1,213	1,107	1.9	1.1	1.0	0.9
24	Australia	757	761	976	1,092	0.6	0.6	0.8	0.9
25	Israel	879	994	1,053	988	0.7	0.8	0.8	0.8

Table E-32.   State Trade by Country: New Mexico, 2012–2015

(Top 25 countries based on 2015 dollar value. Value in millions of dollars.)

U.S. Exports by Origin State

Rank	Country	Value (Millions of dollars)				Percent of Share			
		2012	2013	2014	2015	2012	2013	2014	2015
	Total New Mexico Exports and % Share of U.S. Total	2,958	2,727	3,800	3,772	0.2	0.2	0.2	0.3
	Total, Top 25 Countries and % Share of State Total	2,793	2,494	3,630	3,639	94.4	91.5	95.5	96.5
1	Mexico	593	801	1,549	1,683	20.0	29.4	40.8	44.6
2	Israel	1,295	788	812	1,083	43.8	28.9	21.4	28.7
3	Canada	328	289	232	180	11.1	10.6	6.1	4.8
4	China	77	96	106	117	2.6	3.5	2.8	3.1
5	Belgium	16	45	59	77	0.5	1.7	1.6	2.0
6	Japan	53	41	73	69	1.8	1.5	1.9	1.8
7	Germany	72	68	63	65	2.4	2.5	1.7	1.7
8	Ireland	18	64	101	52	0.6	2.3	2.7	1.4
9	United Arab Emirates	17	5	12	36	0.6	0.2	0.3	1.0
10	United Kingdom	50	38	30	33	1.7	1.4	0.8	0.9
11	India	16	20	26	24	0.5	0.7	0.7	0.6
12	Netherlands	18	27	23	24	0.6	1.0	0.6	0.6
13	Singapore	19	23	26	22	0.6	0.8	0.7	0.6
14	Korea, South	14	21	42	20	0.5	0.8	1.1	0.5
15	Thailand	15	16	21	19	0.5	0.6	0.6	0.5
16	Brazil	41	41	33	19	1.4	1.5	0.9	0.5
17	Hong Kong	17	16	22	18	0.6	0.6	0.6	0.5
18	Australia	31	40	29	16	1.0	1.5	0.8	0.4
19	Italy	17	9	264	14	0.6	0.3	6.9	0.4
20	Czech Republic	9	7	10	14	0.3	0.3	0.3	0.4
21	Saudi Arabia	34	12	72	13	1.1	0.4	1.9	0.3
22	France	20	16	13	11	0.7	0.6	0.3	0.3
23	Sweden	3	4	3	11	0.1	0.1	0.1	0.3
24	Portugal	0	2	3	10	0.0	0.1	0.1	0.3
25	Chile	21	5	6	10	0.7	0.2	0.2	0.3

U.S. Imports by State of Final Destination

Rank	Country	Value (Millions of dollars)				Percent of Share			
		2012	2013	2014	2015	2012	2013	2014	2015
	Total New Mexico Imports and % Share of U.S. Total	2,326	2,016	2,237	2,244	0.1	0.1	0.1	0.1
	Total, Top 25 Countries and % Share of State Total	2,217	1,927	2,142	2,195	95.3	95.6	95.8	97.8
1	China	757	722	781	790	32.5	35.8	34.9	35.2
2	Mexico	496	361	502	632	21.3	17.9	22.4	28.2
3	Canada	252	237	202	198	10.8	11.8	9.0	8.8
4	Germany	100	112	150	103	4.3	5.6	6.7	4.6
5	United Kingdom	89	72	72	68	3.8	3.6	3.2	3.0
6	Netherlands	145	146	156	62	6.2	7.2	7.0	2.8
7	Japan	68	38	41	46	2.9	1.9	1.8	2.0
8	France	21	22	16	45	0.9	1.1	0.7	2.0
9	Korea, South	15	17	29	31	0.6	0.8	1.3	1.4
10	Taiwan	45	25	34	29	1.9	1.2	1.5	1.3
11	Belgium	20	18	32	27	0.9	0.9	1.4	1.2
12	Israel	30	22	16	26	1.3	1.1	0.7	1.2
13	Switzerland	18	10	12	18	0.8	0.5	0.5	0.8
14	India	19	18	18	16	0.8	0.9	0.8	0.7
15	Indonesia	2	1	3	15	0.1	0.0	0.1	0.7
16	Italy	12	15	15	15	0.5	0.7	0.7	0.7
17	Czech Republic	6	6	12	12	0.3	0.3	0.5	0.5
18	Hungary	1	1	7	12	0.0	0.0	0.3	0.5
19	Malaysia	38	56	8	11	1.6	2.8	0.4	0.5
20	Spain	6	7	7	9	0.3	0.3	0.3	0.4
21	Thailand	61	5	6	7	2.6	0.2	0.3	0.3
22	Sweden	6	3	5	7	0.3	0.1	0.2	0.3
23	Turkey	2	1	5	6	0.1	0.0	0.2	0.3
24	Ireland	3	9	7	5	0.1	0.4	0.3	0.2
25	Philippines	5	4	5	5	0.2	0.2	0.2	0.2

Table E-33.　State Trade by Country: New York, 2012–2015

(Top 25 countries based on 2015 dollar value. Value in millions of dollars.)

U.S. Exports by Origin State

Rank	Country	Value (Millions of dollars)				Percent of Share			
		2012	2013	2014	2015	2012	2013	2014	2015
	Total New York Exports and % Share of U.S. Total	81,338	86,312	88,434	80,059	5.3	5.5	5.5	5.3
	Total, Top 25 Countries and % Share of State Total	72,819	76,923	80,547	72,709	89.5	89.1	91.1	90.8
1	Canada	15,395	16,863	17,064	12,411	18.9	19.5	19.3	15.5
2	Hong Kong	8,897	9,310	10,790	9,549	10.9	10.8	12.2	11.9
3	Switzerland	6,498	10,042	8,744	8,314	8.0	11.6	9.9	10.4
4	United Kingdom	6,549	5,009	6,217	5,877	8.1	5.8	7.0	7.3
5	Israel	4,469	5,226	6,367	5,356	5.5	6.1	7.2	6.7
6	Belgium	2,665	2,909	3,898	3,986	3.3	3.4	4.4	5.0
7	China	4,286	5,033	4,291	3,743	5.3	5.8	4.9	4.7
8	Mexico	2,606	2,202	2,875	3,071	3.2	2.6	3.3	3.8
9	India	2,482	2,026	2,520	2,940	3.1	2.3	2.8	3.7
10	Germany	2,300	1,977	2,183	2,168	2.8	2.3	2.5	2.7
11	France	1,793	1,720	1,949	2,026	2.2	2.0	2.2	2.5
12	United Arab Emirates	1,636	2,013	1,921	2,013	2.0	2.3	2.2	2.5
13	Japan	2,254	2,089	1,902	2,012	2.8	2.4	2.2	2.5
14	Korea, South	1,517	1,283	1,350	1,427	1.9	1.5	1.5	1.8
15	Netherlands	1,505	1,491	1,279	1,156	1.9	1.7	1.4	1.4
16	Taiwan	997	763	844	1,048	1.2	0.9	1.0	1.3
17	Singapore	1,206	1,177	1,108	1,019	1.5	1.4	1.3	1.3
18	Italy	997	851	1,024	1,017	1.2	1.0	1.2	1.3
19	Brazil	1,053	833	741	623	1.3	1.0	0.8	0.8
20	Australia	654	932	1,017	605	0.8	1.1	1.2	0.8
21	Turkey	905	761	739	583	1.1	0.9	0.8	0.7
22	Thailand	517	846	502	520	0.6	1.0	0.6	0.6
23	Saudi Arabia	572	599	467	519	0.7	0.7	0.5	0.6
24	Spain	398	386	366	382	0.5	0.4	0.4	0.5
25	Russia	672	581	388	343	0.8	0.7	0.4	0.4

U.S. Imports by State of Final Destination

Rank	Country	Value (Millions of dollars)				Percent of Share			
		2012	2013	2014	2015	2012	2013	2014	2015
	Total New York Imports and % Share of U.S. Total	124,434	129,807	134,580	133,086	5.5	5.7	5.7	5.9
	Total, Top 25 Countries and % Share of State Total	109,700	115,780	120,841	118,956	88.2	89.2	89.8	89.4
1	China	22,617	22,752	23,074	22,976	18.2	17.5	17.1	17.3
2	Canada	18,956	19,407	20,282	18,001	15.2	15.0	15.1	13.5
3	India	8,330	10,456	10,555	10,618	6.7	8.1	7.8	8.0
4	Israel	7,867	8,629	9,580	9,074	6.3	6.6	7.1	6.8
5	France	4,899	6,375	6,115	7,038	3.9	4.9	4.5	5.3
6	Italy	4,893	5,323	5,656	5,765	3.9	4.1	4.2	4.3
7	Switzerland	4,436	5,091	5,451	5,324	3.6	3.9	4.1	4.0
8	United Kingdom	4,555	4,723	5,162	5,211	3.7	3.6	3.8	3.9
9	Germany	3,813	3,957	4,755	5,081	3.1	3.0	3.5	3.8
10	Belgium	4,236	4,714	4,669	4,888	3.4	3.6	3.5	3.7
11	Mexico	2,998	3,350	3,623	3,710	2.4	2.6	2.7	2.8
12	Hong Kong	2,426	2,651	2,698	3,064	1.9	2.0	2.0	2.3
13	Japan	3,125	2,579	2,778	2,858	2.5	2.0	2.1	2.1
14	Korea, South	1,547	1,573	1,859	1,999	1.2	1.2	1.4	1.5
15	Vietnam	1,383	1,552	1,721	1,924	1.1	1.2	1.3	1.4
16	Taiwan	1,973	1,701	1,766	1,723	1.6	1.3	1.3	1.3
17	Ireland	2,781	1,898	1,605	1,459	2.2	1.5	1.2	1.1
18	Spain	1,200	1,180	1,270	1,268	1.0	0.9	0.9	1.0
19	Thailand	1,194	1,241	1,113	1,189	1.0	1.0	0.8	0.9
20	Indonesia	1,293	1,182	998	1,163	1.0	0.9	0.7	0.9
21	Brazil	1,143	1,370	949	1,070	0.9	1.1	0.7	0.8
22	South Africa	1,294	1,321	1,818	1,026	1.0	1.0	1.4	0.8
23	Netherlands	1,027	877	1,714	945	0.8	0.7	1.3	0.7
24	Australia	825	949	873	842	0.7	0.7	0.6	0.6
25	Bangladesh	891	930	754	741	0.7	0.7	0.6	0.6

Table E-34.   State Trade by Country: North Carolina, 2012–2015

(Top 25 countries based on 2015 dollar value. Value in millions of dollars)

U.S. Exports by Origin State

Rank	Country	Value (Millions of dollars)				Percent of Share			
		2012	2013	2014	2015	2012	2013	2014	2015
	Total North Carolina Exports and % Share of U.S. Total	28,839	29,342	31,377	30,018	1.9	1.9	1.9	2.0
	Total, Top 25 Countries and % Share of State Total	24,573	25,136	26,615	26,029	85.2	85.7	84.8	86.7
1	Canada	7,013	6,737	6,797	6,803	24.3	23.0	21.7	22.7
2	Mexico	2,319	2,718	3,011	3,186	8.0	9.3	9.6	10.6
3	China	2,539	2,694	2,661	2,095	8.8	9.2	8.5	7.0
4	Japan	1,773	1,672	1,750	1,468	6.1	5.7	5.6	4.9
5	Saudi Arabia	730	798	1,227	1,435	2.5	2.7	3.9	4.8
6	France	856	1,000	1,138	1,136	3.0	3.4	3.6	3.8
7	United Kingdom	957	899	1,016	1,009	3.3	3.1	3.2	3.4
8	Germany	1,042	998	1,005	1,005	3.6	3.4	3.2	3.3
9	Honduras	757	760	840	861	2.6	2.6	2.7	2.9
10	Belgium	707	800	885	785	2.5	2.7	2.8	2.6
11	Hong Kong	817	774	927	772	2.8	2.6	3.0	2.6
12	Netherlands	679	715	789	723	2.4	2.4	2.5	2.4
13	Korea, South	619	690	649	618	2.1	2.4	2.1	2.1
14	Brazil	784	744	666	562	2.7	2.5	2.1	1.9
15	Australia	465	464	470	482	1.6	1.6	1.5	1.6
16	Singapore	352	343	389	426	1.2	1.2	1.2	1.4
17	India	298	481	422	414	1.0	1.6	1.3	1.4
18	Ireland	162	261	277	380	0.6	0.9	0.9	1.3
19	Dominican Republic	292	256	339	336	1.0	0.9	1.1	1.1
20	Spain	140	155	219	328	0.5	0.5	0.7	1.1
21	El Salvador	255	274	261	265	0.9	0.9	0.8	0.9
22	Taiwan	317	306	273	253	1.1	1.0	0.9	0.8
23	United Arab Emirates	274	162	175	241	1.0	0.6	0.6	0.8
24	Indonesia	203	245	237	229	0.7	0.8	0.8	0.8
25	Turkey	223	189	191	217	0.8	0.6	0.6	0.7

U.S. Imports by State of Final Destination

Rank	Country	Value (Millions of dollars)				Percent of Share			
		2012	2013	2014	2015	2012	2013	2014	2015
	Total North Carolina Imports and % Share of U.S. Total	49,580	49,848	52,864	50,880	2.2	2.2	2.3	2.3
	Total, Top 25 Countries and % Share of State Total	43,315	43,868	46,364	44,497	87.4	88.0	87.7	87.5
1	China	9,450	11,515	12,486	11,063	19.1	23.1	23.6	21.7
2	Mexico	5,188	4,797	4,641	4,507	10.5	9.6	8.8	8.9
3	Canada	3,327	3,443	3,448	3,482	6.7	6.9	6.5	6.8
4	Germany	3,407	3,366	3,377	3,236	6.9	6.8	6.4	6.4
5	Japan	3,236	2,749	3,118	2,944	6.5	5.5	5.9	5.8
6	United Kingdom	2,260	2,150	2,709	2,727	4.6	4.3	5.1	5.4
7	France	1,895	2,744	2,506	2,166	3.8	5.5	4.7	4.3
8	Italy	1,342	1,465	1,870	1,852	2.7	2.9	3.5	3.6
9	India	1,140	1,176	1,300	1,345	2.3	2.4	2.5	2.6
10	Vietnam	661	760	858	1,195	1.3	1.5	1.6	2.3
11	Switzerland	736	1,008	1,471	1,150	1.5	2.0	2.8	2.3
12	Honduras	948	872	833	938	1.9	1.7	1.6	1.8
13	Taiwan	777	865	874	882	1.6	1.7	1.7	1.7
14	Brazil	930	1,027	835	805	1.9	2.1	1.6	1.6
15	Ireland	1,482	362	516	753	3.0	0.7	1.0	1.5
16	Dominican Republic	653	659	581	656	1.3	1.3	1.1	1.3
17	Indonesia	656	684	683	632	1.3	1.4	1.3	1.2
18	Korea, South	1,027	565	703	631	2.1	1.1	1.3	1.2
19	Netherlands	493	735	641	626	1.0	1.5	1.2	1.2
20	Singapore	1,724	932	780	559	3.5	1.9	1.5	1.1
21	El Salvador	562	582	528	544	1.1	1.2	1.0	1.1
22	Thailand	480	427	458	472	1.0	0.9	0.9	0.9
23	Bangladesh	299	362	427	470	0.6	0.7	0.8	0.9
24	Malaysia	212	192	286	445	0.4	0.4	0.5	0.9
25	Haiti	428	431	436	417	0.9	0.9	0.8	0.8

'(Z)' indicates a percent change greater than 500.
Open in Microsoft Excel.

Table E-35. State Trade by Country: North Dakota, 2012–2015

(Top 25 countries based on 2015 dollar value. Value in millions of dollars.)

U.S. Exports by Origin State

Rank	Country	Value (Millions of dollars)				Percent of Share			
		2012	2013	2014	2015	2012	2013	2014	2015
	Total North Dakota Exports and % Share of U.S. Total	4,310	4,402	5,493	3,863	0.3	0.3	0.3	0.3
	Total, Top 25 Countries and % Share of State Total	3,947	4,078	5,207	3,677	91.6	92.6	94.8	95.2
1	Canada	3,088	3,340	4,349	2,725	71.6	75.9	79.2	70.5
2	Mexico	283	238	320	295	6.6	5.4	5.8	7.6
3	Australia	124	82	84	133	2.9	1.9	1.5	3.4
4	Czech Republic	34	23	23	70	0.8	0.5	0.4	1.8
5	Spain	14	25	22	48	0.3	0.6	0.4	1.2
6	Germany	51	40	43	43	1.2	0.9	0.8	1.1
7	Italy	17	8	17	42	0.4	0.2	0.3	1.1
8	Japan	34	32	37	41	0.8	0.7	0.7	1.1
9	India	27	29	35	34	0.6	0.7	0.6	0.9
10	Brazil	31	15	19	24	0.7	0.3	0.3	0.6
11	Panama	1	5	8	20	0.0	0.1	0.1	0.5
12	Korea, South	22	19	31	20	0.5	0.4	0.6	0.5
13	Dominican Republic	34	32	13	19	0.8	0.7	0.2	0.5
14	United Kingdom	30	31	21	19	0.7	0.7	0.4	0.5
15	China	19	24	50	17	0.4	0.5	0.9	0.4
16	Nigeria	12	5	20	15	0.3	0.1	0.4	0.4
17	Guyana	0	3	4	15	0.0	0.1	0.1	0.4
18	United Arab Emirates	9	9	10	14	0.2	0.2	0.2	0.4
19	Algeria	0	0	12	14	0.0	0.0	0.2	0.4
20	South Africa	16	18	15	14	0.4	0.4	0.3	0.4
21	Venezuela	54	58	33	12	1.3	1.3	0.6	0.3
22	Ethiopia	7	7	3	11	0.2	0.2	0.1	0.3
23	Taiwan	8	5	8	11	0.2	0.1	0.1	0.3
24	Kazakhstan	19	11	11	10	0.4	0.2	0.2	0.3
25	France	12	18	20	10	0.3	0.4	0.4	0.3

U.S. Imports by State of Final Destination

Rank	Country	Value (Millions of dollars)				Percent of Share			
		2012	2013	2014	2015	2012	2013	2014	2015
	Total North Dakota Imports and % Share of U.S. Total	3,907	3,601	3,829	3,146	0.2	0.2	0.2	0.1
	Total, Top 25 Countries and % Share of State Total	3,790	3,498	3,703	3,053	97.0	97.1	96.7	97.0
1	Canada	2,689	2,491	2,569	1,927	68.8	69.2	67.1	61.3
2	Korea, South	35	48	145	212	0.9	1.3	3.8	6.7
3	Mexico	144	143	153	148	3.7	4.0	4.0	4.7
4	Germany	125	186	130	132	3.2	5.2	3.4	4.2
5	China	148	145	153	120	3.8	4.0	4.0	3.8
6	India	70	54	59	74	1.8	1.5	1.5	2.4
7	France	84	93	93	69	2.1	2.6	2.4	2.2
8	United Kingdom	39	42	54	45	1.0	1.2	1.4	1.4
9	Saudi Arabia	58	64	37	44	1.5	1.8	1.0	1.4
10	Czech Republic	15	11	5	40	0.4	0.3	0.1	1.3
11	Japan	89	73	49	37	2.3	2.0	1.3	1.2
12	Italy	31	44	39	25	0.8	1.2	1.0	0.8
13	Spain	4	3	13	23	0.1	0.1	0.3	0.7
14	Bolivia	21	26	27	22	0.5	0.7	0.7	0.7
15	Singapore	8	6	18	17	0.2	0.2	0.5	0.5
16	Vietnam	17	12	16	16	0.4	0.0	0.4	0.5
17	Taiwan	15	12	9	15	0.4	0.3	0.2	0.5
18	Poland	1	2	6	14	0.0	0.1	0.2	0.4
19	Denmark	135	10	45	13	3.5	0.3	1.2	0.4
20	Austria	3	6	6	12	0.1	0.2	0.2	0.4
21	Russia	20	2	8	11	0.5	0.1	0.2	0.3
22	Kenya	7	6	8	11	0.2	0.2	0.2	0.3
23	Turkey	7	3	5	11	0.2	0.1	0.1	0.3
24	Peru	8	7	19	8	0.2	0.2	0.5	0.3

Table E-36.   State Trade by Country: Ohio, 2012–2015

(Top 25 countries based on 2015 dollar value. Value in millions of dollars.)

U.S. Exports by Origin State

Rank	Country	Value (Millions of dollars)				Percent of Share			
		2012	2013	2014	2015	2012	2013	2014	2015
	Total Ohio Exports and % Share of U.S. Total	48,819	50,827	52,240	50,694	3.2	3.2	3.2	3.4
	Total, Top 25 Countries and % Share of State Total	43,793	45,163	47,223	46,213	89.70	88.86	90.40	91.16
1	Canada	19,711	20,059	20,832	20,084	40.38	39.47	39.88	39.62
2	Mexico	4,718	5,018	6,005	6,495	9.66	9.87	11.50	12.81
3	China	2,839	3,374	3,882	3,314	5.82	6.64	7.43	6.54
4	France	2,671	2,029	1,382	1,904	5.47	3.99	2.65	3.76
5	United Kingdom	1,459	1,600	1,773	1,791	2.99	3.15	3.39	3.53
6	Germany	1,416	1,404	1,726	1,492	2.90	2.76	3.30	2.94
7	Japan	1,552	1,538	1,371	1,369	3.18	3.03	2.62	2.70
8	Brazil	1,609	1,535	1,392	1,284	3.30	3.02	2.66	2.53
9	Korea, South	865	1,035	956	1,063	1.77	2.04	1.83	2.10
10	Australia	973	846	820	792	1.99	1.66	1.57	1.56
11	Netherlands	810	758	783	657	1.66	1.49	1.50	1.30
12	Singapore	542	560	692	568	1.11	1.10	1.32	1.12
13	Switzerland	466	509	618	565	0.95	1.00	1.18	1.11
14	Belgium	496	465	572	546	1.02	0.91	1.09	1.08
15	Italy	461	507	747	534	0.94	1.00	1.43	1.05
16	Taiwan	394	452	454	512	0.81	0.89	0.87	1.01
17	United Arab Emirates	471	678	571	501	0.96	1.33	1.09	0.99
18	India	553	384	388	445	1.13	0.76	0.74	0.88
19	Hong Kong	427	453	499	431	0.87	0.89	0.96	0.85
20	Thailand	367	327	390	426	0.75	0.64	0.75	0.84
21	Saudi Arabia	454	886	533	332	0.93	1.74	1.02	0.65
22	Malaysia	193	288	277	299	0.40	0.57	0.53	0.59
23	Indonesia	197	279	188	274	0.40	0.55	0.36	0.54
24	Bangladesh	5	11	126	269	0.01	0.02	0.24	0.53
25	Hungary	145	168	247	262	0.30	0.33	0.47	0.52

U.S. Imports by State of Final Destination

Rank	Country	Value (Millions of dollars)				Percent of Share			
		2012	2013	2014	2015	2012	2013	2014	2015
	Total Ohio Imports and % Share of U.S. Total	64,143	66,419	70,269	68,843	2.8	2.9	3	3.1
	Total, Top 25 Countries and % Share of State Total	60,222	62,523	65,657	64,290	93.9	94.1	93.4	93.4
1	Canada	16,284	17,312	17,107	13,828	25.4	26.1	24.3	20.1
2	China	11,738	12,395	12,671	13,355	18.3	18.7	18.0	19.4
3	Mexico	6,659	7,615	7,809	8,188	10.4	11.5	11.1	11.9
4	Germany	4,806	4,591	5,691	5,844	7.5	6.9	8.1	8.5
5	Japan	6,245	5,870	5,794	5,224	9.7	8.8	8.2	7.6
6	France	1,473	1,431	1,512	1,939	2.3	2.2	2.2	2.8
7	Ireland	1,189	964	1,277	1,924	1.9	1.5	1.8	2.8
8	Vietnam	993	1,202	1,359	1,616	1.5	1.8	1.9	2.3
9	India	1,027	1,011	1,345	1,398	1.6	1.5	1.9	2.0
10	Taiwan	1,141	1,086	1,155	1,202	1.8	1.6	1.6	1.7
11	Korea, South	1,121	1,121	1,171	1,142	1.7	1.7	1.7	1.7
12	Italy	1,029	967	1,158	1,133	1.6	1.5	1.6	1.6
13	United Kingdom	953	1,218	1,187	968	1.5	1.8	1.7	1.4
14	Indonesia	669	667	778	882	1.0	1.0	1.1	1.3
15	Sri Lanka	502	639	654	787	0.8	1.0	0.9	1.1
16	Thailand	587	587	557	735	0.9	0.9	0.8	1.1
17	Brazil	591	682	717	585	0.9	1.0	1.0	0.8
18	Netherlands	425	419	545	484	0.7	0.6	0.8	0.7
19	Sweden	485	384	500	475	0.8	0.6	0.7	0.7
20	Austria	302	278	367	471	0.5	0.4	0.5	0.7
21	Switzerland	394	468	492	439	0.6	0.7	0.7	0.6
22	Russia	281	257	453	436	0.4	0.4	0.6	0.6
23	Trinidad and Tobago	685	624	630	428	1.1	0.9	0.9	0.6
24	Malaysia	409	426	408	409	0.6	0.6	0.6	0.6
25	Spain	236	309	320	398	0.4	0.5	0.5	0.6

Table E-37.   State Trade by Country: Oklahoma, 2012–2015

(Top 25 countries based on 2015 dollar value. Value in millions of dollars.)

U.S. Exports by Origin State

Rank	Country	Value (Millions of dollars)				Percent of Share			
		2012	2013	2014	2015	2012	2013	2014	2015
	Total Oklahoma Exports and % Share of U.S. Total	6,579	6,919	6,309	5,258	0.4	0.4	0.4	0.3
	Total, Top 25 Countries and % Share of State Total	5,516	5,661	5,215	4,474	83.8	81.8	82.7	85.1
1	Canada	1,995	1,923	1,858	1,567	30.3	27.8	29.4	29.8
2	Mexico	621	613	612	565	9.4	8.9	9.7	10.7
3	Germany	207	290	211	279	3.1	4.2	3.3	5.3
4	Japan	433	340	311	238	6.6	4.9	4.9	4.5
5	Singapore	230	225	232	227	3.5	3.3	3.7	4.3
6	China	333	428	273	166	5.1	6.2	4.3	3.2
7	Netherlands	115	136	153	161	1.7	2.0	2.4	3.1
8	Australia	174	168	134	122	2.6	2.4	2.1	2.3
9	United Kingdom	146	111	115	113	2.2	1.6	1.8	2.1
10	Saudi Arabia	129	185	121	103	2.0	2.7	1.9	2.0
11	United Arab Emirates	142	103	135	101	2.2	1.5	2.1	1.9
12	Brazil	177	220	139	93	2.7	3.2	2.2	1.8
13	Iraq	20	35	111	87	0.3	0.5	1.8	1.7
14	India	65	82	80	82	1.0	1.2	1.3	1.6
15	Korea, South	77	102	85	80	1.2	1.5	1.3	1.5
16	Colombia	125	104	90	60	1.9	1.5	1.4	1.1
17	Israel	57	89	91	60	0.9	1.3	1.4	1.1
18	Argentina	90	99	79	59	1.4	1.4	1.3	1.1
19	Kuwait	20	26	34	49	0.3	0.4	0.5	0.9
20	Italy	38	36	39	46	0.6	0.5	0.6	0.9
21	France	65	48	43	46	1.0	0.7	0.7	0.9
22	Sweden	31	17	17	44	0.5	0.2	0.3	0.8
23	Malaysia	34	53	68	44	0.5	0.8	1.1	0.8
24	Belgium	91	68	71	42	1.4	1.0	1.1	0.8
25	Russia	101	159	115	39	1.5	2.3	1.8	0.7

U.S. Imports by State of Final Destination

Rank	Country	Value (Millions of dollars)				Percent of Share			
		2012	2013	2014	2015	2012	2013	2014	2015
	Total Oklahoma Imports and % Share of U.S. Total	11,419	12,383	13,589	10,994	0.5	0.5	0.6	0.5
	Total, Top 25 Countries and % Share of State Total	10,944	11,887	13,008	10,522	95.8	96.0	95.7	95.7
1	Canada	5,158	5,907	6,542	4,441	45.2	47.7	48.1	40.4
2	China	2,290	2,298	2,650	2,483	20.1	18.6	19.5	22.6
3	Mexico	886	1,056	1,043	1,021	7.8	8.5	7.7	9.3
4	Japan	472	458	444	340	4.1	3.7	3.3	3.1
5	Germany	346	305	341	265	3.0	2.5	2.5	2.4
6	India	180	166	214	209	1.6	1.3	1.6	1.9
7	United Kingdom	186	208	218	185	1.6	1.7	1.6	1.7
8	Taiwan	228	213	215	181	2.0	1.7	1.6	1.6
9	Italy	101	96	130	155	0.9	0.8	1.0	1.4
10	Thailand	109	118	136	137	1.0	1.0	1.0	1.2
11	France	85	134	149	133	0.7	1.1	1.1	1.2
12	Australia	153	192	139	111	1.3	1.6	1.0	1.0
13	Vietnam	59	67	107	102	0.5	0.5	0.8	0.9
14	Argentina	15	16	13	86	0.1	0.1	0.1	0.8
15	South Africa	151	146	143	85	1.3	1.2	1.1	0.8
16	Switzerland	23	26	43	67	0.2	0.2	0.0	0.0
17	Austria	47	59	95	65	0.4	0.5	0.7	0.6
18	Korea, South	67	67	67	65	0.6	0.5	0.5	0.6
19	Spain	32	11	10	63	0.3	0.1	0.1	0.6
20	Malaysia	56	49	50	62	0.5	0.4	0.4	0.6
21	Hong Kong	13	36	36	60	0.1	0.3	0.3	0.5
22	Indonesia	102	82	68	59	0.9	0.7	0.5	0.5
23	Sweden	46	41	37	53	0.4	0.3	0.3	0.5
24	Belgium	111	112	76	53	1.0	0.9	0.6	0.5
25	Turkey	26	28	42	41	0.2	0.2	0.3	0.4

'(Z)' indicates a percent change greater than 500.

Table E-38.   State Trade by Country: Oregon, 2012–2015

(Top 25 countries based on 2015 dollar value. Value in millions of dollars.)

U.S. Exports by Origin State

Rank	Country	Value (Millions of dollars)				Percent of Share			
		2012	2013	2014	2015	2012	2013	2014	2015
	Total Oregon Exports and % Share of U.S. Total	18,388	18,636	20,889	20,084	1.2	1.2	1.3	1.3
	Total, Top 25 Countries and % Share of State Total	16,138	16,264	18,910	18,697	87.8	87.3	90.5	93.1
1	China	2,662	3,381	4,265	4,818	14.5	18.1	20.4	24.0
2	Canada	3,005	3,143	3,125	2,563	16.3	16.9	15.0	12.8
3	Malaysia	1,952	1,859	2,570	2,499	10.6	10.0	12.3	12.4
4	Japan	1,580	1,525	1,580	1,440	8.6	8.2	7.6	7.2
5	Korea, South	1,102	995	1,234	1,046	6.0	5.3	5.9	5.2
6	Taiwan	745	825	981	836	4.1	4.4	4.7	4.2
7	Vietnam	589	411	538	533	3.2	2.2	2.6	2.7
8	Australia	421	360	414	438	2.3	1.9	2.0	2.2
9	Singapore	365	359	336	424	2.0	1.9	1.6	2.1
10	Hong Kong	434	399	314	414	2.4	2.1	1.5	2.1
11	Mexico	372	336	375	406	2.0	1.8	1.8	2.0
12	United Kingdom	385	287	275	373	2.1	1.5	1.3	1.9
13	Germany	433	371	381	359	2.4	2.0	1.8	1.8
14	Netherlands	198	243	277	302	1.1	1.3	1.3	1.5
15	Ireland	82	114	243	285	0.4	0.6	1.2	1.4
16	Philippines	312	293	457	271	1.7	1.6	2.2	1.3
17	Brazil	408	348	317	268	2.2	1.9	1.5	1.3
18	United Arab Emirates	50	87	191	264	0.3	0.5	0.9	1.3
19	Israel	172	121	196	219	0.9	0.6	0.9	1.1
20	Switzerland	120	62	61	204	0.7	0.3	0.3	1.0
21	Thailand	162	163	192	189	0.9	0.9	0.9	0.9
22	France	201	207	208	184	1.1	1.1	1.0	0.9
23	Italy	119	126	126	145	0.6	0.7	0.6	0.7
24	Belgium	109	115	100	127	0.6	0.6	0.5	0.6
25	India	160	133	154	91	0.9	0.7	0.7	0.5

U.S. Imports by State of Final Destination

Rank	Country	Value (Millions of dollars)				Percent of Share			
		2012	2013	2014	2015	2012	2013	2014	2015
	Total Oregon Imports and % Share of U.S. Total	16,571	14,344	13,788	14,815	0.7	0.6	0.6	0.7
	Total, Top 25 Countries and % Share of State Total	15,574	13,584	13,155	14,152	94.0	94.7	95.4	95.5
1	Canada	2,637	2,878	2,727	2,701	15.9	20.1	19.8	18.2
2	China	2,962	2,578	2,632	2,547	17.9	18.0	19.1	17.2
3	Korea, South	1,607	1,346	1,573	1,587	9.7	9.4	11.4	10.7
4	Japan	3,980	3,053	1,830	1,522	24.0	21.3	13.3	10.3
5	Israel	234	182	150	804	1.4	1.3	1.1	5.4
6	Mexico	638	509	576	710	3.9	3.5	4.2	4.8
7	Netherlands	243	133	284	618	1.5	0.9	2.1	4.2
8	Ireland	15	17	165	571	0.1	0.1	1.2	3.9
9	Germany	532	382	403	450	3.2	2.7	2.9	3.0
10	Vietnam	276	270	346	406	1.7	1.9	2.5	2.7
11	Taiwan	317	311	365	382	1.9	2.2	2.6	2.6
12	Thailand	187	328	310	282	1.1	2.3	2.2	1.9
13	Russia	429	333	501	195	2.6	2.3	3.6	1.3
14	United Kingdom	116	107	151	166	0.7	0.7	1.1	1.1
15	India	195	119	190	141	1.2	0.8	1.4	1.0
16	Italy	107	110	116	132	0.6	0.8	0.8	0.9
17	Malaysia	134	116	126	119	0.8	0.8	0.9	0.8
18	Sweden	52	61	87	116	0.3	0.4	0.6	0.8
19	Switzerland	46	48	80	114	0.3	0.3	0.6	0.8
20	France	129	87	87	109	0.8	0.6	0.6	0.7
21	Singapore	375	221	83	109	2.3	1.5	0.6	0.7
22	Indonesia	184	177	149	105	1.1	1.2	1.1	0.7
23	Brazil	64	86	96	100	0.4	0.6	0.7	0.7
24	Chile	59	75	74	98	0.4	0.5	0.5	0.7
25	Austria	55	55	55	69	0.3	0.4	0.4	0.5

Table E-39.   State Trade by Country: Pennsylvania, 2012–2015

(Top 25 countries based on 2015 dollar value. Value in millions of dollars.)

U.S. Exports by Origin State

Rank	Country	Value (Millions of dollars)				Percent of Share			
		2012	2013	2014	2015	2012	2013	2014	2015
	Total Pennsylvania Exports and % Share of U.S. Total	38,852	41,173	40,355	39,403	2.5	2.6	2.5	2.6
	Total, Top 25 Countries and % Share of State Total	33,444	35,273	35,160	34,739	86.1	85.7	87.1	88.2
1	Canada	11,461	11,724	12,300	11,605	29.5	28.5	30.5	29.5
2	Mexico	2,831	3,450	3,729	4,178	7.3	8.4	9.2	10.6
3	United Kingdom	1,514	1,456	1,850	2,328	3.9	3.5	4.6	5.9
4	China	2,858	2,926	2,398	2,061	7.4	7.1	5.9	5.2
5	Japan	1,477	1,566	1,581	1,669	3.8	3.8	3.9	4.2
6	Germany	1,821	1,681	1,447	1,576	4.7	4.1	3.6	4.0
7	Netherlands	1,268	2,420	1,912	1,407	3.3	5.9	4.7	3.6
8	Belgium	850	1,039	1,215	1,288	2.2	2.5	3.0	3.3
9	Brazil	1,190	1,434	1,153	1,006	3.1	3.5	2.9	2.6
10	Korea, South	879	1,213	1,009	916	2.3	2.9	2.5	2.3
11	India	543	474	706	763	1.4	1.2	1.7	1.9
12	France	627	630	621	643	1.6	1.5	1.5	1.6
13	Australia	833	645	740	585	2.1	1.6	1.8	1.5
14	Italy	609	641	619	584	1.6	1.6	1.5	1.5
15	Ireland	941	553	194	555	2.4	1.3	0.5	1.4
16	Singapore	613	574	705	470	1.6	1.4	1.7	1.2
17	Hong Kong	448	404	471	466	1.2	1.0	1.2	1.2
18	Taiwan	517	422	409	386	1.3	1.0	1.0	1.0
19	Switzerland	409	320	340	379	1.1	0.8	0.8	1.0
20	Turkey	318	332	234	363	0.8	0.8	0.6	0.9
21	Saudi Arabia	304	417	355	355	0.8	1.0	0.9	0.9
22	South Africa	393	275	359	334	1.0	0.7	0.9	0.8
23	United Arab Emirates	238	216	368	332	0.6	0.5	0.9	0.8
24	Colombia	358	273	255	248	0.9	0.7	0.6	0.6
25	Spain	143	189	191	242	0.4	0.5	0.5	0.6

U.S. Imports by State of Final Destination

Rank	Country	Value (Millions of dollars)				Percent of Share			
		2012	2013	2014	2015	2012	2013	2014	2015
	Total Pennsylvania Imports and % Share of U.S. Total	80,772	84,939	83,086	79,675	3.5	3.7	3.5	3.6
	Total, Top 25 Countries and % Share of State Total	68,340	72,466	73,010	71,476	84.6	85.3	87.9	89.7
1	China	16,472	18,092	18,098	20,134	20.4	21.3	21.8	25.3
2	Canada	11,195	11,508	12,624	10,697	13.9	13.5	15.2	13.4
3	Germany	4,988	5,622	6,550	5,798	6.2	6.6	7.9	7.3
4	Israel	4,948	4,859	3,720	5,023	6.1	5.7	4.5	6.3
5	Mexico	2,852	2,989	3,522	4,214	3.5	3.5	4.2	5.3
6	Korea, South	2,793	2,960	4,188	3,677	3.5	3.5	5.0	4.6
7	Switzerland	791	991	2,445	2,630	1.0	1.2	2.9	3.3
8	United Kingdom	2,727	2,404	2,564	2,539	3.4	2.8	3.1	3.2
9	Japan	1,980	2,048	2,067	2,277	2.5	2.4	2.5	2.9
10	Ireland	1,059	811	1,304	1,560	1.3	1.0	1.6	2.0
11	Italy	1,374	1,594	1,558	1,527	1.7	1.9	1.9	1.9
12	India	1,051	1,093	1,176	1,457	1.3	1.3	1.4	1.8
13	Belgium	1,324	1,757	1,512	1,284	1.6	2.1	1.8	1.6
14	France	1,243	1,480	1,232	1,068	1.5	1.7	1.5	1.3
15	Sweden	557	935	1,086	954	0.7	1.1	1.3	1.2
16	Vietnam	572	602	691	803	0.7	0.7	0.8	1.0
17	Russia	996	877	1,400	772	1.2	1.0	1.7	1.0
18	Finland	677	746	831	766	0.8	0.9	1.0	1.0
19	Australia	535	482	720	718	0.7	0.6	0.9	0.9
20	Brazil	955	826	812	709	1.2	1.0	1.0	0.9
21	Taiwan	732	1,075	771	694	0.9	1.3	0.9	0.9
22	Nigeria	5,801	6,305	1,601	597	7.2	7.4	1.9	0.7
23	Chad	1,449	1,239	1,475	581	1.8	1.5	1.8	0.7
24	Netherlands	865	741	669	525	1.1	0.9	0.8	0.7
25	Austria	406	430	396	474	0.5	0.5	0.5	0.6

Table E-40. State Trade by Country: Rhode Island, 2012–2015

(Top 25 countries based on 2015 dollar value. Value in millions of dollars)

U.S. Exports by Origin State

Rank	Country	Value (Millions of dollars)				Percent of Share			
		2012	2013	2014	2015	2012	2013	2014	2015
	Total Rhode Island Exports and % Share of U.S. Total	2,366	2,164	2,389	2,125	0.2	0.1	0.1	0.1
	Total, Top 25 Countries and % Share of State Total	2,089	1,920	2,006	1,877	88.3	88.7	84.0	88.3
1	Canada	576	483	498	522	24.3	22.3	20.8	24.6
2	Mexico	150	166	195	181	6.3	7.7	8.2	8.5
3	Turkey	198	162	124	132	8.4	7.5	5.2	6.2
4	China	90	98	116	130	3.8	4.5	4.9	6.1
5	Germany	192	206	127	108	8.1	9.5	5.3	5.1
6	Ireland	16	21	71	93	0.7	1.0	3.0	4.4
7	Dominican Republic	61	44	60	93	2.6	2.0	2.5	4.4
8	Italy	127	92	79	78	5.4	4.3	3.3	3.7
9	Japan	78	33	62	66	3.3	1.5	2.6	3.1
10	Singapore	77	72	72	63	3.3	3.3	3.0	3.0
11	United Kingdom	93	57	65	59	3.9	2.6	2.7	2.8
12	Hong Kong	29	40	41	44	1.2	1.8	1.7	2.1
13	France	71	68	54	43	3.0	3.1	2.3	2.0
14	Taiwan	66	81	91	40	2.8	3.7	3.8	1.9
15	Korea, South	30	31	40	29	1.3	1.4	1.7	1.4
16	Benin	57	53	57	29	2.4	2.4	2.4	1.4
17	Belgium	35	30	36	25	1.5	1.4	1.5	1.2
18	Netherlands	28	18	15	20	1.2	0.8	0.6	0.9
19	Bahamas	1	6	6	20	0.0	0.3	0.3	0.9
20	Egypt	14	58	101	19	0.6	2.7	4.2	0.9
21	Thailand	19	15	14	18	0.8	0.7	0.6	0.8
22	Costa Rica	23	22	22	17	1.0	1.0	0.9	0.8
23	Austria	11	17	20	17	0.5	0.8	0.8	0.8
24	Guatemala	15	17	19	16	0.6	0.8	0.8	0.8
25	Malaysia	30	28	21	16	1.3	1.3	0.9	0.8

U.S. Imports by State of Final Destination

Rank	Country	Value (Millions of dollars)				Percent of Share			
		2012	2013	2014	2015	2012	2013	2014	2015
	Total Rhode Island Imports and % Share of U.S. Total	9,460	9,568	8,354	8,224	0.4	0.4	0.4	0.4
	Total, Top 25 Countries and % Share of State Total	9,056	9,272	8,027	7,975	95.7	96.9	96.1	97.0
1	Germany	3,337	3,367	2,151	2,356	35.3	35.2	25.7	28.6
2	Mexico	1,297	1,080	946	1,214	13.7	11.3	11.3	14.8
3	China	1,224	1,369	1,136	1,184	12.9	14.3	13.6	14.4
4	United Kingdom	623	752	876	528	6.6	7.9	10.5	6.4
5	Canada	641	384	388	429	6.8	4.0	4.6	5.2
6	Hungary	25	20	257	377	0.3	0.2	3.1	4.6
7	Slovakia	267	236	287	347	2.8	2.5	3.4	4.2
8	Costa Rica	161	155	179	182	1.7	1.6	2.1	2.2
9	Netherlands	196	394	387	169	2.1	4.1	4.6	2.1
10	Spain	11	14	49	160	0.1	0.1	0.6	1.9
11	France	256	406	296	156	2.7	4.2	3.5	1.9
12	Italy	78	90	87	97	0.8	0.9	1.0	1.2
13	Austria	149	140	114	97	1.6	1.5	1.4	1.2
14	Russia	50	165	166	93	0.5	1.7	2.0	1.1
15	Belgium	120	87	120	79	1.3	0.9	1.4	1.0
16	Thailand	102	106	80	76	1.1	1.1	1.0	0.9
17	Switzerland	42	50	49	65	0.4	0.5	0.6	0.8
18	Portugal	64	118	67	64	0.7	1.2	0.8	0.8
19	India	78	118	55	52	0.8	1.2	0.7	0.6
20	Taiwan	53	48	60	50	0.6	0.5	0.7	0.6
21	Japan	198	50	76	47	2.1	0.5	0.9	0.6
22	Norway	27	65	145	46	0.3	0.7	1.7	0.6
23	Korea, South	31	27	27	37	0.3	0.3	0.3	0.4
24	Vietnam	16	21	22	37	0.2	0.2	0.3	0.4
25	Finland	12	10	8	35	0.1	0.1	0.1	0.4

Table E-41.   State Trade by Country: South Carolina, 2012–2015

(Top 25 countries based on 2015 dollar value. Value in millions of dollars.)

U.S. Exports by Origin State

Rank	Country	Value (Millions of dollars)				Percent of Share			
		2012	2013	2014	2015	2012	2013	2014	2015
	Total South Carolina Exports and % Share of U.S. Total	25,115	26,291	29,624	30,861	1.6	1.7	1.8	2.1
	Total, Top 25 Countries and % Share of State Total	21,296	22,372	25,069	27,525	84.8	85.1	84.6	89.2
1	China	3,250	4,878	4,228	4,396	12.9	18.6	14.3	14.2
2	Germany	3,748	3,183	3,874	3,908	14.9	12.1	13.1	12.7
3	Canada	3,972	3,733	3,622	3,667	15.8	14.2	12.2	11.9
4	United Kingdom	1,352	1,363	1,863	2,843	5.4	5.2	6.3	9.2
5	Mexico	1,972	1,838	2,115	2,447	7.9	7.0	7.1	7.9
6	Japan	727	655	916	1,804	2.9	2.5	3.1	5.8
7	Singapore	215	280	377	1,111	0.9	1.1	1.3	3.6
8	Australia	779	748	874	795	3.1	2.8	3.0	2.6
9	Belgium	410	514	719	669	1.6	2.0	2.4	2.2
10	Korea, South	471	598	632	582	1.9	2.3	2.1	1.9
11	United Arab Emirates	491	383	458	544	2.0	1.5	1.5	1.8
12	Saudi Arabia	432	457	387	525	1.7	1.7	1.3	1.7
13	Brazil	716	652	592	485	2.9	2.5	2.0	1.6
14	Colombia	179	195	204	424	0.7	0.7	0.7	1.4
15	Algeria	34	115	1,067	424	0.1	0.4	3.6	1.4
16	France	406	388	454	423	1.6	1.5	1.5	1.4
17	Netherlands	374	436	610	405	1.5	1.7	2.1	1.3
18	India	423	352	386	381	1.7	1.3	1.3	1.2
19	Vietnam	71	115	125	296	0.3	0.4	0.4	1.0
20	Russia	95	191	323	293	0.4	0.7	1.1	0.9
21	Hong Kong	260	286	255	275	1.0	1.1	0.9	0.9
22	Taiwan	226	283	211	219	0.9	1.1	0.7	0.7
23	Chile	246	375	292	214	1.0	1.4	1.0	0.7
24	Italy	276	243	330	200	1.1	0.9	1.1	0.6
25	Honduras	172	110	155	193	0.7	0.4	0.5	0.6

U.S. Imports by State of Final Destination

Rank	Country	Value (Millions of dollars)				Percent of Share			
		2012	2013	2014	2015	2012	2013	2014	2015
	Total South Carolina Imports and % Share of U.S. Total	35,601	32,899	37,729	38,988	1.6	1.5	1.6	1.7
	Total, Top 25 Countries and % Share of State Total	31,149	29,091	33,775	34,662	87.5	88.4	89.5	88.9
1	Germany	7,099	6,925	7,156	7,472	19.9	21.0	19.0	19.2
2	China	5,450	5,008	5,539	5,859	15.3	15.2	14.7	15.0
3	Mexico	2,783	2,222	3,625	3,436	7.8	6.8	9.6	8.8
4	Canada	2,438	2,476	2,845	2,774	6.8	7.5	7.5	7.1
5	Japan	1,803	1,923	2,410	2,616	5.1	5.8	6.4	6.7
6	Italy	1,160	1,194	1,156	1,290	3.3	3.6	3.1	3.3
7	Austria	907	891	1,336	1,195	2.5	2.7	3.5	3.1
8	United Kingdom	1,348	1,324	915	1,101	3.8	4.0	2.4	2.8
9	France	900	956	1,121	1,082	2.5	2.9	3.0	2.8
10	India	793	719	834	921	2.2	2.2	2.2	2.4
11	Vietnam	408	377	467	577	1.1	1.1	1.2	1.5
12	Czech Republic	436	420	511	560	1.2	1.3	1.4	1.4
13	Taiwan	359	387	534	558	1.0	1.2	1.4	1.4
14	Malaysia	442	448	710	543	1.2	1.4	1.9	1.4
15	Hungary	312	253	385	507	0.9	0.8	1.0	1.3
16	Brazil	778	420	556	480	2.2	1.3	1.5	1.2
17	Russia	177	127	585	457	0.5	0.4	1.6	1.2
18	Netherlands	821	468	513	455	2.3	1.4	1.4	1.2
19	Honduras	376	291	434	452	1.1	0.9	1.2	1.2
20	Thailand	462	417	408	433	1.3	1.3	1.1	1.1
21	Indonesia	814	609	437	427	2.3	1.9	1.2	1.1
22	Korea, South	372	428	426	423	1.0	1.3	1.1	1.1
23	Belgium	394	375	401	387	1.1	1.1	1.1	1.0
24	Ireland	61	175	236	343	0.2	0.5	0.6	0.9
25	Spain	256	258	236	312	0.7	0.8	0.6	0.8

Table E-42.   State Trade by Country: South Dakota, 2012–2015

(Top 25 countries based on 2015 dollar value. Value in millions of dollars.)

U.S. Exports by Origin State

Rank	Country	Value (Millions of dollars)				Percent of Share			
		2012	2013	2014	2015	2012	2013	2014	2015
	Total South Dakota Exports and % Share of U.S. Total	1,557	1,584	1,594	1,405	0.1	0.1	0.1	0.1
	Total, Top 25 Countries and % Share of State Total	1,433	1,463	1,465	1,306	92.0	92.3	91.9	93.0
1	Canada	699	694	715	527	44.9	43.8	44.9	37.5
2	Mexico	346	373	344	404	22.2	23.5	21.6	28.8
3	Saudi Arabia	28	70	51	64	1.8	4.4	3.2	4.6
4	Japan	55	41	39	36	3.5	2.6	2.5	2.6
5	China	78	49	39	34	5.0	3.1	2.5	2.4
6	Australia	31	39	29	34	2.0	2.5	1.8	2.4
7	Belgium	44	34	51	23	2.8	2.1	3.2	1.7
8	Korea, South	15	16	34	23	0.9	1.0	2.1	1.6
9	Germany	13	17	19	15	0.8	1.1	1.2	1.1
10	United Arab Emirates	4	4	4	15	0.3	0.2	0.2	1.0
11	Hong Kong	14	17	13	14	0.9	1.1	0.8	1.0
12	Israel	12	13	18	14	0.8	0.8	1.1	1.0
13	Switzerland	1	1	2	14	0.1	0.1	0.1	1.0
14	France	9	7	11	10	0.6	0.4	0.7	0.7
15	United Kingdom	28	9	10	9	1.8	0.5	0.6	0.7
16	Taiwan	6	7	8	8	0.4	0.4	0.5	0.6
17	Ukraine	2	6	2	8	0.1	0.4	0.2	0.6
18	New Zealand	6	8	14	8	0.4	0.5	0.9	0.6
19	Singapore	6	12	15	8	0.4	0.8	0.9	0.5
20	Netherlands	3	5	4	7	0.2	0.3	0.3	0.5
21	Colombia	6	5	9	7	0.4	0.3	0.6	0.5
22	Brazil	19	24	21	6	1.2	1.5	1.3	0.5
23	Argentina	3	3	4	6	0.2	0.2	0.2	0.4
24	Finland	6	5	4	6	0.4	0.3	0.2	0.4
25	Papua New Guinea	1	5	6	6	0.1	0.3	0.3	0.4

U.S. Imports by State of Final Destination

Rank	Country	Value (Millions of dollars)				Percent of Share			
		2012	2013	2014	2015	2012	2013	2014	2015
	Total South Dakota Imports and % Share of U.S. Total	954	999	1,042	1,140	0.0	0.0	0.0	0.1
	Total, Top 25 Countries and % Share of State Total	928	975	1,019	1,124	97.3	97.7	97.8	98.6
1	Canada	452	462	481	543	47.4	46.3	46.2	47.6
2	Brazil	115	111	141	158	12.0	11.1	13.6	13.9
3	China	128	133	143	153	13.4	13.3	13.8	13.4
4	Mexico	58	65	71	70	6.1	6.5	6.8	6.1
5	Japan	13	26	37	32	1.3	2.6	3.5	2.8
6	Taiwan	20	20	23	26	2.1	2.0	2.2	2.2
7	Germany	29	32	22	21	3.0	3.2	2.1	1.9
8	Italy	26	21	13	15	2.7	2.1	1.3	1.3
9	Korea, South	8	5	7	14	0.9	0.5	0.7	1.2
10	Switzerland	2	6	3	12	0.2	0.6	0.3	1.0
11	Malaysia	8	8	13	11	0.8	0.8	1.2	0.9
12	Netherlands	4	7	4	8	0.4	0.7	0.4	0.7
13	Austria	5	10	7	7	0.5	1.0	0.6	0.6
14	India	4	5	6	7	0.4	0.5	0.6	0.6
15	Vietnam	4	4	6	7	0.4	0.4	0.6	0.6
16	United Kingdom	10	5	6	7	1.1	0.5	0.5	0.6
17	Spain	3	5	5	6	0.3	0.5	0.5	0.5
18	Poland	0	0	1	6	0.0	0.0	0.1	0.5
19	Sweden	3	1	3	5	0.3	0.1	0.3	0.4
20	France	16	37	13	4	1.7	3.7	1.2	0.4
21	Philippines	3	5	7	4	0.3	0.5	0.7	0.4
22	Belgium	2	2	1	3	0.2	0.2	0.1	0.2
23	Argentina	0	0	0	3	0.0	0.0	0.0	0.2
24	Ireland	1	1	2	3	0.1	0.1	0.2	0.2
25	Thailand	15	4	2	2	1.6	0.4	0.2	0.2

'(Z)' indicates a percent change greater than 500.

Table E-43. State Trade by Country: Tennessee, 2012–2015

(Top 25 countries based on 2015 dollar value. Value in millions of dollars.)

U.S. Exports by Origin State

Rank	Country	Value (Millions of dollars)				Percent of Share			
		2012	2013	2014	2015	2012	2013	2014	2015
	Total Tennessee Exports and % Share of U.S. Total	31,143	32,307	32,940	32,431	2.0	2.0	2.0	2.2
	Total, Top 25 Countries and % Share of State Total	27,573	28,489	29,230	29,080	88.5	88.2	88.7	89.7
1	Canada	8,660	8,720	9,160	8,648	27.8	27.0	27.8	26.7
2	Mexico	4,232	4,324	4,760	4,785	13.6	13.4	14.5	14.8
3	China	2,180	2,225	2,334	2,228	7.0	6.9	7.1	6.9
4	Japan	1,847	1,984	1,731	1,868	5.9	6.1	5.3	5.8
5	Belgium	1,295	1,232	1,184	1,275	4.2	3.8	3.6	3.9
6	Netherlands	919	1,031	1,024	1,123	3.0	3.2	3.1	3.5
7	Singapore	684	1,004	981	979	2.2	3.1	3.0	3.0
8	United Kingdom	898	886	925	956	2.9	2.7	2.8	2.9
9	Germany	792	731	807	922	2.5	2.3	2.4	2.8
10	Australia	915	925	859	905	2.9	2.9	2.6	2.8
11	Korea, South	594	690	745	794	1.9	2.1	2.3	2.4
12	Brazil	705	750	835	732	2.3	2.3	2.5	2.3
13	United Arab Emirates	562	605	499	542	1.8	1.9	1.5	1.7
14	Chile	440	449	376	436	1.4	1.4	1.1	1.3
15	France	349	367	332	338	1.1	1.1	1.0	1.0
16	Hong Kong	359	289	290	332	1.2	0.9	0.9	1.0
17	India	280	256	262	292	0.9	0.8	0.8	0.9
18	Switzerland	190	261	295	270	0.6	0.8	0.9	0.8
19	Italy	364	291	349	259	1.2	0.9	1.1	0.8
20	Taiwan	316	323	317	255	1.0	1.0	1.0	0.8
21	Colombia	275	289	347	253	0.9	0.9	1.1	0.8
22	Vietnam	118	157	141	253	0.4	0.5	0.4	0.8
23	Philippines	154	181	143	235	0.5	0.6	0.4	0.7
24	South Africa	178	160	161	201	0.6	0.5	0.5	0.6
25	Saudi Arabia	266	360	373	199	0.9	1.1	1.1	0.6

U.S. Imports by State of Final Destination

Rank	Country	Value (Millions of dollars)				Percent of Share			
		2012	2013	2014	2015	2012	2013	2014	2015
	Total Tennessee Imports and % Share of U.S. Total	61,484	65,026	69,754	76,864	2.7	2.9	3.0	3.4
	Total, Top 25 Countries and % Share of State Total	59,089	62,889	67,334	74,354	96.1	96.7	96.5	96.7
1	China	20,580	22,418	25,334	27,150	33.5	34.5	36.3	35.3
2	Japan	10,539	10,333	8,211	7,239	17.1	15.9	11.8	9.4
3	Mexico	4,963	5,686	6,713	7,210	8.1	8.7	9.6	9.4
4	Ireland	2,052	3,040	4,097	7,002	3.3	4.7	5.9	9.1
5	Canada	5,289	5,418	5,458	5,758	8.6	8.3	7.8	7.5
6	Germany	2,647	2,659	2,952	3,181	4.3	4.1	4.2	4.1
7	Vietnam	1,025	1,170	1,321	1,568	1.7	1.8	1.9	2.0
8	Korea, South	481	492	810	1,544	0.8	0.8	1.2	2.0
9	India	1,425	1,307	984	1,431	2.3	2.0	1.4	1.9
10	United Kingdom	1,249	1,381	1,111	1,374	2.0	2.1	1.6	1.8
11	Singapore	191	508	534	1,096	0.3	0.8	0.8	1.4
12	Thailand	692	715	957	1,046	1.1	1.1	1.4	1.4
13	Taiwan	858	851	1,019	1,003	1.4	1.3	1.5	1.3
14	France	1,355	1,013	960	962	2.2	1.6	1.4	1.3
15	Indonesia	996	929	944	924	1.6	1.4	1.4	1.2
16	Belgium	718	966	1,007	920	1.2	1.5	1.7	1.2
17	Italy	777	764	628	884	1.3	1.2	0.9	1.2
18	Switzerland	685	841	882	734	1.1	1.3	1.3	1.0
19	Brazil	405	415	514	630	0.7	0.6	0.7	0.8
20	Malaysia	465	435	573	617	0.8	0.7	0.8	0.8
21	Netherlands	289	349	491	600	0.5	0.5	0.7	0.8
22	Spain	430	397	668	556	0.7	0.6	1.0	0.7
23	Philippines	493	366	476	437	0.8	0.6	0.7	0.6
24	Sweden	340	289	314	297	0.6	0.4	0.5	0.4
25	Cambodia	147	148	178	191	0.2	0.2	0.3	0.2

Table E-44.   State Trade by Country: Texas, 2012–2015

(Top 25 countries based on 2015 dollar value. Value in millions of dollars.)

U.S. Exports by Origin State

Rank	Country	Value (Millions of dollars)				Percent of Share			
		2012	2013	2014	2015	2012	2013	2014	2015
	Total Texas Exports and % Share of U.S. Total	264,665	279,371	288,049	251,087	17.1	17.7	17.8	16.7
	Total, Top 25 Countries and % Share of State Total	224,840	236,889	246,063	216,772	85.0	84.8	85.4	86.3
1	Mexico	94,434	100,930	102,556	94,524	35.7	36.1	35.6	37.6
2	Canada	23,859	26,054	31,295	25,387	9.0	9.3	10.9	10.1
3	China	10,305	10,847	10,948	11,611	3.9	3.9	3.8	4.6
4	Korea, South	7,761	7,878	8,918	8,094	2.9	2.8	3.1	3.2
5	Brazil	10,035	10,847	11,832	7,217	3.8	3.9	4.1	2.9
6	Netherlands	9,597	9,500	8,753	6,839	3.6	3.4	3.0	2.7
7	Colombia	5,631	7,096	7,295	6,028	2.1	2.5	2.5	2.4
8	Japan	4,674	5,111	5,534	5,079	1.8	1.8	1.9	2.0
9	Singapore	6,383	5,736	5,601	4,944	2.4	2.1	1.9	2.0
10	Belgium	4,324	4,664	4,631	4,632	1.6	1.7	1.6	1.8
11	United Kingdom	4,234	3,740	4,425	4,452	1.6	1.3	1.5	1.8
12	Venezuela	6,925	5,368	4,532	3,891	2.6	1.9	1.6	1.5
13	Germany	2,608	2,791	3,185	3,270	1.0	1.0	1.1	1.3
14	Saudi Arabia	3,978	3,846	3,600	3,266	1.5	1.4	1.2	1.3
15	Taiwan	3,471	4,051	4,069	3,248	1.3	1.5	1.4	1.3
16	Chile	4,270	4,564	4,002	3,059	1.6	1.6	1.4	1.2
17	Ecuador	2,448	2,692	3,546	2,770	0.9	1.0	1.2	1.1
18	France	3,827	3,719	3,233	2,726	1.4	1.3	1.1	1.1
19	Argentina	2,594	3,066	3,385	2,678	1.0	1.1	1.2	1.1
20	Peru	2,623	3,060	2,706	2,455	1.0	1.1	0.9	1.0
21	Panama	2,458	2,483	3,224	2,441	0.9	0.9	1.1	1.0
22	United Arab Emirates	2,191	2,676	2,599	2,403	0.8	1.0	0.9	1.0
23	Hong Kong	1,492	1,715	1,931	2,059	0.6	0.6	0.7	0.8
24	Australia	2,702	2,474	2,306	1,921	1.0	0.9	0.8	0.8
25	India	2,016	1,982	1,958	1,777	0.8	0.7	0.7	0.7

U.S. Imports by State of Final Destination

Rank	Country	Value (Millions of dollars)				Percent of Share			
		2012	2013	2014	2015	2012	2013	2014	2015
	Total Texas Imports and % Share of U.S. Total	330,295	311,867	302,277	251,492	14.5	13.7	12.9	11.2
	Total, Top 25 Countries and % Share of State Total	287,094	279,262	274,633	228,518	86.9	89.5	90.9	90.9
1	Mexico	99,868	94,677	90,138	83,473	30.2	30.4	29.8	33.2
2	China	40,697	42,833	45,447	40,932	12.3	13.7	15.0	16.3
3	Canada	16,039	14,659	17,445	15,923	4.9	4.7	5.8	6.3
4	Korea, South	7,242	9,322	10,618	10,333	2.2	3.0	3.5	4.1
5	Germany	6,907	8,075	8,738	8,543	2.1	2.6	2.9	3.4
6	Saudi Arabia	20,101	22,560	19,089	7,644	6.1	7.2	6.3	3.0
7	Venezuela	19,143	16,210	15,226	7,511	5.8	5.2	5.0	3.0
8	Japan	7,373	6,766	6,352	6,351	2.2	2.2	2.1	2.5
9	Vietnam	1,634	1,653	2,370	5,100	0.5	0.5	0.8	2.0
10	United Kingdom	4,867	4,824	5,190	4,758	1.5	1.5	1.7	1.9
11	Brazil	6,391	4,696	5,647	4,380	1.9	1.5	1.9	1.7
12	Malaysia	3,362	3,422	3,492	3,506	1.0	1.1	1.2	1.4
13	Russia	8,339	8,742	6,244	3,473	2.5	2.8	2.1	1.4
14	India	6,211	4,288	4,045	3,332	1.9	1.4	1.3	1.3
15	France	3,112	3,188	3,424	3,302	0.9	1.0	1.1	1.3
16	Thailand	3,108	3,014	2,892	2,946	0.9	1.0	1.0	1.2
17	Italy	3,048	2,619	2,927	2,917	0.9	0.8	1.0	1.2
18	Colombia	8,449	7,453	5,482	2,413	2.6	2.4	1.8	1.0
19	Taiwan	3,003	2,929	2,917	2,350	0.9	0.9	1.0	0.9
20	Netherlands	2,035	1,811	2,297	1,797	0.6	0.6	0.8	0.7
21	Kuwait	4,339	6,435	6,811	1,737	1.3	2.1	2.3	0.7
22	Ireland	926	1,085	1,320	1,610	0.3	0.3	0.4	0.6
23	Iraq	8,803	5,410	3,574	1,598	2.7	1.7	1.2	0.6
24	Belgium	994	1,555	1,616	1,295	0.3	0.5	0.5	0.5
25	Spain	1,102	1,037	1,335	1,291	0.3	0.3	0.4	0.5

Table E-45. State Trade by Country: Utah, 2012–2015

(Top 25 countries based on 2015 dollar value. Value in millions of dollars.)

U.S. Exports by Origin State

Rank	Country	Value (Millions of dollars)				Percent of Share			
		2012	2013	2014	2015	2012	2013	2014	2015
	Total Utah Exports and % Share of U.S. Total	19,260	16,111	12,306	13,282	1.2	1.0	0.8	0.9
	Total, Top 25 Countries and % Share of State Total	18,429	15,232	11,405	12,496	95.7	94.5	92.7	94.1
1	United Kingdom	6,043	1,293	1,415	3,037	31.4	8.0	11.5	22.9
2	Hong Kong	4,178	5,528	1,761	1,947	21.7	34.3	14.3	14.7
3	Canada	1,918	1,324	1,421	1,488	10.0	8.2	11.5	11.2
4	Mexico	487	547	742	854	2.5	3.4	6.0	6.4
5	China	608	1,413	892	841	3.2	8.8	7.2	6.3
6	Taiwan	533	477	677	710	2.8	3.0	5.5	5.3
7	Japan	563	628	553	546	2.9	3.9	4.5	4.1
8	Korea, South	243	341	404	377	1.3	2.1	3.3	2.8
9	Netherlands	165	254	388	364	0.9	1.6	3.2	2.7
10	Singapore	484	644	545	359	2.5	4.0	4.4	2.7
11	Germany	294	228	256	266	1.5	1.4	2.1	2.0
12	Switzerland	99	268	255	219	0.5	1.7	2.1	1.6
13	Australia	324	162	184	190	1.7	1.0	1.5	1.4
14	India	1,056	311	325	182	5.5	1.9	2.6	1.4
15	Italy	142	168	140	167	0.7	1.0	1.1	1.3
16	Thailand	507	835	532	148	2.6	5.2	4.3	1.1
17	France	104	109	114	129	0.5	0.7	0.9	1.0
18	Belgium	222	141	268	127	1.2	0.9	2.2	1.0
19	Philippines	132	156	164	113	0.7	1.0	1.3	0.9
20	Malaysia	84	103	97	98	0.4	0.6	0.8	0.7
21	Brazil	98	118	114	92	0.5	0.7	0.9	0.7
22	United Arab Emirates	50	47	38	69	0.3	0.3	0.3	0.5
23	Chile	47	61	73	66	0.2	0.4	0.6	0.5
24	Indonesia	34	64	37	59	0.2	0.4	0.3	0.4
25	Austria	15	12	11	46	0.1	0.1	0.1	0.3

U.S. Imports by State of Final Destination

Rank	Country	Value (Millions of dollars)				Percent of Share			
		2012	2013	2014	2015	2012	2013	2014	2015
	Total Utah Imports and % Share of U.S. Total	11,150	10,639	11,118	12,093	0.5	0.5	0.5	0.5
	Total, Top 25 Countries and % Share of State Total	10,589	9,971	10,422	11,431	95.0	93.7	93.7	94.5
1	Mexico	4,409	3,470	3,126	3,337	39.5	32.6	28.1	27.6
2	China	1,656	1,887	2,007	2,228	14.9	17.7	18.1	18.4
3	Canada	1,599	1,656	1,682	1,821	14.3	15.6	15.1	15.1
4	Brazil	47	111	579	716	0.4	1.0	5.2	5.9
5	Taiwan	257	326	373	493	2.3	3.1	3.4	4.1
6	Peru	1,066	831	428	357	9.6	7.8	3.8	3.0
7	Colombia	1	84	342	328	0.0	0.8	3.1	2.7
8	Guatemala	549	418	366	309	4.9	3.9	3.3	2.6
9	Nicaragua	0	1	65	206	0.0	0.0	0.6	1.7
10	Germany	173	198	195	188	1.6	1.9	1.8	1.6
11	Japan	125	137	145	174	1.1	1.3	1.3	1.4
12	France	110	111	196	173	1.0	1.0	1.8	1.4
13	Vietnam	39	58	74	133	0.3	0.5	0.7	1.1
14	Italy	72	91	104	127	0.6	0.9	0.9	1.1
15	Korea, South	43	82	80	106	0.4	0.8	0.7	0.9
16	Chile	98	158	75	102	0.9	1.5	0.7	0.0
17	Honduras	1	1	99	98	0.0	0.0	0.9	0.8
18	United Kingdom	77	67	78	91	0.7	0.6	0.7	0.8
19	India	61	65	116	84	0.5	0.6	1.0	0.7
20	Malaysia	37	52	55	69	0.3	0.5	0.5	0.6
21	Austria	68	50	51	66	0.6	0.5	0.5	0.5
22	Hong Kong	18	19	42	62	0.2	0.2	0.4	0.5
23	Romania	25	26	43	57	0.2	0.2	0.4	0.5
24	Spain	31	31	55	54	0.3	0.3	0.5	0.4
25	Ireland	26	37	44	53	0.2	0.3	0.4	0.4

Table E-46. State Trade by Country: Vermont, 2012–2015

(Top 25 countries based on 2015 dollar value. Value in millions of dollars.)

U.S. Exports by Origin State

Rank	Country	Value (Millions of dollars)				Percent of Share			
		2012	2013	2014	2015	2012	2013	2014	2015
	Total Vermont Exports and % Share of U.S. Total	4,139	4,027	3,669	3,176	0.3	0.3	0.2	0.2
	Total, Top 25 Countries and % Share of State Total	3,998	3,894	3,558	3,071	96.6	96.7	97.0	96.7
1	Canada	1,828	1,869	1,637	1,166	44.2	46.4	44.6	36.7
2	Hong Kong	255	334	333	302	6.2	8.3	9.1	9.5
3	Malaysia	171	173	197	232	4.1	4.3	5.4	7.3
4	China	584	491	275	220	14.1	12.2	7.5	6.9
5	Mexico	130	130	212	213	3.1	3.2	5.8	6.7
6	Korea, South	152	136	142	134	3.7	3.4	3.9	4.2
7	Taiwan	145	116	93	110	3.5	2.9	2.5	3.5
8	Netherlands	48	52	94	108	1.2	1.3	2.6	3.4
9	United Kingdom	57	53	75	87	1.4	1.3	2.0	2.7
10	Singapore	105	92	69	86	2.5	2.3	1.9	2.7
11	Japan	179	153	111	81	4.3	3.8	3.0	2.6
12	Thailand	47	58	52	62	1.1	1.4	1.4	2.0
13	Germany	55	56	60	60	1.3	1.4	1.6	1.9
14	France	35	43	58	52	0.8	1.1	1.6	1.6
15	Italy	20	25	23	23	0.5	0.6	0.6	0.7
16	Israel	13	9	10	20	0.3	0.2	0.3	0.6
17	Belgium	24	20	20	18	0.6	0.5	0.5	0.6
18	Switzerland	6	7	9	15	0.1	0.2	0.2	0.5
19	Australia	15	15	13	15	0.4	0.4	0.4	0.5
20	Ireland	49	23	27	15	1.2	0.6	0.7	0.5
21	India	10	16	11	13	0.2	0.4	0.3	0.4
22	United Arab Emirates	7	3	8	13	0.2	0.1	0.2	0.4
23	Brazil	5	7	15	10	0.1	0.2	0.4	0.3
24	Spain	7	9	8	9	0.2	0.2	0.2	0.3
25	Sweden	51	4	5	7	1.2	0.1	0.1	0.2

U.S. Imports by State of Final Destination

Rank	Country	Value (Millions of dollars)				Percent of Share			
		2012	2013	2014	2015	2012	2013	2014	2015
	Total Vermont Imports and % Share of U.S. Total	4,351	4,949	4,760	4,023	0.2	0.2	0.2	0.2
	Total, Top 25 Countries and % Share of State Total	4,176	4,797	4,631	3,900	96.0	96.9	97.3	97.0
1	Canada	3,291	3,776	3,720	2,878	75.6	76.3	78.2	71.5
2	China	243	281	226	265	5.6	5.7	4.7	6.6
3	Vietnam	27	43	48	74	0.6	0.9	1.0	1.8
4	United Kingdom	60	57	62	66	1.4	1.2	1.3	1.6
5	India	63	69	69	65	1.4	1.4	1.4	1.6
6	Korea, South	31	33	39	64	0.7	0.7	0.8	1.6
7	Japan	48	53	38	61	1.1	1.1	0.8	1.5
8	France	20	25	26	54	0.5	0.5	0.5	1.3
9	Indonesia	21	53	44	53	0.5	1.1	0.9	1.3
10	Germany	67	70	67	51	1.5	1.4	1.4	1.3
11	Taiwan	23	33	42	42	0.5	0.7	0.9	1.0
12	Russia	28	34	38	40	0.6	0.7	0.8	1.0
13	Mexico	98	109	46	33	2.3	2.2	1.0	0.8
14	Italy	36	30	28	27	0.8	0.6	0.6	0.7
15	Austria	10	11	10	16	0.2	0.2	0.2	0.4
16	Spain	12	14	15	15	0.3	0.3	0.3	0.4
17	Malaysia	7	16	25	14	0.2	0.3	0.5	0.3
18	Colombia	12	13	19	12	0.3	0.3	0.4	0.3
19	Switzerland	29	26	18	11	0.7	0.5	0.4	0.3
20	Turkey	3	6	6	11	0.1	0.1	0.1	0.3
21	Ecuador	20	16	12	11	0.5	0.3	0.3	0.3
22	New Zealand	6	9	9	11	0.1	0.2	0.2	0.3
23	Brazil	8	5	8	9	0.2	0.1	0.2	0.2
24	Romania	9	13	7	9	0.2	0.3	0.1	0.2
25	Belgium	3	3	11	9	0.1	0.1	0.2	0.2

Table E-47. State Trade by Country: Virginia, 2012–2015

(Top 25 countries based on 2015 dollar value. Value in millions of dollars.)

U.S. Exports by Origin State

Rank	Country	Value (Millions of dollars)				Percent of Share			
		2012	2013	2014	2015	2012	2013	2014	2015
	Total Virginia Exports and % Share of U.S. Total	18,277	17,904	19,255	18,137	1.2	1.1	1.2	1.2
	Total, Top 25 Countries and % Share of State Total	14,449	14,091	15,318	14,748	79.1	78.7	79.6	81.3
1	Canada	3,194	3,227	3,678	3,383	17.5	18.0	19.1	18.7
2	China	2,004	1,871	2,000	1,705	11.0	10.5	10.4	9.4
3	Mexico	1,055	1,051	1,218	1,231	5.8	5.9	6.3	6.8
4	United Kingdom	1,077	991	971	1,049	5.9	5.5	5.0	5.8
5	Germany	922	790	856	844	5.0	4.4	4.4	4.7
6	Japan	476	554	553	582	2.6	3.1	2.9	3.2
7	Taiwan	371	458	520	578	2.0	2.6	2.7	3.2
8	Belgium	384	435	526	557	2.1	2.4	2.7	3.1
9	Netherlands	336	570	504	556	1.8	3.2	2.6	3.1
10	Brazil	800	427	460	522	4.4	2.4	2.4	2.9
11	Korea, South	313	368	429	486	1.7	2.1	2.2	2.7
12	Saudi Arabia	309	371	416	368	1.7	2.1	2.2	2.0
13	Singapore	427	526	528	349	2.3	2.9	2.7	1.9
14	Italy	253	204	283	282	1.4	1.1	1.5	1.6
15	France	309	290	246	281	1.7	1.6	1.3	1.5
16	Australia	450	265	246	262	2.5	1.5	1.3	1.4
17	India	265	214	230	237	1.4	1.2	1.2	1.3
18	Switzerland	172	238	211	235	0.9	1.3	1.1	1.3
19	Indonesia	233	308	308	229	1.3	1.7	1.6	1.3
20	Hong Kong	216	230	214	186	1.2	1.3	1.1	1.0
21	Colombia	176	147	156	183	1.0	0.8	0.8	1.0
22	Turkey	295	169	219	169	1.6	0.9	1.1	0.9
23	Spain	133	121	209	161	0.7	0.7	1.1	0.9
24	United Arab Emirates	165	159	218	156	0.9	0.9	1.1	0.9
25	Malaysia	115	106	118	156	0.6	0.6	0.6	0.9

U.S. Imports by State of Final Destination

Rank	Country	Value (Millions of dollars)				Percent of Share			
		2012	2013	2014	2015	2012	2013	2014	2015
	Total Virginia Imports and % Share of U.S. Total	21,867	22,383	24,287	25,017	1.0	1.0	1.0	1.1
	Total, Top 25 Countries and % Share of State Total	19,051	19,439	21,223	22,224	87.1	86.8	87.4	88.8
1	China	4,160	5,043	5,855	6,917	19.0	22.5	24.1	27.6
2	Canada	1,964	1,838	1,853	1,799	9.0	8.2	7.6	7.2
3	Germany	1,765	1,703	1,692	1,698	8.1	7.6	7.0	6.8
4	Japan	2,158	1,695	1,387	1,260	9.9	7.6	5.7	5.0
5	United Kingdom	843	908	1,327	1,196	3.9	4.1	5.5	4.8
6	Malaysia	187	1,033	1,114	1,189	0.9	4.6	4.6	4.8
7	Mexico	493	573	731	917	2.3	2.6	3.0	3.7
8	Austria	476	664	800	789	2.2	3.0	3.3	3.2
9	India	894	798	728	753	4.1	3.6	3.0	3.0
10	Italy	630	654	840	738	2.9	2.9	3.5	2.9
11	Vietnam	355	472	552	649	1.6	2.1	2.3	2.6
12	Israel	322	343	408	481	1.5	1.5	1.7	1.9
13	Indonesia	506	508	614	478	2.3	2.3	2.5	1.9
14	Brazil	546	504	675	442	2.5	2.3	2.8	1.8
15	France	421	351	373	439	1.9	1.6	1.5	1.8
16	Korea, South	180	191	266	397	0.8	0.9	1.1	1.6
17	Taiwan	247	234	257	311	1.1	1.0	1.1	1.2
18	Singapore	1,641	597	348	290	7.5	2.7	1.4	1.2
19	Turkey	194	226	238	243	0.9	1.0	1.0	1.0
20	Switzerland	293	175	211	222	1.3	0.8	0.9	0.9
21	Belgium	179	163	196	215	0.8	0.7	0.8	0.9
22	Spain	183	226	215	211	0.8	1.0	0.9	0.8
23	Guatemala	62	81	116	208	0.3	0.4	0.5	0.8
24	Thailand	212	210	212	197	1.0	0.9	0.9	0.8
25	Sweden	139	249	217	184	0.6	1.1	0.9	0.7

Table E-48.   State Trade by Country: Washington, 2012–2015

(Top 25 countries based on 2015 dollar value. Value in millions of dollars.)

U.S. Exports by Origin State

Rank	Country	Value (Millions of dollars)				Percent of Share			
		2012	2013	2014	2015	2012	2013	2014	2015
	Total Washington Exports and % Share of U.S. Total	75,654	81,631	90,547	86,353	4.9	5.2	5.6	5.7
	Total, Top 25 Countries and % Share of State Total	65,706	71,068	76,759	76,920	86.9	87.1	84.8	89.1
1	China	14,157	16,711	20,690	19,456	18.7	20.5	22.8	22.5
2	Canada	8,381	8,993	9,291	8,008	11.1	11.0	10.3	9.3
3	Japan	9,026	7,037	7,364	5,993	11.9	8.6	8.1	6.9
4	Korea, South	3,384	2,712	2,754	4,293	4.5	3.3	3.0	5.0
5	United Arab Emirates	5,059	3,870	3,272	3,212	6.7	4.7	3.6	3.7
6	Chile	1,000	1,386	1,102	3,010	1.3	1.7	1.2	3.5
7	Taiwan	1,515	1,443	2,475	2,756	2.0	1.8	2.7	3.2
8	Singapore	910	1,253	1,714	2,567	1.2	1.5	1.9	3.0
9	United Kingdom	1,610	2,702	2,951	2,554	2.1	3.3	3.3	3.0
10	Turkey	856	548	1,340	1,892	1.1	0.7	1.5	2.2
11	Saudi Arabia	1,127	1,661	811	1,876	1.5	2.0	0.9	2.2
12	Mexico	2,864	3,198	2,735	1,871	3.8	3.9	3.0	2.2
13	Thailand	728	1,347	1,943	1,859	1.0	1.6	2.1	2.2
14	Germany	1,877	2,103	2,061	1,850	2.5	2.6	2.3	2.1
15	Qatar	1,180	2,194	2,344	1,809	1.6	2.7	2.6	2.1
16	Indonesia	1,610	2,290	2,173	1,754	2.1	2.8	2.4	2.0
17	Netherlands	916	831	889	1,680	1.2	1.0	1.0	1.9
18	Hong Kong	2,161	2,703	1,968	1,606	2.9	3.3	2.2	1.9
19	Russia	906	1,545	2,135	1,601	1.2	1.9	2.4	1.9
20	France	883	562	679	1,391	1.2	0.7	0.7	1.6
21	Australia	1,698	1,495	1,515	1,350	2.2	1.8	1.7	1.6
22	Ethiopia	947	468	793	1,225	1.3	0.6	0.9	1.4
23	India	1,273	2,221	2,134	1,151	1.7	2.7	2.4	1.3
24	Vietnam	223	328	508	1,080	0.3	0.4	0.6	1.3
25	Philippines	1,412	1,467	1,119	1,074	1.9	1.8	1.2	1.2

U.S. Imports by State of Final Destination

Rank	Country	Value (Millions of dollars)				Percent of Share			
		2012	2013	2014	2015	2012	2013	2014	2015
	Total Washington Imports and % Share of U.S. Total	47,627	49,927	52,379	51,271	2.1	2.2	2.2	2.3
	Total, Top 25 Countries and % Share of State Total	44,112	46,651	49,678	48,771	92.6	93.4	94.8	95.1
1	Canada	13,819	14,565	16,298	13,540	29.0	29.2	31.1	26.4
2	China	8,465	8,801	8,302	10,349	17.8	17.6	15.9	20.2
3	Japan	6,143	7,055	6,931	6,704	12.9	14.1	13.2	13.1
4	Korea, South	2,197	2,161	2,503	2,843	4.6	4.3	4.8	5.5
5	Taiwan	1,949	2,004	2,545	2,117	4.1	4.0	4.9	4.1
6	France	1,690	1,860	2,218	1,510	3.5	3.7	4.2	2.9
7	United Kingdom	1,545	1,758	2,134	1,470	3.2	3.5	4.1	2.9
8	Mexico	556	791	789	1,287	1.2	1.6	1.5	2.5
9	Thailand	582	582	706	1,086	1.2	1.2	1.3	2.1
10	Australia	707	793	934	927	1.5	1.6	1.8	1.8
11	Germany	808	795	774	915	1.7	1.6	1.5	1.8
12	Vietnam	394	430	548	907	0.8	0.9	1.0	1.8
13	Singapore	187	310	192	794	0.4	0.6	0.4	1.5
14	Italy	530	510	499	539	1.1	1.0	1.0	1.1
15	Russia	1,398	697	584	505	2.9	1.4	1.1	1.0
16	Malaysia	427	475	450	502	0.9	1.0	0.9	1.0
17	India	364	342	386	452	0.8	0.7	0.7	0.9
18	Indonesia	352	382	371	398	0.7	0.8	0.7	0.8
19	Netherlands	364	397	524	312	0.8	0.8	1.0	0.6
20	Brazil	269	262	208	302	0.6	0.5	0.4	0.6
21	Argentina	276	91	359	293	0.6	0.2	0.7	0.6
22	Philippines	129	184	265	289	0.3	0.4	0.5	0.6
23	Saudi Arabia	711	1,158	854	283	1.5	2.3	1.6	0.6
24	Chile	105	107	137	239	0.2	0.2	0.3	0.5
25	New Zealand	143	144	167	209	0.3	0.3	0.3	0.4

Table E-49.   State Trade by Country: West Virginia, 2012–2015

(Top 25 countries based on 2015 dollar value. Value in millions of dollars.)

U.S. Exports by Origin State

Rank	Country	Value (Millions of dollars)				Percent of Share			
		2012	2013	2014	2015	2012	2013	2014	2015
	Total West Virginia Exports and % Share of U.S. Total	11,407	8,620	7,486	5,722	0.7	0.5	0.5	0.4
	Total, Top 25 Countries and % Share of State Total	10,459	7,804	6,801	5,364	91.7	90.5	90.9	93.7
1	Canada	1,785	1,845	1,971	1,742	15.6	21.4	26.3	30.4
2	China	887	613	549	453	7.8	7.1	7.3	7.9
3	Netherlands	961	665	548	364	8.4	7.7	7.3	6.4
4	Brazil	686	513	473	304	6.0	6.0	6.3	5.3
5	Japan	773	310	268	302	6.8	3.6	3.6	5.3
6	India	739	314	185	224	6.5	3.6	2.5	3.9
7	Ukraine	359	294	276	219	3.1	3.4	3.7	3.8
8	United Kingdom	566	449	327	211	5.0	5.2	4.4	3.7
9	Belgium	331	286	230	210	2.9	3.3	3.1	3.7
10	Germany	345	286	259	189	3.0	3.3	3.5	3.3
11	Korea, South	612	211	150	185	5.4	2.4	2.0	3.2
12	Mexico	239	324	238	184	2.1	3.8	3.2	3.2
13	Italy	727	470	424	177	6.4	5.5	5.7	3.1
14	France	445	384	200	112	3.9	4.5	2.7	2.0
15	Hong Kong	66	68	93	68	0.6	0.8	1.2	1.2
16	Turkey	410	330	189	63	3.6	3.8	2.5	1.1
17	Sweden	91	56	64	58	0.8	0.6	0.9	1.0
18	Singapore	56	62	47	46	0.5	0.7	0.6	0.8
19	Spain	163	122	82	45	1.4	1.4	1.1	0.8
20	Thailand	28	26	41	38	0.2	0.3	0.5	0.7
21	Switzerland	30	12	38	38	0.3	0.1	0.5	0.7
22	Malaysia	13	27	16	36	0.1	0.3	0.2	0.6
23	Taiwan	39	42	48	33	0.3	0.5	0.6	0.6
24	Australia	48	39	52	33	0.4	0.5	0.7	0.6
25	Argentina	62	57	32	31	0.5	0.7	0.4	0.5

U.S. Imports by State of Final Destination

Rank	Country	Value (Millions of dollars)				Percent of Share			
		2012	2013	2014	2015	2012	2013	2014	2015
	Total West Virginia Imports and % Share of U.S. Total	3,809	3,701	3,811	3,776	0.2	0.2	0.2	0.2
	Total, Top 25 Countries and % Share of State Total	3,703	3,610	3,737	3,715	97.2	97.5	98.0	98.4
1	Japan	982	990	1,116	1,259	25.8	26.7	29.3	33.3
2	Canada	1,476	1,445	1,354	1,158	38.8	39.0	35.5	30.7
3	China	238	284	279	259	6.2	7.7	7.3	6.9
4	Mexico	273	160	253	220	7.2	4.3	6.6	5.8
5	Germany	132	185	166	156	3.5	5.0	4.4	4.1
6	France	59	63	107	113	1.5	1.7	2.8	3.0
7	Italy	53	41	43	66	1.4	1.1	1.1	1.7
8	India	135	127	66	64	3.5	3.4	1.7	1.7
9	Taiwan	31	40	44	47	0.8	1.1	1.2	1.2
10	United Kingdom	38	50	47	45	1.0	1.4	1.2	1.2
11	Kuwait	27	0	0	41	0.7	0.0	0.0	1.1
12	Belgium	22	45	42	40	0.6	1.2	1.1	1.1
13	Poland	22	26	32	38	0.6	0.7	0.8	1.0
14	Brazil	30	25	40	31	0.8	0.7	1.0	0.8
15	Pakistan	29	22	15	24	0.8	0.6	0.4	0.6
16	Switzerland	8	6	14	22	0.2	0.2	0.4	0.6
17	Spain	12	11	25	20	0.3	0.3	0.7	0.5
18	Netherlands	8	13	22	19	0.2	0.4	0.6	0.5
19	Vietnam	36	39	25	18	0.9	1.1	0.7	0.5
20	Israel	8	8	8	15	0.2	0.2	0.2	0.4
21	Korea, South	13	8	10	15	0.3	0.2	0.3	0.4
22	South Africa	9	5	6	12	0.2	0.1	0.2	0.3
23	Thailand	5	7	9	11	0.1	0.2	0.2	0.3
24	Austria	2	3	5	11	0.1	0.1	0.1	0.3
25	Malaysia	56	6	9	10	1.5	0.2	0.2	0.3

Table E-50.   State Trade by Country: Wisconsin, 2012–2015

(Top 25 countries based on 2015 dollar value. Value in millions of dollars.)

U.S. Exports by Origin State

Rank	Country	Value (Millions of dollars)				Percent of Share			
		2012	2013	2014	2015	2012	2013	2014	2015
	Total Wisconsin Exports and % Share of U.S. Total	23,119	23,109	23,428	22,445	1.5	1.5	1.4	1.5
	Total, Top 25 Countries and % Share of State Total	20,246	20,320	20,614	19,976	87.6	87.9	88.0	89.0
1	Canada	7,643	7,527	7,955	7,309	33.1	32.6	34.0	32.6
2	Mexico	2,167	2,515	2,835	2,967	9.4	10.9	12.1	13.2
3	China	1,547	1,659	1,561	1,546	6.7	7.2	6.7	6.9
4	United Kingdom	615	679	849	824	2.7	2.9	3.6	3.7
5	Japan	858	934	897	814	3.7	4.0	3.8	3.6
6	Germany	715	701	731	702	3.1	3.0	3.1	3.1
7	Saudi Arabia	312	396	368	597	1.3	1.7	1.6	2.7
8	Australia	866	676	605	584	3.7	2.9	2.6	2.6
9	Korea, South	403	431	472	507	1.7	1.9	2.0	2.3
10	France	509	460	489	457	2.2	2.0	2.1	2.0
11	Belgium	412	385	332	432	1.8	1.7	1.4	1.9
12	Brazil	498	477	515	403	2.2	2.1	2.2	1.8
13	Netherlands	395	379	427	393	1.7	1.6	1.8	1.7
14	Italy	271	279	309	311	1.2	1.2	1.3	1.4
15	Chile	555	474	290	283	2.4	2.0	1.2	1.3
16	Hong Kong	290	250	252	237	1.3	1.1	1.1	1.1
17	Singapore	330	259	246	221	1.4	1.1	1.0	1.0
18	India	457	289	230	215	2.0	1.3	1.0	1.0
19	Thailand	184	203	211	214	0.8	0.9	0.9	1.0
20	Peru	230	257	264	206	1.0	1.1	1.1	0.9
21	Taiwan	192	174	182	184	0.8	0.8	0.8	0.8
22	United Arab Emirates	305	394	170	177	1.3	1.7	0.7	0.8
23	Philippines	148	138	126	143	0.6	0.6	0.5	0.6
24	South Africa	228	261	178	132	1.0	1.1	0.8	0.6
25	Sweden	117	123	121	117	0.5	0.5	0.5	0.5

U.S. Imports by State of Final Destination

Rank	Country	Value (Millions of dollars)				Percent of Share			
		2012	2013	2014	2015	2012	2013	2014	2015
	Total Wisconsin Imports and % Share of U.S. Total	23,198	22,223	23,525	22,964	1.0	1.0	1.0	1.0
	Total, Top 25 Countries and % Share of State Total	21,177	20,308	21,526	21,273	91.3	91.4	91.5	92.6
1	China	5,772	5,854	6,063	6,205	24.9	26.3	25.8	27.0
2	Canada	4,190	4,213	4,517	4,207	18.1	19.0	19.2	18.3
3	Mexico	3,006	2,452	2,548	2,662	13.0	11.0	10.8	11.6
4	Germany	1,333	1,212	1,433	1,271	5.7	5.5	6.1	5.5
5	Vietnam	628	736	898	960	2.7	3.3	3.8	4.2
6	India	660	639	676	673	2.8	2.9	2.9	2.9
7	Japan	825	733	689	660	3.6	3.3	2.9	2.9
8	Italy	693	697	738	604	3.0	3.1	3.1	2.6
9	Taiwan	499	487	547	577	2.2	2.2	2.3	2.5
10	France	478	451	499	460	2.1	2.0	2.1	2.0
11	Indonesia	419	379	343	372	1.8	1.7	1.5	1.6
12	United Kingdom	266	291	337	345	1.1	1.3	1.4	1.5
13	Korea, South	357	313	337	332	1.5	1.4	1.4	1.4
14	Finland	292	278	287	248	1.3	1.2	1.2	1.1
15	Israel	170	165	177	214	0.7	0.7	0.8	0.9
16	Austria	182	178	194	178	0.8	0.8	0.8	0.8
17	Switzerland	201	174	191	176	0.9	0.8	0.8	0.8
18	Philippines	125	129	145	175	0.5	0.6	0.6	0.8
19	Bangladesh	203	220	165	168	0.9	1.0	0.7	0.7
20	Malaysia	226	130	141	142	1.0	0.6	0.6	0.6
21	Denmark	94	103	122	140	0.4	0.5	0.5	0.6
22	Netherlands	182	147	131	133	0.8	0.7	0.6	0.6
23	Thailand	104	86	95	128	0.4	0.4	0.4	0.6
24	Sweden	98	87	89	123	0.4	0.4	0.4	0.5
25	Cambodia	175	156	163	121	0.8	0.7	0.7	0.5

Table E-51. State Trade by Country: Wyoming, 2012–2015

(Top 25 countries based on 2015 dollar value. Value in millions of dollars.)

U.S. Exports by Origin State

Rank	Country	Value (Millions of dollars)				Percent of Share			
		2012	2013	2014	2015	2012	2013	2014	2015
	Total Wyoming Exports and Perent Share of U.S. Total	1,439	1,351	1,757	1,174	0.1	0.1	0.1	0.1
	Total, Top 25 Countries and % Share of State Total	1,330	1,255	1,662	1,106	92.4	92.9	94.6	94.2
1	Brazil	118	135	153	195	8.2	10.0	8.7	16.6
2	Canada	330	375	727	191	22.9	27.8	41.4	16.3
3	Indonesia	101	74	86	81	7.0	5.5	4.9	6.9
4	Japan	59	44	68	64	4.1	3.3	3.8	5.4
5	Australia	137	88	55	53	9.5	6.5	3.1	4.5
6	United Kingdom	21	23	45	52	1.5	1.7	2.6	4.5
7	Chile	73	65	62	46	5.1	4.8	3.5	3.9
8	Saudi Arabia	23	26	28	43	1.6	1.9	1.6	3.7
9	Taiwan	41	35	41	40	2.8	2.6	2.3	3.4
10	Korea, South	55	61	48	37	3.8	4.5	2.8	3.2
11	Venezuela	48	47	44	35	3.3	3.5	2.5	3.0
12	Mexico	56	49	31	30	3.9	3.6	1.8	2.5
13	Tunisia	26	29	28	25	1.8	2.2	1.6	2.1
14	Thailand	42	30	33	25	2.9	2.2	1.8	2.1
15	Colombia	23	19	41	24	1.6	1.4	2.3	2.1
16	United Arab Emirates	14	18	24	23	1.0	1.3	1.4	2.0
17	Netherlands	45	42	25	20	3.2	3.1	1.4	1.7
18	Argentina	25	18	19	19	1.8	1.3	1.1	1.6
19	South Africa	26	18	15	17	1.8	1.3	0.8	1.4
20	Belgium	9	2	9	16	0.6	0.2	0.5	1.3
21	Vietnam	9	15	20	16	0.6	1.1	1.1	1.3
22	Peru	22	15	24	15	1.5	1.1	1.4	1.3
23	Germany	2	1	8	15	0.1	0.1	0.5	1.3
24	China	13	15	19	12	0.9	1.1	1.1	1.0
25	Philippines	12	12	11	11	0.8	0.9	0.6	1.0

U.S. Imports by State of Final Destination

Rank	Country	Value (Millions of dollars)				Percent of Share			
		2012	2013	2014	2015	2012	2013	2014	2015
	Total Wyoming Imports and % Share of U.S. Total	2,005	2,162	1,902	1,144	0.1	0.1	0.1	0.1
	Total, Top 25 Countries and % Share of State Total	1,981	2,138	1,890	1,130	98.8	98.9	99.4	98.9
1	Canada	1,714	1,885	1,637	815	85.5	87.2	86.1	71.3
2	China	104	121	129	139	5.2	5.6	6.8	12.1
3	Mexico	20	22	29	48	1.0	1.0	1.5	4.2
4	Germany	43	22	12	24	2.1	1.0	0.6	2.1
5	Thailand	1	1	12	15	0.0	0.0	0.6	1.3
6	Singapore	1	2	2	10	0.1	0.1	0.1	0.9
7	United Kingdom	28	16	13	10	1.4	0.8	0.7	0.9
8	Korea, South	7	7	3	9	0.3	0.3	0.1	0.8
9	India	10	22	7	7	0.5	1.0	0.4	0.6
10	Italy	1	3	2	6	0.1	0.2	0.1	0.5
11	Taiwan	4	3	6	5	0.2	0.1	0.3	0.5
12	Czech Republic	1	2	0	4	0.1	0.1	0.0	0.4
13	France	17	7	5	4	0.9	0.3	0.3	0.3
14	Sweden	6	2	2	4	0.3	0.1	0.1	0.3
15	Australia	3	3	11	4	0.1	0.1	0.6	0.3
16	Belgium	1	0	1	4	0.0	0.1	0.0	0.3
17	Japan	8	9	5	3	0.4	0.4	0.3	0.3
18	Brazil	1	0	2	3	0.0	0.0	0.1	0.3
19	Romania	3	1	2	3	0.1	0.0	0.1	0.3
20	United Arab Emirates	0	0	0	3	0.0	0.0	0.0	0.2
21	Vietnam	3	1	1	3	0.1	0.0	0.1	0.2
22	Switzerland	1	2	1	2	0.1	0.1	0.0	0.2
23	Turkey	1	2	1	2	0.0	0.1	0.1	0.2
24	Netherlands	2	3	4	2	0.1	0.1	0.2	0.1
25	Austria	3	3	3	1	0.1	0.2	0.1	0.1

PART II: STATE TRADE BY COMMODITY

Table E-52.   State Trade by Commodity: Alabama, 2014–2015

(Value in millions of dollars.)

U.S. Exports by Origin State

Rank	HS Code	Description	Value 2014	Value 2015	Percent of share 2014	Percent of share 2015
		Total Alabama Exports and % Share of U.S. Total	19,440	19,370	1.2	1.3
		Total, Top 25 Commodities and % Share of State Total	12,012	12,511	61.8	64.6
1	870323	PASS VEH SPK-IG INT COM RCPR P ENG >1500 NOV	2,728	3,160	14.0	16.3
2	870333	PASS VEH COM-IG INT COM ENG > 2500 CC	1,621	1,761	8.3	9.1
3	870324	PASS VEH SPK-IG INT COM RCPR P ENG > 3000 CC	1,916	1,670	9.9	8.6
4	270112	BITUMINOUS COAL, NOT AGGLOMERATED	1,114	698	5.7	3.6
5	880000	CIVILIAN AIRCRAFT, ENGINES, AND PARTS	595	605	3.1	3.1
6	390740	POLYCARBONATES, PR FMS	600	510	3.1	2.6
7	870332	PASS VEH COM-IG INT COM ENG > 1500 NOV 2500 C	383	437	2.0	2.3
8	721914	FR SS 600MM AO W HR CLS UN 3MM THCK	180	412	0.9	2.1
9	470321	CHEMICAL WOODPULP, SODA ETC. N DIS S BL & BL	360	368	1.9	1.9
10	840734	SPARK-IGNTN RECPRCTING PISTON ENGINE ETC > 10	347	348	1.8	1.8

U.S. Imports by State of Final Destination

Rank	HS Code	Description	Value 2014	Value 2015	Percent of share 2014	Percent of share 2015
		Total Alabama Imports and % Share of U.S. Total	22,210	21,880	0.9	1.0
		Total, Top 25 Commodities and % Share of State Total	10,291	10,402	46.3	47.5
1	270900	CRUDE OIL FROM PETROLEUM AND BITUMINOUS MINER	2,646	1,816	11.9	8.3
2	870829	PTS & ACCESS OF BODIES OF MOTOR VEHICLES, NES	808	1,146	3.6	5.2
3	840734	SPARK-IGNTN RECPRCTING PISTON ENGINE ETC > 10	879	944	4.0	4.3
4	870899	PARTS AND ACCESSORIES OF MOTOR VEHICLES, NESO	774	653	3.5	3.0
5	870840	GEAR BOXES FOR MOTOR VEHICLES	455	613	2.0	2.8
6	940190	PARTS OF SEATS (EX MEDICAL, BARBER, DENTAL ET	538	579	2.4	2.6
7	840820	COMPRESSION-IGNTN INT COMBUSTION PISTON ENGIN	396	453	1.8	2.1
8	870894	STEERING WHEELS, COLUMNS & BOXES F MOTOR VEHI	418	443	1.9	2.0
9	840991	SPARK-IGNITION INT COMBUSTION PISTON ENG PTS	511	420	2.3	1.9
10	870830	BRAKES AND SERVO-BREAKS; PARTS THEREOF	344	383	1.6	1.7

Table E-53.   State Trade by Commodity: Alaska, 2014–2015

(Value in millions of dollars.)

U.S. Exports by Origin State

Rank	HS Code	Description	Value 2014	Value 2015	Percent of share 2014	Percent of share 2015
		Total Alaska Exports and % Share of U.S. Total	5,111	4,675	0.3	0.3
		Total, Top 25 Commodities and % Share of State Total	4,745	4,449	92.8	95.2
1	260800	ZINC ORES AND CONCENTRATES	1,068	897	20.9	19.2
2	30499	FISH MEAT, FROZEN, NESOI	347	374	6.8	8.0
3	260700	LEAD ORES AND CONCENTRATES	367	317	7.2	6.8
4	30475	ALASKA POLLOCK FILLETS, FROZEN	319	299	6.2	6.4
5	30312	PACIFIC SALMON, FROZEN, NESOI	208	282	4.1	6.0
6	30363	COD, FROZEN	253	268	4.9	5.7
7	30390	FISH LIVERS AND ROES, FROZEN	225	256	4.4	5.5
8	30389	FISH, FROZEN, NESOI	270	246	5.3	5.3
9	271019	PETROL OIL BITUM MINERAL (NT CRUD) ETC NT BIO	176	221	3.4	4.7
10	271111	NATURAL GAS, LIQUEFIED	217	188	4.2	4.0

U.S. Imports by State of Final Destination

Rank	HS Code	Description	Value 2014	Value 2015	Percent of share 2014	Percent of share 2015
		Total Alaska Imports and % Share of U.S. Total	2,008	2,485	0.1	0.1
		Total, Top 25 Commodities and % Share of State Total	1,460	1,980	72.7	79.7
1	271019	PETROL OIL BITUM MINERAL (NT CRUD) ETC NT BIO	692	703	34.5	28.3
2	890520	FLOATING OR SUBMERSIBLE DRILLING OR PRODCTN,P	0	382	0.0	15.4
3	852351	SOLID-STATE NON-VOL SEMICONDUCTOR STORAGE DEV	9	275	0.4	11.1
4	843143	PARTS FOR BORING OR SINKING MACHINERY, NESOI	16	81	0.8	3.3
5	847130	PORT DIGTL AUTOMATIC DATA PROCESS MACH NOT >	91	77	4.6	3.1
6	260300	COPPER ORES AND CONCENTRATES	88	74	4.4	3.0
7	847150	DIGITAL PROCESSING UNITS, N.E.S.O.I.	21	72	1.0	2.9
8	271012	LT OILS, PREPS GT=70% PETROLEUM/BITUM NT BIOD	92	62	4.6	2.5
9	851762	MACH FOR RECP/CONVR/TRANS/REGN OF VOICE/IMAGE	22	34	1.1	1.4
10	270900	CRUDE OIL FROM PETROLEUM AND BITUMINOUS MINER	310	33	15.4	1.3

Table E-54.   State Trade by Commodity: Arizona, 2014–2015

(Value in millions of dollars.)

U.S. Exports by Origin State

Rank	HS Code	Description	Value		Percent of share	
			2014	2015	2014	2015
		Total Arizona Exports and % Share of U.S. Total	21,248	22,563	1.3	1.5
		Total, Top 25 Commodities and % Share of State Total	10,485	11,674	49.3	51.7
1	880000	CIVILIAN AIRCRAFT, ENGINES, AND PARTS	2,226	2,960	10.5	13.1
2	260300	COPPER ORES AND CONCENTRATES	2,178	2,502	10.2	11.1
3	854231	PROCESSORS AND CONTROLLERS, ELECTRONIC INTEG	878	1,052	4.1	4.7
4	854239	ELECTRONIC INTEGRATED CIRCUITS, NESOI	749	694	3.5	3.1
5	854150	SEMICNDCTR DVICE EX PHOTOSENSITIVE/PHOTOVOLTA	345	428	1.6	1.9
6	853890	PT F ELECT APPR F ELECT CIRCT; F ELCT CONTRL	401	405	1.9	1.8
7	271121	NATURAL GAS, GASEOUS	629	376	3.0	1.7
8	930690	BOMB MINES OT AMMNTION PROJCTIONS ETC AND PAR	413	339	1.9	1.5
9	851762	MACH FOR RECP/CONVR/TRANS/REGN OF VOICE/IMAGE	271	331	1.3	1.5
10	300490	MEDICAMENTS NESOI, MEASURED DOSES, RETAIL PK	215	257	1.0	1.1

U.S. Imports by State of Final Destination

Rank	HS Code	Description	Value		Percent of share	
			2014	2015	2014	2015
		Total Arizona Imports and % Share of U.S. Total	19,716	19,679	0.8	0.9
		Total, Top 25 Commodities and % Share of State Total	7,951	7,578	40.3	38.5
1	880240	AIRPLANE & OT A/C, UNLADEN WEIGHT > 15,000 KG	840	929	4.3	4.7
2	70200	TOMATOES, FRESH OR CHILLED	523	481	2.7	2.4
3	854430	INSULATED WIRING SETS FOR VEHICLES SHIPS AIRC	400	418	2.0	2.1
4	841191	TURBOJET AND TURBOPROLLER PARTS	343	411	1.7	2.1
5	70960	FRUITS OF GENUS CAPSICUM OR PIMENTA, FRESH/CH	462	362	2.3	1.8
6	854231	PROCESSORS AND CONTROLLERS, ELECTRONIC INTEG	897	360	4.5	1.8
7	854140	PHOTOSNSITVE SEMICNDCTR DVICE INC PHTVLTC CEL	265	338	1.3	1.7
8	854239	ELECTRONIC INTEGRATED CIRCUITS, NESOI	255	325	1.3	1.7
9	841199	GAS TURBINE PARTS NESOI	309	310	1.6	1.6
10	740311	REFINED COPPER CATHODES AND SECTIONS OF CATHO	313	279	1.6	1.4

Table E-55.   State Trade by Commodity: Arkansas, 2014–2015

(Value in millions of dollars.)

U.S. Exports by Origin State

Rank	HS Code	Description	Value 2014	Value 2015	Percent of share 2014	Percent of share 2015
		Total Arkansas Exports and % Share of U.S. Total	6,860	5,874	0.4	0.4
		Total, Top 25 Commodities and % Share of State Total	3,744	3,079	54.6	52.4
1	880000	CIVILIAN AIRCRAFT, ENGINES, AND PARTS	1,628	791	23.7	13.5
2	853669	ELECT PLUGS & SOCKETS F VOLTAGE NOT OVER 1000	229	429	3.3	7.3
3	481151	PPR/PBRD,CTD/IMPG/CVR W/PLAST,BLEACH,WT>150G/	174	180	2.5	3.1
4	100630	RICE, SEMI- OR WHOLLY MILLED, POLISHED ETC OR	180	165	2.6	2.8
5	293090	ORGANO-SULFUR COMPOUNDS NESOI	125	139	1.8	2.4
6	40711	EGGS OF CHICKENS, FERTILIZED FOR INCUBATION	73	136	1.1	2.3
7	20714	CHICKEN CUTS AND EDIBLE OFFAL (INC LIVERS), F	213	120	3.1	2.0
8	930690	BOMB MINES OT AMMNTION PROJCTIONS ETC AND PAR	75	100	1.1	1.7
9	842920	GRADERS AND LEVELERS, SELF-PROPELLED	70	83	1.0	1.4
10	390390	POLYMERS OF STYRENE NESOI, IN PRIMARY FORMS	81	81	1.2	1.4

U.S. Imports by State of Final Destination

Rank	HS Code	Description	Value 2014	Value 2015	Percent of share 2014	Percent of share 2015
		Total Arkansas Imports and % Share of U.S. Total	7,603	7,915	0.3	0.4
		Total, Top 25 Commodities and % Share of State Total	3,235	3,417	42.5	43.2
1	880230	AIRPLANE & A/C UNLADEN WGHT > 2000, NOV 15000	1,005	933	13.2	11.8
2	880240	AIRPLANE & OT A/C, UNLADEN WEIGHT > 15,000 KG	579	692	7.6	8.7
3	950300	TRICYCLE, SCOOTR, PEDAL CAR & SIM WHEELED TYS	275	264	3.6	3.3
4	870120	ROAD TRACTORS FOR SEMI-TRAILERS	120	178	1.6	2.3
5	720836	FLT-HOT-ROLL IRN,NONALY STL,COIL,>10MM THICK,	92	152	1.2	1.9
6	930690	BOMB MINES OT AMMNTION PROJCTIONS ETC AND PAR	141	105	1.9	1.3
7	848180	TAPS COCKS ETC F PIPE VAT INC THERMO CONTROL	108	99	1.4	1.3
8	845590	PARTS FOR METAL ROLLING MILLS EXC ROLLS FOR R	3	75	0.0	0.9
9	852872	RECEPTION APPARATUS FOR TELEVISION, COLOR, NE	130	70	1.7	0.9
10	846722	SAWS W/ SELF-CONT. ELECTIRIC MOTORS, FOR WK I	56	67	0.7	0.8

Table E-56.   State Trade by Commodity: California, 2014–2015

(Value in millions of dollars.)

U.S. Exports by Origin State

Rank	HS Code	Description	Value		Percent of share	
			2014	2015	2014	2015
		Total California Exports and % Share of U.S. Total	173,812	165,367	10.7	11.0
		Total, Top 25 Commodities and % Share of State Total	59,321	58,701	34.1	35.5
1	880000	CIVILIAN AIRCRAFT, ENGINES, AND PARTS	7,504	6,508	4.3	3.9
2	851762	MACH FOR RECP/CONVR/TRANS/REGN OF VOICE/IMAGE	5,310	6,284	3.1	3.8
3	710239	DIAMONDS, NONINDUSTRIAL, WORKED	5,367	4,582	3.1	2.8
4	80212	ALMONDS, FRESH OR DRIED, SHELLED	3,505	3,728	2.0	2.3
5	848620	MACHINES FOR MAN. SEMICONDUTOR DEVICES/ELEC I	2,670	3,269	1.5	2.0
6	271019	PETROL OIL BITUM MINERAL (NT CRUD) ETC NT BIO	4,788	3,104	2.8	1.9
7	300210	ANTISERA, BLOOD FRACTIONS & IMMUNOLOGICAL PRO	3,189	2,781	1.8	1.7
8	851712	PHONES FOR CELLULAR NTWKS OR FOR OTH WIRELESS	2,268	2,502	1.3	1.5
9	847330	PARTS & ACCESSORIES FOR ADP MACHINES & UNITS	2,122	2,091	1.2	1.3
10	880260	SPACECRAFT & SUBORBITAL AND SPACE LAUNCH VEHI	560	2,038	0.3	1.2

U.S. Imports by State of Final Destination

Rank	HS Code	Description	Value		Percent of share	
			2014	2015	2014	2015
		Total California Imports and % Share of U.S. Total	403,369	408,180	17.2	18.2
		Total, Top 25 Commodities and % Share of State Total	189,483	191,940	47.0	47.0
1	870323	PASS VEH SPK-IG INT COM RCPR P ENG >1500 NOV	34,025	38,976	8.4	9.5
2	870324	PASS VEH SPK-IG INT COM RCPR P ENG > 3000 CC	15,789	16,172	3.9	4.0
3	270900	CRUDE OIL FROM PETROLEUM AND BITUMINOUS MINER	29,207	16,150	7.2	4.0
4	847130	PORT DIGTL AUTOMATIC DATA PROCESS MACH NOT >	16,994	15,846	4.2	3.9
5	851762	MACH FOR RECP/CONVR/TRANS/REGN OF VOICE/IMAGE	12,550	14,836	3.1	3.6
6	851712	PHONES FOR CELLULAR NTWKS OR FOR OTH WIRELESS	12,022	14,608	3.0	3.6
7	854231	PROCESSORS AND CONTROLLERS, ELECTRONIC INTEG	8,490	10,996	2.1	2.7
8	847330	PARTS & ACCESSORIES FOR ADP MACHINES & UNITS	8,537	8,441	2.1	2.1
9	852872	RECEPTION APPARATUS FOR TELEVISION, COLOR, NE	6,966	7,125	1.7	1.7
10	847170	AUTOMATIC DATA PROCESSING STORAGE UNITS, N.E.	6,067	5,806	1.5	1.4

Table E-57. State Trade by Commodity: Colorado, 2014–2015

(Value in millions of dollars.)

U.S. Exports by Origin State

Rank	HS Code	Description	Value 2014	Value 2015	Percent of share 2014	Percent of share 2015
		Total Colorado Exports and % Share of U.S. Total	8,337	7,978	0.5	0.5
		Total, Top 25 Commodities and % Share of State Total	3,364	3,281	40.3	41.1
1	854239	ELECTRONIC INTEGRATED CIRCUITS, NESOI	304	373	3.7	4.7
2	20130	MEAT OF BOVINE ANIMALS, BONELESS, FRESH OR CH	439	346	5.3	4.3
3	901890	INSTR & APPL F MEDICAL SURGICAL DENTAL VET, N	343	291	4.1	3.6
4	20230	MEAT OF BOVINE ANIMALS, BONELESS, FROZEN	239	217	2.9	2.7
5	880000	CIVILIAN AIRCRAFT, ENGINES, AND PARTS	221	180	2.7	2.3
6	410150	WHOLE HIDES & SKINS, OF A WT >16KG BOVINE/EQU	201	171	2.4	2.1
7	370110	X-RAY PLATES & FLAT FILM, SENS, UNEX	129	158	1.6	2.0
8	902110	ORTHOPEDIC OR FRACTRE APPLIANCES, PARTS & ACC	135	136	1.6	1.7
9	370210	X-RAY FILM IN ROLLS, SENS, UNEX, NO PAPER ETC	173	127	2.1	1.6
10	261390	MOLYBDENUM ORES AND CONCENTRATES NOT ROASTED	164	120	2.0	1.5

U.S. Imports by State of Final Destination

Rank	HS Code	Description	Value 2014	Value 2015	Percent of share 2014	Percent of share 2015
		Total Colorado Imports and % Share of U.S. Total	14,237	13,487	0.6	0.6
		Total, Top 25 Commodities and % Share of State Total	6,683	6,160	46.9	45.7
1	270900	CRUDE OIL FROM PETROLEUM AND BITUMINOUS MINER	2,785	1,765	19.6	13.1
2	847150	DIGITAL PROCESSING UNITS, N.E.S.O.I.	609	585	4.3	4.3
3	300490	MEDICAMENTS NESOI, MEASURED DOSES, RETAIL PK	398	443	2.8	3.3
4	880240	AIRPLANE & OT A/C, UNLADEN WEIGHT > 15,000 KG	119	440	0.8	3.3
5	901890	INSTR & APPL F MEDICAL SURGICAL DENTAL VET, N	268	336	1.9	2.5
6	847170	AUTOMATIC DATA PROCESSING STORAGE UNITS, N.E.	297	254	2.1	1.9
7	880230	AIRPLANE & A/C UNLADEN WGHT > 2000, NOV 15000	195	251	1.4	1.9
8	420299	CONTAINER BAGS, CASES ETC NESOI	164	184	1.2	1.4
9	902190	OTH ARTIFICAL PTS OF THE BODY & PTS & ACCESSO	102	164	0.7	1.2
10	841290	ENGINE AND MOTOR PARTS, NESOI	88	155	0.6	1.1

Table E-58. State Trade by Commodity: Connecticut, 2014–2015

(Value in millions of dollars.)

U.S. Exports by Origin State

Rank	HS Code	Description	Value		Percent of share	
			2014	2015	2014	2015
		Total Connecticut Exports and % Share of U.S. Total	15,931	15,256	1.0	1.0
		Total, Top 25 Commodities and % Share of State Total	9,269	9,040	58.2	59.3
1	880000	CIVILIAN AIRCRAFT, ENGINES, AND PARTS	6,568	6,516	41.2	42.7
2	848690	PARTS & ACCSESORIES FOR MACH TO MAN. SEMICNT,	270	279	1.7	1.8
3	740319	UNWROUGHT REFINED COPPER NESOI	150	236	0.9	1.5
4	293499	NUCLEIC ACIDS & SALTS; OTHER HETEROCYCLIC CMP	4	175	0.0	1.1
5	283620	DISODIUM CARBONATE	126	125	0.8	0.8
6	850239	GENERATING SETS, ELECTRIC, NESOI	378	122	2.4	0.8
7	841191	TURBOJET AND TURBOPROLLER PARTS	127	115	0.8	0.8
8	880212	HELICOPTERS OF AN UNLADEN WEIGHT EXCEEDING 20	218	112	1.4	0.7
9	902780	PHY CHEM INS/APPR;MEAS VSCSTY & HEAT NESOI	83	112	0.5	0.7
10	271019	PETROL OIL BITUM MINERAL (NT CRUD) ETC NT BIO	130	107	0.8	0.7

U.S. Imports by State of Final Destination

Rank	HS Code	Description	Value		Percent of share	
			2014	2015	2014	2015
		Total Connecticut Imports and % Share of U.S. Total	23,892	25,957	1.0	1.2
		Total, Top 25 Commodities and % Share of State Total	10,545	12,840	44.1	49.5
1	293499	NUCLEIC ACIDS & SALTS; OTHER HETEROCYCLIC CMP	312	3,380	1.3	13.0
2	841191	TURBOJET AND TURBOPROLLER PARTS	2,365	2,151	9.9	8.3
3	880240	AIRPLANE & OT A/C, UNLADEN WEIGHT > 15,000 KG	1,368	1,263	5.7	4.9
4	710691	SILVER, UNWROUGHT NESOI	1,056	977	4.4	3.8
5	740311	REFINED COPPER CATHODES AND SECTIONS OF CATHO	499	707	2.1	2.7
6	300490	MEDICAMENTS NESOI, MEASURED DOSES, RETAIL PK	180	594	0.8	2.3
7	880230	AIRPLANE & A/C UNLADEN WGHT > 2000, NOV 15000	543	562	2.3	2.2
8	271012	LT OILS, PREPS GT=70% PETROLEUM/BITUM NT BIOD	967	518	4.0	2.0
9	880330	PARTS OF AIRPLANES OR HELICOPTERS, NESOI	475	331	2.0	1.3
10	790111	ZINC UNWRT NT ALY CNT WGT AT LST 99.99 PERCNT	195	197	0.8	0.8

Table E-59.   State Trade by Commodity: Delaware, 2014–2015

(Value in millions of dollars.)

U.S. Exports by Origin State

Rank	HS Code	Description	Value 2014	Value 2015	Percent of share 2014	Percent of share 2015
		Total Delaware Exports and % Share of U.S. Total	5,267	5,403	0.3	0.4
		Total, Top 25 Commodities and % Share of State Total	3,823	4,125	72.6	76.3
1	300490	MEDICAMENTS NESOI, MEASURED DOSES, RETAIL PK	1,587	1,300	30.1	24.1
2	870324	PASS VEH SPK-IG INT COM RCPR P ENG > 3000 CC	289	796	5.5	14.7
3	870431	MTR VEH TRANS GDS SPK IG IN C P ENG, GVW NOV	16	288	0.3	5.3
4	271019	PETROL OIL BITUM MINERAL (NT CRUD) ETC NT BIO	106	285	2.0	5.3
5	902780	PHY CHEM INS/APPR;MEAS VSCSTY & HEAT NESOI	248	189	4.7	3.5
6	851712	PHONES FOR CELLULAR NTWKS OR FOR OTH WIRELESS	316	183	6.0	3.4
7	880000	CIVILIAN AIRCRAFT, ENGINES, AND PARTS	184	140	3.5	2.6
8	80390	BANANAS, FRESH OR DRIED, NESOI	147	138	2.8	2.6
9	870323	PASS VEH SPK-IG INT COM RCPR P ENG >1500 NOV	101	109	1.9	2.0
10	392690	ARTICLES OF PLASTICS, NESOI	86	85	1.6	1.6

U.S. Imports by State of Final Destination

Rank	HS Code	Description	Value 2014	Value 2015	Percent of share 2014	Percent of share 2015
		Total Delaware Imports and % Share of U.S. Total	10,690	9,194	0.5	0.4
		Total, Top 25 Commodities and % Share of State Total	8,060	7,194	75.4	78.2
1	270900	CRUDE OIL FROM PETROLEUM AND BITUMINOUS MINER	2,919	1,810	27.3	19.7
2	293499	NUCLEIC ACIDS & SALTS; OTHER HETEROCYCLIC CMP	1,271	1,626	11.9	17.7
3	300432	MEDICAMENTS CONT CORTEX HORMONES ETC DOSES	707	913	6.6	9.9
4	300490	MEDICAMENTS NESOI, MEASURED DOSES, RETAIL PK	1,106	906	10.3	9.8
5	80390	BANANAS, FRESH OR DRIED, NESOI	469	500	4.4	5.4
6	271019	PETROL OIL BITUM MINERAL (NT CRUD) ETC NT BIO	496	237	4.6	2.6
7	293399	HETEROCYCLIC COMP W NITROGEN HETERO-ATM ONLY	14	143	0.1	1.6
8	271012	LT OILS, PREPS GT=70% PETROLEUM/BITUM NT BIOD	160	142	1.5	1.5
9	80610	GRAPES, FRESH	156	123	1.5	1.3
10	880240	AIRPLANE & OT A/C, UNLADEN WEIGHT > 15,000 KG	138	122	1.3	1.3

Table E-60.   State Trade by Commodity: District of Columbia, 2014–2015

(Value in millions of dollars.)

U.S. Exports by Origin State

Rank	HS Code	Description	Value 2014	Value 2015	Percent of share 2014	Percent of share 2015
		Total District of Colombia Exports and % Share of U.S. Total	938	1,089	0.1	0.1
		Total, Top 25 Commodities and % Share of State Total	591	920	63.0	84.4
1	854390	PT ELEC MACH & APPR W INDIVIDUAL FUNCTIONS, N	42	360	4.5	33.0
2	880212	HELICOPTERS OF AN UNLADEN WEIGHT EXCEEDING 20	2	156	0.2	14.3
3	880330	PARTS OF AIRPLANES OR HELICOPTERS, NESOI	166	137	17.7	12.6
4	930690	BOMB MINES OT AMMNTION PROJCTIONS ETC AND PAR	222	66	23.7	6.1
5	930120	RKT LAUNCH.,FLAMMTHROW, & SIM. PROJECTORS(MILI	0	33	0.0	3.0
6	880000	CIVILIAN AIRCRAFT, ENGINES, AND PARTS	36	32	3.8	2.9
7	980320	EXPORTS OF MILITARY EQUIPMENT, NOT IDENTIFIED	30	29	3.2	2.7
8	871000	TANK & OT ARMORED FIGHT VEH, MOTORIZED; AND P	15	12	1.6	1.1
9	841182	GAS TURBINES OF A POWER EXCEEDING 5,000 KW	26	10	2.8	1.0
10	930630	CARTRIDGES AND PARTS THEREOF, NESOI	1	9	0.1	0.8

U.S. Imports by State of Final Destination

Rank	HS Code	Description	Value 2014	Value 2015	Percent of share 2014	Percent of share 2015
		Total District of Colombia Imports and % Share of U.S. Total	1,104	912	0.0	0.0
		Total, Top 25 Commodities and % Share of State Total	499	351	45.2	38.5
1	300490	MEDICAMENTS NESOI, MEASURED DOSES, RETAIL PK	171	115	15.5	12.6
2	970110	PAINTINGS, DRAWING AND PASTELS BY HAND	34	52	3.0	5.7
3	220421	WINE, FR GRAPE NESOI & GR MUST W ALC, NOV 2 L	21	19	1.9	2.0
4	970300	ORIGINAL SCULPTURES AND STATUARY, IN ANY MATE	19	18	1.7	1.9
5	300420	ANTIBIOTICS NESOI, IN DOSAGE FORM	29	16	2.6	1.7
6	200811	PEANUTS, PREPARED OR PRESERVED, NESOI	13	14	1.2	1.6
7	220860	VODKA	15	12	1.4	1.3
8	220830	WHISKIES	8	10	0.8	1.1
9	851762	MACH FOR RECP/CONVR/TRANS/REGN OF VOICE/IMAGE	13	8	1.2	0.9
10	300220	VACCINES FOR HUMAN MEDICINE	94	8	8.5	0.9

Table E-61.   State Trade by Commodity: Florida, 2014–2015

(Value in millions of dollars.)

U.S. Exports by Origin State

Rank	HS Code	Description	Value 2014	Value 2015	Percent of share 2014	Percent of share 2015
		Total Florida Exports and % Share of U.S. Total	58,507	53,844	3.6	3.6
		Total, Top 25 Commodities and % Share of State Total	23,441	20,963	40.1	38.9
1	880000	CIVILIAN AIRCRAFT, ENGINES, AND PARTS	4,799	4,716	8.2	8.8
2	851712	PHONES FOR CELLULAR NTWKS OR FOR OTH WIRELESS	2,923	2,486	5.0	4.6
3	710812	GOLD, NONMONETARY, UNWROUGHT NESOI	3,282	1,736	5.6	3.2
4	851762	MACH FOR RECP/CONVR/TRANS/REGN OF VOICE/IMAGE	972	953	1.7	1.8
5	310530	DIAMMONIUM HYDROGENORTHOPHOSPHATE (DAP)	1,058	899	1.8	1.7
6	870324	PASS VEH SPK-IG INT COM RCPR P ENG > 3000 CC	351	791	0.6	1.5
7	310540	AMMONIUM DIHYDROGENORTHOPHOSPHATE	738	788	1.3	1.5
8	847130	PORT DIGTL AUTOMATIC DATA PROCESS MACH NOT >	993	762	1.7	1.4
9	870323	PASS VEH SPK-IG INT COM RCPR P ENG >1500 NOV	937	733	1.6	1.4
10	854231	PROCESSORS AND CONTROLLERS, ELECTRONIC INTEG	920	693	1.6	1.3

U.S. Imports by State of Final Destination

Rank	HS Code	Description	Value 2014	Value 2015	Percent of share 2014	Percent of share 2015
		Total Florida Imports and % Share of U.S. Total	71,782	73,437	3.1	3.3
		Total, Top 25 Commodities and % Share of State Total	26,584	25,901	37.0	35.3
1	710812	GOLD, NONMONETARY, UNWROUGHT NESOI	4,335	3,192	6.0	4.3
2	271019	PETROL OIL BITUM MINERAL (NT CRUD) ETC NT BIO	4,614	3,166	6.4	4.3
3	870323	PASS VEH SPK-IG INT COM RCPR P ENG >1500 NOV	1,370	2,853	1.9	3.9
4	851712	PHONES FOR CELLULAR NTWKS OR FOR OTH WIRELESS	3,049	2,406	4.2	3.3
5	271012	LT OILS, PREPS GT=70% PETROLEUM/BITUM NT BIOD	1,247	1,305	1.7	1.8
6	880240	AIRPLANE & OT A/C, UNLADEN WEIGHT > 15,000 KG	759	1,282	1.1	1.7
7	870324	PASS VEH SPK-IG INT COM RCPR P ENG > 3000 CC	753	1,239	1.0	1.7
8	330300	PERFUMES AND TOILET WATERS	858	838	1.2	1.1
9	890392	MOTORBOATS, OTHER THAN OUTBOARD MOTORBOATS	362	834	0.5	1.1
10	854231	PROCESSORS AND CONTROLLERS, ELECTRONIC INTEG	863	806	1.2	1.1

Table E-62.   State Trade by Commodity: Georgia, 2014–2015

(Value in millions of dollars.)

U.S. Exports by Origin State

Rank	HS Code	Description	Value 2014	Value 2015	Percent of share 2014	Percent of share 2015
		Total Georgia Exports and % Share of U.S. Total	39,377	38,548	2.4	2.6
		Total, Top 25 Commodities and % Share of State Total	17,822	18,292	45.3	47.5
1	880000	CIVILIAN AIRCRAFT, ENGINES, AND PARTS	6,035	6,208	15.3	16.1
2	870323	PASS VEH SPK-IG INT COM RCPR P ENG >1500 NOV	1,293	1,301	3.3	3.4
3	841199	GAS TURBINE PARTS NESOI	981	1,285	2.5	3.3
4	470321	CHEMICAL WOODPULP, SODA ETC. N DIS S BL & BL	1,197	1,153	3.0	3.0
5	870324	PASS VEH SPK-IG INT COM RCPR P ENG > 3000 CC	372	757	0.9	2.0
6	20714	CHICKEN CUTS AND EDIBLE OFFAL (INC LIVERS), F	1,046	731	2.7	1.9
7	480411	KRAFTLINER, UNCOATED UNBLEACHED IN ROLLS OR S	741	686	1.9	1.8
8	250700	KAOLIN AND OTHER KAOLINIC CLAYS, INCL CALCINE	529	492	1.3	1.3
9	880212	HELICOPTERS OF AN UNLADEN WEIGHT EXCEEDING 20	117	490	0.3	1.3
10	520100	COTTON, NOT CARDED OR COMBED	556	488	1.4	1.3

U.S. Imports by State of Final Destination

Rank	HS Code	Description	Value 2014	Value 2015	Percent of share 2014	Percent of share 2015
		Total Georgia Imports and % Share of U.S. Total	83,765	88,545	3.6	4.0
		Total, Top 25 Commodities and % Share of State Total	30,763	33,435	36.7	37.8
1	870323	PASS VEH SPK-IG INT COM RCPR P ENG >1500 NOV	6,989	8,412	8.3	9.5
2	870324	PASS VEH SPK-IG INT COM RCPR P ENG > 3000 CC	6,123	6,727	7.3	7.6
3	300431	MEDICAMENTS CONT INSULIN, NO ANTIBIOTICS, DOS	4,295	3,923	5.1	4.4
4	847130	PORT DIGTL AUTOMATIC DATA PROCESS MACH NOT >	720	1,056	0.9	1.2
5	300490	MEDICAMENTS NESOI, MEASURED DOSES, RETAIL PK	761	895	0.9	1.0
6	950300	TRICYCLE, SCOOTR, PEDAL CAR & SIM WHEELED TYS	957	878	1.1	1.0
7	740311	REFINED COPPER CATHODES AND SECTIONS OF CATHO	528	878	0.6	1.0
8	870190	TRACTORS, NESOI	615	846	0.7	1.0
9	401110	NEW PNEUMATIC TIRES OF RUBBER, FOR MOTOR CARS	742	755	0.9	0.9
10	940510	CHANDELIER CEILNG/WALL LGHTNG FTTNG EX PUBLIC	659	737	0.8	0.8

Table E-63.   State Trade by Commodity: Hawaii, 2014–2015

(Value in millions of dollars.)

U.S. Exports by Origin State

Rank	HS Code	Description	Value		Percent of share	
			2014	2015	2014	2015
		Total Hawaii Exports and % Share of U.S. Total	1,447	1,896	0.1	0.1
		Total, Top 25 Commodities and % Share of State Total	1,211	1,720	83.7	90.7
1	880240	AIRPLANE & OT A/C, UNLADEN WEIGHT > 15,000 KG	0	516	0.0	27.2
2	880330	PARTS OF AIRPLANES OR HELICOPTERS, NESOI	303	347	21.0	18.3
3	880212	HELICOPTERS OF AN UNLADEN WEIGHT EXCEEDING 20	94	307	6.5	16.2
4	271019	PETROL OIL BITUM MINERAL (NT CRUD) ETC NT BIO	292	165	20.2	8.7
5	271012	LT OILS, PREPS GT=70% PETROLEUM/BITUM NT BIOD	128	125	8.9	6.6
6	841182	GAS TURBINES OF A POWER EXCEEDING 5,000 KW	0	32	0.0	1.7
7	270750	AROM HYDC NESOI 65PCT AO DSTLS A 250DC ASTM D	143	25	9.9	1.3
8	720449	FERROUS WASTE & SCRAP NESOI	35	21	2.4	1.1
9	30626	COLD-WATER SHRIMPS AND PRAWNS, NOT FROZEN	26	20	1.8	1.0
10	980320	EXPORTS OF MILITARY EQUIPMENT, NOT IDENTIFIED	34	20	2.4	1.0

U.S. Imports by State of Final Destination

Rank	HS Code	Description	Value		Percent of share	
			2014	2015	2014	2015
		Total Hawaii Imports and % Share of U.S. Total	5,330	3,760	0.2	0.2
		Total, Top 25 Commodities and % Share of State Total	4,456	3,000	83.6	79.8
1	270900	CRUDE OIL FROM PETROLEUM AND BITUMINOUS MINER	3,005	1,798	56.4	47.8
2	880240	AIRPLANE & OT A/C, UNLADEN WEIGHT > 15,000 KG	636	363	11.9	9.7
3	271019	PETROL OIL BITUM MINERAL (NT CRUD) ETC NT BIO	276	269	5.2	7.2
4	870323	PASS VEH SPK-IG INT COM RCPR P ENG >1500 NOV	118	128	2.2	3.4
5	870324	PASS VEH SPK-IG INT COM RCPR P ENG > 3000 CC	92	108	1.7	2.9
6	270112	BITUMINOUS COAL, NOT AGGLOMERATED	46	43	0.9	1.1
7	761010	ALU DOR WIN AND THEIR FRA AND THRES FOR DOORS	5	31	0.1	0.8
8	854140	PHOTOSNSITVE SEMICNDCTR DVICE INC PHTVLTC CEL	30	24	0.6	0.6
9	30487	TUNA, SKIPJACK/STRIPE-BELLIED BONITO FILLET F	13	23	0.2	0.6
10	252329	PORTLAND CEMENT EXCEPT WHITE PORTLAND CEMENT	16	23	0.3	0.6

Table E-64. State Trade by Commodity: Idaho, 2014–2015

(Value in millions of dollars.)

U.S. Exports by Origin State

Rank	HS Code	Description	Value		Percent of share	
			2014	2015	2014	2015
		Total Idaho Exports and % Share of U.S. Total	5,137	4,296	0.3	0.3
		Total, Top 25 Commodities and % Share of State Total	3,352	2,964	65.2	69.0
1	854232	MEMORIES, ELECTRONIC INTEGRATED CIRCUITS	1,407	798	27.4	18.6
2	854140	PHOTOSNSITVE SEMICNDCTR DVICE INC PHTVLTC CEL	0	291	0.0	6.8
3	903082	INST TO CHECK SEMICONDUCT WAFERS &SUCH THAT R	75	268	1.5	6.2
4	847330	PARTS & ACCESSORIES FOR ADP MACHINES & UNITS	202	199	3.9	4.6
5	903090	PTS OF INST F MEAS ELECT QUAT ALPHA BETA INZN	56	135	1.1	3.2
6	370590	PHOTO PLATES & FILM, EXPOS & DEVL, NESOI	79	135	1.5	3.1
7	710691	SILVER, UNWROUGHT NESOI	65	116	1.3	2.7
8	310540	AMMONIUM DIHYDROGENORTHOPHOSPHATE	113	103	2.2	2.4
9	260700	LEAD ORES AND CONCENTRATES	104	89	2.0	2.1
10	280920	PHOSPHORIC ACID AND POLYPHOSPHORIC ACIDS	57	67	1.1	1.5

U.S. Imports by State of Final Destination

Rank	HS Code	Description	Value		Percent of share	
			2014	2015	2014	2015
		Total Idaho Imports and % Share of U.S. Total	5,692	5,166	0.2	0.2
		Total, Top 25 Commodities and % Share of State Total	4,033	3,659	70.9	70.8
1	854232	MEMORIES, ELECTRONIC INTEGRATED CIRCUITS	1,728	1,152	30.4	22.3
2	847330	PARTS & ACCESSORIES FOR ADP MACHINES & UNITS	936	1,047	16.4	20.3
3	847170	AUTOMATIC DATA PROCESSING STORAGE UNITS, N.E.	456	296	8.0	5.7
4	848620	MACHINES FOR MAN. SEMICONDUTOR DEVICES/ELEC I	137	215	2.4	4.2
5	852351	SOLID-STATE NON-VOL SEMICONDUCTOR STORAGE DEV	3	90	0.1	1.7
6	848690	PARTS & ACCSESORIES FOR MACH TO MAN. SEMICNT,	104	85	1.8	1.6
7	440710	CONIFEROUS WOOD SAWN, SLICED ETC, OVER 6 MM T	80	75	1.4	1.5
8	230641	RAPE/COLZA SEED OILCAKE&SOLID RES. LOW ERUCIC	80	64	1.4	1.2
9	903141	OPTICAL INST FOR INSPECTING SEMICONDUCTOR WAF	42	64	0.7	1.2
10	281410	ANHYDROUS AMMONIA	49	55	0.9	1.1

Table E-65.   State Trade by Commodity: Illinois, 2014–2015

(Value in millions of dollars.)

U.S. Exports by Origin State

Rank	HS Code	Description	Value 2014	Value 2015	Percent of share 2014	Percent of share 2015
		Total Illinois Exports and % Share of U.S. Total	68,247	63,402	4.2	4.2
		Total, Top 25 Commodities and % Share of State Total	24,343	22,094	35.7	34.8
1	271012	LT OILS, PREPS GT=70% PETROLEUM/BITUM NT BIOD	4,919	2,648	7.2	4.2
2	870324	PASS VEH SPK-IG INT COM RCPR P ENG > 3000 CC	1,611	1,595	2.4	2.5
3	120190	SOYBEANS, NESOI	1,823	1,556	2.7	2.5
4	300210	ANTISERA, BLOOD FRACTIONS & IMMUNOLOGICAL PRO	555	1,134	0.8	1.8
5	870410	DUMPERS DESIGNED FOR OFF-HIGHWAY USE	1,810	1,054	2.7	1.7
6	300490	MEDICAMENTS NESOI, MEASURED DOSES, RETAIL PK	550	1,031	0.8	1.6
7	901890	INSTR & APPL F MEDICAL SURGICAL DENTAL VET, N	914	1,020	1.3	1.6
8	880000	CIVILIAN AIRCRAFT, ENGINES, AND PARTS	948	991	1.4	1.6
9	870323	PASS VEH SPK-IG INT COM RCPR P ENG >1500 NOV	932	871	1.4	1.4
10	851712	PHONES FOR CELLULAR NTWKS OR FOR OTH WIRELESS	656	847	1.0	1.3

U.S. Imports by State of Final Destination

Rank	HS Code	Description	Value 2014	Value 2015	Percent of share 2014	Percent of share 2015
		Total Illinois Imports and % Share of U.S. Total	140,123	121,252	6.0	5.4
		Total, Top 25 Commodities and % Share of State Total	71,191	55,071	50.8	45.4
1	270900	CRUDE OIL FROM PETROLEUM AND BITUMINOUS MINER	32,478	18,328	23.2	15.1
2	851712	PHONES FOR CELLULAR NTWKS OR FOR OTH WIRELESS	9,889	9,657	7.1	8.0
3	847130	PORT DIGTL AUTOMATIC DATA PROCESS MACH NOT >	3,592	4,327	2.6	3.6
4	300490	MEDICAMENTS NESOI, MEASURED DOSES, RETAIL PK	4,602	3,124	3.3	2.6
5	220300	BEER MADE FROM MALT	1,977	2,171	1.4	1.8
6	950450	VIDEO GAME CONSOLES & MACH, EXC OF SUBHEAD 95	1,605	1,568	1.1	1.3
7	852872	RECEPTION APPARATUS FOR TELEVISION, COLOR, NE	1,058	1,558	0.8	1.3
8	851762	MACH FOR RECP/CONVR/TRANS/REGN OF VOICE/IMAGE	1,364	1,437	1.0	1.2
9	271121	NATURAL GAS, GASEOUS	2,655	1,370	1.9	1.1
10	853710	CONTROLS ETC W ELECT APPR F ELECT CONT NOV 10	1,211	1,156	0.9	1.0

Table E-66.   State Trade by Commodity: Indiana, 2014–2015

(Value in millions of dollars.)

U.S. Exports by Origin State

Rank	HS Code	Description	Value 2014	Value 2015	Percent of share 2014	Percent of share 2015
		Total Indiana Exports and % Share of U.S. Total	35,467	33,652	2.2	2.2
		Total, Top 25 Commodities and % Share of State Total	18,560	18,076	52.3	53.7
1	300490	MEDICAMENTS NESOI, MEASURED DOSES, RETAIL PK	4,304	4,446	12.1	13.2
2	870840	GEAR BOXES FOR MOTOR VEHICLES	2,289	1,786	6.5	5.3
3	300210	ANTISERA, BLOOD FRACTIONS & IMMUNOLOGICAL PRO	808	1,381	2.3	4.1
4	840820	COMPRESSION-IGNTN INT COMBUSTION PISTON ENGIN	1,208	1,215	3.4	3.6
5	880000	CIVILIAN AIRCRAFT, ENGINES, AND PARTS	865	1,105	2.4	3.3
6	870324	PASS VEH SPK-IG INT COM RCPR P ENG > 3000 CC	1,277	960	3.6	2.9
7	871610	TRAILERS AND SEMI-TRAILERS FOR HOUSING OR CAM	1,098	789	3.1	2.3
8	382200	COMPOSITE DIAGNOSTIC/LAB REAGENTS, EXC PHARMA	629	656	1.8	1.9
9	870431	MTR VEH TRANS GDS SPK IG IN C P ENG, GVW NOV	894	628	2.5	1.9
10	293712	INSULIN AND ITS SALTS	419	623	1.2	1.9

U.S. Imports by State of Final Destination

Rank	HS Code	Description	Value 2014	Value 2015	Percent of share 2014	Percent of share 2015
		Total Indiana Imports and % Share of U.S. Total	48,794	48,979	2.1	2.2
		Total, Top 25 Commodities and % Share of State Total	19,056	19,003	39.1	38.8
1	300210	ANTISERA, BLOOD FRACTIONS & IMMUNOLOGICAL PRO	1,834	2,820	3.8	5.8
2	300439	HORMONES ETC. (NO ANTIBIOTICS CONTAINED) DOSA	1,717	2,286	3.5	4.7
3	293359	COMP WITH PYRIMIDINE OR PIPERAZINE RING, NESO	2,776	2,058	5.7	4.2
4	870899	PARTS AND ACCESSORIES OF MOTOR VEHICLES, NESO	1,148	1,203	2.4	2.5
5	300490	MEDICAMENTS NESOI, MEASURED DOSES, RETAIL PK	853	1,102	1.7	2.2
6	902131	ARTIFICIAL JOINTS AND PARTS AND ACCESSORIES T	775	938	1.6	1.9
7	851712	PHONES FOR CELLULAR NTWKS OR FOR OTH WIRELESS	697	755	1.4	1.5
8	870840	GEAR BOXES FOR MOTOR VEHICLES	1,219	729	2.5	1.5
9	293410	HETERCYC CMP, UNFUSED THIAZOLE RING IN THE ST	911	713	1.9	1.5
10	840734	SPARK-IGNTN RECPRCTING PISTON ENGINE ETC > 10	484	527	1.0	1.1

Table E-67.   State Trade by Commodity: Iowa, 2014–2015

(Value in millions of dollars.)

U.S. Exports by Origin State

Rank	HS Code	Description	Value		Percent of share	
			2014	2015	2014	2015
		Total Iowa Exports and % Share of U.S. Total	15,092	13,114	0.9	0.9
		Total, Top 25 Commodities and % Share of State Total	7,453	6,744	49.4	51.4
1	100590	CORN (MAIZE), OTHER THAN SEED CORN	1,161	977	7.7	7.5
2	870190	TRACTORS, NESOI	966	764	6.4	5.8
3	230330	BREWING OR DISTILLING DREGS AND WASTE, W/NT P	210	478	1.4	3.6
4	20319	MEAT OF SWINE, NESOI, FRESH OR CHILLED	530	451	3.5	3.4
5	380893	HERBCD, ANTISPROUT. PROD. & PLANT-GRWTH REG.	374	404	2.5	3.1
6	120190	SOYBEANS, NESOI	515	385	3.4	2.9
7	20329	MEAT OF SWINE, NESOI, FROZEN	518	367	3.4	2.8
8	230400	SOYBEAN OILCAKE & OTH SOLID RESIDUE, WH/NOT G	450	324	3.0	2.5
9	880000	CIVILIAN AIRCRAFT, ENGINES, AND PARTS	284	262	1.9	2.0
10	843351	COMBINE HARVESTER-THRESHERS	144	259	1.0	2.0

U.S. Imports by State of Final Destination

Rank	HS Code	Description	Value		Percent of share	
			2014	2015	2014	2015
		Total Iowa Imports and % Share of U.S. Total	10,081	9,444	0.4	0.4
		Total, Top 25 Commodities and % Share of State Total	3,442	3,223	34.1	34.1
1	271121	NATURAL GAS, GASEOUS	528	355	5.2	3.8
2	843149	PARTS AND ATTACHMENTS NESOI FOR DERRICKS ETC.	268	238	2.7	2.5
3	310420	POTASSIUM CHLORIDE	176	201	1.7	2.1
4	961900	SANITARY TOWELS AND TAMPONS DIAPERS FOR BABIE	215	198	2.1	2.1
5	840890	COMPRESSION-IGNTN INT COMBUSTION PISTON ENG,	263	187	2.6	2.0
6	870120	ROAD TRACTORS FOR SEMI-TRAILERS	191	183	1.9	1.9
7	842952	MECH SHOVELS EXCAVATORS ETC W 360 DEGREE SPRS	29	158	0.3	1.7
8	100490	OATS, NESOI	159	138	1.6	1.5
9	853710	CONTROLS ETC W ELECT APPR F ELECT CONT NOV 10	144	137	1.4	1.5
10	842890	LIFTING, HANDLING, LOADING & UNLOADING MACHY	139	133	1.4	1.4

Table E-68.   State Trade by Commodity: Kansas, 2014–2015

(Value in millions of dollars.)

U.S. Exports by Origin State

Rank	HS Code	Description	Value 2014	Value 2015	Percent of share 2014	Percent of share 2015
		Total Kansas Exports and % Share of U.S. Total	12,046	10,686	0.7	0.7
		Total, Top 25 Commodities and % Share of State Total	6,925	6,237	57.5	58.4
1	880000	CIVILIAN AIRCRAFT, ENGINES, AND PARTS	1,905	2,031	15.8	19.0
2	20130	MEAT OF BOVINE ANIMALS, BONELESS, FRESH OR CH	714	680	5.9	6.4
3	100199	WHEAT AND MESLIN, NESOI	1,054	668	8.8	6.2
4	100790	GRAIN SORGHUM, NESOI	177	262	1.5	2.4
5	880230	AIRPLANE & A/C UNLADEN WGHT > 2000, NOV 15000	168	220	1.4	2.1
6	100590	CORN (MAIZE), OTHER THAN SEED CORN	281	214	2.3	2.0
7	230910	DOG AND CAT FOOD, PUT UP FOR RETAIL SALE	174	198	1.4	1.9
8	20230	MEAT OF BOVINE ANIMALS, BONELESS, FROZEN	247	198	2.0	1.9
9	120190	SOYBEANS, NESOI	395	167	3.3	1.6
10	410150	WHOLE HIDES & SKINS, OF A WT >16KG BOVINE/EQU	160	153	1.3	1.4

U.S. Imports by State of Final Destination

Rank	HS Code	Description	Value 2014	Value 2015	Percent of share 2014	Percent of share 2015
		Total Kansas Imports and % Share of U.S. Total	11,806	11,666	0.5	0.5
		Total, Top 25 Commodities and % Share of State Total	4,838	4,651	41.0	39.9
1	880330	PARTS OF AIRPLANES OR HELICOPTERS, NESOI	1,283	802	10.9	6.9
2	852691	RADIO NAVIGATIONAL AID APPARATUS	826	676	7.0	5.8
3	841112	TURBOJETS OF A THRUST EXCEEDING 25 KN	79	428	0.7	3.7
4	640299	FOOTWEAR, OUTER SOLE & UPPER RUBBER OR PLAST	306	269	2.6	2.3
5	640411	FOOTWEAR TEX UP RUBPLAS SOL SPORT SHOES	124	230	1.0	2.0
6	640419	FOOTWEAR, OUT SOLE RUB OR PLAST & TEXT UPPER	173	173	1.5	1.5
7	110900	WHEAT GLUTEN, WHETHER OR NOT DRIED	199	169	1.7	1.4
8	300490	MEDICAMENTS NESOI, MEASURED DOSES, RETAIL PK	231	157	2.0	1.3
9	903180	MEAS & CHECKNG INSTRUMENT, APPLIANCES & MACH	158	145	1.3	1.2
10	840734	SPARK-IGNTN RECPRCTING PISTON ENGINE ETC > 10	102	135	0.9	1.2

Table E-69.   State Trade by Commodity: Kentucky, 2014–2015

(Value in millions of dollars.)

U.S. Exports by Origin State

Rank	HS Code	Description	Value		Percent of share	
			2014	2015	2014	2015
		Total Kentucky Exports and % Share of U.S. Total	27,651	28,053	1.7	1.9
		Total, Top 25 Commodities and % Share of State Total	16,251	17,488	58.8	62.3
1	880000	CIVILIAN AIRCRAFT, ENGINES, AND PARTS	7,734	8,653	28.0	30.8
2	870323	PASS VEH SPK-IG INT COM RCPR P ENG >1500 NOV	1,678	1,445	6.1	5.2
3	870324	PASS VEH SPK-IG INT COM RCPR P ENG > 3000 CC	1,375	1,062	5.0	3.8
4	300210	ANTISERA, BLOOD FRACTIONS & IMMUNOLOGICAL PRO	678	1,018	2.5	3.6
5	300220	VACCINES FOR HUMAN MEDICINE	121	541	0.4	1.9
6	870894	STEERING WHEELS, COLUMNS & BOXES F MOTOR VEHI	230	359	0.8	1.3
7	870422	MTR VEH TRANS GDS COM-IG INT C P E GVW >5NOV2	290	333	1.0	1.2
8	700490	DRWN/BLWN GLSS SHTS W/WO ABSRB/RFCT LYR N OTH	339	327	1.2	1.2
9	391000	SILICONES, IN PRIMARY FORMS	349	315	1.3	1.1
10	220830	WHISKIES	301	311	1.1	1.1

U.S. Imports by State of Final Destination

Rank	HS Code	Description	Value		Percent of share	
			2014	2015	2014	2015
		Total Kentucky Imports and % Share of U.S. Total	39,266	38,538	1.7	1.7
		Total, Top 25 Commodities and % Share of State Total	17,086	17,238	43.5	44.7
1	841191	TURBOJET AND TURBOPROLLER PARTS	3,077	3,553	7.8	9.2
2	300490	MEDICAMENTS NESOI, MEASURED DOSES, RETAIL PK	2,396	2,586	6.1	6.7
3	300210	ANTISERA, BLOOD FRACTIONS & IMMUNOLOGICAL PRO	967	1,202	2.5	3.1
4	851712	PHONES FOR CELLULAR NTWKS OR FOR OTH WIRELESS	1,641	965	4.2	2.5
5	840820	COMPRESSION-IGNTN INT COMBUSTION PISTON ENGIN	835	917	2.1	2.4
6	847330	PARTS & ACCESSORIES FOR ADP MACHINES & UNITS	724	735	1.8	1.9
7	840734	SPARK-IGNTN RECPRCTING PISTON ENGINE ETC > 10	883	709	2.2	1.8
8	870899	PARTS AND ACCESSORIES OF MOTOR VEHICLES, NESO	578	656	1.5	1.7
9	854430	INSULATED WIRING SETS FOR VEHICLES SHIPS AIRC	507	591	1.3	1.5
10	870829	PTS & ACCESS OF BODIES OF MOTOR VEHICLES, NES	490	533	1.2	1.4

Table E-70.   State Trade by Commodity: Louisiana, 2014–2015

(Value in millions of dollars.)

U.S. Exports by Origin State

Rank	HS Code	Description	Value 2014	Value 2015	Percent of share 2014	Percent of share 2015
		Total Louisiana Exports and % Share of U.S. Total	64,814	49,183	4.0	3.3
		Total, Top 25 Commodities and % Share of State Total	51,342	38,511	79.2	78.3
1	271019	PETROL OIL BITUM MINERAL (NT CRUD) ETC NT BIO	20,309	12,475	31.3	25.4
2	120190	SOYBEANS, NESOI	10,647	9,041	16.4	18.4
3	100590	CORN (MAIZE), OTHER THAN SEED CORN	5,396	4,016	8.3	8.2
4	271012	LT OILS, PREPS GT=70% PETROLEUM/BITUM NT BIOD	3,911	2,130	6.0	4.3
5	230400	SOYBEAN OILCAKE & OTH SOLID RESIDUE, WH/NOT G	1,927	1,934	3.0	3.9
6	230330	BREWING OR DISTILLING DREGS AND WASTE, W/NT P	695	817	1.1	1.7
7	270900	CRUDE OIL FROM PETROLEUM AND BITUMINOUS MINER	398	765	0.6	1.6
8	293190	ORGANO-INORGANIC COMPOUNDS, NESOI	677	664	1.0	1.3
9	843143	PARTS FOR BORING OR SINKING MACHINERY, NESOI	780	655	1.2	1.3
10	100199	WHEAT AND MESLIN, NESOI	816	611	1.3	1.2

U.S. Imports by State of Final Destination

Rank	HS Code	Description	Value 2014	Value 2015	Percent of share 2014	Percent of share 2015
		Total Louisiana Imports and % Share of U.S. Total	57,605	35,226	2.5	1.6
		Total, Top 25 Commodities and % Share of State Total	49,081	27,641	85.2	78.5
1	270900	CRUDE OIL FROM PETROLEUM AND BITUMINOUS MINER	33,898	17,442	58.8	49.5
2	271019	PETROL OIL BITUM MINERAL (NT CRUD) ETC NT BIO	9,403	4,981	16.3	14.1
3	310210	UREA, WHETHER OR NOT IN AQUEOUS SOLUTION	561	765	1.0	2.2
4	90111	COFFEE, NOT ROASTED, NOT DECAFFEINATED	667	566	1.2	1.6
5	281410	ANHYDROUS AMMONIA	341	378	0.6	1.1
6	290511	METHANOL (METHYL ALCOHOL)	560	329	1.0	0.9
7	271012	LT OILS, PREPS GT=70% PETROLEUM/BITUM NT BIOD	673	296	1.2	0.8
8	151190	PALM OIL, REFINED BUT NOT CHEMICALLY MODIFIED	485	293	0.8	0.8
9	290220	BENZENE	471	269	0.8	0.8
10	310420	POTASSIUM CHLORIDE	103	226	0.2	0.6

Table E-71.   State Trade by Commodity: Maine, 2014–2015

(Value in millions of dollars.)

U.S. Exports by Origin State

Rank	HS Code	Description	Value		Percent of share	
			2014	2015	2014	2015
		Total Maine Exports and % Share of U.S. Total	2,712	2,724	0.2	0.2
		Total, Top 25 Commodities and % Share of State Total	1,679	1,824	61.9	67
1	30622	LOBSTERS, LIVE, FRESH,CH, DRIED, SALTD OR IN	349	331	12.9	12.2
2	880000	CIVILIAN AIRCRAFT, ENGINES, AND PARTS	118	237	4.4	8.7
3	854239	ELECTRONIC INTEGRATED CIRCUITS, NESOI	70	225	2.6	8.3
4	440320	CONIFEROUS WOOD IN THE ROUGH, NOT TREATED	145	156	5.4	5.7
5	470329	CHEM WOODPULP, SODA ETC, N DIS S BL & BL NONC	100	134	3.7	4.9
6	481013	PPR/PBRD FOR WRIT/PRING,CLAY CTD,<=10%MEC FBR	161	120	5.9	4.4
7	271121	NATURAL GAS, GASEOUS	210	92	7.8	3.4
8	481190	PAPER, PAPERBD, CELLULOSE WADD ETC, COAT ETC	57	61	2.1	2.3
9	382200	COMPOSITE DIAGNOSTIC/LAB REAGENTS, EXC PHARMA	52	50	1.9	1.8
10	30441	PACIFIC, ATLANTIC, DANUBE SALMON FILLET FRESH	19	46	0.7	1.7

U.S. Imports by State of Final Destination

Rank	HS Code	Description	Value		Percent of share	
			2014	2015	2014	2015
		Total Maine Imports and % Share of U.S. Total	3,867	3,685	0.2	0.2
		Total, Top 25 Commodities and % Share of State Total	1,815	1,581	46.9	42.9
1	271600	ELECTRICAL ENERGY	312	226	8.1	6.1
2	271012	LT OILS, PREPS GT=70% PETROLEUM/BITUM NT BIOD	333	247	8.6	6.7
3	30622	LOBSTERS, LIVE, FRESH,CH, DRIED, SALTD OR IN	161	180	4.2	4.9
4	440710	CONIFEROUS WOOD SAWN, SLICED ETC, OVER 6 MM T	61	62	1.6	1.7
5	470421	CHEM WDPULP SULFITE EX DSSLVNG GR CONIF SEMI/	114	90	2.9	2.4
6	640399	FOOTWEAR, OUTER SOLE RUB ETC & LEATHER UPPER	69	107	1.8	2.9
7	850300	PARTS OF ELECTRIC MOTORS, GENERATORS & SETS	0	15	0	0.4
8	470321	CHEMICAL WOODPULP, SODA ETC. N DIS S BL & BL	134	79	3.5	2.2
9	271112	PROPANE, LIQUEFIED	112	58	2.9	1.6
10	854129	TRANSISTORS, OTHER THAN PHOTOSENSITIVE, NESOI	48	42	1.2	1.1

Table E-72.   State Trade by Commodity: Maryland, 2014–2015

(Value in millions of dollars.)

U.S. Exports by Origin State

Rank	HS Code	Description	Value		Percent of share	
			2014	2015	2014	2015
		Total Maryland Exports and % Share of U.S. Total	12,233	10,030	0.8	0.7
		Total, Top 25 Commodities and % Share of State Total	6,138	4,643	50.2	46.3
1	870324	PASS VEH SPK-IG INT COM RCPR P ENG > 3000 CC	1,540	809	12.6	8.1
2	851762	MACH FOR RECP/CONVR/TRANS/REGN OF VOICE/IMAGE	611	358	5.0	3.6
3	382200	COMPOSITE DIAGNOSTIC/LAB REAGENTS, EXC PHARMA	295	337	2.4	3.4
4	381519	SUPPORTED CATALYSTS, NESOI	277	324	2.3	3.2
5	880000	CIVILIAN AIRCRAFT, ENGINES, AND PARTS	454	310	3.7	3.1
6	300490	MEDICAMENTS NESOI, MEASURED DOSES, RETAIL PK	441	292	3.6	2.9
7	880330	PARTS OF AIRPLANES OR HELICOPTERS, NESOI	129	274	1.1	2.7
8	300210	ANTISERA, BLOOD FRACTIONS & IMMUNOLOGICAL PRO	293	268	2.4	2.7
9	870323	PASS VEH SPK-IG INT COM RCPR P ENG >1500 NOV	655	215	5.4	2.1
10	852610	RADAR APPARATUS	39	162	0.3	1.6

U.S. Imports by State of Final Destination

Rank	HS Code	Description	Value		Percent of share	
			2014	2015	2014	2015
		Total Maryland Imports and % Share of U.S. Total	30,072	31,501	1.3	1.4
		Total, Top 25 Commodities and % Share of State Total	15,048	17,322	50.0	55.0
1	870323	PASS VEH SPK-IG INT COM RCPR P ENG >1500 NOV	3,874	5,796	12.9	18.4
2	870324	PASS VEH SPK-IG INT COM RCPR P ENG > 3000 CC	3,470	3,348	11.5	10.6
3	851762	MACH FOR RECP/CONVR/TRANS/REGN OF VOICE/IMAGE	1,162	1,398	3.9	4.4
4	711311	JEWELRY AND PARTS THEREOF, OF SILVER	594	700	2.0	2.2
5	870190	TRACTORS, NESOI	563	654	1.9	2.1
6	750210	NICKEL, UNWROUGHT, NOT ALLOYED	784	566	2.6	1.8
7	90111	COFFEE, NOT ROASTED, NOT DECAFFEINATED	355	477	1.2	1.5
8	760612	ALUMINUM ALLOY RECT PLATES ETC, OVER .2 MM TH	344	451	1.1	1.4
9	760120	UNWROUGHT ALUMINUM ALLOYS	359	422	1.2	1.3
10	800110	TIN, UNWROUGHT, NOT ALLOYED	600	394	2.0	1.2

Table E-73.   State Trade by Commodity: Massachusetts, 2014–2015

(Value in millions of dollars.)

U.S. Exports by Origin State

Rank	HS Code	Description	Value 2014	Value 2015	Percent of share 2014	Percent of share 2015
		Total Massachusetts Exports and % Share of U.S. Total	27,385	25,282	1.7	1.7
		Total, Top 25 Commodities and % Share of State Total	12,019	11,012	43.9	43.6
1	711291	WASTE & SCRAP GOLD EXCL SWPNGS CNTNG OTH PREC	171	727	0.6	2.9
2	901890	INSTR & APPL F MEDICAL SURGICAL DENTAL VET, N	1,054	1,052	3.8	4.2
3	901839	MED NEEDLES. NESOI, CATHERERS ETC AND PARTS E	974	997	3.6	3.9
4	848620	MACHINES FOR MAN. SEMICONDUTOR DEVICES/ELEC I	721	1,029	2.6	4.1
5	854231	PROCESSORS AND CONTROLLERS, ELECTRONIC INTEG	935	892	3.4	3.5
6	710812	GOLD, NONMONETARY, UNWROUGHT NESOI	1,942	182	7.1	0.7
7	300210	ANTISERA, BLOOD FRACTIONS & IMMUNOLOGICAL PRO	367	508	1.3	2.0
8	300390	MEDICAMENTS NESOI, NOT IN DOSAGE FORM ETC	454	511	1.7	2.0
9	880000	CIVILIAN AIRCRAFT, ENGINES, AND PARTS	715	699	2.6	2.8
10	902780	PHY CHEM INS/APPR;MEAS VSCSTY & HEAT NESOI	393	386	1.4	1.5

U.S. Imports by State of Final Destination

Rank	HS Code	Description	Value 2014	Value 2015	Percent of share 2014	Percent of share 2015
		Total Massachusetts Imports and % Share of U.S. Total	34,525	33,652	1.5	1.5
		Total, Top 25 Commodities and % Share of State Total	12,936	12,375	37.5	36.8
1	851762	MACH FOR RECP/CONVR/TRANS/REGN OF VOICE/IMAGE	1,184	1,472	3.4	4.4
2	300490	MEDICAMENTS NESOI, MEASURED DOSES, RETAIL PK	158	534	0.5	1.6
3	710812	GOLD, NONMONETARY, UNWROUGHT NESOI	1,511	1,324	4.4	3.9
4	271012	LT OILS, PREPS GT=70% PETROLEUM/BITUM NT BIOD	2,501	1,353	7.2	4.0
5	902139	ARTIFICIAL JOINTS & PARTS & ACCESSORIES THERO	768	857	2.2	2.5
6	901890	INSTR & APPL F MEDICAL SURGICAL DENTAL VET, N	724	661	2.1	2.0
7	854239	ELECTRONIC INTEGRATED CIRCUITS, NESOI	819	949	2.4	2.8
8	870323	PASS VEH SPK-IG INT COM RCPR P ENG >1500 NOV	27	13	0.1	0.0
9	901839	MED NEEDLES. NESOI, CATHERERS ETC AND PARTS E	538	564	1.6	1.7
10	901819	ELECTRO-DIAGNOSTIC APPARATUS NESOI, AND PARTS	573	557	1.7	1.7

Table E-74.   State Trade by Commodity: Michigan, 2014–2015

(Value in millions of dollars.)

U.S. Exports by Origin State

Rank	HS Code	Description	Value		Percent of share	
			2014	2015	2014	2015
		Total Michigan Exports and % Share of U.S. Total	55,929	53,171	3.5	3.5
		Total, Top 25 Commodities and % Share of State Total	28,188	27,313	50.4	51.4
1	870431	MTR VEH TRANS GDS SPK IG IN C P ENG, GVW NOV	3,866	3,990	6.9	7.5
2	870324	PASS VEH SPK-IG INT COM RCPR P ENG > 3000 CC	3,486	3,051	6.2	5.7
3	870829	PTS & ACCESS OF BODIES OF MOTOR VEHICLES, NES	3,426	3,019	6.1	5.7
4	870840	GEAR BOXES FOR MOTOR VEHICLES	1,817	2,252	3.2	4.2
5	870899	PARTS AND ACCESSORIES OF MOTOR VEHICLES, NESO	2,287	2,227	4.1	4.2
6	271121	NATURAL GAS, GASEOUS	2,054	1,219	3.7	2.3
7	870323	PASS VEH SPK-IG INT COM RCPR P ENG >1500 NOV	1,640	1,178	2.9	2.2
8	840734	SPARK-IGNTN RECPRCTING PISTON ENGINE ETC > 10	1,171	1,021	2.1	1.9
9	700910	REAR-VIEW MIRRORS FOR VEHICLES	849	934	1.5	1.8
10	870850	DRIVE AXLES WITH DIFFERENTIAL FOR MOTOR VEHIC	724	889	1.3	1.7

U.S. Imports by State of Final Destination

Rank	HS Code	Description	Value		Percent of share	
			2014	2015	2014	2015
		Total Michigan Imports and % Share of U.S. Total	122,739	124,088	5.2	5.5
		Total, Top 25 Commodities and % Share of State Total	81,158	82,648	66.1	66.6
1	870324	PASS VEH SPK-IG INT COM RCPR P ENG > 3000 CC	22,896	20,487	18.7	16.5
2	870323	PASS VEH SPK-IG INT COM RCPR P ENG >1500 NOV	12,847	16,401	10.5	13.2
3	870431	MTR VEH TRANS GDS SPK IG IN C P ENG, GVW NOV	10,055	10,420	8.2	8.4
4	870829	PTS & ACCESS OF BODIES OF MOTOR VEHICLES, NES	2,846	3,067	2.3	2.5
5	840734	SPARK-IGNTN RECPRCTING PISTON ENGINE ETC > 10	2,943	3,002	2.4	2.4
6	870899	PARTS AND ACCESSORIES OF MOTOR VEHICLES, NESO	2,968	2,997	2.4	2.4
7	940190	PARTS OF SEATS (EX MEDICAL, BARBER, DENTAL ET	2,854	2,935	2.3	2.4
8	270900	CRUDE OIL FROM PETROLEUM AND BITUMINOUS MINER	4,899	2,614	4	2.1
9	870421	TRUCKS, NESOI, DIESEL ENG, GVW 5 METRIC TONS	1,994	2,214	1.6	1.8
10	870422	MTR VEH TRANS GDS COM-IG INT C P E GVW >5NOV2	2,041	1,910	1.7	1.5

Table E-75. State Trade by Commodity: Minnesota, 2014–2015

(Value in millions of dollars.)

U.S. Exports by Origin State

Rank	HS Code	Description	Value		Percent of share	
			2014	2015	2014	2015
		Total Minnesota Exports and % Share of U.S. Total	21,408	19,988	1.3	1.3
		Total, Top 25 Commodities and % Share of State Total	6,714	6,284	31.4	31.4
1	901839	MED NEEDLES. NESOI, CATHERERS ETC AND PARTS E	875	864	4.1	4.3
2	880000	CIVILIAN AIRCRAFT, ENGINES, AND PARTS	518	449	2.4	2.2
3	842199	FILTER/PURIFY MACHINE & APPARATUS PARTS	379	409	1.8	2.0
4	854290	ELECTRONIC INTEGRATED CIRCUITS AND MCRSSMBLS	431	348	2.0	1.7
5	851762	MACH FOR RECP/CONVR/TRANS/REGN OF VOICE/IMAGE	322	332	1.5	1.7
6	870321	PASS MTR VEH, SPARK IGN ENG, NOT OV 1,000 CC	418	309	2.0	1.5
7	391990	PLATES, SHEETS, FILM ETC, PLASTICS, SELF-ADH	294	298	1.4	1.5
8	902190	OTH ARTIFICAL PTS OF THE BODY & PTS & ACCESSO	308	297	1.4	1.5
9	900190	LENSES PRISMS MIRRORS OPTCL ELMNT N OPTICALLY	256	278	1.2	1.4
10	870310	PASS VEH FOR SNOW; GOLF CARTS & SIMILAR VEHIC	359	270	1.7	1.4

U.S. Imports by State of Final Destination

Rank	HS Code	Description	Value		Percent of share	
			2014	2015	2014	2015
		Total Minnesota Imports and % Share of U.S. Total	34,693	28,576	1.5	1.3
		Total, Top 25 Commodities and % Share of State Total	15,723	11,269	45.3	39.4
1	270900	CRUDE OIL FROM PETROLEUM AND BITUMINOUS MINER	7,799	3,842	22.5	13.4
2	950300	TRICYCLE, SCOOTR, PEDAL CAR & SIM WHEELED TYS	1,108	1,094	3.2	3.8
3	852872	RECEPTION APPARATUS FOR TELEVISION, COLOR, NE	963	1,076	2.8	3.8
4	902150	PACEMAKERS FOR STIMULATING HEART MUSCLES	916	652	2.6	2.3
5	880240	AIRPLANE & OT A/C, UNLADEN WEIGHT > 15,000 KG	99	595	0.3	2.1
6	271121	NATURAL GAS, GASEOUS	872	355	2.5	1.2
7	310210	UREA, WHETHER OR NOT IN AQUEOUS SOLUTION	531	316	1.5	1.1
8	271600	ELECTRICAL ENERGY	307	301	0.9	1.1
9	310420	POTASSIUM CHLORIDE	220	299	0.6	1.0
10	902140	HEARING AIDS	275	256	0.8	0.9

Table E-76.   State Trade by Commodity: Mississippi, 2014–2015

(Value in millions of dollars.)

U.S. Exports by Origin State

Rank	HS Code	Description	Value		Percent of share	
			2014	2015	2014	2015
		Total Mississippi Exports and % Share of U.S. Total	11,450	10,786	0.7	0.7
		Total, Top 25 Commodities and % Share of State Total	7,928	7,334	69.2	68.0
1	271019	PETROL OIL BITUM MINERAL (NT CRUD) ETC NT BIO	2,970	2,349	25.9	21.8
2	271012	LT OILS, PREPS GT=70% PETROLEUM/BITUM NT BIOD	888	850	7.8	7.9
3	320611	PIGMNTS\PREPS CONT =>80% TITANIUM DIOXIDE, DR	793	649	6.9	6.0
4	470321	CHEMICAL WOODPULP, SODA ETC. N DIS S BL & BL	468	477	4.1	4.4
5	870324	PASS VEH SPK-IG INT COM RCPR P ENG > 3000 CC	202	435	1.8	4.0
6	902131	ARTIFICIAL JOINTS AND PARTS AND ACCESSORIES T	292	349	2.6	3.2
7	520100	COTTON, NOT CARDED OR COMBED	378	297	3.3	2.7
8	870431	MTR VEH TRANS GDS SPK IG IN C P ENG, GVW NOV	251	197	2.2	1.8
9	870323	PASS VEH SPK-IG INT COM RCPR P ENG >1500 NOV	192	187	1.7	1.7
10	901839	MED NEEDLES. NESOI, CATHERERS ETC AND PARTS E	174	187	1.5	1.7

U.S. Imports by State of Final Destination

Rank	HS Code	Description	Value		Percent of share	
			2014	2015	2014	2015
		Total Mississippi Imports and % Share of U.S. Total	17,254	14,063	0.7	0.6
		Total, Top 25 Commodities and % Share of State Total	10,395	7,002	60.2	49.8
1	270900	CRUDE OIL FROM PETROLEUM AND BITUMINOUS MINER	6,496	2,451	37.6	17.4
2	870840	GEAR BOXES FOR MOTOR VEHICLES	689	707	4.0	5.0
3	940190	PARTS OF SEATS (EX MEDICAL, BARBER, DENTAL ET	480	526	2.8	3.7
4	271019	PETROL OIL BITUM MINERAL (NT CRUD) ETC NT BIO	486	424	2.8	3.0
5	300630	OPACIFYING PREPARATIONS FOR X-RAY EXAMINATION	194	243	1.1	1.7
6	840999	SPARK-IGNITION RECIPROCATING INT COM PISTN EN	234	225	1.4	1.6
7	846729	TOOLS FOR WK IN HAND,W/ SELF-CONT ELEC MOTOR	76	221	0.4	1.6
8	901839	MED NEEDLES. NESOI, CATHERERS ETC AND PARTS E	132	187	0.8	1.3
9	620342	MEN'S OR BOYS' TROUSERS ETC, NOT KNIT, COTTON	147	165	0.9	1.2
10	80390	BANANAS, FRESH OR DRIED, NESOI	213	153	1.2	1.1

Table E-77.   State Trade by Commodity: Missouri, 2014–2015

(Value in millions of dollars.)

U.S. Exports by Origin State

Rank	HS Code	Description	Value 2014	Value 2015	Percent of share 2014	Percent of share 2015
		Total Missouri Exports and % Share of U.S. Total	14,141	13,617	0.9	0.8
		Total, Top 25 Commodities and % Share of State Total	5,837	5,603	34.6	38.0
1	870431	MTR VEH TRANS GDS SPK IG IN C P ENG, GVW NOV	1,443	1,150	7.8	9.8
2	880000	CIVILIAN AIRCRAFT, ENGINES, AND PARTS	496	686	1.4	0.7
3	300230	VACCINES FOR VETRINARY MEDICINE	333	337	2.7	2.9
4	230400	SOYBEAN OILCAKE & OTH SOLID RESIDUE, WH/NOT G	240	263	0.6	0.5
5	293399	HETEROCYCLIC COMP W NITROGEN HETERO-ATM ONLY	186	244	0.4	0.9
6	871150	MOTORCYCLES, CYCL,EXCD 800 CC	268	238	1.7	2.0
7	100590	CORN (MAIZE), OTHER THAN SEED CORN	168	232	1.9	0.8
8	410411	BOV/EQ HIDE/SKIN,FUL GRN,UNSPLIT;GRN SPL, WET	198	204	0.7	1.0
9	930690	BOMB MINES OT AMMNTION PROJCTIONS ETC AND PAR	144	200	0.4	0.6
10	270112	BITUMINOUS COAL, NOT AGGLOMERATED	393	186	4.9	4.0

U.S. Imports by State of Final Destination

Rank	HS Code	Description	Value 2014	Value 2015	Percent of share 2014	Percent of share 2015
		Total Missouri Imports and % Share of U.S. Total	18,284	18,444	0.7	0.8
		Total, Top 25 Commodities and % Share of State Total	5,410	5,864	24.8	30.3
1	270900	CRUDE OIL FROM PETROLEUM AND BITUMINOUS MINER	511	714	4.0	7.6
2	760120	UNWROUGHT ALUMINUM ALLOYS	576	539	2.4	2.6
3	840734	SPARK-IGNTN RECPRCTING PISTON ENGINE ETC > 10	693	461	2.8	2.7
4	220300	BEER MADE FROM MALT	291	393	1.3	1.3
5	300490	MEDICAMENTS NESOI, MEASURED DOSES, RETAIL PK	394	364	1.4	2.2
6	850140	AC MOTORS NESOI, SINGLE-PHASE	343	319	1.7	1.7
7	940190	PARTS OF SEATS (EX MEDICAL, BARBER, DENTAL ET	318	299	1.1	1.4
8	870120	ROAD TRACTORS FOR SEMI-TRAILERS	314	271	1.2	1.3
9	870840	GEAR BOXES FOR MOTOR VEHICLES	61	186	0.1	0.1
10	950300	TRICYCLE, SCOOTR, PEDAL CAR & SIM WHEELED TYS	160	180	1.0	0.8

Table E-78.   State Trade by Commodity: Montana, 2014–2015

(Value in millions of dollars.)

U.S. Exports by Origin State

Rank	HS Code	Description	Value		Percent of share	
			2014	2015	2014	2015
		Total Montana Exports and % Share of U.S. Total	1,545	1,386	0.1	0.1
		Total, Top 25 Commodities and % Share of State Total	901	938	58.3	67.7
1	282550	COPPER OXIDES AND HYDROXIDES	122	147	7.9	10.6
2	270119	COAL NESOI, NOT AGGLOMERATED	138	123	8.9	8.9
3	240220	CIGARETTES CONTAINING TOBACCO	53	103	3.4	7.4
4	848620	MACHINES FOR MAN. SEMICONDUTOR DEVICES/ELEC I	35	74	2.3	5.4
5	285000	HYDRIDS/NITRIDS/AZIDS/SILICIDS ETC W/NT CHEM	84	68	5.4	4.9
6	71340	LENTILS, DRIED SHELLED, INCLUDING SEED	38	53	2.4	3.9
7	280461	SILICON CONTAIN BY WT NT < 99.99% OF SILICON	32	39	2.1	2.8
8	252329	PORTLAND CEMENT EXCEPT WHITE PORTLAND CEMENT	43	37	2.8	2.7
9	300290	HUMAN BLOOD; ANIMAL BLOOD PREP, TOXINS, CULTR	25	35	1.6	2.5
10	71310	PEAS, DRIED SHELLED, INCLUDING SEED	49	34	3.1	2.5

U.S. Imports by State of Final Destination

Rank	HS Code	Description	Value		Percent of share	
			2014	2015	2014	2015
		Total Montana Imports and % Share of U.S. Total	6,237	4,067	0.3	0.2
		Total, Top 25 Commodities and % Share of State Total	5,452	3,343	87.4	82.2
1	270900	CRUDE OIL FROM PETROLEUM AND BITUMINOUS MINER	4,503	2,630	72.2	64.7
2	711292	PLAT WST A SCRP NT CNTNG OTH PREC MTLS	229	139	3.7	3.4
3	310210	UREA, WHETHER OR NOT IN AQUEOUS SOLUTION	102	101	1.6	2.5
4	440710	CONIFEROUS WOOD SAWN, SLICED ETC, OVER 6 MM T	58	47	0.9	1.2
5	711299	WASTE AND SCRAP OF PRECIOUS METAL NESOI	21	46	0.3	1.1
6	240220	CIGARETTES CONTAINING TOBACCO	52	43	0.8	1.0
7	100119	DURUM WHEAT, NESOI	36	37	0.6	0.9
8	271121	NATURAL GAS, GASEOUS	40	36	0.6	0.9
9	230641	RAPE/COLZA SEED OILCAKE&SOLID RES. LOW ERUCIC	33	34	0.5	0.8
10	100199	WHEAT AND MESLIN, NESOI	66	30	1.1	0.7

Table E-79. State Trade by Commodity: Nebraska, 2014–2015

(Value in millions of dollars.)

U.S. Exports by Origin State

Rank	HS Code	Description	Value 2014	Value 2015	Percent of share 2014	Percent of share 2015
		Total Nebraska Exports and % Share of U.S. Total	7,863	6,556	0.5	0.4
		Total, Top 25 Commodities and % Share of State Total	5,098	4,074	64.8	62.1
1	20130	MEAT OF BOVINE ANIMALS, BONELESS, FRESH OR CH	532	488	6.8	7.4
2	20230	MEAT OF BOVINE ANIMALS, BONELESS, FROZEN	433	376	5.5	5.7
3	120190	SOYBEANS, NESOI	524	315	6.7	4.8
4	843351	COMBINE HARVESTER-THRESHERS	466	308	5.9	4.7
5	410150	WHOLE HIDES & SKINS, OF A WT >16KG BOVINE/EQU	314	259	4.0	3.9
6	100590	CORN (MAIZE), OTHER THAN SEED CORN	195	230	2.5	3.5
7	842481	AGRICULTURAL OR HORTICULTURAL MECH SPRAYERS E	241	191	3.1	2.9
8	853890	PT F ELECT APPR F ELECT CIRCT; F ELCT CONTRL	89	188	1.1	2.9
9	853690	ELECT APPR F PRTCT TO ELECT CIRCT NOV 1000 V	122	175	1.6	2.7
10	271121	NATURAL GAS, GASEOUS	477	174	6.1	2.6

U.S. Imports by State of Final Destination

Rank	HS Code	Description	Value 2014	Value 2015	Percent of share 2014	Percent of share 2015
		Total Nebraska Imports and % Share of U.S. Total	4,050	4,130	0.2	0.2
		Total, Top 25 Commodities and % Share of State Total	1,482	1,519	36.6	36.8
1	10229	CATTLE, LIVE, OTHER THAN PUREBRED BREEDING	313	202	7.7	4.9
2	870120	ROAD TRACTORS FOR SEMI-TRAILERS	81	133	2.0	3.2
3	293499	NUCLEIC ACIDS & SALTS; OTHER HETEROCYCLIC CMP	66	128	1.6	3.1
4	843390	PARTS FOR HARVESTER, GRASS MOWERS, SORTING EG	126	110	3.1	2.7
5	840890	COMPRESSION-IGNTN INT COMBUSTION PISTON ENG,	116	98	2.9	2.4
6	293410	HETERCYC CMP, UNFUSED THIAZOLE RING IN THE ST	0	96	0.0	2.3
7	293359	COMP WITH PYRIMIDINE OR PIPERAZINE RING, NESO	18	75	0.4	1.8
8	950300	TRICYCLE, SCOOTR, PEDAL CAR & SIM WHEELED TYS	71	71	1.8	1.7
9	843359	HARVESTING MACHINERY, NESOI	67	47	1.6	1.1
10	440710	CONIFEROUS WOOD SAWN, SLICED ETC, OVER 6 MM T	54	47	1.3	1.1

Table E-80.   State Trade by Commodity: Nevada, 2014–2015

(Value in millions of dollars.)

U.S. Exports by Origin State

Rank	HS Code	Description	Value		Percent of share	
			2014	2015	2014	2015
		Total Nevada Exports and % Share of U.S. Total	7,692	8,658	0.5	0.6
		Total, Top 25 Commodities and % Share of State Total	5,636	6,895	73.3	79.6
1	710812	GOLD, NONMONETARY, UNWROUGHT NESOI	2,798	3,941	36.4	45.5
2	950430	GAMES COIN-/TOKEN-OPERATED EXC BOWLING ALLEY	396	444	5.2	5.1
3	710239	DIAMONDS, NONINDUSTRIAL, WORKED	292	403	3.8	4.7
4	854239	ELECTRONIC INTEGRATED CIRCUITS, NESOI	360	370	4.7	4.3
5	260300	COPPER ORES AND CONCENTRATES	560	327	7.3	3.8
6	710691	SILVER, UNWROUGHT NESOI	43	244	0.6	2.8
7	854231	PROCESSORS AND CONTROLLERS, ELECTRONIC INTEG	160	172	2.1	2.0
8	903180	MEAS & CHECKNG INSTRUMENT, APPLIANCES & MACH	187	155	2.4	1.8
9	880000	CIVILIAN AIRCRAFT, ENGINES, AND PARTS	107	115	1.4	1.3
10	854232	MEMORIES, ELECTRONIC INTEGRATED CIRCUITS	88	82	1.1	0.9

U.S. Imports by State of Final Destination

Rank	HS Code	Description	Value		Percent of share	
			2014	2015	2014	2015
		Total Nevada Imports and % Share of U.S. Total	7,850	9,590	0.3	0.4
		Total, Top 25 Commodities and % Share of State Total	3,923	5,306	50.0	55.3
1	847180	AUTOMATIC DATA PROCESSING UNITS, N.E.S.O.I.	40	961	0.5	10.0
2	851712	PHONES FOR CELLULAR NTWKS OR FOR OTH WIRELESS	547	719	7.0	7.5
3	710239	DIAMONDS, NONINDUSTRIAL, WORKED	274	500	3.5	5.2
4	854239	ELECTRONIC INTEGRATED CIRCUITS, NESOI	879	440	11.2	4.6
5	950430	GAMES COIN-/TOKEN-OPERATED EXC BOWLING ALLEY	319	370	4.1	3.9
6	847141	DIGITAL ADP MACH,WITH CP UNIT,INPUT,OUTPUT, N	111	351	1.4	3.7
7	854140	PHOTOSNSITVE SEMICNDCTR DVICE INC PHTVLTC CEL	339	256	4.3	2.7
8	847330	PARTS & ACCESSORIES FOR ADP MACHINES & UNITS	85	190	1.1	2.0
9	847150	DIGITAL PROCESSING UNITS, N.E.S.O.I.	196	184	2.5	1.9
10	620342	MEN'S OR BOYS' TROUSERS ETC, NOT KNIT, COTTON	131	176	1.7	1.8

Table E-81.   State Trade by Commodity: New Hampshire, 2014–2015

(Value in millions of dollars.)

U.S. Exports by Origin State

Rank	HS Code	Description	Value		Percent of share	
			2014	2015	2014	2015
		Total New Hampshire Exports and % Share of U.S. Total	4,227	4,007	0.3	0.3
		Total, Top 25 Commodities and % Share of State Total	1,804	1,973	42.7	49.2
1	851712	PHONES FOR CELLULAR NTWKS OR FOR OTH WIRELESS	503	287	11.9	7.2
2	844399	PTS & ACC OF PRINTERS, COPIERS AND FAX MACH,	173	203	4.1	5.1
3	851770	PTS OF PHONE SETS & OTH APP FOR THE TRANS/REC	125	180	2.9	4.5
4	854470	INSULATED OPTICAL FIBER CABLES WITH INDVULY S	4	157	0.1	3.9
5	846693	PARTS AND ACCESSORIES FOR USE WITH MACH TOOL	158	141	3.7	3.5
6	851762	MACH FOR RECP/CONVR/TRANS/REGN OF VOICE/IMAGE	49	129	1.2	3.2
7	844332	PRINTERS/ COPIERS/FAX MACH, NT COMB, CONNCT T	89	84	2.1	2.1
8	841370	CENTRIFUGAL PUMPS, NESOI	0	81	0.0	2.0
9	880000	CIVILIAN AIRCRAFT, ENGINES, AND PARTS	69	76	1.6	1.9
10	852990	PTS,EX ANTENNA,FOR TRNSMSSN,RDR,RADIO,TV,ETC	100	70	2.4	1.7

U.S. Imports by State of Final Destination

Rank	HS Code	Description	Value		Percent of share	
			2014	2015	2014	2015
		Total New Hampshire Imports and % Share of U.S. Total	11,216	9,283	0.5	0.4
		Total, Top 25 Commodities and % Share of State Total	7,833	5,817	69.8	62.7
1	271012	LT OILS, PREPS GT=70% PETROLEUM/BITUM NT BIOD	3,432	2,344	30.6	25.3
2	271019	PETROL OIL BITUM MINERAL (NT CRUD) ETC NT BIO	1,988	1,329	17.7	14.3
3	271020	PETROLEUM OILS AND PREPS CONTAINING BIODIESEL	558	242	5	2.6
4	640399	FOOTWEAR, OUTER SOLE RUB ETC & LEATHER UPPER	239	225	2.1	2.4
5	271320	PETROLEUM BITUMEN	179	185	1.6	2
6	851770	PTS OF PHONE SETS & OTH APP FOR THE TRANS/REC	203	151	1.8	1.6
7	392119	PLATES, SHEETS ETC. NESOI, CELLULAR PLASTIC N	120	142	1.1	1.5
8	851762	MACH FOR RECP/CONVR/TRANS/REGN OF VOICE/IMAGE	99	127	0.9	1.4
9	950699	ART FOR SPORTS ETC.NESOIF SWIM POOLSF PTS & A	44	115	0.4	1.2
10	901890	INSTR & APPL F MEDICAL SURGICAL DENTAL VET, N	94	104	0.8	1.1

Table E-82. State Trade by Commodity: New Jersey, 2014–2015

(Value in millions of dollars.)

U.S. Exports by Origin State

Rank	HS Code	Description	Value		Percent of share	
			2014	2015	2014	2015
		Total New Jersey Exports and % Share of U.S. Total	36,616	32,076	2.3	2.1
		Total, Top 25 Commodities and % Share of State Total	14,657	11,468	40	35.8
1	271019	PETROL OIL BITUM MINERAL (NT CRUD) ETC NT BIO	2,882	1,249	7.9	3.9
2	711319	JEWELRY AND PARTS THEREOF, OF OTH PRECIOUS ME	1,423	1,090	3.9	3.4
3	880000	CIVILIAN AIRCRAFT, ENGINES, AND PARTS	594	721	1.6	2.2
4	711021	PALLADIUM, UNWROUGHT OR IN POWDER FORM	885	679	2.4	2.1
5	711292	PLAT WST A SCRP NT CNTNG OTH PREC MTLS	868	659	2.4	2.1
6	851712	PHONES FOR CELLULAR NTWKS OR FOR OTH WIRELESS	696	655	1.9	2
7	300490	MEDICAMENTS NESOI, MEASURED DOSES, RETAIL PK	530	553	1.4	1.7
8	720449	FERROUS WASTE & SCRAP NESOI	754	472	2.1	1.5
9	330499	BEAUTY & SKIN CARE PREPARATION, NESOI	430	462	1.2	1.4
10	870324	PASS VEH SPK-IG INT COM RCPR P ENG > 3000 CC	612	438	1.7	1.4

U.S. Imports by State of Final Destination

Rank	HS Code	Description	Value		Percent of share	
			2014	2015	2014	2015
		Total New Jersey Imports and % Share of U.S. Total	126,365	119,490	5.4	5.3
		Total, Top 25 Commodities and % Share of State Total	59,002	49,208	46.7	41.2
1	870323	PASS VEH SPK-IG INT COM RCPR P ENG >1500 NOV	11,855	10,080	9.4	8.4
2	300490	MEDICAMENTS NESOI, MEASURED DOSES, RETAIL PK	5,550	8,485	4.4	7.1
3	270900	CRUDE OIL FROM PETROLEUM AND BITUMINOUS MINER	10,894	6,449	8.6	5.4
4	271012	LT OILS, PREPS GT=70% PETROLEUM/BITUM NT BIOD	9,674	6,268	7.7	5.2
5	870324	PASS VEH SPK-IG INT COM RCPR P ENG > 3000 CC	4,008	2,487	3.2	2.1
6	271019	PETROL OIL BITUM MINERAL (NT CRUD) ETC NT BIO	4,685	2,323	3.7	1.9
7	711021	PALLADIUM, UNWROUGHT OR IN POWDER FORM	1,477	1,293	1.2	1.1
8	851762	MACH FOR RECP/CONVR/TRANS/REGN OF VOICE/IMAGE	1,280	991	1	0.8
9	870322	PASS MTR VEH,SPARK IGN ENG, >1000CC BUT =<150	525	967	0.4	0.8
10	401110	NEW PNEUMATIC TIRES OF RUBBER, FOR MOTOR CARS	759	863	0.6	0.7

Table E-83.   State Trade by Commodity: New Mexico, 2014–2015

(Value in millions of dollars.)

U.S. Exports by Origin State

Rank	HS Code	Description	Value 2014	Value 2015	Percent of share 2014	Percent of share 2015
		Total New Mexico Exports and % Share of U.S. Total	3,800	3,772	0.2	0.3
		Total, Top 25 Commodities and % Share of State Total	2,175	2,796	57.2	74.1
1	854231	PROCESSORS AND CONTROLLERS, ELECTRONIC INTEG	837	1,084	22.0	28.7
2	847330	PARTS & ACCESSORIES FOR ADP MACHINES & UNITS	495	795	13.0	21.1
3	851762	MACH FOR RECP/CONVR/TRANS/REGN OF VOICE/IMAGE	42	104	1.1	2.8
4	901890	INSTR & APPL F MEDICAL SURGICAL DENTAL VET, N	43	67	1.1	1.8
5	848180	TAPS COCKS ETC F PIPE VAT INC THERMO CONTROL	66	64	1.7	1.7
6	880000	CIVILIAN AIRCRAFT, ENGINES, AND PARTS	99	60	2.6	1.6
7	847170	AUTOMATIC DATA PROCESSING STORAGE UNITS, N.E.	36	53	0.9	1.4
8	392690	ARTICLES OF PLASTICS, NESOI	56	53	1.5	1.4
9	930690	BOMB MINES OT AMMNTION PROJCTIONS ETC AND PAR	66	43	1.7	1.2
10	854442	ELEC CONDUCTORS, LT=1000 V, W/ CONNECTORS, NE	18	39	0.5	1.0

U.S. Imports by State of Final Destination

Rank	HS Code	Description	Value 2014	Value 2015	Percent of share 2014	Percent of share 2015
		Total New Mexico Imports and % Share of U.S. Total	2,237	2,244	0.1	0.1
		Total, Top 25 Commodities and % Share of State Total	1,291	1,377	57.7	61.4
1	847330	PARTS & ACCESSORIES FOR ADP MACHINES & UNITS	556	468	24.9	20.9
2	851769	APP FOR THE TRANS/RECEP OF VOICE/IMAGES/DATA	42	103	1.9	4.6
3	853890	PT F ELECT APPR F ELECT CIRCT; F ELCT CONTRL	51	90	2.3	4
4	840120	ISOTOPIC SEPARATION MACHINERY, APARATUS AND P	188	88	8.4	3.9
5	392690	ARTICLES OF PLASTICS, NESOI	64	71	2.9	3.2
6	853690	ELECT APPR F PRTCT TO ELECT CIRCT NOV 1000 V	34	51	1.5	2.3
7	854470	INSULATED OPTICAL FIBER CABLES WITH INDVULY S	19	47	0.9	2.1
8	10229	CATTLE, LIVE, OTHER THAN PUREBRED BREEDING	40	43	1.8	1.9
9	901380	OPTICAL DEVICES, APPLIANCES AND INSTRUMENTS,	14	41	0.6	1.8
10	392490	HOUSEHOLD AND TOILET ARTICLES NESOI OF PLASTI	38	33	1.7	1.5

Table E-84.   State Trade by Commodity: New York, 2014–2015

(Value in millions of dollars.)

U.S. Exports by Origin State

Rank	HS Code	Description	Value 2014	Value 2015	Percent of share 2014	Percent of share 2015
		Total New York Exports and % Share of U.S. Total	88,434	80,059	5.5	5.3
		Total, Top 25 Commodities and % Share of State Total	48,441	45,276	54.8	56.6
1	710239	DIAMONDS, NONINDUSTRIAL, WORKED	14,422	12,657	16.3	15.8
2	970110	PAINTINGS, DRAWING AND PASTELS BY HAND	6,448	6,977	7.3	8.7
3	710812	GOLD, NONMONETARY, UNWROUGHT NESOI	8,007	6,754	9.1	8.4
4	711319	JEWELRY AND PARTS THEREOF, OF OTH PRECIOUS ME	6,538	6,002	7.4	7.5
5	970300	ORIGINAL SCULPTURES AND STATUARY, IN ANY MATE	1,151	1,427	1.3	1.8
6	880000	CIVILIAN AIRCRAFT, ENGINES, AND PARTS	1,276	1,174	1.4	1.5
7	710391	RUBIES, SAPPHIRES AND EMERALDS, OTHERWISE WOR	982	1,080	1.1	1.3
8	300220	VACCINES FOR HUMAN MEDICINE	626	1,022	0.7	1.3
9	851712	PHONES FOR CELLULAR NTWKS OR FOR OTH WIRELESS	1,119	915	1.3	1.1
10	870323	PASS VEH SPK-IG INT COM RCPR P ENG >1500 NOV	1,035	804	1.2	1.0

U.S. Imports by State of Final Destination

Rank	HS Code	Description	Value 2014	Value 2015	Percent of share 2014	Percent of share 2015
		Total New York Imports and % Share of U.S. Total	134,580	133,086	5.7	5.9
		Total, Top 25 Commodities and % Share of State Total	51,004	50,544	37.9	38.0
1	710239	DIAMONDS, NONINDUSTRIAL, WORKED	22,085	21,509	16.4	16.2
2	970110	PAINTINGS, DRAWING AND PASTELS BY HAND	4,697	6,630	3.5	5.0
3	711319	JEWELRY AND PARTS THEREOF, OF OTH PRECIOUS ME	2,593	2,824	1.9	2.1
4	710812	GOLD, NONMONETARY, UNWROUGHT NESOI	3,358	1,998	2.5	1.5
5	271121	NATURAL GAS, GASEOUS	2,858	1,675	2.1	1.3
6	711590	OTH PREC METL ARTCLS OR ARTCLS CLAD W PM, NES	884	1,315	0.7	1.0
7	710691	SILVER, UNWROUGHT NESOI	1,044	1,049	0.8	0.8
8	710391	RUBIES, SAPPHIRES AND EMERALDS, OTHERWISE WOR	1,043	1,013	0.8	0.8
9	220421	WINE, FR GRAPE NESOI & GR MUST W ALC, NOV 2 L	978	927	0.7	0.7
10	300490	MEDICAMENTS NESOI, MEASURED DOSES, RETAIL PK	802	918	0.6	0.7

Table E-85.   State Trade by Commodity: North Carolina, 2014–2015

(Value in millions of dollars.)

U.S. Exports by Origin State

Rank	HS Code	Description	Value		Percent of share	
			2014	2015	2014	2015
		Total North Carolina Exports and % Share of U.S. Total	31,377	30,018	1.9	2.0
		Total, Top 25 Commodities and % Share of State Total	9,795	10,028	31.2	33.4
1	880000	CIVILIAN AIRCRAFT, ENGINES, AND PARTS	1,200	1,267	3.8	4.2
2	300490	MEDICAMENTS NESOI, MEASURED DOSES, RETAIL PK	1,175	951	3.7	3.2
3	240120	TOBACCO, PARTLY OR WHOLLY STEMMED/STRIPPED	747	712	2.4	2.4
4	300210	ANTISERA, BLOOD FRACTIONS & IMMUNOLOGICAL PRO	491	710	1.6	2.4
5	470321	CHEMICAL WOODPULP, SODA ETC. N DIS S BL & BL	641	594	2.0	2.0
6	870120	ROAD TRACTORS FOR SEMI-TRAILERS	466	553	1.5	1.8
7	880330	PARTS OF AIRPLANES OR HELICOPTERS, NESOI	141	525	0.4	1.7
8	854140	PHOTOSNSITVE SEMICNDCTR DVICE INC PHTVLTC CEL	541	409	1.7	1.4
9	520512	COT YARN, 85% COT, NO RETAIL, OV 14NM NOT OV	457	387	1.5	1.3
10	841182	GAS TURBINES OF A POWER EXCEEDING 5,000 KW	37	362	0.1	1.2

U.S. Imports by State of Final Destination

Rank	HS Code	Description	Value		Percent of share	
			2014	2015	2014	2015
		Total North Carolina Imports and % Share of U.S. Total	52,864	50,880	2.3	2.3
		Total, Top 25 Commodities and % Share of State Total	17,232	15,736	32.6	30.9
1	300490	MEDICAMENTS NESOI, MEASURED DOSES, RETAIL PK	2,908	2,840	5.5	5.6
2	841191	TURBOJET AND TURBOPROLLER PARTS	2,064	2,033	3.9	4.0
3	847130	PORT DIGTL AUTOMATIC DATA PROCESS MACH NOT >	3,046	1,437	5.8	2.8
4	611020	SWEATERS, PULLOVERS ETC, KNIT ETC, COTTON	761	835	1.4	1.6
5	620342	MEN'S OR BOYS' TROUSERS ETC, NOT KNIT, COTTON	787	833	1.5	1.6
6	610910	T-SHIRTS, SINGLETS, TANK TOPS ETC, KNIT ETC C	772	827	1.5	1.6
7	847150	DIGITAL PROCESSING UNITS, N.E.S.O.I.	976	807	1.8	1.6
8	870899	PARTS AND ACCESSORIES OF MOTOR VEHICLES, NESO	662	623	1.3	1.2
9	621210	BRASSIERES, KNIT OR CROCHETED OR NOT	429	519	0.8	1.0
10	284420	URANIUM ENRICHED IN U235 ETC. PLUTONIUM ETC.	661	506	1.2	1.0

Table E-86. State Trade by Commodity: North Dakota, 2014–2015

(Value in millions of dollars.)

U.S. Exports by Origin State

Rank	HS Code	Description	Value 2014	Value 2015	Percent of share 2014	Percent of share 2015
		Total North Dakota Exports and % Share of U.S. Total	5,493	3,863	0.3	0.3
		Total, Top 25 Commodities and % Share of State Total	4,490	2,973	81.7	77
1	270900	CRUDE OIL FROM PETROLEUM AND BITUMINOUS MINER	2,353	1,216	42.8	31.5
2	842951	MECH FRONT-END SHOVEL LOADERS, SELF-PROPELLED	296	249	5.4	6.4
3	271012	LT OILS, PREPS GT=70% PETROLEUM/BITUM NT BIOD	300	225	5.5	5.8
4	100199	WHEAT AND MESLIN, NESOI	141	170	2.6	4.4
5	870130	TRACK-LAYING TRACTORS	148	96	2.7	2.5
6	870190	TRACTORS, NESOI	145	94	2.6	2.4
7	100590	CORN (MAIZE), OTHER THAN SEED CORN	28	82	0.5	2.1
8	220720	ETHYL ALCOHOL & OTH SPIRITS DENATURED ANY STR	89	70	1.6	1.8
9	290110	ACYCLIC HYDROCARBONS, SATURATED	34	68	0.6	1.8
10	271113	BUTANES, LIQUEFIED	138	62	2.5	1.6

U.S. Imports by State of Final Destination

Rank	HS Code	Description	Value 2014	Value 2015	Percent of share 2014	Percent of share 2015
		Total North Dakota Imports and % Share of U.S. Total	3,829	3,146	0.2	0.1
		Total, Top 25 Commodities and % Share of State Total	1,794	1,542	46.9	49.0
1	840890	COMPRESSION-IGNTN INT COMBUSTION PISTON ENG,	137	184	3.6	5.8
2	281410	ANHYDROUS AMMONIA	111	163	2.9	5.2
3	310210	UREA, WHETHER OR NOT IN AQUEOUS SOLUTION	96	128	2.5	4.1
4	120510	LOW ERUCIC ACID RAPE/COLZA SEEDS W/NOT BROKEN	283	106	7.4	3.4
5	711292	PLAT WST A SCRP NT CNTNG OTH PREC MTLS	151	97	3.9	3.1
6	120190	SOYBEANS, NESOI	177	94	4.6	3.0
7	730519	PIPE, OIL LINE ETC OV16IN IR OR STEEL, CLOSE	0	75	0.0	2.4
8	271019	PETROL OIL BITUM MINERAL (NT CRUD) ETC NT BIO	204	72	5.3	2.3
9	870210	MV TRNSP >TEN PRSNS COM-IGNTN INTR COMB PIST(	34	52	0.9	1.6
10	100390	BARLEY, NESOI	64	47	1.7	1.5

Table E-87.   State Trade by Commodity: Ohio, 2014–2015

(Value in millions of dollars.)

U.S. Exports by Origin State

Rank	HS Code	Description	Value 2014	Value 2015	Percent of share 2014	Percent of share 2015
		Total Ohio Exports and % Share of U.S. Total	52,240	50,694	3.2	3.4
		Total, Top 25 Commodities and % Share of State Total	18,725	18,844	35.8	37.2
1	880000	CIVILIAN AIRCRAFT, ENGINES, AND PARTS	4,398	4,940	8.4	9.7
2	870324	PASS VEH SPK-IG INT COM RCPR P ENG > 3000 CC	2,123	1,943	4.1	3.8
3	120190	SOYBEANS, NESOI	1,729	1,640	3.3	3.2
4	840734	SPARK-IGNTN RECPRCTING PISTON ENGINE ETC > 10	1,198	1,359	2.3	2.7
5	870323	PASS VEH SPK-IG INT COM RCPR P ENG >1500 NOV	1,302	1,057	2.5	2.1
6	870829	PTS & ACCESS OF BODIES OF MOTOR VEHICLES, NES	1,107	995	2.1	2.0
7	870899	PARTS AND ACCESSORIES OF MOTOR VEHICLES, NESO	715	700	1.4	1.4
8	841182	GAS TURBINES OF A POWER EXCEEDING 5,000 KW	573	480	1.1	0.9
9	870840	GEAR BOXES FOR MOTOR VEHICLES	395	470	0.8	0.9
10	300490	MEDICAMENTS NESOI, MEASURED DOSES, RETAIL PK	384	463	0.7	0.9

U.S. Imports by State of Final Destination

Rank	HS Code	Description	Value 2014	Value 2015	Percent of share 2014	Percent of share 2015
		Total Ohio Imports and % Share of U.S. Total	70,269	68,843	3.0	3.1
		Total, Top 25 Commodities and % Share of State Total	23,397	21,189	33.3	30.8
1	300490	MEDICAMENTS NESOI, MEASURED DOSES, RETAIL PK	1,623	2,500	2.3	3.6
2	270900	CRUDE OIL FROM PETROLEUM AND BITUMINOUS MINER	5,406	2,019	7.7	2.9
3	300440	ALKALOIDS (NO HORMONES OR ANTIBIOTICS), DOSAG	1,954	2,003	2.8	2.9
4	841191	TURBOJET AND TURBOPROLLER PARTS	1,143	1,484	1.6	2.2
5	870829	PTS & ACCESS OF BODIES OF MOTOR VEHICLES, NES	1,202	1,170	1.7	1.7
6	870840	GEAR BOXES FOR MOTOR VEHICLES	1,222	1,118	1.7	1.6
7	870899	PARTS AND ACCESSORIES OF MOTOR VEHICLES, NESO	1,102	1,069	1.6	1.6
8	840991	SPARK-IGNITION INT COMBUSTION PISTON ENG PTS	650	805	0.9	1.2
9	901890	INSTR & APPL F MEDICAL SURGICAL DENTAL VET, N	768	792	1.1	1.2
10	621210	BRASSIERES, KNIT OR CROCHETED OR NOT	621	723	0.9	1.1

Table E-88.   State Trade by Commodity: Oklahoma, 2014–2015

(Value in millions of dollars.)

U.S. Exports by Origin State

Rank	HS Code	Description	Value		Percent of share	
			2014	2015	2014	2015
		Total Oklahoma Exports and % Share of U.S. Total	6,309	5,258	0.4	0.3
		Total, Top 25 Commodities and % Share of State Total	2,420	2,236	38.4	42.5
1	880000	CIVILIAN AIRCRAFT, ENGINES, AND PARTS	385	429	6.1	8.2
2	847170	AUTOMATIC DATA PROCESSING STORAGE UNITS, N.E.	141	128	2.2	2.4
3	870210	MV TRNSP >TEN PRSNS COM-IGNTN INTR COMB PIST(	95	119	1.5	2.3
4	848180	TAPS COCKS ETC F PIPE VAT INC THERMO CONTROL	153	115	2.4	2.2
5	841391	PARTS OF PUMPS FOR LIQUIDS	183	114	2.9	2.2
6	843143	PARTS FOR BORING OR SINKING MACHINERY, NESOI	107	105	1.7	2.0
7	841950	HEAT EXCHANGE UNITS, INDUSTRIAL TYPE	112	98	1.8	1.9
8	20319	MEAT OF SWINE, NESOI, FRESH OR CHILLED	104	90	1.7	1.7
9	854460	ELECTRIC CONDUCTORS FOR VOLTAGE EXCEEDING 100	148	81	2.3	1.5
10	841370	CENTRIFUGAL PUMPS, NESOI	128	76	2.0	1.4

U.S. Imports by State of Final Destination

Rank	HS Code	Description	Value		Percent of share	
			2014	2015	2014	2015
		Total Oklahoma Imports and % Share of U.S. Total	13,589	10,994	0.6	0.5
		Total, Top 25 Commodities and % Share of State Total	8,060	5,985	59.3	54.4
1	270900	CRUDE OIL FROM PETROLEUM AND BITUMINOUS MINER	5,199	3,469	38.3	31.6
2	847170	AUTOMATIC DATA PROCESSING STORAGE UNITS, N.E.	380	306	2.8	2.8
3	841391	PARTS OF PUMPS FOR LIQUIDS	267	262	2.0	2.4
4	880330	PARTS OF AIRPLANES OR HELICOPTERS, NESOI	198	175	1.5	1.6
5	852872	RECEPTION APPARATUS FOR TELEVISION, COLOR, NE	80	126	0.6	1.1
6	870880	SUSPENSION SHOCK ABSORBERS FOR MOTOR VEHICLES	124	113	0.9	1.0
7	950510	ART F CHRISTMAS FESTIVITIES AND PTS & ACCESSO	109	112	0.8	1.0
8	870120	ROAD TRACTORS FOR SEMI-TRAILERS	104	112	0.8	1.0
9	847330	PARTS & ACCESSORIES FOR ADP MACHINES & UNITS	104	109	0.8	1.0
10	848190	PTS F TAPS ETC F PIPE VAT INC PRESS & THERMO	135	105	1.0	1.0

Table E-89.   State Trade by Commodity: Oregon, 2014–2015

(Value in millions of dollars.)

U.S. Exports by Origin State

Rank	HS Code	Description	Value 2014	Value 2015	Percent of share 2014	Percent of share 2015
		Total Oregon Exports and % Share of U.S. Total	20,889	20,084	1.3	1.3
		Total, Top 25 Commodities and % Share of State Total	12,698	13,099	60.8	65.2
1	854231	PROCESSORS AND CONTROLLERS, ELECTRONIC INTEG	4,649	5,410	22.3	26.9
2	848620	MACHINES FOR MAN. SEMICONDUTOR DEVICES/ELEC I	940	1,154	4.5	5.7
3	847150	DIGITAL PROCESSING UNITS, N.E.S.O.I.	896	976	4.3	4.9
4	100199	WHEAT AND MESLIN, NESOI	1,590	930	7.6	4.6
5	310420	POTASSIUM CHLORIDE	792	628	3.8	3.1
6	880000	CIVILIAN AIRCRAFT, ENGINES, AND PARTS	536	450	2.6	2.2
7	854239	ELECTRONIC INTEGRATED CIRCUITS, NESOI	445	434	2.1	2.2
8	851712	PHONES FOR CELLULAR NTWKS OR FOR OTH WIRELESS	180	349	0.9	1.7
9	370242	PHOT FLM NO SPROCKET HLS,OV 610MM& OV200MM EX	254	278	1.2	1.4
10	847170	AUTOMATIC DATA PROCESSING STORAGE UNITS, N.E.	288	265	1.4	1.3

U.S. Imports by State of Final Destination

Rank	HS Code	Description	Value 2014	Value 2015	Percent of share 2014	Percent of share 2015
		Total Oregon Imports and % Share of U.S. Total	13,788	14,815	0.6	0.7
		Total, Top 25 Commodities and % Share of State Total	5,263	6,123	38.2	41.3
1	870323	PASS VEH SPK-IG INT COM RCPR P ENG >1500 NOV	1,010	881	7.3	5.9
2	854231	PROCESSORS AND CONTROLLERS, ELECTRONIC INTEG	50	781	0.4	5.3
3	848620	MACHINES FOR MAN. SEMICONDUTOR DEVICES/ELEC I	611	740	4.4	5
4	310420	POTASSIUM CHLORIDE	611	548	4.4	3.7
5	870324	PASS VEH SPK-IG INT COM RCPR P ENG > 3000 CC	552	486	4	3.3
6	848690	PARTS & ACCSESORIES FOR MACH TO MAN. SEMICNT,	177	317	1.3	2.1
7	720712	SMFD IRN/NAL STL LT .25 PCT CRB RECT CS WID 2	479	231	3.5	1.6
8	847330	PARTS & ACCESSORIES FOR ADP MACHINES & UNITS	209	219	1.5	1.5
9	870120	ROAD TRACTORS FOR SEMI-TRAILERS	105	207	0.8	1.4
10	381800	CHEM ELEM DOPED, USED IN ELECTRON, DISCS WAFE	103	192	0.7	1.3

Table E-90.   State Trade by Commodity: Pennsylvania, 2014–2015

(Value in millions of dollars.)

U.S. Exports by Origin State

Rank	HS Code	Description	Value 2014	Value 2015	Percent of share 2014	Percent of share 2015
		Total Pennsylvania Exports and % Share of U.S. Total	40,355	39,403	2.5	2.6
		Total, Top 25 Commodities and % Share of State Total	11,178	12,166	27.7	30.9
1	270112	BITUMINOUS COAL, NOT AGGLOMERATED	1,561	1,306	3.9	3.3
2	880000	CIVILIAN AIRCRAFT, ENGINES, AND PARTS	1,129	1,112	2.8	2.8
3	300490	MEDICAMENTS NESOI, MEASURED DOSES, RETAIL PK	676	1,105	1.7	2.8
4	300220	VACCINES FOR HUMAN MEDICINE	1,037	1,017	2.6	2.6
5	293499	NUCLEIC ACIDS & SALTS; OTHER HETEROCYCLIC CMP	333	781	0.8	2.0
6	851712	PHONES FOR CELLULAR NTWKS OR FOR OTH WIRELESS	341	616	0.8	1.6
7	871150	MOTORCYCLES, CYCL,EXCD 800 CC	561	542	1.4	1.4
8	847130	PORT DIGTL AUTOMATIC DATA PROCESS MACH NOT >	386	512	1.0	1.3
9	300210	ANTISERA, BLOOD FRACTIONS & IMMUNOLOGICAL PRO	369	477	0.9	1.2
10	860210	DIESEL ELECTRIC LOCOMOTIVES	295	455	0.7	1.2

U.S. Imports by State of Final Destination

Rank	HS Code	Description	Value 2014	Value 2015	Percent of share 2014	Percent of share 2015
		Total Pennsylvania Imports and % Share of U.S. Total	83,086	79,675	3.5	3.6
		Total, Top 25 Commodities and % Share of State Total	36,902	35,516	44.4	44.6
1	300490	MEDICAMENTS NESOI, MEASURED DOSES, RETAIL PK	7,558	9,984	9.1	12.5
2	851712	PHONES FOR CELLULAR NTWKS OR FOR OTH WIRELESS	3,674	4,710	4.4	5.9
3	270900	CRUDE OIL FROM PETROLEUM AND BITUMINOUS MINER	7,936	3,758	9.6	4.7
4	847130	PORT DIGTL AUTOMATIC DATA PROCESS MACH NOT >	3,534	3,134	4.3	3.9
5	870323	PASS VEH SPK-IG INT COM RCPR P ENG >1500 NOV	2,565	1,999	3.1	2.5
6	300220	VACCINES FOR HUMAN MEDICINE	1,572	1,550	1.9	1.9
7	300210	ANTISERA, BLOOD FRACTIONS & IMMUNOLOGICAL PRO	1,123	1,255	1.4	1.6
8	851762	MACH FOR RECP/CONVR/TRANS/REGN OF VOICE/IMAGE	266	739	0.3	0.9
9	901819	ELECTRO-DIAGNOSTIC APPARATUS NESOI, AND PARTS	597	668	0.7	0.8
10	620462	WOMEN'S OR GIRLS' TROUSERS ETC NOT KNIT, COTT	610	664	0.7	0.8

Table E-91. State Trade by Commodity: Rhode Island, 2014–2015

(Value in millions of dollars.)

U.S. Exports by Origin State

Rank	HS Code	Description	Value		Percent of share	
			2014	2015	2014	2015
		Total Rhode Island Exports and % Share of U.S. Total	2,389	2,125	0.1	0.1
		Total, Top 25 Commodities and % Share of State Total	1,338	1,156	56.0	54.4
1	711291	WASTE & SCRAP GOLD EXCL SWPNGS CNTNG OTH PREC	160	179	6.7	8.4
2	720449	FERROUS WASTE & SCRAP NESOI	290	137	12.1	6.5
3	711299	WASTE AND SCRAP OF PRECIOUS METAL NESOI	124	130	5.2	6.1
4	300210	ANTISERA, BLOOD FRACTIONS & IMMUNOLOGICAL PRO	123	129	5.1	6.1
5	710610	SILVER POWDER	154	85	6.4	4.0
6	711719	OTH IMITATION JEWELRY, BASE METAL, INC PR MTL	63	70	2.6	3.3
7	284330	GOLD COMPOUNDS	58	49	2.4	2.3
8	870323	PASS VEH SPK-IG INT COM RCPR P ENG >1500 NOV	77	45	3.2	2.1
9	854390	PT ELEC MACH & APPR W INDIVIDUAL FUNCTIONS, N	31	38	1.3	1.8
10	711311	JEWELRY AND PARTS THEREOF, OF SILVER	23	33	0.9	1.5

U.S. Imports by State of Final Destination

Rank	HS Code	Description	Value		Percent of share	
			2014	2015	2014	2015
		Total Rhode Island Imports and % Share of U.S. Total	8,354	8,224	0.4	0.4
		Total, Top 25 Commodities and % Share of State Total	6,301	6,204	75.4	75.4
1	870323	PASS VEH SPK-IG INT COM RCPR P ENG >1500 NOV	1,995	2,739	23.9	33.3
2	870324	PASS VEH SPK-IG INT COM RCPR P ENG > 3000 CC	960	995	11.5	12.1
3	271012	LT OILS, PREPS GT=70% PETROLEUM/BITUM NT BIOD	1,817	989	21.7	12
4	870332	PASS VEH COM-IG INT COM ENG > 1500 NOV 2500 C	126	193	1.5	2.3
5	950300	TRICYCLE, SCOOTR, PEDAL CAR & SIM WHEELED TYS	142	177	1.7	2.2
6	901839	MED NEEDLES. NESOI, CATHERERS ETC AND PARTS E	122	122	1.5	1.5
7	711719	OTH IMITATION JEWELRY, BASE METAL, INC PR MTL	117	115	1.4	1.4
8	711790	IMITATION JEWELRY NOT OF BASE METAL	117	107	1.4	1.3
9	870333	PASS VEH COM-IG INT COM ENG > 2500 CC	183	105	2.2	1.3
10	900490	SPECTACLES, ETC, CORRECTIVE, PROTECTIVE, NESO	67	75	0.8	0.9

Table E-92.   State Trade by Commodity: South Carolina, 2014–2015

(Value in millions of dollars.)

U.S. Exports by Origin State

Rank	HS Code	Description	Value		Percent of share	
			2014	2015	2014	2015
		Total South Carolina Exports and % Share of U.S. Total	29,624	30,861	1.8	2.1
		Total, Top 25 Commodities and % Share of State Total	16,595	18,894	56.0	61.2
1	870323	PASS VEH SPK-IG INT COM RCPR P ENG >1500 NOV	4,309	4,301	14.5	13.9
2	880000	CIVILIAN AIRCRAFT, ENGINES, AND PARTS	1,389	3,887	4.7	12.6
3	870333	PASS VEH COM-IG INT COM ENG > 2500 CC	2,617	2,679	8.8	8.7
4	870332	PASS VEH COM-IG INT COM ENG > 1500 NOV 2500 C	1,867	2,345	6.3	7.6
5	401120	NEW PNEUMATIC TIRES OF RUBBER, FOR BUSES OR T	958	767	3.2	2.5
6	870840	GEAR BOXES FOR MOTOR VEHICLES	353	607	1.2	2.0
7	401110	NEW PNEUMATIC TIRES OF RUBBER, FOR MOTOR CARS	550	499	1.9	1.6
8	841182	GAS TURBINES OF A POWER EXCEEDING 5,000 KW	1,089	462	3.7	1.5
9	841199	GAS TURBINE PARTS NESOI	602	431	2.0	1.4
10	870324	PASS VEH SPK-IG INT COM RCPR P ENG > 3000 CC	234	410	0.8	1.3

U.S. Imports by State of Final Destination

Rank	HS Code	Description	Value		Percent of share	
			2014	2015	2014	2015
		Total South Carolina Imports and % Share of U.S. Total	37,729	38,988	1.6	1.7
		Total, Top 25 Commodities and % Share of State Total	12,966	13,346	34.4	34.2
1	880330	PARTS OF AIRPLANES OR HELICOPTERS, NESOI	2,059	2,325	5.5	6.0
2	840734	SPARK-IGNTN RECPRCTING PISTON ENGINE ETC > 10	998	1,024	2.6	2.6
3	284420	URANIUM ENRICHED IN U235 ETC. PLUTONIUM ETC.	1,247	901	3.3	2.3
4	870840	GEAR BOXES FOR MOTOR VEHICLES	838	820	2.2	2.1
5	401110	NEW PNEUMATIC TIRES OF RUBBER, FOR MOTOR CARS	746	683	2.0	1.8
6	870829	PTS & ACCESS OF BODIES OF MOTOR VEHICLES, NES	545	587	1.4	1.5
7	840820	COMPRESSION-IGNTN INT COMBUSTION PISTON ENGIN	454	562	1.2	1.4
8	853224	CERAMIC DIELECTRIC, MULTILAYER FIXED CAPACITO	952	535	2.5	1.4
9	870899	PARTS AND ACCESSORIES OF MOTOR VEHICLES, NESO	589	496	1.6	1.3
10	841112	TURBOJETS OF A THRUST EXCEEDING 25 KN	29	479	0.1	1.2

Table E-93. State Trade by Commodity: South Dakota, 2014–2015

(Value in millions of dollars.)

U.S. Exports by Origin State

Rank	HS Code	Description	Value		Percent of share	
			2014	2015	2014	2015
		Total South Dakota Exports and % Share of U.S. Total	1,594	1,405	0.1	0.1
		Total, Top 25 Commodities and % Share of State Total	867	862	54.4	61.4
1	230330	BREWING OR DISTILLING DREGS AND WASTE, W/NT P	64	96	4.0	6.8
2	230400	SOYBEAN OILCAKE & OTH SOLID RESIDUE, WH/NOT G	125	91	7.8	6.4
3	870530	FIRE FIGHTING VEHICLES	63	66	4.0	4.7
4	20312	MEAT, SWINE, HAMS, SHLDRS, BONE IN, FRSH OR C	79	62	4.9	4.4
5	842720	SELF-PROPELLED WORKS TRUCKS AND FORKLIFTS, NE	4	54	0.3	3.9
6	842710	SELF-PROPELLED LIFTING ETC TRUCKS WITH ELECT	8	47	0.5	3.3
7	20319	MEAT OF SWINE, NESOI, FRESH OR CHILLED	65	45	4.0	3.2
8	842951	MECH FRONT-END SHOVEL LOADERS, SELF-PROPELLED	80	45	5.1	3.2
9	20329	MEAT OF SWINE, NESOI, FROZEN	53	37	3.3	2.7
10	250810	BENTONITE, INCLUDING CALCINED	31	35	1.9	2.5

U.S. Imports by State of Final Destination

Rank	HS Code	Description	Value		Percent of share	
			2014	2015	2014	2015
		Total South Dakota Imports and % Share of U.S. Total	1,042	1,140	0.0	0.1
		Total, Top 25 Commodities and % Share of State Total	511	604	49.0	53.0
1	160250	PREPARED OR PRESERVED BOVINE MEAT ETC. NESOI	140	157	13.4	13.8
2	730519	PIPE, OIL LINE ETC OV16IN IR OR STEEL, CLOSE	0	104	0.0	9.2
3	20130	MEAT OF BOVINE ANIMALS, BONELESS, FRESH OR CH	22	25	2.1	2.2
4	440710	CONIFEROUS WOOD SAWN, SLICED ETC, OVER 6 MM T	29	23	2.8	2.0
5	310420	POTASSIUM CHLORIDE	17	23	1.7	2.0
6	10229	CATTLE, LIVE, OTHER THAN PUREBRED BREEDING	46	21	4.4	1.9
7	840890	COMPRESSION-IGNTN INT COMBUSTION PISTON ENG,	25	19	2.4	1.6
8	271112	PROPANE, LIQUEFIED	22	18	2.1	1.6
9	310280	MIXTURES OF UREA AND AMMONIUM NITRATE IN SOLU	10	18	1.0	1.6
10	847130	PORT DIGTL AUTOMATIC DATA PROCESS MACH NOT >	19	17	1.8	1.5

Table E-94.   State Trade by Commodity: Tennessee, 2014–2015

(Value in millions of dollars.)

U.S. Exports by Origin State

Rank	HS Code	Description	Value		Percent of share	
			2014	2015	2014	2015
		Total Tennessee Exports and % Share of U.S. Total	32,940	32,431	2.0	2.2
		Total, Top 25 Commodities and % Share of State Total	15,317	15,375	46.5	47.4
1	901890	INSTR & APPL F MEDICAL SURGICAL DENTAL VET, N	2,125	2,224	6.5	6.9
2	870323	PASS VEH SPK-IG INT COM RCPR P ENG >1500 NOV	1,411	1,385	4.3	4.3
3	880000	CIVILIAN AIRCRAFT, ENGINES, AND PARTS	1,254	1,297	3.8	4.0
4	870324	PASS VEH SPK-IG INT COM RCPR P ENG > 3000 CC	1,225	1,184	3.7	3.7
5	840734	SPARK-IGNTN RECPRCTING PISTON ENGINE ETC > 10	734	889	2.2	2.7
6	847130	PORT DIGTL AUTOMATIC DATA PROCESS MACH NOT >	826	812	2.5	2.5
7	520100	COTTON, NOT CARDED OR COMBED	525	694	1.6	2.1
8	220830	WHISKIES	712	691	2.2	2.1
9	550200	ARTIFICIAL FILAMENT TOW	675	602	2.0	1.9
10	847150	DIGITAL PROCESSING UNITS, N.E.S.O.I.	599	573	1.8	1.8

U.S. Imports by State of Final Destination

Rank	HS Code	Description	Value		Percent of share	
			2014	2015	2014	2015
		Total Tennessee Imports and % Share of U.S. Total	69,754	76,864	3.0	3.4
		Total, Top 25 Commodities and % Share of State Total	32,798	39,649	47.0	51.6
1	847130	PORT DIGTL AUTOMATIC DATA PROCESS MACH NOT >	7,713	7,871	11.1	10.2
2	300490	MEDICAMENTS NESOI, MEASURED DOSES, RETAIL PK	4,372	6,441	6.3	8.4
3	851712	PHONES FOR CELLULAR NTWKS OR FOR OTH WIRELESS	4,121	4,637	5.9	6.0
4	300220	VACCINES FOR HUMAN MEDICINE	1,248	3,376	1.8	4.4
5	851762	MACH FOR RECP/CONVR/TRANS/REGN OF VOICE/IMAGE	1,823	2,128	2.6	2.8
6	870324	PASS VEH SPK-IG INT COM RCPR P ENG > 3000 CC	1,833	1,672	2.6	2.2
7	870323	PASS VEH SPK-IG INT COM RCPR P ENG >1500 NOV	871	1,365	1.2	1.8
8	870840	GEAR BOXES FOR MOTOR VEHICLES	1,160	1,118	1.7	1.5
9	847150	DIGITAL PROCESSING UNITS, N.E.S.O.I.	662	1,082	0.9	1.4
10	300439	HORMONES ETC. (NO ANTIBIOTICS CONTAINED) DOSA	723	1,056	1.0	1.4

Table E-95.   State Trade by Commodity: Texas, 2014–2015

(Value in millions of dollars.)

U.S. Exports by Origin State

Rank	HS Code	Description	Value		Percent of share	
			2014	2015	2014	2015
		Total Texas Exports and % Share of U.S. Total	288,049	251,087	17.8	16.7
		Total, Top 25 Commodities and % Share of State Total	132,563	113,463	46.0	45.2
1	271019	PETROL OIL BITUM MINERAL (NT CRUD) ETC NT BIO	33,283	24,683	11.6	9.8
2	271012	LT OILS, PREPS GT=70% PETROLEUM/BITUM NT BIOD	22,450	17,787	7.8	7.1
3	847330	PARTS & ACCESSORIES FOR ADP MACHINES & UNITS	10,008	9,914	3.5	3.9
4	880000	CIVILIAN AIRCRAFT, ENGINES, AND PARTS	5,914	5,748	2.1	2.3
5	270900	CRUDE OIL FROM PETROLEUM AND BITUMINOUS MINER	7,430	5,614	2.6	2.2
6	851762	MACH FOR RECP/CONVR/TRANS/REGN OF VOICE/IMAGE	4,942	5,151	1.7	2.1
7	854231	PROCESSORS AND CONTROLLERS, ELECTRONIC INTEG	4,738	5,108	1.6	2.0
8	271112	PROPANE, LIQUEFIED	7,108	4,775	2.5	1.9
9	843143	PARTS FOR BORING OR SINKING MACHINERY, NESOI	4,679	3,156	1.6	1.3
10	870899	PARTS AND ACCESSORIES OF MOTOR VEHICLES, NESO	1,708	3,078	0.6	1.2

U.S. Imports by State of Final Destination

Rank	HS Code	Description	Value		Percent of share	
			2014	2015	2014	2015
		Total Texas Imports and % Share of U.S. Total	302,277	251,492	12.9	11.2
		Total, Top 25 Commodities and % Share of State Total	162,019	116,763	53.6	46.4
1	270900	CRUDE OIL FROM PETROLEUM AND BITUMINOUS MINER	76,088	34,057	25.2	13.5
2	851712	PHONES FOR CELLULAR NTWKS OR FOR OTH WIRELESS	15,260	12,709	5.0	5.1
3	851762	MACH FOR RECP/CONVR/TRANS/REGN OF VOICE/IMAGE	8,221	11,544	2.7	4.6
4	847150	DIGITAL PROCESSING UNITS, N.E.S.O.I.	9,069	11,322	3.0	4.5
5	271019	PETROL OIL BITUM MINERAL (NT CRUD) ETC NT BIO	13,472	8,832	4.5	3.5
6	854430	INSULATED WIRING SETS FOR VEHICLES SHIPS AIRC	3,445	3,623	1.1	1.4
7	870323	PASS VEH SPK-IG INT COM RCPR P ENG >1500 NOV	2,861	3,289	0.9	1.3
8	852872	RECEPTION APPARATUS FOR TELEVISION, COLOR, NE	3,352	2,818	1.1	1.1
9	854231	PROCESSORS AND CONTROLLERS, ELECTRONIC INTEG	3,883	2,559	1.3	1.0
10	880240	AIRPLANE & OT A/C, UNLADEN WEIGHT > 15,000 KG	1,914	2,210	0.6	0.9

Table E-96.   State Trade by Commodity: Utah, 2014–2015

(Value in millions of dollars.)

U.S. Exports by Origin State

Rank	HS Code	Description	Value 2014	Value 2015	Percent of share 2014	Percent of share 2015
		Total Utah Exports and % Share of U.S. Total	12,306	13,282	0.8	0.9
		Total, Top 25 Commodities and % Share of State Total	8,458	9,621	68.7	72.4
1	710812	GOLD, NONMONETARY, UNWROUGHT NESOI	3,798	5,098	30.9	38.4
2	854232	MEMORIES, ELECTRONIC INTEGRATED CIRCUITS	1,308	1,115	10.6	8.4
3	210690	FOOD PREPARATIONS NESOI	483	473	3.9	3.6
4	880000	CIVILIAN AIRCRAFT, ENGINES, AND PARTS	403	301	3.3	2.3
5	870895	SAFETY AIRBAGS WITH INFLATOR SYSTEM; PARTS TH	306	291	2.5	2.2
6	901839	MED NEEDLES. NESOI, CATHERERS ETC AND PARTS E	240	227	1.9	1.7
7	902290	X-RAY/HI TNSN GENR CNTR PNL & DSK EXM/TRTMNT	220	203	1.8	1.5
8	740311	REFINED COPPER CATHODES AND SECTIONS OF CATHO	149	197	1.2	1.5
9	681510	NONELECTRICAL ARTICLES OF GRAPHITE OR CARBON	145	168	1.2	1.3
10	300490	MEDICAMENTS NESOI, MEASURED DOSES, RETAIL PK	197	154	1.6	1.2

U.S. Imports by State of Final Destination

Rank	HS Code	Description	Value 2014	Value 2015	Percent of share 2014	Percent of share 2015
		Total Utah Imports and % Share of U.S. Total	11,118	12,093	0.5	0.5
		Total, Top 25 Commodities and % Share of State Total	6,332	6,704	57.0	55.4
1	710812	GOLD, NONMONETARY, UNWROUGHT NESOI	2,942	2,734	26.5	22.6
2	880240	AIRPLANE & OT A/C, UNLADEN WEIGHT > 15,000 KG	595	796	5.3	6.6
3	870895	SAFETY AIRBAGS WITH INFLATOR SYSTEM; PARTS TH	264	418	2.4	3.5
4	710691	SILVER, UNWROUGHT NESOI	498	368	4.5	3.0
5	870120	ROAD TRACTORS FOR SEMI-TRAILERS	228	349	2.1	2.9
6	710813	GOLD, NONMONETARY, SEMIMANUFACTURED FORMS NES	337	329	3.0	2.7
7	871200	BICYCLES & OTH CYCLES (INC DEL TRICYCLE) NO M	144	213	1.3	1.8
8	950691	ARTCL/EQUIP F GEN PHYS EXERC, GYMN ETC NESOI;	245	206	2.2	1.7
9	870894	STEERING WHEELS, COLUMNS & BOXES F MOTOR VEHI	119	194	1.1	1.6
10	880230	AIRPLANE & A/C UNLADEN WGHT > 2000, NOV 15000	71	164	0.6	1.4

Table E-97.   State Trade by Commodity: Vermont, 2014–2015

(Value in millions of dollars.)

U.S. Exports by Origin State

Rank	HS Code	Description	Value 2014	Value 2015	Percent of share 2014	Percent of share 2015
		Total Vermont Exports and % Share of U.S. Total	3,669	3,176	0.2	0.2
		Total, Top 25 Commodities and % Share of State Total	2,847	2,403	77.6	75.7
1	854231	PROCESSORS AND CONTROLLERS, ELECTRONIC INTEG	1,408	1,022	38.4	32.2
2	854239	ELECTRONIC INTEGRATED CIRCUITS, NESOI	803	741	21.9	23.3
3	847330	PARTS & ACCESSORIES FOR ADP MACHINES & UNITS	61	59	1.7	1.9
4	950691	ARTCL/EQUIP F GEN PHYS EXERC, GYMN ETC NESOI;	46	54	1.2	1.7
5	847790	PTS MACH FOR WORK RUBBER/PLAST/MFG RBBR/PLSTC	48	43	1.3	1.4
6	854233	AMPLIFIERS, ELECTRONIC INTEGRATED CIRCUITS	35	43	0.9	1.4
7	880000	CIVILIAN AIRCRAFT, ENGINES, AND PARTS	45	41	1.2	1.3
8	190110	FOOD PREPARATIONS FOR INFANTS, RETAIL SALE NE	34	39	0.9	1.2
9	481092	PPR/PBRD EX KRFT/GRPHC CLAY COATD MULTI-PLY R	38	36	1.0	1.1
10	180620	CHOCOLATE PREP NESOI, IN BLOCKS ETC. OVER 2 K	29	35	0.8	1.1

U.S. Imports by State of Final Destination

Rank	HS Code	Description	Value 2014	Value 2015	Percent of share 2014	Percent of share 2015
		Total Vermont Imports and % Share of U.S. Total	4,760	4,023	0.2	0.2
		Total, Top 25 Commodities and % Share of State Total	3,326	2,670	69.9	66.4
1	271600	ELECTRICAL ENERGY	716	626	15	15.6
2	854231	PROCESSORS AND CONTROLLERS, ELECTRONIC INTEG	859	609	18	15.1
3	854239	ELECTRONIC INTEGRATED CIRCUITS, NESOI	241	246	5.1	6.1
4	180620	CHOCOLATE PREP NESOI, IN BLOCKS ETC. OVER 2 K	184	196	3.9	4.9
5	271019	PETROL OIL BITUM MINERAL (NT CRUD) ETC NT BIO	303	170	6.4	4.2
6	271012	LT OILS, PREPS GT=70% PETROLEUM/BITUM NT BIOD	160	98	3.4	2.4
7	847330	PARTS & ACCESSORIES FOR ADP MACHINES & UNITS	151	73	3.2	1.8
8	271121	NATURAL GAS, GASEOUS	120	67	2.5	1.7
9	620331	M/B SUIT-TYPE JACKETS AND BLAZERS OF WOOL, NT	46	62	1	1.5
10	848180	TAPS COCKS ETC F PIPE VAT INC THERMO CONTROL	63	54	1.3	1.4

Table E-98.   State Trade by Commodity: Virginia, 2014–2015

(Value in millions of dollars.)

U.S. Exports by Origin State

Rank	HS Code	Description	Value		Percent of share	
			2014	2015	2014	2015
		Total Virginia Exports and % Share of U.S. Total	19,255	18,137	1.2	1.2
		Total, Top 25 Commodities and % Share of State Total	7,416	7,296	38.5	40.2
1	854232	MEMORIES, ELECTRONIC INTEGRATED CIRCUITS	780	717	4.1	4.0
2	270112	BITUMINOUS COAL, NOT AGGLOMERATED	500	639	2.6	3.5
3	870120	ROAD TRACTORS FOR SEMI-TRAILERS	588	592	3.1	3.3
4	120190	SOYBEANS, NESOI	786	586	4.1	3.2
5	844399	PTS & ACC OF PRINTERS, COPIERS AND FAX MACH,	511	489	2.7	2.7
6	481032	KRAFT PAPER OV150G/M2, BLEACH, 95% W FIB CH P	414	429	2.1	2.4
7	271019	PETROL OIL BITUM MINERAL (NT CRUD) ETC NT BIO	588	358	3.1	2.0
8	980320	EXPORTS OF MILITARY EQUIPMENT, NOT IDENTIFIED	131	328	0.7	1.8
9	550200	ARTIFICIAL FILAMENT TOW	437	299	2.3	1.6
10	230400	SOYBEAN OILCAKE & OTH SOLID RESIDUE, WH/NOT G	305	268	1.6	1.5

U.S. Imports by State of Final Destination

Rank	HS Code	Description	Value		Percent of share	
			2014	2015	2014	2015
		Total Virginia Imports and % Share of U.S. Total	24,287	25,017	1.0	1.1
		Total, Top 25 Commodities and % Share of State Total	7,626	8,414	31.4	33.6
1	844399	PTS & ACC OF PRINTERS, COPIERS AND FAX MACH,	2,284	2,200	9.4	8.8
2	870324	PASS VEH SPK-IG INT COM RCPR P ENG > 3000 CC	897	918	3.7	3.7
3	851762	MACH FOR RECP/CONVR/TRANS/REGN OF VOICE/IMAGE	529	600	2.2	2.4
4	870323	PASS VEH SPK-IG INT COM RCPR P ENG >1500 NOV	248	512	1.0	2.0
5	950300	TRICYCLE, SCOOTR, PEDAL CAR & SIM WHEELED TYS	375	477	1.5	1.9
6	847150	DIGITAL PROCESSING UNITS, N.E.S.O.I.	215	357	0.9	1.4
7	90111	COFFEE, NOT ROASTED, NOT DECAFFEINATED	353	307	1.5	1.2
8	854140	PHOTOSNSITVE SEMICNDCTR DVICE INC PHTVLTC CEL	67	261	0.3	1.0
9	611020	SWEATERS, PULLOVERS ETC, KNIT ETC, COTTON	204	236	0.8	0.9
10	80132	CASHEW NUTS, FRESH OR DRIED, SHELLED	181	209	0.7	0.8

Table E-99. State Trade by Commodity: Washington, 2014–2015

(Value in millions of dollars.)

U.S. Exports by Origin State

Rank	HS Code	Description	Value 2014	Value 2015	Percent of share 2014	Percent of share 2015
		Total Washington Exports and % Share of U.S. Total	90,547	86,353	5.6	5.7
		Total, Top 25 Commodities and % Share of State Total	71,203	68,880	78.6	79.8
1	880000	CIVILIAN AIRCRAFT, ENGINES, AND PARTS	47,786	51,115	52.8	59.2
2	120190	SOYBEANS, NESOI	5,378	3,768	5.9	4.4
3	100199	WHEAT AND MESLIN, NESOI	1,940	1,836	2.1	2.1
4	271019	PETROL OIL BITUM MINERAL (NT CRUD) ETC NT BIO	2,849	1,532	3.1	1.8
5	100590	CORN (MAIZE), OTHER THAN SEED CORN	1,751	1,418	1.9	1.6
6	870323	PASS VEH SPK-IG INT COM RCPR P ENG >1500 NOV	1,947	1,205	2.2	1.4
7	80810	APPLES, FRESH	838	797	0.9	0.9
8	200410	POTATOES, PREPARED ETC., NO VINEGAR ETC., FRO	731	719	0.8	0.8
9	901812	ULTRASONIC SCANNING APPARATUS	744	703	0.8	0.8
10	440320	CONIFEROUS WOOD IN THE ROUGH, NOT TREATED	1,022	683	1.1	0.8

U.S. Imports by State of Final Destination

Rank	HS Code	Description	Value 2014	Value 2015	Percent of share 2014	Percent of share 2015
		Total Washington Imports and % Share of U.S. Total	52,379	51,271	2.2	2.3
		Total, Top 25 Commodities and % Share of State Total	30,145	25,341	57.6	49.4
1	880330	PARTS OF AIRPLANES OR HELICOPTERS, NESOI	5,627	5,320	10.7	10.4
2	270900	CRUDE OIL FROM PETROLEUM AND BITUMINOUS MINER	6,895	3,924	13.2	7.7
3	271121	NATURAL GAS, GASEOUS	3,478	2,422	6.6	4.7
4	870323	PASS VEH SPK-IG INT COM RCPR P ENG >1500 NOV	2,401	2,358	4.6	4.6
5	841112	TURBOJETS OF A THRUST EXCEEDING 25 KN	2,676	1,818	5.1	3.5
6	852871	RECEPTION APP FOR TV NT DESIGNED TO INC VIDEO	1,272	895	2.4	1.7
7	950450	VIDEO GAME CONSOLES & MACH, EXC OF SUBHEAD 95	503	851	1.0	1.7
8	852560	TRANSMISSION APP INCORP RECEPTION, FOR RADIO	109	666	0.2	1.3
9	880320	UNDCARRGE & PTS GLIDERS & A/C, NON-POWERED/PO	631	646	1.2	1.3
10	851712	PHONES FOR CELLULAR NTWKS OR FOR OTH WIRELESS	1,005	624	1.9	1.2

Table E-100.   State Trade by Commodity: West Virginia, 2014–2015

(Value in millions of dollars.)

U.S. Exports by Origin State

Rank	HS Code	Description	Value 2014	Value 2015	Percent of share 2014	Percent of share 2015
		Total West Virginia Exports and % Share of U.S. Total	7,486	5,722	0.5	0.4
		Total, Top 25 Commodities and % Share of State Total	6,041	4,491	80.7	78.5
1	270112	BITUMINOUS COAL, NOT AGGLOMERATED	3,109	1,719	41.5	30.0
2	848340	GEARS; BALL OR ROLLER SCREWS; GEAR BOXES, ETC	515	522	6.9	9.1
3	848350	FLYWHEELS AND PULLEYS, INCLUDING PULLEY BLOCK	563	511	7.5	8.9
4	760612	ALUMINUM ALLOY RECT PLATES ETC, OVER .2 MM TH	138	206	1.8	3.6
5	880000	CIVILIAN AIRCRAFT, ENGINES, AND PARTS	170	184	2.3	3.2
6	390810	POLYAMIDE-6,-11,-12,-6,6,-6,9,-6,10 OR -6,12	247	181	3.3	3.2
7	391190	POLYSULFIDES, POLYSULFONES & OTHER NESOI, PRI	142	151	1.9	2.6
8	902139	ARTIFICIAL JOINTS & PARTS & ACCESSORIES THERO	162	119	2.2	2.1
9	390720	POLYETHERS NESOI, PR FMS	119	117	1.6	2.0
10	390710	POLYACETALS, PR FMS	99	111	1.3	1.9

U.S. Imports by State of Final Destination

Rank	HS Code	Description	Value 2014	Value 2015	Percent of share 2014	Percent of share 2015
		Total West Virginia Imports and % Share of U.S. Total	3,811	3,776	0.2	0.2
		Total, Top 25 Commodities and % Share of State Total	2,092	2,130	54.9	56.4
1	870899	PARTS AND ACCESSORIES OF MOTOR VEHICLES, NESO	252	339	6.6	9.0
2	291736	TEREPHTHALIC ACID AND ITS SALTS	319	240	8.4	6.4
3	390760	POLYETHYLENE TEREPHTHALATE, PR FMS	202	180	5.3	4.8
4	841191	TURBOJET AND TURBOPROLLER PARTS	130	151	3.4	4.0
5	841112	TURBOJETS OF A THRUST EXCEEDING 25 KN	100	117	2.6	3.1
6	760120	UNWROUGHT ALUMINUM ALLOYS	101	113	2.7	3.0
7	902710	GAS OR SMOKE ANALYSIS APPARATUS	116	99	3.1	2.6
8	841111	TURBOJETS OF A THRUST NOT EXCEEDING 25 KN	122	96	3.2	2.5
9	848120	VALVES F OLEOHYDRAULIC OR PNEUMATIC TRANSMISS	56	75	1.5	2.0
10	902790	PTS OF INST, PHYS/CHEM ANALYSIS ETC, NESOI	52	59	1.4	1.6

Table E-101.   State Trade by Commodity: Wisconsin, 2014–2015

(Value in millions of dollars.)

U.S. Exports by Origin State

Rank	HS Code	Description	Value 2014	Value 2015	Percent of share 2014	Percent of share 2015
		Total Wisconsin Exports and % Share of U.S. Total	23,428	22,445	1.4	1.5
		Total, Top 25 Commodities and % Share of State Total	5,666	5,646	24.2	25.2
1	293729	ADRENAL CORTICAL HORMONES AND DERIV NESOI	301	421	1.3	1.9
2	880000	CIVILIAN AIRCRAFT, ENGINES, AND PARTS	365	381	1.6	1.7
3	870899	PARTS AND ACCESSORIES OF MOTOR VEHICLES, NESO	365	358	1.6	1.6
4	902212	COMPUTED TOMOGRAPHY APPARATUS	241	355	1.0	1.6
5	901819	ELECTRO-DIAGNOSTIC APPARATUS NESOI, AND PARTS	336	311	1.4	1.4
6	847149	DIGITAL ADP MAC & UNITS,ENTERED AS SYSTEMS, N	193	248	0.8	1.1
7	840721	OUTBOARD ENGINES FOR MARINE PROPULSION	216	246	0.9	1.1
8	902290	X-RAY/HI TNSN GENR CNTR PNL & DSK EXM/TRTMNT	232	232	1.0	1.0
9	392690	ARTICLES OF PLASTICS, NESOI	200	211	0.9	0.9
10	842952	MECH SHOVELS EXCAVATORS ETC W 360 DEGREE SPRS	308	211	1.3	0.9

U.S. Imports by State of Final Destination

Rank	HS Code	Description	Value 2014	Value 2015	Percent of share 2014	Percent of share 2015
		Total Wisconsin Imports and % Share of U.S. Total	23,525	22,964	1.0	1.0
		Total, Top 25 Commodities and % Share of State Total	4,690	4,881	19.9	21.3
1	611020	SWEATERS, PULLOVERS ETC, KNIT ETC, COTTON	547	517	2.3	2.3
2	901819	ELECTRO-DIAGNOSTIC APPARATUS NESOI, AND PARTS	345	323	1.5	1.4
3	611030	SWEATERS, PULLOVERS ETC, KNIT ETC, MANMADE FI	253	301	1.1	1.3
4	840991	SPARK-IGNITION INT COMBUSTION PISTON ENG PTS	244	261	1.0	1.1
5	470321	CHEMICAL WOODPULP, SODA ETC. N DIS S BL & BL	293	261	1.2	1.1
6	870120	ROAD TRACTORS FOR SEMI-TRAILERS	215	246	0.9	1.1
7	950300	TRICYCLE, SCOOTR, PEDAL CAR & SIM WHEELED TYS	226	242	1.0	1.1
8	902290	X-RAY/HI TNSN GENR CNTR PNL & DSK EXM/TRTMNT	213	196	0.9	0.9
9	850780	STORAGE BATTERIES NESOI	1	194	0.0	0.8
10	850440	STATIC CONVERTERS; ADP POWER SUPPLIES	189	183	0.8	0.8

Table E-102. State Trade by Commodity: Wyoming, 2014–2015

(Value in millions of dollars.)

U.S. Exports by Origin State

Rank	HS Code	Description	Value 2014	Value 2015	Percent of share 2014	Percent of share 2015
		Total Wyoming Exports and % Share of U.S. Total	1,757	1,174	0.1	0.1
		Total, Top 25 Commodities and % Share of State Total	1,154	1,079	65.7	91.9
1	283620	DISODIUM CARBONATE	891	833	50.7	71.0
2	280429	RARE GASES, OTHER THAN ARGON	53	61	3.0	5.2
3	250810	BENTONITE, INCLUDING CALCINED	33	35	1.9	3.0
4	271012	LT OILS, PREPS GT=70% PETROLEUM/BITUM NT BIOD	45	16	2.6	1.4
5	843149	PARTS AND ATTACHMENTS NESOI FOR DERRICKS ETC.	12	14	0.7	1.2
6	680919	PLSTER BOARDS PANELS ETC NOT ORNAMENTED NESOI	10	12	0.6	1.0
7	681510	NONELECTRICAL ARTICLES OF GRAPHITE OR CARBON	14	11	0.8	0.9
8	843143	PARTS FOR BORING OR SINKING MACHINERY, NESOI	8	11	0.5	0.9
9	283630	SODIUM HYDROGENCARBONATE (SODIUM BICARBONATE)	10	9	0.6	0.8
10	250840	CLAYS NESOI, INCLUDING BALL CLAYS, INCL CALCI	10	9	0.6	0.8

U.S. Imports by State of Final Destination

Rank	HS Code	Description	Value 2014	Value 2015	Percent of share 2014	Percent of share 2015
		Total Wyoming Imports and % Share of U.S. Total	1,901	1145	0.1	0.1
		Total, Top 25 Commodities and % Share of State Total	1,402	678	73.7	59.3
1	270900	CRUDE OIL FROM PETROLEUM AND BITUMINOUS MINER	1,178	445	62.0	38.9
2	847150	DIGITAL PROCESSING UNITS, N.E.S.O.I.	0	11	0.0	0.9
3	271012	LT OILS, PREPS GT=70% PETROLEUM/BITUM NT BIOD	0	38	0.0	3.3
4	281410	ANHYDROUS AMMONIA	29	34	1.5	2.9
5	851762	MACH FOR RECP/CONVR/TRANS/REGN OF VOICE/IMAGE	3	1	0.1	0.1
6	841810	COMBINED REFRIGERATOR-FREEZERS W SEPARATE DOO	10	12	0.5	1.0
7	720837	FLT-HOT-ROL IRN,NONALY,COILS,4.75MM N/O 10MM	0	4	0.0	0.3
8	310230	AMMONIUM NITRATE, WHETHER/NOT IN AQUEOUS SOLU	42	39	2.2	3.4
9	940151	SEATS OF BAMBOO OR RATTAN	1	4	0.1	0.3
10	940510	CHANDELIER CEILNG/WALL LGHTNG FTTNG EX PUBLIC	5	6	0.3	0.5

INDEX

ACQUISITIONS
Foreign direct investment in the U.S., 12
ADVANCED TECHNOLOGY
Commodity trade highlights
trade balance, 202
U.S. trade in products, 203
AFFILIATION
Foreign trade in goods and services
trade in services by type of service and by country or
affiliation, 131
AFRICA
Foreign direct investment in the U.S., 14
AGRICULTURE
Commodity trade highlights
exports, 176
imports, 177
Foreign trade in goods and services
balance of payments by regions and individual
countries, 118
imports by NAICS from regions and individual
countries, 110
top 30 purchasers and suppliers of agricultural products
by NAICS, 126
top 30 suppliers of agricultural products by NAICS, 128
AIRCRAFT, SPACECRAFT, AND PARTS
Commodity trade highlights
exports and imports by country, 190
ALABAMA
State trade by commodity, 263
State trade by country, 212
ALASKA
State trade by commodity, 264
State trade by country, 213
ARAB EMIRATES
Commodity trade by geographic area, 156
ARIZONA
State trade by commodity, 265
State trade by country, 214
ARKANSAS
State trade by commodity, 266
State trade by country, 215
ASIA AND PACIFIC
Foreign direct investment in the U.S., 14
ASSETS
International transactions and investment position
net acquisition of financial assets, 6
net international investment position, 10
AUSTRALIA
Commodity trade by geographic area, 157
Foreign direct investment in the U.S., 14

BALANCE OF PAYMENTS
Foreign trade in goods and services
agricultural balance of payments by regions and individual
countries, 118
NAICS balance of payments by region and individual
countries, 94

NAICS balance of payments with world, 49
total balance of payments of goods by region and
individual country, 78
total exports, imports, and balances by area, 130
trade in goods-balance of payments basis vs. census
basis, 28
BELGIUM
Commodity trade by geographic area, 150
Foreign direct investment in the U.S., 14
BERMUDA
Foreign direct investment in the U.S., 14
BEVERAGES AND SPIRITS
Commodity trade highlights
exports and imports by country, 178
BIOTECHNOLOGY
Commodity trade highlights
U.S. trade in products, 203
BRAZIL
Commodity trade by geographic area, 152
Foreign direct investment in the U.S., 14

CALIFORNIA
State trade by commodity, 267
State trade by country, 216
CANADA
Commodity trade by geographic area, 141
Foreign direct investment in the U.S., 14
CAPITAL TRANSFER PAYMENTS
International transactions and investment position, 6
CAPITAL TRANSFER RECEIPTS
International transactions and investment position, 6
CARIBBEAN ISLANDS
Foreign direct investment in the U.S., 14
CENSUS BASIS
Foreign trade in goods and services
trade in goods-balance of payments basis vs. census
basis, 28
CENTRAL AMERICA
Foreign direct investment in the U.S., 14
CEREALS AND GRAINS
Commodity trade highlights
exports and imports by country, 179
CHEMICALS
Commodity trade highlights
exports and imports by country, 195
CHILE
Commodity trade by geographic area, 163
CHINA
Commodity trade by geographic area, 143
Foreign direct investment in the U.S., 14
COCOA
Commodity trade highlights
exports and imports by country, 180
COFFEE AND TEA
Commodity trade highlights
exports and imports by country, 181
COLOMBIA

Commodity trade by geographic area, 162
COLORADO
State trade by commodity, 268
State trade by country, 217
COMMODITY TRADE BY GEOGRAPHIC AREA
Arab Emirates, 156
Australia, 157
Belgium, 150
Brazil, 152
Canada, 141
Chile, 163
China, 143
Colombia, 162
France, 151
Germany, 146
Hong Kong, 149
India, 158
Israel, 161
Italy, 160
Japan, 144
Malaysia, 164
Mexico, 142
Netherlands, 148
Saudi Arabia, 159
Singapore, 153
South Korea, 147
State trade by commodity
        see **STATE TRADE BY COMMODITY**
Switzerland, 155
Taiwan, 154
Thailand, 165
Top U.S. trade partners ranked by 2015 export value for
        goods, 140
United Kingdom, 145
COMMODITY TRADE HIGHLIGHTS
Advanced technology
        trade balance, 202
        U.S. trade in products, 203
Agriculture
        exports, 176
        imports, 177
Aircraft, spacecraft, and parts
        exports and imports by country, 190
Beverages and spirits
        exports and imports by country, 178
Biotechnology
        U.S. trade in products, 203
Cereals and grains
        exports and imports by country, 179
Chemicals
        exports and imports by country, 195
Cocoa
        exports and imports by country, 180
Coffee and tea
        exports and imports by country, 181
Crude oil
        exports by country, 200
        imports by country, 199
Dairy products

exports and imports by country, 182
Diamonds
        exports and imports by country, 197
Drugs
        exports and imports by country, 196
Electric machinery
        exports and imports by country, 191
Flowers and live trees
        exports and imports by country, 184
Fruits and nuts
        exports and imports by country, 183
Furniture
        exports and imports by country, 192
Live trees and cut flowers
        exports and imports by country, 184
Meat
        exports and imports by country, 185
Medical or surgical instruments
        exports and imports by country, 194
Motor vehicles and parts
        exports and imports by country, 198
Nuclear reactors
        exports and imports by country, 193
Nuts and fruits
        exports and imports by country, 183
Oil
        exports by country, 200
        imports by country, 199
Oilseeds and soybeans
        exports and imports by country, 186
Optic-photo instruments
        exports and imports by country, 194
Organic chemicals
        exports and imports by country, 195
Petroleum products
        exports by country, 200
        imports by country, 199
Pharmaceutical products
        exports and imports by country, 196
Precious stones
        exports and imports by country, 197
Rare earth elements
        sources of imports, 201
Soybeans and oilseeds
        exports and imports by country, 186
State trade by commodity
        see **STATE TRADE BY COMMODITY**
Sugar
        exports and imports by country, 187
Surgical instruments
        exports and imports by country, 194
Tea and coffee
        exports and imports by country, 181
Technology
        trade balance, 202
        U.S. trade in products, 203
Tobacco
        exports and imports by country, 188
Trees and cut flowers

exports and imports by country, 184
Vegetables
exports and imports by country, 189
Vehicles and parts
exports and imports by country, 198
CONNECTICUT
State trade by commodity, 269
State trade by country, 218
COUNTRIES
Commodity trade by geographic area
see **COMMODITY TRADE BY GEOGRAPHIC AREA**
Commodity trade highlights
see **COMMODITY TRADE HIGHLIGHTS**
Foreign trade in goods and services
agricultural balance of payments by regions and individual countries, 118
agricultural imports by NAICS from regions and individual countries, 110
balance of payments of NAICS manufactures by region and individual countries, 94
exports by NAICS by region and country, 102
exports of goods to regions and individual countries, 74
exports of NAICS manufactures by region and individual country, 82
exports of total merchandise to individual countries by HS, 54
imports of goods from regions and individual countries, 70
imports of NAICS manufactures by region and individual countries, 86
imports of total merchandise from individual countries by HS, 62
total balance of payments of goods by region and individual country, 78
trade in services by type of service and by country or affiliation, 131
State trade by country
see **STATE TRADE BY COUNTRY**
CREDITS
International transactions and investment position
capital transfer receipts and other credits, 6
exports of goods and services and income receipts, 6
CRUDE OIL
Commodity trade highlights
exports by country, 200
imports by country, 199
CURRENCY
Foreign exchange rates, 15

DAIRY PRODUCTS
Commodity trade highlights
exports and imports by country, 182
DEBITS
International transactions and investment position
capital transfer payments and other debits, 6
imports of goods and services and income payments, 6
DEFICITS
Foreign trade in goods and services
top 10 exports, imports, deficit, and surplus by SITC, 46

top 10 imports, exports, deficit, and surplus by NAICS, 51
top imports, exports, deficit, and surplus for total merchandise, 36
DELAWARE
State trade by commodity, 270
State trade by country, 219
DENMARK
Foreign direct investment in the U.S., 14
DIAMONDS
Commodity trade highlights
exports and imports by country, 197
DISTRICT OF COLUMBIA
State trade by commodity, 271
State trade by country, 220
DRUGS
Commodity trade highlights
exports and imports by country, 196

ELECTRIC MACHINERY
Commodity trade highlights
exports and imports by country, 191
END-USE CODES
Foreign trade in goods and services
exports to world total by 5-digit End-Use Code, 40
imports from world total by 5-digit End-Use Code, 37
ESTABLISHMENTS
Foreign direct investment in the U.S., 12
EUROPE
Foreign direct investment in the U.S., 14
EXCHANGE RATES
Foreign exchange rates, 15
EXPANSIONS
Foreign direct investment in the U.S., 12
EXPORTS
Foreign trade in goods and services
see **FOREIGN TRADE IN GOODS AND SERVICES**
International transactions and investment position
goods and services and income receipts (credits), 6
State trade by commodity
see **STATE TRADE BY COMMODITY**
State trade by country
see **STATE TRADE BY COUNTRY**

FINANCE AND INSURANCE
Foreign direct investment in the U.S., 13
FINANCIAL DERIVATIVES
International transactions and investment position
net transactions, 6
FINLAND
Foreign direct investment in the U.S., 14
FLORIDA
State trade by commodity, 272
State trade by country, 221
FLOWERS AND LIVE TREES
Commodity trade highlights
exports and imports by country, 184
FOREIGN DIRECT INVESTMENT IN THE U.S.
Acquisitions, 12
Countries of UBO by type of investment, 14

Establishments, 12
Expansions, 12
Finance and insurance, 13
Information services, 13
International transactions and investment position
    first-year expenditures for new direct investment, 12-14
Manufacturing, 13
Professional, scientific, and technical services, 13
Real estate and rental and leasing, 13
Retail trade, 13
Wholesale trade, 13

FOREIGN EXCHANGE RATES
List of countries, 15

FOREIGN TRADE IN GOODS AND SERVICES
Affiliation
    trade in services by type of service and by country or
        affiliation, 131
Agriculture
    balance of payments by regions and individual
        countries, 118
    imports by NAICS from regions and individual
        countries, 110
    top 30 purchasers and suppliers of agricultural products
        by NAICS, 126
    top 30 suppliers of agricultural products by NAICS, 128
Balance of payments
    agricultural balance of payments by regions and individual
        countries, 118
    NAICS balance of payments by region and individual
        countries, 94
    NAICS balance of payments with world, 49
    total balance of payments of goods by region and
        individual country, 78
    total exports, imports, and balances by area, 130
    trade in goods-balance of payments basis vs. census
        basis, 28
Census basis
    trade in goods-balance of payments basis vs. census
        basis, 28
Countries
    agricultural balance of payments by regions and individual
        countries, 118
    agricultural imports by NAICS from regions and
        individual countries, 110
    balance of payments of NAICS manufactures by region
        and individual countries, 94
    exports by NAICS by region and country, 102
    exports of goods to regions and individual countries, 74
    exports of NAICS manufactures by region and individual
        country, 82
    exports of total merchandise to individual countries by
        HS, 54
    imports of goods from regions and individual countries, 70
    imports of NAICS manufactures by region and individual
        countries, 86
    imports of total merchandise from individual countries by
        HS, 62
    total balance of payments of goods by region and
        individual country, 78

trade in services by type of service and by country or
    affiliation, 131
Deficits
    top 10 exports, imports, deficit, and surplus by SITC, 46
    top 10 imports, exports, deficit, and surplus by NAICS, 51
    top imports, exports, deficit, and surplus for total
        merchandise, 36
End-Use Codes
    exports to world total by 5-digit End-Use Code, 40
    imports from world total by 5-digit End-Use Code, 37
Exports by NAICS by region and country, 102
Exports of goods by principal end-use category, 30
Exports of goods to regions and individual countries, 74
Exports of NAICS manufactures by region and individual
    country, 82
Exports of total merchandise by NAICS, 47
Exports of total merchandise to countries by Harmonized
    System, 54
Exports to world total by 5-digit End-Use Code, 40
Exports with world by Harmonized System, 32
Exports with world by SITC, 42
Harmonized System
    exports of total merchandise to countries by HS, 54
    exports with world by Harmonized System, 32
    imports of total merchandise from countries by HS, 62
    imports with world by Harmonized System, 34
Imports from world total by 5-digit End-Use Code, 37
Imports of goods by principal end-use category, 30
Imports of goods from regions and individual countries, 70
Imports of NAICS manufactures by region and individual
    countries, 86
Imports of total merchandise by NAICS, 48
Imports of total merchandise from countries by Harmonized
    System, 62
Imports with world by Harmonized System, 34
International trade in goods and services, 26, 27
North American Industry Classification System
    agricultural imports by NAICS from regions and
        individual countries, 110
    balance of payments of NAICS manufactures by region
        and individual countries, 94
    balance of payments with world by NAICS, 49
    exports by NAICS by region and country, 102
    exports of NAICS manufactures by region and individual
        country, 82
    exports of total merchandise by NAICS, 47
    imports of NAICS manufactures by region and individual
        countries, 86
    imports of total merchandise by NAICS, 48
    top 10 imports, exports, deficit, and surplus by NAICS, 51
    top 30 purchasers and suppliers of agricultural products
        by NAICS, 126
    top 30 suppliers of agricultural products by NAICS, 128
Principal end-use category
    exports and imports of goods by, 30
    real exports of goods by principal end-use category, 52
    real imports of goods by principal end-use category, 53
Real exports of goods by principal end-use category, 52
Real imports of goods by principal end-use category, 53

Regions
    agricultural balance of payments by regions and individual
        countries, 118
    agricultural imports by NAICS from regions and
        individual countries, 110
    balance of payments of NAICS manufactures by region
        and individual countries, 94
    exports by NAICS by region and country, 102
    exports of goods to regions and individual countries, 74
    exports of NAICS manufactures by region and individual
        country, 82
    imports of goods from regions and individual countries, 70
    imports of NAICS manufactures by region and individual
        countries, 86
    total balance of payments of goods by region and
        individual country, 78
Standard International Trade Classification
    exports with world by SITC, 42
    top 10 exports, imports, deficit, and surplus by SITC, 46
    top 10 trade with world for SITC total all merchandise, 45
Surpluses
    top 10 exports, imports, deficit, and surplus by SITC, 46
    top 10 imports, exports, deficit, and surplus by NAICS, 51
    top imports, exports, deficit, and surplus for total
        merchandise, 36
Top 10 exports, imports, deficit, and surplus by SITC, 46
Top 10 imports, exports, deficit, and surplus by NAICS, 51
Top 10 trade with world for SITC total all merchandise, 45
Top imports, exports, deficit, and surplus for total
    merchandise, 36
Total all merchandise exports to world, 44
Total balance of payments of goods by region and individual
    country, 78
Total exports, imports, and balances by area, 130
Trade in goods-balance of payments basis vs. census basis, 28
Trade in services by type of service, 29
Trade in services by type of service and by country or
    affiliation, 131
FRANCE
    Commodity trade by geographic area, 151
    Foreign direct investment in the U.S., 14
FRUITS AND NUTS
    Commodity trade highlights
        exports and imports by country, 183
FURNITURE
    Commodity trade highlights
        exports and imports by country, 192

GEORGIA
    State trade by commodity, 273
    State trade by country, 222
GERMANY
    Commodity trade by geographic area, 146
    Foreign direct investment in the U.S., 14
GOODS
    Foreign trade in goods and services
        see **FOREIGN TRADE IN GOODS AND SERVICES**
HARMONIZED SYSTEM
    Foreign trade in goods and services

    exports of total merchandise to countries by HS, 54
    exports with world by Harmonized System, 32
    imports of total merchandise from countries by HS, 62
    imports with world by Harmonized System, 34
HAWAII
    State trade by commodity, 274
    State trade by country, 223
HONG KONG
    Commodity trade by geographic area, 149
    Foreign direct investment in the U.S., 14

IDAHO
    State trade by commodity, 275
    State trade by country, 224
ILLINOIS
    State trade by commodity, 276
    State trade by country, 225
IMPORTS
    Foreign trade in goods and services
        see **FOREIGN TRADE IN GOODS AND SERVICES**
    International transactions and investment position
        goods and services and income payments (debits), 6
    State trade by commodity
        see **STATE TRADE BY COMMODITY**
    State trade by country
        see **STATE TRADE BY COUNTRY**
INDIA
    Commodity trade by geographic area, 158
    Foreign direct investment in the U.S., 14
INDIANA
    State trade by commodity, 277
    State trade by country, 226
INFORMATION SERVICES
    Foreign direct investment in the U.S., 13
INSURANCE
    Foreign direct investment in the U.S., 13
INTERNATIONAL TRADE IN GOODS AND SERVICES
        see **FOREIGN TRADE IN GOODS AND SERVICES**
INTERNATIONAL TRANSACTIONS AND
        INVESTMENT POSITION
    Assets
        net acquisition of financial assets, 6
        net international investment position, 10
    Capital transfer payments, 6
    Capital transfer receipts, 6
    Credits
        capital transfer receipts and other credits, 6
        exports of goods and services and income receipts, 6
    Debits
        capital transfer payments and other debits, 6
        imports of goods and services and income payments, 6
    Exports
        goods and services and income receipts (credits), 6
    Financial derivatives other than reserves,
        net transactions, 6
    Foreign direct investment in the U.S.
        first-year expenditures for new direct investment, 12-14
    Foreign exchange rates, 15
    Imports

goods and services and income payments (debits), 6
International transactions, 6
Investment position
  net international investment position, 10
Liabilities
  net incurrence of liabilities, 6
  net international investment position, 10
Net acquisition of financial assets, 6
Net borrowing, 6
Net incurrence of liabilities, 6
Net international investment position, 10
Net lending, 6

INVESTMENT POSITION
International transactions and investment position
  net international investment position, 10
IOWA
State trade by commodity, 278
State trade by country, 227
IRELAND
Foreign direct investment in the U.S., 14
ISRAEL
Commodity trade by geographic area, 161
Foreign direct investment in the U.S., 14
ITALY
Commodity trade by geographic area, 160
Foreign direct investment in the U.S., 14

JAPAN
Commodity trade by geographic area, 144
Foreign direct investment in the U.S., 14

KANSAS
State trade by commodity, 279
State trade by country, 228
KENTUCKY
State trade by commodity, 280
State trade by country, 229

LATIN AMERICA
Foreign direct investment in the U.S., 14
LEASING
Foreign direct investment in the U.S., 13
LIABILITIES
International transactions and investment position
  net incurrence of liabilities, 6
  net international investment position, 10
LIVE TREES AND CUT FLOWERS
Commodity trade highlights
  exports and imports by country, 184
LOUISIANA
State trade by commodity, 281
State trade by country, 230

MAINE
State trade by commodity, 282
State trade by country, 231
MALAYSIA
Commodity trade by geographic area, 164
MANUFACTURING

Foreign direct investment in the U.S., 13
MARYLAND
State trade by commodity, 283
State trade by country, 232
MASSACHUSETTS
State trade by commodity, 284
State trade by country, 233
MEAT
Commodity trade highlights
  exports and imports by country, 185
MEDICAL OR SURGICAL INSTRUMENTS
Commodity trade highlights
  exports and imports by country, 194
MEXICO
Commodity trade by geographic area, 142
Foreign direct investment in the U.S., 14
MICHIGAN
State trade by commodity, 285
State trade by country, 234
MIDDLE EAST
Foreign direct investment in the U.S., 14
MINNESOTA
State trade by commodity, 286
State trade by country, 235
MISSISSIPPI
State trade by commodity, 287
State trade by country, 236
MISSOURI
State trade by commodity, 288
State trade by country, 237
MONTANA
State trade by commodity, 289
State trade by country, 238
MOTOR VEHICLES AND PARTS
Commodity trade highlights
  exports and imports by country, 198

NEBRASKA
State trade by commodity, 290
State trade by country, 239
NET ACQUISITION OF FINANCIAL ASSETS
International transactions and investment position, 6
NET BORROWING
International transactions and investment position, 6
NETHERLANDS
Commodity trade by geographic area, 148
Foreign direct investment in the U.S., 14
NET INCURRENCE OF LIABILITIES
International transactions and investment position, 6
NET INTERNATIONAL INVESTMENT POSITION
International transactions and investment position, 10
NET LENDING
International transactions and investment position, 6
NEVADA
State trade by commodity, 291
State trade by country, 240
NEW HAMPSHIRE
State trade by commodity, 292
State trade by country, 241

NEW JERSEY
State trade by commodity, 293
State trade by country, 242
NEW MEXICO
State trade by commodity, 294
State trade by country, 243
NEW YORK
State trade by commodity, 295
State trade by country, 244
NORTH AMERICAN INDUSTRY CLASSIFICATION SYSTEM (NAICS)
Foreign trade in goods and services
agricultural imports by NAICS from regions and individual countries, 110
balance of payments of NAICS manufactures by region and individual countries, 94
balance of payments with world by NAICS, 49
exports by NAICS by region and country, 102
exports of NAICS manufactures by region and individual country, 82
exports of total merchandise by NAICS, 47
imports of NAICS manufactures by region and individual countries, 86
imports of total merchandise by NAICS, 48
top 10 imports, exports, deficit, and surplus by NAICS, 51
top 30 purchasers and suppliers of agricultural products by NAICS, 126
top 30 suppliers of agricultural products by NAICS, 128
NORTH CAROLINA
State trade by commodity, 296
State trade by country, 245
NORTH DAKOTA
State trade by commodity, 297
State trade by country, 246
NUCLEAR REACTORS
Commodity trade highlights
exports and imports by country, 193
NUTS AND FRUITS
Commodity trade highlights
exports and imports by country, 183

OHIO
State trade by commodity, 298
State trade by country, 247
OIL
Commodity trade highlights
exports by country, 200
imports by country, 199
OILSEEDS AND SOYBEANS
Commodity trade highlights
exports and imports by country, 186
OKLAHOMA
State trade by commodity, 299
State trade by country, 248
OPTIC-PHOTO INSTRUMENTS
Commodity trade highlights
exports and imports by country, 194
OREGON
State trade by commodity, 300

State trade by country, 249
ORGANIC CHEMICALS
Commodity trade highlights
exports and imports by country, 195

PACIFIC
Foreign direct investment in the U.S., 14
PENNSYLVANIA
State trade by commodity, 301
State trade by country, 250
PETROLEUM PRODUCTS
Commodity trade highlights
exports by country, 200
imports by country, 199
PHARMACEUTICAL PRODUCTS
Commodity trade highlights
exports and imports by country, 196
PRECIOUS STONES
Commodity trade highlights
exports and imports by country, 197
PRINCIPAL END-USE CATEGORY
Foreign trade in goods and services
exports and imports of goods by, 30
real exports of goods by principal end-use category, 52
real imports of goods by principal end-use category, 53
PROFESSIONAL, SCIENTIFIC, AND TECHNICAL SERVICES
Foreign direct investment in the U.S., 13

RARE EARTH ELEMENTS
Commodity trade highlights
sources of imports, 201
REAL ESTATE AND RENTAL AND LEASING
Foreign direct investment in the U.S., 13
REGIONS
Foreign trade in goods and services
agricultural balance of payments by regions and individual countries, 118
agricultural imports by NAICS from regions and individual countries, 110
balance of payments of NAICS manufactures by region and individual countries, 94
exports by NAICS by region and country, 102
exports of goods to regions and individual countries, 74
exports of NAICS manufactures by region and individual country, 82
imports of goods from regions and individual countries, 70
imports of NAICS manufactures by region and individual countries, 86
total balance of payments of goods by region and individual country, 78
RETAIL TRADE
Foreign direct investment in the U.S., 13
RHODE ISLAND
State trade by commodity, 302
State trade by country, 251

SAUDI ARABIA
Commodity trade by geographic area, 159

Foreign direct investment in the U.S., 14
SCIENTIFIC SERVICES
Foreign direct investment in the U.S., 13
SERVICES
Foreign trade in goods and services
see **FOREIGN TRADE IN GOODS AND SERVICES**
SINGAPORE
Commodity trade by geographic area, 153
Foreign direct investment in the U.S., 14
SOUTH AFRICA
Foreign direct investment in the U.S., 14
SOUTH AMERICA
Foreign direct investment in the U.S., 14
SOUTH CAROLINA
State trade by commodity, 303
State trade by country, 252
SOUTH DAKOTA
State trade by commodity, 304
State trade by country, 253
SOUTH KOREA
Commodity trade by geographic area, 147
Foreign direct investment in the U.S., 14
SOYBEANS AND OILSEEDS
Commodity trade highlights
exports and imports by country, 186
SPAIN
Foreign direct investment in the U.S., 14
**STANDARD INTERNATIONAL TRADE
CLASSIFICATION (SITC)**
Foreign trade in goods and services
exports with world by SITC, 42
top 10 exports, imports, deficit, and surplus by SITC, 46
top 10 trade with world for SITC total all merchandise, 45
STATE TRADE BY COMMODITY
Alabama, 263
Alaska, 264
Arizona, 265
Arkansas, 266
California, 267
Colorado, 268
Connecticut, 269
Delaware, 270
District of Columbia, 271
Florida, 272
Georgia, 273
Hawaii, 274
Idaho, 275
Illinois, 276
Indiana, 277
Iowa, 278
Kansas, 279
Kentucky, 280
Louisiana, 281
Maine, 282
Maryland, 283
Massachusetts, 284
Michigan, 285
Minnesota, 286
Mississippi, 287

Missouri, 288
Montana, 289
Nebraska, 290
Nevada, 291
New Hampshire, 292
New Jersey, 293
New Mexico, 294
New York, 295
North Carolina, 296
North Dakota, 297
Ohio, 298
Oklahoma, 299
Oregon, 300
Pennsylvania, 301
Rhode Island, 302
South Carolina, 303
South Dakota, 304
Tennessee, 305
Texas, 306
Utah, 307
Vermont, 308
Virginia, 309
Washington, 310
West Virginia, 311
Wisconsin, 312
Wyoming, 313
STATE TRADE BY COUNTRY
Alabama, 212
Alaska, 213
Arizona, 214
Arkansas, 215
California, 216
Colorado, 217
Connecticut, 218
Delaware, 219
District of Columbia, 220
Florida, 221
Georgia, 222
Hawaii, 223
Idaho, 224
Illinois, 225
Indiana, 226
Iowa, 227
Kansas, 228
Kentucky, 229
Louisiana, 230
Maine, 231
Maryland, 232
Massachusetts, 233
Michigan, 234
Minnesota, 235
Mississippi, 236
Missouri, 237
Montana, 238
Nebraska, 239
Nevada, 240
New Hampshire, 241
New Jersey, 242
New Mexico, 243

New York, 244
North Carolina, 245
North Dakota, 246
Ohio, 247
Oklahoma, 248
Oregon, 249
Pennsylvania, 250
Rhode Island, 251
South Carolina, 252
South Dakota, 253
Tennessee, 254
Texas, 255
Utah, 256
Vermont, 257
Virginia, 258
Washington, 259
West Virginia, 260
Wisconsin, 261
Wyoming, 262

SUGAR
Commodity trade highlights
    exports and imports by country, 187
SURGICAL INSTRUMENTS
Commodity trade highlights
    exports and imports by country, 194
SURPLUSES
Foreign trade in goods and services
    top 10 exports, imports, deficit, and surplus by SITC, 46
    top 10 imports, exports, deficit, and surplus by NAICS, 51
    top imports, exports, deficit, and surplus for total
        merchandise, 36
SWEDEN
Foreign direct investment in the U.S., 14
SWITZERLAND
Commodity trade by geographic area, 155
Foreign direct investment in the U.S., 14

TAIWAN
Commodity trade by geographic area, 154
Foreign direct investment in the U.S., 14
TEA AND COFFEE
Commodity trade highlights
    exports and imports by country, 181
TECHNICAL SERVICES
Foreign direct investment in the U.S., 13
TECHNOLOGY
Commodity trade highlights
    trade balance, 202
    U.S. trade in products, 203
TENNESSEE
State trade by commodity, 305
State trade by country, 254

TEXAS
State trade by commodity, 306
State trade by country, 255
THAILAND
Commodity trade by geographic area, 165
TOBACCO
Commodity trade highlights
    exports and imports by country, 188
TRADE IN GOODS AND SERVICES
    see **FOREIGN TRADE IN GOODS AND SERVICES**
TREES AND CUT FLOWERS
Commodity trade highlights
    exports and imports by country, 184

UNITED ARAB EMIRATES
Foreign direct investment in the U.S., 14
UNITED KINGDOM
Commodity trade by geographic area, 145
Foreign direct investment in the U.S., 14
UTAH
State trade by commodity, 307
State trade by country, 256

VEGETABLES
Commodity trade highlights
    exports and imports by country, 189
VEHICLES AND PARTS
Commodity trade highlights
    exports and imports by country, 198
VENEZUELA
Foreign direct investment in the U.S., 14
VERMONT
State trade by commodity, 308
State trade by country, 257
VIRGINIA
State trade by commodity, 309
State trade by country, 258

WASHINGTON
State trade by commodity, 310
State trade by country, 259
WEST VIRGINIA
State trade by commodity, 311
State trade by country, 260
WHOLESALE TRADE
Foreign direct investment in the U.S., 13
WISCONSIN
State trade by commodity, 312
State trade by country, 261
WYOMING
State trade by commodity, 313
State trade by country, 262